ISBN 978-1-331-15646-8
PIBN 10151711

1 MONTH OF
FREE
READING

at

www.ForgottenBooks.com

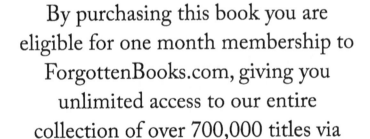

By purchasing this book you are eligible for one month membership to ForgottenBooks.com, giving you unlimited access to our entire collection of over 700,000 titles via our web site and mobile apps.

To claim your free month visit:

www.forgottenbooks.com/free151711

History of Buchanan County and St. Joseph, Mo.

FROM THE TIME OF THE PLATTE PURCHASE TO
THE END OF THE YEAR 1915

C. L. Rutt

PRECEDED BY A SHORT HISTORY OF MISSOURI

SUPPLEMENTED BY BIOGRAPHICAL SKETCHES OF
NOTED CITIZENS, LIVING AND DEAD

By The History Publishing Company

PRESS OF
MIDLAND PRINTING COMPANY
ST. JOSEPH, MISSOURI

E. L. McDONALD   W. J. KING

1151710

Introduction

The first history of Buchanan County was published in 1881. The second was in 1899, when C. L. Rutt, managing editor of the News-Press, compiled a very satisfactory book, using the 1881 publication as a ground work. In order that the highest possible degree of accuracy might be obtained the chapters were published serially in the Daily News and the public was invited to make corrections. In this way many errors that would otherwise have marred the usefulness of the book were obviated. The present volume is intended to bring the work down to date, using the matter compiled by Mr. Rutt up to 1899, and adding the essential facts in the history of the county since that time. To all who have aided in the preparation of this work, the compilers extend their sincere thanks.

THE COMPILERS.

History of Missouri

CHAPTER I.

HERNANDO DE SOTO—THE NAME OF MISSOURI—EARLY SETTLEMENTS—FRENCH AND SPANISH RULE— LOUISIANA PURCHASE—TERRITORIAL GOVERNMENT —ADMITTED AS A STATE—FIRST REPRESENTATIVES IN CONGRESS—GOVERNORS McNAIR, BATES, MILLER, DUNKLIN, BOGGS, REYNOLDS, EDWARDS, KING, PRICE, POLK, HANCOCK, JACKSON AND STEWART— 1541 TO 1857.

The first white man to put foot on the soil of Missouri was Hernando de Soto, the Spaniard. This was in 1541. He led a small band of soldiers of fortune as far north as the region now known as New Madrid County, and then moved west across the Ozark Mountains and went into Arkansas. He sought gold, but finding none, returned to the Mississippi and died. He was buried at midnight in the river he had discovered, and his priests chanted over his body the first requiem ever heard in the Mississippi Valley. The Indians believed him to be the son of the sun, who could not die, and his body was consigned to the waters to conceal his death and keep the Indians in awe.

The Spanish, however, did not colonize Missouri. In 1662 Robert Cavalier de la Salle, a Frenchman from Quebec, came down the Mississippi and took possession of the whole country in the name of Louis XIV., the reigning King of France. Within the next fifty years various settlements were projected, all in the interest of gold and silver mining. It is said that in 1705 a prospecting party of Frenchmen ascended the Missouri River as far as where Kansas City is now located.

In his school history, Perry S. Rader of Brunswick states that this river was first called Pek-i-ta-nou-i by Marquette, which is an Indian word meaning "muddy water." About 1712, says Mr. Rader, it was first called Missouri, from the name of a tribe of Indians who inhabited the country at its mouth and along a considerable portion of its banks. There is no authority, according to Mr. Rader, for the often-repeated assertion that "Missouri means muddy." This definition of the word was given to it after the name of the river was changed from Pekitanoui to Missouri.

The first place settled in Missouri was Ste. Genevieve, in about 1735, and the next settlement of consequence was St. Louis. The latter place owes its existence to Pierre Laclede Ligueste, more generally known in history as Pierre Laclede.

The first settlement north of the Missouri River was at St.

Charles, called Village des Cotes (Village of the Hills) then, and most of the Indian wars and adventures which figure in the early history of the state occurred in this vicinity.

When France lost Canada she gave up all her possessions in America. Canada and the country east of the Mississippi, except New Orleans, went to England in 1763, and Spain was indemnified for losses in the war with the territory west of the river, which included Missouri. Spanish governors ruled until 1800, when Louisiana was transferred to France, through the efforts of the first Napoleon, who had planned a monarchy in the new world. Both the people of the United States and the government of England objected to this. Negotiations were opened by President Jefferson for the Louisiana purchase. Napoleon, who was getting into close quarters, accepted an offer of $15,000,000, and the country was ceded to the United States. The French had not yet taken possession. On March 9, 1804, the American troops crossed the Mississippi and entered St. Louis, where Don Carlos Delassus, the Spanish commandant, delivered Upper Louisiana to Captain Amos Stoddard of the United States army, who received it as the agent of France and transferred it to himself as the agent of the United States. By this transaction Missouri was under the flags of three nations in as many consecutive days.

Congress divided Louisiana into two parts soon after the transfer. All that is now within the State of Louisiana was called the Territory of New Orleans, the rest was called the District of Louisiana. The district was attached, for administrative purposes, to the then Territory of Indiana, whose governor was General William Henry Harrison. This was unsatisfactory, and upon a petition from the people the territory was separated from Indiana and given a governor and three judges.

The first governor appointed under the new order of things was General James Wilkinson, who was succeeded by General Meriwether Lewis, of the famous Lewis-and-Clark expedition. General Lewis committed suicide in Tennessee in 1809, while on his way to Washington, and President Madison appointed General Benjamin Howard of Lexington, Ky., to succeed him.

In 1812 Congress passed a law by which Louisiana was raised from a second-grade to a first-grade territory, with a governor and general assembly, and its name was changed to Missouri.

Governor Howard resigned in 1812, and was succeeded by Captain William Clark, the companion of General Lewis in their exploration, and who was known as "Redhead" by the Indians, over whom he exercised great influence. Captain Clark was the first and only governor of the Territory of Missouri. Edward Hempstead of St. Louis was elected the first delegate to Congress from the new territory, and was the first delegate to that body from west of the Mississippi River. He was succeeded in 1815 by Rufus Easton, and he, in 1817, by John Scott, who served until Missouri became a state.

The first general assembly of the new territory met on December 7, 1812, at St. Louis, in the house of Joseph Robidoux, the father of the founder of St. Joseph.

In 1818 Missouri applied for admission to the Union as a state. Two years of bitter controversy ensued, which convulsed the country and threatened the dissolution of the Union. This controversy followed a resolution introduced into Congress which intended to prohibit slavery in Missouri. The momentous question was finally settled by the adoption of the "Missouri Compromise," which forbade slavery in all that portion of the Louisiana purchase lying north of 36 degrees 30 minutes, except in Missouri, and on July 19, 1820, the law passed admitting Missouri to the Union.

A convention to frame a constitution had already been called, and the constitution then adopted remained without material change until 1865. The population of Missouri in 1820 was 66,000, of which number 10,000 were slaves..

Captain Clark and Alexander McNair were rival candidates for the first gubernatorial honors of the new state. McNair was elected, with William H. Ashley of St. Louis as lieutenant-governor. Governor McNair served four years. He was a Pennsylvanian by birth and had been United States commissary at St. Louis for a number of years before he was elected governor. He died in 1826.

The first general assembly of the state, composed of fourteen senators and forty-three representatives, met at St. Louis in September of 1820, and elected David Barton and Thomas H. Benton United States senators. John Scott was the first congressman, the state being entitled to but one member of the lower house at that time. Scott had been the territorial delegate, and was an able man.

Until 1851 the judges of the supreme court were appointed by the governor. The first members of the supreme court were Mathias McGirk of Montgomery County, John D. Cook of Cape Girardeau, and John Rice Jones of Pike.

At its first session the legislature organized the following ten counties: Boone, Callaway, Chariton, Cole, Gasconade, Lafayette, Perry, Ralls, Ray, and Saline.

The second governor was Frederick Bates, who died before completing his first year of service. Benjamin Reeves, the lieutenant-governor, having resigned shortly after his election, the executive office fell to the president pro tem. of the senate, Abraham J. Williams of Columbia, who at once called a special election, which brought John Miller of Howard County to the head of the administration. Governor Miller was elected in 1828, with Daniel Dunklin of Potosi as lieutenant-governor.

Spencer Pettis was the second congressman. He was killed in a duel on Bloody Island by Major Biddle. In his canvass he had sharply criticized Major Biddle's brother, president of the United States Bank, for which Major Biddle severely chastised him. Mr. Pettis issued a challenge, and both combatants were killed. This was in 1831. William H. Ashley was elected to succeed Mr. Pettis.

Daniel Dunklin was elected governor in 1832. He resigned one month before the expiration of his term to become surveyor-general of Missouri, Arkansas and Illinois. He was an ardent advocate of the public school and did much toward the development of the system in this state.

Lilburn W. Boggs of Jackson County, the Democratic candidate, was elected to succeed Governor Dunklin, with Franklin Cannon of Cape Girardeau as lieutenant-governor. William H. Ashley of St. Louis, a Whig, who had been his opponent, was elected to Congress in the same year.

It was during the administration of Governor Boggs that the Mormon troubles occurred. The part taken by the governor caused an attempt upon his life. He was shot at Independence in 1841. Three bullets lodged in the victim's neck and head; another passed through and came out at the mouth. Nevertheless, Governor Boggs recovered, and died in California in 1861. Peter Rockwell, a Mormon, was charged with the crime, but was acquitted, the evidence being insufficient.

Thomas Reynolds of Howard County, a Democrat, was elected governor in 1840, with Meredith M. Marmaduke of Saline County as lieutenant-governor. The presidential campaign of this year was attended with deep interest in Missouri, as in other states. The Whig candidate was General William Henry Harrison of Indiana, and the Democratic candidate was Martin Van Buren. Harrison was called the "log cabin candidate." The contest was called the "log cabin, coon skin and hard cider campaign," and the emblems were displayed in reality at the public meetings.

At this election the Whigs for the first time assumed a distinct organization in Missouri. Before that some Whigs had been prominent in politics, and had been elected to important offices, but they were chosen often on account of their personal popularity and worth, rather than because of their politics. But for the next twelve years the party made bold and aggressive campaigns at every election, although at no time did they gain control of the state.

Governor Reynolds committed suicide at the executive mansion on February 9, 1844, whereupon Lieutenant-Governor Marmaduke took charge and served until the 20th of November.

John C. Edwards of Cole County was elected governor in 1844, with James Young, of Lafayette County, as lieutenant-governor. There were then, as now, two factions in the Democratic party of Missouri, and they were divided then, as now, upon the money question. One faction, which favored silver and gold money, headed by Senator Benton, had nominated and elected Governor Edwards. The other faction favored a liberal use of paper money and opposed the re-election of Senator Benton.

In 1848 Austin A. King, of Ray County, Democrat, was elected governor over James S. Rollins, of Boone, a Whig. Thomas L. Price, of Cole County, was elected lieutenant-governor. Mr. King, who, prior to his nomination for governor, had been judge of the Fifth judicial circuit, held the first term of court in Buchanan

County. When the war broke out he denounced the secession movement and was elected to Congress by the Union party in 1862. He died in 1870 at Richmond.

Sterling Price was elected governor in 1852. He was from Chariton County, and his name figures prominently in the history of the nation, both as a soldier in the war with Mexico and as a brilliant leader of Confederate forces during the rebellion. After the war he embarked in business in St. Louis, and died there in 1867.

Trusten Polk, a St. Louis lawyer of great ability, was elected governor in 1856, as the Democratic candidate, over Robert C. Ewing, the "American," or "Know-Nothing," candidate. He served less than a month, however, having been elected by the legislature to the United States senate, from which body he and his colleague were expelled by the Republican members early in the war, for disloyal utterances. He died in St. Louis in 1876.

Hancock Jackson, the lieutenant-governor, served until August of 1857, when Robert M. Stewart, of St. Joseph, was elected.

CHAPTER II.

MISSOURI IN VARIOUS WARS.—TROOPS FOR' THE
BLACK HAWK WAR.—THE MORMON DIFFICULTIES.—
COLONEL GENTRY'S TROOPS IN THE SEMINOLE WAR.
—THE WAR WITH MEXICO.

Six wars figure in the history of Missouri—the Black Hawk war, the Mormon difficulties, the Seminole war. the war with Mexico, the civil war, and the war with Spain, in 1898.

On the 14th day of May, 1832, a bloody engagement took place between the regular forces of the United States and a part of the Sacs, Foxes and Winnebago Indians, commanded by Black Hawk and Keokuk, near Dixon's ferry, in Illinois. The governor (John Miller) of Missouri, fearing these savages would invade the soil of his state, ordered Major-General Richard Gentry to raise one thousand volunteers for the defense of the frontier. Five companies were at once raised in Boone, Callaway, Montgomery, St. Charles, Lincoln, Pike, Marion, Ralls, Clay, and Monroe counties. These companies went to Fort Pike, but finding that Black Hawk had not crossed the Mississippi River, returned home and disbanded.

* * *

Upon the present town site of Independence the Mormons located their "Zion" and gave it the name of "The New Jerusalem." They published here The Evening Star and made themselves generally obnoxious to the Gentiles, who were then in the minority, by their denunciatory articles through their paper, their clannishness, and their religious intolerance. Dreading the demoralizing influence of a paper which seemed to be inspired only with hatred and malice toward them, the Gentiles threw the press and type into the Missouri River, tarred and feathered one of their bishops, and otherwise gave the Mormons and their leaders to understand that they must conduct themselves in an entirely different manner if they wished for peace. After the destruction of their paper and press, they became furiously incensed, and sought many opportunities for retalliation. Matters continued in an uncertain condition until the 31st day of October, 1833, when a deadly conflict occurred near Westport, in which two Gentiles and one Mormon were killed. On the 2d of November following the Mormons were overpowered and compelled to lay down their arms and agree to leave the country with their families by January 1, on the condition that the owner would be paid for his printing press. Leaving Jackson County, they crossed the Missouri and located in Clay, Carroll, and other counties.

In 1837 they selected in Caldwell County a town site. which they called "Far West," and where they entered more land for their future homes. The printing press mentioned above was taken from the river, brought to St. Joseph, and used in producing the first issue of The Gazette.

In 1838 the discord between the citizens and Mormons became so great that Governor Boggs issued a proclamation ordering Major-General David R. Atchison to call the militia of his division to enforce the laws. He called out a part of the First Brigade of the Missouri state militia, under command of General A. W. Doniphan, who proceeded to the seat of war. The Mormon forces numbered about 1,000 men, and were led by G. W. Hinkle. The first engagement occurred at Crooked River, where one Mormon was killed. The principal fight took place at Haughn's Mills, where eighteen Mormons were killed and the remainder captured, some of them being killed after they had surrendered. Only one militiaman was wounded. In the month of October, 1838, Joseph Smith, the leader of the Mormons, and the chosen prophet and apostle of the church, surrendered the town of Far West to General Doniphan, agreeing to his conditions, viz: That they should deliver up their arms, surrender their prominent leaders for trial, and the remainder of the Mormons should, with their families, leave the state. Indictments were found against a number of these leaders, including Smith, who, while being taken to Boone County for trial, made his escape, and was afterward, in 1844, killed at Carthage, Ill. The others were acquitted.

* * *

In September, 1837, the Secretary of War issued a requisition on Governor Boggs of Missouri for six hundred volunteers, for service in Florida against the Seminole Indians, with whom the Creek nation had made common cause under Osceola. The first regiment was chiefly raised in Boone County by Colonel Richard Gentry. Arriving at Jackson Barracks, New Orleans, they were from there transported in brigs across the gulf to Tampa Bay, Florida. General Zachary Taylor, who then commanded in Florida, ordered Colonel Gentry to march to Okee-cho-bee, one hundred and thirty-five miles inland by the route traveled. Having reached the Kissimee River, seventy miles distant, a bloody battle ensued, in which Colonel Gentry was killed, on Christmas day of 1837. The Missourians then fought without a leader until they had completely routed the Indians. They returned home in 1838.

* * *

The Missourians also distinguished themselves in the war with Mexico in 1846-48. Not waiting for the call for volunteers, the "St. Louis Legion" hastened to the field of conflict. The Legion was commanded by Colonel A. R. Easton. During the month of May, 1846, Governor Edwards of Missouri called for volunteers to join the "Army of the West," an expedition to the Santa Fe—under command of General Stephen W. Kearny. Fort Leavenworth was the appointed rendezvous for the volunteers. By the 18th of June the full complement of companies to compose the First Regiment had arrived from Jackson, Lafayette, Clay, Saline, Franklin, Cole,

Howard, and Callaway counties. Of this regiment A. W. Doniphan
was made colonel, C. F. Ruff lieutenant-colonel, and William Gilpin
major. The battery of light artillery from St. Louis was commanded by Captains R. A. Weightman and A. W. Fischer, with
Major M. L. Clark as field officer; battalions of infantry from Platt
and Cole counties, commanded by Captains Murphy and W. Z. Aug-
ney, respectively, and the "Laclede Rangers," from St. Louis, by
Captain Thomas B. Hudson, aggregating, all told, from Missouri
1,658 men. In the summer of 1846 Hon. Sterling Price resigned
his seat in Congress and raised a mounted regiment to reinforce
the "Army of the West." He was made colonel, and D. D. Mitchel
lieutenant-colonel. Shortly afterwards an independent battalion
went under Lieutenant-Colonel Willock from Hannibal. In August
1847, Governor Edwards made another requisition for one thousand men, to consist of infantry. The regiment was raised at once.
John Dougherty, of Clay County, was chosen colonel, but before the
regiment marched the President countermanded the order. A company of mounted volunteers was raised in Ralls County, commanded by Captain William T. Lalfland. Conspicuous among the
engagements in which the Missouri volunteers participated in
Mexico were the battles of Brazito, Sacramento, Canada, El Em-
budo, Taos, and Santa Cruz de Rosales. The forces from Missouri
were mustered out in 1848.

CHAPTER III

THE CIVIL WAR.—AGITATION OF THE ABOLITION OF
SLAVERY.—GOVERNOR STEWART'S AIM.—GOVERNOR
JACKSON'S UTTERANCES.—THE CONVENTION OF
1861.—LYON AND BLAIR AT ST. LOUIS.—LIBERTY
ARSENAL AND CAMP JACKSON.—THE GOVERNOR
ABANDONS THE CAPITAL.—STERLING PRICE.—THE
FIRST BATTLE.—SKIRMISH AT CARTHAGE.—WIL-
SON'S CREEK.

Governor Stewart was succeeded by Claiborne F. Jackson of
Saline County, who was elected as a Douglas Democrat in 1860.
He received 77,446 votes. Opposed to him were Sample Orr, a
"Know-Nothing," who received 64,583 votes, and Hancock Jack-
son, a Breckenridge Democrat, who received 6,135 votes.

Public feeling was at unrest, for the agitation of the abolition
of negro slavery had stirred the people as nothing before had ever
done. The North and South were divided, and secession from the
Union was urged in slave states, that the people therein might hold
their property in peace, for slaves were valuable chattels. Others
advised arbitration and the perpetuation of the Union.

The fugitive slave law did much to aggravate the troubles.
This law gave the owner of a fugitive slave the right to pursue the
fugitive into any state and take him out without any verdict of
court. In the celebrated Dred Scott decision the supreme court
said this law was constitutional.

As a result of this decision, the legislatures of a number of
Northern states passed laws nullifying the fugitive slave law, and
the United States authorities found themselves powerless. At this
assertion of state's rights on the part of the Northern states, the
Southern states argued that if the Northern states could nullify one
law of the Union, the Southern states could, by application of the
same principle, nullify all of the laws of the Union and withdraw
from the Union entirely.

In the presidential campaign of 1860 the Breckenridge party
declared if the Republican party (which had come into existence in
1856, after the passing of the Whig party) were successful at the
polls, the Southern states would withdraw from the Union. Abraham Lincoln was elected, and subsequent events show how the
Southern states made good their threat. Missouri was the only
state that gave Stephen A. Douglas its electoral vote.

When the Southern states seceded, in 1860, Missouri was confronted with a grave problem, being at the time the most populous
of the slave-holding states. Governor Stewart, who was then retiring from office, sincerely desired to keep Missouri in the Union, but

he was opposed to forcing the seceded states back into the Union and was opposed to Missouri's taking part in such a project; so also, was he opposed to the introduction of troops, either to force Missouri out of the Union or to keep her in.

Governor Jackson, though he had been elected as a Douglas Democrat, now expressed different views. "The destiny of the slave-holding states is one and inseparable," he declared in his inaugural, "and Missouri," he concluded, "will, in my opinion, best consult her own interests, and the interests of the whole country by a timely determination to stand by her sister states." Lieutenant Governor Reynolds, who presided over the senate, favored secession, because he believed it impossible for Missouri to preserve an "armed neutrality."

A bill providing for a state convention to consider what position Missouri should take with regard to secession was passed by the legislature soon after it convened. This convention met at St. Louis on the last day of February, 1861.

In the election of delegates the people had divided into three parties—Secessionists, Conditional Union men and Unconditional Union men. Governor Jackson, Lieutenant-Governor Reynolds, Senators Polk and Green and ex-Senator David R. Atchison led the Secessionists. Judge Hamilton R. Gamble of St. Louis, Alexander W. Doniphan, Sterling Price and ex-Governor Stewart led the Conditional Union men. They were for union, provided the federal government would not attempt to force the seceded states back and attempt to coerce them into submission. The Unconditional Union men were for the Union, come what might, and they were in favor of forcing the seceded states back into the Union. They were led by Frank P. Blair of St. Louis, Judge Fagg of Pike County, Arnold Krekel of St. Charles, General John D. Stephenson of Franklin County, and Sam Breckenridge of St. Louis, and were most ardently supported by the German-Americans of the state.

Sterling Price presided over the convention. Buchanan County was represented by ex-Governor Stewart, ex-Congressman Willard P. Hall and Robert W. Donnell. Secession was defeated, the convention declaring that there was "no adequate cause to compel Missouri to dissolve the connection with the federal Union." The convention perpetuated itself, after a session of twenty-three days, by adjourning subject to the call of the executive committee.

A measure making provision for arming the state militia was defeated in the legislature, and that body adjourned without making arrangements for war. In fact, neither war nor armed neutrality were desired by the people.

When Fort Sumter fell, on April 13, 1861, President Lincoln called for 75,000 troops. In response to a requisition for four regiments, Governor Jackson replied that Missouri would not furnish a man to "carry on an unholy crusade upon the seceded states."

In the meantime Captain Nathaniel Lyon and Francis P. Blair were preparing for trouble at St. Louis. Captain Lyon, a West Point graduate, had enlisted and drilled five regiments and armed them from the St. Louis arsenal. General Frost, who had returned with 700 state troops from the Kansas troubles, was quartered at the edge of St. Louis, in Camp Jackson.

When the call for troops came Lyon and Blair were to a considerable extent prepared for business. Under a special order from the Secretary of War to enroll ten thousand loyal citizens of St. Louis and vicinity, five new regiments were formed, known as the "Home Guards." The first five regiments were known as Missouri Volunteers. Of the ten regiments, nine were made up largely of German-Americans.

There was a government arsenal about four miles south of Liberty, in Clay County. It was in charge of Major Nathaniel Grant and two other men and contained about 11,000 pounds of powder, about 1,500 guns and twenty or thirty small cannon. On April 20, 1861, two hundred men, under Colonel H. L. Routt, most of them from Clay and Jackson counties, quietly took possession of this arsenal, without interruption. The guns and ammunition were removed, some of the supplies being brought to St. Joseph and ultimately reaching the Confederate army. General Lyon drove through Camp Jackson, disguised in female attire, and convinced himself that some of the supplies had been brought there. He had been hoping for an opportunity to break up General Frost's command, and lost no time in setting about his work.

Camp Jackson was attacked on May 10th, and General Frost surrendered without a struggle. It was a case of 700 to 7,000, and he did the best he could. General Lyon's troops were frightened by a mob of citizens while returning with their prisoners, and fired several volleys into the crowd, leaving some forty people dead and wounded in the streets.

General Harney, who was in command at St. Louis, justified the attack upon Camp Jackson, but many people disagreed with him, and the breach between the Union and Secession classes was at once widened. Among those who differed with General Harney was General Price, who now offered his services to Governor Jackson for what he declared to be in defense of the state, and he was at once appointed major-general of the Missouri state guards.

On June 11, 1861, Governor Jackson and General Lyon met in a conference at St. Louis to agree, if possible, upon a plan for the restoration of order. No agreement was reached, however, after five hours, and General Lyon, who was an impetuous man, suddenly broke up the conference and gave the governor an hour to get ready to be conducted out of his lines.

General Jackson hastened to Jefferson City and issued a proclamation, calling for fifty thousand volunteers "for the purpose of repelling the attack that has been made on the state, and for the protection of the lives, liberties and property of her citizens." On the following day he and General Price, together with the state officers and state papers, left for Boonville.

Here the first battle of the rebellion in Missouri was fought, on June 17, 1861, between the forces of General Lyon and Colonel John

S. Marmaduke, resulting in a victory for Lyon. Marmaduke had two killed and five wounded, while Lyon's loss was two killed and nine wounded.

Jackson retreated southward with an army of 7,000 men, so poorly organized and wretchedly equipped that it was little better than a mob. At Carthage General Sigel was encountered, with a loss to Jackson of ten killed and sixty-one wounded, and to Sigel of thirteen killed and thirty-one wounded; but Jackson carried the day and Sigel retreated to Sarcoxie.

Governor Jackson went to Memphis and induced Governor Polk to send General Pillow with 6,000 men to Missouri, but General Fremont checked this invasion at Bird's Point, on the Mississippi. It was planned that Pillow should co-operate with General Jeff Thompson, who had gone from St. Joseph.

However, Price received aid from McCulloch and Pearce, who were stationed in the Indian Territory. On August 10, 1861, was fought the terrific battle of Wilson's Creek. Lyon was at Springfield and Price and McCulloch were pressing him. He felt that his only chance was to turn and fight. The armies met nine miles southeast of Springfield. A hill that rises from the ford of Wilson's Creek was the scene of action, and this has since been known as "Bloody Hill." Of the 5,400 Union men who took part in the fight 1,317 officers and men were killed, wounded or missing. General Lyon was killed, and every Union brigadier-general and colonel engaged on Bloody Hill was either killed or wounded, and the defeated Union forces were led off by a major. The total loss to the Confederate and state troops was 1,230 killed, wounded and missing.

Price pleaded with McCulloch to follow up the attack, but McCulloch argued that he was a Confederate officer, in command of a Confederate army; that he had been stationed in Arkansas to defend the Indian Territory; that it was his duty to defend, not to attack; that he had aided in repelling General Lyon because Lyon was about to invade the Indian Territory; that having done this, his mission was ended. Price was unable to alone follow the retreating troops, and before he could undertake it the Union army had increased to many times larger than his own.

CHAPTER IV.

SECOND SESSION OF THE CONVENTION.—HAMILTON R. GAMBLE MADE GOVERNOR, WILLIARD P. HALL, SR., LIEUTENANT-GOVERNOR, AND MORDECAI OLIVER SECRETARY OF STATE.—BATTLE OF LEXINGTON.— GOVERNOR JACKSON CONVENES THE LEGISLATURE AT NEOSHO.—SENATORS AND REPRESENTATIVES TO THE CONFEDERATE STATES CONGRESS.—BATTLE OF PEA RIDGE.—PRICE'S RAID.—LAWRENCE MASSACRE AND ORDER NO. 11.—McNEILL AT PALMYRA AND ANDERSON AT CENTRALIA.

The convention which had met at St. Louis in March and adjourned subject to call, met at Jefferson City on July 22, 1861. General Robert Wilson of Andrew County, who at that time lived on his farm at "Jimtown," three miles northeast of St. Joseph. was elected president in the place of Sterling Price. The convention declared the offices of governor, lieutenant-governor and secretary of state vacant, and selected Hamilton R. Gamble of St. Louis to succeed Governor Jackson. Willard P. Hall of St. Joseph was elected to succeed Lieutenant-Governor Reynolds, and Mordecai Oliver of Springfield was appointed secretary of state. The convention also declared vacant the seats in the legislature, and for seventeen months it exercised the duties of the general assembly.

The next battle of importance in Missouri was fought at Lexington, where Price besieged General James Mulligan, commanding three thousand men, one-half from Missouri and the other half comprising the "Irish Brigade" of Chicago. After fifty-two hours, Mulligan surrendered.

Governor Jackson issued a proclamation at New Madrid declaring the independence of Missouri. He also issued a call for the general assembly to meet October 1, 1861, at Neosho. The legislature, or a part of it, at least, met and declared that Missouri had withdrawn from the Union. John B. Clark, Sr., and R. L. Y. Peyton were elected senators to the Confederate States senate. Senator Peyton was succeeded by George G. Vest. Eight members of the lower house were also elected. The Confederate Congress, which met at Richmond, Va., recognized these proceedings and admitted Missouri to the Confederacy. But the United States Congress recognized the convention in all future dealings, and thus Missouri remained a Union state.

Governor Jackson went south after this and died at Little Rock, December 6, 1862. Thomas C. Reynolds, his lieutenant-governor, continued to act, however, in dispute of the right of Governor Gamble, until the election of Governor Fletcher in 1864. But.

he was governor in name only. He was killed by falling through an elevator shaft at St. Louis, March 30, 1887.

The next important battle in which Missouri figured was at Pea Ridge, in Arkansas, about thirty miles from Cassville, Mo. Price, McCulloch and Pike had a combined force of 20,000 men, who were placed under the command of General Van Dorn. The Federal forces were under Curtis. It was a desperate battle, skillfully fought on both sides, and continued for three days. Victory finally fell to the Federals. Over thirteen hundred men were killed or wounded on either side. Generals McCulloch, McIntosh and Slack fell, and Price was wounded. After this engagement, which opened early in the morning, March 16, 1862, and closed on March 19, Price, with about 5,000 state troops, joined the Confederacy and his command was transferred to the east side of the Mississippi.

The slaughter of ten innocent men by General John H. McNeill at Palmyra on October 8, 1862, is classed as one of the horrors of the civil war. Some of the troops of Colonel Porter, a Secessionist marauder, had captured one Andrew Allsman, a disabled Union soldier, and doubtless put him to death. McNeill notified Porter that if Allsman was not safely returned in ten days he (McNeill) would put to death ten citizens of that section whom he held in captivity at Palmyra upon the suspicion that they were in sympathy with the South. Allsman was not returned and, at the end of ten days, McNeill fulfilled his threat. The ten victims, some of whom were connected with the best families of the community, were taken from the Palmyra prison and placed in wagons, each man sitting upon his coffin. Half a mile east of town they were shot, each victim kneeling beside his coffin.

It is not within the scope of this brief history to present the details of the numerous clashes at arms during the war period; however, some mention of the sacking of Lawrence and General Ewing's consequent "Order No. 11" should be made. But a short digression is necessary.

The border troubles that arose over the Kansas question are well remembered by older people who lived in Platte and Buchanan counties before the war. Both the North and South wished to be triumphant in Kansas, and the Missourians who desired that Kansas be admitted as a slave-holding state took an active part in regulating the affairs of the neighboring territory. In order to carry the state for abolition, Massachusetts sent out men under the auspices of "Emigration Aid Companies," "Kansas Societies," and the like. These men brought more guns and powder than agricultural implements. Missouri formed "Blue Lodges," to counteract the Massachusetts companies.

In 1855 the pro-slavery party elected the territorial legislature in Kansas, and it was charged that 5,000 Missourians had crossed the border from Buchanan, Platte, Jackson and Cass counties. and voted. As a counter charge, the pro-slavery people claimed that a company of immigrants had voted at Lawrence on the day of their arrival. The election of six pro-slavery candidates was contested and sustained by the territorial governor, who gave certificates to the anti-slavery candidates.

But the anti-slavery men were still dissatisfied. They refused to acknowledge the authority of the legislature or to obey its laws. Active troubles now began, and the contending factions soon learned to rob each other, burn each other's houses, and destroy property. The inhabitants of Missouri border counties now began to suffer severely also.

John Brown of Osawatomie instigated raids and headed some of them himself. In one of these raids, made in December of 1858, he carried off eleven slaves. The general assembly of Missouri appropriated $30,000 to be used by Governor Stewart as he thought best. He offered $3,000 as a reward for John Brown, all of whose raids into Missouri were marked with blood.

The efforts put forth by the legislature, the governors of Missouri and Kansas, and the United States army, partially quieted the "Jayhawkers," as these marauders were called, for two years, but in 1860 they broke out afresh, under the leadership of a desperado named James Montgomery. Governor Stewart sent General Frost with 7,000 men to the border, but General Harney of the United States army had preceded him.

Historians declare that the depredations of the "Jayhawkers" and other raids of Kansas troops and freebooters into Missouri led to the destruction of Lawrence by Quantrell and his band of guerrillas on August 21, 1863. Stores, banks, hotels and dwellings were sacked and burned, and one hundred and eighty-three men, women and children were killed. It was a most cruel and inhuman deed, even in warfare.

General Ewing, stationed at Kansas City, issued Order No. 11 on August 25, four days after the massacre. All persons then living in Jackson, Cass and Bates counties, except those dwelling in the principal towns, were ordered to remove from their places of abode within fifteen days. Those who could show that they were loyal were permitted to remove to the military stations or to Kansas. All others were to remove entirely out of these counties. Their grain and hay were to be taken to the nearest military station, where the owners were to be granted certificates showing their value, and all produce not so delivered was to be destroyed. The whole district soon presented a scene of desolation. In 1866, when the inhabitants returned, they found their homes destroyed by fire, with nothing left but the blackened chimneys. Thus did General Ewing square up accounts for the sacking of Lawrence.

That Missouri was the scene of much bloodshed during the war is easily proven by the fact that 450 battles and skirmishes were fought from the time of the capture of Liberty Arsenal until the end of the great struggle. It is estimated that Missouri furnished to Governor Jackson and the Confederate service about 40,000 men. The number of Union enlistments reaches nearly 110,000, of which number about 8,000 were negroes.

That feature of the war in Missouri known as Price's raid began in September of 1864. Price entered Southeastern Missouri with a large force and was making for Jefferson City, where the Union forces from every part of the state were rapidly concentrated to defend the capital. Price evaded Jefferson City, upon information of the formidable resistance to be made there, and moved toward Boonville and Lexington, hotly pursued by Generals A. J. Smith and Pleasanton. At Independence he was defeated by Pleas anton and retreated to Arkansas.

The Centralia massacre, which also lives in history as a war horror, occurred on September 27, 1864. Bill Anderson, a notorious guerilla and a band of two hundred cut-throats, surrounded a train aboard which were some twenty-five Federal soldiers who were on furlough and unarmed. Anderson's men opened fire and the soldiers made desperate efforts to escape, leaving the cars and running, only to be shot down. Some sought protection under the depot platform, others in outhouses and barns, but the ferocious guerillas permitted none to escape. On the same day, in a battle between Major John son's forces and Anderson's band, sixty-eight of Johnson's men were killed. Johnson's forces scattered and were pursued, seventy more being killed by the guerillas before these terrors ended their bloody work. A month later Anderson was killed in Ray County.

CHAPTER V.

LAST SESSION OF THE CONVENTION.—DEATH OF GOV-
ERNOR GAMBLE.—WILLARD P. HALL AS GOVERNOR.
THOMAS C. FLETCHER AS GOVERNOR.—THE DRAKE
CONSTITUTION AND TEST OATH.—GOVERNOR Mc-
CLURG.—THE LIBERAL REPUBLICANS.—B. GRATZ
BROWN FOR GOVERNOR.—REPEAL OF THE TEST
OATH.—GOVERNORS WOODSON AND HARDIN.—THE
NEW CONSTITUTION.—GOVERNORS PHELPS, CRIT-
TENDEN, MARMADUKE, MOREHOUSE, FRANCIS,
STONE AND STEPHENS.

The famous "convention of '61" met for the last time in June
of 1863, and among other work, passed an ordinance providing for
the emancipation of slaves after July 4, 1870. This was accomplished earlier, however, by another method, as will be seen below.
The convention adjourned *sine die* on July 1, 1863.

Governor Gamble died on January 21, 1864, and Lieutenant-
Governor Hall of St. Joseph became governor and served about one
year, when he yielded to Thomas C. Fletcher, the first Republican
governor elected in Missouri, who had received 71, 531 votes, over
Thomas L. Price, Democrat. Mr. Fletcher was born in Jefferson
County, Mo., January 22, 1827, and was serving as brigadier-
general under Sherman in Georgia when elected. At the same
time Francis Rodman of St. Joseph was elected secretary of state.
He served six years.

At the election of 1864 the people had voted for a convention to
amend the constitution, and sixty-six delegates were elected. These
delegates met in the Merchants' Library Hall at St. Louis in January of 1865, and adopted what is known in history as the "Drake
Constitution," from the fact that Charles D. Drake was the leading
spirit in the convention and practically the author of the law.

This convention, on January 11, 1865, passed an ordinance
abolishing slavery. Governor Fletcher did not wait to have this
ratified, but on the following day issued a proclamation that "hence-
forth and forever no person shall be subject to any abridgement of
liberty, except such as the law shall prescribe for the common
good, or know any master but God." Buchanan County was not
directly represented in this convention. Each senatorial district
was entitled to two representatives. This county was then in the
twelfth senatorial district, composed of Buchanan, De Kalb, Gentry and Worth counties. Dr. L. H. Weatherby, of De Kalb, and
Eli Smith, of Worth County, represented the district in the convention.

The Drake constitution soon became odious because of the

test oath, which declared that no person should vote or hold off
who had "ever" engaged in hostilities or given aid, comfort, cou
tenance or support to persons engaged in hostilities against t
governmnt of the United States," etc. By this oath one-half of t
people were prevented from voting until 1872, and many mc
doubtless would have been had they told the truth.

In 1868 Joseph McClurg of Camden County, Republican, c
feated John S. Phelps of Springfield, Democrat, for governor,
19,000, out of a total vote of 145,000. E. O. Stannard of St. Lou
was elected lieutenant-governor. Under the Drake constitution t
term of office of the governor was two years.

In 1870 an effort was made to have a new constitution. T
Republican party was divided upon the subject into "Liberal" a
"Radical" factions. The liberal element believed in repealing t
test oath, and the radicals declared for its perpetuation. The latt
nominated Governor McClurg for re-election. The liberals wit
drew from the convention and nominated B. Gratz Brown of ,
Louis, who was elected by 41,000 majority. The people voted
repeal the test oath by a majority of 111,000. At the same time t
Liberal Republicans and Democrats obtained control of the legisl
ture. As soon as possible all obnoxious laws were repealed and
disabilities removed, as a result of which the vote in 1872 w
112,276 greater than in 1870.

When confidence had been restored an era of prosperity f
lowed, and on every side the people began to efface the traces of t
war. The Liberal Republican movement, which began in 187
continued until 1874. In 1872 the Liberal Republicans and Dem
crats met in convention at Jefferson City. The Democrats non
nated Silas Woodson of St. Joseph for governor; also candidat
for treasurer, attorney-general and auditor and eight of the pre
dential electors. The Liberals nominated Charles P. Johnson of S
Louis for lieutenant-governor, candidates for secretary of stat
register of the land office and seven presidential electors. Th
ticket was elected and the entire electoral vote cast for Greeley a
Brown. The regular Republicans had nominated John B. Hende
son for governor.

In 1874 the Democrats nominated Charles H. Hardin
Audrain County for governor and Norman J. Colman of St. Lou
for lieutenant-governor. The Republicans did not make any nor
inations, but William Gentry of Pettis County was nominated b
the People's party, which had grown out of the Granger movemen
This party was organized on the basis that nearly all of the fina
cial troubles that followed the crash of 1873 were due to bad legi
lation, and its mission was to unite farmers, laborers and mecha
ics in an attempt to repeal all bad laws and make good ones. Bu
Governor Woodson's administration had forestalled the Grange
by passing the desired laws and cutting down expenses. Governc
Hardin was elected by a majority of 37,463.

At the same election the people voted for a constitutional co
vention. James C. Roberts was elected to represent Buchana

County in this convention, which met at the Capitol May 15, 1875. The new constitution went into operation on January 1, 1876. By this constitution the terms of the governor and nearly all of the state officers and many of the county officers were lengthened to four years.

In 1876 John S. Phelps of Springfield and Henry C. Brockmeyer of St. Louis were elected governor and lieutenant-governor by 50,000 majority over G. A. Finkelnburg of St. Louis. At the same time Colonel Elijah Gates of St. Joseph was elected state treasurer.

In 1880 Thomas T. Crittenden, Democrat, of Warrensburg, was elected governor, over D. P. Dyer of St. Louis, Republican. Robert A. Campbell of St. Louis was elected lieutenant-governor. Under the last Cleveland administration ex-Governor Crittenden was consul-general at the City of Mexico. It was during his administration that the James and Younger bandits, who had made Western Missouri infamous for some years, were broken up, Jesse James being killed in St. Joseph by Bob and Charley Ford, who were soon afterward pardoned by the governor.

In 1884 John S. Marmaduke of St. Louis, Democrat, was elected governor, and Albert P. Morehouse of Maryville was elected lieutenant-governor. The Republicans nominated ex-Congressman Nicholas Ford, who at that time lived in Andrew County. During Governor Marmaduke's administration St. Joseph became a city of the second class, and he appointed the first local board of police commissioners.

Governor Marmaduke died on December 28, 1887, and Lieutenant-Governor Morehouse served the unexpired term. Ex-Governor Morehouse committed suicide at his home in Maryville September 31, 1891.

In 1888 David R. Francis, Democrat, of St. Louis was elected over E. E. Kimball of Nevada. Stephen Claycomb of Jasper County was elected lieutenant-governor. William J. Stone, Democrat, of Nevada, was elected governor in 1892, over Major William Warner of Kansas City, Republican. John B. O'Meara of St. Louis was elected lieutenant-governor. Lon V. Stephens of Boonville, the elected lieutenant-governor. Lon V. Stephens of Boonville, who had been state treasurer under Governors Francis and Stone, was elected governor in 1896, over Robert E. Lewis of Henry County. August H. Bolte of Franklin County was elected lieutenant-governor. Alexander M. Dockery was elected governor in 1900; Joseph W. Folk in 1904; Herbert S. Hadley in 1908, and Elliott W. Major in 1912.

CHAPTER VI.

MISSOURI'S REPRESENTATIVES IN THE UNITED STAT] SENATE FROM BENTON AND BARTON TO THE PRE ENT.—FIRST MEMBERS OF THE LOWER HOUSE (CONGRESS.—MEMBERS WHO HAVE REPRESENTI THE DISTRICT TO WHICH BUCHANAN COUNTY W/ ATTACHED FROM HALL (1846) TO COCHRAN (1898). STATE SENATORS FROM VARIOUS DISTRICTS 1 WHICH BUCHANAN COUNTY HAS BEEN ATTACHE SINCE 1840.—BUCHANAN COUNTY'S REPRESENT TIVES IN THE LEGISLATURE FROM 1840 TO TE PRESENT TIME.

The first two men to represent Missouri in the United Stat senate were David Barton of Howard County, who served 1820-£ and Thomas H. Benton of St. Louis, who served 1820-51. Th were elected by the legislature, which met in its first session at £ Louis in September of 1820, but were not permitted to take the seats until 1821, because the state was not yet formally admitt into the Union.

Mr. Barton was a native of Tennessee and a soldier of the w of 1812. He was quite a popular public man in the state wh elected, but during his last term lost prestige because of his pref ence of John Quincy Adams over General Jackson for the pre dency, General Jackson being a great favorite with the Missou ans. He was stricken with insanity and died at Boonville in 183

Senator Benton was not elected without opposition, because a difficulty he had had with Andrew Jackson, who attempted horsewhip Benton in the streets of Nashville, and was shot in t arm by Benton's brother. Benton afterwards killed Charles Luc. at that time United States attorney for Missouri, in a duel, a was regarded by many as a murderer. He served thirty years, a became unpopular because of his domineering disposition. He re resented St. Louis one term in Congress in 1852-54, and was c feated for re-election by Luther M. Kennett, a Know-Nothing.] then made an independent effort to become governor, and was al defeated. He was a man of strong character; in fact, one of t remarkable men of the nation.

Senator Barton was succeeded by Alexander Buckner of Ca Girardeau, who served 1830-33, and died of cholera. Govern Dunklin appointed Dr. Lewis F. Linn of Ste. Genevieve to t vacancy, who served until 1843, and died in office. Dr. Linn wa most useful man to Missouri, and it was largely through his effo that the Platte purchase was made. Upon his death Governor R nolds appointed Judge David R. Atchison of Platte County, w was at that time judge of the Twelfth Judicial Circuit and w held court regularly in Robidoux's store and at the house of Richard Hill, in Buchanan County.

Senator Benton was succeeded in 1851 by Henry S. Geyer of St. Louis. Senator Geyer was a Marylander, who came to Missouri in 1815, and who was speaker of the House for the first five years after the admission of Missouri into the Union. He was a famous lawyer and did much to systematize the Missouri code. He was the only avowed Whig ever elected to the United States senate from Missouri. He died in 1859.

In 1855 the legislature ballotted in vain for a successor to Senator Atchison, and the election went over to the next session. In 1857 there were successors to both Senators Atchison and Geyer to choose. Governor Trusten Polk and James S. Green of Lewis County were elected.

Governor Polk was a native of Delaware and a graduate of Yale College. In 1862 he was expelled for disloyalty, and died in St. Louis in 1876. James S. Green was a Virginian, and a strong state's rights man. He was a powerful debater and had few peers. He, like Polk, was expelled in 1861 for secession utterances.

Waldo P. Johnson of Osceola, St. Clair County, was elected to succeed Senator Green. He cast his lot with the South and resigned his seat soon after taking it.

Lieutenant-Governor Hall of St. Joseph, who was acting for Governor Gamble, appointed J. B. Henderson of Pike County and Robert Wilson of Andrew to fill the vacancies. In November of 1863 the legislature elected Mr. Henderson to serve until March 4, 1869, and elected B. Gratz Brown for a term expiring March 4, 1867. Senator Brown was elected governor in 1870 and served two years. In 1872 he was a candidate for Vice-President with Horace Greeley.

Charles D. Drake, the author of the Drake constitution, was elected to succeed Senator Brown. He served until 1871, when he resigned to become judge of the court of claims at Washington, and was succeeded by Daniel F. Jewett of St. Louis, who served one year, and who was in turn succeeded by General Frank P. Blair, who served out the remainder of the term, until 1873.

Carl Schurz was elected to succeed Senator Henderson for a term of six years, 1869-75. He was succeeded by Francis M. Cockrell of Johnson County, who has succeeded himself continuously until 1905, when he was succeeded by William A. Warner. James A. Reed followed Warner in 1911 and is still serving.

Lewis V. Bogy of St. Louis was elected to succeed Senator Blair and served 1873-77, dying in office. Governor Phelps appointed David H. Armstrong of St. Louis to serve until the legislature met. The legislature elected General James Shields of Carroll County for the unexpired term, and George Graham Vest of Warrensburg for the full term. Vest was succeeded in 1903 by William J. Stone.

* * *

Up to 1845 the congressmen from Missouri were elected at

large. The last member from this section under the old syste
was James M. Hughes of Clay County, a nephew of General Andre
S. Hughes and the father of Mrs. Calvin F. Burnes of St. Josep

The first man to be elected when the state was divided in
districts was Willard P. Hall. This was then, as now, the Fourt
Congressional district, though it has undergone several transform
tions since the first organization.

General Hall was the regular Democratic nominee in 1846, ar
against him was pitted James H. Birch of Clinton County, a bri
liant man, but one who vacillated politically. Judge Birch was tl
independent candidate. General Hall, who was plain Willard i
those days, left the campaign to take care of itself and went wit
General Doniphan's expedition to Mexico. The people liked h
spirit and patriotism, and elected him in his absence.

After serving two terms, General Hall was succeeded by Mo:
decai Oliver, a Whig, who was then living at Richmond. Judg
Oliver was afterward secretary of state, and in 1884-6 served a
police judge in St. Joseph.

In the Thirty-fifth and Thirty-sixth Congresses (1857-61) th
Fourth District was represented by General James Craig, Dem(
crat, of St. Joseph. Judge Elijah H. Norton of Platte Count)
Democrat, succeeded General Craig and served one term.

The state had meanwhile been redistricted and St. Joseph wa
in the Seventh Congressional District. General Ben F. Loan o
St. Joseph, Republican, represented the district in the Thirt
eighth, Thirty-ninth and Fortieth Congresses (1863-69).

In the Forty-first Congress (1869-71) the district was repr
sented by Hon. Joel F. Asper, Republican, of Livingston County.

Judge Isaac C. Parker, Republican, of St. Joseph represent
the district in the Forty-second and Forty-third Congress
(1871-75). During the last term of Congressman Parker the sta
was again redistricted and Buchanan County fell into the Nint
Congressional District.

Judge Parker was succeeded by Judge David Rea, Democra
of Andrew County, who served two terms (1875-79). Hon. Nicl
olas Ford, Greenback, of Andrew County, succeeded Judge Re
defeating General Craig, and served two terms (1879-83).

In 1881 the state was again redistricted and the entire Plat
Purchase—Platte, Buchanan, Andrew, Holt, Nodaway and Atch
son counties—formed into the Fourth Congressional District. Tl
first man to represent the new district was the late James ,
Burnes, Democrat, who defeated Morris A. Reed of St. Josep
Republican, and Nathaniel Sisson of Maryville, Greenback-Labc
in November of 1882, by a majority of 569. In 1884 Colonel Burn
defeated Judge Henry S. Kelly, Republican, then of Andre
County, by 2,176 votes. In 1886 Colonel Burnes defeated Byr
A. Dunn of Maryville, Republican, by 3,087 votes. In 1888 Colon
Burnes defeated H. R. W. Hartwig of St. Joseph, Republican,
3,177 votes.

Colonel Burnes died January 24, 1889, at Washington.

had yet to serve his unexpired term in the Fiftieth Congress. Governor Francis ordered a special election to be held February 21, 1889, to fill the vacancy in the Fiftieth Congress and also for the election of a successor to Colonel Burnes in the Fifty-first Congress. The Republicans nominated Francis M. Posegate of St. Joseph for both places. The Democrats nominated Charles F. Booher of Savannah for the short term and Robert P. C. Wilson of Platte County for the long term. Captain Posegate was defeated by 618 votes. Mr. Booher served only about two weeks.

In 1890 Mr. Wilson defeated Nicholas Ford, Republican, of Andrew County, and W. H. Whipple, Populist, of Buchanan County, receiving a majority of 1,118. In 1892 Daniel D. Burnes, Democrat, defeated George C. Crowther, Republican, of St. Joseph, and J. B. Wilcox, Populist, of Andrew County, receiving a majority of 1,259. In 1894 Mr. Crowther defeated William C. Ellison of Maryville, Democrat, and William S. Missemer of St. Joseph, Populist, his majority being 1,661. In 1896 Charles F. Cochran of St. Joseph, Democrat, defeated Mr. Crowther, his plurality being 3,829. Frank B. Fulkerson, of St. Joseph, was elected in 1904, and Charles F. Booher, of Savannah, the present incumbent, in 1906.

* * *

The act authorizing the creation of Buchanan County attached it to the Twelfth State Senatorial District, which was represented at that time by Cornelius Gillam and James T. V. Thompson. Subsequently Buchanan County was a part of the Tenth District, which, in 1842, was represented by Cornelius Gillam, and in 1844 by Jesse B. Thompson. In 1846 it was part of the Seventh District and was represented by Robert M. Stewart, who served until 1858 and was succeeded by John Scott. Buchanan County was then in the Twelfth District. Senator Scott was succeeded in 1862 by Colonel John Severance, who in 1864 was succeeded by J. N. Young. Colonel Thomas Harbine succeeded Senator Young, the county having meanwhile become part of the Second District. Senator Harbine served until 1871, and was succeeded by Daniel Ransom, who served one term, and was succeeded in 1875 by Waller Young, who also served one term. Ahira Manring of DeKalb County succeeded Senator Young and served two terms. In 1882 Randolph T. Davis was elected and resigned, his unexpired term being filled by Waller Young, who was succeeded in 1886 by Michael G. Moran. Senator Moran was succeeded in 1890 by Charles F. Cochran, who served four years and was succeeded by Arthur W. Brewster in 1894. William H. Haynes was elected in 1898, Lawrence A. Vories in 1902, Charles H. Mayer in 1906, Thomas J. Lysaght in 1910, James A. Campbell in 1914. During Senator Cochran's term the state was redistricted and Buchanan County now constitutes the Twelfth District alone. The senatorial term is four years.

* * *

The first man to represent Buchanan County in the house was Jesse B. Thompson, who served 1840-44. The second was Richard

Roberts, who served 1844-46. Then came James B. Gardenhirc. who served two years, and was followed by John Bretz, who served until 1850.

Buchanan County was now entitled to two representatives, and Henry S. Tutt and Sinclair K. Miller were elected. In 1852 A. J. Vaughan and E. F. Dixon were the representatives, each serving one term. Then came Wellington A. Cunningham and W. J. Everett, who served in the session of 1854. In the session of 1856 Buchanan County was represented by John Bretz and Alexander Davis, and in the session of 1858 and the special session of 1859 by Cornelius Day and Alexander Davis. In the session of 1860 J. C. Roberts and J. H. Ashbaugh were representatives; in 1862 J. L. Bittinger and Robert Brierly. In 1864 Buchanan County was represented by Robert Brierly and Joseph Thompson.

Three years elapsed between the Twenty-third and Twenty-fourth general assemblies, and when the latter met in 1867 Buchanan County was represented by Charles B. Wilkinson and Washington Bennett, who were succeeded in the session of 1867 by Samuel Hays and Oscar Kirkham. In the session of 1871 our representatives were J. L. Bittinger and William Randall, and in the following two sessions, in 1873 and 1875, they were J. L. Bittinger and W. S. Wells of Rushville.

For the Twenty-ninth general assembly, which met in 1877, Buchanan County elected three representatives—W. S. Wells, George W. Sutherland and Dr. E. A. Donelan. In the session of 1879 our representatives were Thomas Crowther, John T. Riley and John Saunders. The session of 1881 found Dr. Donelan, John T. Riley and Benjamin J. Woodson representing Buchanan County, and the following session, 1883, Alex D. Vories, Michael G. Moran and A. A. Whittington. In the session of 1885 our representatives were William H. Haynes, Dr. Donelan and William S. Wells; in the session of 1887, William H. Haynes, Dr. Donelan and G. W. Johnson; in 1889, Waller Young, Abraham Davis and B. F. Stuart; in 1891, Abraham Davis, Dr. E. A. Donelan and B. F. Stuart; in 1893, Abraham Davis, Granville G. Adkins and B. F. Stuart; in 1895, John L. Bittinger, James Moran and Oliver P. Smith; in 1897, John L. Bittinger, Joseph A. Piner and James Shewmaker; in 1899, W. K. Amick, Joseph A. Piner and James P. Shewmaker; in 1901, R. M. Abercrombie, W. S. Connor, Albert B. Duncan. Beginning with the session of 1903, Buchanan County had four representatives: Charles S. Shepherd, John G. Parkinson, Albert B. Duncan, W. S. Connor; 1905, Joseph Albus John L. Bittinger, Charles H. Watts, W. S. Connor; 1907, E. L. Hart, Richard D. Garvey, W. S. Connor, W. H. Sherman; 1909, E. L. Hart, Dr. U. G. Crandall, H. C. Yates, W. H. Sherman; 1911, W. S. Willard, John E. Webster, H. C. Yates, George T. Claiborne; 1913, Phillip McCollum, E. N. Peterson, Jacob L. Bretz, George T. Claiborne; 1915, Phillip McCollum, Frank J. Staedtler, Jacob L. Bretz, Jack D. Robinson.

CHAPTER VII.

THE STATE CAPITAL—SOME FIRST THINGS IN MISSOURI —LEWIS AND CLARK—NEW MDRID EARTHQUAKE— DANIEL BOONE — CHOLERA — IMPRISONMENT FOR DEBT—GASCONADE BRIDGE DISASTER—RAILROAD BONDS AND STATE AID—IOWA BOUNDARY LINE— "IMPERIAL MISSOURI."

The first seat of government of the State of Missouri was at St. Louis. In 1821 the capital was changed to St. Charles, but this was not satisfactory, for immigration was pushing to the broad prairies of the west. By a revision of the constitution it was provided that the capital be located on the Missouri River, within forty miles of the mouth of the Osage. A commission was appointed and after examining many localities, they decided upon the spot where Jefferson City now stands. The town was named after Thomas Jefferson, the third President of the United States. The capitol was located upon four sections of land donated by the United States government. It was large enough to meet the needs of the state at the time, and stood until 1837, when it was destroyed by fire. The legislature met in the new state building in 1826. The oldest portion of the second capitol was erected after the destruction of the original building. This structure was destroyed by fire February 5, 1911. A new state capitol to cost $3,500,000 is now being built.

* * *

The following are some of the first things that occurred in Missouri: The first marriage took place April 20, 1766, at St. Louis. The first baptism was performed in May, 1776, at St. Louis. The first house of worship (Catholic) was erected in 1775 at St. Louis. The first ferry was established in 1805 on the Mississippi River at St. Louis. The first newspaper was established in 1808. This was the Missouri Gazette, and the St. Louis Republic represents the perpetuation of this pioneer in journalism. The first postoffice was established at St. Louis in 1804, with Rufus Easton as postmaster. The first Protestant church (Baptist) was erected at Ste. Genevieve in 1806. The first bank was established at St. Louis in 1814. It was called the Bank of St. Louis. The first college was built at St. Louis in 1814. The first market house was opened at St. Louis in 1811. The first steamboat on the Upper Mississippi River was the General Pike, which landed at St. Louis in 1817. The first steamboat that came up the Missouri River was the Independence, which touched at Franklin in 1819. The first court house was erected at

St. Louis in 1823. The first line of telegraph reached St. Louis December 20, 1847.

* * *

Lewis and Clark, the explorers, began their ascent of the Missouri River in May of 1804. Captain Meriwether Lewis and Willilam Clark were accompanied by forty-three men and a servant. The party stopped off frequently and explored the surrounding country, collected information concerning the Indians, the soil, the tributaries to the rivers, etc.

* * *

The earthquake that destroyed New Madrid occurred after midnight of December 16, 1811. By this terrific convulsion vast tracts of land were plunged into the Mississippi River, large lakes were made in an instant, trees split in the middle, great fissures were formed where the earth had burst, and hundreds of them remained for years afterward. After the earthquake the country about New Madrid exhibited a melancholy aspect. Congress enacted laws permitting the earthquake sufferers to locate the same amount of lands in other parts of the territory, but owing to their ignorance of the ways of the world many of them were cheated out of their claims by unscrupulous speculators.

* * *

Daniel Boone, the famous pioneer, came to Missouri in 1794 and settled forty-five miles north of St. Louis in what is now Warren County. He spent most of his latter days with his son, Major Nathan Boone, in St. Charles County. He died September 26, 1820, aged eighty-eight years. In 1845 both his body and that of his wife were disinterred and taken to Frankfort, Ky. Boone had two sons, Nathan and Daniel M., who, like their father, were noted for their courage and enterprise. They were among the first to manufacture salt, building furnaces at what was afterward called Boone's Lick, in what is now Howard County. Wonderful salt springs existed there, and the Boones brought kettles in which the water was evaporated and the salt retained. The country about Boone's Lick was settled rapidly when the fame of the salt spring and the beauty of the locality became known.

* * *

Asiatic cholera appeared at St. Louis in 1832, and for a time the death rate averaged thirty-two per day. When it finally disappeared a reckoning showed that one out of every twelve of the population had fallen a victim. In the spring of 1849 it appeared again, and between April and August 4,060 persons died. In 1850 and 1851, and again in 1867, there was cholera at various points along the Missouri and Mississippi Rivers. St. Joseph had but little of it, while Weston and other points farther down suffered more severely. Those who were crossing the plains and Indians along the trails fell victims in large numbers.

* * *

Imprisonment for debt was permissible under the statutes of

Bird's Eye View of St. Joseph

Missouri until 1843. The enforcement of this worked great hardships and created much dissatisfaction. There were but few things that the sheriff could not sell for debt, and if there was not enough to satisfy the avaricious creditor, he could have the unfortunate debtor cast into prison. The act abolishing the law was written by Governor Reynolds. It contained but six words: "Imprisonment for debt is hereby abolished." Yet those few words brought great joy to all but the unscrupulous creditor.

* * *

On November 1, 1855, there occurred the first railroad wreck in the history of Missouri. The completion of the Missouri Pacific railroad from St. Louis to Jefferson City was being celebrated and an excursion train of nine cars crowded with notables was speeding to the capital. The bridge spanning the Gasconade River was not completed and a temporary scaffolding had been erected. A furious storm was raging while the train was crossing this bridge, and, amid the fiercest lightning and thunder, the timbers of the temporary structure parted and several cars went down. Forty-three lives were lost and many persons were injured.

* * *

The Drake constitution permitted counties to subscribe any sum of money to aid in building railroads, and county courts were authorized to issue bonds binding the county for the payment of these subscriptions wherever two-thirds of the qualified voters should assent thereto. These courts, in some cases, were characterless or ignorant men, and the "qualified" voters were not the people who owned property and who had to shoulder the burden. Bonds to the amount of over $15,000,000 were issued by various counties. In some instances the roads were not built, only a few miles being graded. But the bonds were marketed in New York and passed into the hands of the "innocent purchaser" as soon as possible. The county courts of Lafayette, Cass, Knox and St. Clair Counties refused to pay such bonds at maturity, but the United States court held that they were legally issued and must be paid. The people of Cass and St. Clair Counties were particularly stubborn in their opposition, and are to this day. County judges are firm upon this issue and cheerfully go to jail rather than levy taxes for the payment of these bonds.

* * *

At different times prior to the war the state had granted aid to various railroad companies by issuing bonds to the amount of $23,701,000. For this aid the companies agreed to pay interest. During and soon after the war the Missouri Pacific, the Iron Mountain, the North Missouri, and what was then the Kansas City, St. Joseph & Council Bluffs road, now the Burlington system, from St. Joseph to Weston, were sold for non-payment of interest on these bonds. The entire debt at the time of the sale was over $31,000,-000, and the state realized from the various sales only about $8,000,000, thus leaving a deficit of $23,000,000, which the state had to pay, besides several millions in interest.

The contest over the boundary line between Iowa and Missouri, which was settled by the supreme court of the United States in 1845, was due to a mistake on the part of John Sullivan, the United States surveyor, who ran the lines. Missouri claimed that the northern border should be a parallell of the latitude which passed through the rapids of the Des Moines River, and Iowa claimed it should be a line which passed through the rapids of the Mississippi River, some twenty miles south. Unfriendly and revengeful feelings grew out of the dispute between the people who resided on the borders. Sullivan, the surveyor, began on a meridian one hundred miles north of Kansas City, and, instead of running due east, varied to the north, having varied four miles when he reached the Des Moines River. The United States had recognized Sullivan's survey in a number of Indian treaties, and now held that it should be forever the dividing line, and Missouri lost a strip of territory ten miles wide from the northern line.

* * *

Having briefly sketched the history of Missouri from its beginning, it will be appropriate to quote from the 1915 Report of Labor Commissioner Fitzpatrick as to the present condition of the state:

"The resources and advantages which nature has so freely scattered about in Missouri with practically half the large area south of the Missouri River still to be closely settled and developed, makes it the leading state of the Union for opportunities open to manufacturers, capitalists, farmers, dairymen, miners, horticulturists, live stock and poultry raisers and timbermen.

"With two-fifths of the state still open for development and Missouri already ranking first among all states for its annual poultry production, third in corn, seventh in wheat, first for both lead and zinc, ninth for building stone, first in manufactured plug tobacco, first in cadmiun, first for red gum cooperage, first for tripoli, first for barytes, first in corn-cob pipes, fourth in mineral paints, fifth in the manufacture of lime, seventh in clay products, seventh in portland cement, seventh in sand and gravel, and second for mules, there is no limit to the future prosperity of the commonwealtlh and its inhabitants.

"Among the other commodities Missouri holds high rank for in annual production are: Shoes and boots, walnut timber, watermelons, strawberries, tomatoes, big red apples, Elberta peaches, flour, feed, meal, cooperage, packing house products, malt liquor (beer), street and railway cars, small fruit, brick and tiling, canned goods, livestock, frogs, fresh water fish, nursery products, sycamore lumber, railroad ties, sand and gravel, glass, natural mineral waters, mushrooms, red gum and maple lumber, honey and beeswax, granite and other building stone, pearl buttons, printing and publishing, furs, clothing, drugs, chemicals and bakery products.

"Located between the 36th and 41st parallels of north latitude and between the 89th and 96th meridians of west longitude, Missouri is a part of the temperate zone in which the work of the world is done. Its climate conduces to health and physical strength.

The Bureau of Ethnology of the federal government has pointed out that the native Missourians are stronger and taller than the native citizens of any other state. The average mean temperature of Missouri, 54 degrees, is higher than the average mean temperature in any other state of the same latitude eastward.

"Health in Missouri is promoted by the pure air and bright sunshine and by the good water with which the state is abundantly supplied. Vital statistics taken from the federal census make plain that the claim for the health feature of Missouri is not an idle boast. The annual death rate in the United States per thousand population, is 16.3, while in Missouri the annual death rate is only 12.2. To express it differently, one-third more deaths occur annually in the other states of the Union, in proportion to the population, than in Missouri. While the annual birth rate in the United States exceeds the annual death rate 11 per cent, the excess in Missouri is 13.8 per cent. Missourians are born more numerously and die less rapidly than the citizens of the other states."

The Platte Purchase

ORIGINAL WESTERN BOUNDARY—PLATTE COUNTRY
OCCUPIED BY INDIANS—THE WHITE MAN NEEDED
IT — MUSTER DAY AT DALE'S FARM — GENERAL
HUGHES' SPEECH AND ITS EFFECT—THEPURCHASE
MADE—CONSIDERATIONS AND STIPULATIONS OF
THE TREATY—EXIT THE INDIAN, ENTER THE WHITE
MAN.

When Missouri was admitted to the Union the western line of
the state passed from the corner of Arkansas directly north through
the mouth of the Kansas River to the Iowa line. This left a section
embracing what are now Platte, Buchanan, Andrew, Holt, Nodaway and Atchison Counties in the Indian territory, of which both
Kansas and Nebraska formed a part.

This section of the territory, between the Missouri River and
the west line of Missouri, was ceded to the Sac-and-Fox and Ioway
Indians, in the treaty of Prairie du Chien, ratified in 1830, in
exchange for certain lands in Wisconsin. These two tribes, and
also a band of Omahaws and a few Sioux, located along the banks
of the larger streams in the upper part of the strip, while the lower
portion was occupied by the Pottawatomies, who were removed
from Indiana in 1833, after the Black Hawk war.

The government had places of supply at Rock-house, near what
is now the town of Agency, in Buchanan County, and at Beverly, in
Platte, and General Andrew S. Hughes was the government agent.
General Hughes made his headquarters with Joseph Robidoux in
the Blacksnake hills, going among the Indians only on issue days.
He had warehouses near the Ford and at Beverly, but these were in
charge of guards.

The Indians were particularly undesirable neighbors to the
people of the old Missouri border. They were drunken, lazy, quar-
selsome, and altogether unworthy to occupy so valuable and so
beautiful a territory. So argued the white man, who believed the
heritage to be his, and who went systematically to work to secure it.

It was customary in those times to have militia muster on certain days, and so it came to pass that muster was held at the farm
of Weakly Dale, near Liberty, in Clay County, in April of 1835. At
these musters there were speeches, and measures for the general
welfare were publicly debated. The Indian neighbor was the theme
on a speech by General Hughes on this particular occasion, and the
effect of his oration was immediate.

Recent correspondence between Major John Dougherty of Clay
County, then an Indian agent, and Senator Linn, in reference to
coveted territory, was also read. Major Dougherty had shown how

the formation of the boundary had inconvenienced persons settling along the border, in what are now DeKalb, Gentry or Worth Counties, from reaching the river (then the only mode of transportation) without traveling over a hundred miles to get below the mouth of the Kansas River, when the Missouri could be reached at twenty, thirty or fifty miles at Robidoux's or Weston, which were the most important river points in the Platte country.

The many streams capable of furnishing water and power, the rich soil, valuable forests, luxuriant grasses, wild fruits, thousands of wild flowers, well-filled bee trees, flocks of wild deer and turkey, all had been voiced aloud until the old Kentuckians, Tennesseeans and North Carolina forming that military array, resolved that they must have the strip without delay. In fact, they started to obtain it in Western style, resolving that they ought and would have it, and E. M. Samuel, David R. Atchison, Alexander W. Doniphan, W. T. Wood and Peter H. Burnett were appointed a committee to obtain it. But some of those same muster-men, being doubtful about the efficacy of negotiation and red-tape, moved into the new country that fall. The government had them removed by soldiers, but they went back again, and like the Sooners of the present day, kept themselves in evidence so as hasten the inevitable.

The result was that on September 17, 1836, William Clark of the famous expedition of Lewis and Clark, of 1804, then agent for all of the Indians west of the Mississippi River, held a council with the Sacs-and-Foxes and Ioways at Fort Leavenworth, and made a treaty whereby the Platte country passed into the hands of the white man.

The Indians received $7,500 in cash and four hundred sections of land in what are now Doniphan and Brown Counties, Kansas. The government agreed to erect five comfortable houses for the Ioways and three for the Sacs-and-Foxes; to provide for each tribe an interpreter, a farmer, a blacksmith, and a schoolmaster; to break up two hundred acres of ground for each tribe and to furnish each with a ferryboat; also to provide rations for one year and agricultural implements for five years.

The treaty was signed by William Clark, superintendent of Indian affairs, for the United States. For the Ioway Indians it was signed by the following chiefs and braves: Mo-hos-ca (or White Cloud), Nau-che-ning (or No Heart), Wa-che-mo-ne (or the Orator), Ne-o-mo-ne (or Raining Cloud), Ne-wan-thaw-chu (Hair Shedder), Man-haw-ka (Bunch of Arrows), Cha-tau-the-ne (Big Bull), Man-o-mo-ne (Pumpkin), Con-gu (Plumb), Wau-thaw-ca-be-chu (One that Eats Rats), Cha-tea-thau (Buffalo Bull), Cha-ta-ha-ra-wa-re (Foreign Buffalo).

The following signed for the Sacs-and-Foxes: Ca-ha-qua (Red Fox), Pe-shaw-ca (Bear), Pe-cau-ma (Deer), Ne-bosh-ca-na (Wolf), Ne-squi-in-a (Deer), Ne-saw-au-qua (Bear), Qua-co ousi-si (Wolf), Suquil-la (Deer), As-ke-pa-ke-ka-as-a (Green Lake), Wa-pa-se (Swan), No-cha-tau-wa-ta-sa (Star), Can-ca-car-mack (Rock Bass), Sea-sa-ho (Sturgeon), Pe-a-chim-a-car-mack (Bald-

Headed Eagle), Pe-a-chim-a-car-mack, Jr., (Bald-Headed Eagle).

The following citizens of Missouri signed as witnesses: S. W. Kearney, John Dougherty, A. S. Hughes, George R. H. Clark, Willian Duncan, Joseph V. Hamilton, Joseph Robidoux, Jr., William Bowman, Jeffry Dorion, Peter Constine, Jacques Mette, Louis M. Davidson.

Thus was the Platte Purchase made. The red man was told to move on, and resumed his pilgrimage toward the setting sun, and the white man promptly built his cabin where the Indian's tepee erst had stood.

Buchanan County and St. Joseph

CHAPTER I.

FIRST SETTLERS—LOCATION AND NATURAL ADVAN-
TAGES—RIVERS, CREEKS AND LAKES—PIONEER
LIFE—FIRST DWELLINGS—PRIMITIVE FURNITURE
AND FRUGAL HABITS—ONE-LEGGED BEDSTEAD—
WILD MEAT AND WILD HONEY—RYE COFFEE, THE
HORSE-POWER MILL, THE HOMINY BLOCK AND THE
GRITTER—LABORIOUS AND OTHER AMUSEMENTS.

When in the summer of 1826 Joseph Robidoux pushed the nose
of his keel boat into the mouth of the creek now called Roy's
Branch, he began the history of Buchanan County, as far as concerns the white man, at least. The red man had made history, too,
in his own way, among the Blacksnake hills and valleys, but he took
it with him when he crossed the river, and it is buried with him
forever, as are his weapons and his wampum.

Robidoux remained undisturbed while the soldiers from Fort
Leavenworth were raiding this section for squatters, prior to the
purchase. As soon as the treaty was made, and even before the
Indians had taken up their march to other hunting grounds, the
tide of immigration to Buchanan County set in.

History mentions only a few settlers who escaped the vigilance
of the soldiers. Robidoux and his men were here by permission of
the government. One of the trespassers was John Elliott, who
came from Kentucky in 1833 and located this side of the former
state line, in what is now Platte Township. When driven off he
moved over the line, but continued to cultivate the land on this side.
Another was Hiram Roberts, who located in the vicinity of what is
now DeKalb, in 1836, and who was overlooked by the soldiers. He
remained in undisturbed possession until the annexation and resided in the neighborhood until his death, in 1881. Absalom
Enyard of Clay County located in what is now the center of Platte
Township in 1836 and built a small cabin, but was soon ejected.
He had been visited by Judge Weston J. Everett of Clay County,
who was seeking a location, and who was so favorably impressed
that when the Platte purchase was completed he bought Enyard's
cabin, and, in the February of 1837, took possession under the
homestead law. Judge Everett was followed in a few weeks by
Absalom Munkers.

1151710

From 1837 to 1840 there was a steady influx of settlers and the development of the country progressed rapidly. Immigrants came from the neighboring counties and from Kentucky, Ohio, Indiana, Tennessee, North Carolina and Virginia.

Because of their early environments, most of these took naturally to the timbered districts that skirt the streams. This was practical, too, for the early settler required wood for his houses, his fences and his fuel. Transportation was an item of great moment, for there were no railroads and few steamboats in those days.

Among the most abundant trees of all originally found was the black walnut. However, the later demand for this wood in the manufacture of furniture was so great that the forests fell before the axe, and now there is but little of it left. A line of timber still follows the course of all streams, and detached groves, natural and artificial, are found throughout the country.

Buchanan is situated in latitude 39 degrees 47 minutes north, and longitude 4 degrees 55 minutes west. Its altitude is about 1,000 feet above sea level, and it is about 400 feet above Chicago and 600 feet above St. Louis. The highest point in the county is the hill upon which are located the reservoirs of the St. Joseph Water Company. It is 320 feet above low water mark in the Missouri River and is situated two and one-half miles north of St. Joseph.

The surface away from the streams is gently undulating prairie, and there is a wonderful diversity of country for so small an area. Few, if any, counties in the state possess better natural drainage, and there is consequently but little waste land. Nor could any improvement be made over nature in the distribution of the water courses. Platte River is a fine stream, as is also the One-Hundred-and-Two River. The name of this stream is somewhat of a puzzle. One authority asserts that it is 102 miles in length. Another authority claims that it was so named because when the river was first seen by the surveyors who were locating a military road, the distance from Fort Leavenworth was 102 miles, and they named it so, as is the custom—the name of Ten-mile Creek, Forty-mile Creek, etc., being similar instances. Bee Creek, Castile, Malden, Sugar and Contrary Creeks and their various forks and feeders are all valuable and never-failing streams.

Besides these, there are numerous lakes, bordering the Missouri River. Contrary, the most extensive and beautiful of these, is located about three miles southwest of St. Joseph. It receives its name from Contrary Creek, which empties into it, Contrary Creek being so called because it flows north, contrary to the course of the Missouri River. Sugar Lake, in Rush Township, is partly in Buchanan and partly in Platte County. It is a picturesque sheet of water. Then there are Singleton, Horseshoe, Muskrat, New Made and Mud Lakes. Contrary and Sugar Lakes are fruitful ice fields. The meat-packing concerns of Kansas City and St. Joseph formerly drew their supplies largely from them.

That the climate is healthful is best known to those who dwell here. In fact, almost the whole of the Platte Purchase is singularly free from consumption, asthma, bronchitis and the diseases most dreaded in the Eastern states. The air is dry and pure and the malarial fevers so common to Western and Southern states are confined to the river bottoms and are comparatively mild.

The early settlers found, besides timber and water, an easy and productive soil. To these advantages the sturdy pioneer had but to apply his energies, and the reward was certain. Hence the wealthy farmers of today, whose broad acres and ample houses, whose grand orchards and blooded livestock are but the primitive establishments of the early settler amplified and developed, step by step, from generation to generation, by industry and thrift, aided by natural conditions and a constant benediction in the climate. It can be truthfully said that there has never been a total failure of crops in Platte Purchase.

Pioneer life in Buchanan County was no different from pioneer life elsewhere in the West. The first settlers were plain, hospitable, brave, generous people. They were good neighbors, bound together with a strong bond of sympathy, which made one man's interest every other man's interest also, and every man's protection lay in the good will and friendship of those about him.

The first dwellings of the white man in this country were a cross between Indian bark huts and "hoop cabins," for it took a number of men to build a log house. The settlers generally located in bunches, for mutual protection, and when three or four families had formed a community, they began the building of log houses, each assisting the other. The logs were round, notched together at the corners. The cabins were ribbed with poles and covered with split boards. A puncheon floor was then laid, a hole cut in the end and a chimney made of sticks and mud. The door was of clapboard, and a window was provided by cutting out a log in the side and inserting glass or covering it with greased paper. The house was then chinked and daubed with mud, and was ready for the occupant.

The furniture consisted generally of the one-legged bedstead, a rude table, a few plain chairs and an assortment of pots and pans for cooking the food at the fire-place, there being no stoves. The one-legged bedstead was made by cutting a stick the proper length and boring holes in the edge to correspond with holes in a log of the cabin. Rounds of woods were inserted into the corresponding holes, and what resembled a ladder in a horizontal position was supported on one corner by a leg, the other end and one side being fastened to the walls. Bark was woven into the rounds, and upon this primitive structure the bed was laid.

The manner of living was extremely simple. For some years the only mills were propelled by horse power, each customer furnishing his own power. There were no roads and the grain was carried in sacks, horseback. In the first years very little wheat was grown, corn being the only grain. The hominy block, an improvised mortar, made by cutting a hole into the stump of a large tree, and using a heavy timber as a pestle, was one way of producing meal for bread. Another instrument was the "gritter," made by punching holes into a piece of tin, which was then nailed to a board, rough side out, and upon which green or previously softened corn was rubbed into a pulp and then baked into bread or ash cakes.

Rye and cornmeal parched were often a substitute for coffee and sassafras root produced a palatable substitute for "store tea." Game was plenty, especially deer, elk, wild turkeys, prairie chickens, and even bear, so there was no scarcity of meat until the hog could be turned into pork.

The clothing was homespun, made by the women of the household—"jeans" for the men and 'linsey-woolsey" for the maids and matrons. Hunting shirts and pantaloons of dressed buckskin were also worn by the men. The linsey and jeans for every-day use were colored with hickory or walnut bark, and those for Sunday wear were dyed in indigo. A fell suit of blue jeans was considered a fine dress.

It required great industry and rigid economy to make a plain living in those times. Iron and salt, two very necessary articles, were high and difficult to obtain. The pioneers had no money, as a rule, and for the first few years had nothing to sell except skins, wild honey and beeswax. Along the streams there were many hollow trees in which wild bees had deposited their honey, and these were eagerly sought.

. There were amusements, too. Log-rolling was a laborious sport. Rail-splitting was another. The women had quilting parties while the men enjoyed themselves with the logs and the rails, and in the evening there was generally a dance, if a fiddler could be had, or games of various kinds, as in all primitive communities. In fact, the history of the early settlers of Kentucky, Tennessee and Indiana was repeated in Missouri.

In a few years the settlers of Buchanan County had made great progress, and in five years after the country was opened for settlement there were several saw and flouring mills, roads and other improvements.

CHAPTER II.

BUCHANAN COUNTY FORMED AND NAMED — FIRST COUNTY COURT, SHERIFF AND SURVEYOR—FORMA-TION OF TOWNSHIPS — FIRST ELECTION — FIRST COUNTY SEAT AND COURT HOUSE—REMOVAL OF COUNTY SEAT FROM SPARTA TO ST. JOSEPH.

In December, 1838, the General Assembly of Missouri passed an act providing for the organization of Platte and Buchanan Counties. James Buchanan, afterwards President, at that time represented the United States at the court of St. Petersburg. He was a popular idol at home, and this county was named in his honor.

The creative act authorized the governor to appoint three judges of the county court and a sheriff, to serve until the general election in 1840; also a surveyor. The act provided for a commission to locate a permanent seat of government, naming Peter B. Fulkerson and Armstrong McClintock of Clinton and Leonard Brassfield of Clay County as commissioners. It provided also that until this commission had acted the seat of government should be at the house of Richard Hill. The regular terms of the county court were fixed for the first Mondays in February, May, August and November, but the court was permitted to hold special sessions.

Buchanan County was made part of the Twelfth senatorial district, part of the First judicial district and part of the Twelfth judicial circuit, and the regular terms of the circuit court were fixed for the second Mondays of April, August and December. County and district courts were authorized to appoint clerks.

Governor Lilburn W. Boggs appointed Samuel Johnson, William Harrington and William Curl as the first judges of the Buchanan County court, and Samuel Gilmore as the first sheriff. This court met at the house of Richard Hill, near the site of old Sparta, on the first Monday in April, 1839, and organized by electing Mr. Johnson as presiding judge and appointing William Fowler clerk.

The first business of the court was the subdivision of the county into municipal townships. This was no small task and underwent remodeling several times before it was found satisfactory. Platte, Tremont, Marion, Lewis, Noble, Jefferson, Nodaway, Atchison, Bloomington, Washington, Crawford, Wayne and Center are mentioned in the early records. However, the court, at its first session, ordered an election of two justices of the peace and one constable for each township, and specifically mentions the following: Platte, Tremont, Marion, Bloomington, Crawford, Noble, Lewis, Nodaway and Jefferson. In 1842 we find ten townships: Bloomington, Crawford, Platte, Tremont, Marion, Jackson, Washington, Rush, Wayne and Center. As the population increased it became necessary from time to time to change the boundaries, until the present subdivision into twelve townships was reached. We

have now Washington, Marion, Lake, Wayne, Center, Agency, Tremont, Rush, Bloomington, Crawford, Jackson and Platte. The
county court met alternately at Mr. Hill's house and at the house of
Joseph Robidoux.

Matthew M. Hughes, who had been appointed by Governor
Boggs to survey Buchanan County, made his report to the county
court on January 8, 1840. "I commenced on the northwest corner
of Platte County," he says, "in the center of the main channel of the
Missouri River, and ran up the same, with its various meanders,
forty-two miles and fifty-two chains, which constitutes the western
boundary of your county; thence I ran a due east course, marking
each fore and aft tree with a blaze and two chops, and trees on
each side in the way pointing to the line, of fourteen miles and
twenty-seven chains to a stake in the old state line, or the line of
Clinton County, which constitutes your northern boundary; then
south twenty miles and fifty-two chains along said line to the northeast corner of Platte County, which constitutes your eastern boundary; thence west along the line of Platte County twenty-seven miles
and forty-seven chains, which constitutes your southern boundary,
containing four hundred square miles." For all this work the court
paid Mr. Hughes ninety-four dollars."

The commissioners appointed by Governor Boggs to select a
seat of justice did not act until May 26, 1840. On that day they
met the county court at Mr. Hill's house, and, after going carefully
over the ground, selected for the seat of justice the southeast
quarter of section 21, township 56, range 35. This land is now
owned and cultivated by William McCauley.

Anticipating the decision of the commissioners, a small settlement had been made. The commissioners named the new county
seat Benton, in honor of Senator Thomas H. Benton, but this did
not meet with popular approval, and at the August term the county
court changed the name to Sparta.

Having a seat of justice, Buchanan County must, of course,
have a court house. A log structure was erected, which is mentioned more extensively in another chapter. In 1842 $6,000 was
appropriated for a substantial court house, but this was never built
at Sparta.

While Sparta was near the center of the county, the principal
trading point was at Blacksnake Hills. A petition, signed by 956
(being three-fifths) of the taxable citizens, asking for the removal
of the county seat, was presented to the county court at the February term in 1843, and the court appointed Winslow Turner, James
Hull and James Kuykendall to select a site. These gentlemen reported on July 4, 1843, stating that they had selected the southwest
quarter of section 8, township 57, range 35, 'the same being on the
Missouri River at the Blacksnake Hills.''

This quarter section had been pre-empted by Joseph Robidoux
and he lost no time in platting the town of St. Joseph after this
report. At the election that followed a majority voted for the
removal of the county seat to the Blacksnake Hills, but the measure

failed because the claim of the county to the quarter section above mentioned was not sustained by the circuit court. Robidoux had a prior right.

In the fall of 1844 a majority of all the voters in the county petitioned the legislature, and an act was passed in March, 1845, under which succeeding elections were held for the removal of the county seat.

The commissioners provided by the legislature met in St. Joseph on May 24, 1845. Joseph Robidoux, who objected to giving his entire townsite to the county, was inclined to be liberal, however, and donated all of block 48, the site of the present court house. This was accepted by the commissioners.

The legislature had also provided for the reimbursement of the holders of lots in Sparta. To assist in doing this Frederick W. Smith donated one block of ground in St. Joseph and Elias F. Wells donated two lots. John Patee donated three acres of land and Samuel C. Hall twenty acres. To further aid this movement the citizens of St. Joseph subscribed about $1,000 in money.

The lands donated were sold for $1,370.50. They are today among the best property in St. Joseph and are easily worth $300,-000. The amount thus secured covered the liability to the Spartans by a narrow margin, for of the $2,370.50, it required $2,185.

On December 24, 1845, an election was held to ratify the action of the commissioners. St. Joseph received 1,037 votes and Sparta 541. The county court held that this vote did not decide the question in favor of St. Joseph, contending that a majority of all free white male inhabitants taxable, over the age of twenty-one, was required, and hold that there was no such majority for St. Joseph.

The court at once ordered another election for February 28, 1846. The Spartans had been inspired with new hope and worked vigorously to defeat the aspirations of St. Joseph. There were speeches, the press was brought into active use, and people made a personal matter of the contest. Fortune favored St. Joseph this time with 1,164 votes against 455 for Sparta. The county seat was at once removed to St. Joseph. The lot owners in Sparta, having been reimbursed, moved off and the land reverted to the legal holder.

CHAPTER III.

THE COURTS OF BUCHANAN COUNTY—FIRST SESSION
OF THE CIRCUIT COURT—JUDGES FROM 1839 TO 1898
—THE COURT OF COMMON PLEAS—THE COUNTY
COURT AND ITS ORGANIZATION FROM 1839 TO 1898—
SUPREME COURT SESSIONS AT ST. JOSEPH—JUSTICE
COURTS AND A LIST OF THOSE WHO HAVE SERVED
AS MAGISTRATES IN VARIOUS TOWNSHIPS FROM
1839 TO 1898.

As stated in the previous chapter, Buchanan County was attached to the Fifth judicial circuit, and it therefore became the distinguished duty of the Honorable Ausutin A. King of Ray County, the judge of the Fifth district aforesaid, to hold the first session of the circuit court.

On February 16, 1839, Judge King commissioned Edwin Toole of Blacksnake Hills as clerk of the circuit court, to hold said office until his successor should be elected at the general election in 1840.

On July 15, 1839, Judge King opened court at the house of Joseph Robidoux at Blacksnake Hills, through the proclamation of Samuel Gilmore, "high sheriff in and for said county."

Both civil and criminal cases were considered at this term, the first case docketed being Andrew S. Hughes vs. Ishmael Davis, a petition in debt. This case was dismissed at the plaintiff's cost. There was also an assault and battery case, and the grand jury returned indictments against twenty-three pioneers who had whiled away monotony and money in the national game of poker. Several merchants were indicted for doing business without license.

Little was accomplished, however, at the first term of court, most of the cases being continued to the November term, when the gamesters were fined five dollars each.

Two applications for citizenship were made during the first session of the court. Gottfried Rentel, a native of Poland, and Rudolph Mill of Hesse-Darmstadt, Germany, renounced allegiance to their respective princes and potentates and declared intention to support the constitution of the United States.

During the November term much business was disposed of. Among other things, one William Williams was indicted by the grand jury for rape. He was remanded to the sheriff of Clay County for keeping, there being no jail in Buchanan County as yet, and, at the March term of 1840, was found guilty and sentenced to the penitentiary for five years. He was the first criminal taken to that institution from this county.

The first three terms of court were held at Robidoux's house, and the July and November terms of 1840 were held at the house of Richard Hill, near Sparta.

During the session of 1840-41 the legislature erected the

Twelfth judicial circuit, composed of the Platte Purchase and Clinton County.

Governor Reynolds appointed Hon. David R. Atchison of Platte County as judge of this circuit, and Peter H. Burnett, also ,of Platte County, as circuit attorney.

On March 31, 1841, Judge Atchison convened his court at the house of Richard Hill, and the next term, in July, was held in the log court house at Sparta, which had just been completed.

In 1843, Henderson Young of Lafayette County succeeded Judge Atchison, who had been appointed United States Senator by Governor Reynolds to fill the unexpired term of Dr. Linn.

Judge Young resigned one year after Judge Atchison, and the governor appointed Solomon L. Leonard of Buchanan County, who served until 1852, and was succeeded by William B. Almond of Platte County. Judge Almond held the office only one year, when he resigned to go to California, where he had previously accumulated a considerable fortune, and Elijah H. Norton, also of Platte County, was appointed to fill the vacancy.

Judge Norton served until 1860, when he was succeeded by Silas Woodson of Buchanan County, who, during the war, became a member of General Willard P. Hall's staff as colonel and inspector-general. There was little business in the circuit court in those stormy days. In 1864, Judge Woodson was a candidate for re-election and was defeated by William Herron of Andrew County, who served for the following four years.

Isaac C. Parker of St..Joseph served from 1868 to 1870, when he resigned to go to Congress. Judge Parker's term was completed by Bennett Pike. Joseph P. Grubb was elected to succeed Judge Pike, and served from 1872 to 1880, when he was in turn succeeded by William Sherman. Judge Sherman died after two years, and Judge Grubb was appointed to fill the vacancy.

The Twelfth judicial circuit diminished in size as the territory became populated. During the war the circuit was composed of the Platte Purchase only. From 1872 to 1889 the circuit was composed of Buchanan and DeKalb Counties. By considering that twenty-five years ago one circuit judge was able to meet the requirements of these two counties and that it now requires three circuit judges for Buchanan County alone, one gets some idea of the growth of this community in that period.

In 1885 it was deemed necessary to establish a criminal branch of the circuit court, and the legislature of that year provided for this. Governor Crittenden appointed Silas Woodson to the post and Judge Woodson served until June 11, 1895, when he resigned, owing to ill health. Governor Stone appointed Romulus E. Culver to fill the vacancy and Judge Culver was elected to succeed himself at the general election of November, 1896. He resigned in April, 1899, and was succeeded by Benjamin J. Casteel, who was appointed by the governor to fill the unexpired term. He was elected to succeed himself in November, 1902, and again in 1906. Judge Thomas F. Ryan was elected in 1910 and still holds the office. The legislature in 1915 abolished the criminal court and created a third division of the circuit court. This act takes effect January 1, 1917.

Oliver M. Spencer was elected circuit judge November, 1886, and served until May of 1890, when he resigned. Governor Francis appointed Archelaus M. Woodson to fill the vacancy. Judge Woodson was re-elected November 8, 1898, and in 1904 Judge C. A. Mossman was elected. He was succeeded by Judge W. D. Rusk in 1910. Judge Rusk died in February, 1914, and Judge W. H. Haynes was appointed by the governor. Judge T. B. Allen was elected in November, 1914, to fill the unexpired term of six years.

The legislature of 1889 passed a bill establishing two civil branches of the Buchanan County circuit court, and Governor Francis appointed Henry M. Ramey judge of Division No. 2, Judge Woodson's court being Division No. 1. Judge Ramey was elected for a full term in November, 1890. He was succeeded in 1896 by Thomas H. Parrish, who died in October, 1897. Governor Stephens appointed Charles F. Strop to fill the vacancy until the general election, November, 1898. Judge Strop failed of nomination at the Democratic primaries in May of 1898, being defeated by William K. James, who was elected November 8, 1898, to fill out the unexpired term of Judge Parrish, which ended in 1902, when he was succeeded by Judge Henry M. Ramey. L. J. Eastin was elected in November, 1908. He served two years, when he resigned and W. K. Amick was appointed to serve until the election in 1912. At that time Charles H. Mayer was elected for the unexpired term. He was re-elected in 1914 for the term ending in 1920.

*　*　*

COURT OF COMMON PLEAS—A tribunal within the recollection of comparatively few of the younger people was the Buchanan County court of common pleas, which existed from 1853 to 1873. This court was created to relieve the circuit judge, whose territory was too large and who often did not reside in the county.

The court of common pleas had concurrent jurisdiction with the circuit court except as to criminal cases, and its records tell the history of a large volume of the litigation that was had here during the twenty years of its existence.

This court opened for its first term on Monday, September 12, 1853, with William C. Toole as judge, who served until September 15, 1855, when he was succeeded by Washington Jones. Judge Jones only served one year, resigning, and was succeeded by Joseph J. Wyatt September 18, 1856. Judge Wyatt served for ten years, being succeeded in October of 1866 by E. J. Montague, who served until December of 1870. Judge Toole again came upon the bench at that time and served until December of 1873.

The court was abolished by the legislature, and when Judge Toole adjourned without date the pending litigation was transferred to the circuit court, the Twelfth judicial circuit having meanwhile been contracted to Buchanan and DeKalb Counties. The clerk of the circuit court was also clerk of the common pleas court.

THE COUNTY COURT—William Harrington, Samuel Johnson and William Curl were appointed by Governor Boggs as the first county court of 1839. In 1840, Stephen Jones, Richard Roberts and Upton Rohrer were judges. From that time to this the court has been organized as follows, the first named being the presiding judge: Stephen Jones, Richard Roberts, Thomas A. Brown, 1841-42; Richard Roberts, Thomas A. Brown, William Dunning, 1843-44; William Dunning, Robert Irwin, Robert Duncan, 1845-48; William Dunning, Robert Irwin, T. S. Talbot, 1849; T. S. Talbot, William Dunning, Robert Jesse, 1850-52; Aaron Lewis, Nelson Witt, Hiram Rogers, 1853-54; Aaron Lewis, Nelson Witt, Cornelius Roberts, 1854-55; William M. Carter, Nelson Witt, Cornelius Roberts, 1855-56; Joseph H. Crane, Cornelius Roberts, John J. Pullins, 1856-57; John J. Pullins, James A. Anthony, Cornelius Roberts, 1857-59; James A. Anthony, John J. Pullins, William Dunning, 1860-61; P. B. Locke, Cornelius Roberts, Ransom Ridge, 1862-63; Cornelius Roberts, Ransom Ridge, Charles Schreiber, 1863-64; Cornelius Roberts, Charles Schreiber, William Ridenbaugh, 1865; James Pettigrew, Charles Schreiber, J. R. Bell, 1866; Philomen Bliss, Jacob Boyer, Charles Schreiber, 1867-68; William M. Albin, Charles Schreiber, Jacob Boyer, 1869-70; John Pinger, W. B. Gilmore, John Bretz, 1871-72; John Pinger, William B. Gilmore, Benjamin B. Frazer, 1872-73; John Bretz, Michael Fitzgerald, John Taylor, 1873-74.

During 1874-78, the county court consisted of five members. In that period the organization was: Michael Fitzgerald, John Taylor, Fred W. Smith, John L. Wade, John L. Sutherland, 1874-75; Bernard Patton, S. D. Cowan, John E. Wade, John Rohan, John Taylor, 1875-76; Bernard Patton, William Roberts, John Pryor, Cornelius Roberts, Patrick McIntyre, 1876-78.

From 1878 to the present time there have been but three judges and the organization of the court has been: Thos. A. Brown, P. McIntyre, John H. Carey, 1878-80; Thomas A. Brown, P. McIntyre, L. F. Carpenter, 1880-82; Thomas A. Brown, John Kelley, William Buntin, 1882-84; Thomas A. Brown, John Kelly, A. F. Greenard, 1884-86; A. M. Dougherty, John Kelly, James Ferrill, 1886-88; A. M. Dougherty, W. B. Smith, Harry Keene, 1888-90; Thomas A. Brown, James W. Mansfield, W. B. Smith, 1890-92; Thomas A. Brown, William M. Stanton, James A. Millan, 1892-94; Harry Keene, Edgar Sleppy, William M. Stanton, 1894-96; Harry Keene, Augustus Saltzman, Jason B. Landis, 1896-98; William M. Stanton, T. J. Hill, Augustus Saltzman, 1898-1900; William M. Stanton, T. J. Hill, Edgar Sleppy, 1900-02; William M. Stanton, John H. Duncan and Harry D. Bassett formed the court January 1, 1903. Judge Bassett died August 27, 1903, and John Kelly, a former member of the court, was appointed by Governor Dockery to fill the unexpired term. Judge Stanton died March 14, 1904. The governor appointed John T. Chestnut to serve until the election of a successor in November of that year.

H. R. W. Hartwig was elected presiding judge in 1904, and

the district judges were J. H. Duncan and Edgar Sleppy. Judge Hartwig died December 30, 1905, and John L. Leonard was appointed by the governor to succeed him. Judge Leonard was elected in 1906, and his associates were Lee Jackson and George W. Akers. Since that time the court has been composed of John L. Leonard, Julius Meyer, Lee Jackson, 1908-10; Thomas J. Hill, John H. McClanahan, James H. Leonard, 1910-12; Thomas J. Hill, J. H. McClanahan, William Bubb, 1912-14; Thomas J. Hill, Marion Kirkman, William Bubb, 1914——

* * *

THE PROBATE COURT—Prior to 1851, the county court was also the probate court. The first regular probate judge was Joseph J. Wyatt, who served 1851-59. Henry S. Tutt succeeded him and served 1859-65. For the next ten years the county court was again the probate court. In 1875, the probate court having been restored, the judgeship was held by Henry S. Tutt, who served until 1890, when he was succeeded by John M. Stewart, who held the office four years. From 1894 up to the time of his death James P. Thomas filled the place. Governor Dockery appointed Sterling P. Reynolds to fill the vacancy. Reynolds was elected in 1904. John F. Imel was elected in 1906, and A. B. Duncan in 1914.

* * *

THE SUPREME COURT—Under the provisions of the Drake constitution a law was passed making the supreme court a migratory tribunal. The state was divided into districts, and St. Joseph was the seat of justice for northwest Missouri. From 1866 to 1876 two sessions of the supreme court were held here each year. Litt R. Lancaster, for many years a prominent attorney here, but who later became a resident of California, was clerk of the St. Joseph sessions.

Judge A. M. Woodson of St. Joseph was elected to the supreme court in 1906 for a term of ten years. Stephen S. Brown of St. Joseph was appointed a commissioner of the supreme court by Governor Hadley in 1911, and is still serving (1915).

COUNTY OFFICES AND THE INCUMBENTS THEREOF, FROM THE EARLIEST DAYS TO THE PRESENT TIME. —PROSECUTORS, CLERKS OF CIRCUIT COURT, SHERIFFS AND CONTESTS FOR THE OFFICE, COUNTY CLERKS AND CONTESTS, CORONERS, RECORDERS OF DEEDS, TREASURERS, ASSESSORS, PHYSICIANS, SURVEYORS AND PUBLIC ADMINISTRATORS.

Prior to 1872 the public prosecutor was styled circuit attorney and was elected, as the judge, by the votes of the judicial circuit. When the Twelfth circuit was created by the legislature, in 1841, Governor Reynolds appointed Peter H. Burnett of Platte County as circuit attorney. In 1843 Mr. Burnett resigned and was succeeded by Willard P. Hall, Sr., of Buchanan, who in turn was succeeded by J. M. Jones of Andrew. The office was also held by James Craig of Buchanan, James N. Burnes of Platte, Joseph P. Grubb of Buchanan, Thomas Thoroughman of Buchanan, Jonathan M. Bassett of Buchanan, and Isaac C. Parker of Buchanan. The last incumbent was B. K. Davis of Maryville.

Of those named, Mr. Burnett was afterwards governor of California, Willard P. Hall was governor of Missouri, and Isaac C. Parker, James Craig and James N. Burnes went to Congress. Judge Parker ended his days as United States judge at Fort Smith, Arkansas.

In 1872, S. Alexander Young, brother of the late Waller Young, and of the then existing law firm of Woodson, Vineyard & Young, was elected the first prosecuting attorney of Buchanan County. He resigned before the expiration of his term, and James P. Thomas, now probate judge, was appointed to serve out the unexpired period.

Judge Henry M. Ramey held the office for four years, 1874-78, and was succeeded by Willard P. Hall, Jr. Oliver M. Spencer prosecuted during 1880-82, Thomas F. Ryan, 1882-84; James W. Boyd, 1884-86; Benjamin J. Woodson, 1886-88; William M. Sherwood, 1888-90; Lawrence A. Vories, 1890-92; Romulus E. Culver, 1892-94; Albert B. Duncan, 1894-96; William B. Norris, 1896-98; James W. Mytton, 1898-1902; Lewis C. Gabbert, 1902-04; John D. McNeely, 1904-06; C. F. Keller, 1906-10; C. E. Ferrell, 1910-14; Oscar D. McDaniel, 1914——

* * *

CIRCUIT CLERKS—The first entry on the record of the circuit court for Buchanan County recites the appointment, by Judge Austin A. King, of Edwin Toole as "clerk of the circuit court," with power and authority to discharge the duties of said office until the general election in the year 1840. This order was made on February 13, 1839, and Mr. Toole at once began the work of preparing for the first term of court, to be held the following July. In 1840, Mr. Toole was succeeded by William Fowler, who held the position until 1852, being at the same time county clerk.

William Ridenbaugh was clerk of the circuit court from 1852 to 1862, when he was succeeded by William C. Toole, who served two years. Frank G. Hopkins served from 1864 to 1870 and wa succeeded by William Ridenbaugh, who held the place for thre years, dying in office. C. C. Colt served out Mr. Ridenbaugh' term and was succeeded by J. H. R. Cundiff, who held the offic from 1874 to 1878, and was in turn succeeded by Samuel D. Cowan who held the office until 1894. John T. Chestnut, the next incum bent, was elected for a second term of four years in November 1898. He was succeeded by Ambrose Patton, 1902-10; Ross C Cox, the present incumbent was elected in 1910 and again in 1914.

* * *

SHERIFFS—When Governor Boggs appointed the first judges of the Buchanan county court he also appointed a sheriff, Samuel M. Gilmore. Mr. Gilmore held the office until 1843, when he wa, succeeded by George W. Taylor, who served until 1846. The nex four years saw William B. Reynolds in the office, who was suc ceeded in 1850 by Leander T. Ellis. Joseph B. Smith served fron 1852 to 1856, when Solomon N. Sheridan took the office. Mr Sheridan did not serve out his term, and was succeeded by Jame A. Matney. Michael D. Morgan served from 1858 to 1861, when h resigned to go to war. Samuel Ensworth was appointed to serve out the term. Enos Craig was elected and served 1862-64. In 1864-66, Ransom Ridge was sheriff. Irvin Fish served in 1866-68. Dr. R. P. Richardson filled the office for the next two years and was succeeded by Col. Elijah Gates, who served in 1870-74. James L. Spencer, better known as "Fay" Spencer, succeeded Colonel Gates with four years, and Robert H. Thomas followed Mr. Spen- cer, serving four years also.

In 1884, John H. Carey took the office. In November of 188t he was defeated for a second term by Joseph Andriano, the vote being 295 in favor of the latter. Mr. Carey refused to give up the office on the ground that Mr. Andriano was ineligible, and, on November 13, notified Mr. Andriano that he intended to contest the election, for the reason that he (Carey) had been creditably in- formed that Andriano was an alien and not a citizen of the United States. This was a surprise of Mr. Andriano, who had lived in St. Joseph thirty-six years, held city offices and served three years in the Union army. However, he engaged counsel and prepared for the contest. The case came up before Judge Oliver M. Spencer in the Buchanan County circuit court, who, on January 23, 1887, de- cided in favor of Mr. Carey. The first paragraph of Judge Spen- cer's decision reads as follows:

"The decision in this case depends alone upon the citizenship of the defendant. From the testimony of the defendant himself, who was the only witness examined, it appears that he was born at

Heidelberg, Germany, on the 15th day of October, 1841. When he reached the age of seven, he, together with his parents, immigrated to the United States. In 1854, while the defendant was still a minor, his parents were naturalized. The defendant never at any time declared his intention to become a citizen of the United States; never renounced his allegiance to the government of Germany, or took the oath of allegiance to this country. He depends alone upon the naturalization of his parents to make him a citizen."

Judge Spencer decided at length, and with numerous citations, that Andriano was not a citizen of the United States under the evidence and the circumstances. The case was at once appealed to the supreme court and the decision reversed.

Sheriff Andriano took the office early in May of 1887 and held it until January, 1889, when he was succeeded by Eugene H. Spratt, who subsequently served four years. Charles W. Carson then served two years and was succeeded in January, 1893, by Joseph Andriano, who in turn was succeeded January, 1895, by James Hull, who served until the end of 1900 when he was succeeded by Martin L. Spencer. He was followed by James M. Sampson, 1904, Otto Theisen, 1908; C. H. Jones, 1912 to date.

* * *

COUNTY CLERKS—William Fowler was appointed county clerk at the first meeting of the Buchanan county court, held at the house of Richard Hill, on the first Monday in April, 1839, and served under this appointment until the election in 1840, when he was elected and thereafter was re-elected repeatedly until 1852, being succeeded by Milton H. Wash, who served until 1858. From 1858 to 1864 the office was held by Isaac Van Riley. Willis M. Sherwood succeeded Mr. Riley, serving until 1870, when John B. Harder took the office. Mr. Harder served three years and some months and died while in office. His unexpired term was filled by John T. Ransom. I. Van Riley was again elected in November, 1874, and took charge January, 1875. In the following April he died, and his son, Edward Van Riley, was appointed. E. Van Riley served out the remaining portion of his father's term and was then elected, holding the office until 1884. Phillip Rogers was the next clerk, serving in 1884-92. He was succeeded by T. Ed Campbell, who died May 3, 1893. Waller Young was appointed by Governor Stone to serve until the next election, November, 1894.

The opposing candidates at the election of 1894 were Enos Craig, Republican, and Robert M. Nash, Democrat. The returning board showed that Mr. Craig had a majority of one vote. Mr. Nash was satisfied, but the leaders of his party urged him to contest the election. He declined to do this until various defeated candidates of the Republican ticket had instituted proceedings for a recount of votes. As a result of this recount Nash had a majority of eighty votes over Craig. On January 7, 1895, Craig took charge of the office under his certificate from the governor, based upon the first count. On February 19, 1895, Judge A. M. Woodson of the circuit

court decided that Nash was entitled to the office. Craig filed
notice of appeal and gave an appeal bond. Nash applied for a writ
of ouster, but Craig's attorneys set up the claim that the appeal
bond constituted a supersedeas to the writ of ouster and appealed
to the supreme court for a writ of prohibition upon the writ of
ouster. Judge McFarland of the supreme court decided that the
appeal bond was not a supersedeas to the writ of ouster and that
the writ of ouster must prevail. Thereupon Judge Woodson ordered
the sheriff to place Nash in office. This was done, but Nash's
troubles were not over yet, for the two Republican members of the
county court, Judges Keene and Sleppy, refused to approve his
bond or to recognize him as clerk. However, it was soon legally
decided that the county court could not sit without a clerk, and so
the judges bowed to the inevitable. The case which Craig had
appealed to the supreme court was afterward decided against him.

Craig and Nash again opposed each other for this office in
November, 1898, and Nash was elected by 900 majority. Sterling
Price Smith was elected in 1902, and Joseph E. Hunt, the present
(1915) incumbent, succeeded to the office in 1910.

* * *

COLLECTORS—The sheriff was *ex-officio* county collector and
tax gatherer until 1864. Thomas Harbine was the first incuumbent
of the office, serving 1864-68. The office was then filled as follows:
John Pinger, 1868-70; Robert F. Maxwell, 1870-72; Talbot Fairleigh, 1872-74; Thomas J. Burgess, 1874-76; Milton M. Clagett,
1876-78; Randolph T. Davis, 1878-82; Tandy H. Trice, 1882-88;
James Hull, 1888-92. George H. Hall, Jr., served 1892 to April 23,
1895, when he resigned, having defaulted. Governor Stone appointed Edward J. Breen to serve out the term. Eugene H. Spratt
was elected November, 1896, and again in November, 1898. Benjamin L. Helsley was elected in 1898; William M. Dougherty in
1904; Richard D. Fulks in 1910. He was re-elected in 1914.

* * *

CORONERS—Up to 1852 this office was held at different times
by William H. Ridenbaugh, Benjamin B. Hartwell and David V.
Thompson. The following were the other incumbents: David J.
Heaton, 1852-54; Wm. R. Penick, 1854-58; Josiah H. Crane,
1858-60; R. F. Maxwell, 1862-64; John A. Dolman, 1862-64;
Thomas Young, 1864-66; Dr. John T. Berghoff, 1866-70; Dr. C. J.
Siemens, 1870-72; Dr. Samuel Goslee, 1872-74; Dr. Hugh Trevor,
1874-80; Dr. J. W. Heddens, 1880-82; Dr. P. J. Kirschner, 1882-86;
Dr. J. W. Stringfellow, 1886-88; Dr. W. L. Whittington, 1888-92;
Dr. S. D. Reynolds, 1892-94; Dr. J. W. Islaub, 1894-96; Dr. W.
Spier Richmond, 1896-1900; Dr. John M. Doyle, 1900-04; Dr. J. J.
Bansbach, 1904-06; Dr. C. F. Byrd, 1906-12; Dr. Thomas J. Lynch,
1912——

* * *

RECORDERS—The circuit clerk was recorder of deeds up to
1865. The first recorder was George A. Pearcy, who served 1865-

74; Thomas Kelly served 1874-75; Michael Crawford, 1875-78; James Millan, 1878-80; Thomas N. Finch, 1880-90; Joel E. Gates, 1890-98; Joseph N. Karnes, 1898-1906; John J. Downey, 1906-14; Harry C. Yates, 1914——

* * *

TREASURERS—The following have filled the office of county treasurer in the past: James A. Anthony, 1840-50; John Curd, 1850-62; George Lyon, 1862-70; Gustavus H. Koch, 1870-74; John Williams, 1874-78; James Hull, 1878-80; John T. Ransom, 1880-82; James Hull, 1882-86; T. Ed Campbell, 1886-90; Joseph Andriano, 1890-92; John B. Corbett, 1892-94. Harry Cox was elected for 1894-96, but the office was filled by Richard Horigan, who furnished the bond for Cox. Ishmael Davis served 1896-1900; Nathan D. Goff, 1900-04; S. W. Starrett, 1904-06; G. M. Allison, 1906-10; W. H. Frans, 1912——

* * *

ASSESSORS—W. W. Reynolds was the first assessor of Buchanan County, having been appointed by the county court in 1839. He served until 1843, since which time the office has been held as follows: Hiram Roberts, 1843-45; Zachariah Garten, 1845-46; Mathew C. Ferrell, 1846-47; Leander T. Ellis, 1847-51; H. M. Beauchamp, 1851-52; Henry Smith, 1852-53; Hiram Roberts, 1853-55; James A. Matney, 1855-63; William Fitton, 1863-65; John B. Harder, 1865-67; J. A. Matthews, 1867-69; Joseph Mathers, 1869-71; Cyrus J. Missemer, 1871-73; John S. Tutt, 1873-75; George Garrett, 1875-77; John S. Tutt, 1877-85. Tutt died in office. John P. Boyle was appointed to fill out the unexpired term. He did this and was elected to succeed himself, but died shortly after qualifying. John C. Landis was appointed by Governor Marmaduke to serve Boyle's term. Harry D. Bassett served 1888-94. William H. Croy followed Bassett and served until his death, in February of 1898. His brother, James B. Croy, was appointed by Governor Stephens to serve out the unexpired term, and then elected to serve until 1902, when he was again elected, and again in 1904. George W. Akers was elected in 1908 and is still serving.

* * *

COUNTY PHYSICIANS—Dr. Samuel Goslee was the first county physician of whom there is record. He attended the county's poor when they were located on the farm near Sparta. Dr. William Bertram was county physician from 1868 to 1870, when he was succeeded by Dr. A. S. Long. Dr. Gray succeeded Dr. Long in 1872, but served only a few months and died. Dr. Goslee was again appointed and served until June, 1873, when he died also. Dr. E. A. Donelan was the next appointee and served until 1877, when he was succeeded by Dr. J. M. D. France, who served until 1886. Dr. P. J. Kirschner, Dr. C. R. Woodson, Dr. W. B. Davis and Dr. F. G. Thompson have held the office in turn since 1886. Dr. F. G. Thompson was succeeded in 1898 by Dr. Daniel Morton. Dr. J. K. Graham succeeded to the office in 1901; Dr. W. J. Hansen, 1905;

Dr. J. F. Owen, 1906; Dr. E. A. Holley, 1907; Dr. J. M. Doyle, 1909; Dr. J. K. Graham, 1911; Dr. W. J. Hunt, 1915. During the year 1913 two physicians were appointed, Dr. J. I. Byrne serving with Doctor Graham.

* * *

COUNTY SURVEYORS—Simeon Kemper was the first county surveyor. He and Elijah McCrary held the office until 1857, when M. Jeff Thompson was elected. W. B. Johnson was elected in 1861, S. P. Hyde in 1868, Lemuel Peters in 1872, Theodore Steinacker in 1880, Harry Fardwell in 1888, W. B. Hazen in 1892, Theodore Steinacker in 1896, Peter H. Jones in 1904, L. M. Stallard in 1908, Ray L. Cargill, 1912. He is the present incumbent.

* * *

COUNTY AUDITORS—The office of county auditor was created by the legislature in March, 1901. Emmett Wells was the first incumbent. He served until January 1, 1903, when he was succeeded by John H. Watson. James S. Burris, the present officer, took the office January 1, 1911.

* * *

PUBLIC ADMINISTRATORS—Prior to 1874 this office was held by William Ridenbaugh, William M. Albin, James H. Ashbaugh, Henry Smith and Eugene Ayres. From 1874 to 1896 it was held by Thomas R. Smith, who was succeeded by James A. Gibson, who died October 8, 1913. Clay C. Macdonald was appointed to serve until the election in 1914, when Miss Mary A. Williams was elected.

* * *

CONSTABLE—Each township elects one constable every even numbered year. The constable is a peace officer and is also empowered to serve writs issued by justices of the peace. The records afford so little satisfaction that no effort will be made to present a list of those who have held this office in the various townships during the past. In 1882, Charles W. Carson was elected constable of Washington Township, but resigned shortly after taking the office. In 1884, Louis Eggert was elected. He resigned in 1885, and Stephen Sale served out the term. In 1886, James Mansfield was elected and served two terms. He was succeeded in 1890 by W. R. Womach, who also served two terms, and was succeeded by George Nixon in 1912, who was succeeded by David Hatfield in 1904; Samuel Byers, 1906; Ben L. Arnholdt, 1908; John Gordon, 1910; W. R. Parrish, 1912.

* * *

TERMS AND EMOLUMENTS—Circuit judges, six years; salary, $4,500. Circuit clerk, four years; salary, $4,000. County clerk, four years; salary, $3,500. Collector, four years; salary, $5,000. Sheriff, four years; salary, $5,000. Prosecuting attorney, two years; salary, $5,000. Surveyor, four years; salary, $2,000. Probate judge, four years; salary, $3,500. Public administrator, four years; salary, fees. Assessor, four years; salary, $3,500. Recorder, four years; salary, $4,000. Auditor, four years; salary,

county court, four years; salary, $5 per
, two years; salary, $5 per day. County
year; salary, $1,200. County coroner,
. County treasurer, four years; salary,

CHAPTER V.

TOWNSHIPS AND TOWNS OF BUCHANAN COUNTY, AND
THE NAMES OF SOME OF THE FIRST SETTLERS—
POPULATION, BOUNDARIES, AND VOTING PRECINCTS
OF THE VARIOUS TOWNSHIPS—THE TOWNS OF
AGENCY, DeKALB, WALLACE, TAOS, WINTHROP,
RUSHVILLE, HALLS, EASTON AND ST. GEORGE—
SPARTA, THE FIRST COUNTY SEAT — TRADING
POINTS AND POSTOFFICES.

PLATTE TOWNSHIP—The first settlers came by wagon from
Clay County, and Platte Township, which forms the southeast
corner of Buchanan County, was the scene of the earliest struggles
of the pioneers, though the other southern townships were populated so near the same time that there is little difference as to age.
However, the Enyards, the Everetts and the Munkers are among
the first who came to the new country, and they settled in Platte
Township.

The following are the names of some of the pioneers of Platte
Township and the dates of their coming: Absalom Enyard, 1836;
Weston J. Everett and Absalom Munkers, February, 1837; David
Munkers, first white child born in the township, April, 1838; Jack-
son Erickson, 1837; James Williams, 1837; John Huntsucker, Ten-
nessee, 1837; Peter Bledsoe, 1837; William Cobb, Tennessee, 1837;
John Fletcher and Jesse Rockhold, 1837; John Tobin, Kentucky,
1838; John Dryden, Thompson Burnham, Charles Kennaird, Morris
Pile, James Anderson, 1838; Dr. Samuel Trower, Kentucky, 1838;
Nelson Witt, Kentucky, 1838; John Berryhill, James Courtney,
James Fidler, John G. Elliott, John Cummins, Eli Cummins, Harrison Whitson and John Rohan, 1838.

The first church in the township was built by Judge Nelson
Witt. It was of logs and octagonal in shape, with a considerable
seating capacity. It was called the Witt meeting house and was
used by the Calvinistic Baptists.

According to the last census Platte Township has a population
of 794. The voting precinct is at Burnett school house and the post
office is at Platte River, where there is a general store, a mill, and
a bridge over the river.

* * *

JACKSON TOWNSHIP—Pleasant Yates came in the spring of
1837; Isaac Farris, Kentucky, 1837; Levi Jackson, Kentucky, 1837;
John Johnson, North Carolina, 1837; Robert Prather, Kentucky;
1837; Phillip Walker, 1837; Robert Wilson, Ohio, 1837; John Ray,
North Carolina, 1838; Christopher Cunningham, 1838; Benjamin
McCrary, 1838; Charles Grable, 1840; Eli Arnold, 1840.

Jackson is the first township of the southern tier, west of
Platte. Its population, according to the last census, was 593.

Arnoldsville was at one time a trading point and postoffice. Eli Arnold built a mill there in 1847. Matney's mill and store are on the Jackson Township side of the bridge.

* * *

CRAWFORD TOWNSHIP—History has preserved the names of the following early settlers of Crawford Township, the second of the southern tier west of Platte: William Fowler, Delaware, 1837; William Harrington, 1837; Caleb Bailey, 1837; William Guinn and William Lockhart, Illinois, 1837; Bartlett Curl, Kentucky, 1837; James B. O'Toole, Illinois, 1837; Harvey Jones, North Carolina, 1837; O. M. Spencer, father of Judge Spencer, Kentucky, 1837; James Curl, William Payne, Guian Brown, Turpin Thomas, Matt Ferril, 1837; Thomas A. Brown, late judge of the county court, Tennessee, 1838; H. W. Baker, Virginia, 1837; John Hickman, St. Louis, 1837; Levi Judah, Indiana, 1837; Columbus Roundtree, Kentucky, 1837; Dr. Silas McDonald, Kentucky, 1838, first physician in the county; Major Sandford Feland, Kentucky, 1839; Guilford Moultrie, 1839; Nathan Turner, 1839.

Crawford Township had, according to the last census, a population of 1153. There are three voting precincts, Halleck, Wallace and Faucett, and each of these has a postoffice.

Halleck, which is also called "Old Taos," was originally known as Fancher's Cross Roads. In 1848 a saloon was kept there, in which was sold whisky of so villainous a character that those who had returned from the Mexican war compared it to Taos whisky, which was mescal, and considered the worst in New Mexico; so, when a drunken soldier galloped through the village yelling "Hurrah for Old Taos!" the name was fixed. The place was afterward called Birming, but during the civil war it was rechristened in honor of General Halleck. It has no railroad. There is a population of about 200. There is a blacksmith shop and a general store. There was formerly a mill and Halleck flour was famous.

Wallace, on the Atchison branch of the Rock Island railroad, is the most important business point in Crawford Township. It was platted in 1872, and the last census gives the population at 300. There are two general stores, churches, school, blacksmith shop, hotel and livery.

Faucett was platted when the Chicago Great Western railroad extended its line, in 1890, from St. Joseph to Kansas City, and named in honor of Robert Faucett, the miller. There is a population of about 200, a school, depot, two general stores, a church, school and a large grain elevator.

BLOOMINGTON TOWNSHIP—Among the first settlers of what is now Bloomington Township was Hiram Roberts, who came in 1836, and who escaped the military raiders. Bloomington is the second township of the southern tier west of the river. The population is about 1,445. Other early settlers were Cornelius Roberts, 1837; Isom Gardner, Amos Horn, John Underwood, Holland Jones, Thomas Hickman, William Hickman, William Ballow, Matt Geer,

Hardin Hamilton, Mrs. Sally Davis, F. D. Davis, Thomas Hill, Major Francis Drake Bowen, Stephen Field, James Hamilton and Isaac Van Hoozier, 1837; Zachariah, Uriah, John, William and Lewis Garten, 1838; Michael Gabbard, 1838; Benjamin Yocum, Kentucky, 1839; Richard Murphy, 1839; Robert M. Stewart, New York, afterward governor of Missouri, 1839; Joel Hedgepeth, 1839; James Ellison, William Moore, David Brown, William Clasby, John Sampson, 1837; Benjamin Sampson, Abraham and William Womack, J. P. Pettigrew, Fountain and Rice McCubbin and James G. Finch,. 1839.

DeKalb, the postoffice, trading point and voting precinct, is a prosperous town, nicely located on the Atchison branch of the Rock Island railroad, and well equipped with schools, churches, etc. The town was platted by James G. Finch in 1839, and is the oldest in the county, Sparta not having been platted until 1840 and St. Joseph not until 1843. Finch had an idea that the county seat would be located there, and so he laid off his town around a contemplated court house square. When Sparta was chosen as the seat of justice Finch left in disgust. The quarter section containing the town site was afterward entered by Oliver Norman, who deeded to each settler the lot he occupied.

DeKalb was always a good trading point, and is so today. The town is not incorporated, though there is a population of about 600. There is a newspaper (The Tribune), a bank, two general stores, hotel, an extensive hardware and implement house, drug store, blacksmiths, harnessmakers, barbers. etc.

* * *

RUSH TOWNSHIP—This is the extreme southwestern township in the county, and its western boundary is the Missouri River. William Allison, John Allison and James Canter located in 1837; John Seips, Eli Seips, Mitchell Owen, John Utt, Colonel Wells, Henry Hayes, Sylvester Hays, Morris Baker, James Carpenter, Anthony Graves, John Flannery, 1839.

There are two postoffices and voting precincts in the town-ihsp—Rushville and Winthrop—and the population of the township is given in the last census at 1,472.

Rushville was platted in 1847 by Perman Hudson and James Leachman upon a quarter section that had been entered in 1830 by John Flannery. Five railroads pass through the town—the Chicago, Rock Island & Pacific, Atchison, Topeka & Santa Fe, Hannibal & St. Joseph, Kansas City, St. Joseph & Council Bluffs and Missouri Pacific. There is a population of about 500 and the town is incorporated. There are three general stores, an implement house, drug store, hotel, blacksmith, etc.; also schools and churches.

Winthrop was once a prosperous place, but the ravages of the river and the departure of the industries that once flourished have reduced it to a comparatively insignificant point. The quarter section upon which Winthrop is located was entered by George Million in 1839. Million operated a ferry across the river to the point where Atchison is now located. The town company was formed in 1857, and Senator Pomeroy of Kansas was one of the incorporators. The place was named in honor of Governor Winthrop of Massachusetts colony. There were at one time two extensive pork packing plants in operation. The larger one was erected by Fowler Brothers in 1879, at a cost of $150,000, and the smaller one by Smith, Farlow & Co., of Quincy. The Fowlers moved their plant to Kansas City after operating for something over a year. There were several causes for this—one that the bridge rates were exorbitant, another the flings of an Atchison newspaper at the peculiarities of the resident Fowler, whose manners were European, and a third that Kansas City offered high inducements. Perhaps all three reasons are entitled to weight, but the last was doubtless the prime cause of the removal. Kansas City was making a special offer for packing houses. The Fowlers were offered ground and buildings, and the offer was accepted. The Winthrop house was dismantled and afterward destroyed by the elements. As the Fowlers killed about 3,000 hogs daily, the loss by their departure was great, not only to Winthrop, but to Atchison as well.

The packing house of Smith, Farlow & Co. was built in 1880 at a cost of $60,000, and had a capacity of about 1,000 hogs daily. It was operated for about four years by the builders, and at different times subsequently by other parties. The plant is idle now.

There were stockyards, freight depots, lumber yards, saloons and numerous business houses in those days, and there was quite a speculation in Winthrop town lots in 1879 and 1880.

Prior to the construction of the Atchison bridge, which was opened in September of 1874, there was a steam ferry, the Ida, owned by Dr. Challiss of Atchison, and also a railroad transport boat, the Wm. M. Osborn.

In 1884, the northern portion of Winthrop went into the river, and the ravages of the flood were so great as to necessitate the abandonment of a railroad station between Winthrop and Rushville, called "Paw-Paw." For over three years trains were run to Sugar Lake, where Armour station was erected, and thence to Atchison. In 1897 the Rock Island and Santa Fe companies built tracks along the old route and their trains no longer go to Armour.

The census of 1890 shows a population of 490 for Winthrop, but there are not that number now by half. The postoffice is called East Atchison. There are two general stores, blacksmiths, saloons and drug store.

* * *

LAKE TOWNSHIP—This is the smallest township in the county. It lies north of Rush and west of Wayne, and has the Missouri River for its western boundary. The earliest settlers were from Bartholomew County, Indiana, and the following came in 1841: William McHammer, Henry Siebert, Nathaniel Wilson, James McKinney, John, James and Thomas McGalliard, James Wilson and Eli Gabbert.

The population of Lake Township is about 147. The voting

precinct is at Wilson's school house, and the postoffice at Hall's, in Wayne Township.

* * *

WAYNE TOWNSHIP—Peter Price was among the first settlers, coming in 1837, and Isaac Lower of Tennessee came at about the same time. Samuel Hawley and Jesse Hawley of Indiana came in 1839; William Dunning, North Carolina, 1839; Daniel Devorss, Ohio, 1839.

Wayne Township is bounded on the west by Lake Township and the river, on the south by Bloomington, on the east by Center and on the north by Washington. There are three voting precincts —Hall's, Lake Station and Yeakley's school house. The population of the township is about 1,048.

Hall's, the principal trading point in the township, is about midway between St. Joseph and Atchison. There are two railroad depots, two general stores, postoffice, church, blacksmith, etc. The place was formerly called Eveline. The population is about 100.

Kenmoor is a small point of the Rock Island road, two miles northeast of Hall's. It was founded by Warren Samuel of St. Joseph. There is a depot and general store.

Lake Station, about four miles south of St. Joseph, was formerly a flourishing point, but since the extension of business to South St. Joseph there is little doing at the station.

* * *

CENTER TOWNSHIP—This was at one time the most promising township in the county, for within its confines were located the first seat of justice and court house. Among the early settlers were Richard Hill, Jesse Reames, Zachariah Waller, Elijah W. Smith, Thomas More, Lucas Dawson and John Martin, who located in 1837. Robert Duncan, William Hunter, Andrew J. Hunter, John Ritchie, James Donovan, John, Samuel and Joseph Hill came in 1839; William C. Connett, Kentucky, 1839; William Farris, Indiana, 1840; Samuel McCauley, Pennsylvania, 1840; H .G. Gordon, James Woodward, Evan Jordan, Ransom Ridge, Robert W. Donnell, James Woodward, Martin Hirsch, Samuel and Elbert Gann, John Copeland, 1842.

Center Township is bounded by Wayne, Washington, Agency and Crawford, and has a population of about 1,231. The voting precinct and postoffice, called Adams, is about eight miles south east of St. Joseph.

Sparta, which was the name of the first county seat, exists on the map only, the ground being now a part of the McCauley farm. Sparta had a brief existence of six years. It was platted in 1840 and its streets were named Hazel, Prune, Olive, Vine, Market, Chestnut, Cedar, Cherry, Walnut, Main and Harrison. There was the log court house, a tavern, kept by Robert Duncan, several general stores, a saloon and wagon and blacksmith shops. It was only a small town when at the height of its prosperity. During the struggle between Sparta and St. Joseph over the county seat, a newspaper called The Rooster, was published at Sparta. When th county seat was moved to St. Joseph Sparta faded out of existence.

Bee Creek is a point about nine miles southeast of St. Joseph, where the Santa Fe and Chicago Great Western railroads join, both using the same track from St. Joseph to this point.

Willow Brook is a station on the Chicago Great Western about twelve miles from St. Joseph. A general store and postoffice existed there for some time prior to the coming of the railroad.

* * *

AGENCY TOWNSHIP—The population of this township is about 888. It is bounded by Washington, Center, Jackson and Tremont, the latter being divided by Platte River. James and Robert Gilmore, Samuel Poteet and William McDowell settled in 1837; James J. Reynolds, 1838; Jacob Reese, North Carolina, 1838; Benjamin Moore, Virginia, 1838; Littleberry Estes and Bright Martin, 1838; John Lamb, Robert Gilmore and Richard Fulton, 1839.

In the early days there was a road from Clay County to the Blacksnake Hills which crossed the Platte River where the town of Agency now stands. The river was shallow here and could be forded by teams. The agency of the Sac and Fox Indians was located on the west side of the Platte, about where the town now stands, and the point became known as Agency Ford. In 1839, Robert Gilmore established a ferry, which was afterwards operated by William B. Smith, and continued until the county built a wagon bridge, in 1868.

The town of Agency was platted in 1865 by William B. Smith, and the building of the railroad from St. Joseph to Lexington, now a part of the Santa Fe system, gave an impetus to business. Agency is now incorporated, and is in a flourishing condition, the population being about 400. There is a bank, two mills, six general stores, school, churches, etc.

* * *

TREMONT TOWNSHIP—One of the first settlers of Tremont Township was Ishmael Davis, father of the late R. T. Davis, who located in the spring of 1837 at the edge of Rock House Prairie. The late R. T. Davis is said to have been the first white child born in the county. The following are mentioned as having located prior to 1840: Ambrose McDaniel, George Jeffers, Harold Miller, Robert Irwin, Samuel D. Gilmore, Stephen Bedford, Daniel McCreary, Jacob Schultz, Henry Jones, Creed Herring, M. D. Finch and William P. Mudgett, who was the first postmaster in the township.

The Rock House Prairie, in the southern part of this township, was so named from the following circumstances: While the Indians still occupied the county, the route traveled between Clay County and the Indian agency, near Agency Ford, after crossing the Platte River, led over the prairie. On a rocky point of ground, near the residence of Ransom Ridge, the Indians had erected a huge pile of stones, shaped as much as possible in the form of a house. This was known as the Rock House. It stood directly on the road traveled from Agency Ford to Liberty, Clay County, and attracted the attention of every white man who traversed that region, and from this fact, at an early date, the prairie came to be called the Rock House Prairie.

Tremont is the extreme eastern of the center tier of townships, and is bounded by Platte, Agency and Marion. Its population is about 865. There are two voting precincts—Garretsburg and Frazer—both of which have postoffices. Garretsburg is on a wagon road from St. Joseph, and there is a general store. Frazer is a station on the Lexington branch of the Santa Fe railroad, and also has a general store.

* * *

MARION TOWNSHIP—This township forms the northeastern portion of the county. It is separated from Washington Township by the Platte River and bounded on the south by Tremont.

Calvin James, of barbecue fame, was one of the first settlers of Marion, locating near the present town of Easton in 1837. Benjamin Cornelius, Peter Boyer, James Blakely, Thomas McGowan, Jesse Clark and Barnes Clark came in 1837 and 1838; Caleb Hasenmeyer and the Markers came in 1838; Nicholas Roberts, James Roberts, James McCorkle, 1838; Jacob Kessler, Jacob Wiedmayer, John Wunderlich, Wolfgang Beck, John Slaybaugh, David Davis, Dr. John Minor, Isaac Gibson, William P. Shortridge, Augustus and James Wiley, 1840 and 1844.

Marion Township has a population of about 1,607. There are two voting precincts—Easton and San Antonio.

Easton, which is one of the three incorporated towns in the county, is located about twelve miles from St. Joseph on the Hannibal & St. Joseph railroad. The town was platted in 1854 by E. Don McCrary, who owned four hundred acres of land and who had for some time been operating a general store. The present population is about 400, and there a mill, several general stores, drug store, Catholic and Protestant churches, school and other conveniences.

San Antonio is an old trading point near the central portion of the township. There is a general store and church, and there was formerly a postoffice.

New Hurlingen is the trading point of a thriving German community, located in the northeastern portion of the township. There is a general store, postoffice and Catholic church.

Platte River bridge and Stockbridge are points on the Chicago, Rock Island & Pacific railroad, the latter being a postoffice. Clair is at the Platte River crossing of the St. Joseph & Des Moines railroad, there being a general store and siding.

* * *

WASHINGTON TOWNSHIP—Some of the early farms in Washington Township now form a part of the city of St. Joseph. The following persons are mentioned in history as having settled prior to 1840: John H. Whitehead, William Whitehead, Henry W. Hanson, James Cochran, Frederick Waymire, William Pugh, Clayborne F. Palmer, A. C. Hyde, Thomas, John and Elisha Sollars, Stephen

Corby-Forsee Building

Parker, Isaac and Michael Miller, James G. Karnes, Alexander Fudge, Leroy Kauffman, Benjamin Williams, Jacob Groschon, Logan Jones, Edward Maxwell, John H. Cox, David Ewing, William Sallee, Joseph Davis, George Coughern, Michael Rogers, F. B. Kercheval, Simeon Kemper, Frederick W. Smith, Dr. Daniel Keedy, Bela M. Hughes, Robert I. Boyd, William T. Harris, Joseph Gladden, Samuel C. Hall, John B. Hundley, Richard Gilmore, William P. Richardson and Isadore Poulin.

Washington Township has four justices of the peace and one constable, who are stationed at St. Joseph. There are three post-offices besides St. Joseph—Vories (South Park), Inza (Hyde Valley), South St. Joseph and Saxton.

Saxton is located six miles east of St. Joseph on the Hannibal & St. Joseph railroad. It was named after the late Albe M. Saxton, who donated the ground for a railroad station. A depot, general store and postoffice, church and school are the equipments.

There are six voting precincts in the township: Felling, near the mouth of Roy's Branch; New Ulm school house, Woodbine school house, east of the asylum; Oak Hill school house, Saxton station and Parnell.

When the stockyards were opened, what had been St. George became South St. Joseph and soon developed into a populous suburb. It was taken into the city by an extension of the limits in 1899, and has lately come to be known as the South Side.

CHAPTER VI.

EARLY HISTORY OF ST. JOSEPH—THE FUR COMPANIES —ROBIDOUX AT ROY'S BRANCH AND BLACKSNAKE HILLS—FIRST SETTLERS—THE TOWN PLATTED AND LOTS SOLD—FIRST BUSINESS HOUSES, HOTELS, CHURCHES, NEWSPAPERS, ETC.—FIRST MUNICIPAL GOVERNMENT, AND ORDINANCES OF THE TOWN BOARD—POPULATION AT VARIOUS PERIODS—THE TRADING POST, THE SETTLEMENT, THE VILLAGE AND THE TOWN UP TO 1849.

The French were the earliest and most successful Indian traders. They settled Canada and the northwestern part of the United States, and also the country about the mouth of the Mississippi. Pierre Laclede Liguest, who is better known in history simply as Pierre Laclede, held by charter from the French government, the exclusive right to trade with the Indians in all the country as far north as St. Peter's River. In 1764 he established a colony, out of which grew the present city of St. Louis. His followers consisted of daring frontiersmen, who made trading and trapping incursions to the wilderness before them, establishing posts at interior points, where peltries were collected and shipped to headquarters.

In 1808 the Chouteaus of St. Louis, and others, organized the Missouri Fur Company. In 1813 the Missouri company was merged into the American Fur Company, and the Chouteaus became connected with the latter.

A vigorous effort was at once made by this company to drive out the independent traders, and Francis Chouteau was sent forth to establish a chain of posts. Among the first posts thus established by Chouteau was one on the Kaw River, about twenty miles from its mouth, and known as the "Four Houses"; also one at the "Bluffs," the present site of Council Bluffs.

Joseph Robidoux, of French parentage, born at St. Louis, was a rival trader at the "Bluffs," but in 1822 sold out to the company and agreed to remain away for three years. At the end of that period he announced his intention of again going into business at the old stand, but the Fur Company proposed to establish him at the mouth of what is now called Roy's Branch, just above the "Blacksnake Hills," upon a salary of $1,800 per year, provided he would not interfere with the trade at the "Bluffs." This proposition he accepted, and, with a stock of goods, he landed his keel boats at the mouth of the branch in the fall of 1826.

Robidoux soon recognized the superiority of a location at the mouth of Blacksnake Creek, and, in the following spring, moved to this point, where he continued to work for the Fur Company until 1830, when he became the sole proprietor of the trading post which formed the nucleus of the present city of St. Joseph.

For many years the solitary log house of Joseph Robidoux was the only evidence of civilized man within a radius of fifty miles. Robidoux's first house stood near the mouth of Blacksnake. His second, and more pretentious one, occupied the spot where the Occidental Hotel now stands, at the northeast corner of Main and Jule streets. It faced the south, was one and one-half stories high, contained nine rooms, six on the first floor and three on the second, and a covered porch extended along the entire front. Besides, there was a shed on the north side, divided into three rooms, in one of which Robidoux slept. The entire structure was of logs, chinked with mud, and was substantially and correctly built, insuring comfort in all seasons, and being sufficiently formidable to withstand an attack of hostile Indians, should one be made.

Robidoux, however, was a man of peace, and, so far as known, never had difficulties with the red man. He had in his employ about twenty Frenchmen, who made regular trips with mules to the Grand River country and across the Missouri River into what is now Kansas and Southern Nebraska, taking with them beads, mirrors, brilliant cloth and other flummery dear to the heart of the savage, and bringing home peltries and buffalo hides. These were stored and packed, and were shipped to St. Louis in keel boats before the days of the steamboat.

In time travelers came and saw the beauties of this section and, as the tiding went abroad, others came to see and locate. In 1834 several families from Franklin County, consisting of Thomas and Henry Sollars, Elisha Gladden, Mrs. Jane Purget and others, settled near the post. Elisha Gladden, who is still a resident of the city, was at once employed by Robidoux and remained in his service for many years.

For the convenience of those in his employ and the Indians, Robidoux operated a small ferry, consisting of a flat boat. The landing at this side was about where Francis street originally struck the river, and the road led from there southeast to the Agency Ford of the Platte River, where it forked, one branch leading to Liberty, Clay County, and the other to the Grand River country.

There were few, if any, additions to the population of the "Blacksnake Hills," as Robidoux's post was called, until the completion of the Platte purchase in 1837. When the country was opened for settlement there was a rush of immigration, and the trading post was naturally the objective point. Robidoux secured two quarter sections, embracing what is now designated on the map as Original Town and the various Robidoux additions.

Rival trading points sprang up all over the new country between 1837 and 1840. Of Savannah, Amazonia, Bontown, Elizabethtown, Boston and Jimtown, all in Andrew County, the two former alone remain. However, Blacksnake Hills continued to prosper and the population steadily increased.

In the fall of 1839 Robidoux agreed to sell the site of Blacksnake Hills to Warren Samuel and two other parties from Inde-

pendence, Mo., for sixteen hundred dollars in silver. They went
home and returned in due time with the money, and also with a
plat of the future town. They were Robidoux's guests. During the
evening a dispute arose over a trivial matter, which caused Robidoux to decline further negotiations. He had doubtless regretted
his part of the bargain and gladly availed himself of this opportunity to cancel the deal at the critical time.

However, Robidoux gave or leased ground in small parcels to
all who desired to locate, and so there developed quite a settlement.
Robidoux engaged in general merchandise and built a flouring
mill near the mouth of Blacksnake Creek. Dr. Daniel Keedy, who
was the first physician, built a sawmill south of the settlement.

In June of 1840 a postoffice was established here and called
Blacksnake Hills, with Jules C. Robidoux, a son of Joseph, as postmaster.

Among those who came prior to 1840 were Frederick W.
Smith, a surveyor, whose name is prominently identified with the
subsequent history of the city; Dr. Daniel Keedy, Joseph Gladden,
Polly Debard, Samuel Hull, John Freeman, John Patchen, James
B. O'Toole, William C. Toole, Edwin Toole, and others. Of these
Judge William C. Toole still lives in the city, and Edwin Toole lives
in Montana. The others are dead.

Among those who came prior to 1843 were William P. Rich-
ardson, Simeon Kemper, Dr. D. Benton, John Corby, Joseph C.
Hull, Elias Perry, Charles and A. M. Saxton, Rev. T. S. Reeves,
Isadore Poulin, James W. Whitehead, Lawrence Archer, Benjamin
C. Powell, John D. Richardson, Jonathan Levy, Isaac and John
Curd, William H. Edgar, Robert G. Boyd, Thomas Mills, Joseph
Davis, Joseph Fisher, Michael Miller, J. G. Kearns, James Highly,
Christopher Carbry, Robert W. Donnell and David J. Heaton.

Josiah Beattie kept a tavern, where the gospel was also
preached by Reverend Reeves. Louis Picard is mentioned as the
first carpenter, William Langston as the first plasterer, two brothers named Belcher as the first brickmakers, and Jacob Mitchell as
the first blacksmith, though Robidoux had a blacksmith regularly
employed for many years previous to this time.

Though the population was small, Blacksnake Hills was the
best trading point in this region, and farmers came long distances
to the mills and stores. Sparta was the county seat, but the people
were never attracted there, always preferring this point. When
the county court appropriated $6,000 for the second court house, in
November of 1842, the enterprising people of the Hills at once
began to agitate the county seat question, urging that it be moved
here.

Robidoux was alive to the importance of that matter and began
preparations to form a town. The population was about two hundred at that time, and the business was along the river bank, near
the mouth of the Blacksnake. The larger portion of the proposed
townsite was then used as a hemp field. As soon as the crop was
harvested Robidoux had surveys and plats made by two rival sur-

veyors, Frederick W. Smith and Simeon Kemper. Smith named his plat St. Joseph and Kemper named his Robidoux. Smith's plat was selected, taken to St. Louis and recorded on July 26, 1843; returned and recorded here August 2, 1843. The history of St. Joseph therefore begins with July 26, 1843.

The town as then platted included all of the territory between Robidoux street on the north, Messanie on the south, Sixth street on the east and the river on the west—fifty-two whole and twelve fractional blocks, the dimensions of each whole block being 240 by 300 feet, bisected by a twelve-foot alley. Robidoux named the streets running back from the river Water, Levee, First (Main), Second, Third, Fourth, Fifth and Sixth. Those running at right angles he named after members of his family, beginning with Robidoux, then Faraon, Jules, Francis, Felix, Edmond, Charles, Sylvanie, Angelique and Messanie.

The town lots were immediately put upon the market, though Robidoux's title was not perfected until 1847. At that time the land office was located at Plattsburg. The first conveyance of lots was made on July 25, 1843, the day before the plat was recorded, and was a deed of trust to secure to the Chouteaus the payment of a loan of $6,372.57, with interest at the rate of 10 per cent per annum. The education of Mrs. Robidoux seems to have been neglected, for the deed of trust was signed:

JH. ROBIDOUX. (Seal.)

her

ANGELIQUE   X   ROBIDOUX. (Seal.)

mark

As sales were made, the money received was applied to the payment of the Choteau mortgage.

The population now increased rapidly, and at the end of the year 1843 there were five hundred people here, as compared with two hundred in the June previous. In the fall there occurred a public sale of town lots, which had been extensively advertised and had attracted a large number of men from the surrounding country. The property was put up at auction. One hundred and fifty lots were sold, and more would have been purchased, but Robidoux wisely closed the sale. The corner lots brought $150 and inside lots $100 each at this sale.

It was not until 1845, however, that the town of St. Joseph had a municipal government, as will be shown by the following, which is a copy of the first entry made in the original minute book of the board of trustees:

"St. Joseph, Mo., May 8, 1845.

"At a meeting of the trustees of the town of St. Joseph, who were elected on Monday, May the 5th, 1845, there were present Joseph Robidoux, Isidore Barada, John F. Carter, Johnson Copeland, Wiley W. English, Sinclair Miller and Benjamin C. Powell. The meeting was organized by calling Joseph Robidoux to the chair and appointing Benjamin F. Loan clerk pro tem. The certificate of election of each of said trustees was submitted to the inspection and action of said meeting. After a careful examination of each of said certificates by said meeting, they were severally received and each of said trustees declared duly elected. Whereupon the said trustees were each sworn to the oath of office and their respective certificates filed with the clerk. The meeting then went into an election of a chairman of the Board, and upon the first ballot Joseph Robidoux received six votes, he was duly declared elected chairman of said Board. Said Board then went into an election of officers, which resulted in the election of Benjamin F. Loan for clerk and attorney; Howell Thomas for constable and collector; Benjamin C. Powell, treasurer; Charles White, inspector and assessor, and Frederick W. Smith, surveyor. On motion of John F. Carter, esq., the chair appointed Messrs. Carter, Barada and Powell a committee to draft and report at the next meeting of the Board of Trustees for adoption, such by-laws and regulations as they shall think proper. Ordered that the Board of Trustees adjourn to meet Thursday, the 15th of May, at 2 o'clock p. m."

Joseph Robidoux had a monopoly of the trade until 1843, when Charles and Elias Perry leased from him the small log house which stood on the west side of Blacksnake, and opened a stock of general merchandise. In the fall of that year they built a two-story brick house on Main street, fronting east, where the Sommer-Richardson cracker factory now stands. The brothers Perry became prominent factors in the early commerce of this point.

In 1844 Hull & Carter and E. Livermore & Co. also built business houses on Main street, between Jule and Francis. Benjamin C. Powell and Jonathan Levy each built a business house on Levee street, and Archie McDonald erected a small brick house on Edmond near Water street, in a portion of the original town which has long been in the river. Robidoux also was a builder, and provided several brick tenements.

Israel Landis came in 1844 and opened a saddle and harness shop, west of Blacksnake Creek, but soon moved over to Main street, where business was rapidly centering. William Carter and Aquilla Morrow are recorded as early smiths and plowmakers. Philip Werthwine was the village barber; Allendorff & Rhodes kept a meat market, and Horatio Glasgow was the shoemaker. All of these were in the same neighborhood, except Glasgow, who isolated himself and kept a shop on the west side of Blacksnake, at the terminus of the bridge. There was also a ten-pin alley, kept by John Kennedy, and liquor could be bought at several places. The first permanent organization of the Methodist church was perfected in 1844 by Rev. Edward Robinson.

In 1845 the first three-story building, the Edgar House, was erected at the corner of Main and Francis streets. It is still in a good state of preservation. At about the same time Rev. T. S. Reeves, a Presbyterian clergyman, who was the pioneer Protestant minister, erected the first church edifice on a lot now occupied by the John S. Brittain wholesale house at Fourth and Jule streets. John Corby opened an office as money lender and general speculator ; about the same time. Hull & Welding opened a wagon shop and ,adore Barada a bakery.

Jonathan Copeland built the first warehouse, near the river bank, between Jule and Water streets. Steamboats, other than those owned and run by the American Fur Company, generally passed about twice a month. The staple product in those days was hemp, and much of it was shipped to St. Louis.

How the foundations of some fortunes were laid in the early days may be seen from three transactions. In 1844 John Corby purchased the tract of land now known as Corby's Grove, consisting of eighty acres, for the sum of $200. In the same year Albe M. Saxton purchased a section of land one.and one-half miles east of the Patee house for 1¼ cents per acre. John Patee purchased the tract, 320 acres, which became Patee's addition, for $3,200.

In April, 1845, the following were in business here: E. Livermore & Co., general merchandise; Jules C. Robidoux, who had succeeded his father in business, general merchant; Ross & Harper, general merchants; Hull & Carter, drugs and sundries; Middleton, Perry & Co., general merchants; Israel Landis, saddler; John Patee, drugs and medicines; E. Kemp, gunsmith; Henry McKee, wines and liquors. There were five physicians—Drs. D. G. Keedy, B. V. Teel, J. Lawrence Page, J. H. Crane and D. Benton. There were four lawyers—Theodore D. Wheaton, George Brubaker, Benjamin Hays and H. L. Routt.

It is interesting to note the prices for necessaries that prevailed in those primitive days, when everything not produced at home was shipped from St. Louis by boat. Coffee was 9 cents per pound, flour $4.50 per barrel, corn meal, 50 cents per bushel; glass, 8 by 10, the common size of window panes in those days, $3.75 per box; gunpowder, $6.50 to $7.50 per keg; molasses, 40 cents per gallan; bacon and hams, 7 cents per pound; lard, 6¼ cents per pound; butter, 7 to 8 cents per pound; cheese, 6 to 12 cents per pound; eggs, 6 cents per dozen; salt, $2.25 per sack; whisky, 23 to 25 cents per gallon; Louisiana sugar, 7 to 8 cents per pound; leaf tobacco, $1.75 per 100 pounds; manufactured tobacco, 10 to 16 cents per pound; tea, 60 cents to $1 per pound.

The year 1845 saw the first newspaper issued in St. Joseph. William Ridenbaugh commenced the publication of the Weekly Gazette, the first number of which appeared on April 25. The paper was first edited by Lawrence Archer, a lawyer of ability, and the terms of subscription were $2 per annum if paid in advance, or $3 if paid at the end of the year.

The Fourth of July was celebrated by the St. Joseph Sunday school in .1845. There was a procession to a grove near the city, where there was music, oratory and feasting.

During that year the county seat question was uppermost, the people of St. Joseph making every effort to secure the prize. After several elections, the last of which was held on February 28, 1846,

St. Joseph finally triumphed, and the future of the city was assured.

Amusements in those days were "home made." The "St. Joseph Thespian Society," composed of local amateurs, presented theatricals, and there were occasional lectures and magic lantern shows. However, in May of 1846, the circus of Hawes & Mabie visited the village and was well patronized. St. Joseph is to this day partial to the circus.

Quite a number of Mormons had located in St. Joseph and vicinity in 1845, and that their presence was not desirable is evident from a notice, signed by Samuel C. Hall, which was served upon them, and in which they were advised to "seek some other home,' as there is considerable excitement existing against them."

In *The Gazette* of July 17, 1846, are published several ordinances which are of interest. By Ordinance No. 37 the Board of Trustees ordains: "(1) That there shall be levied, in addition to the taxes imposed by the provisions of the second section of Ordinance No. 35, a tax of one-third of 1 per cent on the assessed value of all livestock, including horses, cattle, hogs and kine of every description, without distinction of age, which may be found within the corporate limits at the time of assessment and belonging to persons living in the corporate limits of the town of St. Joseph. (2) All manner of mules, horses and stock kept in the town of St. Joseph, though without the limits of the town at the time of assessment, for temporary purposes, are hereby declared subject to the above tax.   (3) Every slave which is hired in the town of St. Joseph shall be liable to a tax of one-third of 1 per cent on his or her assessed value, to be collected of the owner."

By Ordinance No. 37 the Board of Trustees ordains: "(1) That all the space of ground lying on the east bank of the Missouri River in the town of St. Joseph, commencing at the north side of Jule street, where it strikes said river, and extending one hundred and fifty feet south, and back east to a line parallel with the front of Johnson Copeland's, is hereby declared a steamboat landing. (2) That hereafter no flat or wood boat, raft or water craft of any description (except steamboats) shall lie or be stationed within the limits above specified, nor shall any load or loads of freight of any kind be landed from any such craft upon the shore within said limits.   A penalty of not less than $5 is provided."

The Gazette supports Willard P. Hall of Buchanan County as the regular nominee for Congress in 1846.   James H. Birch of Plattsburg was an independent candidate, and of the two men *The Gazette* warns the Democrats to stand by the regular nominee. "To the Democrats of this district we have this to say," quoth the editor, "that the nominee must be sustained; the organization of the party must be maintained; union and harmony must prevail, or we must inevitably at every election realize trouble and at very many suffer defeat. Shall it be so?"   Though this sentiment appeared in *The Gazette* over half a century ago, it still does good service during campaigns.

In the same issue of *The Gazette* a number of candidates are announced. The election was held in August then. Dr. Daniel G. Keedy, James H. Ashbaugh, Captain Henry McKee and A. D. McDonald are candidates for the legislature. Captain Henry H. ·Moss, Captain Augustus Wylie and J. F. Hamilton are candidates for sheriff. William A. McDonald and Milton H. Wash are candidates for the office of clerk of the circuit court, and Captain F. B. Kercheval is a candidate for the county clerkship. Benjamin F. Loan, Levi T. Carr, Joseph J. Wyatt, James B. Hull and V. Tullar are candidates for the office of justice of the peace of Washington Township. Allen Mansfield, P. N. Smith and Samuel Martin offer themselves for constable, and William Ridenbaugh, the editor, closes the list with the modest statement that he has yielded to the solicitations of his friends and become a candidate for the office of coroner.

The advertisements of the following firms appear in the same issue of *The Gazette:* Israel Landis, saddles and harness; Todd & Richardson, drugs; Holladay & Somerville, drugs; E. Livermore & Co., general; M. M. & G. T. Moss, general; David S. Skaggo, saddles and harness; Thomas H. Larkin, forwarding and commission merchant; C. F. Emery, painter and paper hanger; Wylie M. English, saddler; L. Halloran, general; I. Barada, fancy groceries and liquors; William P. Flint, physician; Hull & Carter, drugs. J. W. Glasgow advertises for sale his tannery, which was located on Blacksnake. Joseph Robidoux warns his debtors that if they do not pay up promptly their accounts will be put into the hands of an officer for collection. Two weddings are announced in that issue. John Angel was married to Miss Eugenia Robidoux by Rev. J. T. Higginbotham, and Mansfield Carter was married to Miss McClelland by Justice Hall. Among the news items it is stated that the "Clermont No. 2" passed up the river for the mouth of the Yellowstone, and that seven Mackinaw boats passed down, loaded with furs, etc., for the American Fur Company.

In December of 1846 a census of St. Joseph was taken, which showed a population of 936. Of these 142 were males under ten years of age, 81 males between ten and twenty-one years, 257 males over forty-five years, 124 females under ten years, 85 females between ten and twenty-one years, 175 females over twenty years, 27 male slaves, 43 female slaves, and two free negroes.

Times were quite lively in St. Joseph in 1847. New mercantile houses had been established and all old firms had enlarged; the spirit of internal improvement came over the people, and they were looking forward to considerable industrial progress. The first Catholic church was built in 1847 at Fifth and Felix streets.

The years 1848 and 1849 saw many hopes fulfilled, and it is recorded that from March to September of the latter year one hundred and forty-three buildings were erected. Among them was the first brewery, built by Joseph Kuechle. *The Adventure,* a Whig newspaper, was started in 1848 by E. Livermore.

CHAPTER VII.

THE DAYS OF '49 AND THE OVERLAND PERIOD—CALIFORNIA EMIGRATION—ST. JOSEPH AS THE STARTING POINT AND SUPPLY DEPOT—WAITING FOR GRASS—LINING UP FOR DINNER—A LANDLORD WHO KNEW HIS BUSINESS—FREIGHTING BY WAGON—THE OVERLAND STAGE AND THE PONY EXPRESS.

St. Joseph was now on the eve of the next important period in its history. Early in the spring of 1849 began the rush to California. As a starting point St. Joseph offered advantages which no other place possessed. There was at that time a population of 1,000, and there were nineteen well-equipped stores in operation, with an aggregate stock of $400,000. Among the merchants of that period was the late Milton Tootle. In addition there were two flouring mills, two steam saw mills, nine blacksmith shops, four wagon shops, two tinners, two extensive saddle and harness manufactories, etc. There were also two ferries.

Scarcely a day in February and March passed that did not bring a large number of emigrants, and *The Gazette* of March 30, 1849, states that at that time there were upwards of five hundred people camped about the city, awaiting the appearance of grass. The next month saw this number doubled. Grass came early that year, and the emigrants got away promptly.

On May 7, 1849, the St. Joseph Mining Company, the first regularly organized company of men, left for California. Samuel Johnson, A. D. McDonald, Joel Ryan, John Lewis, James Andrews, John and James Somerfield, B. D. Ellett, Edward Banall, J. W. Jones, Thomas Faucett, Michael Cameron, Samuel Wilson, Francis Brubaker, John F. McDowell, T. F. Warner, D. H. and M. F. Moss and James Kirkwood were among the number and all did well.

From April 1st to June 15th, 1849, 1,508 wagons crossed on the ferries from St. Joseph. Estimating four men to the wagon, this would make 6,032 emigrants. At Duncan's ferry, four miles above St. Joseph, 685 wagons crossed. At other ferries as far north as Council Bluffs, 2,000 crossed, and 10,000 crossed at Independence. It is estimated that 27,000 men and 38,000 mules and oxen left these points during that time.

In 1850 the overland emigration exceeded 100,000, and it is estimated that over one-half of the emigrants left from St. Joseph. As the spring was later by a month than was expected, forty to fifty thousand people were encamped in and for miles around the town, in tents and wagons.

In the fall of 1849 the Occidental Hotel was built by William Fowler, and rented to Major James Vaughn. In his reminiscences Colonel John Doniphan describes Major Vaughn as a jolly, rubicund landlord, who extended a Virginia welcome to all his guests;

who, apparently, never slept, and who never permitted a stranger to drink alone. He had an inexhaustible stock of stories and was a marvelous raconteur. The line from the dining room often extended across Jule street and curved up Second, and dinner often continued from 12 to 4 o'clock. Meals were one dollar each, as . this was the best hotel in town, and a man stood at the dining room door to collect in advance.

In 1849 the emigrants by steamboat brought cholera here, but although a few isolated cases occurred, there were no deaths. The disease was, however, communicated to the Indians across the river, and claimed many victims among the Sacs and Foxes and other tribes. In 1851 cholera was epidemic at many of the towns on the Missouri, and there were several cases in St. Joseph in May of that year.

By 1851 the California fever had considerably abated. The increase of steamers on the Missouri River caused a competition in prices to such an extent that emigrants and freight were carried to Council Bluffs and Florence, a Mormon settlement six miles above Council Bluffs, on the west side of the river, at the same figures which had obtained to St. Joseph during the two previous years. Those going by Florence saved over two hundred miles of land travel and avoided crossing both the Missouri and Big Platte Rivers. The route was generally via Kearney, Laramie, Echo Canyon and Webber River, through Salt Lake. After 1850, oxen were largely used to draw the heavy trains, as experience had taught that they were less liable to loss from stampede and alkali water, stood travel better, and were more valuable at the end of the trip. The number of emigrants leaving St. Joseph in 1851 and 1852 was comparatively small. The Indians, too, had proved more annoying, and great care and vigilance were required.

St. Joseph and Savannah sent out large ventures. Among those interested were the late James McCord, Richard E. Turner and the late Dudley M. Steele, all of whom figured prominently in the later commercial history of St. Joseph. Many cattle were driven from this state and sold for beef in the mining camps and at San Francisco. A few months' grazing in the Sacramento bottoms generally put them in fine condition for slaughter. In 1852 Charles A. and Elias H. Perry crossed over 1,000 head at Amazonia, and the latter accompanied them to California, realizing large profits.

Many wagon trains were loaded at St. Joseph with provisions and wares of various kinds and taken to Salt Lake and other Western points. The freighting business soon grew to immense proportions, St. Joseph being the supply depot for the outlying civilization. From this grew the wholesale business of St. Joseph, which is today among the greatest in the West.

The necessities of the case brought forth the overland stage. People who travel to California in cushioned cars in these days can have but little conception of this gigantic enterprise and its offspring, the pony express. The first contract to transfer the mails.

to Salt Lake from the Missouri River was let to Samuel Woodson of Independence, in 1850. The intervening country was a wilderness more than a thousand miles in breadth, occupied by Indians and buffalo, and it required a high quality of nerve to invest money in such an undertaking.

The next contract was let to John M. Hockaday, also of Missouri, who ran stages out of St. Joseph, striking the government road at Kennekuk, Kansas, near the site of Horton. Hockaday received $190,000 annually for carrying a weekly mail. He sold out to Russell, Majors & Waddell. The "Pony Express" was inaugurated and operated by this firm. The following facts concerning this celebrated venture are taken from a sketch by W. T. Bailey, which appeared in *The Century Magazine* of November, 1898, and from an article prepared by Colonel John Don'phan for *McClure's Magazine*.

In the fall of 1854, United States Senator W. M. Gwin of California made the trip from San Francisco east en route to Washington, D. C., on horseback, by the way of Salt Lake and South Pass, then known as the Central Route. For a part of the way he had for company Mr. B. F. Ficklin, general superintendent of the freighting firm of Russel, Majors & Waddell.

Out of this traveling companionship grew the pony express. Mr. Ficklin's enthusiasm for closer communication with the East was contagious, and Senator Gwin became an untiring advocate of an express service via this route and on the lines suggested by Mr. Ficklin.

While at this time there were three transcontinental routes to California, the great bulk of the mail was sent by way of Panama on a twenty-two-day schedule from New York to San Francisco. The Butterfield Route carried some through mail, while the Central Route and Chorpenning lines carried only local mail.

California by this time held a large and enterprising population. While the Union men were in the majority, the Southern sympathizers were numerous and aggressive, and were making every effort to carry the state out of the Union. To the Union men the existing arrangements were far from satisfactory; for it was evident that both the Southern Stage Route and the Panama Route would be liable to interruption upon the opening of hostilities, and, besides, it was of the utmost importance that quicker communication be had with the Washington authorities.

Called to Washington in connection with their government contracts, Mr. Russell, the head of the firm of Russell, Majors & Waddell, met Senator Gwin, and was approached by him on the subject of increased mail facilities via the Central Route.

Mr. Russell hurriedly returned West. Meeting his partners, Mr. Majors and Mr. Waddell, at Fort Leavenworth, he laid the project before them. These gentlemen, while appreciating the force of the arguments advanced, could not see even expenses in the undertaking, and consequently objected to it. But Mr. Russell still insisted that the project would eventually lead up to a paying proposition, and, further, said that he was committed to Senator Gwin and his friends.

This latter settled the matter, for the word of this firm, once given, was to them as binding as their written obligation, and they unitedly threw their whole energy and resources into the carrying . out of the pledge made by one of their members. Committed to the enterprise, the firm proceeded to organize the Central Overland California and Pike's Peak Express Company, obtaining a charter under the State laws of Kansas. The stage line from Atchison to Salt Lake City was turned over by the firm to the new company, who purchased Chorpenning's mail contract and stage outfit, then operating a monthly line between Salt Lake City and Sacramento, and the franchise and equipment of the Leavenworth and Pike's Peak Express, organized in 1859, then operating a daily stage line between Leavenworth and Denver, via the Smoky Hill Route, now covered by the Kansas division of the Union Pacific.

The company had an established route with the necessary stations between St. Joseph and Salt Lake City. Chorpenning's line west of Salt Lake City had few or no stations, and these had to be built; also some changes in the route were considered advisable. The service comprised sixty agile young men as riders, one hundred additional station-keepers, and four hundred and twenty strong, wiry horses. So well did those in charge understand their business that only sixty days were required to make all necessary arrangements for the start. April 3, 1860, was the date agreed upon, and on that day the first pony express left St. Joseph and San Francisco. In March, 1860, the following advertisement had appeared in the *Missouri Republican* of St. Louis, and in others papers:

"To San Francisco in eight days by the C. O. C. & P. P. Ex. Co. The first courier of the Pony Express will leave the Missouri River on Tuesday, April 3d, at ―― p. m., and will run regularly weekly hereafter, carrying a letter mail only. The point on the Mo. River will be in telegraphic connection with the east and will be announced in due time.

"Telegraphic messages from all parts of the United States and Canada in connection with the point of departure will be received up to 5 p. m. of the day of leaving and transmitted over the Placerville & St. Jo to San Francisco and intermediate points by the connecting express in eight days. The letter mail will be delivered in San Francisco in ten days from the departure of the express. The express passes through Forts Kearney, Laramie, Bridger, Great Salt Lake City, Camp Floyd, Carson City, The Washoe Silver Mines, Placerville and Sacramento, and letters for Oregon, Washington Territory, British Columbia, the Pacific Mexican ports, Russian possessions, Sandwich Islands, China, Japan and India will be mailed in San Francisco.

"Special messengers, bearers of letters to connect with the express of the 3d of April, will receive communications for the courier of that day at 481 10th St., Washington City, up to 2:45

p. m. of Friday, March 30th, and New York at the office of J. B. Simpson, Room 8, Continental Bank Building, Nassau St., up to 6:50 p. m. of 31st of March.

"Full particulars can be obtained on application at the above places and from the agents of the company."

The start from St. Joseph was made at 5:30 o'clock p. m., directly after the arrival of the Hannibal & St. Joseph train from the East. There is some dispute as to who was the first rider. Mr. Bailey says that it was Henry Wallace, and Charles Cliff of this city, who was one of the regular riders of the Pony Express, says that it was Johnny Fry. The popular belief in St. Joseph is that Fry is entitled to the credit. The start proper was made from the original Pike's Peak Stables, which stood south of Patee Park, and which have since been replaced by a structure bearing the same name. A large crowd was collected about the stables and the Patee House. The rider started for the local office of the express company on north Second street, at the firing of a cannon. Here he received his dispatches and, without delay, rode to the ferryboat in waiting. At Elwood he met with another popular ovation, and galloped westward, followed by the cheers of the multitude. From San Francisco the start was made at the same hour, a steamer being used to Sacramento, where the pony service really began. From there the first rider, Harry Roff, left at 12 midnight.

The distance between St. Joseph and Sacramento was covered in 232 hours. Riders out of St. Joseph went as far as Seneca, making the sixty miles in eight hours, and stopping for meals at Kennekuk. There were four stations between St. Joseph and Seneca. John Fry, John Burnett, Jack Keetly, Charles Cliff, and Gus Cliff rode out of St. Joseph. Of these but two survive. Keetly lives in Montana and Charles Cliff in this city. They received $400 per annum and maintenance. While in St. Joseph they were quartered at the Patee House.

All the riders were young men selected for their nerve, light weight and general fitness. No effort was made to uniform them, and they dressed as their individual fancy dictated, the usual costume being a buckskin hunting shirt, cloth trousers tucked into a pair of high boots, and a jockey cap or slouch hat. All rode armed. At first a Spencer rifle was carried strapped across the back, in addition to a pair of army (Colt's) revolvers in their holsters. The rifle, however, was found useless, and was abandoned. The equipment of the horses was a light riding saddle and bridle, with the saddle-bags, or "mochila," of heavy leather. These had holes cut in them so that they would fit over the horn and tree of the saddle. The mochilas had four pockets, called "cantinas," one in each corner, so as to have one in front and one behind each leg of the rider; in these the mail was placed. Three of these pockets were locked and opened enroute at military posts and at Salt Lake City, and under no circumstances at any other place. The fourth was for way-stations, for which each station-keeper had a key, and also contained a way-bill, or time-card, on which a record of arrival and departure was kept. The same mochila was transferred from pony to pony and from rider to rider until it was carried from one terminus to the other. The letters, before being placed in the pockets, were wrapped in oiled silk to preserve them from moisture. The maximum weight of any one mail was twenty pounds; but this was rarely reached. The charges were originally $5 for each letter of one-half ounce or less, but afterward this was reduced to $2.50 for each letter not exceeding one-half ounce, this being in addition to the regular United States postage. Specially made light-weight paper was generally used to reduce the expense. Special editions of the Eastern newspapers were printed on tissue-paper to enable them to reach subscribers on the Pacific Coast. This, however, was more as an advertisement, there being little demand for them at their necessarily large price.

At first, stations averaged twenty-five miles apart, and each rider covered three stations, or seventy-five miles, daily. Later, station were established at intermediate points, reducing the distance between them, in some cases, to ten miles, the distance between stations being regulated by the character of the country. This change was made in the interest of quicker time, it having been demonstrated that horses could not be kept at the top of their speed for so great a distance as twenty-five miles. At the stations, relays of horses were kept, and the station-keeper's duties included having a pony ready briddled and saddled half an hour before the express was due. Upon approaching a station, the rider would loosen the mochila from his saddle so that he could leap from his pony as soon as he reached the station, throw the mochila over the saddle of the fresh horse, jump on, and ride off. Two minutes was the maximum time allowed at stations, whether it was to change riders or horses. At relay-stations where riders were changed the incoming man would unbuckle his mochila before arriving, and hand it to his successor, who would start off on a gallop as soon as his hand grasped it. Time was seldom lost at stations. Station-keepers and relay-riders were always on the lookout. In the daytime a few well-known yells would bring everything into readiness in a very short time. As a rule, the riders would do seventy-five miles over their route west-bound one day, returning over the same distance with the first east-bound express.

The great feat of the pony-express service was the delivery of President Lincoln's inaugural address in 1861. Great interest was felt in this all over the land, foreshadowing as it did the policy of the administration in the matter of the rebellion. In order to establish a record, as well as for an advertisement, the company determined to break all previous records, and to this end horses were led out from the stations so as to reduce the distance each would have to run, and get the highest possible speed out of every animal. Each horse averaged only ten miles, and that at its very best speed. Every precaution was taken to prevent delay, and the result stands without a parallel in history: seven days and seventeen hours—one hundred and eighty-five hours—for 1,950 miles, an average of 10.7 miles per hour. From St. Joseph to Denver, 665 miles were made in two days and twenty-one hours, the last ten miles being accomplished in thirty-one minutes.

After running for seventeen months, the Pony Express closed in 1861, Edward Creighton having completed a telegraph line from Omaha to Sacramento. At the time of its death the express was owned by Ben Holladay, who had acquired the stage line of Russell, Majors & Waddell, and was operating out of St. Joseph. ·

CHAPTER VIII.

A REVIEW OF THE PROGRESS OF ST. JOSEPH FROM THE OVERLAND PERIOD TO THE PRESENT TIME—THE EFFORTS IN BEHALF OF "PATEETOWN"—EFFECTS OF THE CIVIL WAR AND SEVERAL FINANCIAL DISTURBANCES—THE BOOM OF 1886 AND THE RESULTS. THE NEW ERA AND WHAT IT PROMISES.

The impetus given St. Joseph by the overland emigration and freighting caused the town to make rapid strides up to 1861, at which time a population of 11,000 was claimed and many substantial public improvements were shown. The streets were paved with macadam, bridges had been built across the different creeks that coursed through the city, and considerable grading had been done in the hills. Besides being a supply point for overland freighters, St. Joseph was a hemp and grain market of prominence, and pork packing had become an important industry.

When the Hannibal & St. Joseph road became a fact, business, which had heretofore closely hugged the river and market square, began to look to the southeast. John Patee was one of the foremost citizens of the place. He had platted his land in an early day, and when the Hannibal & St. Joseph road was projected had donated a strip of forty acres for terminal and depot purposes. This land stretches from Olive street south to Mitchell avenue, west of Eighth street. In the firm belief that the future St. Joseph would build up around the railroad terminals, and with the assurance that the depot would be located at Penn street, Mr. Patee built a magnificent hotel, which cost him about $180,000, and which was then the second largest and best appointed hostelry in the United States. However, he was somewhat disappointed, for the depot was located at Eighth and Olive streets.

"Pateetown," as that section of the city was nick-named, grew rapidly after the completion of the railroad in 1859. A market house was built at Tenth and Lafayette streets, which still stands; business houses and hotels sprang up on Eighth and Tenth streets, south of Olive, and there was lively traffic. But the people up town were not idle either, for prosperity was ruling there too. Many brick business houses were built, among them the Pacific House, the Odd Fellow building at Fifth and Felix streets, Turner Hall, and several blocks on Felix, Edmond, Francis and Fourth streets. The town was spreading out. Graders were busy leveling the hills and filling up the valleys, and the residence portion was being beautified with good homes.

Public improvements were confined mostly to grading the streets and to building bridges over the crooked creeks that coursed through the city. Smith's branch, which headed near the upper end of Frederick avenue, came down that street, crossed lots to and followed the course of Buchanan avenue, touched Faraon and Jule streets and flowed southwest to Eighth near Edmond street, thence across lots between the Kuechle brewery and Turner Hall to Sixth and Messanie streets, thnce south to where the gas plant is located, below Olive street, and thence west to the river. Though there was not much water ordinarily, there was a deep ravine which was often filled with a wild torrent when the rains were heavy. This creek was bridged wherever the travel demanded, and so likewise were Blacksnake and Liniment creeks.

St. Joseph had progressive men at the head of affairs in those days. The people responded to every call, both from their private resources and with the public funds, and bonds were voted with a recklessness that is astonishing in these conservative days. Any project that knocked for admittance was welcomed heartily, and led at once to the open purse. Some of this liberality is still being atoned for by the innocent taxpayer.

From 1861 to 1865—the rebellion period—St. Joseph, like other cities and the country in general, went backwards. Business was paralyzed, labor was unemployed and all conditions were disturbed. The growth and decline of the city is best illustrated by the values of real estate. In 1851 the assessed valuation was $651,-000; in 1852, $784,000; in 1856, $1,040,653; in 1857, $3,313,000, and in 1860, $5,126,249. From the depressing effects of the rebellion the values fell in 1861 to $1,859,224 below 1860. In 1862 a decline of $810,384 from the previous year was noted, and in 1864 the entire assessed valuation was only $3,384,145. Subsequently matters began to look up again. In 1866 the valuation reached $5,426,600, and in 1868 it was $7,000,000.

After the war St. Joseph made marvelous progress. During the first two years 3,000 buildings were erected. The era of prosperity continued until the panic of 1873. During that period the Kansas City, St. Joseph & Council Bluffs railroad was extended north, the St. Joseph & St. Louis (now Santa Fe) road was built from Richmond, the St. Joseph & Denver City (Grand Island) was extended west, and the St. oseph & Topeka was built from Wathena to Doniphan. This road was operated by the Burlington company for a time and was afterwards abandoned. The first street car line was also built in 1866, from Mitchell avenue and Eleventh street to the Pacific Hotel.

, In the latter sixties there was much street improvement and many miles of macadam were laid. During the same period the first attempt at sewering was made. The creek known as Bush branch, which meandered from the neighborhood of Hall and Bush streets by a devious course to Fifth and Francis, was partially covered. Among the prominent manufacturing industries was the starch factory, which has long since disappeared.

Recovering from the stagnation caused by the panic of 1872 and the grasshopper years, St. Joseph began a steady march of progress, which has continued up to the present. However, notwithstanding the fact that business the country over was paralyzed by the panic of 1873, there are local monuments to activity in building during the period of depression. The Missouri river bridge was completed in May of 1873. The court house, city hall, Tootle's opera house and asylum No. 2 were built in 1873-74.

In 1874 the first telephones were put in. In the same and during subsequent years the Charles street and Smith branch sewers were built and the Bush branch sewer extended down Fifth to Charles street.

In 1876 the Union street railway was built to New Ulm park, from Market Square, and in 1878 the narrow gauge street cars were put upon Frederick avenue. Matters generally were looking up again by this time. In 1877-78 the St. Joseph & Des Moines narrow gauge road was built. In 1878 the Board of Trade was organized. At the close of the decade the Krugs, Hax Bros., A. O. Smith, David Pinger and Connett Bros. were packing pork on a large scale, and at the Union stock yards, on South Tenth street, there was a market in lively competition with Kansas City.

In 1880 the Missouri Pacific began to run trains into St. Joseph, and the next four years marked a period of steady progress. In 1880 the site of the old Odd Fellows' hall and Hax's furniture store at Fifth and Felix streets, which had been destroyed by fire, were covered with the splendid buildings of the present. The Odd Fellows' building and Hax's faced Fifth street before the fire, the former being occupied by Bailey, Townsend & Co. The Faulhaber, Bergman and Stone buildings soon completed this block. R. L. McDonald built on Fourth and Francis streets at about the same time, and the imposing block of wholesale houses on Fourth street, north of him, followed at short intervals. The Turner-Frazer building, at Third and Charles streets, went up in 1881, and Nave & McCord built in 1882. The Tootle building on Fourth, between Felix and Francis streets, the large building at the northwest corner of Fifth and Edmond streets, and the Union depot, were built during the first eighties. The Chamber of Commerce, the Saxton building at Fourth and Francis streets, the Tootle building at Sixth and Francis streets, and the general offices of the Burlington railroad were built during 1883-84.

Real estate values were remarkably low in St. Joseph up to 1886. A wave of speculation swept the country at about that time, and, though St. Joseph did not escape the craze, she suffered less than her neighbors from the reaction. On the contrary, the city was, generally speaking, benefited. From a complaisant lethargy there sprang energy, progressiveness and confidence. Values went up, outside capital was attracted, and to the conservatives there was unfolded a future of which there had been many early prophecies.

The first five months of 1886 saw real estate speculation at its height. Addition upon addition was platted and people scrambled to obtain lots at the first sale—to "get in on the ground floor," as the saying was. Real estate agents were without number, and on Francis street there was a Real Estate Exchange, where property was listed on the blackened walls of a store room. Among the first new additions upon the market early in the boom was St. Joseph Eastern Extension, then came Saxton Heights, Wyatt Park, McCool's, Walker's and others.

Suburban property had the call of the speculators. As an evidence of the permanent benefits of the real estate flurry one need but to compare the city of 1886 with the city of the present. At that time there were not more than fifty houses east of Twenty-second street, and few between that and Eighteenth street. All was in grass and of no value except to the dairymen, who pastured their cows thereon. McCool's and Walker's additions, on the north, were in small farms or vacant. Now Wyatt Park is a populous suburb of modern dwellings; there is a street railway, there are paved streets, city water, churches, schools, fire protection, etc. The other additions likewise show up well. As a result of the boom the Wyatt Park, the Jule street and the Messanie street lines of electric cars are running today. As a result of the boom Krug Park and the city parks were opened and beautified. As a result of the boom St. Joseph has now many miles of streets paved with asphaltum, brick and macadam. And there is much more that might be added.

From 1885 to 1893 was the most momentous period in the city's history. To what has been mentioned above may be added the Rock Island railway, east and west; the Chicago Great Western north and south; the Atchison, Topeka & Santa Fe, and the St. Joseph Terminal Company. The Y. M. C. A. building, the Commercial block, Center block, Carbry block, Zimmerman buildings, Irish-American building, Ballinger building, C. D. Smith building, Van Natta-Lynds building, Wyeth building, Crawford theatre, the Podvant and Donovan buildings, Coulter Manufacturing Company's building, France building, Central police station, Turner Hall, the Moss building, Samuels block, the Saxton & Hendricks building; also those massive piles of architecture occupied by the Richardson, Roberts & Byrne Dry Goods Company; Tootle, Wheeler & Motter; the Wood Manufacturing Company; the Michau block, the Hughes building, and the block on the north side of Felix, west of Sixth street—all are to the credit of that prosperous era.

Blacksnake and Mitchell avenue sewers were built and the drainage system of the city perfected, the city electric lighting plant erected and the entire street railway system placed upon an electrical basis. Numerous manufacturing ventures were launched, some of which did not survive, however; notably the steel car works, the stove works and the nail mills.

A bureau of statistics and information did much during 1889-90 to attract the attention of eastern capital, and the Board of Trade was then, as now, a prominent factor for the commercial advancement of the city. The foundation of the present pretentious live stock market and meat packing industry was laid in 1887, and during the following five years three packing plants were established.

The financial depression of 1893 checked the progress of St.

Joseph somewhat, and but little of magnitude was done until 1897, when a fresh impetus was given the city by a revival on a gigantic scale of the meat-packing industry. The stock yards passed into the control of Swift & Co. of Chicago, and two of the largest plants in the world—one by Swift & Co. and one by Nelson Morris & Co.— were erected in 1897 and placed in operation in April of 1898.

A couple of years later a large and modern plant was built by the Hammond Packing Company. It has since passed to the control of the Armours. The livestock market has developed wonderfully, and St. Joseph is one of the principal packing centers of the United States.

Real estate values, which fell during the period of depression, are looking up; many tenements are building, and the season of 1897-98 is marked as one of the most active in the history of the city for mechanics and laborers. There is, indeed, much in the prospect which the future historian may tell.

CHAPTER IX.

THE MUNICIPAL GOVERNMENT OF ST. JOSEPH—THE OLD CITY CHARTER AND THE EVILS THAT WERE WROUGHT UNDER ITS PROVISIONS—BONDS ISSUED WITH ASTONISHING RECKLESSNESS — THE CITY SCRIP AND OTHER METHODS OF RELIEF—THE NEW CHARTER, ITS PROVISIONS AND VALUE—HOW THE CITY IS GOVERNED.

As the community progressed and developed, the scope of the town charter became too narrow, and the people sought relief at the hands of the legislature. Accordingly, a new charter was obtained, early in 1851. The following, from the minutes of the town trustees, shows how the way was paved for the new municipal government:

"March 24, 1851.

"Board met at the call of the chairman for the purpose of laying the city into convenient wards and for the ordering of election of city officers. Present: James A. Anthony, R. W. Donnell, Lewis Tracy, A. Dillon, W. M. Carter, James A. Cochran.

"On motion, ordered that the town be laid off for the purpose of elections into the following wards: First Ward is all that portion of the town lying south of Edmond street; Second Ward, all that portion of the town lying north of Edmond and south of Jule street; Third Ward is all that portion of the town lying north of Jule street, extending from the river to the eastern boundary of the city.

"On motion, ordered that an election be held on the first Monday in April, 1851, for the election of a mayor of the city, six councilmen, two from each ward, and a city marshal. And that John A. Devorss, William Langston and Conrad Crawley be appointed judges of election for the First Ward, and that said election be held for the First Ward at the Missouri Hotel; that John Cargill, Joseph B. Smith and William Dillon be appointed judges of said election for the Second Ward, to be held at the office of Lewis Tracy, Esq.; that John H. Whitehead, David Frank and Neely Fitzgerald be appointed judges of said election for the Third Ward, to be held at the steam mill of John Whitehead."

The following is a copy of the minutes of the first meeting of the mayor and council of the City of St. Joseph:

"Monday, April 14, 1851.

"City council met and took the oath of office and was duly organized. Present: His Honor the mayor, Israel Landis, William M. Carter, John Angel, James B. Pendleton, James A. Anthony and John H. Whitehead.

"On motion, the council proceeded to choose from their num-her a president *pro tem,* whereupon William M. Carter was declared duly elected.

"On motion, the council adjourned until 2 o'clock p. m."

The mayor, councilmen and marshal were the only officers elected at first. The mayor and council appointed the following other officers at the ensuing meetings: Milton H. Wash, city register; Alexander W. Terrell, city attorney; John Curd, treasurer; Isadore Poulin, assessor; Charles Schreiber, city engineer; Johnson Copeland, street commissioner; Dr. J. H. Crane, health officer; V. Tullar, market master; R. L. McGhee, wharf master.

There were no municipal buildings of any kind in those days, and the council paid one-half of Lawyer Terrell's office rent for quarters for the mayor and a meeting place for the council. F. M. Wright, who was the first marshal, had to look out for himself, as did also several of his successors.

The mayor had jurisdiction as a justice and the marshal was the sole guardian of the peace at first. Offenders were brought before the mayor and tried. A room in the old county jail, that stood on the court house hill, was used as a workhouse, and the street commissioner had charge of the city prisoners, who were generally employed on the streets.

In 1852-53 a market house was built on the site of the present city hall. In August of 1855 the workhouse was established in a two-story stone building that gave way, in 1884, to the present structure. The market house was supplanted by the present city hall in 1873.

In January of 1858 the office of city recorder was established and the mayor relieved of the judicial power. A police department was also created at the same time and the marshal was given six policemen. As the marshal was also the tax collector, the police duty fell largely to his deputy and assistants, who were styled the "city guard." This order continued until 1866, when a collector was provided by an amendment to the charter. In 1885 the offices of collector and treasurer were combined. The recorder was *ex-officio* justice of the peace until 1889, and the name of the office was changed to "police judge" in 1893. The marshal's office continued until St. Joseph became a city of the second class.

The city had three wards until 1864. The First Ward was all of the corporate territory south of Edmond street, the Second Ward was bounded by Edmond and Jule streets, and the Third Ward was north of Jule street. When, by an increase of population and an extension of the boundaries, five wards became necessary, the territory was divided as follows: First Ward, north of a line extending through Poulin, Corby and Colhoun streets; Second Ward, between Faraon street and the southern boundary of the First Ward; Third Ward, between Faraon and Edmond street; Fourth Ward, between Edmond and Olive streets; Fifth Ward, south of Olive. When the limits were again extended in 1889 the territory was divided into eight wards.

The municipal history of St. Joseph is unique in more ways than one, and offers a rare field, especially for the students of pioneer city financiering.

The provisions of the charter were good—too good to suit the people, because it restrained the council from creating an indebtedness exceeding $1,000. In 1853 and 1855 other descents were made upon the legislature, and amendments secured authorizing the city to "subscribe for the capital stock of railroads, and for erecting wharves and protecting the banks of the Missouri" against the encroachments of that changeful stream. This was well enough for a year or two, and thousands of dollars were voted by the people for the above purposes. But as the Western country settled up new schemes for investing city funds were devised, and a fourth call on the legislature, in 1857, secured the passage of another bill, authorizing the mayor and councilmen "to subscribe for the capital stock of any railroad terminating at or near said city, or for the stock of any other improvement tending to promote the general interest and prosperity of the city."

The people apparently voted yes on almost every proposition submitted to them, for the records of the defeat of measures of this kind are few and far between. The people evidently reasoned that the only great city in the West must give a certificate to that effect in the shape of an indebtedness of a million or so. They also probably argued that future generations would pay these debts so contracted.

With laws such as the above, and in the swift times in which they prevailed, it is no wonder that the question of voting a few thousands of bonds was regarded so lightly. Bonds were voted for almost any purpose, and the interest was almost invariably fixed at from 8 to 10 per cent. Some of these bonds went for railroad which were never built; others for a road which was built and afterwards abandoned; others still for the bridge, for river improvements, for building macadamized roads, and other schemes supposed to benefit the city—all given with a free hand for the asking.

Of course there were halts called now and then by thinking men—but usually they were of short duration—and the jolly giving of gold went merrily on, until the state constitution of 1870 put limit to city indebtedness, prohibiting its exceeding 5 per cent of the city's assessed valuation.

In those days the council proceedings, instead of being dull and prosy accounts of resolutions ordering sidewalks repaired or ordinances ordering district sewers, as in these days, were in the nature of a meeting of railroad builders, resolutions directing superintendent this or manager that to buy flat cars, hire engines, or buy railroad ties, being of frequent occurrence.

Further amendments to the charter later on prohibited the expenditure of money beyond the receipts of the city. It was thought for a time that this provision would at least prevent the incurring of further indebtedness, but this was a false hope, and soon a scheme was devised that circumvented the law. The council estimated the receipts at the beginning of the year, and went on appropriating from this estimate, totally regardless of whether it was collected or not. As a consequence, city warrants were soon below par, although bearing interest at 6 per cent.

Something else must be done, and in 1878 Mayor Joseph A. Pinger brought relief with a city scrip. One and two-dollar warrants, resembling government bills, non-interest bearing, were issued to the extent of $100,000 for home circulation, which contained upon their face the city's promise of redemption. The "ones and twos," as they were called, served a good purpose. Though there was some question as to the legality of the city's action in the premises, the people took them and they passed at par, and were finally redeemed. The redemption, however, was not brought about until the business men of the city, harassed beyond forbearance by the necessity of continuous handling of this city "money," its delapidated condition, and the urgency for exchanging it for money for use in all outside business transactions, insisted that the council should provide ways for retiring the scrip. In 1885-6, the first year of the city under its new charter, $35,000 worth of scrip was redeemed by the city and destroyed; the following year $25,000 was called in and burned, and in two years more it was practically all in. A city "bill" or scrip is now regarded as a curiosity. The first city pills paid out in each denomination were secured by William B. McNutt, then chief of the first department.

Use of this "money" being confined to the city, little else was seen in ordinary transactions. This constant circulation soon reduced it to a dilapidated condition, necessitating the renewal of a large portion of it, under Mayor Posegate, in 1882. An attempt to replace it again in 1885 was frustrated by Gen. James Craig, then comptroller, who refused to certify to the ordinance carrying an appropriation of $800 for that purpose, on the ground that the entire transaction was illegal. The appearance of government officials on the ground to investigate the matter about this time, together with the demand of the merchants, settled the fate of city scrip. In the matter of interest the scrip saved the taxpayers between $65,000 and $75,000.

But times grew harder and harder for the city. People began to refuse to pay taxes, and in the latter part of the 70's and early 80's the council tried to evade part of the city's debt, declaring it invalid, but better judgment finally prevailed, the means were found to pay the interest falling due, and steps were taken in 1882 to refund all that was left of the high interest bearing bonds. This only partly succeeded at the time, but it was the entering wedge to the settlement of the debt.

In 1884 the indebtedness of the city was, in round numbers, about $2,250,000, of which $210,000 was a floating debt in the shape of warrants, one-half of which was interest bearing, the other half being sham money; $40,000 in judgments, interest and claims against the city. Then there was a bonded debt of about

$2,000,000. The city had issued bonds for the following purposes: River and improvement, $200,000; gas plant, $25,000; macadam road from Elwood to Wathena, $25,000; St. Joseph & Denver Railroad, $500,000; bridge, $500,000; Kansas City, St. Joseph & Council Bluffs Railroad, $210,000; Missouri Valley Railroad, $150,000; St. Joseph & Topeka Railroad, $50,000. The other figures necessary to round out the two millions are furnished by bonds issued to provide money to grade streets and cover deficiencies in the treasury. At the same time there was due the city in back taxes about $150,000.

It was at this time that the howl, loud and long, went up for a change of some sort. Taxation was doubly onerous, the city's credit was *nil*, interest-bearing warrants were at a discount of from 10 to 20 per cent, and the "ones and twos" were in such a wretchedly dilapidated and worn condition that merchants were refusing to receive them.

The agitation thus commenced resulted in deserting the patched-up old charter and starting anew in April, 1885, as a city organized under the laws of the state governing cities of the second class.

When the legislature met in January of 1885 a committee went to Jefferson City with such amendments to the existing state laws governing cities of the second class as would permit the adjustment of St. Joseph's affairs so that the city could be brought under the provisions of the desired charter. The amendments were not material so far as the organic law was concerned, and the delegation from Buchanan County in the house and senate had no difficulty in securing their adoption. At the April election of 1885, the people voted upon the proposition and it was carried, the vote standing 2,925 for the adoption of the charter, and 192 against it.

On Monday, April 21, 1885, the transition took place, and St. Joseph became a city of the second class, under H. R. W. Hartwig as mayor. Mr. Hartig had been elected in the previous year.

The disposition of the "ones and twos" gave great concern, for they were a problem of proportions. The best business men of the city met with the council and a solution of the problem was found in accepting the "ones and twos" in payment for back taxes. This was done, and as the scrip came in it was cancelled and burned.

St. Joseph was dressed up in a new charter again in 1909. The legislature that year passed an act that considerably enlarged the organic law of the city. It contains practically all of the features of the charter of 1885, with the addition of some important features. These are:

More power to compel the construction of viaducts and subways.

A public utilities commission, which has since been superceded by the state public service commission.

Enlarged powers of the park department, and provision for the building of a park and boulevard system.

A city council of five members.

The initiative and referendum.

Under the charter no debts can be made, no contract can be entered into for a period longer than one year, no public work can be ordered, and no purchase made for which the money is not in · the treasury.

The component parts of the city's machinery are the mayor and council, the comptroller, auditor, collector and treasurer, city clerk, engineer, assessor, building inspector, license inspector, health department, keeper of the workhouse, superintendent of streets, the park commissioners, board of public works, market master, chimney sweep, boiler inspector, superintendent of electric light, a library board, weighmaster, fire department, police department, police judge and city counselor.

The assessor lays the foundation for the municipal works. In January of each year he begins to make his assessment. The real estate values are taken from the county assessment, to which they must conform. Personal property, merchandise, banks, etc., are within his jurisdiction. When the tax books are completed the mayor, assessor, comptroller, clerk and president of the council sit as a board of equalization. Some assessments are raised and others lowered by this board, according to circumstances.

The tax books are ready by the third Monday in April, the beginning of the fiscal year. On that day the council meets and the city clerk announces the total valuation of property. Under the charter not more than 1 per cent on each one hundred dollars' valuation can be assessed for general administration purposes, and as much as is necessary may be assessed for the purpose of paying interest on outstanding bonds, and the creation of a sinking fund for the payment of these bonds. Under the charter of today no new bonded indebtedness can be created until the present bonded indebtedness of the city has been reduced to within 5 per cent of the assessed valuation of property.

Upon the first assessment under the charter of 1885 the tax levy was two dollars, one dollar for administration purposes and one dollar for the interest and sinking fund. The levy has since been reduced to $1.35 on the one hundred dollars.

Aside from the one dollar tax, there are other sources of revenue to the city—licenses upon various occupations, and the police court. Of the saloon license, however, the city retains but 47 per cent, the county receiving 53 per cent.

The comptroller makes an estimate of receipts from all sources at the beginning of each fiscal year, and this is apportioned in advance by the finance committee of the council. For instance, at the beginning of the present fiscal year (1915-16) the funds were apportioned as follows: City officers' salaries, $33,500; city officers' assistants' salaries, $18,000; common council salary, $15; fire department salaries, $91,563.33; police department salaries, $124,760; fire department expense, $11,300; police department expense, $3,000; board of public works assistants, $18,000; health department, $16,000; workhouse expense, $800; city hall expense,

$2,500; street lighting department, $25,000; water service, $50,-
000; street, sewer and bridge department, $7,000; park improve-
ment department, $17,000; Krug Park improvements, $4,000; contingent and incidental department, $24,600; Washington Park
library, $3,250; public library, Carnegie branch, $3,250; public
library, main, $19,000; police and fire alarm system, $2,200; street
maintenance and repairs, $60,000; board of public welfare, $10,-
000; band concerts, $3,800; asphalt plant, $7,000; rest rooms,
$2,500.

City taxes are not properly due until August, but the tax
books are ready on May 1, and on all taxes paid during that month
a rebate of 6 per cent is allowed; on all paid in June, a rebate of 4
per cent; in July, 2 per cent. After August a penalty of 2 per cent
per month is charged. Under this wise law an average of 65 per
cent of the entire taxes levied for the given year is paid in May,
this year the collections being 66 per cent of the entire levy. Practically speaking, all the taxes levied by the city are collected. De-
inquent property is sold to the highest bidder in November, and is
redeemable within four years.

As the money is received it is credited by the comptroller to the
various funds as prescribed by the apportionment ordinance. Each
department is required to live within its means. Bills are audited,
and, if allowed, the money for their payment is appropriated by
ordinance, as are also salaries. The auditor draws a warrant upon
the treasurer, which must be countersigned by the comptroller,
who has previously certified that the money is in the treasury to the
credit of the fund upon which the warrant is drawn. The police
department, however, which is under the metropolitan system,
draws one-twelfth of its apportionment each month and the funds
are expended at the discretion of the commissioners.

The mayor, aldermen, collector, auditor and police judge are
elected, and hold office for two years. The engineer, counselor,
comptroller, clerk, superintendent of street lighting, keeper of the
workhouse, superintendent of streets, assessor, market-master,
weighmaster, and license inspector are appointed by the mayor
and confirmed by the council for two-year term. The chief of the
fire department is appointed by the mayor and confirmed by the
council; firemen are appointed by the chief, and are removed for
cause only. Three police commissioners are appointed by the governor for three years each, one term expiring each year. They
appoint the chief and all other attaches to the police department.
The public library and the city parks are managed by boards appointed by the mayor, and these boards appoint the various employes of their departments. The building inspector is appointed
by the mayor, and holds his office during good behavior.

When the charter of 1885 took effect, an agreement was made
with those officials who had been elected for two years that they
would, upon resignation, be appointed to serve out the unexpired
portions of their terms. Under this agreement Harry Carter, who
had been elected collector in 1894, was made treasurer for one

year; William B. Tullar, who had been elected city marshal, was made chief of police for one year, and Francis M. Tufts, who had been elected as register, was made auditor for one year. All fees were abolished.

The following new officers were appointed: General James Craig, comptroller; Purd B. Wright, clerk; James Limbird, counselor; M. M. Kane, chief of fire department; Patrick McIntyre, street commissioner; M. J. McCabe, engineer; Dr. J. A. French, health officer; Ishmael Davis, assessor; Anton Dalhoff, keeper of the workhouse. Policemen, firemen and market-master were also appointed. Officials other than these who are now in the government have been added since then.

That the adoption of the charter of 1885 was wise is best known by those who experienced the workings and trembled for the city from the dangers of the old system. Since 1885 the city has paid its way out of the revenues, has completely wiped out the floating debt and city scrip, and has materially reduced the bonded burden. As evidences of improvement we have the parks, the sewers, the streets, the electric lighting plant, the central police station, the free public library, and excellent fire and police departments.

CHAPTER X.

THE POLICE DEPARTMENT OF ST. JOSEPH, ITS HISTORY
AND THE VARIOUS CHIEFS FROM THE BEGINNING
TO THE PRESENT TIME—THE POLICE JUDGE AND
CITY ATTORNEY, AND THE MEN WHO HAVE HELD
THESE PLACES—HISTORY OF THE FIRE DEPART-
MENT FROM THE DAYS OF THE BUCKET BRIGADE
TO THE PRESENT TIME—THE VARIOUS CHIEFS.

Up to 1851 the peace of St. Joseph was preserved by a constable, who, when the times were lively, as during the California
period, had a force of deputies and was assisted by the sheriff.
The constable was also the collector of town taxes and was withal
an important functionary.

When St. Joseph was incorporated as a city, a marshal was
provided, who, like the constable, was the tax collector; but it was
not until 1858 that the police department was created, at which
time the marshal was given a deputy and six men. These were
pompously styled the city guard, and the deputy marshal was the
captain thereof. The marshall received fees only, but had a lucrative place. In 1866 the collector's office was established and the
marshal gave his entire attention to police work. The fee system
continued until the city adopted the charter of 1885, when the title
of the office was changed to that of chief of police and a salary of
$1,500 per annum provided.

In 1887 the metropolitan system was adopted. Under this the
governor appoints three commissioners, whose duty it is to manage the police department. The commissioners elect on their number as treasurer. At the beginning of each fiscal year they certify
to the council the amount necessary for the department during the
year, which the council is required to provide. This amount is
paid in monthly installments to the treasurer of the board, and
expended for salaries and other necessaries.

Howell Thomas, the first contable, was appointed in 1845.
Henry S. Smith, Edward Searcy and V. Tullar succeeded each
other until 1851.

Francis M. Wright was the first marshal, serving 1851-52.
Then came the following: Allen McNew, 1852-54; George Merlatt,
1854-57; Shad R. Wages, 1857-60; Allen McNew, 1860-62; R. J. S.
Wise, 1862-64; E. H. Saville, 1864-66; Enos Craig, 1866-68; Allen
McNew, 1868-70; Louis Stroud, 1870-72; Thos. H. Ritchie, 1872-74;
John Broder, 1874-76; B. F. Buzard, 1876-78; Phil Rogers, 1878-80;
Enos Craig, 1880-82; Thomas H. Ritchie, 1882-84; William B.
Tullar, 1884-85.

The first chief of police was William B. Tullar, who had been
elected marshall for two years, but who resigned when the new

charter went into effect and was made chief of police for one year. He was succeeded by John Broder in 1886, who was retained by the board of commissioners when the metropolitan system went into effect, and who filled the place continuously until June 1, 1901, when he resigned and was succeeded by W. H. Frans eight months. later. He resigned after the election of Governor Hadley in 1902. J. J. McNamara was appointed for a few months, when Charles H. Haskell was named for a term of three years. He was succeeded by James A. Clouser, the present (1915) chief, Feb. 2, 1914.

Under the present system a captain of police and two sergeants are provided for. Solomon Broyles was captain from June 1, 1887, to March 3, 1888, when he died. He was succeeded by John Bloomer, promoted from sergeant, and who has been constantly on duty to this date. The first two sergeants were John Bloomer and William J. Lovell. When Sergeant Bloomer was made captain, J. Fred Henry, who held the honorary title of corporal, was advanced. Sergeant Lovell was succeeded May 7, 1892, by Corporal Edward L. Cutler, who served until June 1, 1893. Corporal John J. Neenan was advanced and served until his death, August 29, 1896. Patrolman Wm. H. Frans was then made sergeant. Sergeant Henry died in August, 1898, and was succeeded by Robert Maney, who served until June 1, 1901, and was succeeded by William P. Gibson. On June 1, 1899, Sergeant Frans was made captain and James T. Allee was appointed sergeant. Captain Frans succeeded John Broder as chief June 1, 1901, and at the same time John J. McNamara was made captain and Charles Kelley was advanced to the grade of sergeant, succeeding James Taylor Allee. The present captain is William T. Gray and the Sergeants are Martin Shea, J. P. O'Brien, W. P. Gibson and Cecil James. The last two named serve in South St. Joseph.

The metropolitan force was organized June 1, 1887, with the chief, captain, two sergeants, two turnkeys, two drivers and thirty-two patrolmen. At present (1915) there are seventy-two patrolmen, nineteen detectives, one humane officer, three signal service operators, six chauffeurs, one matron and four motorcycle officers.

The chief, captain and sergeants are appointed for one year. Patrolmen are appointed for six months as specials, on probation, at $60 per month. If confirmed they are appointed for three years from the date of the first appointment. The humane officer is selected by the Humane Society and commissioned and paid as a regular patrolman by this department, he being under the direction of the chief. Regular patrolmen receive $70 per month salary.

A telephone signal service, the first to exist, was introduced in 1891, leased from the Missouri & Kansas Telephone Company. The city has since installed its own signal system.

On April 28, 1887, Governor Marmaduke appointed Bernard Patton, John Donovan, Jr., and Thos. P. Maupin commissioners, the first for three years, the second for two, and the last for one year. The regular terms of commissioners after the first appointment are for three years, a vacancy occurring annually. Mr. Patton was president for three years. He was succeeded as commissioner by Geo. H. Hall, Jr. Mr. Donovan was re-appointed at the expiration of two years, and Mr. Maupin was re-appointed at the expiration of his year. Mr. Donovan was treasurer for the first three years and was succeeded by Mr. Hall in 1890, when Mr. Maupin was elected president. This organization continued until August 11, 1892. Mr. Maupin's term had expired in April, 1891, Mr. Donovan's, April, 1892, and Mr. Hall had become ineligible because he was a candidate for office. At that time Governor Francis appointed an entire new board, consisting of Thos. F. Ryan to succeed Mr. Donovan, Samuel M. Nave to succeed Mr. Maupin and Harris Ettenson to succeed Mr. Hall. Mr. Nave served as president until the expiration of his term. Mr. Ryan was elected treasurer and served continuously in that capacity for six years. Mr. Ettenson was succeeded in 1893 by T. F. Van Natta, and Mr. Nave was succeeded in 1894 by John H. Trice. Mr. Van Natta was elected to succeed Mr. Nave as president. Both Mr. Ryan and Mr. Van Natta were re-appointed. Mr. Trice was re-appointed April 29, 1897, and Mr. Ryan was succeeded September 6, 1898, by Walter H. Robinson. Mr. Van Natta was succeeded in 1899 by Frank Freytag, Jr., who served two terms. Mr. Trice was succeeded in 1901 by William H. Utz. Mr. Robinson was succeeded in 1903 by Joseph H. Tullar. Utz was reappointed in 1904, and the following named have since held the office of police commissioner: Dr. T. H. Doyle, 1905; Judge W. K. James, 1906; Col. James H. McCord, 1907; Frank B. Fulkerson and G. L. Zwick, 1909; Maj. John D. McNeely, 1910; Carl Weigel and·Edward L. Hart, 1911. After the election of Governor Major the commissioners resigned, and the following named were appointed: Dr. U. G. Crandall, Henry Vogelman and Joseph I. McDonald. They are still serving.

Chris L. Rutt was appointed secretary at the first organization of the board in 1887, and served until May 1, 1900, when he resigned to become managing editor of *The Gazette*. He was succeeded by Richard S. Graves, now managing editor of a newspaper in Oklahoma City. Fred.Lauder was appointed to this position June 1, 1910, and served until June 15, 1913, when he was succeeded.by John E. Webster, the present incumbent.

The police court is the tribunal to which offenders against the city ordinances are bought. When St. Joseph was a town offenders were brought before a justice of the peace. When St. Joseph became a city, in 1851, the mayor was, under the charter, the police judge, and so continued until 1855. The office of recorder was then introduced, the first incumbent being A. A. Dougherty, who served one year. The position was subsequently held as follows: Felix Robidoux, 1856-58; John A. Dolman, 1858-62; M. L. Harrington, 1862-64; Wm. C. Toole, 1864-66; J. B. Hawley, 1866-68; Charles M. Thompson, 1868-70; Wm. Drumhiller, 1870-72; Charles M. Thompson, 1872-76; R. B. Fleming, 1876-78; Samuel B. Green, 1878-80; George W. Belt, 1880-82; John A. Dolman, 1882-84; Mordecai Oliver, 1884-86; John A. Dolman, 1886-90; William B. San-

Y. M. C. A. Building

ford, April, 1890, to September, 1891, died in office; John A. Dolman, September 1, 1891, to February 9, 1896, dying in office; Peter J. Carolus, February 10, 1896, to April, 1898, when succeeded by Col. John Doniphan, who served two years, when Judge Carolus returned to the bench. He was followed in 1906 by John W. Muir. James Taylor Allee was elected in 1908 and he's still there.

The office depended upon fees until 1885, when the fees were abolished and a stated salary provided. The recorder was also *ex-officio* justice of the peace, up to 1889, when this perquisite was cut off. In 1893 the name of the office was changed to "police judge."

Prior to 1884, the recorder provided his own clerk. Harry Angel was the first appointee, serving until April, 1891, when he was succeeded by Albe M. Tracy, who served until April, 1895, and was succeeded in turn by John T. Warburton. The mayor appointed these clerks. In 1897, the office was abolished, and the duties thereof delegated to the secretary of the board of police commissioners.

The city attorney prosecutes offenders against the ordinances before the police judge. This office was created under the first charter and Alexander W. Terrell was the first incumbent, serving 1851-52. He was succeeded by John Scott, who served until 1856. The office was held subsequently in the following order: Alexander M. Davis, 1856-57; Thomas Thoroughman, 1857-58; W. R. Likens, 1858-60; Joseph P. Grubb, 1860-61; Isaac Parker, 1861-64; James Hunter, 1864-66; Jeff Chandler, 1866-72; Wm. D. O'Toole, 1872-74; John T. Baldwin, 1874-76; Willard P. Hall, Jr., 1876-78; William Fitzgerald, 1878-80; Enos J. Crowther, 1880-82; Augustus Saltzman, 1882-84; William E. Sherwood, 1884-86; Fred J. Lufler, 1886-88; George P. Rowe, 1888-90; Peter J. Carolus, 1890-92; Wm. R. Hoffman, 1892-94; James W. Mytton, 1894-96; Joshua A. Graham, 1896-98, succeeded by Fred W. Heyde, who served two years and was succeeded by John S. Boyer. In 1902 Charles H. Mayer was elected for two years and was succeeded by Milton J. Bauer, who gave way to Burr N. Mossman in 1906. Phil A. Slattery was elected in 1908 and served until the office was abolished in 1910 and the duties performed by an attache of the city legal department.

A number of men who held this humble office afterwards distinguished themselves in the legal profession, among them Alexander Terrell, who was United States minister to Turkey; Alexander Davis, Thomas Thoroughman, John T. Baldwin, Isaac Parker, Jeff Chandler, Willard P. Hall, Jr., and Joseph P. Grubb. Messrs. Davis, Thoroughman and Chandler achieved fame at St. Louis and John T. Baldwin in Montana. Willard P. Hall was one of the first judges of the court of appeals at Kansas City and Joseph P. Grubb was circuit judge here for many years. Isaac C. Parker went to congress from this district and was appointed by President Grant as United States judge at Fort Smith, Arkansas, where he died.

THE FIRE DEPARTMENT.—First, there was the bucket brigade, then organizations of volunteer firemen; next a combination of volunteer and paid firemen, and then an all-paid department, which has grown into one of the best equipped and most efficient in the West.

The late General William R. Penick is credited with having been the most ardent promoter of organized and systematic protection from fires. He began his efforts in 1860, when a member of the city council, but was unsuccessful until 1864, when, as mayor of the city, he earnestly recommended an appropriation of $5,000 for the purchase of a steam engine. The provision was made in August of 1864. At the same time Mayor Penick urged that the citizens subscribe means for the purchase of hose and hook-and-ladder equipments. The people responded promptly and sufficient money was soon pledged. In May of 1865 the steam engine arrived, was tested, accepted and named "Blacksnake." The hook-and-ladder truck and hose-reels were also on hand, and the next step was the formation of a volunteer corps. The Blacksnake engine company and the Rescue hook-and-ladder company were promptly organized. In the following year the German-Americans organized a third volunteer company and purchased a hand engine, which was named the "Water-witch." The steamer was drawn by horses, but the trucks and hand engine were drawn by the firemen and volunteer citizens, there being ropes to accommodate all who desired to "run wid de masheen." Cisterns were built at important points in the business district. There were thirteen of these when the introduction of waterworks supplanted them, and the average capacity of each was about twelve hundred barrels.

There was great rivalry among the firemen, both for efficiency and splendor in parade, and the annual turn-out was always the occasion of a public holiday. The first of these parades occurred on Washington's birthday. The first of these parades occurred on Washington's birthday, 1868, when the late Edward R. Brandow was chief of the department. The procession was composed as follows: "Blacksnake" Steam Engine Company, Hardin Ellis, foreman, 25 men; "Waterwitch" Hand Engine Company, Henry Lund, foreman, 45 men; "Rescue" Hook-and-Ladder Company, Hugh Symmonds, foreman, 55 men. The engine companies had a contest at Market Square and the affair concluded with a general drenching, the rivals turning their nozzles upon each other.

In 1870, a paid fire department was established. Seven men were stationed in a house at the foot of Edmond street. The apparatus consisted of the "Blacksnake" engine and three one-horse reels.

The hook-and-ladder company's apparatus was stationed in a building at the alley east of Tootle's opera house. The ground was donated to the city by the late Milton Tootle, and the Rescue company built the house with money secured by means of entertainments. In 1871 two paid men and two horses were placed on duty here.

The zeal of the volunteers naturally began to wane with the introduction of paid firemen, and the companies disbanded. The "Waterwitch," which had been stationed on Edmond street, west of where the Ballinger building now stands, gave way to a second steamer, named "Bluebird," which was purchased in 1872, and the "Waterwitch," which was sold in 1875 to a party in Wyandotte. The "Blacksnake" was sold to Shenandoah, Iowa, some years ago, and the "Bluebird" is still in service.

The introduction of waterworks gave an impetus to improvement and expansion of the fire department. In 1879 a hose reel was located in the Patee market house, which remained there until 1886, when the present house was built at Tenth and Olive streets. In 1881 a reel was located at Tenth and Francis streets, in a building leased from the O. M. Smith estate. In 1895 this company was removed to Seventh and Charles streets. In the same year a company was stationed on North Third street. In 1882, the house at the foot of Felix street was built and the apparatus removed there from Second and Edmond, to make room for the Davis mill. In 1884, Mr. Tootle exchanged ground at Seventh and Charles streets for that which he had donated adjoining the opera house, the hook-and-ladder trucks were moved, and the old "Rescue" house was merged into the Tootle theater. In 1895, the building at Seventh and Charles streets was enlarged, so as to accommodate new apparatus, and that which was moved from Tenth and Francis streets. In 1889, a house was built at Ninth and Doniphan avenue; in 1891, one at Eighteenth and Felix streets; in 1892, one at Tenth and Powell streets, and in the following year the company on North Third street was moved to a new house which had been built at Third and Franklin streets. Since 1896, at Twenty-seventh and Penn streets; on Frederick avenue near Twenty-first street; on St. Joseph avenue; in Walker's addition; in South Park, and in South St. Joseph. Motor trucks were introduced in January, 1915.

The fire department is now composed of the chief, assistant chief, sixteen foremen, ten lieutenants and fifty-eight firemen. There are in service two steam engines, one aerial truck, one water tower, two chemical engines and fourteen hose wagons. There are forty horses and about 50,000 feet of hose. There are located about the city 483 fire hydrants. The cisterns of the olden days have all been filled up.

Dr. Robert Gunn was the first chief of the fire department. He was appointed October 13, 1865. The position had been tendered to Charles W. Davenport, who declined, however, because he was an insurance agent. Dr. Gunn served until April, 1867, when he was succeeded by Edward R. Brandow, who served until April, 1870, and who was in turn succeeded by Robert J. S. Wise. In 1871, Harry Carter was elected and served one year, being succeeded by Egid Wagner, and he in turn by Augustus Saltzman, each serving one year. In April of 1874, Wm. B. McNutt was elected, served six years, and was succeeded by Henry Gibson, who served one year.

In 1881, W. B. McNutt was again made chief and served until 1885. In 1882, Michael M. Kane was made assistant chief, and in 1885 he was made chief, with William D. Smith as assistant. In 1892, Oliver M. Knapp and P. P. Kane were made assistant chiefs. In 1895, Oliver M. Knapp was made acting chief, owing to the illness of Mr. Kane, who resigned in 1897, and was succeeded by his brother, P. P. Kane, the present chief.

CHAPTER XI.

THE PARKS OF ST. JOSEPH, THEIR HISTORY AND DEVEL-
OPMENT—LAKE CONTRARY AS CITY PROPERTY—
THE FREE PUBLIC LIBRARY; ITS ORIGIN AND EX-
PANSION—STREET LIGHTING; FROM GAS TO ELEC-
TRICITY AND MUNICIPAL OWNERSHIP—THE CITY'S
SEWER SYSTEM; ITS HISTORY AND CONDITION—
STREET PAVING; VARIOUS PERIODS OF PROGRESS.

There are seven public parks in the city proper. Krug Park
is the largest and most beautiful. All of these parks were donated.
Smith Park was the gift of the late Frederick W. Smith, Patee
Park the gift of the late John Patee; Mitchell Park, the gift of
A. M. Mitchell, and Washington Park the gift of those who placed
St. Joseph Extension Addition on the market.

These were all dedicated when the additions containing them
were platted. Krug Park, containing ten acres, was the gift of
Henry and William Krug, made in February of 1889, the conditions being that the council spend annually the sum of $1,500 in
beautifying and maintaining the park, and the restrictions being
that no intoxicating liquors be permitted to be sold. In 1914 Henry
Krug, Jr., donated an addition of twenty acres to Krug Park.

Smith and Patee parks were rough ground in the beginning,
but the grader made all things even. Up to 1879 Smith Park was
occupied by a florist. When the Smith branch sewer, which cut
through the northeastern portion of the park, was completed the
place was graded and filled. In 1882 an iron fence was built. In
1884, Dr. Henry D. Cogswell, of San Francisco, a noted advocate
of temperance, presented the city with his statue, to be placed in
the park. Dr. Cogswell was engaged in perpetuating himself by
the means of these statues, which were mounted upon a drinking
fountain. The statue was removed in 1909, as well as the old iron
fence, adding greatly to the appearance of the grounds.

Patee Park was opened to the public at about the same time
as Smith Park. The ground was low, and a fill of five feet was
made when Messanie street was graded. Cottonwood trees grew
there in profusion for a time, but these were cut out and other
shade provided.

Mitchell Park was used for some years as a potato patch, and
then occupied by a florist, who remained until 1891.

Washington Park, which was originally dedicated for a market
place, was beautified in 1894, and has since been greatly appreciated by the people of the northwestern portion of the city.

Smith, Patee and Mitchell parks each occupy a block of ground.
Washington Park is triangular, and not quite as large as the others.

Bartlett Park, about twenty acres in extent, was donated to the city in 1907 by Barlett Brothers Investment Company.

Gordon Park, in South St. Joseph, was dedicated when the plat of that addition was filed.

Calvin Hyde filed a deed in 1915 for a considerable tract in the southeastern part of the city to be known as Hyde Park.

St. Joseph owes much to the energy and perseverance of the park board. Before 1890 there was a council committee on parks. Mayor Shepherd appointed the first board of commissioners, naming H. M. Garlichs, Wm. E. Jamieson and N. P. Ogden. These commissioners employed a superintendent, Rudolph Rau, a skillful florist and landscape gardener, who is still in his place. The council provided liberally, and the result is that Krug Park is one of the most picturesque places in the West, and in ten years will surpass any public park of its size and kind in the country.

There were those who believed, and with good reason, that if the city owned Lake Contrary that body of water and the surroundings would be greatly improved and beautified. Congressman R. P. C. Wilson was appealed to, and, in 1890, secured the passage of an act of congress granting to the city of St. Joseph Lake Contrary and the shores thereof. Early in 1891, the city ordered a canal cut to unite the upper and lower lakes. The farmers in the neighborhood protested and obtained an injunction. The cause was tried, and it was found that the United States, having previously given to the state of Missouri all of the territory embracing Lake Contrary, had no right to give the property to the city, having, in fact, no title. Had the result of the trial been favorable to the city Lake Conrary would appear to better advantage than it does now.

The park board has been composed as follows since 1890: For 1890-93, H. M. Garlichs, Wm. E. Jamieson, N. P. Ogden; for 1893-94, Joseph Hansen, Charles F. Bacon, F. G. Hopkins; for 1894-96, Chas. F. Bacon, F. G. Hopkins, John L. Bittinger; for 1896-98, Frank G. Hopkins, Charles F. Bacon, Sol Ehrman; for 1898-99, Frank G. Hopkins, Sol Ehrman, Henry Uhlinger. Appointments to membership on the park board have since been made as follows: Adolph Schrader, 1899; Robert McGowan, 1900; Henry Uhlinger, 1901; L. D. W. Van Vleit, 1902; J. R. McKillop (Schrader resigned), 1902; J. M. Austin, 1903; Henry Uhlinger, 1904; E. L. Phipps, 1905; W. H. Griffith, 1906; Dr. E. H. Bullock (succeeded Phipps, resigned), 1907; Henry Uhlinger, 1907; Dr. F. G. Weary (succeeded Dr. Bullock, resigned), 1907; W. D. Webb, 1908; John D. Richardson, 1909; Henry Uhlinger, 1910; W. D. Webb, 1911; Rudolph Janicke, 1912; Fred Neudorff, 1913 (succeeded Janicke, resigned); Henry Uhlinger, 1913; W. D. Webb, 1914; John D. Richardson, 1915.

The powers of the park board were considerably enlarged by the charter of 1909. The board now maintains its own engineering staff and has its own secretary, J. H. Barnes being the present (1915) incumbent. An important innovation was made in May, 1915, when H. G. Getchell, was made supervisor of parks. Rudolph

G. Rau, who has been in active charge of the work in the various parks since the first park board was organized, is still on the job.

An attempt was made to give St. Joseph an extensive park and boulevard system shortly after the charter of 1909 went into ·effect. The first important project, Prospect Park, was initiated· by an ordinance passed in 1911. Strenuous opposition developed, and after the matter had been in litigation for a couple of years, a supreme court decision stopped the work. It has never been revived. However, there are other projects of importance under way, notable among them being the building of Noyes Boulevard.

* * *

THE PUBLIC LIBRARY—Prior to 1887 there were several circulating libraries in St. Joseph. In May of that year Warren Samuel announced through the newspapers that he would give the free use of a room in his building at Tenth and Charles streets for library purposes, provided a certain sum of money could be raised for the purchase of books. Mrs. T. F. Van Natta and Mrs. George C. Hull took the matter in hand, and, ascertaining from Mr. Samuels that if $5,000 was raised he would give the use of a room for five years, plans were at once outlined for securing the sum required. These ladies, together with Mrs. John S. Lemon, successfully solicited seventy-five life memberships at $50 each, and they had collected a total of $3,000 by the August following. When the financial work had progressed thus far, Mr. Samuels executed a lease of the large room on the second floor of his building for three years, with the understanding that the lease would be extended to five years when the remainder of the fund should have been collected.

The library was formally opened on the 8th day of November, 1887, Miss Nellie Millan acting as librarian.

The first board of directors and officers consisted of Mrs. John S. Lemon, president; Mrs. Winslow Judson, vice-president; Mrs. T. F. Van Natta, treasurer; Mrs. George C. Hull, secretary, and Mrs. M. A. Reed, Mrs. John D. Richardson, Jr., Mrs. John I. McDonald and Mrs. B. F. Colt.

The library opened with 2,200 volumes of well-selected books, and during the first year of its existence 1,000 additional volumes were added. Under these auspices it did excellent work, but a lack of funds prevented the success desired. The small yearly sum charged for the use of the library, $2, proved inadequate to its needs, but the library was by no means permitted to languish. The ladies in charge worked hard and through their efforts alone the institution was kept intact.

In January, 1890, Edward S. Douglas suggested the idea of taking advantage of the state law which authorized cities to establish free public libraries by a vote of the people, and the suggestion met with hearty support. Purd B. Wright, then city clerk, united with Mr. Douglas in the movement, and these two pushed the matter. Petitions were prepared asking that the question of voting·

a tax of three-tenths of a mill be submitted to the voters of the city, as authorized by law. Only one hundred names were necessary, but many times this number were secured. When presented to the mayor and council for official consideration the petition contained not only the name of the mayor, George J. Englehart, but those of nine of the ten aldermen as well, in their capacity as citizens. The question being submitted to the voters, such was the interest that had been aroused that it carried by a vote of more than six to one.

In April, 1890, the then mayor-elect, Wm. M. Shepherd, appointed as the first board of directors Rev. H. L. Foote, Prof. E. B. Neeley, Willard P. Hall, H. G. Getchell, Dr. J. Francis Smith, B. Newburger, G. W. Hendley, Mrs. J. S. Lemon and Mrs. George C. Hull. Rev. Foote was at the first meeting elected president and Mr. Getchell, secretary; Prof. E. B. Neeley at the next meeting being elected vice-president. After a few months' service, Mrs. Hull and Mrs. Lmon and Dr. Smith resigned from the board, Mr. Johnson, George C. Hull and J. L. Bittinger succeeding them. Mr. Foote remained the president of the board until he left the city in 1895. Prof. E. B. Neeley acted as president during the remainder of the term and was succeeded by Rev. Henry Bullard, who in turn gave way in 1896 to John DeClue, an old member of the board.

Soon after organizing Henry J. Carr, of Grand Rapids, Mich., was employed as librarian, and remained with the library until July, 1891, when he resigned to accept a more lucrative position as head of the Scranton, Pa., public library, just organizing.

Meantime, the old library association, by a vote of a majority of its directors and life members, donated the books owned by it to the free public library, numbering 3,272 volumes, and went out of existence, having accomplished its real purpose in providing the nucleus of the present successful institution. Mrs. Russel¹, who had succeeded Miss Millan as librarian, was continued in the employ of the free library under Mr. Carr. The remainder of the force was Miss C. L. Rathbun, Miss L. C. Senter, who was appointed assistant librarian in April; and Miss Agnes Van Volkenburg. Miss A. M. Perry was the next employe.

Large purchases of books were made as soon as a librarian was employed, but the work of classifying and cataloguing required so much time that the library was not opened for the issue of books for home use until March 16, 1891, with 5,510 volumes; the reference and reading rooms, however, having been opened two months previously. On the resignation of Mr. Carr, George T. Wright, formerly of this city, but then of California, was offered the position, but declined on account of his health, and William H. Culver was appointed, continuing in charge until the following year in May, when he resigned. Miss L. C. Senter assumed charge of the library and conducted it until July 1, when H. L. Elmendorf was appointed to the position of librarian. He remained with the library until October 1, 1896, when he, too, resigned and was succeeded by

Purd B. Wright, who resigned in 1910 to accept a position as librarian in Los Angeles, Calif. Mr. Wright was succeeded by C. E. Rush of Jackson, Mich., who took charge July 15, 1910. He has done and is still doing excellent work for the library.

During the administration of Mr. Culver the library was removed from Sixth and Charles streets to Tenth and Sylvanie streets. During the incumbency of Mr. Wright the present handsome library building at Tenth and Felix streets was erected. It was formally opened March 13, 1902, and is used jointly by the school and library boards.

At this time (1915) the library board is organized as follows: James H. McCord, president; Rabbi Louis Bernstein and Samuel I. Motter, vice-presidents; Henry Krug, Jr., secretary-treasurer; Charles E. Rush, assistant secretary.

Some idea of the development of St. Joseph's free public library may be gained from the number of volumes in circulation. In 1898 it was 15,000; now it is 72,000, housed in three buildings— the main library, Carnegie branch in South St. Joseph, and Washington Park branch library in North St. Joseph. Besides these there are various stations in different parts of the city and about seventy-five traveling libraries in the public schools.

* * *

STREET LIGHTING—As early as 1856 the city aided in the erection of a plant for the manufacture of illuminating gas, but this proved an unprofitable investment. In 1861 a second concern secured the contract and the city was lighted, after a fashion, with gas, until 1889. In 1887 gasoline lamps mounted on wooden posts, supplied by a Chicago concern, were added to the system.

In 1889 the city embarked in municipal ownership as to street lighting. A contract was made with the Excelsior Electrical Company of Chicago for a $60,000 plant, to be paid for in two years. The city built a power house at Fifth and Olive streets. Walter C. Stewart superintended the construction of the plant and managed it for the Excelsior company. Frank P. Yenawine was the first city electrician, succeeding Mr. Stewart in 1891. He served until May of 1896 and was in turn succeeded by Mr. Stewart, who gave way to William E. Gorton in 1908; M. C. Hunter in 1912; Amos L. Utz in 1913; C. D. Fox in 1915.

Since its erection various improvements have been added to the plant, making the total cost nearly $175,000.

* * *

THE SEWERAGE SYSTEM—St. Joseph has a well-planned sewer system of considerable extent. In the early days the creeks that coursed through the city from the hills formed the only drainage. Blacksnake, Bush branch, Smith branch and Liniment (or Patee branch) were all creeks of consequence, especially when the rains were heavy. In planning the sewerage system of the city these natural water courses were followed wherever possible. The first effort at sewering was made in 1867, when a section was built between Fifth and Sixth streets, covering Bush branch. In 1870 an extension of 160 feet was added, which brought the sewer to a point on Fifth street about where the side entrance to the Tootle Theater is. This is a five-foot sewer and its mouth was then above ground. There was a trap-door, hinged at the top, which opened automatically when the volume of water was great enough. The street was paved in the shape of a gutter, and during heavy rains was impassable.

The sewer-building era properly began in 1874, when a nine-foot solid limestone sewer was constructed on Charles street, from the river to Seventh street. This was followed by the completion of the Smith branch sewer, which had been started at an earlier period, and which now extends from Twentieth street and Frederick avenue to Seventh and Charles streets. The Bush branch sewer was next continued down Fifth street to Charles. The combined length of these sewers is 16,523 feet.

Messanie street was sewered from the river to Eighth street in 1879. This is a round brick culvert, five feet in diameter. The total length of the sewer now is 1,856 feet.

The building of the Union Depot at Sixth street and Mitchell avenue made it necessary to sewer Liniment creek. In 1880 a section reaching from Fifth to Eighth streets was built. In 1886 it was completed to the river. This is called the Mitchell avenue sewer. It is thirteen to fifteen feet in diameter, and built of brick. The Patee branch sewer, ranging in diameter from eight and one-half to ten and one-half feet, oval, brick, joins the Mitchell avenue sewer at Eighth street. It was built in sections and completed to Twenty-second street in 1894. The combined length is 8,188 feet.

The first section of Blacksnake sewer was built in 1883 across Main street. In 1889 it was carried east to Third street. In 1891 the city and the Chicago Great Western Railway Company jointly built the sewer from the Main street section to the river. In 1894 the sewer was extended from Third street, along the course of Blacksnake creek, to Pendleton street; and in 1896, to Middleton street. This is a brick sewer, egg-shaped. The dimensions of the western portion are 14½x17 feet. At the time of its building it was the largest brick sewer in the world.

By an issue of bonds in 1908, $250,000 was voted for main sewers. Provision was made for: Blacksnake sewer extension to Broadway, Highland avenue sewer, Grand avenue sewer, Brookdale sewer, Eastern Extension addition sewer, Hall's addition sewer, Sycamore sewer, Patee street and Thirty-first street and Thirty-second street branches of Oak Hill sewer, Wyatt Park sewer, Atchison street sewer, South Park sewer, Eleventh street sewer, Gordon avenue sewer, Barbara street sewer, and Lake avenue sewer.

There are more than five miles of main sewers and sixty miles of district sewers that drain into these main sewers. In all, there are nearly sixty-five miles of sewers in St. Joseph.

Prior to 1885 property owners who desired sewerage had to build at their own expense. Now, however, the city is divided into sewer districts, and when a sewer is desired in a certain neighborhood, to drain into a main sewer, three or more property owners petition the council, and an ordinance is passed ordering the sewer. The city engineer advertises for bids, and when the work is completed the cost is assessed against all of the real estate in the district, in proportion to the number of square feet contained in each lot. Special tax bills are issued, which bear 6 per cent interest after thirty days. The contractor is placed under bond to keep his work in repair for one year. By this method the burden of sewer building has been lightened, and, as a consequence, the drainage of St. Joseph is excellent.

* * *

STREET PAVING—From 1866 to 1873 the topography of the city underwent a great transformation. The grader opened streets, leveled hills and filled hollows; many miles of macadam were put down in the business and residence portions of the city. There had been street paving in the neighborhood of the Market square before the war, but the streets in general were in bad condition. Nor did the enterprising people of St. Joseph stop at home in their zeal for paving, but they went across the river—or at least their money did—and aided in the building of a rock road from Elwood west. Bonds in the sum of $25,000 were voted for this purpose, and the money was doubtless returned indirectly by the farmers who came to the city over the highway. Portions of the rock road are still in existence, though in bad repair.

The panic of 1873 checked all public improvements, and for the next thirteen years little paving was done. By 1886 the business streets were in wretched condition. The macadam was worn in many places beyond repair. Omaha was putting down asphaltum pavements. Dr. Thomas H. Doyle, who had been elected mayor upon the issue of good streets, was a strong advocate of asphaltum, and a committee that visited Omaha brought back satisfactory reports. The real estate boom was on and the prospects seemed brilliant. There was no difficulty in securing signers for street paving, and so the work began in the summer of 1886. Felix and Edmond streets were paved with asphaltum, and Francis street to Frederick avenue; as were also Fourth street, from Felix to Olive, and Third street, from Jule street to Messanie. In 1887 Sixth street was paved with asphaltum from Atchison street to Hall, and Frederick avenue from Eighth street to its terminus. In 1888 cedar blocks were put down on Twentieth and on Faraon streets, and during the same year many miles of macadam were laid in the residence districts. In 1890 vitrified brick was introduced, and with this material Francis street was paved from Frederick avenue to Thirteenth street, Main street from Felix to Isidore, and Fifth street from Patee to Antoine. In 1891 brick paving was laid on Messanie street from Second to Eighth streets, on Lafayette street from Twenty-second to Twenty-eighth, and on Olive from Twenty-sixth to Twenty-eighth. In 1892 Charles street, from Second street to Twelfth, was paved with brick; in 1893 Jule street, from Main street to Sixth, and Fourth street, from Francis street to Faraon, were similarly paved.

For the next four years no paving except macadam was put down, and not much of that. In the fall of 1897 Third street was paved with asphaltum from Jule street to Franklin. Seventh street, from Olive to Robidoux, was paved with asphaltum also.

Activities in street paving began again in 1901 and since that time many substantial improvements of this character have been made each year. Concrete has come into favor as a paving material, while few streets are laid with brick, which for many years was the popular material. There one hundred and twenty-five miles of paved streets in St. Joseph at this time.

CHAPTER XII.

MUNICIPAL OFFICES AND THEIR INCUMBENTS—THE BOARD OF TOWN TRUSTEES, AND THE CITY COUNCIL —PRESIDENT AND MAYOR, CLERK, REGISTER AND AUDITOR, COLLECTOR AND TREASURER AND COMPTROLLER—THE ENGINEER—THE HEALTH DEPARTMENT—ASSESSOR, COUNSELOR, STREET COMMISSIONER, LICENSE INSPECTOR, SUPERINTENDENT OF BUILDING, BOILER INSPECTOR, AND MINOR OFFICERS—SALARIES, TERMS OF OFFICE AND DUTIES.

The municipal affairs of St. Joseph, like those of other incorporated communities, have always been administered by men chosen by the people. As a town the administrative function was vested in a board of sevent trustees, who selected on of their number as president. The first board, elected in 1845, was composed of Joseph Robidoux, president; Isadore Barada, John F. Carter, Johnson Copeland, Wiley M. English, Sinclair K. Miller and Benjamin Powell. The next board, in 1846, was composed of Wiley M. English, president; Preston T. Moss, Johnson Copeland, Allen G. Mansfield, Posey N. Smith, Henry S. Creal and Joseph Robidoux. The board for 1847 was composed of Henry S. Creal, president; Wiley M. English, Johnson Copeland, Preston T. Moss, Edward Searcy, William H. High, Aaron Lewis and James B. Gardenhire. The board for 1848 was composed of Lewis Tracy, president; Joseph Smith, William Ridenbaugh, Preston T. Moss, Samuel D. Overstreet, Thomas Wildbahn and James A. Anthony. The board for 1849 was composed of James A. Anthony, president; John Whitehead, Henry S. Creal, Thomas Price, Wiley M. English, Thomas Wildbahn and Lewis Tracy. The last board was composed of James A. Anthony, president; Lewis Tracy, John Rhode, William M. Carter, James B. Pendleton, Abraham M. Dillon and Lewis Stigers.

* * *

MAYORS—Thomas Mills, the first mayor, was elected in April, 1851, and served one year. His successors were as follows: Robert Lamdin, 1852-53; James A. Anthony, 1853-54; Robert Boyle, 1854-55; Jonathan M. Bassett, 1855-56; John Corby, 1856-57; Armstrong Beattie, 1857-59; M. Jeff Thompson, 1859-60; Armstrong Beattie, 1860-61; Frederick W. Smith, 1861-62; Thomas Harbine, 1862-64; W. R. Penick, 1864-66; Armstrong Beattie, 1866-67; Dr. Francis J. Davis, 1867-68; George H. Hall, 1868-70; John Severance, 1870-74; Isaac T. Hosea, 1874-78; Armstrong Beattie, 1878-80; Joseph A. Piner, 1880-82; Francis M. Postegate, 1882-84; H.

R. W. Hartwig, 1884-86; Dr. Thomas H. Doyle, 1886-88; George J. Englehart, 1888-90; William M. Shepherd, 1890-96; Lawrence A. Vories, 1896-98; Dr. Peter J. Kirschner, 1898-1900; John Combe, 1900-02; Charles J. Borden, 1902-04; William E. Spratt, 1904-08; A. P. Clayton, 1908-12; Charles A. Pfeiffer, 1912-14; Elliot Marshall, 1914.

* * *

THE COUNCIL—The first council, elected in 1851, was composed as follows, there being but three wards: First ward, John Angel, James Pendleton; Second ward, William M. Carter, James Pendleton; Third ward, James A. Anthony, John H. Whitehead. For the ensuing years the representation was as follows:

For 1852-53—First ward, John Angel, James B. Pendleton; Second ward, Joel J. Penick, W. M. Carter; Third ward, John H. Whitehead, B. F. Loan.

. For 1853-54—First ward, H. D. Louthen, B. O'Driscoll; Second ward, W. M. Carter, Joel Penick; Third ward, John H. Whitehead, Thomas Wildbahn.

For 1854-55—First ward, John C. Cargill, Emery Livermore; Second ward, Robert W. Donnell, Joseph C. Hull; Third ward, Thomas Wildbahn, Robert L. McGhee.

For 1855-56—First ward, H. D. Louthen, James B. Pendleton; Second ward, Joseph C. Hull, Preston T. Moss; Third ward, Armstrong Beattie, J. O. Fisher.

For 1856-57—First ward, John Angel, James B. Pendleton; Second ward, Preston T. Moss, O. K. Knode; Third ward, Armstrong Beattie, John O. Fisher.

For 1857-58—First ward, Frederick W. Smith, N. J. McAshan; Second ward, O. B. Knode, Charles Kearney; Third ward, John J. Johnson, Samuel Floyd.

For 1858-59—First ward, J. N. McAshan, John Rhode; Second ward, O. B. Knode, J. A. Chambers; Third ward, John J. Johnson, Samuel G. Floyd.

For 1859-60—First ward, Michael McGee, William Lennox; Second ward, Thomas Keys, Wm. J. Taylor; Third ward, James Highly, Samuel G. Floyd.

For 1860-61—First ward, Wm. R. Penick, John Rhode; Second ward, D. J. Heaton, Robert F. Maxwell; Third ward, J. J. Johnson, P. L. McLaughlin.

For 1861-62—First ward, Michael McGee, Louis Hax; Second ward, A. G. Clark, John Saunders; Third ward, James A. Storm, Samuel H. Boyd.

For 1862-63—First ward, James Tracy, Elias Eppstein; Second ward, George T. Hoagland, William Fowler; Third ward, Joseph C. Hull, John Colhoun.

For 1863-64—First ward, J. D. McNeely, G. W. H. Landon; Second ward, Anton Klos, R. Fisher; Third ward, Henry Boder, Joseph Steinacker.

For 1864-65—There were now five wards, represented as follows: First ward, Thos. H. Ritchie, Wm. Z. Ransom; Second ward, John R. Bell, W. L. Chadwick; Third ward, John Corby, George T. Hoagland; Fourth ward, J. D. McNeely, A. Andriano; Fifth ward, ·H. N. Turner, Jeremiah Whalen.

For 1865-66—First ward, W. Z. Ransom, Wm. M. Albin; Second ward, W. L. Chadwick, John Colhoun; Third ward, John Corby, George T. Hoagland; Fourth ward, J. D. McNeeley, A. Andriano; Fifth ward, H. N. Turner, Isaac Wilkins.

For 1866-67—First ward, W. Z. Ransom, Wm. M. Albin; Second ward, W. L. Chadwick, Edward R. Brandow; Third ward, George T. Hoagland, Samuel Hays; Fourth ward, A. Andriano, Bernard Patton; Fifth ward, Jeremiah Whalen, Isaac Wilkins.

For 1867-68—First ward, W. Z. Ransom, Phillip Pinger; Second ward, J. H. Dayton, Robert Gunn; Third ward, John Corby, John A. Dolman; Fourth ward, J. D. McNeely, David H. Winton; Fifth ward, Patrick H. Early, M. Fitzgerald.

For 1868-69—First ward, W. Z. Ransom, Florence Kiley; Second ward, I. Van Riley, O. M. Smith.; Third ward, John A. Dolman, Thomas E. Tootle; Fourth ward, David H. Winton, Michael McGee; Fifth ward, Patrick Early, M. Fitzgerald.

For 1869-70—First ward, Florence Kiley; J. C. Kessler; Second ward, Robert Gunn, I. Van Riley; Third ward, John A. Dolman, J. A. V. McNeal; Fourth ward, D. H. Winton, Phillip Pinger; Fifth ward, Patrick Early, M. Fitzgerald.

For 1870-71—First ward, J. C. Kessler, Seymour Jenkins; Second ward, Robert Gunn, George Buell; Third ward, A. C. V. McNeal, C. W. Davenport; Fourth ward, Phillip Pinger, George Hildebrant; Fifth ward, M. Fitzgerald, Henry Blum.

For 1871-72—First ward, Seymour Jenkins, Joseph Diedrich; Second ward, George Buell, Fred Westpheling; Third ward, C. W. Davenport, Edwin Toole; Fourth ward, George R. Hildebrant, John Burnside; Fifth ward, Henry Blum, James Bowen.

For 1872-73—First ward, Seymour Jenkins, Joseph Diedrich; Second ward, Fred Westpheling, Oscar Schramm; Third ward, Edwin Toole, Isaac Curd; Fourth ward, John Burnside, John Kieffer; Fifth ward, James Bowen, E. W. Ray.

For 1873-74—First ward, Seymour Jenkins, Joseph Diedrich; Second ward, Oscar Schramm, J. H. Dayton; Third ward, Isaac Curd, James M. Street; Fourth ward, George R. Hildebrant, John Kieffer; Fifth ward, Joseph Hermann, E. W. Ray.

For 1874-75—First ward, Seymour Jenkins, Joseph Diedrich; Second ward, Oscar Schramm, J. H. Dayton; Third ward, James M. Street, Donald M. McDonald; Fourth ward, George R. Hildebrant, Wm. Sidenfaden; Fifth ward, Joseph Hermann, Michael Kiley.

For 1875-76—First ward, Seymour Jenkins, Joseph Diedrich; Second ward, Oscar Schramm, J. H. Dayton; Third ward, James M. Street, Wm. H. Wood; Fourth ward, George R. Hildebrant, Wm. Sidenfaden; Fifth ward, Michael Kiley, Joseph Hermann.

For 1876-77—First ward, Seymour Jenkins, Jacob Arnholt; Second ward, Oscar Schrämm, J. H. Dayton; Third ward, Wm. H. Wood, Thomas H. Hail; Fourth ward, J. D. McNeely, Wm. Sidenfaden; Fifth ward, Michael Kiley, Charles Michaelis.

For 1877-78—First ward, Jacob Arnholt, Charles Howe; Second ward, J. H. Dayton, George W. Morris; Third ward, Thomas H. Hail, H. C. Cockrill; Fourth ward, Wm. Sidenfaden, Joseph H. McInerny; Fifth ward, John Kieffer, Thomas Aylesbury.

For 1878-79—First ward, Seymour Jenkins, Charles Howe; Second ward, George W. Morris; Third ward, Thomas H. Hail, H. C. Cockrill; Fourth ward, J. D. McNeely, Joseph McInerny; Fifth ward, Thomas Aylesbury, Maurice Hickey.

For 1879-80—First ward, Seymour Jenkins, John Newcum; Second ward, George W. Morris, I. B. Thompson; Third ward, Chas. W. Campbell, Samuel Westheimer; Fourth ward, Joseph McInerny, J. D. McNeely; Fifth ward, Thomas Aylesbury, Maurice Hickey.

For 1880-81—First ward, Seymour Jenkins, John Newcum; Second ward, George W. Morris, I. B. Thompson; Third ward, Samuel Westheimer, Chas. W. Campbell; Fourth ward, Joseph McInerny, J. W. Atwill; Fifth ward, Thos. Aylesbury, Maurice Hickey.

For 1881-82—First ward, Seymour Jenkins, Stephen Geiger; Second ward, John S. Lemon, I. B. Thompson; Third ward, Chas. W. Campbell, Samuel Westheimer; Fourth ward, J. W. Atwill, Egid Wagner; Fifth ward, R. Womach, Wm. O'Hara.

For 1882-83—First ward, Seymour Jenkins, Willis M. Sherwood; Second ward, Simon Stern, I. B. Thompson; Third ward, Jacob Geiger, Samuel Westheimer; Fourth ward, Joseph McInerny, Egid Wagner; Fifth ward, Thos. Winston, John Kieffer.

For 1883-84—First ward, Seymour Jenkins, Willis M. Sherwood; Second ward, Simon Stern, J. M. Austin; Third ward, Samuel Westheimer, Jacob Geiger; Fourth ward, Joseph McInerny, Egid Wagner; Fifth ward, Thomas Winston, Wm. Valentine.

For 1884-85—First ward, Seymour Jenkins, Ben B. Turner; Second ward, Simon Stern, J. M. Austin; Third ward, Stephen F. Carpenter, Samuel Westheimer; Fourth ward, Joseph McInerny, John Giller; Fifth ward, Thomas Winston, Wm. Valentine.

For 1885-86—First ward, Charles Nowland, B. B. Turner; Second ward, Simon Stern, J. M. Austin; Third ward, S. F. Carpenter, Ewald Padberg; Fourth ward, Charles T. Nicholls, John Giller; Fifth ward, Thomas Winston, Wm. Valentine.

For 1886-87—First ward, Charles Nowland, Thos. R. Ashbrook; Second ward, James H. Lewis, George W. Morris; Third ward, Justus C. Gregg, Ewald Padberg; Fourth ward, William H. Jones, Oscar M. Spalsbury; Fifth ward, William E. Jamieson, John B. Ryan.

For 1887-88—First ward, Chas. Nowland, Thos. R. Ashbrook; Second ward, George W. Morris, (Mr. Lewis resigned and his place was left vacant) ; Third ward, J. C. Gregg, Ewald Padberg; Fourth ward, Wm. H. Jones, O. M. Spalsbury; Fifth ward, W. E. Jamieson, John B. Ryan.

For 1888-89—First ward, Wilfred McDonald, Henry Luchsinger; Second ward, Nelson J. Riley, Samuel Ostrander; Third ward, Jacob Geiger, Henry Ellinger; Fourth ward, Rufus Todd, S. O. Brooks; Fifth ward, Wm. E. Jamieson, John B. Ryan.

For 1889-90—First ward, Wilfred McDonald, David E. Marshall; Second ward, N. J. Riley, Samuel Ostrander; Third ward, Jacob Geiger, Henry Ellinger; Fourth ward, Rufus Todd, Edward Felling; Fifth ward, Wm. E. Jamieson, A. E. Arnell.

For 1890-91—In 1890 the city limits were extended and the territory divided into eight wards. There were sixteen aldermen as follows: First ward, Hans Nielson, Wm. Dersch; Second ward, James M. Hall, D. E. Marshall; Third ward, Samuel Ostrander, J. W. Lancaster; Fourth ward, John L. Zeidler, T. W. Hackett; Fifth ward, Patrick Martin, Henry Ellinger; Sixth ward, Joseph Hermann, Edward B. Felling; Seventh ward, Stephen T. Pendleton, A. E. Arnell; Eighth ward, Charles A. Pfeiffer, James W. Mansfield.

For 1891-92—First ward, Hans Nielson, Wm. Dersch; Second ward, James M. Hall, Thomas N. Finch; Third ward, Albert B. Duncan, J. W. Lancaster; Fourth ward, F. K. Doniphan, John Zeidler; Fifth ward, Patrick Martin, Henry Ellinger; Sixth ward, Joseph Hermann, John Combe; Seventh ward, S. T. Pendleton, W. E. Jamieson; Eighth ward, Charles A. Pfeiffer, Wm. M. Rush, Jr.

For 1892-93—First ward, James Burlington, Wm. Dersch; Second ward, C. F. Meyer, Thos. N. Finch; Third ward, A. B. Duncan, Thos. R. Bretz; Fourth ward, F. K. Doniphan, Robert Baker; Fifth ward, Patrick Martin, George M. Goode; Sixth ward, Wm. L. Buechle, John Combe; Seventh ward, J. W. Stouffer, W. E. Jamieson; Eighth ward, Charles J. Borden, Wm. M. Rush, Jr.

For 1893-94—First ward, James Burlington, Horace Wood; Second ward, C. F. Meyer, John D. Clark; Third ward, Thos. R. Bretz, Daniel Ransom; Fourth ward, R. E. Baker, R. M. Abercrombie; Fifth ward, Geo. M. Good, George L. Jewett; Sixth ward, W. L. Buechle, J. W. Powers; Seventh ward, J. W. Stouffer, M. M. Duggan; Eighth ward, Chas. J. Borden, Samuel Gosnell.

For 1894-95—First ward, John Custer, Horace Wood; Second ward, John D. Clark, Stephen F. Geiger; Third ward, Daniel Ransom, Andrew J. Smith; Fourth ward, R. M. Abercrombie, W. J. Browne; Fifth ward, George M. Good, George Geiwitz; Sixth ward, W. L. Buechle, J. W. Powers; Seventh ward, M. M. Duggan, E. H. Giles; Eighth ward, Chas. J. Borden, Samuel Gosnell.

For 1895-96—First ward, John E. Custer, Hans Nielson; Second ward, S. F. Geiger, Wm. H. Finch; Third ward, A. J. Smith, F. M. Lemmon; Fourth ward, R. M. Abercrombie, W. J. Browne; Fifth ward, J. G. Geiwitz, G. D. Berry; Sixth ward, W. L. Buechle,

Louis Prawitz; Seventh ward, L. H. Giles, W. E. Jamieson; Eighth ward, C. J. Borden, A. S. Long.

For 1896-97—First ward, John E. Custer, Hans Nielson; Second ward, James M.. Cline, W. H. Finch; Third ward, John W. Bruce, F. M. Lemmon; Fourth ward, R. M. Abercrombie, W. J. Browne; Fifth ward, C. A. Tygart, G. D. Berry; Sixth ward, D. H. Schmidt, Louis Prawitz; Seventh ward, W. J. Robertson, W. E. Jamieson; Eighth ward, C. J. Borden, A. S. Long..

For 1897-98—First ward, John E. Custer, Fred E. Ernst; Second ward, James M. Cline, W. H. Finch; Third ward, John W. Bruce, F. C. Kuehl; Fourth ward, G. V. Koch, W. J. Browne; Fifth ward, C. A. Tygart, George W. Akers; Sixth ward, Richard Garvey, D. H. Schmidt; Seventh ward, W. J. Robertson, J. L. Meyer; Eighth ward, C. J. Borden, A. M. Twedell.

For 1898-99—First ward, Fred E. Ernst, Phil Hall; Second ward, Wm. H. Finch, Wm. H. Smith; Third ward, F. C. Kuehl, John W. Bruce; Fourth ward, E. M. Birkes, G. V. Koch; Fifth ward, Gorge W. Akers, John H. Kelly; Sixth ward, Richard Garvey, E. G. Chandlee; Seventh ward, J. L. Meyer, Henry Felling; Eighth ward, A. M. Twedell, Niels P. Sommer.

For 1899-1900—First ward, Phil Hall, W. A. Bodenhausen; Second ward, William H. Finch, Fred M. Smith; Third ward, John W. Bruce, Fred Hoefer; Fourth ward, G. V. Koch, E. M. Birkes; Fifth ward, George W. Akers, John H. Kelly; Sixth ward, Richard Garvey, Ed. G. Chandlee; Seventh ward, J. L. Meyer, Henry Felling; Eighth ward, Neils P. Sommer, A. S. Long.

For 1900-01—Early in 1900 the Ninth ward was created, embracing the territory in South St. Joseph which has been developed by the packing industries. The council for 1900-01 was: First ward, William Liebig, W. A. Bodenhausen; Second ward, William H. Finch, William F. Bode; Third ward, John W. Bruce, Fred Hoefer, L. O. Weakley (Hoefer resigned); Fourth ward, G. V. Koch, E. M. Birkes; Fifth ward, George W. Akers, O. M. Spalsbury; Sixth ward, Richard J. Garvey, Charles F. Ogden; Seventh ward, J. L. Meyer, W. E. Pamieson; Eighth ward, A. S. Long, C. J. Pohle; Ninth ward, Louis R. Sack, A. K. Pickle.

For 1901-02—The legislature in 1901 amended the charter so as to give St. Joseph a legislative body composed of two houses, a house of delegates, consisting of one member from each ward, elected locally, and a council, composed of five members elected at large. Each body was organized independent of the other. Joint sessions were held to consider appointments and, similar matters. These were known as session of the municipal assembly. At the beginning of this new order of things the council was composed of nine members who had one year yet to serve, the membership of this body being William Liebig, William F. Bode, John W. Bruce, E. M. Birkes, O. M. Spalsbury, Charles F. Ogden, William E. Jamieson, C. J. Pohle and L. R. Sack. The house of delegates was composed of James E. Gates, representing the First ward; Benjamin B. Turner, Second ward; L. O. Weakley, Third ward; F. C. Barrington, Fourth ward; Joseph Andriano, Fifth ward; John Wisniewski, Sixth ward; J. L. Meyer, Seventh ward; A. W. Horn, Eighth ward; J. W. Fleeman, Ninth ward.

For 1902-03—Council: Joseph Andriano, John O. Barkley, John W. Bruce, Louis R. Sack, Brant C. Thayer; House of Delegates: First ward, E. O. Hicks; Second ward, John F. Imel; Third ward, Edward W. Klos; Fourth ward, Joseph A. Fullerton; Fifth ward, Ulysses G. Crandall; Sixth ward, Thomas Cannon; Seventh ward, Daniel J. Barrett; Eighth ward, A. W. Horn; Ninth ward, David C. Reeves.

For 1903-04 — The double-house system was abolished this year, a merger being effected in April, 1903, but all of the details of the new plan were not worked out until the following year, when a council of nine members, elected at large, with a president, also elected, was provided for. The council for 1903-04 was composed of Louis R. Sack, E. O. Hicks, Edward W. Klos, Joseph A. Fullerton, John O. Barkley, Brant C. Thayer, John W. Bruce, Ulysses G. Crandall, Thomas Cannon, Daniel J. Barrett, David C. Reeves, Joseph Andriano, John F. Imel and August W. Horn.

For 1904-06—President, David C. Reeves; First ward, John O. Barkley; Second ward, J. H. Mitchell; Third ward, John W. Bruce; Fourth ward, Brant C. Thayer; Fifth ward, Joseph Andriano; Sixth ward, D. W. Henderson; Seventh ward, Loarn Randall; Eighth ward, Charles Whalen; Ninth ward, Louis R. Sack. Thayer retired in October, 1905, and Jesse I. Roberts was appointed.

For 1906-08—It was also provided in the change in the charter made in 1903 that councilmen and president of the body should be elected for four years, elections being held every two years, when approximately half of the members were chosen. The council for 1906-08 was composed of David C. Reeves, president; First ward, Thomas Shaffer; Second ward, Thomas J. Clark; Third ward, J. C. Schopp; Fourth ward, Jesse I. Roberts; Fifth ward, Vincent Gilpin; Sixth ward, John W. Bennett; Seventh ward, John Egli; Eighth ward, Dr. P. I. Leonard; Ninth ward, Hugh J. Bowen.

For 1908-10—President, Vincent Gilpin; First ward, George O. Meisner; Second ward, Thomas J. Clark; Third ward, W. D. Morrison; Fourth ward, Jesse I. Roberts; Fifth ward, Herman J. Gehrs; Sixth ward, John W. Bennett; Seventh ward, Julius H. Eckhardt; Eighth ward, Dr. P. I. Leonard had resigned during his term, and Henry Grosser was appointed to serve until the election of 1908, when he was elected for the remainder of the term; Ninth ward, S. J. Ackerly. The seat of Herman J. Gehrs was declared vacant in May, 1909, and J. B. Moss was appointed to the vacancy.

For 1910-12—The charter passed by the legislature of 1909 reduced the number of councilmen to five members, elected at large, and abolished the office of president of the council as an elective office, one member of the body being chosen presiding officer by the members thereof. As a result of this change an entirely new council was elected in 1910, as follows: John Egli, John W. Holtman, C. L. Kennedy, E. A. King, J. C. Wyatt. Mr. Wyatt died in November, 1911, and C. D. Radford was appointed to serve out his term.

For 1912-1914—John Brendel, John Egli, John W. Holtman, W. D. Morrison, C. D. Radford.

For 1914-1916—John Brendel, Henry E. Grosser, John W. Holtman, W. D. Morrison, C. D. Radford. Mr. Morrison resigned in September, 1915.

The council passes laws for the government of the city, authorizes the expenditures of money, levies taxes, grants franchises, confirms or rejects appointments, and exercises a general legislative power over the corporation. One of the members is elected president, who is authorized to act as mayor in the absence of that official.

* * *

CLERK, RÉGISTER AND AUDITOR — The late General Ben. F. Loan was appointed clerk and attorney at the first session of the town trustees, in 1845. Levi T. Carr was clerk in 1846, James B. Gardenhire, afterwards attorney general of Missouri, in 1847; Ben F. Loan in 1848, A. D. Madeira in 1849. In 1850-51, the late Joseph J. Wyatt, father of J. C. and George Wyatt, held the office. He was the last clerk of the town board.

Under the city charter which went into operation in 1851, the city register's office was created. The register was a combination of secretary to the council and city accountant. The office was first held by Milton H. Wash, who served 1851-56, and who compiled and published the first city ordinances. William C. Toole succeeded Mr. Wash and served 1856-64, when the late John A. Dolman was elected. Major Dolman served 1864-66 and was succeeded by Thos. H. Ritchie, who served 1866-68. Col. Robert C. Bradshaw, who had distinguished himself in the war, was elected in 1868, and served two years. In 1870 W. W. Brown was elected and served four years, being succeeded by Hardin A. Davis, who served until 1877, when he was succeeded by Enos J. Crowther, who served until 1880. The late James H. Ringo was elected in 1880 and was succeeded in 1882 by the late Francis M. Tufts. Mr. Tufts was the last register. He was elected in 1884, for two years. When the new charter was adopted he resigned and was made auditor.

Purd B. Wright was the first city clerk. He was appointed in April, 1885, and served continuously until April, 1896. Mr. Wright created numerous features of this office and brought order out of a wilderness. His work, his indices and his classifications are of immeasurable value to the city. He was succeeded by Charles S. Shepherd, who was succeeded by John J. Downey in 1899. He was followed by Frank W. Beach, in 1901, who served until August, 1905, when Joel E. Gates, the present clerk, took charge of the office. The city clerk is appointed by the council.

Mr. Tufts was succeeded as auditor by Harry C. Carter, in 1888. Oswald M. Gilmer was elected in 1890, and served four years. He was succeeded in April, 1894, by Thomas R. Ashbrook, who served until April, 1900, when he was succeeded by Caleb B. Lucas, who served until 1906, when Charles Whalen was elected. Frank H. Allen succeeded to the office in 1910, and Robert J. Kennard in 1914.

COLLECTOR AND TREASURER—The constable collected the taxes under the town organization, and the marshal under the city organization, up to 1866. Thomas Henry was the first collector, serving 1866-70. He was succeeded by H. R. W. Hartwig, who served 1870-72. George M. Hauck served 1872-74; Daniel T. Lysaght, 1874-76; James A. Millan, 1876-78; H. N. Turner, 1878-80; Joseph Andriano, 1880-84; Harry C. Carter, 1884-85.

The collector paid the moneys over to the city treasurer, who was generally connected with one of the local banks. Robert I. Boyd and John Curd kept the city's moneys in the town days, and John Curd was city treasurer from 1851 to 1863. George Lyon succeeded Mr. Curd and served three years. In 1866-68 Samuel McGibbens was treasurer, and was succeeded by W. H. Collins, who served one year. Ignatz G. Kappner served 1870-73; H. N, Turner, 1873-74; W. B. Johnson, 1874-77; George C. Hull, 1877-79; George W. Belt, 1879-81; Christian Frenger, 1881-82; Thomas W. Evans, 1882-84; John Colhoun, 1884-85. The collector was elected by the people and the treasurer appointed by the mayor. Under the charter of 1885 these offices were merged. Harry Carter, who had been elected collector in 1884, for two years, resigned and was appointed collector and treasurer for the year 1885-86. The collector received fees under the old system and the treasurer received a salary. The office is now elective and the salary is fixed by the council. Harry Carter was elected to succeed himself, and served 1886-88, when he was succeeded by George C. Crowther, who served 1888-92. Joseph Albus served 1892-96, and was succeeded by Rice D. Gilkey, who was succeeded in 1900 by William A. Dolman. In 1906 he gave way to George H. Wyatt, who was succeeded in 1914 by Frank H. Allen, the present incumbent.

* * *

THE COMPTROLLER—This office is a check upon the auditor and treasurer. Nor can any money be appropriated by the city unless the comptroller certifies that the amount is in the treasury to the credit of the fund from which it is to be drawn. He also countersigns all warrants upon the treasury, redeems outstanding bonds, pays interest coupons, and is the city's fiscal officer.

Gen. James Craig was the first comptroller, the office having been created under the new charter. He was appointed in April of 1885 and served two years. In 1887 he was succeeded by William

B. Johnson, who served until 1895, when he was succeeded by John P. Strong, who served two years, and was succeeded in 1897 by M. M. Riggs, who in turn was succeeded by John F. Johnson. The legislature, in 1899, made the office elective, and Mr. Johnson was elected for a term ending April 18, 1904, when he was succeeded by Thomas R. Ashbrook, who resigned August 20, 1906, and was succeeded by Hiram H. Barnes, who resigned September 30, 1907. Hickman B. Harris was appointed to fill the vacancy. Thomas Shaffer was elected in April, 1908. The charter of 1909 made this office appointive. Shaffer continued to serve until the spring of 1914, when he was succeeded by Frank M. Lemmon, the present incumbent.

* * *

THE CITY ENGINEER—In the early days there was a town surveyor. The first man to hold this position was Capt. F. W. Smith, whose plat of the town Robidoux had accepted. He was succeeded in 1846 by Simeon Kemper, who had also made a plat, that was rejected, which is to be deplored, more at this late day than ever, as Mr. Kemper's plat is said to have been provided with wider streets than Captain Smith's plat. Mr. Kemper served until St. Joseph became a city. Charles Schreiber was the first city engineer, serving 1851-54, when he was succeeded by M. Jeff Thompson, who served 1854-56. Simeon Kemper served in 1856-57, and was succeeded by Charles Hausding, who served 1857-59. P. K. O'Donnell was engineer in 1859-62, and was in turn succeeded by Mr. Hausding, who served 1862-66. John Severance served 1866-70, when he was elected mayor. John Quigly succeeded Colonel Severance, serving 1870-76, and was succeeded by Thomas Long, who served 1876-77. M. J. McCabe was engineer 1877-82, and was succeeded by Frank Fanning, who served 1882-85, when he was in turn succeeded by M. J. McCabe, who served until 1891, when Charles W. Campbell, Jr., took the office. Mr. Campbell served until May of 1898, when he was succeeded by J. R. Rackliffe, who served until the spring of 1901, when William H. Floyd, Jr., was appointed by Mayor Combe. Floyd was succeeded in 1906 by David L. Lawlor, and he by Charles W. Campbell, in April, 1912. Mr. Campbell died in December, 1914. Carl P. Hoff, the present engineer, was appointed January 1, 1915. This office is now under the jurisdiction of the board of public works.

* * *

THE HEALTH DEPARTMENT—During the California emigration days, when St. Joseph was filled with a miscellaneous population that lived principally out-of-doors, waiting for the grass to come, it became necessary to have a health officer to enforce sanitation. Dr. Daniel G. Keedy was appointed by the board of town trustees in 1849 and served one year. He was succeeded by Dr. Josiah H. Crane, who held the office for two years, being the first appointee of the mayor and council when St. Joseph became a city. The place has been held by the following physicians since then: Dr. James Sykes, 1852-55; Dr. John A. Chambers, 1855-56; Dr. Crane, 1856-57; Dr. C. F. Knight, 1857-58; Dr. J. G. Meacher, 1858-60; Dr. Knight, 1860-61; Dr. Hugh Trevor, 1861-62; Dr. W. I. Heddens, 1862-64; Dr. James F. Bruner, 1864-66; Dr. F. T. Davis, 1866-67; Dr. A. V. Banes, 1867-69; Dr. J. D. Smith, 1870-71; Dr. Knight, 1871-72; Dr. J. A. Gore, 1872-73; Dr. Knight, 1873-74; Dr. J. M. D. France, 1874-75; Dr. D. I. Christopher, 1875-77; Dr. Thos. H. Doyle, 1877-79; Dr. Gore, 1879-80; Dr. P. J. Kirschner, 1880-82; Dr. F. C. Hoyt, 1882-84; Dr. J. A. French, 1884-86; Dr. Charles O'Ferrall, 1886-88; Dr. Wm. H. Geiger, 1888-90; Dr. J. T. Berghoff, 1890-92; Dr. Thos. K. Sawyer, 1892-94; Dr. Wm. H. Geiger, 1894-96; Dr. W. B. Davis, 1896-98. Dr. J. K. Graham served two years, and was succeeded by Dr. J. F. Owen in 1900; Dr. C. A. Tygart, 1902; Dr. W. B. Deffenbaugh, 1904; Dr. E. S. Ballard, 1908; Dr. G. M. Boteler, 1912. At this time the office was abolished and the duties of city physician were assumed by officials of the social welfare board.

In 1890-92, Dr. W. T. Elam was assistant health officer to Dr. Berhoff. In 1894-96, Dr. J. R. A. Crossland (colored) was assistant to Dr. Geiger. In 1896-97, Dr. Levi Long was assistant to Dr. Davis, and in 1897-98, Dr. Graham was Dr. Davis' assistant. During the term of Dr. Graham as city physician there was no assistant. Dr. M. F. Hall was Dr. Tygart's assistant; Dr. Spier Richmond served with Dr. Owen, and Dr. E. S. Ballard with Dr. Deffenbaugh. Dr. J. H. McCoy was named for this office April 27, 1908, and Dr. T. J. Stamey, March 3, 1910. It was abolished with the office of city physician.

In 1890 a city dispensary was established and the office of city chemist created. The dispensary was located at the city hall. The duties of the chemist were to analyze milk and food, to compound charity prescriptions, to act as clerk of the board of health, issue burial permits and to keep vital statistics. Logan D. Currin was the first city chemist. He was succeeded by Ed E. Hunter, who held the place continuously until the office was abolished in the first part of the fiscal year of 1898-99. The steward of the hospital, who was required to be a physician, filled the offices of city chemist and assistant health officer. In 1902 the office of clerk of the board of health and city chemist was again established, and William H. Hartigan was appointed to fill it. He was succeeded by Joseph Quinliven, September 19, 1907. W. B. Kelling was appointed in 1908. He was succeeded by William E. Harrington, the present incumbent, September 15, 1912.

THE ASSESSOR—There has always been an assessor, for where taxes are to be levied there must be a valuation of property. Charles White was the first assessor of the town of St. Joseph, serving in 1845. The office was held in 1846 by George W. Waller, in 1847 by Milton H. Wash, in 1848 by Simeon Kemper, who was also surveyor at the same time; in 1849 by H. S. Smith, and in 1850 by James

O'Donoghue. The first assessor under the city charter was Isador Poulin, who served 1851-52. This office has since been held as follows: F. M. Wright, 1852-53; James A. Owen, 1853-54; Felix Robidoux, 1854-55; Wm. C. Toole, 1855-56; John A. Dolman, 1856-57; James A. Owen, 1857-59; Charles M. Thompson, 1859-60; Preston T. Moss, 1860-61; Joseph McAleer, 1861-62; Cyrus E. Kemp, 1862-63; E. H. Saville, 1863-64; John Angel, 1864-65; John B. Harder, 1865-66; James A. Matney, 1866-67; John E. McGinty, 1867-68; John O'Donoghue, 1868-69; James A. Matney, 1869-70; E. H. Saville, 1870-71; J. B. Hawley, 1871-72; Wm. Drumhiller, 1872-73; James H. Ringo, 1873-75; James A. Millan, 1875-77; John T. Baldwin, 1877-78; Robert C. Bradshaw, 1879-82; Joseph Thompson, 1882-84; Thomas Kelly, 1884-85; Ishmael Davis, 1885-86; D. M. McDonald, 1886-87; Joseph E. Cook, 1887-89; John P. Strong, 1889-95; Caleb B. Lucas, 1895-97; George B. Allee, 1897-1901; Perry Noland, 1901-03; George F. Casey, 1903-1905; A. W. Horn, 1905-1915; George C. Toel, 1915—.

* * *

COUNSELOR—Prior to 1877 it was the duty of the city attorney to give advice to the mayor and council and to defend suits against the city. The first regular counselor, as near as can be ascertained, was Benjamin R. Vineyard, who was appointed by Mayor Beattie in 1877. Mr. Vineyard served until the spring of 1879 and was succeeded by Andrew Royal, who served 1879-80. Mordecai Oliver was counselor to Mayor Piner in the first year of his administration, 1880-81; and Samuel B. Green in the second year, 1881-82. Vinton Pike held the position under Mayor Posegate, 1882-84, and was succeeded by James Limbird, under Mayor Hartwig, 1884-87. Under Mayor Doyle, 1887-89, Thomas F. Ryan was counselor, and he was succeeded by Morris A. Reed, who served 1889-91, two years under Mayor Englehart and one year under Mayor Shepherd. Samuel P. Huston served 1891-95 and was succeeded by William K. Amick, who served 1895-97 and was succeeded by Benjamin J. Casteel, who resigned in April, 1899, and was succeeded by R. E. Culver, who served two years and was succeeded by Kendal B. Randolph, who gave way to James M. Wilson in 1903. W. B. Norris was appointed in 1905. He served until April, 1913, when he was succeeded by Frank B. Fulkerson. Charles L. Faust, the present counselor, was appointed in April, 1915.

STREET COMMISSIONER—In 1846 the board of trustees of the town of St. Joseph found it necessary to have the streets looked after and repaired, so they appointed William King street commissioner. It was a one-year office in those days and was held in 1847 by David J. Heaton, in 1848 by William King, in 1849 by V. Tullar, and in 1850 by William Langston. Johnson Copeland was the first street commissioner under the city charter, serving 1851-52. Then came the following incumbents: James Connell, 1852-54; Jesse B. Lowe, 1854-55; A. L. Creal, 1855-56; Robert Dixon, 1856-57; A.

. Creal, 1857-59; Thomas Byrne, 1859-60; Charles Lehman, 1860-61; John Sheehan, 1861-62; John B. Harder, 1862-65; Wm. B. Gilmore, 1865-66; J. L. Bowen, 1866-67; John Sheehan, 1867-68; John Bloomer, 1868-69; G. B. Skinner, 1869-70; Wm. Frick, 1870-72; Nat Hammond, 1872-74; John Clark, 1874-77; Florence Kiley, 1877-80; Isaac N. Brooks, 1880-81; Henry W. Dunn, 1881-82; H. N. Turner, 1882-84; Patrick McIntyre, 1884-86; Thomas A. Carson, 1886-88; W. G. W. Ritchie, 1888-90; Henry Luchsinger, 1890-91; J. B. Vance, 1891-92; Peter Bowen, 1892-93; Samuel J. Jeffries, 1893-94; Francis M. Posegate, 1894-96; Henry Gibson, 1896-98; Abraham Furst, 1898. The street commissioner formerly superintended the workhouse and fed the prisoners, but such has not been the case since 1885. The street commissioner's duties are now performed by an attache of the board of public works. Charles G. Gates has the position now (1915).

* * *

LICENSE INSPECTOR—This office was created in 1885, and James W. Fowler was the first incumbent. He was succeeded in 1889 by Joseph E. Cook, who served until 1893. Edward Burns served 1893-95. John D. Clark served 1895-97, and was succeeded by Louis Herwig, who was followed by Charles Craighill in 1899. Two years later John P. Remelius was appointed. He was followed by Harry Lucksinger in 1906; James J. McGreevy, 1909; E. M. Gilpin, 1912; Thomas Dear, 1914. In 1905 the license inspector was attached to the auditor's office, the incumbent being appointed by the auditor. It has since been restored to the mayor's list of appointive offices. This office is charged with the enforcement of the license ordinances and the incumbent is also the inspector of weights and measures.

SUPERINTENDENT OF BUILDING — This office was created in 1886 and Seymour Jenkins was the first inspector, serving two years. He was followed by Myron Lytle, 1888-90; Joseph Massard, 1890-92; Thomas Winn, 1892-94; George W. Bulger, 1894-96; Lyman W. Forgrave, 1896-1902; William Fredericks, 1902-04; Thomas W. Stamey, 1904-06; Daniel J. Semple, 1906-08; L. W. Forgrave, 1908-12; E. Gray Powell, 1912-14; Frank Siemens, 1914. This officer issues permits for the erection of buildings. He is charged with the enforcement of the ordinances relating to construction, and has the power to condemn unsafe or insanitary buildings. He is appointed, holds his office during good behavior, and receives $1,800 per annum salary.

* * *

BOARD OF PUBLIC WORKS—When the two-house legislative body was abandoned in 1903, a board of public works was created, having general supervision over public works and such matters. The board appoints the city engineer, superintendent of city light plant, street commissioners, sidewalk and other inspectors that formerly were named by the mayor. The following named have constituted the board since its creation: 1903-04, John C. Landis, B. F. Buazard, August Nunning; 1904-05, John C. Landis, B. F. Buazard, W. A. Bodenhausen; 1905-06, B. F. Buazard, W. A. Bodenhausen, John F. Johnson; 1906-07, John F. Johnson, John B. Ryan, Harry Hansen (appointed to fill the unexpired term of W. A. Bodenhausen, resigned); 1907-08, John F. Johnson, John B. Ryan, Harry Hansen; 1908-09, John B. Ryan, Harry Hansen, Alfred Meier; 1909-10, Harry Hansen, Alfred Meier, J. W. Haight; 1910-11, Harry Hansen, Alfred Meier, J. W. Haight; 1911-12, Harry Hansen, Alfred Meier, J. W. Haight; 1912-13, Harry Hansen, Alfred Meier, Charles Nowland; 1913-14, Charles Nowland, Alfred Meier, Rudolph F. Heim; 1914-15, Charles Nowland, Alfred Meier, Rudolph F. Heim; 1915-16, A. W. Horn, Alfred Meier, Rudolph F. Heim. In September, 1915, the entire board resigned. W. D. Morrison, C. E. Dickey and ———————— were appointed by the mayor to fill the vacancies.

Until 1909 the members of the board were appointed by a committee consisting of the mayor, comptroller and auditor; since that time the appointive power has been vested in the mayor.

George F. Barnes was the first clerk of the board. He served until September, 1910, when he was succeeded by J. P. Srite, who gave way to Fred W. Lauder, the present clerk, in April, 1913.

MINOR OFFICERS—The city weighmaster is stationed at Patee market. At one time there were public scales at the workhouse, at the east end of Frederick avenue, at Tenth and Francis streets, and at Seventh and Messanie streets. These have all been abandoned.

The market-master and the city chimney sweep are appointed by the mayor, as is also the public impounder.

The boiler inspector, appointed by the mayor, is charged with the inspection of steam apparatus. Phillip Hart, the first inspector, was appointed in 1886 and served until 1892, when he was succeeded by George Zipf, who served two years and was in turn succeeded by Phillip Hart, who served until 1898, when he was succeeded by Gustav Geis, who was succeeded in 1900 by William Horigan; Joseph Williams, in 1901; Phillip Hart, in 1906, the present incumbent. In connection with this office there is a board of two examiners, appointed by the mayor, who pass upon the qualifications of steam engineers.

During the days of steamboat traffic there was a wharfmaster, whose duty it was to regulate affairs at the landing. During the latter 60's and 70's there was also a wood inspector, whose duty it was to certify to the quantity of wood in a load.

* * *

TERMS AND SALARIES—There is a city election on the first Tuesday after the first Monday in April every alternate year. The mayor, city treasurer, auditor and police judge are elected for two-year terms. The councilmen are elected for four-year terms. The other city officers are appointed by the mayor and council. The terms of all officials except the building inspector and attaches of the fire and police departments, are two years. The salaries are fixed by ordinance before the term of office begins. At this time the mayor receives a salary of $3,600 per annum. The treasurer receives a salary of $2,400 and 5 per cent on all delinquent taxes he collects; he is authorized to employ one deputy and one clerk. The auditor receives $2,400 per annum and is provided with a clerk. The police judge receives $1,200 per annum. The aldermen are paid at the rate of $10 for each meeting they attend, but cannot draw to exceed $300 per annum.

The following are the officers appointed in the even years, together with their compensation: Superintendent of workhouse, $600 and 15 cents per meal; license inspector, $1,200; comptroller, $2,400; impounder, $300 and fees; market-master, $780; weigh-master, $600.

The following are appointed in the odd years: Counselor, $3,600; assessor, $1,800; boiler inspector, $1,000; two examining engineers, $75 each; chimney-sweep, fees.

One park commissioner and three members of the library board are appointed each year, the terms being three years. No salaries or emoluments are attached to these places.

The chief of the fire department is appointed by the mayor and holds his office during good behavior, as do also the employes of the fire department. He receives a salary of $2,400 per annum, and his assistant receives $1,800.

The superintendent of electric light is appointed by the board of public works. His salary is $1,800 per annum.

Workhouse guards are selected by the superintendent of that institution. They receive $50 per month.

The superintendent of streets employs the men engaged in cleaning streets. The repair of streets, however, is with the engineer's department.

The park board employs those engaged in the public parks, and the library board those engaged at the free public library.

CHAPTER XIII.

MUNICIPAL EQUIPMENT — THE WATERWORKS — ELECTRIC LIGHTING—GAS COMPANIES OF THE PAST AND PRESENT—TELEPHONE COMPANIES—STREET RAILWAYS—OMNIBUS AND HERDIC COACH LINES—HISTORICAL FACTS CONCERNING THE ABOVE MENTIONED INSTITUTIONS.

In 1875 an unsuccessful effort was made to secure a public water system for St. Joseph. The matter was not permitted to slumber, however, and the close of 1879 saw the project well under way to success. On December 1, 1879, the council passed an ordinance agreeing to contract with W. S. Fitz, John W. Rutherford and their associates for waterworks, when these men had formed a corporation to build such works. The sum of $5,000 was deposited with the city treasurer as a guarantee that this company would be formed and incorporated within ten days.

On December 10, 1879, the council passed an ordinance granting the St. Joseph Water Company the right to construct works on the reservoir gravitation plan, to lay mains, etc. The city reserved the right, at its option, at the expiration of ten years from the date of the approval of the ordinance, to purchase the waterworks, including all pipes, attachments, extensions, franchises, etc., upon giving six months' previous notice in writing; the city and water company each to appoint a person and the two to select a third to appraise the property. The city contracted for one hundred and sixty hydrants for a period of twenty years, the company agreeing to place ten additional hydrants for every mile of pipe to be laid in the future extension of the service. This contract was, as provided for in the ordinance, ratified by the people at a special election, held on December 23, 1879, and only four votes were cast in the negative.

The water company was organized as follows: W. Scott Fitz, president; T. J. Chew, Jr., secretary; J. W. Rutherford, chief engineer. The company agreed to have sixteen miles of pipe laid and the system in operation in one year. One hundred acres of land, some miles north of the city, were purchased and work was begun on January 4, 1880. There was but one reservoir at first, located on a hill 320 feet above the river at low water mark, and 112 feet higher than any point in St. Joseph. The pumping station was located at the river. The original cost of the works was estimated at $300,000, but before they were offered for acceptance the company had expended $700,000.

On January 12, 1881, the works were accepted by the mayor and council, and placed into active service. Theodore W. Davis was the first superintendent and was succeeded by Louis C. Burnes, who served until the spring of 1897, when he was succeeded by Charles H. Taylor, the present superintendent. In October of 1889 the stock and franchise of the company were sold to the American Waterworks and Guarantee Company of Pittsburg, Pa., a combination of capitalists owning and controlling the water systems of thirty-one other cities. The stockholders at the time of the sale were Col. James N. Burnes, Calvin F. Burnes, T. J. Chew, Jr., and William M. Wyeth.

The system has grown and expanded materially since the beginning. The water is pumped from the river, through filters, to the reservoir on the hill, and thence it flows to the city through pipes. The pumping plant consists of two Worthington pumps, each of three million gallon capacity in twenty-four hours; one Gaskill high duty pumping engine, of six million gallons capacity in twenty-four hours; one Northberg engine of eight million gallons capacity, and an Epping-Carpenter pump of six million gallons capacity. The water is lifted to the filters by a Worthington low service pump of eight million gallons capacity, an Epping-Carpenter and a Lawrence pump of ten million gallons capacity. There is also in service a rotary pump with a capacity of eight million gallons. The filtering plant consists of fifteen O. A. H. Jewel filtering tanks, each fifteen feet high and twelve feet in diameter, and eight concrete filters of six million gallons capacity every twenty-four hours. There are now four reservoirs with a combined capacity of twenty-one million gallons. The company has 140 miles of pipe, ranging from four to thirty inches in diameter, and there are 1,153 double nozzle hydrants on the streets for fire protection.

The period of the city's first contract with the water company expired in December, 1899, and negotiations for a renewal were started about that time. After much agitation, including the unsuccessful attempt on the part of the Seckner Contracting Company to build for the city a water plant on the installment plan, the present contract was ratified at a special city election March 24, 1900. This contract will expire in 1920.

* * *

ELECTRIC LIGHT—In 1883 The St. Joseph Electric Light Company, composed of J. F. Barnard, L. D. Tuttle, Joseph A. Corby, A. N. Schuster and R. E. Turner, secured a franchise for stringing wires through the streets, and erected a plant at Fourth street and Mitchell avenue for the production of electric light. Walter C. Stewart, later city electrician, was the superintendent. Only arc lights were furnished, and no attempt was made at street lighting. This plant was absorbed by the People's Street Railway, Electric Light and Power Company, in 1887, which company had a contract to furnish a small number of arc lights to the city. This company introduced the incandescent light. It is now known as the

S. Joseph Railway, Light, Heat and Power Company (see street railways), and its plant is located near the river, between Francis and Felix streets.

* * *

GAS COMPANIES—In 1856 the city went into partnership with J. B. Ranney and others for the purpose of manufacturing illuminating gas. The capital stock of the concern was $50,000, one-half of which was owned by the city. A plant was erected at Fifth and Angelique streets, in a building now used as a stable. Gas came high in those days, at least to private consumers, who were charged $5 per thousand cubic feet.

The people were soon sick of the city's bargain. The treasury being empty, the city's stock in the company was sold to James M. Wilson for 20 per cent of its face value. In 1861 the interest of Ranney & Co. was sold under execution to Thomas B. Weakly, who, with James M. Wilson, operated the works until 1864, when Weakly purchased the interest of Wilson, paying therefor $8,000. Previous to this the works were burned to the ground, but had been rebuilt. At this time Weakly advanced the price of gas to $6 per thousand feet to private consumers, at which price it was held until the purchase of the works in 1871 by James Clements and associates of Detroit, Mich., under the name of Citizens' Gas Light Company, at the sum of $50,000. This company at once enlarged and improved the works and secured the contract for lighting the street lamps, which had remained unlighted for several years. They supplied private consumers at $4.50 per thousand feet, and afterwards reduced the price to $4. For street lamps the city paid $30 per year for each light.

In 1878 the Mutual Gas Light Company came before the city authorities and, through their president, Charles H. Nash, offered to supply private consumers at $2.50 per thousand feet and the street lamps at $25 per annum. They were awarded the contract and granted franchises in the streets equal to the other company. The beginning of work was but the commencement of hostilities between the rival companies, which finally resulted in the sale of the entire works and franchises of the Citizens' to the Mutual Gas Light Company. This company was reorganized some years ago and called the St. Joseph Gas and Manufacturing Company up to the summer of 1897.

In 1890 a franchise to lay gas mains in the streets was granted to the late Charles McGuire of St. Joseph, his heirs and assigns. Upon this was founded the St. Joseph Light and Fuel Company, with Samuel Allerton of Chicago as president and L. C. Burnes of St. Joseph as vice-president and general manager. This company manufactured what was called "water gas." It was used for illuminating purposes also, but required a magnesium burner, shaped like a comb, to produce the desired result. The gas burned against the teeth of the burner, heating them to an incandescent point and producing a brilliant light. The process was afterward changed, and the gas was used for illumination as the ordinary coal product. The works of this company were located at Fourth and Cedar streets. There was lively competition, rates went down, and previously unheard-of concessions were made to consumers.

In the summer of 1897 both of the existing companies were absorbed by the St. Joseph Gas Company, of which Emerson McMillan of New York is president, W. A. P. McDonald of St. Joseph, vice-president; V. L. Elbert, general manager, and A. V. Schaeffer, secretary and treasurer.

The price of gas in St. Joseph for many years to ordinary consumers was $1.25 per thousand cubic feet, with a discount of 25 cents per thousand if the bill was paid before the tenth day of the month. In 1905 natural gas was brought here from the fields in southern Kansas. The price was 30 cents for a while, but has since been raised to 40 cents.

* * *

TELEPHONES—Within a year after the first general public exhibition of the telephone at the Centennial Exposition in Philadelphia, in 1876, this invention was practically applied in this city. John Kenmuir, a jeweler, who is generally remembered, first used the telephone in St. Joseph. His place of business was at No. 509 Felix street, and he connected this with his residence at 1211 Frederick avenue. In the same year a line was strung that connected the two fire department houses—one at the foot of Edmond street, and the other east of the Tootle theater—with the residence of W. B. McNutt, who was then chief of the department. In February of 1878 another fire alarm line was built from the engine house to the International Hotel, at Eighth and Olive streets.

The St. Joseph Telephone Company, a partnership consisting of John Kenmuir, P. LeB. Coombes and Joseph A. Corby, was formed in April of 1879. Work was begun soon thereafter, and on August 12th of the same year an exchange with 150 subscribers was opened, the central office being in the rear of Kenmuir's jewelry establishment. At about the same time the Western Union Telegraph Company opened an exchange with about the same number of subscribers, the central office of which was located in the third floor of what was then known as the Board of Trade building, and which is now part of the Hotel Lee, on Third street. A lively fight ensued, and rates ranged from nothing up to $2 per month. This continued until 1879, when both rivals were absorbed by the National Bell Telephone Company under the name of St. Joseph Telephone Company. The exchange was moved to the third floor of the Fairleigh building, at the southeast corner of Third and Felix streets. In 1882 the Missouri & Kansas Telephone Company purchased the system and maintained its exchange in the Fairleigh building until December 12, 1896, when it was moved into a fireproof building erected by the company on Seventh street between

Felix and Edmond streets.

"The Citizens' Telephone Company was organized in 1893, the incorporators being C. M. Shultz, E. J. Peckham, A. B. Sowden and M. M. Riggs. A franchise was secured from the council, and in 1894 an exchange was opened in the Hughes building. In 1909 a new exchange was built on Tenth street north of Frederick avenue and the plant was improved and extended. In 1912 the Missouri & Kansas and the Citizens' telephone companies were consolidated.

* * *

STREET RAILWAYS—St. Joseph has over sixty miles of street railway, operated by electricity. Like all other public conveniences of this kind that existed prior to 1885, St. Joseph street railways were first equipped with horses and mules.

The first street railway line in St. Joseph was built in 1866 by Richard E. Turner, Thomas J. Chew, Jr., Arthur Kirpathrick, John S. Lemmon and others, and extended from Eleventh street and Mitchell avenue to Third and Felix streets. The barns were located on Eighth street near Seneca. In 1881 the line was extended down Eleventh street to Atchison street.

In 1876 Adolph Steinacker, the Krugs, Seymour Jenkins, Louis Streckebein and others built a line from Market Square to New Ulm Park. In 1880 this line was extended to Sixth street and down Sixth to Atchison street. This was the best street railway in the city, its horses being of a high quality and its cars being equipped with stoves.

At about the same time that the Sprague electric motor was being placed into practical operation at Richmond, Va., the late Adolph Steinacker was experimenting upon the Union line with the same machine. Electric cars were run between the power house at Highland and St. Joseph avenues, and New Ulm Park, in the fall of 1887. In the spring of 1888 they were run to Market Square. The Union was the first electric line in the West. It was a horse line from its southern terminus to Market square, where passengers changed to the motor cars. The southern line formerly ran down Second street to Charles, and thence east to Fifth street.

The Frederick avenue line was built in 1878, when a charter was granted to the St. Joseph & Lake Railway Company. The road was narrow gauge, and the iron and rolling stock had been brought by August Kuhn and Charles A. Perry from Leavenworth, where it had been the equipment of an unsuccessful venture between the city and the state penitentiary. The line began at Eighth and Edmond streets and ran to the end of Frederick avenue, where the barns were located. The company went into bankruptcy shortly after the line opened, and was acquired by Thomas E. Tootle, Joseph A. Corby and others. In 1887 a franchise was secured to run down Edmond street to Market Square. In the same year both this line and the Citizens' line were acquired by the People's Street Railway, Electric Light and Power Company, a corporation composed of Eastern capitalists, and at once equipped with electricity.

Hotel Robidoux

In 1888 Charles W. Hobson, Dr. J. M. Huffman and others built the Wyatt Park line, which began at Seventh and Edmond streets and ran south on Seventh street to Olive street and thence, to the power house on Thirty-sixth street. At the same time the People's company built the Jule street line, which began at Seventh and Felix streets, ran north to Jule, and thence east. In 1889 the People's company built the Messanie street line. In that year the Wyatt Park, the Messanie and the Jule street lines were extended to the New Era Exposition grounds.

In 1890 the People's company absorbed the Union line, which was now fully equipped with electricity, and also the Wyatt Park line, gaining control of the entire street car system of St. Joseph. The gap on Seventh street between the Wyatt Park and Jule street lines was at once filled, and a delightful trip could be made around what was called the belt. People could start, say, at Seventh and Felix streets, and go north and east on the Jule street line, pass through the eastern suburbs and the ruined New Era park, and return through Wyatt Park to the starting point. A line was also extended to Vineyard Heights, located on eastern Michell avenue, but neither the belt line nor this spur proved remunerative, and were discontinued.

The Citizens' line was extended to South Park and Gladstone Heights in 1890, but runs only to South Park now. A spur was run from Frederick avenue north on Twenty-second street to Highland Park at about the same time, and is still in operation. In January of 1898 the Union line was extended to the stock yards, over a track leased from the Atchison, Topeka & Santa Fe Railway Company. The following year, upon the completion of the viaduct connecting South Sixth street with King Hill avenue, the Union line was built from Atchison street south on Sixth street and King Hill avenue through South St. Joseph to the stock yards, and thence one branch was extended to Lake Contrary and another to Hyde Valley. In 1900 the Grand Avenue line was built from Francis street north on Sixth, east to Eleventh and north to Grand avenue. In 1904 the Messanie street line was extended from Twenty-sixth and Messanie streets through Wyatt Park to Jackson street. In 1908 a line was built from the northern terminus of the Union line at Krug Park to Industrial City, two miles north.

The Prospect avenue line was built in 1909. It is on Main and Franklin streets, Dewey and Prospect avenues. A franchise was granted for an extension of the Frederick avenue line to State Hospital for Insane No. 2, in 1909, and another in 1914, but the line has never been built. The Jule street and Twenty-second street lines were extended at their termini in 1912.

The People's company was reorganized in 1895 as the St. Joseph Railway, Light, Heat and Power Company, being at that time part of the Harriman interests. It furnishes electric light and power and heats a number of buildings in the city. W. T. VanBrunt was general manager for fourteen years. Early in 1903 he resigned to enter a broader field of activity in New York. He was succeeded by his brother, J. H. VanBrunt, who now holds the position. Extensive improvements and extensions have been made to the company's power plant near the river front.

* * *

OMNIBUS LINE—In February, 1859, upon the opening of the Hannibal & St. Joseph railroad, Major Holman and Samuel Jerome started the St. Joseph Omnibus Line. In the spring following Messrs. John L. Motter and C. D. Smith bought out the line and built omnibus stables near the Patee House. They continued to operate this line until George W. McAleer bought out the interests of J. L. Motter. The business was conducted by these gentlemen for some time, when Colonel J. L. Motter bought out C. D. Smith. Motter and McAleer ran the business in partnership for some time, when Colonel Motter sold his interest to McAleer. The line subsequently became the property of William Medaugh, by whom it was sold, in 1867, to Thomas Christopher. The stock then consisted of five omnibuses, one carriage, four buggies and thirty-six horses. Smith Adams afterward became a partner in the omnibus line with Major Christopher. Joseph A. Piner purchased the line in 1871 and associated with him Thomas A. Massey. Upon the death of Massey, Colonel Elijah Gates became Major Piner's associate, and this firm continued until 1894, when the stock and equipment were purchased by the Brown Transfer Company. Omnibuses are no longer seen on the streets. They have given place to the modern taxicabs and jitney busses.

* * *

HERDIC COACHES—The Herdic coaches were intended for service upon streets that had no tramways. They were a sort of carryall, with seats along the sides, and were quite successfully operated in eastern cities. In July of 1881 a company was established in St. Joseph with Dr. John T. Berghoff as president, Joseph A. Corby as secretary, and E. F. Mitchell as superintendent. There were eight coaches and fifty-six horses. There were two lines. The first ran from Market Square east on Felix street to Ninth street, north to Frederick avenue, east to Thirteenth, south to Sylvanie street, east to Fifteenth street, north to Edmond street, east to Seventeeth street, and north to Francis street, returning by the same route. The second line ran from Felix street north on Sixth street to Hall, east to Ninth street, north to Powell street, and thence to Mount Mora Cemetery. The venture proved unsuccessful and was abandoned after a year's efforts.

CHAPTER XIV.

BUCHANAN COUNTY'S THREE COURT HOUSES—THE COURT HOUSE FIRE IN MARCH OF 1885—THE FIRST MARKET HOUSE AND CITY HALL AND THE PRESENT STRUCTURE—PATEE AND OTHER MARKETS—THE CITY WORKHOUSE AND CENTRAL POLICE STATION—COUNTY JAILS OF THE PAST AND THE PRESENT INSTITUTION.

The first court house of Buchanan County was made of logs and stood at Sparta. It is yet in existence, being used as a granary upon the McCauley farm, which embraces the site of Sparta. The courts, county and circuit, met at the house of Richard Hill and at the house of Joseph Robidoux, as related before, up to the summer of 1841. In January of that year the county court ordered that a building be erected on lot No. 1, block 1, in the town of Sparta. This was a log house, containing two rooms—one 18x20, the other 16x18. The contract was let to Guilford Moultray, and the building was finished by the following July. This house served more than one purpose, for, aside from being the "palace of justice," it was also the academy of learning, the temple of worship, the forum of the people, and the opera house. It was lighted by day through two twelve-light windows in each room below, while the second floor, a half-story, was lighted by a six-light window in each gable. When it became necessary to use the building by night, as for worship or entertainment, tallow candles were used.

On November 9, 1842, the county court appropriated the sum of $6,000 to erect such a court house and jail, to be built at Sparta, as the necessities of the community demanded. But Sparta never saw this pretentious structure. When the new court house was provided for, the question of moving the county seat to Blacksnake Hill took formidable shape. As a result of the agitation Sparta lost, and the $6,000 was invested in St. Joseph. The block occupied by the present court house was the original site. It was a high hill that had been donated by Robidoux, and its apex was fully fifty feet above the present grade of Jule street. A brick house, of which Louis S. Stigers and N. J. Taylor were the architects and builders, was erected on this hill, fronting south. It was a two-story building, the dimensions being 50x74 feet, including a portico, and the people were quite proud of it. In 1871 this structure was condemned as unsafe, after twenty-five years of service, and, in October of that year it was vacated. The county offices were for a time located in the parsonage of what had been the first Catholic church in the city, on the east side of Fifth street, between Felix and Francis streets. In the summer of 1873 the circuit court, circuit clerk's and sheriff's offices were moved to Brady's hall, on Felix, near Fourth street.

The next court house, of which the present one forms a part, was begun in 1873. Its architect was P. F. Meagher and its builder was John De Clue. The cost was $173,000. The cornerstone was laid August 25, 1873, the Masonic rite being performed by Captain Joseph S. Browne, acting grand master of the state. It was a momentous event and the people entered into the spirit thereof with pride and enthusiasm; and well they might, for they were laying the corner stone of the grandest county building in the West at that time. The plan, so far as external appearances go, is preserved in the present court house. It has a frontage of 235 on Jule street, with a depth of 205 feet. It is of brick, with cut stone foundation and trimmings. The building was completed in August, 1876, though some of the county offices occupied rooms as they were finished, as early as January of that year.

On the morning of March 28, 1885, this magnificent building was severely damaged by fire, and much valuable public property was destroyed. The origin of the conflagration is enshrouded in mystery. The building was heated by stoves at that time, and it is a generally accepted theory that from some neglect or accident the fire was transferred from either a stove or an ash receptacle to the floor. Shortly after three o'clock on the morning in question, Wm. H. Mitchell, a compositor on *The Gazette,* was going north on Fourth street, home from his work. When near Robidoux street he looked back toward the court house, his attention having been attracted by crackling noise, and he saw smoke and flames issuing from a window on the north side of the first floor of the west wing. He gave the cry, which was taken up by persons within hearing distance. An effort to reach the fire department by telephone failed and there was an unusual delay in getting the alarm to all of the stations. So fierce was the fire, and such tremendous progress did it make, that before the first apparatus arrived the dome had collapsed and crashed into the burning mass. The only thing left for the department to do was the salvation of the main walls, and this was accomplished by hard and heroic work.

Aside from the county offices, the building was occupied for various other purposes. On the first floor were the offices of the recorder of deeds, the county collector, the prosecuting attorney, the county clerk, the county court, the probate court, assessor and public administrator. There were also the law offices of B. R. Vineyard, Ryan & Stewart, M. G. Moran, A. D. Kirke, Vories & Vories, Moss & Shortridge, Judge Sutherland and Pitts & Porter. The Latter Day Saints occupied a large room for purposes of worship, and several rooms were used for sleeping. On the second floor was the circuit court room and judge's office, circuit clerk's office, sheriff's office, Col. John Doniphan's law office, jury rooms, etc. What is now the criminal court room was used as a lecture room by the Northwestern Medical College, and where the grand jury room and assembly room now are was a large concert hall, used by the Mendelssohn Society.

The losses sustained by the lawyers and roomers were severe, many valuable books and manuscripts being consumed. The county lost nearly all property that was not in vaults. The recorder's office, which is a vault in itself, was unharmed, and those records of the county clerk, circuit clerk, probate court and collector, which were in vaults, were left intact.

Twenty-eight prisoners were incarcerated in the county jail, and these were ascorted without delay by Sheriff Carey and a posse of citizens to the city hall, where they were guarded until the following day, when they were returned to their old quarters, the jail not having been damaged.

There was an insurance of $95,500 on the court house, the adjustment of which began as soon as possible. Quarters for the county officers were provided at once. The circuit court, circuit clerk, sheriff and prosecuting attorney were located in the Tootle building at Sixth and Francis streets, and the others, except the recorder, occupied a building at the corner of Second and Charles streets that had been used as general offices by the Kansas City, St. Joseph & Council Bluffs Railroad Company.

After considerable parleying with the insurance adjusters, an agreement was reached whereby the companies restored the structure. R. K. Allen was awarded the contract, and Judge Bernard Patton was employed by the county court to superintend the work. The end of the year 1885 saw the court house restored and better equipped, so far as heat, lighting and other conveniences go, than before the fire.

* * *

MARKET HOUSES AND CITY HALL—When Joseph Robidoux platted the original town he dedicated half a block, bounded by Second, Felix and Edmond streets, for a market house. The space was occupied by sheds and shanties until 1853, when the first market house was built. This was a brick structure, about 50x50 feet in dimension. The lower floor was occupied as a market, and all vendors of fresh meat were compelled to locate therein. Grocers were prohibited from dealing in vegetables, and huckstering was forbidden until after market hours. This made the market a busy place, and the merchants located on the square enjoyed the best patronage. The upper floor of the original building, at the south end, was occupied by city officials. It was first reached by an outside stairway on the south side, but when an addition was built on the north a covered stairway was provided.

Early in the seventies the building showed signs of decay and the owners of property on the square began to agitate a new market house. However, there was no money in the treasury for such purpose. Finally, in 1873, a plan was developed which brought about the desired result. The sum of $50,000 was subscribed, for which the city issued certificates of indebtedness bearing 6 per cent interest. These were redeemable for city taxes at the rate of on-fifth of the face per year.

The present City Hall and market house is the result of this subscription. The building was begun in the fall of 1873 and finished in July 1874. The plans were by Bottner & Stigers and the work by R. K. Allen, at a cost of $50,000. It was the most pretentious building of its kind in the West at that time. The upper floor was a public hall and was formally opened by St. Patricks' Benevolent Society with a grand ball on July 18, 1874. It served as such until 1888. The two upper floors were then remodeled and the engineer, city clerk and boiler inspector were quartered on the third floor, where a commodious council chamber was also provided. In 1908, $10,000 was expended for a new iron stairway and an elevator.

Patee market house was built first in 1859 upon a square dedicated in Patee's addition. There was never much of a market there, except for hay, wood and country produce. At different times the building has been occupied by butchers and produce dealers. The city scales are located there. In 1908, $25,000 was secured by an issue of bonds to complete the present handsome market house at Tenth and Olive streets. A start had previously been made from appropriations from the general fund.

There was formerly a live stock market located at Seventh and Messanie streets, where the Central Police Station now stands, where there was also a public weighmaster. This was abandoned in 1890.

In 1874 an effort was made to establish a public market on North Sixth street, and the city erected a frame building in the center of the street, south of the City Brewery. This was not a success, however, and he building was torn down in 1884.

* * *

THE WORKHOUSE—Prior to August, 1855, the city's prisoners were kept in a room in the old county jail, which stood on the hill with the old court house. They were in charge of the street commissioner and were generally worked on the highways by him. In 1855 the first workhouse was established in a two-story stone building on the site of the present institution. In 1884 the stone building was torn down and the workhouse of today erected.

Up to 1855 the street commissioner fed and cared for the prisoners. The first superintendent of the workhouse was Anton H. Dalhoff, who served 1885-88. He was succeeded by Peter Reiplinger, 1890; the next superintendent was Charles Johnson, who served 1890-94 and was succeeded by William H. Dersch, 1894-96. In 1896-98, Bert Martin was superintendent, who was succeeded by Andrew Arnell. Henry Raid was appointed in 1902; Gottleib Bandel, 1904; Charles Paulette, 1906; William H. Finch, 1908; Charles Paulette, 1910; Ben L. Arnholdt, the present incumbent, 1912.

The prisoners were worked upon the streets up to 1891, when this practice was abolished. There are sheds in the enclosure about the workhouse where prisoners are employed at breaking rock, which is used by the engineer's department in the repair of streets. The superintendent of the workhouse receives a salary of $600 per annum and fifteen cents per meal for feeding prisoners.

* *·*

CENTRAL POLICE STATION—A holdover cell was provided in the workhouse for city prisoners held for trial, during the early days and up to 1891. It was necessary to walk or cart them to police headquarters at the city hall, where they were searched and booked; thence they were marched or carted through the streets to the workhouse to be detained until the following morning, when they were marched back to the city hall for trial. Those who were sentenced to the workhouse were returned to that institution after court. One of the first steps of the board of police commissioners, when he department had been reorganized under the metropolitan system, was in the direction of a central police station. In 1890 the council appropriated $10,000 for the present central station; located on the site of the old hay scales at Seventh and Messanie streets. With this money the walls and roof were built. In the following year the council appropriated $10,000 additional, and the building was completed and occupied in November, 1891. An addition costing $10,000 was built in 1908. It is one of the most substantial and best appointed buildings of its kind in the West.

* * *

THE COUNTY JAIL—The first jail was at Sparta, and was built of logs. It was a small affair and stood in the public square of the first county seat. The structure survived the town, but was afterward destroyed by fire. It was used as a hold-over. Prisoners of importance were taken to Liberty jail pending trial. When the first court house was built in St. Joseph, a brick jail and residence for the jailor was also constructed. This did service until the night of January 21, 1850, when it was destroyed by fire. Another was built, which was replaced in 1859 by a building which, at the time was considered modern. But it was woefully and wonderfully designed, and for nearly forty years was condemned regularly by grand juries, building inspectors and humanitarians. After repeated attempts, the proposition to issue bonds for a new jail finally was successful at and election held in 1908. The present building, costing nearly $100,000, was erected the following year.

CHAPTER XV.

THE PUBLIC AND PRIVATE CHARITIES OF BUCHANAN
COUNTY AND ST. JOSEPH—HISTORY OF ASYLUM No.
2—THE COUNTY PAUPERS AND HOW THEY HAVE
BEEN MAINTAINED SINCE THE EARLIEST DAYS—
THE CITY HOSPITAL—ST. MARY'S ORPHANAGE ASY-
LUM—MEMORIAL HOME AND THE HOME FOR LITTLE
WANDERERS—THE ASSOCIATED CHARITIES—THE
CHARITY BOARD.

The most important public charity in Buchanan County, and
one of the most important in the entire West, is State Hospital for
Insane, No. 2, just within the eastern city limits. Up to March,
1872, Missouri had but one insane asylum, that located at Fulton.
The necessity for additional accommodations for the afflicted had
long been felt, and the legislature, on March 9, 1872, appropriated
$200,000 for a "Northwestern or Southwestern Lunatic Asylum,"
at the same time providing for a board of commissioners to carry
the act into effect. These commissioners were William H. McHenry,
St. Louis; Zach J. Mitchell, Lafayette County; Joseph K. Rickey,
Calloway; Louis Hax, St. Joseph, and William Gilmore, Springfield.
On June 14 of the same year the commissioners, after a tour of
inspection, located the asylum in Buchanan County, purchasing 120
acres of land from H. R. W. Hartwig and O. M. Loomis for $28,000.
Thomas Walsh of St. Louis was appointed architect, and in the following September N. H. Fitzgibbons of St. Louis was awarded the
contract for building the asylum for $188,897.

There were two north and south wing of 115½ feet each, and
the entire edifice was four stories in height, with a Mansard roof,
and there was a bell tower in the center 115 feet high. The building was of brick, trimmed with Milwaukee brick and cut stone.

The asylum was opened in September, 1874, with sixty pa-
tients. The first board of managers was: Allen H. Vories, R. L.
McDonald, J. C. Roberts, Dr. E. A. Donelan, Elijah H. Norton, Dr.
J. M. Malin and John C. Evans, who were appointed by the gov-
ernor for four years. Mr. Vories was the first president of the
board and Dr. Malin the first secretary. Dr. George C. Catlett of
St. Joseph was the first superintendent and his assistant was Dr. A.
P. Busey, who later was first assistant.

This building, which stood for over five years, was destroyed
by fire January 25, 1879, at about 1 o'clock in the afternoon. The
alarm was given, but the flames spread so rapidly that the attendants had a difficult task in rescuing the inmates. The building was
improperly and inconveniently designed as to stairways, and the
managers had vainly besought the legislature to remedy this impor-

tant defect. The loss was total, there being not a cent of insurance. Luckily there was no loss of life. The patients were brought to the city and quartered at the court house, where the males remained for three months, while the females were taken to a building on Louis. street used as a railroad hospital. Afterward the males were removed to temporary quarters on the asylum grounds and the females were placed in a house nearby.

The people of St. Joseph took immediate steps looking to the ..ding of the asylum, and also for the relief of the distressed. so happened that the legislature was in session at the time of the disaster, and every energy was bent toward securing the necessary appropriation. A commission of architects and builders examined the walls and reported that these could be used to the extent of three-fourths of the entire building and estimated that the sum of $75,000 would cover the expense of rebuilding. There were other claimants, however, for the institution. Legislative committees visited different localities, with much waste of time and money, but the result was favorable to St. Joseph, and, in May of 1879, the legislature appropriated $75,000. The work of rebuilding began at once, the architect being S. V. Shipman of Chicago, and the contractors Lehman & Olson, also of Chicago. The work was superintended by Louis S. Stigers of St. Joseph.

April 1, 1880, the patients were removed to the new building. Since then many improvements have been made. Several wings have been added to the main house, hospitals, a laundry and other buildings have been erected. An electric lighting plant is one of the recent additions.

Dr. Catlett was the superintendent until his death, which occurred in May of 1886. He was succeeded by Dr. R. E. Smith, who served four years and was succeeded August 11, 1890, by Dr. Charles R. Woodson, who held the position until July 1, 1907, when he was succeeded by Dr. William F. Kuhn. He served until July 1, 1909, and was followed by Dr. F. A. Patterson, who was acting superintendent until his death, February 18, 1910. Dr. A. H. Vandivert was acting superintendent until March 20, 1910, when he was succeeded by Dr. Abra C. Pettijohn, who had been appointed to the position. He served until June 5, 1914, when he was followed by Dr. George R. Thompson, the present incumbent. The present board of managers consists of Dr. J. A. Castlewait, Tarkio, Mo., president; Smith A. Penny, St. Joseph; Earnest M. Lindsay, St. Joseph; George B. Baker, Maryville, and Edwin T. Villmoare, Kansas City.

September 24, 1915, there were 1,721 patients in the hospital. The entire number of officers, attendants and employes is about 245. The annual cost of running the institution now is about $350,000.

Since the hospital was rebuilt in 1879 about $250,000 has been expended in improvements and extensions, most of them having been effected since 1885. In 1896 the board of managers purchased another tract of land containing 110 acres, situated just north of the original site. The price paid for this land was $192 per acre, or a total of $21,000. The ground and buildings at this time are valued at $535,802.

*   *   *

THE COUNTY FARM—Buchanan County provides well for its indigent charges. The county farm, situated northeast of the city, about two miles from the corporate limits, is a modern institution, there being quarters for sane and insane patients, a hospital, proper separation of sexes, medical attention and other comforts.

The first pauper mentioned in the history of Buchanan County was Henry Fulks, who petitioned the county court for relief in October, 1840, stating that rheumatism had deprived him of the use of his hands. At that time there was no county farm, and the court made an order granting him $15 a month for three months. This method of providing for the indigent, of whom there were few in those days, was continued until 1850, when Elias Richardson, a farmer residing near the One Hundred and Two River, was authorized to maintain paupers at the rate of $5 per months each, the county providing clothing and medical attention. Richardson kept the paupers for two years. Judge Cornelius Roberts of Bloomington Township then kept the unfortunates until 1857, receiving $80 per annum for each. The county then purchased the Leroy Bean tract of 140 acres, two miles southwest of Sparta, for $3,500. This farm was maintained until 1868. John Peter was superintendent until 1861, when he was succeeded by Henry Utz, who served three years and was succeeded by George Peter, who served until December, 1865. He in turn was succeeded by Isham Wood, who held the place until January, 1868, when he purchased the farm for $4,200. The superintendents received as compensation the use of the farm and $75 to $80 per annum for each pauper, the county providing clothing and medical attention.

The paupers were next brought to the city and kept for three years by Dr. William Bertram, who had been appointed superintendent of the poor and county physician, by the court court. Dr. Bertram was succeeded in January, 1871, by Dr. A. S. Long, who held the place until September, 1871. The county court purchased, August 16 of that year, a quarter section from Matilda S. and Martin Hughes, paying $11,000 for the same, and, as soon as possible, had the paupers removed. Dr. Bertram and Dr. Long received as compensation 50 cents per day for each pauper, the county furnishing everything but the food.

In September of 1871 the new institution was opened, with seven male and six female patients. John Spellman was appointed superintendent at a salary of $100 per month, the county providing for the inmates, and Dr. A. S. Long was retained as physician. There was a good, roomy, frame house on the farm, which had been erected by Kit Todd before the war and intended for use as a summer resort, a railroad from St. Joseph to Savannah having passed through the farm.

In 1873 a frame building was erected for the insane. These unfortunates had been kept at the state insane asylum at Fulton, but were returned owing to the crowded condition of that institution. They were cared for in the temporary quarters until the completion of Asylum No. 2. When that institution burned, January, 1879, they were again placed in the temporary quarters. The necessity of a permanent institution for the county insane was so pressing that, in August, 1880, the judges appropriated $10,000 for this purpose. A building with modern equipments and with a capacity of 150 patients was completed in February of 1881. In this building the incurably insane are kept. The county still maintains a number of patients at Asylum No. 2 considered curable.

Improvements were made at various times as the necessities arose until today the county has an asylum for indigent and insane that is both adequate and comfortable.

* * *

THE CITY HOSPITAL—For many years St. Joseph maintained a city hospital on the high bluffs on West Robidoux street. The building was inadequate in nearly every essential, and there was little to commend it except the fresh air the patients were able to get. Of this there was an abundance.

There is no record of a city hospital prior to 1861. In that year the city acquired the site of the old hospital, upon which stood an old-fashioned building, which had been used during the pioneer days as a combination storehouse and dwelling. This building is still in existence.

The hospital building was forty feet square, two stories high, of brick. This building marks the struggles for an adequate city hospital that has been going on during the past thirty years. In 1875 the council set aside the dog tax for hospital improvement and extension purposes. With the proceeds of this revenue a one-story brick building, 20x40, was erected in 1878. In 1880 a second section, of similar dimensions, was joined to the first. In 1890-91 a second story was placed over the ground work and other improvements, such as water, lighting, etc., were added. This building served the purpose of a city hospital until early in 1902. A contract was then made with St. Joseph Hospital (in charge of the sisters of charity) for the maintenance of charity patients.

* * *

ST. MARY'S ORPHAN ASYLUM—This was for orphaned boys only, conducted by the Sisters of St. Joseph, and which depends entirely upon charity for its existence. It was established by Mother Clements, a lady of great energy and business tact, in 1879, at Corby Chapel, northwest of the city. In 1880 the late Francis Brown donated a substantial house and forty acres of ground, desirably located, about three miles from the eastern city limits. The institution was abandoned early in 1900 for lack of support. The property is still in the possession of the Sisterhood of St.

Joseph, and there is a lingering hope that some day the orphanage
may be reopened.

* * *

MEMORIAL HOME—The Ladies' Union Benevolent Association
is a charitable organization that has accomplished a world of good
in a practical Christian manner since its organization in 1874.
Forty-one years ago this society was organized in a quiet, unos-
tentious way, by the Protestant Evangelical churches of St. Joseph.
The society at the time of its organization had no funds nor a home
in which to shelter the unfortunates, but it was composed of a band
of earnest women who were willing to work. By soliciting contri-
butions, by giving entertainments and by various other means, a
little money was secured, a frame house at the corner of Antoine
and Levee streets was rented, and the work begun. From that time
to this the association has performed a charitable work that has
commanded the respect and aid of the Christian and business ele-
ments of the city.

In 1880 money was raised by private subscription to purchase
what was then known as the Armstrong Beattie homestead, at Main
and Poulin streets, which property has ever since remained in the
possession of the association. The sum of $3,985 was raised by sub-
scription to purchase the Beattie place, and since that time until the
new building was erected, in 1895, it was twice remodeled and enlarged, at considerable expense, to accommodate the homeless and
distressed.

This institution was for many years known as the Home for
the Friendless, but October 1, 1895, it was converted into the Memorial Home for Aged People, both male and female. Since the
property was purchased, eighteen years ago, the old family residence has been supplanted by an entirely new structure, no part of
the original building remaining.

In 1896 the new building was remodeled and enlarged just
before it was converted into a home for aged people. It is a solid,
substantial brick building, heated by steam, supplied with gas and
water and other modern conveniences, and is comfortable in every
respect. This institution is supported largely by "The Hoagland
Endowment Fund," created by George T. Hoagland in honor of his
wife, and consisting of $25,000. This endowment is, however, not
sufficient to entirely support the institution, and the publi con-
tributes the remainder. In April, 1904, Mr. Hoagland's widow
added $5,000 to the endowment.

* * *

HOME FOR LITTLE WANDERERS—The Home for Little Wanderers, located at Twenty-eighth and Colhoun streets, in the extreme
eastern portion of the city, is also controlled by the Ladies' Union
Benevolent Association. This home was erected at a cost of
$25,000, including the site. The home was a gift to the association
from Charles W. Noyes, of the local shoe manufacturing firm of
Noyes, Norman & Co. Mr. Noyes spent most of his life in St.

Joseph and this section, but later moved to Boston. The Home for Little Wanderers is a love tribute to the memory of his daughter, who died in early womanhood.

The gift was made in 1892, accompanied by an endowment of . real estate on North Third street valued at $65,000. The building is of pressed brick, three stories, steam-heated, modern in every respect, and has a capacity of one hundred inmates. The ground consists of eight and one-half acres and the site is commanding and healthful. From the income of the endowment made by Mr. Noyes the home is supported entirely. Children of both sexes, from two years up to nine, are taken here and well cared for.

* * *

THE HOME FOR EX-SLAVES—The idea of a home for dependent ex-slaves originated in Charles S. Baker, an intelligent young negro. By persistent solicitation both at home and abroad he and those of his race who were interested with him in the work, secured enough money to build a structure at Seventeenth street and Highland avenue. This was under roof, but was destroyed by a hurricane in September of 1894. For a time the future of the project seemed gloomy, but Dr. P. J. Kirschner came generously to the rescue. In December of 1887 he donated one-half of the purchase price of a tract of two acres, with a substantial brick house, at Twenty-fourth street and Mitchell avenue, and gave the promoters long and easy terms on the balance, which amounted to $1,500. The project failed after an experiment covering a period of two years.

* * *

THE NOYES HOSPITAL—The Noyes Hospital, at Frederick avenue, Twenty-fourth street and Jones street, is a lasting tribute to the memory of the late C. W. Noyes, who had already done much to perpetuate his name in the city in which he lived. At his death, January 26, 1912, he provided that $275,000 of his estate should be devoted to the erection of a hospital. Provision is made for the care of those unable to pay, although a portion of the building is conducted similar to other general hospitals.

OTHER CHARITIES—The poor were always well cared for in St. Joseph. Up to the fall of 1897 distress was relieved by the county court and by the mayor. At various times organizations have existed for the purpose of systematizing the charity work and preventing impositions. For several years the Associated Charities, representing a consolidation of the various societies, did much good work in behalf of the needy. The Associated Charities kept a list of needy, and relieved those found worthy.

In 1897 a state law was passed authorizing the formation of a Board of Charities. This board was composed of members appointed by the county court and by the mayor, and its business was the distribution of funds supplied by the city and county for charity. A secretary was employed, whose duty it was to investigate all applications and prevent imposition.

In 1911 the present Social Welfare Board was created by **state** law.   It is an amplification of the Charity Board idea and is supposed to put all charity work on a higher level.   Some new, **modern** ideas were introduced with the creation of this **board.**

CHAPTER XVI

THE SCHOOLS OF BUCHANAN COUNTY AND ST. JOSEPH —PRIMITIVE SCHOOLS OF EARLY DAYS—THE PUBLIC SCHOOLS; HOW THEY ARE SUPPORTED AND MANAGED—THE SCHOOL BUILDINGS OF ST. JOSEPH —FINANCIAL STRUGGLES AND VICISSITUDES OF THE SCHOOL BOARD — DENOMINATIONAL AND PAROCHIAL SCHOOLS OF THE PAST AND PRESENT.

The first school of any kind in Buchanan County, as near as can be learned at this time, was a private institution kept by Francis Ferguson, in 1839, on the southwest corner of section 16, in what is now Crawford Township, near Halleck. It was in a log house, with a puncheon floor.

The court house at Sparta was also used for school purposes in 1841-44. Various academies were established in the country, all of which were eventually supplanted by the district school.

According to the constitution under which Missouri was admitted into the Union, the sixteenth section of each congressional township was set aside for school purposes. In Buchanan County about $100,000 was realized from this source and the money is now loaned out by the county court to individuals upon real estate security, the interest going to the districts in proportion to the capital to their various credits. This, however, is a small item in the support of the public schools, the main source of revenue coming from direct taxation. The requirements of the school districts are certified to the county court and are considered in the tax levy. Besides, there is support from the state.

Each district elects directors whose province it is to employ teachers and manage the schools; and there is a county superintendent of public instruction, whose duty it is to pass upon the qualifications of teachers, and, also, to certify to the state the number of children entitled to school support, the school age being from six years to twenty years.

In 1847, the first year in which Buchanan county participated in the apportionment of state school moneys, there was an enumeration of 547, and the amount apportioned was $481.36. In 1857 the enumeration was 5,099, and the amount $3,977.22; in 1867 the enumeration was 12,471, and the amount $6,584.69; in 1877 the enumeration was 10,736, and the apportionment $7,983. In 1897— a span of twenty years—the enumeration was 30,827, and the apportionment $28,767.

Other sources of revenue for school purposes are: An average bridge and right-of-way tax upon railroads, the sale of swamp lands, and various penalties.

There are now seventy-five school districts in Buchanan county outside of the district in which the city of St. Joseph is located. In many of these districts there are substantial and modern brick school houses. The last enumeration in the county shows 5,253 persons within the school age. The county schools are of a high grade and there is commendable rivalry for excellence among the teachers. One month of each year is devoted to an institute, where lecturers and masters of reputation are heard; where the teacher is taught and brightened for the next season's work.

Until the year 1860, no attempt at any system of public schools had been made in St. Joseph. "Occasionally," to quote Professor Neely, "a free school would be taught for a month or two, or for a sufficient length of time to absorb what was not wasted or lost of the city's share of the public school fund." But there was no public school system, and St. Joseph had merely the organization of a country school district. In 1860 a few enterprising citizens obtained from the legislature a charter by which the St. Joseph Board of Public Schools was incorporated. Section 1 of the act provided that "all free white persons residing within the limits of school district No. 1, in township ,No. 8, in Buchanan county, are hereby constituted a body politic and corporate by the name and style of 'the St. Joseph Board of Public School.' " It was provided that there should be two members from each ward and a president, to be elected at large, the term of office in each case to be three years. The charter was made perpetual and the corporation given power to sue and be sued, to purchase, hold or sell property, real and personal, etc.

The war having changed the social condition of the negro, his education by the state was provided for in 1866 by striking out in the St. Joseph charter the words "fre white males" and inserting the words "resident taxpayers." Another change in the charter provided that the terms of the directors should be for two years and that one-half of the number should go out of office at the expiration of every school year. The president's term, however, was continued at three years.

When the first board was elected there were but three wards in the city. This board was constituted as follows: Dr. J. H. Crane, president. Directors, First ward, Louis Hax, John Sheehan; Second ward, James A. Millan, John J. Abell; Third ward, William M. Albin and Erasmus Dixon. The First ward at that time comprised the southern part of the city, the Second ward the central part, and the Third ward the northern part. James A. Millan was elected secretary and Joseph C. Hull, treasurer.

A small school house was provided for each ward as soon as possible. That in the First ward was built at the southeast corner of Third and Charles street. The property was sold to John P. Fink in 1865 for $12,000 and converted into a shoe factory. It is now used for warehouse purposes. The Second ward was provided with a school on the east side of Twelfth street. It was afterward enlarged, and for many years was called the Franklin school, but was abandoned some years ago. The Third ward school was built at Second and Cherry streets. It was afterward enlarged and called the Madison school. Later it was known as the First Colored school, and now it is the Humboldt. The three houses were built from the same plans. They were of brick, 34x25 feet in dimension, two stories high. Each had two school rooms, one on each floor, with a narrow stairway in front. They were furnished with common double desks of pine, and had a capacity of 120 pupils each. There were no cloakrooms or other conveniences.

The schools were opened on April 23, 1860. William H. Marmion was principal of the First ward school, and his assistant was Miss Annie Webster. Sidney P. Cunningham had charge of the Second ward school, and had for his assistant Miss Annie Banes (now Mrs. John Townsend). The principal of the Third ward school was J. W. H. Griffin, and his assistant was Miss Lizzie Brand (afterward Mrs. Carder). Salaries were not high in those days, the principal receiving $50 per month and the assistants $25.

In the winter of 1861 it was found that there were in each of the ward schools quite a number of pupils who had mastered more or less thoroughly the branches prescribed, and who were prepared to take up advanced studies. It was accordingly proposed to open a school of a higher order for their accommodation. Prof. Edward B. Neely had been conducting a classical school in St. Joseph for six years, and had recently erected a school building on Tenth street, between Felix and Francis streets. The school board arranged with Professor Neely to take charge of the proposed higher branch, and on the first Monday in March, 1861, Professor Neely opened in his building what afterward developed into the St. Joseph High School. He had about forty scholars of both sexes, who had brought certificates of qualification from the ward schools.

In consequence of the disturbed condition of society from the impending civil war, the school board, at a meeting on May 21, 1861, resolved to summarily close all primary and grammer schools, but continue the advanced school until the end of June. From this time until 1864, there were no public schools in the cityy, although the board met occasionally and maintained at least a partial organization. The buildings were sometimes rented for private schools and sometimes occupied by the military.

On August 12, 1864, the board of public schools—then consisting of Louis Hax, president; and David Pinger, William M. Wyeth, R. F. Maxwell, John Colhoun, J. P. Adolph and Bernard Patton, as members—resolved to reopen the schools. Professor Neely was, by unanimous vote, elected superintendent, a position which he filled without interruption until his death in 1904.

The board offered $80 per month salary to principals and $50 per month to assistants, and also decided to establish a high school, with the superintendent as principal, and one assistant at $80 per month. The schools were not entirely free. A matriculation fee of 50 cents per month was charged each pupil in the primary and intermediate grades, and $1 per month in the high school. The rate of taxation allowed by the charter was so small that full terms could not have been maintained without the aid of the tuition fee. On February 3, 1872, this practice was abolished, and since that time the schools have been entirely free.

October 3, 1864, the schools were reopened, with Professor Neely as principal of the high school, and Nelson Wilbur, a graduate of Dartmouth College, as his assistant. Nathan Somerville was principal of the First ward school, with Miss Jennie Parson) as assistant. Benjamin R. Vineyard was principal of the Second ward school, with Miss Alice Bruner as assistant, her place being afterward filled by Mrs. Annie R. Townsend. H. C. McLaughlin was principal in the Third ward school, and his assistant was Miss India Cowden (later Mrs. Evan W. Ray).

The schools were immediately crowded and many applicants who applied were unable to gain admission for want of room. This condition continued until the school board found relief through a charter amendment in 1866, permitting an increase in the rate of taxation, which gave the board the means for building two additional houses. With the proceeds of the sale of the First ward property and the yield of the additional tax, the Everett school, at Twelfth and Olive streets, and the old High School building at Tenth and Edmond streets, were erected. The buildings were identical in plan, and the cost of each, exclusive of ground, was about $36,000. Labor and material in those days were both extremely high, as the older people will remember.

The High School was opened in 1866, with John S. Crosby as principal, and was used as such until 1896. The building was damaged by fire in 1889, rebuilt and enlarged. In 1895 it was remodeled for grammar schools and offices of the board of education, and is now known as Robidoux School. It has since been rebuilt on more pretentious lines. The Everett has also been enlarged and is still in service.

In 1867 a house was provided for colored school children at Fourth and Michel streets. It was a one-story frame building, of which no trace remains.

In 1868 the school board found it necessary to issue bonds to provide additional buildings, and the sum of $40,000 was obtained from this source. As a result, the Washington School, at Fifth and Poulin, and the Webster, at Nineteenth and Beattie streets, were built in 1869, the former costing $11,658 and the latter $9,928. Both have since been enlarged to meet the demands. Outstanding indebtedness was liquidated with the balance of the sum realized from the bond sale.

Still the provisions were inadequate, and buildings were rented where possible, to relieve the congested conditions. More school houses were necessary, and in 1872 the board found itself compelled to again issue bonds to erect buildings and make necessary improvements upon property already owned.

At this time the board purchased the property now known as the German-English School, for $8,500. This school had been founded and maintained for some years by an association of German-English citizens, formed for the purpose of perpetuating their language in their children. In the conveyance of the property to the school board it was expressly provided that instruction in the "German as well as English language shall be given in equal proportions in all departments of instruction to meet the demands of the pupils from the whole city for such instruction, according to the capacity thereof."

The sum of $36,000 was realized from the bond issue of $40,000. With this money the board paid debts, built the Neely School at Twelfth and Scott streets, at a cost of about $10,000, erected an addition to the Everett School at a cost of $6,000, repaired the Webster, which had been unroofed by a tornado, and made other substantial and necessary improvements.

In April of 1877 the people voted, by a large majority, to increase the rate of taxation for general school purposes from three to five mills, and the county court ordered a five-mill levy for that year. But in 1878, when the board asked again for a five-mill levy, the county court refused to make it, contending that the people had voted for the five-mill levy for the year 1877 only. The board applied for a writ of mandamus to compel the court to make the five-mill levy, and a judgment was rendered in the circuit court in favor of the board. Through some neglect the judgment was not recorded and it became necessary to go to trial again. The second trial resulted unfavorably to the schools, and the five-mill levy was not again made, it being the judgment of the court that the people must vote for such a levy each year. In 1878 the county court also questioned the legality of the school board's bonds by refusing to levy a sinking fund and interest tax. The question was tested in the United States court and the legality of teh bonds fully sustained.

In 1879 a school was built at Sixth and Jackson streets and named the Floyd. This was sold in 1888 to the Holy Rosary congregation and is now used as a Catholic church. The Crosby School, at Savannah avenue and Richardson street, was built in 1880, at a cost of $7,400. The Steinacker School, at Second and Louis streets, was built in 1883, and the present estimated value of the building is $16,500. The other schools were built in the following order, and the amount represents the present estimated value of the buildings: Hall, Twenty-sixth and Duncan streets, 1887, $5,450; South Park, 1888, $7,600; Colored High School, Eighteenth and Angelique, 1888, $17,690; Young, Ninth and Mary, 1889, $25,725; new Floyd, Third and Hickory, 1889, $18,920; Bliss, Thirtieth and Olive, 1890, $7,500; Ernst, Walker's Addition, 1891, $7,500; Grant, North Eleventh street, 1894, $7,550; Lincoln (colored), St. Joseph avenue and and Pendleton streets, 1894, $10,600; Jackson, Twenty-fourth street, 1894, $6,550. The Avenue School, at Frederick avenue and Thirteenth street, was formerly a store building. It was rented for some years by the board and purchased for $10,000 in 1892.

After various unsuccessful efforts, the school board secured the consent of the taxpayers to erect an adequate and substantial High School building. The funds having been provided, the question of a site for the prospective new structure at once became paramount, and a lively rivalry ensued. The people in general would have been satisfied with an accessible and central location. However, the school board seems to have been actuated by high motives, so far as location and price went, for it purchased for $23,500 a piece of ground 125x200, on the highest point of Carpenter's hill, fronting on Thirteenth and Fourteenth street, about 200 feet north of Olive street. There was much popular indignation at this deal, for the location was considered out of range and inaccessible, and the price exceedingly high.

Plans, prepared by Edmond J. Eckel, were adopted by the board during the winter of 1894-95, and the corner stone of the present building was laid with Masonic ceremony and a popular demonstration, together with oratory and music. The building was occupied in the spring of 1896, the term being finished there. The contractors were Bernard Feeney and William Rupert and John DeClue, and the cost about $90,000.

In 1900 the Eugene Field School was built at Sixteenth and Sacramento streets at a cost of $32,500, and the free public library and school office building was erected at a cost of $121,000. The Wyatt School, at Eleventh and Henry streets, was built the same year; cost, $30,000.

In 1901 three substantial houses were built on the South Side— the Hosea School, at a cost of $26,700; the Hyde School, at a cost of $17,000, and the Florence School in Florence addition, at a cost of $4,800. The Wyatt School, at Eleventh and Henry streets, was also built in 1901, at a cost of $36,500.

In 1902 the Noyes School at Twenty-sixth and Delaware streets, in Saxton Heights, was built at a cost of $16,700; the Krug School, at the entrance to Krug Park, was built at a cost of $17,000, and the Pellipier School at a cost of $3,000.

In 1904 the Sherwood School, at Twenty-ninth and Edmond streets, was built. It was a two-room affair at first, but is now one of the best school buildings in the city.

In 1905 the Benton High School, in South St. Joseph, was begun. It was completed in 1907. The cost was $91,000.

In 1907 the Blair School, at Thirty-fourth and Renick streets, was built at a cost of $11,300.

As the number of wards increased in the city so the number of school directors increased. Up to 1864 there were six members, in 1865 there were ten, and from 1890 to October, 1895, there were sixteen. The members of the school board have always served without pay, but there was frequently spirited rivalry at the elections, which were held in June. And the sessions of the board were often so animated that the reports of the proceedings made spicy reading in the newspapers.

The conviction that the board was unwieldy had been growing upon the people for some time, and a movement to have the charter amended by the legislature met with hearty popular support. This was done at the session of 1895. Under the provisions of the present charter the school board is composed of six members, two of whom are chosen at each general city election and each of whom serves six years. It is customary for each of the political parties to select a candidate, who is endorsed by the opposing party, thus taking the school board practically out of politics. At the April election of 1895, according to the emergency clause of the bill, six members were chosen—Messrs. B. R. Vineyard, I. T. Hosea, Dr. E. A. Donelan, B. Newberger, K. M. Mitchell and David Marshall. The board did not, however, take charge of affairs until October 1, 1895.

When the new board took charge of the schools the members elected Mr. Donelan as president and drew lots for terms. Directors Hosea and Mitchell were placed for six-year terms, Dr. Donelan and Mr. Newberger for three years, and Messrs. Vineyard and Marshall for one year. In April of 1896 Mr. Vineyard was elected to succeed himself and A. C. Hinkley was elected to succeed Mr. Marshall. In April of 1898, Dr. Donelan was elected to succeed himself and Charles J. Borden was elected to succeed Mr. Newberger. Mr. Borden served until he was elected mayor, in April, 1902, when he was succeeded by Elijah M. Birkes, who served until April, 1904. Dr. Donelan was succeeded in April, 1904, by John P. Strong, and James E. McEvoy was elected to succeed Mr. Birkes. In 1899, J. C. Wyatt was elected to succeed Mr. Hosea, and in 1900, Henry W. Burke was elected to fill the unexpired term of B. R. Vineyard. Since that date members of the board have been elected as follows: J. M. Wilson and E. M. Birkes, 1902; J. P. Strong and J. A. McEvoy, 1904; L. O. Weakley and W. E. Warrick, 1906; Carroll Connett, 1908; D. E. Curtin, 1910; Jerome G. Wing, Orestes Mitchell and R. E. Dewitt, 1912; Samuel I. Motter, 1914.

From August, 1864, to August, 1883, Superintendent Neely was *ex-officio* clerk of the school board, and the buildings, supplies, etc., were looked after by committees. August 7, 1883, Frederick C. Parker was appointed secretary and superintendent of buildings. This gentleman held the position until March 1, 1897, when he was succeeded by Harry H. Smith, who in turn gave way to A. L. Long, the present incumbent, in April, 1910.

For many years the board officed and met in the Kirschner building, corner of Felix street and Market square. In 1892 quarters were secured in the Burnes building at Third and Felix, and these were occupied until August of 1896, when quarters in the Robidoux school building were taken. The present offices, in the public library building, were occupied in 1902.

The following are the names of the various president of the school board: Dr. J. H. Crane served 1860-63; John Colhoun, 1863-67; Samuel Hays, 1867-70; Wm. H. Floyd, 1870-79; Adolph Steinacker, 1879-85; Waller Young, 1885-94; C. A. Mosman, 1894-95; Dr. E. A. Donelan, 1895-1904; K. M. Mitchell, 1904-06; J. M. Wilson, 1906-08; H. W. Burke, 1908-12; Carroll Connett, 1912-14; John P. Strong, 1914—.

The following is a list of the members of the old school board, from 1860 to 1895: John Shehan, Louis Hax, John J. Abell, Jas. A.

Millan, E. F. Dixon, W. M. Albin, Thos. Harbine, A. Andriano, David Pinger, W. M. Wyeth, James Tracey, Robt. F. Maxwell, J. B. Adolph, Bernard Patton, J. M. Hawley, H. Nash, P. Bliss, Joseph Steinacker, T. Whiting, H. N. Turner, E. Sleppy, L. M. Lawson, J. J. Wyatt, D. C. Anderson, Otto Behr, Geo. Lyon, Elias Eppstein, Chas. F. Ernst, John T. Ransom, Jas. B. Johnson, Samuel Reynolds, Wm. Drumhiller, W. B. Johnson, John C. Evans, John B. Albrecht, F. T. Davis, D. H. Winton, Isaac Wilkins, J. H. Lewis, R. L. McDonald, W. A. P. McDonald, Samuel Russell, Louis Fuelling, John A. Dolman, J. B. Bernard, John Broder, W. Z. Ranson, John S. Crosby, R. R. Calkins, George C. Hull, F. G. Hopkins, Jo. Hansen, J. M. Armstrong, Robert Musser, Christ. Mast, C. H. Foote, D. F. Bombeck, A. J. Redding, George P. Dixon, John Townsend, Waller Young, Alex A. Vories, O. E. Vandeventer, U. Schneider, C. C. McDonald, J. H. Bulling, C. B. Claggett, George M. Good, C. L. Groscup, Frederick Neudorff, John S. Andrews, A. E. La Brunerie, H. G. Getchell, H. W. Burke, Samuel Hilpp, Joseph Albus, C. B. Lucas, William H. Floyd, Jr., Thomas Winston, W. E. Sullivan, John Jester, H. C. Twedell, John Albus, Jr., W. L. Reynolds, C. C. Crowley, M. M. Crandall, F. M. Atkinson, I. T. Dyer, H. B. Shale, Dr. J. B. Riley, C. J. Pohl, John D. Preston, George E. Acklam, Oscar M. Spalsbury, George Voltz, and B. C. Thayer.

As the directors were generally re-elected, many of them having retained their seats ten and twelve years, the roster is not larger considering the number of elections and members. Among those who served longest are the following: H. N. Turner, twenty years; John Broder, sixteen years; George C. Hull, sixteen years; Char'es F. Ernest, twelve years; H. Nash, eleven years.

Professor Edward B. Neely was superintendent of schools from 1864 until his death, April 29, 1904. He was succeeded by Prof. J. A. Whiteford of Moberly, Mo., the present incumbent.

PRIVATE SCHOOLS—Reference was made to the first school in the county in the opening lines of this chapter. Others of perhaps equal importance existed in different parts of the county from that time to the permanent establishment of the public school system. In 1845 Mrs. Israel Landis opened a female seminary in St. Joseph, which prospered for several years. Contemporaneous with this Mrs. Mary Stone, a Roman Catholic lady of culture, taught a private school in the city. In 1850 Rev. T. S. Reeve, a minister of the New School Presbyterian church, opened a female seminary in the basement of a church that stood on a hill upon the site of the Saxton National Bank building, at Fourth and Francis streets. Mr. Reeves taught successfully for four years and then withdrew from the profession.

The St. Joseph Female High School opened at Fifth and Faraon streets in September of 1854. It was conducted by three ladies named Lesueur.

F. X. Stuppy, Wm. O'Toole, James Hart, Wm. M. Albin, Professor Charles C. Byrne and Mrs. Burr also taught private and subscription schools. In the fall of 1854 Edward B. Neely, afterward superintendent of the St. Joseph public schools, arrived from Virginia, accompanied by R. F. Maxwell. They established a school in the rooms vacated by Mr. Reeves. Mr. Maxwell soon retired and the school was successfully conducted by Mr. Neely until that gentleman closed it.

In 1855 Professors Davis and Rogers opened a female academy in what was afterward the Saunders House, at Third and Faraon streets. Professor Davis retired in 1858 and Professor Rogers in the following year. Rev. A. V. C. Schenck conducted the school for a brief period and sold out to William Cameron of Lexington, Mo., who remained until the building was converted into a hotel.

In 1858, Alonzo W. Slayback, who afterward figured prominently in the history of St. Joseph and of Missouri, taught a private school in what was the Cumberland Presbyterian church, at Sixth and Edmond streets, and which was afterward used as a synagogue. In 1859 J. P. Caldwell taught a school in the same building.

Miss India Cowden (Mrs. E. W. Ray) and Miss Sarah Bell (Mrs. Tiernan) also conducted school before and during the civil war.

At DeKalb, before the war, Professor Charles S. Raffington conducted the Bloomington Academy, a school of high reputation. During the war Professor Raffington came to St. Joseph and opened the St. Joseph Classical Institute in the Franklin school building. It ceased to exist when that house was required by the public schools.

The Patee house was twice used for school purposes. Rev. James H. Robinson, a minister of the M. E. church, South, opened a female academy there in September, 1865, which continued to January 1, 1869. In 1877, Rev. E. S. Dulin, D.D., L.L.D., a prominent minister of the Baptist church, opened the St. Joseph Female College in the building. This institution had a high reputation and was successfully conducted for four years.

A prominent factor in education in the early days was the German School Society (Deutscher Schul-Verein), a chartered organizationzation of German-American citizens of St. Joseph. This association was founded in 1855. Up to 1869, the late Joseph Dreis taught in a building on North Sixth street. The society, by means of entertainments, accumulated a considerable fund. With this money ground was purchased at Tenth and Felix streets and a building erected. The corner stone was laid with great ceremony on July 4, 1868. Professor Dreis was succeeded by William Beneke and Ernst Kuehl. Instruction was given in both German and English. In 1872, the St. Joseph school board purchased the property for $8,500 and agreed to perpetually give instruction in equal proportion in both English and German in all branches taught.

Bryant's Business College, which was established in November of 1864 by Prof. Thomas J. Bryant and continued up to the date of Professor Bryant's death several years ago, was a commercial school of reputation and had pupils from almost every point in the

West. Professor Chapman and Professor Ritner were also successful for many years during the seventies and eightiees with commercial schools.

In 1868 the Sisters of St. Vincent de Paul (Sisters of Charity) opened a school for girls on the south side of Felix street, between Seventh and Eighth, in a building owned by Dr. Long. This continued until 1883, when the Sisters moved to Tenth and Powell streets, where a hospital building had been erected upon a block of ground donated by Joseph Corby. A school was maintained here until 1891, when it gave way to the present hospital.

Of the schools other than public which are still in existence, the Academy of the Sacred Heart is the oldest. In June of 1853 four members of this order came to St. Joseph from St. Louis. They at once established a school, and during the first month enrolled about one hundred pupils. In 1856 the foundations of the present convent were laid, and in the following year the academy was opened. As the establishment flourished the building was enlarged and equipped until today it is one of the best owned by the order of the Sacred Heart in the West.

The Christian Brothers College is another of the older institutions. In 1858 Father James Powers, a pioneer priest, erected a three-story building at Thirteenth and Henry streets and placed it in charge of the Christian Brothers. The school was discontinued during the war and the building used as barracks by federal soldiers, for which the government, through the mediation of Congressman James N. Burnes, made an adequate allowance some years ago. In 1867 the school was reopened by Brother Noah. In 1886 the old building was made part of the present commodious modern structure.

In 1865 Dr. Charles Martin established a female academy at Fifth and Antoine streets, which he conducted until 1893. It continued for some time under various managements. Doctor Martin died March 7, 1896. His daughters conducted a preparatory school in the building for some years.

A parochial school has been maintained at the church of the Immaculate Conception since the creation of the parish. German and English are taught here by Sisters of the Order of St. Joseph. At St. Patrick's church a school for boys has been in existence for many years under the direction of the Christian Brothers, and one for girls under the direction of Sisters of St. Joseph. Holy Rosary, St. Mary's, SS. Peter and Paul, South St. Joseph and Wyatt Park Catholic parishes all have schools attached. A parish school is also maintained in connection with the German-Evangelical church, on South Tenth street.

* * *

MEDICAL COLLEGES—At one time there were three medical colleges in St. Joseph. The St. Joseph Hospital Medical College was founded in 1876. It was located on Second street, north of Francis.

Among the faculty were Dr. C. F. Knight, Dr. Joseph D. Smith, Dr. J. M. D. France, Dr. Thos. H. Doyle, Dr. J. M. Richmond, Dr. C. J. Siemens and Dr. A. V. Banes.

The College of Physicians and Surgeons was founded in 1879, and was located in the old Christian church building at Third and Robidoux streets. Among the faculty were Drs. W. I. Heddens, Jacob Geiger, E. A. Donelan, J. W. Heddens and P. J. Kirschner.

These two colleges were merged and the name was changed to Ensworth Hospital Medical College, in honor of Samuel Ensworth, deceased, who left $100,000 for this purpose. The Ensworth building, at Seventh and Jule streets, was erected in 1888. The hospital has recently been placed in charge of the Order of Deaconnesses, under the auspices of the Fifth Street Methodist Church.

The Northwestern Medical College was founded in January, 1881, by Drs. F. A. Simmons, S. F. Carpenter, J. P. Chesney and J. T. Berghoff. Until the burning of the court house the college was quartered in the second story of that building. Subsequently it was located at Eighth and Sylvanie streets. In 1895 Dr. T. E. Potter, Dr. O. B. Campbell and others of the faculty withdrew and formed the Central Medical College, which is located at Ninth and Felix streets. The Northwestern continued for a short time and was subsequently converted into a school for the training of nurses, under the direction Dr. J. A. French, owner of the property. There are no medical colleges in St. Joseph at the present time, owing to the rather oppressive state law.

CHAPTER XVII.

ST. JOSEPH BRANCHES OF FEDERAL SERVICE—THE FED-
ERAL BUILDING—HISTORY OF THE ST. JOSEPH POST-
OFFICE—RAILWAY MAIL SERVICE—THE INTERNAL
REVENUE OFFICE—ST. JOSEPH AS A PORT OF ENTRY
—SURVEYORS OF THE PORT—THE FEDERAL COURT.

The first appropriation for a federal building in St. Joseph
was made by congress August 5, 1882, while the late Nicholas Ford
represented the Fourth congressional district. Of the original appropriation $50,000 was set aside to purchase a site and inaugurate
the work of construction. After a long delay the lots at Eighth and
Edmond streets were purchased for $11,750. There was or less
objection by down-town merchants, who argued that the proposed
location was too far removed from the business district of the city.
The growth of business since that time, however, has been in the
d'rection of the Federal building until now it is conceded that excellent judgment was displayed in selecting the site.

When the late James N. Burnes entered Congress he took up
the work of pushing the completion of the custom house where his
predecessor in office had left off. Congressman Burnes secured a
second appropriation of $40,000 July 7, 1884, and, on March 3,
1885, another appropriation of $50,000. August 4, 1886, Congress-
man Burnes succeeded in getting $50,000 additional, and March 3,
1887, the last appropriation of $127,000 for the building proper was
made. August 29, 1890, Congressman R. P. C. Wilson obtained an
appropriation of $3,600 for the purchase of a clock for the tower of
the building, making the total appropriations $345,000.

Seven years were occupied in building the custom house, there
being much vexatious delay, as is usual in such cases. The principal loss of time was caused, however, by the sinking of the building at the northwest corner. Much of the masonry had to be taken
down and rebuilt after the foundation had been properly strength-
ened. The latter part of 1890 saw the building completed, and it
was occupied in January of 1891.

* * *

THE POSTOFFICE—In 1840 a postoffice was established at
Blacksnake Hills, with Jules C. Robidoux in charge. The office
continued under this name until 1843, when it was changed to St.
Joseph, the town having meanwhile been platted and christened.
Robidoux, George Brubaker and Captain Frederick W. Smith were
the postmasters under the old name, and Captain Smith was the
first postmaster under the new name. The mails were not very
heavy in those days, coming mostly by boat from the outer world
and by pony and stage from neighboring points. Captain Smith

wore an old-style, bell-crowned beaver hat, which he used as the repository of postal matter. He was personally acquainted with every inhabitant of the village, and it was his custom to deliver mail to parties as he met them. Thus it will be seen that St. Joseph had free postal delivery long before many of the now populous cities of the West were even thought of.

William B. Almond succeeded Captain Smith in November of 1844, and served until September of 1845, when he was succeeded by William Irvin, who served until September, 1848. Joseph Wyatt then filled the office for one year, and was succeeded by Jesse Holladay, who served until September, 1849, when he was succeeded by Henry S. Creal in January of 1852. Charles Dutszchky was appointed April, 1853. Henry Clark was appointed April, 1854, but did not take the office. Henry Slack was appointed in the same month and held the office until October, 1855, when William A. Davis was appointed. Mr. Davis invented the railway postal car. The office was made presidential in March of 1858 and Mr. Davis continued as postmaster until April of 1861. He was succeeded by John L. Bittinger, who served until March, 1865, and was succeeded by William Fowler.

In March of 1866 George H. Hall was appointed. This appointment was rescinded and James M. Graham was appointed October 31, 1866. However, the friends of Colonel Hall prevailed at Washington and he was given the office in the following month, holding it until April of 1867, when he was succeeded by Joseph J. Wyatt, who served until April of 1869. James M. Hunter served from that time until March of 1871, and was succeeded by Phillip Arnholdt, who served until February of 1875. John Severance held the office until May of 1876, and was succeeded by Dr. Robert P. Richardson, who served only a few months, however. He was succeeded in the following August by James T. Beach, who served until December of 1877, and was succeeded by Francis M. Posegate, who served until June of 1881. Frank M. Tracy succeeded Captain Posegate and served until April of 1885, when he was succeeded by John S. Evans, who served four years and was succeeded by Charles F. Ernst. Captain Ernst died August 2, 1892. From that time until September 30 the office was in charge of Deputy Postmaster Joseph S. Browne, when Frank M. Atkinson took charge, served four years, and was reappointed for another four-year term in April of 1897. He was succeeded by A. W. Brewster in 1901. In March, 1910, L. O. Weakley took charge. He was succeeded by the present postmaster, Frank Freytag, April 1, 1914. Berent Springsted is assistant postmaster.

As long as the business of the city centered in the neighborhood of Market Square the postoffice was located in close proximity to that point. For many years it was in the Beatty bank building, on the east side of Second street, north of Francis. Under Hunter and Arnholdt it was located in the Constable building, on Fourth street, south of Edmond. Under Severance, Richardson, Beach, Posegate and Tracy it was located at the southeast corner of Second and Francis streets. Under Tracy, in 1881, the office was moved to a room under Tootle's opera house, the theater at that time occupying the upper floors only. The business of the office soon outgrew the accommodations here, and under Tracy, also, the first floor of the new Tootle building, east of the opera house, was taken. The office remained there until January 26, 1891, when, under Postmaster Ernst, it was removed to its present permanent quarters in the Federal building.

The office force consists of assistant postmaster, superintendent of mails, sixty-seven mail carriers, money order cashier and three clerks, three stamp clerks, two registry clerks, two general delivery clerks, six special delivery boys, and three messengers, making a total of fifty-seven regular clerks and thirteen contract clerks in stations. Seven rural routes are operated from the main postoffice. The receipts of the office for the year ending June 30, 1915, were $379,651.56.

* * *

THE RAILWAY MAIL SERVICE—The St. Joseph division of the railway mail service, which is embraced in the Seventh division of the service, has headquarters in the Federal building. There are two hundred clerks employed under the direction of the chief clerk of the St. Joseph office, fifteen of whom live in this city. The lines under the jurisdiction of the St. Joseph office extend into Iowa, Kansas and Nebraska.

* * *

THE INTERNAL REVENUE OFFICE—A branch of the Sixth Internal Revenue district of Missouri has been located in the Federal building since its completion. A deputy, appointed by the collector at Kansas City, is in charge, and his jurisdiction extends over seventeen counties: Buchanan, Atchison, Holt, Nodaway, Andrew, Clinton, DeKalb, Gentry, Worth, Harrison, Daviess, Caldwell, Livingston, Grundy, Mercer, Putnam and Sullivan. There are in this division 700 retail liquor dealers, including druggists who have permits to sell whiskey and alcohol. In addition there are thirty-two wholesale liquor dealers, three breweries, seven fruit distilleries, five grain distilleries and fifty-two cigar manufactories. The business of all these concerns with the internal revenue department is transacted through the St. Joseph office and consequently it makes a vast amount of work. The deputy has stamp clerk, gauger, and storekeeper to assist him.

In 1862 St. Joseph was headquarters of the Third Revenue district of Missouri, embracing all of the state lying north of the Missouri River, and including forty-four counties. The taxes collected amounted to about one million dollars per annum. Charles B. Wilkinson was the first collector. In 1865 W. A. Price of Savannah was collector and A. N. Schuster was his deputy. In 1869 Mr. Schuster was appointed collector, the district then embracing twenty-five counties. Schuster served until 1871. The boundaries of the district were subsequently changed and it was called the

Sixth. Schuster was succeeded by General James Craig, and he by W. Z. Ransom. In 1875, when Charles B. Wilkinson was collector a second time, irregularities and complications were discovered in the office. Wilkinson went to Australia and was brought back; tried and convicted of embezzlement on a technicality, the irregularities having been traced to some of his employes. Such was the nature of the case, however, that, after a careful examination of the same by the United States attorney-general and the president, a full pardon was granted Wilkinson.

R. T. Van Horn of Kansas City, having meanwhile been appointed collector, the principal office was moved to Kansas City, and Christ. Mast was made deputy at St. Joseph. John G. Walker of Savannah followed Mast, and then came Charles Groscup, H. G. Getchell, John Harnois and John B. Rodgers. The latter was succeeded in November, 1898, by William M. Shepherd, who in turn was succeeded by George L. Jewett, whose successor, George C. Toel, served from July, 1902, until April, 1915, when Wiley O. Cox, Jr., was placed in charge.

* * *

THE PORT OF ENTRY—St. Joseph was made of port of entry January of 1883, through the efforts of Congressman James N. Burnes. Major James Hunter was the first surveyor and he had for his deputy James T. Beach. John Vanderlinde was appointed surveyor January 30, 1887, and was succeeded by James M. Limbird, who was appointed March 21, 1890. It was during his term, in January, 1891, that the customs office, which had previously been quartered in store buildings, moved to the Federal building. President Cleveland appointed Clay C. Macdonald surveyor of the port in 1893, and Captain McDonald was succeeded, March 2, 1898, by William L. Buechle, who served until 1901, when he was succeeded by John Albus. He in turn gave way to Elliot Marshall, June 1, 1911. He served until July 1, 1913. The office was then placed under the district of St. Louis, with Thomas R. Dumont, deputy, in charge. John H. Wittmaack succeeded Mr. Dumont, May 1, 1915. The surveyor was also custodian of the Federal building until April, 1911, when the duties of that office were transferred to the postmaster.

* * *

THE FEDERAL COURT—Through the efforts of Congressman James N. Burnes a branch of the western division of the United States circuit court was established at St. Joseph. The first session of this court was held at the court house on April 4, 1887, with the late Arnold S. Krekel as judge. Channing M. Dunham was appointed clerk. Judge Krekel and Mr. Dunham both died in the summer of 1888. Judge John F. Philips was appointed to succeed Judge Krekel and served until June 10, 1910, when he was succeeded by Arba S. Van Valkenburgh. Judge Philips appointed Charles M. Thompson as clerk. Mr. Thompson served until October of 1891, when he was succeeded by Charles E. Pollock, who was followed by C. C. Colt, the present incumbent. The clerk also fills the office of commissioner and as such officer has authority to give preliminary hearings in cases of violation of Federal laws and to certify to his findings to the district court.

CHAPTER XVIII.

RELIGION IN BUCHANAN COUNTY AND ST. JOSEPH—THE FIRST PREACHERS AND THE FIRST CHURCHES—A REVIEW OF THE PROGRESS OF THE VARIOUS DENOMINATIONS IN ST. JOSEPH—HISTORY OF THE CONGREGATIONS AND THEIR CHURCH BUILDINGS.

During the first ten years of the county's history but few churches were erected. Public religious services were generally held in private houses, until school houses were built, after which these buildings were used for religious purposes on Sundays. The log court house at Sparta was also used. One of the first sermons preached in the county was by the late Bishop Marvin of the Methodist Episcopal church, in a log structure called "Wood's school house," located in what is now Agency Township. This was early in 1838. "Mount Moriah" was the name of a log church located near Frazer. The "Witt Meeting House" was on the farm of Judge Nelson Witt in Platte Township, and was used by the Calvinistic Baptists. The Missionary Baptists subsequently erected in the same township a frame edifice which was called "Hebron."

The Christians were also among the earliest denominations that organized in the Platte Purchase. Archibald Stewart formed a congregation three miles south of DeKalb, in 1839, and preached his first sermon under a buckeye tree. This denomination was known at that time as the "New Light." The Christians also established a church in Crawford Township, in 1842, which was called "Antioch." The Presbyterians organized a church called "Walnut Grove," and also built a church at Easton when that town was platted. The first camp meeting in the county was held in 1842 near Valley Chapel school house in 1842.

* * *

THE CATHOLICS—In 1838, a wandering Jesuit priest visited the obscure and lonely trading post at Blacksnake Hills. Here, in a rude log house of Joseph Robidoux, a primitive altar was extemporized from a common table, and, in the presence of the wondering red man and the scarcely more cultivated pioneer, mass was celebrated. This was the small beginning of the march of Christianity in our midst.

In 1840, another transient priest made his appearance at the settlement, who elicited no small degree of comment, from the singular mark of a cross on the back of his coat. This was the Rev. Father Vogel. On the 17th of June, 1847, the foundation of the brick church on the corner of Felix and Fifth streets was laid. Services were held in this building, before its completion, and in the same year, in September, the house was dedicated by Bishop Kenrick of St. Louis. In 1848, the two-story parsonage was erected (brick), and in 1853 an addition of twenty-two feet was made to the church. The lot was donated by Joseph Robidoux.

At the organization of the church there were about twenty families, two of which were Irish and the other Canadian French. The first permanent pastor in the church was Rev. Thomas Scanlan, who began his labors in 1847. His first service was in a frame building, belonging to Joseph Robidoux, on Jule street, beyond the Blacksnake. He was succeeded by the Rev. D. F. Healy. Rev. Francis Russie succeeded Father Healy, and he, in turn, was succeeded by the Rev. S. A. Grugan.

In 1859, the Rev. James Powers assumed the duties of assistant pastor, which position he filled until the removal of Father Scanlan, in 1860. In 1860, Rev. John Hennessey took charge and continued the same until he was promoted to the See of Dubuque. He was later an archbishop. His successor in St. Joseph was the Rev. James Power. The church at Fifth and Felix streets was abandoned in 1871.

In 1868, the diocese of St. Joseph, comprising all of the territory north of the Missouri River and west of the Chariton River, was erected, and Rt. Rev. John Joseph Hogan consecrated as its bishop. In 1882 Bishop Hogan took charge of the diocese of Kansas City, but continued as administrator of the diocese of St. Joseph. In the fall of 1893 Bishop Maurice F. Burke, who had been stationed at Cheyenne, took charge of this diocese.

There are seven Catholic churches in St. Joseph. The Cathedral was erected in 1868 by Bishop Hogan. Father Ignatius Conrad, O.S.B., was in charge of the parish after Bishop Hogan's departure, until he was abbot of Subiacco monastery in Arkansas, in 1890.

The Church of the Immaculate Conception, Tenth and Angelique streets, was built in 1868, the first priest being Father Hartman, who was succeeded by the present pastor, Father Linnenkamp. This parish is German.

St. Patrick's, Twelfth street and Doniphan avenue, was built in 1873 by Father Eugene Kenny, who remained as pastor until the close of the year 1879, when he died. He was succeeded by Rev. Thomas Walsh, who served about two years and died also. Rev. Francis F. Graham, who died a few years ago, then took charge. Rev. Edward A. Bolger is now in charge of this congregation.

The Polish Catholics organized a congregation in 1883, and purchased the old home of General Willard P. Hall, at Twentieth and Messanie streets, which was converted in a church called SS. Peter and Paul. Father Wenzeslaus Krzywonos was the first pastor. He was succeeded in 1894 by Father Moron, who served two years and was succeeded by Father Reinert. A modern church, costing about $25,000, was erected in 1905 under the direction of Rev. W. Rakowski. The present priest is Rev. Paul Gora.

Holy Rosary congregation, at Sixth and Scott streets, was

Live Stock Exchange Building

City Hall

formed in 1888 by Rev. James Sheehan. The Floyd school was purchased from the school board and converted into a church. Father Sheehan died in 1892, and was succeeded by Rev. Richard J. Cullen. Rev. Andrew Newman succeeded him.

St. Francis Xavier church, on Seneca street, near Twenty-seventh, in Wyatt Park, was built in the summer of 1891 by the confraternity of the Precious Blood. Rev. Seraphim Kunkler, who was placed in charge, was succeeded by Rev. Louis Hefele, who is now in charge.

St. Mary's church, at Main and Cherry streets, was built in the summer of 1891 by the Benedictine Monks of Conception, Mo. The property passed into the hands of the bishop, however, in 1895. Rev. Adolph Schaefer served as pastor until 1904, when he was followed by Rev. James P. Brady.

St. James church, in South St. Joseph, was completed in 1902, under the direction of Father James O'Reilly. Rev. J. D. O'Donnell is the present pastor.

There are several Catholic churches in the county—at Easton, at New Hurlingen, and at Saxton. Corby Chapel (St. John the Baptist church), north of the city, is seldom used for services and no congregation is attached to it. The remains of the late John Corby repose therein.

There was at one time a Catholic church in the French Bottom, known as St. Roche, but this has not been in existence since 1880.

* * *

PRESBYTERIANS—The first Protestant minister to preach the gospel in St. Joseph was Rev. T. S. Reeve, a New School Presbyterian. He held services at the tavern of Josiah Beattie, which stood on Main street, above Francis. In the spring of 1844 Rev. Reeves built the first church in St. Joseph. It was a log structure, 20x30 feet in dimensions, and stood near the corner of Third and Francis streets. Parson Reeve assisted in cutting the timber and erecting the building.

The log church was used by the Presbyterians until 1847, when a brick church was built at the northeast corner of Fourth and Francis streets. This structure stood on a hill, which was cut down when the Saxton bank building was erected. The log church was purchased by the First Missionary Baptist Society. It gave way many years ago to business houses.

In February of 1854 twenty-two people met in the old market house, and, under the sanction of the Presbytery of Upper Missouri, organized what they called the First Presbyterian church. They were of the old school. Here they worshipped for some time, and various halls were occupied until 1858, when they commenced the erection of the Sixth Street church. They built the first story, covered it and worshipped there until after the war. Then there was division in the church. One part of the membership built, in 1867, the present Seventh Street church, for their use, and the others remained in the Sixth Street church. The first minister was the

Rev. A. V. C. Schenck, who remained with the church until 1858, when the Rev. J. G. Fackler became pastor. In 1864 Rev. Fackler resigned on account of ill health and the Rev. A. P. Foreman was called to the charge. He remained with the church six years, doing much good, and ministering well to the spiritual wants of his flock. In 1870 Rev. J. G. Fackler was again called to the charge and occupied the pulpit until 1874, when he was succeeded by the Rev. R. S. Campbell, who held the pastorate for fifteen years. The Rev. A. A. Pfanstiehl occupied the pulpit as temporary supply minister after Rev. Campbell vacated it until Rev. George A. Trenholm took charge, in November, 1891. Rev. Mr. Trenholm died in 1899, and on December 1st, that year, Rev. W. R. Dobyns, the present pastor, took charge.

The Westminster Presbyterian church was organized on May 9, 1863, with twenty members. In May, 1864, Rev. B. B. Parsons of Illinois was installed as pastor. In October, 1866, the stone chapel, directly west of the Hughes building, on Felix street, was completed. This was intended as the wing of a greater church in contemplation. The chapel is a small but massive stone structure of the Gothic type, and had the edifice been completed as originally planned, it would have been one of the most attractive architectural features of the city. In February, 1868, Rev. Henry Bullard, then pastor in Wayland, Mass., supplied the pulpit for two Sundays, and upon the 1st of May following, assumed full charge as pastor. In 1872, the plan of completing the stone church was abandoned and the property of the Old School Presbyterians, at Sixth and Faraon streets, was purchased and completed. In 1892, a new church was erected at Twentieth and Jule streets. The Sixth street property was sold and the site of the church is now occupied by modern dwellings.

The Third Street Presbyterian church grew out of a Sabbath school organized in 1869. The church, located on Third street at the junction of Savannah avenue, was built in 1889.

The Cumberland Presbyterian church had a congregation in the early fifties. They had a church at Sixth and Edmond streets, where a business block now stands. This was afterward used as a Jewish synagogue and was destroyed by fire. The church edifice on the corner of Sixteenth and Edmond streets was erected in 1882 by the members and friends of the Platte Presbytery. Rev. W. B. Farr, D.D., was the first pastor, and the first congregation was organized November 16, 1883, with nineteen charter members, nine being of one family and three of the pastor's family. The church was rebuilt in 1904, and in 1909 the congregation was merged with that of the Westminster church. The property of the Cumberland church was sold and the site is now occupied by modern residences.

The Second Presbyterian church is located at 1124 South Twelfth street, and Hope chapel on Thirteenth and Highly streets.

* * *

THE METHODISTS—In the year 1843-44, Rev. Edwin Robinson,

preacher in charge of the St. Joseph (Savannah) circuit, Weston district, Missouri Annual Conference of the M. E. church, organized the first class in the town of St. Joseph. The leader of this class was John F. Carter; the other members were Rufus Patchen, Clara Patchen, Mrs. Jane Kemper and Mrs. Sarah Jeffries. At the time of the organization W. W. Redman was presiding elder of the district, which included St. Joseph. The first permanent organization of the church was effected during the early part of the year 1844, Edwin Robinson being preacher in charge. The building in which the congregation worshipped at that time was a small frame on Main street, used once by David J. Heaton as a furniture store and cabinet shop; and for nearly two years they worshipped in this humble and primitive structure. The old log church was afterward occupied one Sunday each month by courtesy of the Presbyterians.

This may be the proper place to state that the General Conference of the M. E. Church, held in the city of New York in May, 1844, failing to harmonize the Northern and Southern sections of the country in regard to the disciplinary legislation concerning "slavery," provided a plan of peaceable separation, the important details of which need not be mentioned here; but under the provisions of which the charges and conferences within the territory of the slave holding states proceeded with great unanimity to adjust themselves and were by the delegated convention, held at Louisville, Ky., in May, 1845, organized into the Methodist Episcopal Church, South. So that after this transition period we are speaking of the M. E. Church, South, in St. Joseph.

In 1846, when the Rev. John A. Tutt was in charge, a brick church, 40x60 feet in dimensions, was erected at Third and Felix streets. In 1857 this property was sold, and a new church built at Seventh and Francis streets. It is interesting to note that there was great objection to the new location because it was considered too far out. Rev. Edwin Robinson was in charge in 1847-48, and was succeeded by Rev. Wm. M. Rush, who served until 1852 and was succeeded by Rev. Wm. Holmes. Mr. Holmes did not remain long, giving place to Rev. C. J. Vandeventer, who served two years. In 1854-55 the pulpit was filled by Rev. B. A. Spencer, who was succeeded by Rev. Samuel W. Cape. From 1856 to 1858 Rev. E. R. Miller was pastor, and was succeeded by Rev. John Bull, and he in turn by Rev. E. G. Nicholson. Rev. George T. Hoagland supplied the pulpit also until the return of Rev. Rush. In 1862, Rev. Rush was prohibited from preaching to his congregation by the military order of General Loan. From 1864 to 1865 Rev. Wm. H. Leftwich was pastor. In 1868 Rev. Vandeventer was again placed in charge, remaining until 1872, when he was succeeded by Rev. Eugene R. Hendrix, afterward bishop. Rev. Hendrix remained until 1876. Since then the following ministers have been in charge: 1876-78, Rev. G. T. Gooch; 1878-82, Rev. E. K. Miller; 1882-86, Rev. W. G. Miller; 1886-88, Rev. J. C. Brown; 1888-90, Rev. A. G. Dinwiddie; 1892-94, Rev. J. A. Beagle; 1894-97, Rev. Frank Siler; September, 1897 to 1901, Rev. W. F. Packard; 1901-05, Rev. C. M. Bishop;

1905-08, Rev. S. P. Cresap; 1908-11, Rev. U. G. Foote; 1911-15, Rev. B. P. Taylor; 1915, Rev. Robert E. Goodrich. The handsome stone church at Twelfth and Francis streets was built a few years ago.

The Olive Street M. E. Church, South, was completed in 1870. The building is at the northwest corner of Tenth and Patee streets. It has for some years been used by the Swedish Lutherans. The congregation now owns a commodious edifice at Fifteenth and Olive streets, built in 1894.

Hundley Church, South, at Twenty-second and Colhoun streets, grew out of a mission commenced by Rev. C. I. Vandeventer in 1872. A frame chapel stood on Union street until 1892, when the present building was erected.

Spruce Street church is located at 2922 North Ninth street, and Hyde Park church at Eighth street and Hyde Park avenue.

Centenary M. E. Church, South, dates back to 1883. The building is located on Tenth street, between Pacific and Sycamore streets.

Gooding chapel, at Colorado and Pryor avenues, named in honor of John Gooding, its principal benefactor, is also a branch of the M. E. Church, South.

The following relates to the Methodist Episcopal, or, as it is commonly called, the North Methodist Church: In 1849 Rufus Patchen, John Brady, N. B. McCart and the Rev. A. J. Armstrong, local preacher, withdrew from the parent congregation and organized the "Methodist Episcopal Church," without any geographical distinction. They held meetings, sometimes at the house of Mr. McCart and sometimes at the log church. In 1852 a brick church was erected on Fifth street, below Sylvanie. In 1863 this property was sold for debt. Up to that time the following pastors were consecutively in charge: Revs. J. W. Taylor, J. M. Chivington, Walter Perry, M. T. Kleffer, D. H. May, A. C. Clemens, J. H. Hopkins, J. V. Caughlin, Wm. Hanley, Richard Haney and Alpha Wright. A reorganization took place after the loss of the property. Quarters were fitted up in the Odd Fellows' building, then at Fifth and Felix streets, and Rev. T. H. Hagerty became pastor, remaining until 1865, when Rev. J. T. Boyle took charge. In 1866 their house of worship, on Fifth street, between Jule and Francis streets, was built. Rev. W. G. Mattison succeeded Rev. Boyle, and was in turn succeeded by Rev. J. W. Flowers, who served until March of 1869, when he was succeeded by Rev. J. S. Barwick. In 1870 Rev. C. H. Stocking took the pastorate, served three years and was succeeded by Rev. D. J. Holmes. In 1875 Rev. S. W. Thornton took charge, served two years and was succeeded by Rev. John Wayman, who also served two years and was succeeded in 1880 by Rev. J. M. Greene, who was succeeded by Rev. J. J. Bentley. Following Rev. Bentley came Rev. Eli S. Brumbaugh, who remained until 1894, and was succeeded by Rev. C. H. Stocking, who remained until May of 1898, when he was succeeded by Rev. S. B. Campbell. Rev. B. F. Crissman succeeded to the pastorate in 1903. He was followed by

Rev. C. J. English in 1907, Rev. Frank E. Day in 1910, and Rev. C. O. Kimball in 1914.

The other Methodist Episcopal churches in the city are: Huffman Memorial, at Twenty-eighth and Seneca streets; Oakland Park church, corner of Twentieth and Highly streets; St. Paul's, 419 Dolman street; Wesley church, at 2136 South Eleventh street; Grace church, at 5801 King Hill avenue, and the South Park church.

The congregation of the German Methodist Episcopal church was organized in March of 1849. The communicants numbered ten and the first pastor was Rev. William Eliers. At a quarterly conference held January 13, 1851, a committee was selected to secure a lot on which to build. The site selected was on Edmond street, west of Sixth, on which a church was soon thereafter erected, which was wrecked in 1857 in an attempt to raise it. The old site was sold and a location purchased at Third and Robidoux, on which a brick structure was built, under the supervision of Jacob Hauck, Peter Hammer and John Fink, which served the wants of the congregation for about twenty years. In 1867 a parsonage was built at the rear of the church at an expense of about $2,500, which is still the home of the pastor. For many years the congregation sought to build a new edifice more suited to the times, but it was not until 1887 that the old church was taken down, and the present handsome structure completed, the lot adjoining the old church on the south having been purchased in 1885. The new church was dedicated in the spring of 1888 by Dr. Leibhart of Cincinnati. Rev. Samuel Buechner is now the pastor.

Of the African Methodist Episcopal Church there are two parishes. Ebenezer chapel, corner of Third and Antoine streets, is the principal edifice. Holsey chapel, Eighteenth and Beattie streets, is a modest frame structure.

* * *

THE BAPTISTS—The first records that can be found bearing upon the Baptist church in St. Joseph are dated September 28, 1844, and refer to an "arm of the Dillon Creek Baptist Church." On March 22, 1845, a sermon was preached by Elder William Woreley. Thereupon the first Baptist congregation was organized. Elder Woreley was succeeded in July, 1847, by Elder James I. Robinson, who at first received $50 per annum and his board, and subsequently received $100 per annum and paid his own expenses. During all of this period there was no permanent place of worship. Meetings were held in private houses and rented halls. In 1848 the "old log church" was purchased from the Presbyterians for $100. This purchase did not include the ground. In January of 1852 the log church was sold at auction for $16.25. From this time until 1856 the Baptists worshipped in various places. A movement for a church building was begun in 1850, when the church was incorporated under the laws of the state. Real estate was acquired at the southeast corner of Sixth and Francis, and in 1856 a commodious structure was erected. In 1895 work was begun upon the present massive structure at Thirteenth and Francis streets, and in the spring of 1897 the basement of this building was occupied, the church at Sixth and Francis streets being abandoned.

Rev. Isaiah T. Williams was chosen pastor in 1848. In 1851 Rev. J. Hickman of Kentucky was called, and in March of 1853 Rev. W. F. Boyakin of Illinois assumed the pastorate. When the church at Sixth and Francis streets was completed Rev. Wm. Price was pastor. In November, 1859, Rev. Wm. I. Gill accepted a call and served until June, 1860, when he was succeeded by Rev. E. S. Dulin, who served until March, 1864. Rev. T. W. Barrett of Leavenworth served one year after Dr. Dulin, and in July, 1865, was succeeded by Rev. Joseph R. Manton of Providence, R. I., who remained until April, 1868. Rev. James Dixon of Milwaukee followed and served until November, 1868. Rev. J. M. C. Breaker then took charge and remained until May, 1877, being succeeded by Rev. William Harris of Louisville, Ky. Rev. J. L. Lawless succeeded Mr. Harris in March, 1884, and served until January 1, 1891, when he was succeeded by Rev. W. J. Coulston, who remained until March 15, 1893. The pastorate remained vacant until September, 1893, when Rev. R. P. Johnston of Chilesburg, Ky., accepted a call. Rev. Johnston remained until 1898, when he went to St. Louis. He was succeeded by Rev. J. E. Cook, who resigned July 31, 1903. Rev. T. W. O'Kelly took charge February 7, 1904; Rev. W. M. Vines, September 1, 1911; Rev. Arthur C. Archibald, November 1, 1913; Rev. J. E. Dillard, February 1, 1915.

In 1890 the First Baptist church built a fine edifice in Wyatt Park at Twenty-eighth and Seneca streets, and presented it, paid for in full, to the congregation. Rev. A. D. Cooper is now the pastor.

The Savannah Avenue Baptist church, situated at the corner of Savannah avenue and Woodson street, was the direct outgrowth of the Young People's Mission Society of the First Baptist church, which caused the erection of a neat brick chapel in the fall of 1885. Two years later this building was enlarged to twice its seating capacity, it having been found entirely inadequate to the accommodation of the congregation.

The Patee Park Baptist church was built in 1889-90. As early as 1871 a congregation worshiped in a building at Twelfth and Penn streets. Under the pastorate of Rev. N. R. Pittman the present substantial and modern edifice was erected on Tenth street, opposite Patee Park. Rev. Pittman resigned in 1894 and was succeeded by Rev. J. L. Lawless. The present pastor is Rev. Charles Durden.

Copeland Baptist church was established at 2600 South Eighteenth street a few years ago.

In 1901 the King Hill Baptist church was organized.

The negro Baptists have two churches. The Francis Street Baptist church was organized in 1865 by Rev. B. F. Marshall, with seventeen members. For seven years they worshiped in a frame building on their present location, Francis street, between Tenth and Eleventh streets. In 1873 Rev. W. W. Stewart was called to the pastorate, in which he remained until 1889, during which time the present building was erected and the church increased in membership to 350. In the fall of 1889 Rev. J. J. Lyons was settled as pastor. He remained nine months. Rev. A. M. Lewis was then settled as pastor supply. In August, 1891, Rev. E. M. Cohron was called to the pastorate, since which time the present building has been completed. Mr. Cohron is still the pastor.

New Hope chapel, on Sixteenth street, a frame building, was erected in 1884.

* * *

THE CHRISTIANS—In 1844 Elder Duke Young of the Christian church preached a discourse in the residence of Mrs. Northcutt. The growth of this church was slow and meetings were held at various places until 1847, when Elder Young instituted a revival at the court house, where the congregation continued to hold its meetings until 1858. A church was built at Third and Robidoux streets. This structure is still in existence, though not used as a church. The present Christian church, at Tenth and Edmond streets, was built in 1870. Dr. S. D. Overstreet and Allen G. Mansfield were the elders when the Third Street church was erected. Upon the death of Dr. Overstreet, Judge Joseph J. Wyatt was elected elder and filled the pulpit until Elder Moses E. Lard became pastor of the church. Rev. Lard resigned at the breaking out of the war and Elder Wyatt again took charge. Mr. Lard subsequently became prominent in the ministry in Kentucky and was one of the great lights of the Christian church. In 1866 Elder W, C. Rogers was called, remaining two years. Elder Wyatt again served until the arrival of Elder John Lindsay, in 1869. Elder Lindsay resigned in 1870 and Elder Wyatt for the fourth time filled the vacancy, serving two years, and resigning to give way to Elder Thomas P. Haley. In December of 1876 Elder John H. Duncan succeeded Elder Haley. Elder John B. Corwine succeeded Elder Duncan, and was in turn succeeded in March, 1881, by Elder M. M. Goode, who, after a few years, was succeeded by Elder C. M. Chilton, the present pastor.

The Wyatt Park Christian church is located at Twenty-seventh and Olive streets; Woodson chapel at 2525 St. Joseph avenue; Mitchell Park church at Eleventh and Jackson streets; King Hill church at King Hill avenue and Ohio street; Frederick avenue church at 1912 Frederick avenue.

* * *

PROTESTANT EPISCOPAL—The first missionary service of the Episcopal church in St. Joseph was held in September of 1851. In the following year a parish was organized by Rev. M. M. McNamara. A small building at the northwest corner of Third and Jule streets was purchased and equipped. In 1856 the site of Christ church, at Seventh and Francis streets, was purchased and in August of 1857 the erection of a frame building, which fronted on

Francis street, was begun. This structure was destroyed by fire on Christmas eve, 1876. The present church was erected as soon as possible.

Rev. McNamara remained in charge until March of 1854, when he was succeeded by Rev. W. N. Irish, who served until 1858, when Rev. W. R. Pickman took charge. In October of 1860, Rev. R. H. Weller succeeded Rev. Pickman and served until October 13, 1866, being succeeded by Rev. W. C. Hopkins, who served one year. In November, 1867, Rev. Pickman again took charge and served until April, 1869, being succeeded by Rev. Wm. Phillips, who served until January, 1871. The parish was vacant until June of 1871, when Rev. Dr. James Runcie was installed as pastor. Dr. Runcie served until his death, May 12, 1889. In the fall of 1889 Rev. H. L. Foote took charge and served six years. He was succeeded by Rev. John Henry Hopkins, who was followed by Rev. G. Heathcote Hills, in 1899; Rev. John D. LaMothe, in 1903; Rev. E. H. Eckel, in 1905; Rev. G. Hely Molony, 1914.

* * *

EVANGELICAL AND LUTHERAN—The German Evangelical Zion's church was organized in 1865, with Rev. A. H. Kirchoff as pastor. The old brick church at the northeast corner of Fourth and Francis streets was purchased and services were held there until October, 1881, when the present church, at Ninth and Jule streets, was completed. Rev. Kirchoff was succeeded by Rev. Carl Nestel in 1874. Rev. Nestel gave way to Rev. Max Habeker, who died in 1899, and was succeeded by Rev. William Hackman. Rev. F. C. Klick is now the pastor.

The Second German Evangelical church was organized in 1874 and a building erected at Thirteenth and Monterey streets. Rev. Julius Kramer was pastor until 1876, when he was succeeded by Rev. F. Grabeau. Rev. F. Wellge succeeded Rev. Grabeau in 1880. A substantial brick church was built in 1893 at Fifteenth and Lafayette streets.

The German Evangelical Lutherans organized a church in August, 1881, and erected St. Paul's church at No. 1019 South Tenth street. A new church building was erected at Fourteenth and Lafayette streets in 1902.

St. Peter's German Lutheran church is located at 2104 North Fourth street, and Emmanuel Church German of the Evangelical Association is located at Twelfth and Lafayette streets.

The First English Lutheran church was organized in August of 1894 by Rev. Edward F. Treffz. Until the erection of a building, east of the custom house in 1895, services were held in the Y. M. C. A. auditorium. This congregation built a handsome new church at Tenth and Charles streets in 1913.

There is also a Swedish Lutheran congregation, located in the building at Tenth and Patee streets, formerly used by the Methodists.

CONGREGATIONAL — On May 12, 1867, the Congregational Church of St. Joseph came into existence with only ten members. In October of that year Rev. W. L. Bray was called to the pastorate. He remained three years and was succeeded by Rev. Jonathan Crane, who served only a short time, however, being succeeded in the same year by Rev. F. L. Kenyon, who remained eight years. From 1878 until 1882 no permanent pastor was maintained. Rev. Frederick S. Hayden served from 1882 until 1888, being succeeded by Rev. Albert Bushnell, who began his work February 1, 1889. He resigned in 1899, and the pulpit was filled by Rev. J. G. Dougherty of Kansas City, as supply pastor, until the call of Rev. W. W. Bolt, in the fall of 1900. Rev. Bolt was succeeded in 1904 by Rev. J. B. Kettle of Avon, Ill., who remained pastor until June, 1910. Rev. William M. Jones accepted the pastorate a few months later, taking active charge January 1, 1911. He was followed by the present pastor, Rev. Robert Porter, January 1, 1915.

In 1870 a frame chapel was erected on the south side of Edmond street, between Ninth and Tenth streets. This was abandoned in 1891, the present substantial edifice at Thirteenth and Jule streets having meanwhile been erected.

Plymouth church, at Thirty-third and Penn streets, is an active suburban congregation. Rev. Duncan Brown is the pastor.

* * *

UNITARIAN—In November of 1867 those who were inclined to the Unitarian belief held their first meeting. The service was read by John S. Crosby. For several years various clergymen came and preached to the society. Rev. Mr. Finney served one year as pastor, and Rev. E. H. Danforth served two years. Rev. Joseph A. Chase, Rev. A. F. Abbott, Rev. Charles B. Roberts, Rev. J. F. C. Grumbine served successively until 1891. The pulpit was supplied for a time by Rev. J. E. Roberts of Kansas City, and others. Services.were held in various halls and churches until 1888, when a modern building was erected on Ninth street, between Felix and Edmond street, which gave way to make room for *The News-Press* building in 1912.

* * *

THE Y. M. C. A.—On May 2, 1882, at a meeting in the Baptist church, the St. Joseph branch of the Young Men's Christian Association was formed with forty members. Quarters were rented in the building at the northwest corner of Fifth and Edmond streets, and John W. Hansel of Peoria, Illinois, was installed as general secretary. In October of 1885 Rev. Sam Jones and Rev. Sam Small held a revival in the city. Sunday, October 11, was set apart as Y. M. C. A. day. A movement for a building had been in progress for a year or more. Upon this occasion Rev. Jones made an especial plea for a permanent home for the association, and before the meeting adjourned $39,000 had been subscribed. Later this sum was increased to about $60,000. As a result the Y. M. C. A. building at Seventh and Felix streets was occupied in 1887. The association outgrew this building in time, and the present modern building at Tenth and Faraon streets is the result of the efforts of some of St. Joseph's noble men. The building cost $145,000 exclusive of furnishings, and the ground on which it stands cost $15,000. It was opened August 1, 1912.

* * *

THE Y. W. C. A.—In the summer of 1887 the Young Women's Christian Association was formed. The object of this association is to unite all young women interested in physical, social, business, intellectual and spiritual development. The physical department includes a gymnasium, where proper instructions are imparted by a thorough teacher. A reading room, with a rapidly increasing library, is a feature. The business department seeks the advancement of young women in the business world, and an employment bureau, for the benefit of the employer and employe, is established and successfully conducted. The special features are the gospel meetings, participated in by members of the association. From 1891 to 1905 the organization occupied quarters in the Carbry block at Seventh and Edmond streets. It moved to the Bartlett building, at Ninth street and Frederick avenue, in 1905 and remained there until the new building at the northwest corner of Eighth and Jule streets was occupied, October 5, 1914. The building cost $150,000 and the lot $20,000.

* * *

JEWISH—In 1859 the congregation Adath Joseph erected the synagogue at Sixth and Jule streets. In the beginning services were held in a hall on Felix street. In 1857 a church building, which stood upon the site of the Hotel Donovan at Sixth and Edmond streets, was purchased and fitted up. This building was destroyed by fire. Rev. S. Kauffman was rabbi in charge of the synagogue until 1875, when he was succeeded by Rev. S. Gerstman, who served until 1879, when he gave way to Rev. Isaac Schwab, who was followed by Rabbi Louis Bernstein in 1906. The handsome new synagogue at Seventeenth and Felix streets was built in 1910 at a cost of $60,000.

There is also an orthodox congregation, known as Shaare Sholem. The faithful worshipped in a rented hall at Sixth and Angelique at first, but in 1900 a synagogue was built at Seventh and Patee streets at a cost of $17,000.

* * *

OTHERS—The St. Joseph branch of the Reorganized Church of Latter Day Saints was organized in 1870. Services were held in public halls and at the court house until the erection of the church building on Seventeenth street, north of Faraon street, in 1890.

In 1892 Rev. H. S. Gekeler formed a congregation of the Reformed church. Meetings were held in the Y. M. C. A. auditorium for some time, until the church formerly used by the Congregationalists, on Edmond street, was secured. A modern brick structure was erected at the corner of Tenth and Lincoln streets in 1903 by Rev. A. O. Reiter, who succeeded Rev. Mr. Gekeler.

The First Church of Christ Scientists was formed in 1902. Rev. Charles M. Howe conducted meeting for a time in the Tootle theater; later in Unity chapel. This congregation owns one of the handsomest church buildings in St. Joseph. It is situated at Twelfth and Felix streets.

The Second Church of Christ, Scientists, was organized in 1902. This congregation worships in the building formerly used by the Congregational church, on Edmond street.

The Salvation Army has maintained barracks in St. Joseph since the summer of 1885. During 1898 a detachment of "Volunteers of America" was also quartered in the city.

CHAPTER XIX.

BUCHANAN COUNTY AND ST. JOSEPH IN WAR.—THE WAR WITH MEXICO.—DONIPHAN'S EXPEDITION.— THE OREGON BATTALION.—THE CIVIL WAR.—A MOB DESTROYS THE UNITED STATES FLAG.—SOME OF THE MEN WHO WENT SOUTH AND DISTINGUISHED THEMSELVES AS SOLDIERS.—THE UNION REGIMENTS THAT WERE ORGANIZED IN ST. JOSEPH, THEIR OFFICERS AND WHERE THEY FOUGHT.—THE "PAWPAW MILITIA"; ITS HISTORY AND HOW IT CAME INTO EXISTENCE.—THE MISSOURI MILITIA AFTER THE WAR.—THE NATIONAL GUARD OF MISSOURI.— THE WAR WITH SPAIN AND THE COMPANIES THAT WENT FROM ST. JOSEPH TO THE FOURTH REGIMENT OF MISSOURI VOLUNTEERS.

Having reviewed the political history of Buchanan County and St. Joseph, and touched incidentally upon commercial and social progress, it is deemed proper, at this point, to make a digression and to consider the various war periods. The war with Mexico, the Civil war and the struggle with Spain will be touched upon as far as they are related to the people of this county.

During the month of May, 1846, Governor Edwards called for volunteers to join the Army of the West in an expedition to Santa Fe under command of General Stephen W. Kearney. General Kearney was the father of Charles W. Kearney, later a resident of St. Joseph, and the uncle of General Phil Kearney. A number went from here, among them Willard P. Hall, who was then a candidate for congress. Mr. Hall left a law practice and the campaign to take care of itself and joined the First regiment of Missouri cavalry as a private. This regiment assembled at Fort Leavenworth and elected as its colonel Alexander W. Doniphan of Liberty, who had also enlisted as a private. The regiment went with Colonel Kearney as far as Santa Fe. From that point its operations became known as "Doniphan's Expedition," an achievement that is famous in history, and that is frequently compared with the military feats of Xenophon, Hannibal and the first Napoleon.

The entire Army of the West, at the beginning of the campaign, numbered 1,658 men. The army, composed of dragoons and cavalry, marched across the plains in detachments, the first leaving Fort Leavenworth on June 29, and the last on July 6, 1846. They rendezvoused at a famous trading post on the Arkansas river in Colorado, the present site of Fort Lyon, known then as Bent's Fort. After resting several days the reunited forces proceeded south, crossed the Raton mountains through the Raton pass and entered the city of Las Vegas without opposition on August 15. The alcalde and all other citizens of the place took the oath of allegiance to the United States. Here Colonel Kearney received his commission as general, forwarded by messenger from Washington.

Learning that Armijo, the governor of New Mexico, had fortified Apache pass, through which led the road to Santa Fe, and was occupying it with a considerable force, General Kearney marched to meet him, in the expectation of battle. But at his approach the Mexicans retired without offering resistance, and the army went through the pass and on to Santa Fe, which they occupied unopposed on August 18, 1846.

General Kearney at once proceeded to organize a provisional government for the Mexican state, the capital of which he held. To Colonel Doniphan and to Willard P. Hall was assigned the duty of constructing and formulating laws for the newly acquired territory. They were given quarters in the "palace," as the residence of the governor of New Mexico has always been called, and went to work, each with four clerks and interpreters, in the room in which General Lew Wallace wrote "Ben Hur" a third of a century afterward. The result of their labors is known as the "Kearney code," which forms an important constituent of the laws of New Mexico today.

It was while thus engaged that Willard P. Hall was notified by Colonel Doniphan, who had received dispatches, that he had been elected to congress over Judge Birch of Plattsburg.

On September 26, General Kearney started with his column of regulars for California, leaving Colonel Doniphan in command of Santa Fe. On September 28, General Sterling Price arrived in Santa Fe, followed by a force of 1,700 volunteers from Missouri. Colonel Doniphan, who, at his own request, had been ordered to join General Wool in Chihuahua, was preparing to move south, when an order reached him, sent back by General Kearney, to make a campaign against the Navajo Indians, who had been attacking Mexican villages on the Rio Grande. Turning his authority as governor of New Mexico over to General Price, Colonel Doniphan at once proceeded to execute General Kearney's order.

The Navajos were at that time a powerful tribe, numbering some 17,000, and inhabited what is now northeastern Arizona. They had long been the terror and scourge of the civilized inhabitants of New Mexico. Colonel Doniphan divided his forces, dispatching Major Gilpin with 200 men northwest into the San Juan country, while he himself, with the remainder of his regiment, marched to Albuquerque and thence west up the River Puerco to its headwaters. The Navajos were encompassed and surrounded by this movement and made a treaty in which they bound themselves to cease their depredations and become friends of the United States.

On December 14, 1846, Colonel Doniphan commenced his march to Chihuahua. His route lay through a barren desert of ninety miles, known as the Jornata del Muerto (Journey of the

Dead). No water is to be found the entire distance. Over this plain Colonel Doniphan successfully marched his troops in detachments, each requiring about thirty hours in the passage, and occupied the town of Dona Ana without resistance.

Leaving half his regiment here to guard the river crossing, Colonel Doniphan pushed south, and at Brazito met a Mexican force from Chihuahua that had advanced to oppose him. A sharp skirmish followed in which the Mexicans were routed and followed to El Paso, which was captured with its military supplies.

In the enemy's baggage here taken were found dispatches imparting the information that General Wool, instead of proceeding west to Chihuahua, had gone south to join General Taylor at Monterey. Colonel Doniphan was therefore confronted with the alternative of returning to Santa Fe or marching 1,200 miles through a hostile country to Monterey to effect a junction with Wool. He decided to go on and sent back for artillery. In response he was joined by a Missouri battalion of artillery and by the Laclede rangers of St. Louis, increasing his force to about 1,000 men and six pieces of artillery.

Before him lay the city of Chihuahua, rich, populous and protected by a strong garrison. Colonel Doniphan marched south without serious opposition to the pass of Sacramento, sixteen miles north of the city of Chihuahua, which the Mexicans had fortified and where they were awaiting his coming with 4,200 men, cavalry and artillery. The Mexican flank was protected by a deep and precipitous ravine, difficult of passage.

Colonel Doniphan gave the order to advance as soon as possible. He crossed the ravine, above mentioned, under fire, with his mounted troops, and on the other side was met by the Mexican cavalry, which was repulsed. Then he ordered a counter charge, which was successfully made, and drove the Mexicans from the field. He captured eleven pieces of artillery, forty prisoners and the enemy's baggage, and entered the city of Chihuahua in triumph. The Mexican loss was 300 killed and wounded, while Doniphan's loss was one killed and eight wounded.

Reports were sent to Generals Taylor and Wood and the march to join the former at Monterey began. This expedition, in a hostile country, far from any base of supplies, had to rely wholly upon its own resources for existence, exposed equally to the attacks of the Mexicans, whose country they were invading, and of the predatory band of Indians which roamed over Northern Mexico. Over arid plains, through mountain passes, in which Mexican guerillas lay in ambush, and through fertile valleys as well, the expedition continued its triumphal march, defeating and dispersing all who opposed it, until on the first of May, 1847, it moved into Saltillo with banners flying, and joined Taylor.

But General Taylor was not prepared to utilize these reinforcements. There were reports of a change of commanders in Mexico and all operations were at a standstill. Colonel Doniphan's troops remained with Taylor about one month, when, their terms of enlistment having expired, and there being no prospect of active operations at an early date, he marched his command to Brazos de Santiago and embarked for New Orleans, where the men were mustered out.

From New Orleans to their homes in Missouri the progress of Colonel Doniphan's command was a continuous ovation. The expedition indeed had been a wonderful one. In thirteen months the command had marched, mainly in a hostile country, 3,600 miles by land and traveled 2,500 miles by water. On his arrival in Missouri Colonel Doniphan received the well-earned brevet of brigadier-general. Willard Hall did not participate in the campaign beyond Santa Fe.

In the spring of 1847 Governor Edwards called for a battalion of five companies for service on the Indian frontier, and the routes to Santa Fe and Oregon, to protect traders and emigrants. Lieut.-Col. L. E. Powell, of St. Charles, organized the battalion, among the companies being one formed at St. Joseph. Our company was officered by Robert M. Stewart, captain; Henry Smith, first lieutenant; Howell Thomas, second lieutenant; John Searcy, third lieutenant. The battalion was formed at Fort Leavenworth. Beside Col. Powell there were the following officers: Dr. S. Todd, St. Joseph, adjutant; James McDowell, St. Joseph, sergeant-major; quartermaster, Capt. Stewart Van Vliet; commissary of subsistence, Frank Warmcastle, Atchison County. The late Gen. James Craig commanded a company raised in Holt County. Captain Stewart was stricken with rheumatism at Fort Leavenworth and returned home. After faithfully performing the mission upon which it was sent, doing business over a vast region of country between the Missouri River and the Rocky Mountains, the battalion returned home and the men were mustered out late in the fall of 1848.

* * *

After the war with Mexico interest in military matters lagged. In 1853, the Robidoux Grays existed, under command of Capt. Bela M. Hughes. In 1860 the Fourth Military District, in which St. Joseph was located, was commanded by Col. M. Jeff Thompson, and the First battalion, consisting of three companies, under Major F. W. Smith, was organized in St. Joseph. Company A, Jackson Guards, was commanded by Capt. Reuben Kay. Company B, Emmett Guards, was commanded by Capt. T. J. Rafftery. Company C, German Rifles, was commanded by Capt. George Landry.

* * *

The Civil War period was in some respects the most momentous in the history of the community. Buchanan County was settled largely by people who had come from the Southern States and the fact that over 2,000 slaves, valued at $1,500,000, were owned here will readily explain why there was a strong feeling against abolition on the part of a considerable portion of the community. In the election of 1860, Bell and Everett, the Presidential candidates representing the remnants of the old Whig and Know-Nothing parties, under the name of Constitution-Union party, received 1,287 votes; Stephen A. Douglas, representing that wing of the Democratic party which opposed secession and the interference of the National government with the local affairs and institutions of any State, received 1,226 votes; John C. Breckinridge, representing that wing of the Democratic party known as strict State's Rights men, received 614 votes; Abraham Lincoln, the Republican candidate, received 452 votes, of which number 410 were cast in the city of St. Joseph.

On February 18, 1861, an election was held to choose three delegates to the convention which was to decide the course of Missouri upon the question of secession or loyalty. Ex-Governor Robert M. Stewart, Willard P. Hall and Robert W. Donnell were elected. The first two were strong, outspoken Union men, while the latter sympathized with the South. Public sentiment was fairly reflected in the vote for these delegates.

Prominent among the local followers of Governor Jackson, who had declared that the destiny of all slave-holding states was alike, were M. Jeff Thompson, Alonzo W. Slayback, J. H. R. Cundiff, then the editor of *The Gazette,* and others. A delegation from St. Joseph assisted in the sacking of Liberty arsenal and a portion of the arms and military equipments there taken were brought here and secreted in cellars. The Emmett Guards and the Jackson Guards were disbanded, there being strong division of sentiment. Capt. John C. C. Thornton and Capt. Reuben Kay then formed companies of Jackson sympathizers and went into camp near the Patee house.

Excitement now ran high in St. Joseph and there was great uneasiness, as threats had been uttered against the loyalists, those who had voted for Lincoln being especially unpopular with the Southern sympathizers. At this time an incident occurred which hastened the impending crisis. John L. Bittinger, a prominent Republican, who had been appointed postmaster by President Lincoln, raised the United States flag over the postoffice, which was then located in a building on the east side of Second street, just north of Francis. This incensed the Southern sympathizers and was construed by the military companies as a direct affront to them. One morning in May, 1861, several days after the flag had been raised, a mob collected at Market Square and an angry discussion of the affair took place. Colonel Thompson, who was then engaged in the real estate business with Thomas Harbine, opposite the postoffice, went down and addressed the mob, denouncing the postmaster's course, but counseling moderation. Then, as if seized by a sudden impulse, he did the exact opposite. Proceeding to the rear of the postoffice building, he ascended the roof by a shed, and when his associates saw him again he had torn the flag from its pole and was waving it to the mob at Market Square and excitedly blowing a tin horn. The mob charged up Second street and swarmed upon the roof to join Colonel Thompson. The flag was torn to shreds, the pole was broken off and carried in triumphant procession by the mob to the river, where it was demolished and cast into the water. No resistance was offered to this piece of violence and the frenzied rabble had clear field.

A contingent, headed by Alonzo W. Slayback, proceeded to Turner Hall, where the United States colors were also displayed. Several members of the Turnverein, guarded by Robert Bradshaw, saved the flag here by taking it down in the face of danger. Rebel flags were raised in various parts of the city.

As a result of this outburst a company of United States dragoons, under command of Captain Sully, was sent here to protect loyal citizens. The dragoons broke up the camp near the Patee house and the State troops scattered.

Colonel Thompson joined the Confederacy and rose to the rank of brigadier-general. He was known as the "Swamp Fox," and his career in the great struggle is now a part of the nation's history.

Capt. John C. Landis had secretly formed a company for the South. In July, of 1861, he had the Liberty arsenal arms and ammunition secretly loaded into wagons, covered with hay, and taken through the Federal camp in the daytime to avert suspicion. Outside of the city Captain Landis' company received them and carried them successfully to Price's army, then encamped near Springfield.

This was the only company that went to the South from St. Joseph. The others who fought on that side went singly or in small, unorganized squads. Among these was A. W. Slayback, mentioned above, who, after the battle of Lexington, was elected colonel of a cavalry regiment and served under Kirby Smith. He was killed some years ago by John A. Cockerill, then the editor of the St. Louis *Post-Dispatch*. Captain Landis fought at Corinth, Champion Hills and Vicksburg, where he surrendered and was exchanged. Subsequently he commanded a battery and surrendered at the close of the war with the Army of the Gulf.

Elijah Gates went out as a private in a company formed at Easton and joined Governor Jackson in the summer of 1861. He served with distinction at Lexington and Elkhorn, also at Corinth, was promoted step by step for bravery and retired only after the guns had been silenced. He came out a brigedier-general, but left an arm upon the battlefield.

A regiment to join Price at Lexington was organized from Buchanan, Andrew, Nodaway and Atchison counties, in August, of 1861. John Saunders was colonel, J. H. R. Cundiff lieutenant-colonel, and J. C. C. Thornton major. These troops fought heroically under Colonel Green at Lexington. Thornton's men rolled a bale of hemp before them as they ascended the hill to attack the Union breastworks. The bullets did not penetrate the hemp bales. and the cannon balls only bounced from them to the ground. Thus they reached and took the entrenchments.

It is estimated that between 1,600 and 2,000 men "went South" from Buchanan County during the war. As there are no records to refer to it is impossible to give details of their achievements in the field. Reuben Kay of St. Joseph was in command of a company in the Confederate service, as was also Thomas P. Penick, a brother of Col. William R. Penick, who was an extreme Union man. The late John S. Tutt, county assessor, lost a leg at the battle of Corinth. John Kemper, son of Simeon Kemper, also a captain, was killed in battle, as was also George Baxter, an attorney, who went from St. Joseph and joined Stonewall Jackson. John R. Boyd, another attorney of St. Joseph, was killed at Independence. Sidney Cunningham, who had taught in the public schools of St. Joseph, joined John Morgan, was with that leader throughout his career, and escaped capture by swimming the Ohio River. Ephraim Kelly of the county commanded a battery under General Price and also distinguished himself. It will be impossible to state more in this brief work concerning the sons of Buchanan County who fought and suffered and gave their lives for the cause that was lost. · But there is no doubt about the valor and the heroism of these men, nor of the loyalty and patriotism of those who live to see the nation reunited and prosperous.

Matters grew worse instead of better in St. Joseph after the arrival of the dragoons. These were supplanted by the Second Iowa Infantry under Colonel Curtis. This regiment remained from June until August, 1861. In September, the Sixteenth Illinois, under Colonel Smith, was here for a short time. This regiment and the Fifty-second Illinois returned and spent the winter of 1861-62 in camp on Prospect Hill. Some of the breastworks erected there are still in existence.

Early in September of 1861, St. Joseph was visited by a Confederate regiment, under Boyd and Patton. These troops were on their way South from the upper counties and remained in the city several days, levying tribute and helping themselves to whatever they fancied. There was a reign of terror during their stay, beside which the ordinary run of local dissension was mild and welcome.

Following them, and before the arrival of the Illinois troops, came Major Cranor and a battalion of raw militiamen from the Grand River country. These remained only a short time and created much amusement by their grotesque awkwardness. They soon learned how to fight, however.

In the spring of 1862, Benjamin F. Loan of St. Joseph was appointed brigadier-general and placed in command of Northwestern Missouri, with headquarters at St. Joseph. In the fall of that year he was put into active service in an effort to run the "bushwhackers" from the central part of the State, and finally took command of the Jefferson City district, where he remained until after he was elected to Congress. On his staff were the following from Buchanan County: John Severance, major and aide-de-camp; Joseph Penny, major and quartermaster; James M. Wilson, major and aide-de-camp; Nicholas J. Schlupp, lieutenant and aide; Dr. R. P. Richardson, brigade surgeon.

General Loan was succeeded by Brigadier-General Willard P. Hall in the fall of 1862, as commander of the Seventh Military District, which embraced Buchanan and Platte counties. He remained until February, 1864, when, as lieutenant-governor, he succeeded Governor Gamble, who had died. On General Hall's staff were: Silas Woodson, colonel and inspector-general; Jonathan M. Bassett, colonel and inspector; Allen P. Richardson, colonel and aide-de-camp; Mordecai Oliver, colonel and aide-de-camp; Thomas J. Chew, Jr., major and quartermaster; Dr. William Bertram, major and brigade surgeon; John L. Bittinger, major and aide-de-camp; James Hunter, major and aide-de-camp; Peter W. Fredericks, lieutenant and inspector.

Col. John F. Williams of the Ninth Cavalry was in charge of the district after General Hall. In the spring of 1864 General Clinton B. Fisk was in command of the forces in this county and remained until he was succeeded by Col. Chester Harding, in the fall.

In the winter of 1864-65, General James Craig was in command. On General Craig's staff were these from the neighborhood: Isaac B. Halsey, major and aide-de-camp; E. S. Castle, major and aide-de-camp.

Colonel John Pinger was in command in the spring of 1865, and when the year closed William R. Penick was in command of the Missouri militia in this section as brigadier-general.

Among other citizens of St. Joseph and the county who held general staff positions are the following: John F. Tyler, colonel and aide-de-camp to General Schofield; James Rainsford, major and assistant aide-de-camp on the staff of General Guitar; William Kemper, major and quartermaster on the staff of General Guitar. George H. Hall, brother to Governor Hall, and afterwards mayor of St. Joseph, also rose to the rank of brigadier-general, as did also Colonel Chester Harding and Robert Bradshaw.

Major William M. Albin was provost marshal under General Loan, Jonathan M. Bassett and Silas Woodson under Generals Willard P. Hall and Guitar. General Bassett was also under General Fisk, and was followed by Captain Hardin, Captain Walser and Armstrong Beattie.

St. Joseph was a prominent base of military operations during the Civil War, and a number of regiments were organized here. In June, of 1861, the Thirteenth Regiment, Missouri Volunteers, was formed, of home guard battalions, under Major Everett Peabody, Major Robert T. Van Horn and Major Berry. The regiment was employed in guarding a portion of the Hannibal & St. Joseph railroad and upon garrison duty, until ordered to Lexington, in September. Colonel Mulligan, who commanded at Lexington, surrendered to Sterling Price on September 16, 1861, who paroled the officers of the Thirteenth and released the men upon their oaths. Exchanges were subsequently effected and the regiment was reorganized as the Twenty-fifth Regiment, Infantry, Missouri Volunteers, with Everett Peabody as colonel, R. T. Van Horn as lieutenant-colonel, James E. Powell and Fred C. Nichols as majors, and Dr. J. T. Berghoff as surgeon. There were ten companies and the aggregate strength of the regiment was about 600. Among those from St. Joseph who held commissions were Capt. Joseph Schmitz, Capt. B. F. Buzard, Capt. Robert C. Bradshaw, Capt. Joseph Thompson, Lieut. Litt R. Lancaster and Lieut. Augustus Salzman. In 1862 the regiment was sent to General Grant at Pittsburg Landing and was brigaded in McKean's brigade, Prentiss' division. It participated in the battle of Shiloh, losing very heavily in killed and wounded, among thé former Colonel Peabody and Major Powell. Chester Harding, Jr., was appointed colonel. In the advance upon Corinth the regiment was constantly on picket duty or engaged in the construction of earthworks. During the summer of 1862 the regiment constructed a chain of forts south and west of Corinth. It was ordered to Missouri in 1862, for the purpose of recruiting, but on its arrival at St. Louis was sent to Pilot Knob, Mo. Subsequently it was assigned to General Patterson and became a part of the Army of Southeast Missouri. Upon returning to Iron Mountain in 1863, it was ordered to St. Joseph and actively employed in clearing the district of Northwest Missouri from bushwhackers until June, when it was ordeded to New Madrid, where it reconstructed the fortifications and constituted the garrison of the post. In November, of 1863, it was consolidated with the Engineer Regiment of the West.

Under Governor Gamble's call for 42,000 volunteers for six months' service, August 24, 1861, William M. Albin directed the formation of three companies of infantry at St. Joseph. These were mustered into service on September 19, 1861, as the First Battalion, under Major Albin, and assigned to guard duty and scouting in Gentry, Worth, Andrew, Buchanan and DeKalb counties; also attached to General Prentiss's river expedition. The battalion was never in any general engagement, but had many skirmishes with the enemy, killing a number and taking over 200 prisoners. The officers were: William M. Albin, major; John M. Sullivan, adjutant; Thomas Evans, commissary; Company A had forty-eight men. James Stockton was captain, Philip Huggins first lieutenant and Alex R. Stockton second lieutenant. Company B had fifty-four men, under Captain Horace Hunter, with Jackson Dye and Isaac Phillips as lieutenants. Company C had forty-three men, under Capt. Henry B. Rust, with Edwin N. Storms and John Ray as lieutenants.

Joseph's battalion of six months' militia was also organized in St. Joseph in September of 1861. It was commonly known as the "Third," and was also engaged in scout duty. It was mustered out February 11, 1862. Peter A. Joseph was major, R. B. Linville adjutant, George W. H. Landon surgeon, Willis M. Sherwood quartermaster and Samuel Rosenblatt commissary. There were four companies. Capt. John Pinger commanded Company A, sixty-four men, with John Watson and Henry Kelling as lieutenants. Company B, Capt. William Drumhiller and Lieuts. Elezier S.

Castle and Aaron Widdle, had eighty-four men. Company C, sixty-four men, was under Alex McLarer and Frederick Downey. Company D, fifty-four men, was under Capt. D. H. David and Lieuts. Christian Cook and Thurston Chase.

The Fourth Cavalry, Missouri State Militia, was organized in St. Joseph, April 28, 1862, with· eight companies, and two companies were afterwards added. George H. Hall commanded as colonel, William M. Albin as lieutenant-colonel, George W. Kelly as senior major, Douglas Dale as junior major and Lieuts. Joseph K. Robinson and David Bonham, Jr., as battalion adjutants. In 1863 Lieutenant-Colonel Albin was succeeded by Lieutenant-Colonel Walter King. The regiment did service in Southwest Missouri and was attached to General Brown's brigade, taking part in the battles of Springfield, Marshal, Huntsville, Ark., and in many skirmishes. Colonel Hall was made brigadier-general. The regiment remained in service until 1865.

The Fifth Cavalry Regiment, Missouri State Militia, was also organized in April of 1862. There were ten companies. The regimental organization was as follows: William R. Penick, colonel; Phillip A. Thompson, lieutenant-colonel; William Drumhiller and Thomas B. Biggers, majors; Lyman W. Densmore, adjutant; Josiah C. Spring, commissary; Joel H. Warren, Henry Douglass and Henry Frasse, surgeons; Joseph H. Hopkins, chaplain. The companies were officered, during the life of the regiment, as follows: A. William Drumhiller, captain, promoted to major; John G. Woods and David E. Shannon, ·captains, successively; Morgan Jerman, Charles W. Leach, William Castle and Washington Bennett, lieutenants. B, Daniel H. David, captain; Benjamin T. Henry and William H. Bixby, lieutenants. C, Joseph H. Richards, captain; Don Alfonso Colvin and John W. Enoch, lieutenants. D, George W. Fitzpatrick and John S. Minick, captains; Henry S. Hill and George W. Fairbrother, lieutenants. E, George Wakerle, captain; Nicholas Schlupp and Herman Springer, lieutenants. F, John B. Van Zant, captain; Edward N. Roberts and Theron W. Crandall, lieutenants. G, Robert G. Hubbard, captain; William F. Miller, Henry Ogle, Joseph Penney and John B. Magers, lieutenants. H, John Pinger, captain; Peter Lanenger and George Weber, lieutenants. I, William McCarthy and Luther Tillotson, captains; John W. Coughlin, Peter Simpson, Thomas Wilson, lieutenants. K, J. D. M. Thompson, captain; Frederick Dony, George D. Tolle, L. Densmore and William Fowler, lieutenants. Lieutenant Densmore was made adjutant and Lieutenant Fowler quartermaster. This regiment was employed in fighting the bushwhackers and guerrillas in Northwest Missouri. In July of 1862 the regiment was ordered broken up and the companies attached to the First and Ninth Cavalry regiment of the Missouri State Militia.

In 1862 Buchanan and Platte counties formed the Seventh Military District of Missouri, and three independent companies were· organized for duty at home. One of these, commanded by Capt.. William ·Randall, with Benjamin F. Larkin and Jonas D. Butts as:

lieutenants, was organized August 9, 1862. Another, commanded
by Capt. G. E. Dandry, with Henry Harding and William Backer as
lieutenants, was organized August 21, 1862. These were afterward
merged into the militia. A third company organized among railroad employes for the protection of railroad property was officered
by John S. Kellogg as captain and John Broder and Horatio N.
Turner as lieutenants.

The Twenty-fifth Regiment of Enrolled Missouri Militia was
organized in St. Joseph in July of 1862, with John Severance as
colonel, Thomas Harbinue as lieutenant-colonel, Peter Walter and
John T. Ross as majors, Gustave H. Koch as adjutant, C. W. Davenport as quartermaster, Alfred H. Starr as surgeon and Rev. A. H.
Wright as chaplain. Colonel Severance resigned April 22, 1863,
and was succeeded by Col. John Scott, who was transferred to the
Eighty-first Regiment shortly afterward, and was succeeded by Col.
Thomas Harbine. James Hunter commanded Company A, with
Thomas Young and Ed Freeman as lieutenants. John R. Snyder
commanded Company B, with James S. Barnes and E. E. Cramer as
lieutenants. James Brierly commanded C, with Peter Davis and
William Simmons as lieutenants. Louis Hax commanded D, with
John Kieffer and Fred Riesenmy as lieutenants. Charles Mast com-
manded E, with Charles F. Ernst and Phillip Arnholdt as lieuten-
ants. Jonathan M. Bassett commanded F, with John A. Dolman
and G. W. Davenport as lieutenants. He was succeeded by Captain
Dolman, with Robert S. Gunn and Henry T. Gore as lieutenants.
G was commanded by Capt. George Lyon, with William C. Toole
and R. J. S. Wise as lieutenants. H was commanded by William
Loving, with Joseph S. Browne, J. T. Ross and Anthony Volls as
lieutenants. I was commanded by Ephraim Perry, with Peter A.
Jones and Hamilton Wilson as lieutenants. K was commanded by
James H. Davis, with Francis M. Hall, William S. Tyler and H. G.
Goss as lieutenants. There were also three battalion companies,
one under Capt. O. G. McDonald, another under Capt. Elias Parrott
and a third under Capt. G. M. Brown. This regiment was stationed
in Buchanan County. In consequence of an extraordinary reduc-
tion in numbers, the regiment was disbanded November 1, 1863,
and the commissions of the officers revoked, with the exception of
those in charge of companies F and K. Colonel Scott was instructed
by the same order to reorganize the militia of Buchanan County,
which had become demoralized. He organized the Eighty-first regiment of Enrolled Missouri Militia, and used companies F and K as
the nucleus. This regiment formed a component part of what was
called the "Paw-Paw Brigade."

* * *

The border was overrun with outlaws of all sorts—bushwhackers, Southern recruiting officers, thieves and robbers, without regard to politics. In addition to local troubles of that sort, great
excitement prevailed in Kansas on account of the Lawrence massacre, and an invasion of Missouri was threatened by Jim Lane
and Jennison's "Red-Legs." The militia service hereabouts was in

a very demoralized condition. Feuds that had been engendered between the border residents of Kansas and Missouri in 1854-57, were reopened or made pretexts by marauders and freebooters. A number of citizens of the county had returned from Price's army and were, of course, classed as disloyal. They were, however, fully as anxious to protect life and property from the marauders as were the loyal men. It was proposed by Gen. Willard P. Hall that all of these be organized into militia companies, and President Lincoln, who sanctioned the proposition, saw in it the possibility of keeping many from re-enlstment in the Confederate service. A knowledge of the condition that existed at that time can be gathered from the testimony of Col. John F. Williams, who was in command of the district, with headquarters at St. Joseph, before a committee appointed by the legislature to investigate the militia. Colonel Williams testified as follows:

"When I took command (in July of 1863) I found portions of the district in a lawless condition; mobs and riots were common in a number of counties in my district; I found also that a number of the troops then in service in the district were disobedient, and rather mutinous; were under no discipline or control. I urged upon the officers to subject their men to the observance of the rules and articles of war; some succeeded, others failed. The condition of the troops was improving until Quantrell made his raid on Lawrence; that created great excitement in the country, both among the troops and citizens; numbers of them openly declared they would not resist an invasion by General Lane, or anybody else, made in retaliation from Kansas.

"Both before and after the Lawrence raid, raids from Leavenworth city and other portions of the Kansas border were daily and nightly made into Missouri, the troops stationed at Weston failing or refusing to protect them. Those raids were made by armed negroes, assisted by white outlaws, called 'Red-Legs'; they were not in the military service, with the exception, perhaps, of some negroes. Just after Lane's speech at Leavenworth city, immediately after the Lawrence massacre, an expedition was gotten up at Leavenworth city, of some magnitude, to invade Platte County, composed of 'Red-Legs,' outlaws, runaway negroes, etc. They took the ferryboat to start across. General Ewing telegraphed to the commander of the post at Fort Leavenworth to take the boat and prevent the raid, which he did.

"When I took command in St. Joseph and the district there, there were refugees in the city from several counties in the district, having been ordered to leave the state by a band calling themslves 'Midnight Rangers.' Their mode of operations was about this: They would leave a written notice, three or four matches enclosed in it, at a party's house, notifying him that he did not leave in five days, with his whole family, he would be hanged and his house burned. Then some other members of the gang, who were on friendly terms with the victim, would call and condole with him, and advise him to stay. But the victim had already made up his mind to go, which they knew, and they would take advantage of his fear and buy his property at nominal figures. Thus a system of wholesale robbery was carried on. The reorganization of the militia, or the arming of the Paw-Paws, has entirely stopped this species of lawlessness.

"When I first took command at St. Joseph, countrymen who came in to trade were pulled off their horses, sometimes by soldiers and sometimes by citizens, and threatened with death if they ever came back. An old man from the country was knocked down by a soldier. The fact was reported to me and I had the soldier placed under arrest. The next day the old man came to me and begged that I do not compel him to testify against the soldier before the provost marshal, as he was afraid of being killed by the companions of the soldier. There were hundreds of such instances. * * * Most of the troops in the district are now concentrated on the border along the river to prevent raids into Missouri from the thieves and outlaws of Kansas, assisted by their friends in Missouri. * * * I sent a squad of ten men over the river at St. Joseph to recover two mules stolen from a citizen of Buchanan County, having learned that they were secreted in a cornfield just back of Elwood. The squad recovered the mules, but were fired upon by citizens of Kansas on their return to the river. At another time I ordered Major Garth of the Ninth Cavalry with forty-two men across the river to recapture some horses, guns and money that were stolen from Judge Woodson and another citizen of Buchanan County. The military and civil authorities of Kansas drew up their forces—some hundred and fifty strong, composed of negroes and whites together —in line of battle, and resisted the crossing of my men. I then sent the major across with one man; he had a conference with the commander of the post at Elwood, who promised to recapture the property, but who failed to do so. These raids were frequent."

The Eighty-first Regiment was organized by Col. John Scott and there were many remonstrances to the arming of men who were known or suspected to have been at one time in sympathy with the South. Col. William R. Penick, who was an intense and uncompromising Unionist, in his statement to the legislative committee, said of a portion of the Paw-Paws:

"The two companies I saw were notoriously disloyal. They were in our city last election to guard the polls. I placed myself in a position to look every man in the face as they marched up the street. These were the first Secessionists I ever saw carrying arms under the authority of the government, and I gave them a close inspection. I am almost confident that there was not a loyal man in either company. I saw men who had belonged to Price's army— some were there in the rebel ranks at Lexington and Blue Mills who never joined the army. Some who have assisted in raising rebel flags. Some who had often cheered for Jeff Davis. Some who had acted as recruiting officers for Price's army, but who were too old to go themselves. Nearly all of them are notoriously disloyal and are enrolled as sympathizers on the provost marshal's book."

This, of course, was an extreme view, particularly so in the light of what the late Judge Henry M. Vories said to the committee, among other things being the following:

"Those called Paw-Paws, in my part of the state, have behaved themselves very well; in fact, exceedingly well—as far as I either know or have been informed, and the county has been more quiet and seemed to be more secure since about the time of their organization. But I do not attribute this change for the better so much to the change of the militia organization as to the fact that an election took place about the same time as their organization. My judgment is that a great deal of the trouble we had in our county last summer was caused by the excitement produced by politicians who were running for office, who were haranguing the soldiers and others, by which they were kept in a constant state of excitement, and that of these excitements quarrels arose, and that persons were embittered against each other so as to induce them to commit lawless acts. I think that after the election these acts of violence would, in a great measure, have ceased without any change in the militia. Yet I think that the late militia called the Paw-Paws have exerted themselves to keep the peace of the county. I think they have been anxious to make a good character, knowing that they were charged with disloyalty; at least, they have done well, and we have during this winter had more peace and quiet than we have had since the rebellion."

It is not the purpose of this history to sit in judgment upon the merits or demerits of the militia system, but as there is little known of the "Paw-Paws," it is thought proper to present the matter as gathered from official sources. The organization of the Eighty-first was as follows: John Scott, colonel; Charles West, adjutant. Company A, George J. Lucas, captain; D. L. Irvine, first lieutenant; Thomas L. Crumpacker, second lieutenant. B, F. J. Stratton, captain; W. L. Hyatt, first lieutenant; T. J. Bracken, second lieutenant. C, Jacob B. Cox, captain; Cornelius Day, first lieutenant; Robert B. Thomas, second lieutenant; D, Milton M. Clagget, captain; Jacob T. Child, first lieutenant; Thomas C. Roberts, second lieutenant. E, Harrison W. Davis, captain; James Dye, first lieutenant; Joseph H. Dicken, second lieutenant. F, John A. Dolman, captain; Robert S. Gunn, first lieutenant; Henry T. Gore, second lieutenant. G, Anthony Grable, captain; Daniel A. Meadows, first lieutenant; John T. Ferrill, second lieutenant. H, John W. Smith, captain; William A. Cornelius, first lieutenant; Thomas L. Blakely, second lieutenant. I, Miller Woodson, captain; Urial Griffen, first lieutenant; Jacob Schultz, second lieutenant. K, James H. Davis, captain; William S. Tyler, first lieutenant; H. B. Goss, second lieutenant. L, James Noland, captain; B. F. Catlett, first lieutenant; D. C. Hart, second lieutenant. M, Milton R. Singleton, captain; John L. Stanton, first lieutenant; Isaac Hays, second lieutenant.

* * *

The Forty-third Infantry, Missouri Volunteers, was organized in St. Joseph in June of 1864, with Chester Harding as colonel,

John Pinger as lieutenant-colonel, B. K. Davis as major, Joseph Thompson as adjutant, Francis Rodman as quartermaster and J. Q. Eggleston and E. W. Dill as surgeons. The regiment was on duty in this state during its term of service. Six companies participated in the battle of Glasgow, October 15, 1864. In the spring of 1865 the whole regiment was assigned to the district of Central Missouri and was actively engaged keeping down bushwhackers, so long as its services were needed. The regiment was mustered out June 30, 1865, at Benton Barracks. The companies were organized as follows: A, Captain, Andrew Dusold; lieutenants, Augustus Saltzman and Horace Sayre. B, captain, John B. Edwards; lieutenants, Henderson Edwards and John P. Herren. C, George M. Brown, captain; A. M. Chesmore and A. J. Bulberson, lieutenants. D, Henry W. Ogle, captain; Walter C. Gantt, Richard Buis and Charles S. Pickett, lieutenants. E, Simeon Sutton, captain; William Caneday and Daniel Boyce, lieutenants. F, William F. Flint, captain; John W. Johnson and Thomas Flint, lieutenants. G, Oscar Kirkham, captain; Ebenezer Wickham and Griffith Davidson, lieutenants. H, Marcus Morton, captain; W. J. Porter and Elijah Brunck, lieutenants. I, George Walser, first captain; Robert B. Stockton, second captain; John S. Morgan and Austin F. Tiffany, lieutenants. K, Perry A. Wright, captain; Andrew J. Wray and Martin V. Baker, lieutenants.

In July of 1864 the Eighty-seventh Regiment of Enrolled Missouri Militia was organized in St. Joseph. This was a home guard regiment and was mustered out in March of 1865. Thomas Harbine had been elected colonel, but declined. Robert C. Bradshaw was then elected and served until October. James W. Strong was promoted from lieutenant-colonel and O. G. McDonald was made lieutenant-colonel. The following were staff officers during the life of the regiment: William Drumhiller and Robert F. Maxwell, majors; Joseph Thompson and W. W. Bernard, adjutants; Joseph Schmitz and John B. Harder, quartermasters; Dr. John T. Berghoff, surgeon. Company A was Captain Kellogg's railroad guards, reorganized under Capt. Joseph Truex. Company B had been Captain Landry's detached company, now under Capt. John A. Dolman, and when Captain Dolman was commissioned as aide-de-camp to General Hall he was succeeded by Robert S. Gunn, who had been first lieutenant. Other lieutenants were H. R. W. Hartwig, Henry T. Gore and H. H. Goodheart. C was captained at first by Hamilton S. Wilson, who was killed by bushwhackers and succeeded by Irvin Fish. These were lieutenants at various times: Francis Goodby, Irvin Fish, Amos K. Jones and Oscar Kirkham. D was captained by James C. Karnes, with Washington Bennett, E. Shootner and John S. Smith as lieutenants. E was led by Capt. John Snyder, with Joseph Mathew and Thomas D. Ridge as lieutenants. F was under Capt. Louis Hax, with John Kieffer, Christian Mast, Ulrich Schneider and Louis Fuelling as lieutenants at various times. G was first captained by James W. Strong, then by Robert Maxwell, both of whom were sent to the head of the regiment, and last by

David Pinger, whose lieutenants were Anson Whitney and Elisha Foote. H was officered by Peter A. Jones, captain, and Henry F. Goss and Wiley H. Chapman as lieutenants. This company was consolidated with C in October, 1864. I was organized by Capt. O. G. McDonald, who was afterward lieutenant-colonel. The next captain was William H. Lifers, whose lieutenants were Charles C. Vance, George W. Howard and A. J. Culberson. K was organized. by Capt. George M. Brown, who was shortly afterward transferred to the Forty-third Infantry. He was succeeded by Edward L. Titcomb, whose lieutenant was George Schuckman.

The Forty-fourth Infantry Missouri Volunteers was recruited in St. Joseph by Col. Robert C. Bradshaw and Lieut.-Col. A. J. Barr, in the month of August, 1864, and shipped on cars to Rolla. In November it arrived at Paducah, Ky., and was placed on active duty, though yet in a very raw condition. In the battle of Franklin Colonel Bradshaw was pierced by seven bullets, but not killed. Lieutenants Dunlap, Warren and Kirgan and thirty-five privates were killed in the first charge of the enemy, but the regiment held its position. The regiment fought continuously for three days and nights from November 29th, and during the last two days lost 300 men and officers. "On December, 15th 1864," says Lieutenant-Colonel Barr, in his report, "we were ordered to take a position on the right of Charlotte Pike and engaged the enemy, participated in the battle on the 15th, 16th and 17th insts., and then followed in the pursuit of Hood's demoralized army. On the 27th we reached Columbia, where we first met the enemy. On the 28th we reached Pulaski, with two-thirds of the command barefooted. In this condition the regiment was compelled to march on the ice and snow to Clifton, sixty miles, where we arrived on the 23d of January, 1865 —men worn out and feet terribly mangled." The regiment also participated in the siege of Spanish Fort, Alabama, and went from there to Vicksburg and thence to St. Louis, where it was mustered out on August 15, 1865, after having traveled 5,703 miles, of which 743 was on foot, and after having been for one-third of its term of service under fire and in the midst of the carnage of battle."

The regiment was organized as follows. Robert C. Bradshaw, colonel; A. J. Barr, lieutenant-colonel; Roger A. De Bolt, major; Wm. Drumhiller, adjutant; J. M. Hoskinson, quartermaster; Henry Schoenich, Levi A. Wilson and Isaac Schatz, surgeons. Hanson W. Ware succeeded Captain Drumhiller as adjutant.

The various companies were officered as follows during the life of the regiment: A, John C. Reid, captain; James A. Trussell, Wm. D. Schooler, Francis Audsley, lieutenants. B, Wm. Drumhiller, captain; John McKissock and Miles Bristow, lieutenants. C, Frank G. Hopkins, captain; Wm. M. Goodson and Thomas J. Twidell, lieutenants. D, Wm. B. Rogers, captain; Robert Pixler, Aaron McIntosh and George H. Combs, lieutenants. E, Ephraim Webb, captain; James S. Dunlap and J. C. Webb, lieutenants. E, Isaac M. Henry, captain; James M. Steele, W. C. Halstead, Benjamin Kirgan, lieutenants. G, A. L. Bowen, captain; John Desha and Washington Bennett, lieutenants. H, Wm. D. Fortune, captain; J. D. McBride, John H. Williams and J. D. Snyder, lieutenants. J, A. Muck, captain; A. F. Higgins, Dennis Adams and D. W. McDonald, lieutenants. K, N. A. Winters, captain; James Overman and Samuel Worner, lieutenants.

A military organization which existed in St. Joseph during the war was Hartwig's Independent Company of Artillery, formed by Captain H. R. W. Hartwig in October of 1864. Captain Hartwig was commissioned by Governor Hall to form this company, the strength of which consisted of eighty-four men and four four-pound pieces. Joseph Andriano was first lieutenant, John Riplinger, second lieutenant, and Charles Barrington orderly. The company was on duty in this section and in Platte County, and was mustered out at the close of the war.

* * *

Under Governor Fletcher three regiments of militia were organized in October of 1865—the Second, Third and Fourth Regiments of Missouri Militia. Col. Wm. R. Penick commanded the Second regiment. He was appointed brigadier-general and placed in command of this district. Robert Gunn was lieutenant-colonel; H. R. W. Hartwig, major; Dr. Wm. Bertram, Dr. John S. Logan and Dr. Harvey Bradley, surgeons. W. W. Bernard was captain of Company A and Henry Gore of Company B. David Pinger was captain of Company C, with A. V. Whiting and Elisha Foot, Jr., as lieutenants. Company D was commanded by Captain Greenfield H. Davis, who had Isaac Wilkins and Thomas Early for his lieutenants. Company E was commanded by Joseph Andriano, and Company F by Wm. L. Chadwick, with L. L. Landon and George Hildebrand as lieutenants. Company G was under Captain Joseph S. Browne, with George Buell and Wm. B. French as lieutenants. Company H was under Captain Phillip Arnholdt, with Theodore Kroll and A. Burgmeister as lieutenants. Company J was commanded by M. Gordon Ruby, with Wm. M. Clark and John Stuppy as lieutenants.

Colonel Cyrus J. Missemer commanded the Third regiment. Wm. Randall was lieutenant-colonel, James M. Witt adjutant and James F. Bruner and G. M. Loomis surgeons. Company A was commanded by Irvin Fish; Company B by James G. Karnes, with Edvin A. Guinn as lieutenant; Company C by C. E. Cummings; Company D by C. F. Schoeneck, with Benjamin F. Boyer and Wm. H. Boyer as lieutenants; Company F by N. R. Wakefield, with Henry Myers and L. J. Smith as lieutenants; Company G by W. H. Slaybaugh, with J. S. Blankenship and B. F. Missemer as lieutenants.

The Fourth regiment had but five companies. It was commanded by Major Joseph Thompson. Company A was commanded by R. J. S. Wise, with Thos. H. Ritchie and Fred Amerine as lieutenants. Company B was commanded by Simeon Bell. Company C was under Captain Augustus Salzman, with Theodore F. Gross and Charles Frederick as lieutenants. Company D was commanded by Wm. Drumhiller, with D. M. Stillians as lieutenant, and B. F. Larkin was captain of Company E, with William Arthur as lieutenant.

These regiments did service in enforcing order at the polls during the turbulent political times that followed the war. The test oath was particularly obnoxious, even to many who had been loyal, and politicians were not slow to grasp the advantages it afforded. The oath was as follows:

"I do on oath declare that I have not during the present rebellion wilfully taken up arms or levied war against the United States nor against the provisional government of the state of Missouri, nor have wilfully adhered to the enemies of either, domestic or foreign, by giving them aid and comfort, but have always in good faith opposed the same; and, further, that I will support, protect and defend the constitution of the United States and of the state of Missouri against all enemies and opposers, whether foreign or domestic, any ordinance, order or resolution of any state convention or legislature, or of any order or organization, secret or otherwise, to the contrary notwithstanding, and that I do this with an honest purpose, pledge and determination faithfully to perform the same without any mental reservation or evasion whatsoever, so help me God."

This oath was proscriptive to many, and there was much bitterness. There were those who had been in the service of the South, but who had surrendered and become loyal, those who had honestly sympathized with the lost cause, and those who had taken advantage of General Order No. 24 to escape service in the militia. Under this order anyone who declared that he sympathized with the South was exempt from military duty. When it came to voting after the war this declaration was held against them.

The supreme court of the United States set aside that part of the test oath which disfranchised so many men. However, the ruling politicians in Missouri did not give up so easily and the legislature, in 1868, passed a very stringent registration law. The governor was given power to appoint three registrars in each county and a superintendent for each senatorial district. These four officers were authorized to make a list of all the loyal voters in the county. They were forbidden to enroll any person who would not take the oath of loyalty, and besides were given the power to refuse to enroll any others than those they chose. No one was allowed to vote whose name was not enrolled by these registrars. This law, perhaps, disfranchised more voters than the original test oath. It opened anew the sore places that had begun to heal, and there are many instances where men have not forgiven each other yet, politically speaking, for the trespasses committed under the license of this law. There was more or less turbulence until the constitution was amended in 1870 and these objectionable features eliminated.

Following the dissolution of the Missouri Militia, interest in military matters waned until 1880. Meanwhile, however, there had existed during the Centennial year a company organized by Capt. Aug. Saltzman, called "Continental Rifles." They were dressed as Continental soldiers, in knee-breeches, etc., and wore wigs. In 1880 two battalions, one commanded by Major Joseph A. Hansen and the other by Major Condon. In 1882 the Fourth regiment, National Guard of Missouri, was organized, with Joseph Hansen as colonel, Joseph A. Corby as lieutenant-colonel, Augustus Saltzman as major, Capt. Charles F. Ernst as adjutant, Capt. John Wilson as quarter-master, Dr. Thos. H. Doyle as surgeon and Dr. J. A. French as assistant surgeon. Company A was commanded by Capt. Wm. Osborn, Company B by Capt. John Donovan, Company C by Capt. Dowe, Company D by Capt. Wm. Muehleisen and Company E by Capt. Hazlet. Companies F and G were located at Brookfield. Companies A, B and C were known as "Saxton Rifles," and Captain Muehleisen's company as "Turner Rifles," being made up mostly of members of the Turnverein. These companies were uniformed according to taste, the state providing arms only. After an existence of several years the companies disbanded.

Subsequently there was little interest in militia matters until October, 1890, when Capt. Max Manheim organized the St. Joseph Light Guards. April 2, 1891, the Fourth regiment was reorganized, with Col. Arbuthnot of Brookfield as commanding officer and Capt. Manheim as lieutenant-colonel. A brigade encampment was held in August of that year at Lake Contrary. Subsequently Capt. Clay C. MacDonald organized Company K, known as the "Wickham Rifles." The name was afterward changed to "Macdonald Rifles." Company F existed until 1895 under various captains, and was disbanded.

Captain Manheim organized Company C in December, 1897. When President McKinley called for volunteers to fight Spain, in April, 1898, the Fourth regiment, of which Joseph A. Corby was colonel, responded promptly, and two additional companies were at once formed in St. Joseph—I, by Capt. Charles F. Keller, and G by Capt. Jacob S. Casey. These companies left for Jefferson Barracks May 9th and 10th, 1898, and were mustered into the United States volunteer service. From Jefferson Barracks the Fourth regiment went to Falls Church, Va., into Camp Alger; from there into Camp Meade, at Middletown, Pa., and from there to Greenville, S. C. The regiment did not see service during the war. Each company left St. Joseph with eighty-four enlisted men. Under the second call for volunteers the companies were recruited up to their full strength of 106 enlisted men. Captain Macdonald was advanced to major and Lieut. Niel T. Sommer was promoted to the command of Company K.

St. Joseph was represented in the Fourth regiment as follows: Colonel, Joseph A. Corby; majors, Wm. E. Stringfellow, Wilson S. Hendricks and Clay C. Macdonald; adjutant, George L. Rollins; assistant surgeon, Wm. L. Whittington. Company K was organized as follows: Niel T. Sommers, captain; Charles E. Foster, first lieutenant; John E. O'Donnell, second lieutenant. Company C was organized as follows: Max Manheim, captain; Frank R. Hinds, first lieutenant; Atel H. Knutson, second lieutenant. Company I: Charles F. Keller, captain; Wm. H. Cocke, first lieutenant; Victor C. Sommer, second lieutenant. Company G: Jacob S. Casey, captain; John D. McNeeley, first lieutenant; Mortimer P. Waldron, second lieutenant. Major Hendricks resigned at Camp Alger and Captain Manheim at Greenville.

The Fourth regiment was disbanded in 1900 and reorganized in 1901. It was officered as follows: William E. Stringfellow, colonel; Wilson S. Hendrick, lieutenant-colonel; Clay C. Macdonald, major 1st battalion; John D. McNeely, major 2nd battalion; Dr. Daniel Morton, major and surgeon; Dr. Daniel L. Humfreville, captain and surgeon; Dr. H. L. Walker, lieutenant and surgeon. Regimental headquarters were in St. Joseph, where all the above officers reside. There were nine companies located in St. Joseph, Unionville, Tarkio, Kirksville, Trenton, Milan, Mexico, Jefferson City and Mound City. Company K, located in St. Joseph, was officered by E. K. Stewart, captain; George Graha, first lieutenant; Louis Browne, second lieutenant. The regiment was afterward disbanded.

James H. McCord, who has done much to promote the National Guard interests in Missouri, was for many years attached to the staff of Brigadier-General Clarke, as assistant inspector general with the rank of lieutenant-colonel.

CHAPTER XXI.

THE RAILROADS OF ST. JOSEPH—EARLY STRUGGLES OF RAILROAD PROJECTORS AND BUILDERS.—THE HANNIBAL & ST. JOSEPH, THE K. C., ST. J. & C. B., THE ST. JOSEPH & GRAND ISLAND, THE ST. JOSEPH & TO PEKA, THE SANTA FE SYSTEM, THE ROCK ISLAND, THE ST. JOSEPH & DES MOINES, THE MISSOURI PACIFIC, THE CHICAGO GREAT WESTERN, THE UNION PACIFIC. — INTERURBANS. — THE BRIDGE. — UNION TERMINAL STATION.—TELEGRAPH LINES.

Agitation for railroad connection with Mississippi River points began in St. Joseph as early as 1846. One of the most ardent advocates of the then new mode of transportation was the late Judge Birch of Clinton County, who was at that time stumping this district as a candidate for congress. His opponent, the late Willar P. Hall, was not favorable, and after he had left the campaign t its fate and entered Doniphan's regiment to fight Mexico, he issue a circular letter warning the people not to be tricked by such im practicable things as railroads. Judging from the enthusiasm ar' enterprise afterwards exhibited by this gentleman in the promotic and development of railroads, he atoned well for this error. A. there was no railroad west of Ohio in those days he may be easily pardoned.

Another enthusiast was Robert M. Stewart, then a lawyer at St. Joseph, who was afterwards governor of Missouri. He went actively to work, organized meetings, talked railroad, interested the people, and as a member of the state senate, aided by James Craig and Judge Gardenhire, who represented Buchanan County in the house, secured, in February of 1847, the passage of an act to incorporate the Hannibal & St. Joseph Railroad Company.

The incorporators were Joseph Robidoux, John Corby and Robert J. Boyd, of St. Joseph; Samuel J. Harrison, Zachariah G Draper and Erasmus M. Moffett, of Hannibal; Alexander McMurtry, Shelby County; George A. Shortridge and Thomas Sharp, of Macon County; Wesley Halliburton, Linn County; John Graves Livingston County; Robert Wilson, Daviess County; George W Smith, Caldwell County. The capital stock was two million dollar

A railroad convention was held at Chillicothe in June of 184 at which resolutions were adopted, recommending the following a the best method to procure means for the construction of the Hanni r bal & St. Joseph road: "(1) To appoint a committee of three members to draft an address in the name of this convention, to th people of Western Missouri, setting forth the advantages to t derived from the contemplated railroad from St. Joseph to Hai nibal; (2) to appoint a committee of three, whose duty it shall l

East on Felix Street from Third Street

First National Bank Building

to petition the legislature of Missouri for such aid in the undertaking as can be afforded consistently with the rights of other sections of the state; (3) to appoint a committee of three to petition Congress for a donation of alternate sections of land, within six miles on each side of said road, when located; (4) to appoint a committee whose duty it shall be to superintend the publication and distribution of the proceedings of the convention, and the address to the people of Northern Missouri."

There was considerable enthusiasm among the people as the result of this convention, but material aid came slowly. A few dollars were raised in St. Joseph for a preliminary survey and a surveying corps was organized, with Simeon Kemper and James O'Donoghus as engineers in charge. Six months after their departure from St. Joseph they returned and reported having found a practicable route for a railroad. A meeting of citizens was held, at which the two heroic surveyors made their report, and a banquet was spread in their honor. A subscription paper was circulated and enough money secured to purchase each of the engineers a handsome suit of clothes. This is all they received for their six months' work, except meager expenses and glory.

The first survey was complpeted to Hannibal on Christmas Day, 1850, by Simeon Kemper and James O'Donoghue. The two surveyors were accompanied by Colonel Robert M. Stewart, Colonel M. F. Tiernan and a newspaper correspondent from Baltimore named Brennan, besides some chainmen, etc. Later on the final surveys were made under charge of Colonels M. F. Tiernan and M. Jeff Thompson.

In 1852 the building of the road was assured. Willard P. Hall, who had, in 1846, argued against railroads on general principles, now became the good angel of the despondent enterprise. As chairman of the committee on public lands in Congress he secured the passage of a bill granting six hundred thousand acres of land to the Hannibal & St. Joseph Railroad Company, and the work of construction began at Hannibal as soon as possible.

The state loaned its credit to aid the work in the sum of 1,-500,000 bonds to be issued and used conditioned on proof that the sum of $50,000 had been actually expended in construction. John Corby of St. Joseph, agent of the road, borrowed the first $50,000, and this enabled the work to continue until funds were secured from sales and bonds issued by the counties through which the line passes.

Again, in 1855, the company having exhausted all its resources, the state loaned an additional $1,500,000, making in all the sum of $3,000,000, which was liquidated, with interest, in about seventeen years after the completion of the road.

The contract for building the entire line was let to John Duff & Co., August 10, 1852, its construction being subject to various parties. Work was commenced first on the eastern line, and progressed slowly

In August, 1857, the steamboat Saranak brought an engine and cargo of rails to St. Joseph. Some grading was done, a track laid, and the engine hauled out on the bank, with all the people in town and vicinity as lookers-on. It was a great curiosity.

Work proceeded very rapidly for those days, and progress was reported all along the line. John Corby of St. Joseph was a director and a heavy contractor in the construction of the road. When the two ends of the line were a hundred miles apart stages were put on to carry passengers from one point to the other, and a lively business was done.

Large warehouses were constructed at Hannibal and at St. Joseph, and steamboat lines started up and down the river to transact the immense business done in connection with the road.

On February 14, 1859, the first through passenger train arrived at St. Joseph from Hannibal, with Edgar Sleppy as engineer and Benjamin H. Colt as conductor. A great celebration in honor of the completion of the road was held on Washington's birthday, at the old Odd Fellows' Hall. A jug of water from the Mississippi was emptied into the Missouri River at the mouth of Blacksnake, the ceremony of mingling the waters being performed with great solemnity by Broaddus Thompson, a prominent citizen in those days, and a most unique character withal.

John Patee had donated a strip of ground containing forty acres, from Olive street west of Eighth south to Mitchell avenue, for terminal facilities. A depot was built at Eighth and Olive streets. In 1857, before the completion of the road, shops were established, with C. F. Shivels as master mechanic. In the summer of 1872 a branch was built from St. Joseph to Atchison. The Hannibal & St. Joseph road became part of the Burlington system in 1884.

* * *

THE K. C., ST. J. & C. B.—The consolidtion of several pioneer railroads is represented in the Kansas City, St. Joseph & Council Bluffs line. February 24, 1853, the legislature of Missouri granted a charter for a road to extend from St. Joseph to Kansas City. A company under the name and style of the Platte County Railroad was organized in 1857 by William Osborne, Davis Carpenter, M. Jeff Thompson and others. Under the auspices of this company a line was surveyed from St. Joseph southward through DeKalb, in Buchanan County, Platte City and Parkville in Platte County, to Kansas City. The legislature of 1856-57 granted aid to this road in the sum of 700,000. A subsequent act provided that none of the bonds of this road should be available till the year 1859. The charter also authorized the extension of the road to the northern boundary of the state, under which provision it was completed to Savannah in 1860, and graded to Forest City.

December 11, 1855, the Atchison & St. Joseph railroad was incorporated. The articles of association provided that Benjamin Stringfellow, John H. Stringfellow, Peter T. Abell, John Doniphan, Stephen Johnson, Elijah H. Norton, Harvey Collier, Robert W.

Donnell, Reuben Middleton, Bela M. Hughes, James H. Lucas, John Simon, or any five of them, constitute the first board of directors.

In the summer of 1858, General Benjamin Stringfellow, Dr. J. H. Stringfellow, Peter T. Abell, Harvey Collier, Reuben Middleton, John Doniphan and Robert W. Donnell met in St. Joseph, in the Methodist church, which then stood on the northeast corner of Third and Felix streets, and there organized the company. At this meeting Samuel C. Pomeroy, of Atchison, was elected a director and president of the company. Charles West, of St. Joseph, was also at this meeting elected a director. Stock was taken by the parties present, and in a short time after the city of Atchison subscribed $100,000; Abel Q Stringfellow, $10,000; John Doniphan, $1,600, and Samuel C. Pomeroy, $10,000. Other parties contributed liberally, swelling the aggregate of subscriptions over and above the city stock, to about $60,000. Contracts for grading were immediately let along the entire line of the road, and work commenced at Winthrop, opposite Atchison. By July 1, 1859, this grading was completed between St. Joseph and Winthrop.

In March, 1859, the Weston & Atchison Railroad Company was incorporated under the general laws of the state. The officers of this incorporation were John Doniphan, president; James N. Burnes, vice-president; Fielding H. Lewis, secretary, and Daniel D. Burnes, treasurer. Private subscriptions were forthwith made to the road to the amount of $44,000, and the city of Weston issued her bonds to the amount of $50,000 in aid of the building of the same. Ground was broken at Weston April 27, 1859.

July 15, 1859, the Weston & Atchison and Atchison & St. Joseph companies, finding that their means would be inadequate to accomplish more than the work of grading the road, for the purpose of an early completion of the same, made a contract with the Platte County road by which they transferred to that corporation the roadbed, franchises and right-of-way from St. Joseph to Weston. This company was enabled on the work so done, during the year 1859, to draw most of the state aid, and in January, 1860, the road was completed and in operation from St. Joseph to Atchison. In December of the same year the road was finished to Iatan, and by April 4, 1861, trains were running through to Weston. In 1863 the name of this road was changed, the style "Platte Country" being substituted for the original "Platte County."

In 1864 the road was seized by Governor Hall for non-payment of interest on state bonds. Immediately the Weston & Atchison and the Atchison & St. Joseph railroad companies commenced suits for their road-bed on the ground that the original contract was illegal. The legislature of 1867 acquiesced on condition of a reorganization under the name and style of the Missouri Valley Railroad Company, and a completion of the road from Savannah, through Maryville to the northern boundary of the state. Under this act the road was completed to Hopkins in 1869.

The road from Council Bluffs to Hamburg, Iowa, fiftyy-two miles in length, was built by Willis, Phelps & Co., and completed in

1867. It was styled the Council Bluffs & St. Joseph Railroad. Hon. James F. Joy and his friends came to the front and built the road from St. Joseph to Hamburg, seventy-nine miles long, opening it for traffic in 1868. This was called the St. Joseph & Council Bluffs' Railroad. In 1870 the Missouri Valley and the St. Joseph and Council Bluffs railroads were consolidated and the road called the Kansas City, St. Joseph & Council Bluffs.

The Missouri Valley road ran from St. Joseph to Savannah, via Jimtown, up to 1871, when this roadbed was abandoned, a cut-off to Savannah having been built from Amazonia. In 1884 the K. C., St. J. & C. B. road became part of the C., B. & Q. system.

Davis Carpenter was superintendent in 1866; Col. A. G. Gower from 1866 to 1869; Maj. A. L. Hopkins from 1869 to 1870. Col. J. F. Barned was superintendent from 1870 to 1884, when he was made general manager of the K. C., St. J. & C. B. and H. & St. J. roads under the C., B. & Q. system, serving as such until the summer of 1887, when he was succeeded by W. F. Merrill, who remained until August of 1889, being succeeded by W. C. Brown. Mr. Brown remained until January, 1896, when he was succeeded by Howard Elliott.

* * *

THE ST. JOSEPH & GRAND ISLAND—This is the successor of the Marysville or Palmetto & Roseport, the first railroad projected in Kansas, which was chartered February 17, 1857. In 1856 a party of South Carolinians, who had moved to Kansas with the expectation that slavery would be perpetuated, purchased a claim adjoining Marysville and founded a town, which they called Palmetto, but which has long since disappeared. The projectors of the road, anxious to please the people of both Palmetto and Marysville, blended both names into the title of the railroad. Roseport was the original name of Elwood, opposite St. Joseph, named for Richard Rose, a prominent promoter in those days, who lived in St. Joseph. Roseport, however, gave way to Elwood, and Elwood has since given way to the tawny and turbulent current of the Missouri River. There remain, however, the postoffice, the depot and the name.

In April of 1860, when M. Jeff Thompson was president of the road, a small engine, named "Albany," and three flat cars were crossed on the ferryboat "Ida." In June of 1860 the track-laying began. John Broder, later chief of police of this city, drove the first spike. Sinclair Miller was superintendent, George Lewis superintendent of track-laying, and James Whitney engineer of the "Albany." By July 19, 1860, the road was completed to Wathena, and on that day there was an appropriate celebration at that place. The Jackson Guards of St. Joseph and many citizens assisted. They crossed the river on the ferry and rode to Wathena on the flat cars.

Work was suspended owing to disturbed political conditions, and the engine was brought back to St. Joseph. During the war the farmers in the Kansas bottoms used the flat cars, drawing wood and produce to the ferry landing with oxen. In time, however, the track rotted and cottonwood trees grew profusely among the ties.

In 1862 the name was changed to the St. Joseph & Denver City Railroad Company, the purpose still being the building of a line to Marysville. The Northern Kansas Railroad Company was authorized to build an extension from Marysville to the Nebraska line, and acquired the lands granted by an act of congress approved July 23, 1866. The two companies were consolidated August 11, 1866, under the name of the St. Joseph & Denver City Railroad Company, with a capital stock of $10,000,000. The city of St. Joseph aided this enterprise to the extent of $500,00.

The work of extension was begun in 1867, and the road opened to Hastings, Neb., in 1872. The portion of the road in Nebraska was built under the general railroad law of that state. The total amount expended in construction $5,449,620.77, of which $1,400 was from stockholders, $782,727.10 from the state and county subsidies, and $4,665,493.67 from the sale of $6,755,900 mortgage bonds. The property was placed in the hands of a receiver in 1874, and sold under foreclosure in November, 1875. Under the scheme of reorganization two companies were formed—the St. Joseph & Pacific Railroad Company owning and operating the road from Elwood westward to Marysville, and the Kansas & Nebraska Railroad Company owning and operating the road from Marysville, Kan., west to Hastings, Neb. On the 29th of March, 1877, those two companies were again consolidated under the title of the St. Joseph & Western Railroad Company.

The Hastings & Grand Island Railroad Company was incorporated May 9, 1879. Its road extending from Hastings to Grand Island, Neb., twenty-five miles, was opened October 1, 1879, and bought by the St. Joseph & Western Railroad Company February 18, 1880. By the terms of the sale the stock was exchanged for an equal amount of the St. Joseph & Western stock. Of the land grant, 300,000 acres were placed in the hands of trustees for the benefit of the stockholders of land script.

In January, 1880, the roads came under the control of the Union Pacific Railroad Company. From February, 1880, to January, 1884, the road was operated by the Union Pacific Railroad Company. On the latter date it began to be again operated independently.

On the 11th of June, 1885, the St. Joseph & Western road was sold under foreclosure, the sale of the Hastings & Grand Island railroad following on the 19th of the same month, both lines being bought by a committee of the bondholders. The St. Joseph & Marysville Railroad Company and the Grand Island & Marysville Railroad Company, two new corporations, were organized in the states of Kansas and Nebraska and consolidated into the St. Joseph & Grand Island railroad. The property of the company includes the St. Joseph bridge and the entire line between St. Joseph and Grand Island, 252 miles.

John F. Barnard was superintendent in 1871-72, and was succeeded by Wm. H. Sheridan, who served only a short time and was succeeded by L. D. Tuthill. Mr. Tuthill remained until June, 1885, when he was succeeded by Daniel McCool, who served until January, 1888. Wm. Lush was then made general manager, remaining until May, 1888, when he was succeeded by G. M. Cummings, who served until December, 1888, when E. McNeill took charge. Mr. McNeill was succeeded in August, 1890, by W. P. Robinson, Jr. During 1891 the office was abolished, the road being under the Union Pacific system. In January, 1892, Mr. Robinson returned and remained eight years, being succeeded by Raymond DePuy. The road is now a part of the Union Pacific system.

During the summer of 1898 the Grand Island began running trains into Kansas City over leased lines, but this service has since been discontinued.

* * *

THE ST. JOSEPH & TOPEKA—In 1858 the St. Joseph & Topeka Railroad Company obtained a charter from the Kansas legislature. The St. Joseph city directory of 1860 shows that Willard P. Hall was president; John Corby, vice-president; M. Jeff Thompson, secretary; Joseph C. Hall, treasurer, and Adam Brenner, of Doniphan, assistant treasurer. The city of St. Joseph issued bonds to the amount of $50,000 to aid this enterprise. It was not until 1872, however, that anything materialized. In that year a line was built from Wathena to Doniphan, via Palermo and Geary City, by George H. Hall, John L. Motter, O. B. Craig, Wm. Craig and George W. Barr. The road was leased to the K. C., St. J. & C. B. company and operated until 1876. Trains were run from St. Joseph to Atchison, the St. Joseph & Western tracks being used to Wathena and the Atchison & Nebraska tracks from Doniphan to Atchison. The road had been bonded and the bonds placed with a firm of New York brokers. Before the bonds were disposed of the firm failed and the bonds were taken by its creditors as assets and foreclosed. The line was acquired by the St. Joseph & Western Company. After a time the rails were taken up and relaid on that road. The Hannibal & St. Joseph would have purchased the line had it been possible to acquire the city's interest in the bridge. The St. Joseph & Topeka was also known as the George Hall road and as the "Corkscrew" route.

* * *

THE SANTA FE SYSTEM—The Atchison, Topeka & Santa Fe Company enters the city from two directions—from the southeast and from the southwest. The branch from the southeast was begun in 1867 and completed in the winter of 1869-70. It was then called the St. Louis & St. Joseph railway. Shortly after the completion of the road the company went into bankruptcy. Under a sale in the bankruptcy court the road was bought by the bondholders, who leased it to the North Missouri Railroad Company. Subsequently it was controlled by the Wabash Company. In 1886 it passed into the hands of the late Winslow Judson and others, and was called the St. Joseph & St. Louis. In 1888 the road passed into the control of the Santa Fe system and was called the St. Joseph, St. Louis & Santa Fe.

At about the same time the "Santa Fe" Company built a line from Atchison to St. Joseph, via Rushville. This company also built a line to Lake Contrary shortly after the completion of the Atchison ine.

The St. Joseph Terminal Company was organized in 1889. The "Santa Fe" and "Grand lsland" companies are jointly interested. Shops and a round house were built on lower Sixth street, and, in 1890 a freight depot was erected at Fourth street, south of Olive. Formerly the Grand Island and St. Joseph & St. Louis companies jointly used a freight depot that stood near where the shops and round house are now located. Before the erection of the Union Depot this was used as a passenger station also for these roads.

* * *

THE "ROCK ISLAND"—In 1872 a branch of the Chicago, Rock Island & Pacific railroad was built from Edgerton Junction, in Platte County, through Crawford, Bloomington and Rush Townships, Buchanan County, to Winthrop. Bloomington Township voted bonds to aid this enterprise. This was not accomplished without opposition, however, and the majority was so small that there was a protest. The bonds were certified to by the county court, but for some years there was objection to paying the levy called for by these bonds; there was also litigation, but without avail.

In 1885 the people of St. Joseph subscribed $50,000 to secure a branch of the "Rock Island" from Altamont, Daviess County. Trains began running over this line in May, 1886.

Early in 1886 the "Rock Island" projected a line west of the Missouri River. The Chicago, Kansas & Nebraska Railroad Company was chartered in Kansas and the people of St. Joseph subscribed for stock to the amount of $300,000. The road was bonded and built. Shops were located at Horton, where a prosperous town soon sprang up. At Horton the road forks, one branch going through Topeka and Wichita to Oklahoma and Texas and another through northern Kansas to Denver. Trains began running into St. Joseph in November, 1889. After several years the bondholders foreclosed and the stockholders lost what money they had invested.

* * *

THE ST. JOSEPH & DES MOINES—The St. Joseph & Des Moines Railroad Company was organized in this city in 1877, with Col. John L. Motter as président. In November of the same year a contract for the grading was let, work was commenced at once, and by the first of April, 1878, the first twenty miles of roadbed was ready for the rails. Track-laying was commenced June 1, the first engine placed on the road June 26, and the line was in operation by October. This was a narrow-gauge road while under the control and ownership of John L. Motter, James H. Pickering, F. L. McLean, Wm. B. Johnson, Isaac T. Hosea, A. N. Schuster, R. L. McDonald and John B. Hundley. The first officials of the road were: John L. Motter, president and general manager; James H. Pickering, superintendent; F. L. McLean, general freight and ticket agent; W. B. Johnson, secretary and treasurer.

In 1880 the line was purchased and became a branch of the Chicago, Burlington & Quincy. The gauge was at once widened. It thus added one more important feeder to the great "Burlington system." A depot was located on Mitchell avenue, near Fifteenth street. A few years ago this station was closed and all trains now use the Union Depot exclusively.

* * *

THE MISSOURI PACIFIC—In January of 1880, when it was learned that Jay Gould desired the entrance of the Missouri Pacific railroad to St. Joseph, a number of citizens, interested directly or indirectly in reviving the St. Joseph & Topeka road, offered him a bonus of $30,000 to enter the city over that line. The offer was accepted and the money paid over. Gould, however, disappointed these people by leasing a right-of-way over the Hannibal & St. Joseph tracks. In 1905 the Missouri Pacific secured its own terminal facilities in St. Joseph, a franchise being granted in the name of the St. Joseph & Central Branch. The company built a new freight house between Third and Fourth streets, south of Angelique street, in 1907. The first train of the Missouri Pacific reached St. Joseph on February 23, 1880. Until the completion of the Union Depot the old Hannibal & St. Joseph depot at Eighth and Olive streets was used.

* * *

THE CHICAGO GREAT WESTERN—This road was built to St. Joseph from Des Moines in 1889. It was then called the Chicago, St. Paul & Kansas City, and known as the "Diagonal" route. In 1890 the road was completed to Kansas City. It name was changed to Chicago Great Western some years ago and it is familiarly known now as the "Maple Leaf" route, the emblem being a maple leaf. For many years the company's trains did not use the Union Station, because satisfactory terms could not be secured. In 1905 all obstacles were overcome and Union Station service commenced.

A modern passenger station was built at Third and Antoine streets in 1896. The management has always dealt liberally with the people, asking no bonus, paying for everything and aiding the city by large expenditures in the building of the Blacksnake sewer.

* * *

THE UNION PACIFIC—Up to the war period St. Joseph was generally regarded as the logical starting point of the Union Pacific railroad. The Hannibal & St. Joseph road connected the Mississippi and Missouri Rivers; the Kansas legislature had chartered the Palmetto & Roseport, from Elwood to Marysville, and this road was completed to Wathena; the Pony Express was operated out of St. Joseph over what was supposed to be the route of the future transcontinental railroad. When the Union Pacific was projected two branches were contemplated, one from Memphis by the southern route, and one from the Missouri River. When the road was chartered by congress, in 1862, two branches were provided for, but both were to start from the Missouri. River and meet at the 100th parallel, about where North Platte, Neb., is located. Wyandotte secured the southern branch, and there was a contest between St. Joseph and Omaha for the northern branch. The senators from Missouri—Wilson and Henderson—strongly advocated the cause of St. Joseph. The prospects of success seemed good until an Omaha champion recited in fervid eloquence the fact that the United States flag had been torn down from the postoffice here in May of 1861, and that the people of St. Joseph had been so disloyal as to require the constant presence of United States troops to preserve order and protect those who held Union sentiments. In conclusion he urged that such conduct deserved a rebuke and the proper way of administering this was to start the northern branch of the Union Pacific railroad from Omaha. He carried off the honors, though he did this community a gross injustice.

* * *

UNION TERMINAL—In 1901 a charter was granted the Union Terminal Company, an organization formed by John Donovan and others interested in the St. Joseph Stock Yard. The principal line extends from the stock yards to a point near Jule street, where a connection is made with the Chicago Great Western. The purpose of the project was to facilitate traffic to the stock yards and packing plants, and also to afford terminals for other roads which might desire to enter St. Joseph. In connection with this enterprise twenty-two acres of reclaimed land have been added on the river front.

* * *

INTERURBANS—The first interurban built into St. Joseph, or out of the city, as you may prefer, was by the St. Joseph and Savannah Interurban Railway Company, which began operating the line from this city to Savannah April 4, 1911. The line is owned by the street railway company and represents an investment of $400,000.

The Kansas City, Clay County & St. Joseph Railway Company, an enterprise promoted by George Townsend and C. F. Enwright, is one of the most important interurban railway projects in the West. It built the line from St. Joseph to Kansas City, with a mileage of 52 miles. A branch extends from North Kansas City to Excelsior Springs 30 miles in length. The first car to enter St. Joseph over this line was February 17, 1913, drawn by a locomotive. The first car under regular power—electricity—came April 29, 1913. This enterprise represents an investment of about $5,000,-000, and has been a decided success from the start.

* * *

THE BRIDGE—In 1870 there was incorporated the St. Joseph Bridge Building Company, composed of General Willard P. Hall, J.

M. Hawley, J. H. R. Candiff, J. B. Hinman, John L. Bittinger, James A. Matney, O. M. Smith, I. G. Kappner, John Pinger, J. D. McNeely, W. Z. Ransom, Mordecai Oliver and Isaac C. Parker. A bridge across the river had long been a necessity, and the people were willing to give all possible aid. Hence, on January 25, 1871, they ratified an ordinance, at a special election, authorizing a subscription for five thousand shares of the capital stock of the company above mentioned, to be paid for in the city's bonds, twenty years after date, and bearing 10 per cent interest per annum. This practically meant a donation of $500,000. But nineteen negative votes were cast.

The company at once secured the services of Col. L. D. Mason, an engineer of national reputation, who, after having fixed the location of the bridge, was empowered to advertise for bids for its construction. The highest bid received was from the Baltimore Bridge Company, $1,175,000; the lowest from the Detroit Bridge and Iron Works, $716,000. The latter company was awarded the contract. On July 25, 1871, the first material arrived, and on September 26, the first stone was laid, on the Kansas side, in the presence of a large assemblage of people. In 1872, while the work was in progress, a proposition to transfer the bridge to the Hannibal & St. Joseph Railway Company, according to the proposition of Mr. B. F. Carver, was presented at a meeting of the Manufacturers' Aid Association, held March 20, 1872. The proposition, as may be supposed, caused a great deal of excitement among the people.

Mr. Carver's proposition was to furnish the money to complete the bridge under the present direction, as fast as Chief Engineer Mason would estimate for the required funds; that he would extend the St. Joseph & Topeka Railroad to Atchison, Kan., and connect it with the various roads at that town; that he would remove the machine shops, car works and general offices of the Hannibal & St. Joseph railroad, located at Hannibal, to St. Joseph; that he would fix the tariff on highway travel on the bridge at rates one-half lower than those of any similar structure on the Missouri or Mississippi rivers; and that he would make the tariffs to railroads equal as between his and all others, and that rates guarded and liberal be assured to all. In consideration of his doing these things, he asked that the city transfer to him its entire stock of $500,000, and that the machine and car shops should be exempt from taxation, as they were in Hannibal, for twenty years.

There was much debate and a great variety of opinions delivered. Some wanted the bridge made absolutely free for highway travel, while others thought it was better to allow the owners of it to collect a low rate of tariff and return to the city a portion of the bonds voted to the work. All appeared to favor the proposition in one form or other, and adopted a resolution, unanimously, that it was the sense of the meeting that the city's stock ought to be sold whenever judicious terms could be made. The council submitted the transfer to the vote of the people, but before the election day had arrived the ordinance was withdrawn.

There are six piers. Wooden caissons were sunk to bed rock. The work in the interior of these caissons was carried on under pneumatic pressure and the masonry of the piers progressed upward as the caisson was sunk. Nearly one and one-half million feet of lumber and 16,000 cubic feet of concrete were required for the caissons, and 172,000 cubic feet of masonry for the piers. The superstructure consists of three fixed spans of the quadrangular Pratt truss, each 300 feet long, one fixed span at the east approach of 80 feet, and a draw span of 365 feet, making the entire length of the bridge 1,345 feet.

On the 20th of May, 1873, the first locomotive crossed the bridge. This was engine No. 6, of the St. Joseph & Denver City railroad, in charge of Edgar Sleppy, master mechanic of the shops of that road and the man who ran the first passenger train out of St. Joseph on the opening of the Hannibal & St. Joseph road more than fourteen years before. Charles Stine, now a passenger engineer on the St. J. & G. I. road, performed the duties of fireman on this engine.

On Saturday, May 31, 1873, occurred the grand celebration of the completion of the bridge. This was, beyond doubt, the most magnificent pageant ever displayed in the city. Not only was every civic association and benevolent society represented in the vast procession, but the German citizens of the Northwest had selected St. Joseph as the place for holding their annual saengerfest, and May 31 was selected as the time. The procession which traversed the streets of St. Joseph on that day had never been equaled west of the Mississippi. Every trade was represented.

Dr. Robert Gunn, who served as secretary of the company from the beginning of the second year of its organization, was superintendent of the bridge for many years.

June 16, 1879, the control of the bridge was transferred to Jay Gould and associates. It is now the property of the St. Joseph & Grand Island Railroad Company.

* * *

THE UNION STATION — In .October, 1868, the county judges voted an appropriation of $10,000 to aid the citizens of Buchanan County to procure grounds for a Union Depot, the same to be erected between the foot of Jule street and the foot of Edmond street, for the use of the Hannibal & St. Joseph, the St. Joseph & Council Bluffs, and all other railroads thereafter centering in St. Joseph. Machine shops were also to be maintained. This scheme, though urgently advocated by a number of St. Joseph's most prominent citizens, never materialized.

In April, 1880, the St. Joseph Union Depot Company was formed, the following railroad companies being incorporators and bondholders: Hannibal & St. Joseph, Missouri Pacific, St. Joseph & Western, Kansas City, St. Joseph & Council Bluffs, Wabash, St. Louis & Pacific, and St. Joseph & Des Moines. A building was erected across Mitchell avenue, with a frontage of 405 feet on Sixth street, which was completed on April 30, 1882. Major Joseph Hansen was place'd in charge as superintendent. The upper story was arranged for a hotel. The first train to leave the Union Depot was over the Missouri Pacific route, and was called at an early hour on May 1, 1882, by Isaac Veitch, who for many years served as chief depot master.

On the night of February 9, 1895, the depot was destroyed by fire. The hotel was at that time kept by Major John B. Laughlin.

During the same year a new building was erected upon the site of the old one, with many improvements. This new Union Station was opened for business early in January of 1896.

* * *

TELEGRAPH LINES—The first telegraph line built to St. Joseph was completed on March 3, 1853. The first message received was the inaugural address of President Franklin Pierce. Peter Lovell was the operator and his office was at the southwest corner of Second and Jule streets. There were two newspapers in St. Joseph at that time—*The Gazette* and *The Adventurer*—and the forces were combined in putting the message into type. Captain F. M. Posegate was among the compositors of *The Adventure*, and Charles M. Thompson was of *The Gazette* force. The Stebbens line, from St. Louis to St. Soseph, via Atchison, was built in 1860. In 1880 three telegraph companies had offices in St. Joseph—the Western Union, the American Union, and the Atlantic and Pacific. In 1884 there were three companies—the Union Pacific, the Mutual Union and the Pacific Mutual. The latter line was built from St. Louis to Sioux City by Joseph A. Corby of this city, and was absorbed by the Postal Telegraph and Cable Company. This and the Western Union are the only companies now having offices in St. Joseph.

CHAPTER XXII.

CRIMINAL INCIDENTS—ROBIDOUX ROBBED—THE KILL-ING OF WHITTLE AT SPARTA—MURDER OF DR. JONES—TOM FARRIS—KILLING OF CHARLES ROBI-DOUX—BURNING OF THE FRIEND FAMILY—RESCUE OF DR. DOY—THREE WAR-TIME TRAGEDIES—KILL-ING OF JESSE JAMES—THE BOND ROBBERY—MUR-DER OF COLONEL STRONG—HOLD-UP AT M-DON-ALD'S FACTORY—SEVERAL TRAIN ROBBERIES.

The criminal history of Buchanan County dates back to the summer of 1842. Joseph Robidoux had received $4,000 in silver, in payment for merchandise sold to the Sac and Fox Indians. This money was placed in four strong wooden boxes and stored by Robidoux under a counter in his place of business. Some nights afterward an entrance was effected and the money carried away. Circumstances fastened suspicion upon a party of people who had recently come into the county, and who had located on the east side of One-Hundred-and-Two River. There were three families, named Spence, Scott and Davis. A search was instituted. One of the Spence boys had purchased a pair of new shoes of Robidoux shortly before the robbery. The fact that one of these shoes was found in the mud at the crossing of Blacksnake Creek, confirmed the suspicion. A posse was organized, and efforts were stimulated by a reward of $500 which Robidoux offered for the recovery of the silver. The suspects were surrounded, but stoutly and defiantly denied guilt. The man Davis was taken by a portion of the posse to a secluded spot, and threatened, but he stubbornly refused to confess. As had been prearranged, a pistol was fired, and several of the posse rushed to where the man Scott was in custody, declaring that Davis had been killed, and that they now proposed to treat Scott likewise. Scott begged for mercy, and agreed to tell where the money was. He was promised immunity, and at once led his captors to a spot where $1,000, wrapped in a blanket, had been buried. But Scott's knowledge did not extend beyond the first cache. The vigilantes now resorted to strategy. Davis, who was still in custody, was informed that Scott had confessed, and was told that he would be given his liberty if he did likewise. After much profanity and defiance, he yielded, upon being shown an ominous rope. The remainder of the silver had been buried as the first, and in close proximity. The money was all recovered except $27. Scott and Davis were brought to Blacksnake Hills as prisoners. Davis escaped and Scott was given his liberty. The Spence boys disappeared at once.

In his "Recollections of an Old Pioneer," the late Peter H. Burnett, the first circuit attorney who prosecuted in Buchanan County, and who was afterward governor of California, relates the following incident:

"A celebrated counterfeiter of the name of Whittle went from the county in which he resided to an adjoining county and passed upon a plain farmer some counterfeit gold coin in payment for a horse. Having been indicted in the proper county, he applied for a change of venue; and the case, upon a proper showing, went to Buchanan County.

"When the case was called the prisoner was ready for trial, and I asked the court to order the sheriff to call the trial jurors. The moment I heard their names called I was satisfied that it was mainly a packed jury. I knew that some of them belonged to the band of criminals in that county, or they were unfortunate in reputation and association. I promptly rose and said: 'If the court please, it is now very near dinner time, and I think it very likely I will dispose of this case without troubling the court.' Judge Atchison seemed to understand what I was driving at, and readily adjourned court.

"When the court met again there was a large crowd present, as it must have been anticipated that some decisive step in the case would be taken. When the case was called I said: 'With the leave of the court, I will enter a *polle prosequi* and let the prisoner go. I do not mean to make a farce of justice by trying this prisoner before such a jury.' The prisoner was wholly taken by surprise, and looked exceedingly mortified. He evidently expected to be tried and acquitted. I intended to have the witnesses again subpoenaed before the grand jury of the proper county, and they would no doubt have found another indictment; and, upon another change of venue, I should have opposed successfully any effort of the defendant to have the case sent to Buchanan County. But the prisoner was killed in a private quarrel before the next term of court.

"He was a man of Herculean frame and of desperate character. His death happened in this wise: He forced a quarrel upon a peaceable, awkward, innocent young man, about the age of twenty-one, for the purpose, most likely, of showing off his prowess before his friends. At all events, when the young man had hitched his horse to the rack, Whittle went out and cut off the horse's tail, and came into the room where the young man was sitting, and thrust it rudely into his face. Upon the young man's remonstrating, Whittle chased him into the street; and several times afterward during the day he followed him into other places and forced him hastily to leave. The poor young man became desperate at last, and armed himself with a pistol. Whittle again drove him from the house, and was pursuing him into the street, when the young man turned upon him and shot him through the heart. Though fatally wounded, Whittle picked up a large stone and threw it at the young man with such force that had it struck him it would have killed him instantly. After throwing the stone, Whittle fell upon his face dead."

The History of Buchanan County, published in 1881, refers to this incident, and states that it occurred at Sparta. The name of Whittle's slayer is given as Gillett and the event is said to have occurred in 1842. Whittle's body was the first to be buried in the Sparta graveyard, and his taking off is said to have caused general satisfaction. Gillett left the county soon afterward, though it is doubtful if he would ever have been punished for slaying Whittle.

* * *

The murder of Dr. Jones, which occurred on the morning of June 18, 1848, was one of the notable criminal episodes in the county. Dr. Jones lived on Rock House Prairie. He was sitting with his family upon the porch of his residence. A man named Gibson came and quarreled with Dr. Jones. In an altercation which ensued Gibson fatally stabbed Dr. Jones with a knife. The murderer escaped and was never captured.

* * *

Tom Farris was one of the pestiferous petty criminals of St. Joseph during the overland period. His career extended from 1849 to 1851. His specialty was stealing wheels and chains from the wagons of the emigrants, and then selling the stolen articles back to their owners, in disguised form, at a good price. Many stores were robbed from time to time by Farris and his gang, but notwithstanding the leaders were well known, they always managed to evade the law, and it was impossible to fasten any evidence upon them. One fine May day the good people of St. Joseph became so tired of these things that Old Tom and his first lieutenant, a handsome and finely-dressed man, were conducted to the top of Prospect Hill, given one hundred lashes each and ordered to leave. This broke up the thieving gang.

* * *

The excitement and public indignation caused by the tragic death of Charles Robidoux is well remembered by the survivors of those days. Charles was the youngest son of Joseph Robidoux. He·was a handsome, light-hearted young man, in his twentieth year, who was generally beloved. The circumstances connected with his death are as follows:

On the night of September 8, 1850, at about 11 o'clock, young Robidoux, in company with other young men of the town, were on the street, engaged in some harmless sport. They were rapping at the doors of the business houses, to awaken clerks and others sleeping there. They rapped on the door of D. & T. D. S. MacDonald, which was located on Main street, where the Sommer-Richardson cracker factory now stand; and, after leaving it, they went to a post set in the ground at the edge of the pavement opposite the building, and pulled it up. Young Robidoux placed the post on his shoulder and started toward the opposite side of the street. When he had gone about one-third of the distance, a gun was fired from the window of the second story of MacDonald's store. The load, which consisted of shot of large size, took effect in the back of Robidoux's head and he expired in a few minutes.

Duncan MacDonald confessed that he had fired the gun, but with no intention of injuring any person. The deed created an intense feeling, and there was strong talk of violence on the part of young Robidoux's friends. This was stimulated by the grewsome act of one of these. He procured a quantity of blood from a slaughter-house, with which, during the night, he covered the entire sign in front of the MacDonald store, and then dotted the hideous red ground with black paint, in imitation of bullet marks. Wiser counsel prevailed, however, and the meditated violence was prevented. MacDonald was tried and acquitted, it having been shown that there was no intention to commit murder.

* * *

On May 28, 1856, the family of Jacob Friend, consisting of father, mother and four children, residing about four miles south of St. Joseph, were burned to death in their dwelling. The general supposition was, borne out by circumstances, that the family was first murdered and then the residence burned to destroy evidence of crime. Five men, residing in the neighborhood, were arrested on suspicion. They were indicted and tried, but the evidence was not of sufficient weight to convict, the main point being that it was known that an enmity existed between the parties. Only one member of the family, a daughter, who was away on a visit, escaped, and was not aware of the calamity until the next day.

* * *

In 1859, at the time the slave question was agitated and secession was threatened in several of the Southern states, Kansas was recognized as the haven of slaves; that is, when a slave in Missouri was missing, the supposition was that he had been stolen and transported to Kansas. In January of that year a party of Missourians from Platte County, in pursuit of a negro named "Dick," belonging to a man named Niedman in Platte County, caught up with two wagons near Lawrence, Kan. In those wagons, driven by Dr. John Doy and his son, they found their negro, besides several more who had been taken from Jackson County, Missouri. The Doys were returned to Platte City, where an indictment was found against them, tried for the offense, found guilty and placed in jail. J. M. Bassett, the circuit attorney, being sick, Judge Elijah H. Norton, before whom the cases were tried, appointed Col. John Doniphan, later a prominent citizen of St. Joseph, to prosecute. A change of venue was taken from Platte to Buchanan County, and on May 25 they were put on trial. A hung jury was the result, circumstantial evidence being the main hindrance. In June the cases were again considered, the indictment against young Doy having been dismissed in the meantime. The news of Doy's arrest and the earnest desire of the people of Kansas to see justice done impelled the legislature of Kansas to employ the best legal talent in the country to defend him, and for that purpose Wilson Shannon of Ohio and A. C. Davis, attorney-general of the state of Kansas, were secured. The trial continued for three days amidst the most intense excitement. The jury, composed of Samuel B. Tolin, George Boyer, Jacob Boyer, H. D. Louthen, Merill Willis, Henson Devorss, George Clark, Henry P. Smith, John Madrill, O. M. Loomis, William W. Mitchell and James Hill, after a few moments' deliberation, returned a verdict of guilty.

An appeal was taken to the supreme court, and while pending an episode occurred which not only startled this community, but was noted extensively all over the country. On a dark night a party of Kansans crossed the river. Under pretext of having a prisoner whom they desired to commit, they entered the jail, secured the jailer, released the prisoner, locked the door, threw the key away and escaped with him to Kansas.

* * *

On May 19, 1863, Captain Charles Mast, a prominent German citizen of St. Joseph, and captain of a militia company, who kept a saloon on Second street, was killed in his place of business by Gideon Hudson, a private in a company of Colorado volunteers. Hudson was drunk and threatened several persons with his pistol. Captain Mast remonstrated, and while endeavoring to disarm Hudson, was fatally shot. An arrest followed. The commander of the Colorado troops took the ground that Hudson was acting on the lines of duty. There was much local indignation at this finding, and the papers in the case were then sent to department headquarters, but no one seems to know what finally became of them or Hudson.

* * *

On Sunday evening, September 21, 1862, a desperado named John Young, without cause or provocation, shot and killed D. W. Fritzlein, proprietor of the Avenue brewery in this city. The murder occurred in the bottoms between Elwood and Wathena. About 6 o'clock that evening a wagon was seen coming from the Elwood ferry boat. It was at once driven up Frederick avenue to the brewery. One of the men in the wagon was covered with blood, and around his neck was a rope, held by one of the other occupants. This attracted general attention, and thousands of people followed. Fritzlein's friends were going to lynch Young. He was taken to the cottonwoods on the hills east of the city, where the mob seized the rope, pulled the murderer from the wagon and dragged him to a tree. After beating and pounding him severely he was tied to the trunk of a tree and preparations were made to burn him. Coroner Maxwell used his best endeavors, being seconded in his efforts by the military, to let the law take its course. They were successful, and the man was turned over to the civil authorities. While in the hands of the crow'd he begged piteously to be shot rather than hanged. The following Monday night the prisoner requested to be removed to the post hospital for the purpose of having his wounds dressed. This was granted, and the surgeon, after an examination, ordered the prisoner returned to jail, being convinced that he was feigning, evidently with the hope that he could thereby effect his escape. As the guards, consisting of a sergeant and two men, were returning the man to jail, he was fired upon by parties concealed in the lumber yard, unknown to the guard, the ball inflicting only a flesh wound in his arm. So great was the indignation of the citizens against the murderer that a special guard of militia had to be stationed at the jail to protect him. The murderer was, upon a requisition from the governor of Kansas, turned over to the Doniphan County, Kansas, authorities and placed in jail at Troy. Some months afterward his body was found in the river. Bullet holes indicated that he had been shot before being consigned to the water.

* * *

On the night of August 13, 1878, when the passenger train going south on the Kansas City, St. Joseph & Council Bluffs railroad, Conductor George Brown, arrived at Winthrop Junction, four men boarded it. They seemed unconcerned, cool and deliberate, and it did not take them long to make their purpose known. They entered the express and baggage car, in charge of Frank Baxter. The men were not masked and were strangers to all the railroad men. With drawn revolvers they compelled Baxter to open the express safe, from which they secured about $5,000. They then commanded the conductor to stop the train, whereupon they deliberately took their leave, going into the brush. Subsequently Mike Roarke, Dan Dement, Hillman and Frank Brooks were arrested and punished for other work of the same nature, and circumstances pointed strongly to their connection with this affair.

* * *

Jesse James, outlaw, upon whose head the state had put a price and to whose captors or slayers immunity had been promised, was killed in St. Joseph April 3, 1882, at about 10 o'clock in the morning. James had been living in St. Joseph since November 9, 1881, under the alias of "James Howard." His wife, two children and Charley Ford, a fellow-bandit, whose alias was Charles Johnson, composed the household. For a short time they lived at Twenty-first and Lafayette streets, but the tragedy took place at No. 1318 Lafayette street. The house is still in a good state of preservation, though it has been lowered.

The identity of James was known to but a few persons in St. Joseph, who, for reasons best known to themselves, kept it concealed. He mingled very little with the outside world, seldom going to the business portion of the city, making few acquaintances and keeping his own counsel.

Tempted by a $10,000 reward and the promised immunity, Charley Ford entered into a plan to trap and slay his friend and protector. Feeling the need of an accomplice, he persuaded James to give shelter to his brother Robert, commonly called "Bob." These two worthies only awaited a favorable opportunity. This came on the morning of April 3, 1882. Bob Ford assisted Mrs. James in the housework, while Charley Ford assisted James in the stable. The morning chores accomplished, the three men entered the front room, leaving Mrs. James in the kitchen to prepare dinner. James opened the front door. He remarked that if the people in the street saw him heavily armed they might become suspicious, and he thereupon removed his belt and pistols, throwing them upon a bed. Then he mounted a chair and began to dust a picture that hung against the wall. This was the first time in their long association that the Ford boys had seen James off his guard. He was unarmed and his back was turned. Simultaneously they grasped the situation, and drew their pistols. The click of the trigger caused James to turn his head slightly, but in that instant Bob fired and James fell backward to the floor a corpse. The bullet entered the back of his head near the right ear.

The Fords replaced their revolvers in their belts and hastily left the house, going to the Western Union Telegraph office, where they at once wired Governor Crittenden, as well as Sheriff Timberlake of Clay County and the marshal of Kansas City, that they had killed Jesse James. Thence they went in search of City Marshal Enos Craig, but he had heard of the affair and had gone to the scene of the tragedy. They then secured the protection of a policeman and returned to the house. Meeting the officials, they imparted the fact that they had done the shooting, at the same time disclosing the identity of the victim. They requested to be taken into custody, which was done. Subsequently Mrs. James swore out a warrant charging them with the murder of her husband.

The body of James was buried at Kearney in Clay County, the family home.

Judge O. M. Spencer, who was state's attorney for Buchanan County at that time, insisted upon prosecuting the Fords. They were indicted for murder in the first degree, and, upon arraignment before Judge Sherman, on April 18, 1882, pleaded guilty to the charge. Judge Sherman sentenced them to be hanged on May 19th. On April 19th a pardon, signed by Governor Crittenden, arrived and the Fords were released. They were at once re-arrested by an officer from Ray County and taken to Richmond to answer to the char e of having murdered one Wood Hite. Of this they were also cleared.

The reward of $10,000, which had been offered by express and railroad companies that had been troubled by the depredations of the James gang, was paid over to the Fords, and they lived in debauchery until they perished—Charley as a suicide and Bob by a pistol ball in a Colorado dance hall.

* * *

April, 1882, was replete with sensations in St. Joseph. While the incidents in connection with the killing of Jesse James were being discussed in every household, on every street corner, and even in the pulpit, the startling information was imparted that the city treasury of St. Joseph had been robbed.   The first intimation the officers or citizens had of such a condition of affairs was conveyed by wire from New York in a telegram dated April 8, 3:50 p. m., received by John S. Lemon and Charles W. Campbell, and sent by Robert W. Donnell, formerly of St. Joseph, then a banker of New York and fiscal agent of the city.   The telegram was brief, stating that Pinkerton detectives had arrested two men, giving their names as Irwin and Fish, both of St. Joseph, who were trying to dispose of 4 per cent funding bonds of the city of St. Joseph to the amount of $100,000.

Messrs. Lemon and Campbell, being members of the finance committee of the city council, immediately caused a hasty examination of the city register's office to be made, and it was discovered that bonds numbered 901 to 1,000, inclusive, were missing.   During the afternoon and evening a number of telegrams were exchanged, and at a special session of the city council that evening an appropriation was made to send a delegation to New York City to investigate the matter.   Mayor J. A. Piner, Register James H. Ringo and Marshal Enos Craig were selected.   The delegates at once left the city, Marshal Craig going to Jefferson City for requisition papers.

From the tenor of the dispatches immediate action on the part of St. Joseph officials was necessary, as efforts were being made there to release the bond thieves.   It appears that these men had been in New York for over a week, endeavoring to dispose of the bonds.   Their actions and liberal offers excited suspicion, although the bonds were pronounced genuine by the city's financial agent. They claimed that they had secured the bonds from a man in Missouri, but the story was doubted, and Mr. Donnell expressed the opinion that if the having the bonds in their possession were not guilty of theft they were acting as an agent of a disreputable city official at St. Joseph.

A new city administration having now assumed control, with F. M. Posegate as mayor, it was deemed advisable to send Thos. H. Ritchie, the newly-elected city marshal, to New York City to aid in securing and bringing back to St. Joseph the bond thieves.   Upon the arrival of the St. Joseph parties in New York the prisoners were turned over to Marshal Ritchie and ex-Marshal Craig, while the bonds were placed into the custody of Mr. Donnell.   It was discovered that $4,000 of the coupons attached to the bonds were missing.   The man who gave the name of Fish when arrested proved to be W. W. Scott, who was engaged in the roofing business while here.

Register Ringo submitted to an interview while in New York, in which he said: "It was one of the coolest burglaries ever committed in St. Joseph.   The bond were lying on a little bench in the vault, a large pile of them, and the robber or robbers would have to turn the pile over, which was done, they taking the lower part of them, and a robbery would not have been suspected unless it became necessary to count all of the bonds.   These men must have watched me and taken an impression of the keys, as no person has a key except myself and the chairman of the finance committee."

Scott and Irwin were brought back to St. Joseph, tried and acquitted.

* * *

The jewelry store of Saxton & Hendrick, then located on the north side of Felix street, between Fifth and Sixth streets, was robbed of jewelry to the value of $4,000 at about 6:30 o'clock on the evening of April 23, 1885. Four men entered the store. One engaged the only salesman present, Alfred E. Daniels; the other three sneaked behind the counters, robbed the show cases of gold watches, diamonds and other jewelry, and escaped. No arrests were ever made, nor was the property recovered.

* * *

The murder of Col. J. W. Strong and Dr. S. A. Richmond, on June 18, 1886, shocked the community. Colonel Strong, who had been prominently identified with public enterprises in St. Joseph, was at that time publisher of *The Herald,* the office being located at the southwest corner of Sixth and Edmond streets. Dr. Richmond was the proprietor of a patent medicine. He had failed in business and had previously created a sensation by mysteriously disappearing and having himself "discovered" in Chicago. On the morning of June 29, Colonel Strong was in his office, on the first floor of *The Herald* building. Richmond came up in a carriage, alighted and walked rapidly into Colonel Strong's presence. Without a word he fired three shots from a pistol into Colonel Strong's body. Death resulted in a few minutes. Richmond was tried and the jury found that he was insane at the time the deed was committed. He was sent to Asylum No. 2, from which he escaped. For many years he lived in Illinois, no effort having ever been made to return him to the asylum.

* * *

A bold daylight robbery occurred on the afternoon of Saturday, February 21, 1891. W. T. Kershaw, paymaster at the McDonald overall factory, in the Patee building, arrived with a sack of money, amounting to $1,600, to pay the employes. As he entered the vestibule he saw a man bearing a parcel wrapped in paper, who was apparently waiting for someone. The man proved to be robber and the parcel a club. He struck Mr. Kershaw upon the head. A struggle ensued in which Mr. Kershaw was worsted, being stunned by the blow. The robber had an accomplice ready with a horse and buggy. They drove rapidly away, and though given a hot chase, escaped. No clew was ever found to them or the money.

* * *

Train robberies were quite common in the vicinity of St. Joseph some years ago. A plan to rob a train on the Kansas City, St. Joseph & Council Bluffs railroad was formulated in September of 1893. A point in the vicinity of Roy's Branch, about one mile, north of the city, was selected for the scene of operations. Those implicated in the plot were N. A. Hearst, Charles Fredericks, William Garver, Fred Kohler, Henry Gleitze and Hugo Engel. Some days previous to the attempt the railroad officials had received pointers. Superintendent Hohl, having learned that the attempt was to be made on the night of September 23, so arranged that the train marked by the robbers was enabled to slip by. The robbers then arranged for Sunday night, September 25. The railroad officials were again informed, and in connection with Chief of Police Broder and Sheriff Charles W. Carson, again arranged to frustrate the attempt. The two officers each furnished a quota of men. Those in the police squad were Sergeant J. Fred Henry, Patrolmen John Roach, Robert Maney, Daniel Shea, E. L. Keiffer, John Kendrick, John L. Claiborne, Charles S. Scott, John H. Martin, George W. Hays, Jeff Carson, William Halley, Ed Long and Wm. H. Rice. Sheriff Carson was accompanied by Deputy Sheriff John Brown. T. H. Ritchie, General Manager Brown and Superintendent Hohl were also of the party.

Instead of sending out the regular train, for fear of endangering the lives of passengers, a dummy train, an exact counterpart of the regular, was dispatched, the two rear coaches being darkened to give them the appearance of sleepers. The armed men were mostly placed in the baggage car. To make it appear that a large amount of baggage was on board, empty boxes were taken on at the Francis Street depot. The train was in charge of Conductor Jake Hardenstein. W. L. Wright was engineer and Victor Wise fireman.

There were several traitors in the robbers' camp. Prior to the attempt, Hearst, Frederick and Garver had agreed with the officers that as soon as firing began they were to fall down flat on the ground and to remain unmolested. This plan was carried out to the letter. When the train arrived at Roy's Branch bridge a red light appeared on the track and a signal was given to stop. The train stopped, and as it did so the bandits were discovered, all heavily armed, ranged along the side of the track. Beside their guns, they were supplied with dynamite and fuse. Kohler, who seemed to be the leader, in company with Henry Gleitze, rushed up to the engineer and fireman, covered them with revolvers, and ordered them to climb down and open the express car door. They obeyed with alacrity. When the door was reached, Kohler, with an oath, demanded that the door be opened, threatening at the same time to blow the inmates up with dynamite. Those inside obeyed, and when Kohler saw the head of a man he fired at it. The police then fired a volley and Kohler fell backward to the ground. Although badly wounded in a number of places he kept shooting until his revolver was empty. The other bandits, except those who gave the scheme away, also continued shooting, and soon Hugo Engel went down with his body full of bullets. Henry Gleitze made his escape, while the accomplices were made prisoners.

Gleitze was arrested the next day. He was arraigned at the December term of court. The grand jury had indicted him for an attempt to rob R. E. Calicotte, who acted as express messenger, of a watch valued at $25, and not for an attempt to rob an express train, the train being a dummy and not an express. The prisoner was allowed, by agreement, to plead guilty, and was sentenced to two years in the penitentiary. Garver, Fredericks and Hearst were not prosecuted.

* * *

At about 6:40 p. m. on January 10, 1894, the Chicago fast train, better known as the "Eli," on the Burlington system, was held up about four miles east of the city by five men. As the train reached the summit of the heavy grade a torpedo on the track warned Engineer Gross that something was wrong, and almost at the same instant a red light in the hands of one of the bandits was swung in front of the train. This caused the engineer to immediately apply the airbrakes and stop the train. He was promptly covered with revolvers. The robbers ordered the engineer and fireman to accompany them to the express car, which they did. Messenger G. B. Wetzel, in charge of Adams Express Company's safe, being covered with revolvers, opened the car door and also the safe. The robbers secured all the valuables therein contained. They also took the mail pouches. Having secured what booty they desired, they ordered the engineer and fireman to resume their respective places. The passenger were warned to secrete their treasures by Conductor Frank Murray, but this was unnecessary.

* * *

At an early hour Thursday morning, January 18, 1894, five men, presumably those who figured in the foregoing case, robbed passenger train No. 3 on the K. C., St. J. & C. B. railroad at Roy's Branch. In less than five minutes from the time the train halted the express car had been looted and the bandits disappeared. Express Messenger C. E. Baxter was powerless, and was compelled to stand and witness one of the three men in the car hand the booty to his pals, who placed the parcels in sacks, after which they departed.

The torpedo and red lantern were the means employed to halt the train. The mail coach in this instance was not molested, neither were the passengers. The firing of a number of shots by the bandits warned the postal clerks and passengers that something was wrong, whereat the clerks fastened all the doors of their car and hid under the pouches, while the passengers kept inside the coaches and were busy in secreting their money and jewelry.

Th job being completed, the trainmen were stood in line on the west side of the track and the robbers took to the willows. Instead of pursuing its course, the train backed down to the Francis street depot, when the railroad and county officials were notified of the robbery. Investigation proved that the men did not remain in the willows, but returned to the city, two of them riding in a buggy, while three walked. The vehicle was tracked for some distance. A notorious character named Pat Crowe pleaded guilty to complicity in this robbery and was sent to the penitentiary for two years.

The fourth attempt to rob a train in this vicinity was made on the night of March 2, 1894, the St. Joseph hill, three miles east of the city, being selected as the place and passenger train No. 18 on the Chicago, Rock Island & Pacific being the victim. The same plan was adopted by the bandits as had been successfully carried out in the two last escapades—the torpedo and the red lantern. The engineer, J. D. McKinney, slowed up his train when he observed the danger signal, but when he looked out and saw the armed and masked men, he pulled the throttle wide open and ran the train through. While the train was in rapid motion the engineer was commanded to halt the train, but instead he dodged down in the cab, at the same time calling to the fireman to do the same thing. An examination, when the train reached Stockbridge, showed that the robbers had shot to kill, as the windows of the cab were broken and five bullets were buried in the woodwork near the spot where the engineer's head would have been had he not dodged.

* * *

A Burlington train, southbound, was robbed on the night of August 11, 1898, a short distance north of Francis Street station, about 9 o'clock, by five boys—James Hathaway, William Hathaway, Charles Cook, Alonzo Arterburn and Herbert Donovan. Part of them had been employed as messengers by a local telegraph company, and the dime novels they read told of daring exploits by bandits. They took the safe from the express car, but were scared away by an approaching freight train, and secured no booty. The boys were arrested and punished.

* * *

On the night of September 3, 1903, the Denver express of the Burlington road, southbound, was stopped at Dillon Creek, near the waterworks, by four masked men, who blew open the express company's safe and secured booty valued at $40,000. They have not yet been caught.

* * *

One of the most brutal crimes that the history of Buchanan county records is the murder of Mrs. Sarah Gay, wife of George Gay, a farmer living near Taos, November 23, 1904. While her husband was engaged in the cornfield, Mrs. Gay was bound hand and foot, and her throat cut in a shocking manner. Cassius W. Brown, an aged negro with a prison record, who was seen near the house shortly before the crime, was arrested and tried four times. He was twice convicted, but the case was reversed by the supreme court because of trivial technicalities. Brown was finally given his liberty.

* * *

Paul P. Druckmiller, a government inspector at the packing plants, was fatally shot in the bank, April 1, 1915, by Grace V. Vest, at her home on South Fourth street. Her subsequent trial and acquittal of first degree murder attracted much attention at the time.

James M. Sego, a wealthy farmer in the southern part of the county was shot and killed on the streets of Winthrop, March 24, 1906. John R. Crook and his son Willie were arrested, charged with the crime. It appears that Sego objected to young Crook's attentions to his daughter.

*   .   *

Thomas Harris, a street car conductor, fatally cut the throat of his sweetheart, Madeline Rowbotham, at the entrance to Krug Park, Sunday afternoon, July 13, 1913. He is now serving a life sentence for the crime.

On the afternoon of January 19, 1915, the office of the Aunt Jemima Mill Company, Second and Edmond streets, was held up by a lone robber. The money with which the employes were to be paid in a few hours, amounting to $1,085, was secured. Joe Miller, Irene Smith and F. F. Hotchkiss were arrested for the crime, and subsequent confessions indicated that Miller was the robber. He was taken to the mill in a buggy believed to have been driven by the Smith woman. A short time before this robbery, D. Godsey, a saloon keeper on Frederick avenue, was held up, and when he showed signs of resisting, was shot dead. Miller was tried for this crime and given a life sentence.

CHAPTER XXIII.

LEGAL EXECUTIONS—OTIS JENNINGS, THE FIRST MAN
TO DIE UPON THE SCAFFOLD IN BUCHANAN COUNTY
—EXECUTION OF GREEN, THE SLAVE, AND OF WIL-
LIAM LINVILLE—JOSEPH LANIER TAKEN FROM ST.
JOSEPH TO SAVANNAH AND SHOT—HANGING OF A.
J. BOWZER AND HENRY GRIFFIN—JACKSON JEFFER-
SON PUBLICLY SHOT—GREEN WILLIS, A NEGRO
HANGED FOR MURDER—THE EXECUTION OF JOHN
GRABLE — EXECUTION OF PETER HRONEK, THE
FIRST PRIVATE HANGING IN THE COUNTY—LOUIS
BULLING HANGED AT SAVANNAH—EXECUTION OF
JOE BURRIES AND JIM POLLARD.

The first legal execution to take place in Buchanan County was
that of Augustus Otis Jennings, which occurred on September 2,
1853. Sheriff Joseph B. Smith was the executioner, a scafford having been erected southeast of the Patee House.

Jennings and three others had murdered Edward E. Willard.
The others were Wm. Langston, —— Jones and —— Anderson, but
none of them suffered the extreme penalty of the law except Jennings. Langston was convicted of complicity, sentenced to the
penitentiary, but was subsequently pardoned by Governor Robert
M. Stewart. Of the others, the records only show that a change of
venue was taken to neighboring counties.

The murder of Willard, which occurred on July 27, 1852, in the
brush north of the city, the location being at present in the corporate limits, was most atrocious. The victim was a man of family, a
carpenter by trade, and also an auctioneer. He became indebted to
the parties named above, and to others, and a supposition was en-
tertained that he was about to leave the country. These men, solely,
it seems, with the idea of extorting the money from him—he claiming to have money buried in the woods adjacent to a graveyard—
took him to the brush. They were amply prepared, having in their
possession rope, a pair of handcuffs and a cowhide. Upon arriving
at the point where it was said the money was secreted, Willard was
threatened with torture provided the money was not forthcoming.
Willard, according to the confession of Jennings, seemed to be
indifferent, and finally declared he had no money. Upon this admission, Langston, who took a leading part in the affair, commanded
Willard to remove his shirt, which he did. They placed handcuffs
upon him, and with a rope, procured by Jennings, the victim was
bound to a tree and the cowhide and switches applied until life was
extinct.

Arrests followed, and Jennings made a full confession, detailing all the events connected with it. His trial resulted in a verdict of guilty of murder in the first degree within thirty minutes after the evidence was given to the jury. An appeal was taken to the supreme court of the state, which tribunal sustained the action of the lower court. Many friends, among whom were Revs. Vandeventer and Boyakin, interceded with Governor Sterling Price in his behalf, but without avail.

Sheriff Smith summoned Captain Hughes of the Robidoux Grays, the only militia organization in the city, to escort the procession to the scaffold to preserve order. About 8,000 people were present at the execution. The prisoner firmly ascended the scaffold, expressed the hope that he would die easy, and also a firm faith in Christ. Contrary to his hope, however, he struggled long and died hard.

* * *

In the early part of July, 1859, a young negro slave, who had been purchased in the section of country northeast of St. Joseph, killed Francis Marion Wright, a slave buyer, who was bringing him to St. Joseph. Green was tried, convicted and sentenced to hang. The execution took place on December 2, 1859. Jonathan M. Bassett was state's attorney and Judge Elijah Norton was on the bench. Michael Morgan was sheriff and executioner, with Wash Brown and Sam D. Cowan assistants.

It appears that while en route to the city in a buggy, the negro, by some means, came into possession of a pistol belonging to Wright, shot him through the head, the wound proving fatal at once. The deed was committed on the road running through a heavy body of timber between Rochester and St. Joseph. Wright's corpse remained in the buggy and in a short time the horse, with its ghastly burden, swerved from the main road and stopped at the residence of Thomas Hubbard, in the vicinity. The alarm was given and it was soon learned who was the guilty party.

December 2, 1859, was a cold and bleak day, but notwithstanding that fact a large number of curious spectators gathered at Fowler's Grove, south of the city, to witness the execution. A rude scaffold had been erected, four poles having been sunk into the frozen ground and a rickety platform placed thereon. Among those who mounted the insecure structure were Sheriff Morgan, Deputy Wash Brown, Rev. Fackler, who conducted religious services, and several physicians. The Emmet Guards, under Daniel T. Lysaght, formed an escort from the jail.

The executioner was a bungler. When the trap was sprung the condemned man secured a hold upon the rope, and braced himself against the side of the trap with his elbows. Sheriff Morgan pried the victim loose, and after admonishing him to "behave like a gentleman," forced his body through the trap.

Green cared little for this life or for future existence. He was a great lover of the good things of the earth. especially of liquor and eatables. Several physicians in the city took a fancy to him and gratified his every want. When those who had buried the body in the county cemetery, north of the city, were returning they met the physicians en route to the graveyard. Green had sold his body to them.

* * *

One dark night in July, 1863, a number of men, said to have belonged to Joe Hart's gang of bushwhackers, entered the home of a man by the name of Burns, in Andrew County. During an altercation which ensued, George Henry, son-in-law of Burns, was killed, Burns and another man were wounded, and the marauders escaped. Subsequently a young man by the name of William Linville, only nineteen years of age, was apprehended as one of the gang, and charged with the murder. The military authorities had possession of the city and surrounding country, but young Linville was, from some reason or other, turned over to the state authorities for trial. Judge Silas Woodson was on the circuit court bench at that time, having control of civil as well as criminal cases. A trial was held in September, and on the 29th of the same month a verdict of murder in the first degree was returned. Sentence of death upon the gallows was at once imposed, and Friday, November 6, set for the day of execution.

The hanging took place at noon a few rods southeast of the Patee House, now McDonald's factory. The hills adjacent were covered by many witnesses of the sad scene.

The cortege left the jail, preceded by two companies of the Ninth cavalry, followed by Captain Dolman's company, guarding the prisoner. The condemned youth rode in a light double-seated carriage, seated between the Rev. Dr. Dulin, his spiritual adviser, and Barnes, the jailer, with Deputy Sheriff Matney in the same conveyance. He was followed by Sheriff Enos Craig and his assistants, and an express wagon, wherein was an empty coffin.

The young man was calm and self-possessed to a remarkable degree. Being granted permission to speak, he said:

"The witnesses who swore against me swore to the wrong man. You hang an innocent man. You take the life of the wrong person. I left the Confederate army on the 20th of May, last, and since then have never fired a gun or pistol at any human being. The witnesses who swore that I killed that man were mistaken. I did no crime, but it can't be helped now. Remember, all of you, I die innocent. I am perfectly willing and ready to die, for I expect to find rest in another world. I die an innocent man."

When the time approached for the execution, a prayer was offered, after which, with unfaltering step, Linville approached the drop in the platform and stood unmoved while the sheriff, assisted by the physician, adjusted the fatal noose. A glove was placed in his fingers, which was to be dropped by him to indicate his readiness, the black cap was drawn over his face, the minister and all on the platform bade him goodby. At a few minutes before 12 o'clock he dropped the glove, the cord was cut and all was over. In four minutes life was extinct.

The corpse was taken to the H. & St. J. depot, delivered to his mother, and taken to Chillicothe for burial.

* * *

Joseph Lanier, who was tried by a military commission in this. city, was executed at Savannah, June 10, 1864. The crimes for which he was convicted, under three charges and specifications, were: "Encouraging and aiding rebellion against the United States," "violating allegiance to same," and "violating laws and customs of war." It was charged that he, with other marauders, burned a mill belonging to a Mr. Caldwell at Rochester, Andrew County.

Lanier was a native of Tennessee, and became an orphan at an early age. In the fall of 1861 the Confederates under Colonels Boyd and Patton formed a camp near Rochester, which Joseph and his two brothers joined. Tiring of life in camp, he returned and became a member of the celebrated Hart gang. He was subsequently arrested by Major Bassett and Captain Davenport of this city, tried by military commission and sentenced to be shot. He was sent to the Alton penitentiary, where he remained nearly two years, awaiting a final decision in his case. The verdict was affirmed and he was sent back to be executed.

A military escort accompanied the condemned man to Savannah from the H. & St. J. depot in this city. The details were all arranged and carried out under the directions of Captain Theodore Griswold. At noon the prisoner walked between two ministers of the gospel to the place of execution, a few rods northeast of the depot. A coffin was placed before him, and facing the coffin and his executioners, Lanier uncovered his head while Rev. A. H. Powell uttered a prayer. He was unmoved and unconcerned when the death warrant was read, and when he was asked if he desired to be blindfolded, he replied, "Just as you please." He was requested to kneel by his coffin, which he did. Six bullets pierced his body. Upon the breast of the corpse, suspended by a black string around the neck, was a picture of the Virgin Mary, and in his pocket a crucifix, given him by a Catholic priest who had visited him in jail.

* * *

In the case of A. J. Bowzer of Linn County, charged with being a robber and guerilla, a member of Holtsclaw's band, the work of the military commission was quick. The evidence, in their minds, was conclusive of guilt. If it is true, as is said, that the testimony of one side only was taken, a decision was not difficult to arrive at. Bowzer was tried on September 8, 1864, and his execution was ordered to take place on the 9th—the next day.

The gallows was erected a short distance below where the Burlington roundhouse is now located. When the prisoner mounted the platform his step was firm and not a gleam of fear was depicted on his countenance. Lieutenant Harding, provost marshal, officiated, and at a signal from him the trap was sprung.

On the 23d day of the same month, in accord with the finding of the same tribunal, Henry A. Griffith, said to have been a member of the same company of soldiers as Bowzer, was executed on the same scaffold.

* * *

On August 27, 1864, while drinking in a saloon in the southern part of the city, known as the "Cottage Home," a soldier by the name of Jackson Jefferson became enraged at a fellow soldier and struck him over the heart with a stick of cordwood, death resulting at once.

Jefferson was sentenced by the court-martial to be executed on October 22, the place of execution being arranged for in the vicinity of the Patee House. When the guards arrived at the jail to take him, they found the door barricaded by the prisoner. He threatened death to the first one who entered. After some time, however, he yielded peacefully. He was placed in an ambulance, and, sitting on his coffin, was conveyed to the fatal spot. At 4:30 o'clock p. m. the prisoner marched to the center of the square, where his coffin had been arranged. When all preparations had been made, the man having given up all hope, a message was hurriedly delivered, giving him one week's respite.

At 2 o'clock on Friday, October 29, the time of the respite expired, and he was again escorted to the execution grounds. At the provost marshal's office he entrusted to a friend a number of letters, among which was one to his mother. Some difficulty was experienced by the officials in adjusting the handcuffs, when the prisoner, with composure, assisted in placing them in position. Having been blindfolded, he knelt beside his coffin. A platoon of soldiers leveled their muskets. Four bullets penetrated the condemned man's frame—two almost severing his head, one passing through his breast, and one through the left shoulder.

* * *

November 9, 1865, Jacob T. Kuhn, a tenant of J. C. Roberts, about four miles east of the city, on the One-Hundred and Two River road, was killed while en route home from the city, his body being discovered a few rods from his house. It was found that Kuhn had been murdered and robbed, an axe which he had taken to town being near him, covered with blood and hair. No clue was discovered as to the guilty party until December 20, 1865, when Green Willis and Charles Clark, negroes, were arrested, charged with the murder of John Lohr, on the Brierly farm in Marion Township, a short time previous. Upon being examined before Justice J. C. Robidoux, Clark, the younger of the two, made a confession, which cleared up both the murder of Kuhn and Lohr, fastening the guilt upon Green Willis. The testimony was to the effect that Clark and Willis overtook John Lohr on the public highway, and Green Willis made a proposition to kill him, saying he had money. Clark assented, whereupon Willis struck Lohr upon the head with a stone, after which both dragged the body to a slough in Brierly's field. Clark had heard of the killing of Kuhn, and at that time Willis told him that he (Willis) had committed the act with an axe, and that he had thereby secured the sum of $25.

A special session of the circuit court was convened on Monday, January 22, when the jury, within five minutes after the evidence was closed, returned a verdict of guilty against Green Willis, convicting him of both the murder of Jacob Kuhn and John Lohr and fixing the punishment at death.

The date of execution was set for March 1, 1866. On that day a large number of people came to the city. The scaffold, which was located on the bottom land in the southern part of the city, was surrounded by at least 5,000 people. The prisoner was attended by Rev. J. M. Wilkerson and Rev. Adam Dimitt, both ministers of negro churches in this city. Sheriff Ransom Ridge was the executioner. The prisoner was informed that he had but a few minutes to live and was urged to make a full confession, which he did. He requested that his body be given to his wife for burial.

Charles Clark, the young negro associated with Willis, was convicted as an accessory and imprisoned for life, but it is said that he was later pardoned.

* * *

August 22, 1870, John Grable was executed for the murder of Joel Drake, Sheriff Irving Fish being the executioner. Although neither the evidence nor the confession established the exact locality in which the murder was committed, the defendant was indicted, tried and convicted in Buchanan County, Judge I. C. Parker being upon the bench.

On January 6, 1870, John Grable went to Parkville, Mo., for the purpose of securing a coffin in which to bury Joel Drake, first making arrangements with neighbors for the grave, etc. Statements made by him as to the manner in which deceased came to his death caused suspicion in the minds of some, and on January 9 an affidavit was filed before Justice Saltzman in this city by one Daniel Bender, in which he stated that he believed that on or before January 2d John Grable had murdered Joel Drake.

Grable and Drake were brothers-in-law, both residents of Platte County, and the former had accompanied the latter to Gentry County in a wagon to secure money due Drake for property sold by him in that county, he having formerly resided there. The evidence tended to show that the deceased secured a check for $475 on a St. Joseph bank; that the parties were seen together at several points between Albany, Gentry County, and St. Joseph; that the check was cashed by Grable on the 3d day of January; that Drake was not seen alive in St. Joseph; that Grable put his team in a feed lot in the city, at the same time warning the owner thereof that it would be dangerous to venture near the wagon, as a vicious dog was kept therein; that he drove the team to Halls Station, at which place Mary Nolan, a sister of Grable's wife, got into the wagon, the dead

man meanwhile lying in the rear portion of the vehicle; that they
then drove to their home near Parkville, where the body was buried.

John Grable made a statement to his brother, sister-in-law and
others that he and Drake arrived in St. Joseph on Saturday, January 1; that Drake cashed the check, giving him $120 to hand t'
Drake's wife; that they stopped at a boarding house not far fror.
the Blacksnake; that he saw nothing of Drake until Sunday afternoon, when he found him dead in a questionable house in the vicinity; that the body was rolled into a blanket and placed in the wagon
by three women, who threatened, in case he divulged anything, tc
swear the crime of murder against him.

Acting upon the statement in the affidavit, a coroner's inques
rendered a verdict that the deceased came to his death at the hand
of unknown parties, and on the Sunday following, armed with .
warrant sworn out before Justice Saltzman, Sheriff Fish went tc
Platte County after Grable, and brought him to St. Joseph.

A preliminary examination was held and the accused bounc
over to await the action of the grand jury, which found a true bil
against him. The trial was set for Wednesday, May 25, 1870.
change of venue was asked, but denied by Judge Parker, and tl
case went to trial. Circumstantial evidence proved Grable's gui'
and a verdict of murder in the first degree was rendered June 1. F
was sentenced to be executed on Friday, August 20, 1870, but Judge
Henry S. Tutt, his lawyer, petitioned Governor J. W. McClurg for
a respite, which was granted until September 9. Before the day o'
execution arrived the condemned man made a confession of guilt, in
which he admitted the killing, detailing every fact in connectioj
therewith, and when on the scaffold he reiterated the substance oj
his previous statement.

When the hour for leaving the jail arrived, at noon, Grable
accompanied by Sheriff Fish, with his deputies, Charles Springe·
and Captain Lund, marched out of the jail yard and entered an oper
wagon in waiting to convey him to the place of doom. At this
juncture the sheriff remarked that it was about the noon hour, and
asked Grable if he did not desire his dinner. The prisoner readil:
accepted the invitation, remarking, "I always eat when I can ge·
it." He ate a hearty meal. The repast completed, he again entered
the wagon, seated himself upon his coffin, and was conveyed to the
place of execution, located in the southern part of the city.

The cortege was accompanied by mounted guards, under com·
mand of Captain Saltzman, who, upon arrival at the grounds
formed a cordon around the scaffold.

Grable asked for whisky, which was furnished him, and als·
asked permission to make a statement, as untruthful reports ha
been published about him. He openly confessed the murder, an
gave a warning to those within his hearing to avoid the use of intox·
icants, as by that means he was brought to his present position
During the preparations for the final act he gave instructions as t

German-American Bank Building

View at Lake Contrary

the placing of the rope around his neck. Soon the body shot down, the drop being about eight feet, and within a few second life was extinct.

* * *

The first private execution in the county occurred on June 30, 1888. On April 16, 1887, Peter Hronek, a Bohemian, who lived with his wife and one little child at 1705 Olive street, cruelly murdered the woman by shooting her with a pistol. Hronek was drunk when he committed this crime.

He was convicted and sentenced to be hanged, August 19, 1887, being fixed as the day of execution; but the case was taken to the supreme court. The lower court was sustained, and the condemned man was legally put to death on the scaffold in the jail yard on June 30, 1888, at 1:30 o'clock p. m. Sheriff Joseph Andriano was the officer in charge. Hronek was attended by Father Kryzwonos of the Polish Catholic Church.

* * *

On Sunday afternoon, March 8, 1888, a tragedy occurred at the Herbert House, corner of Fourth and Charles streets, this city. Louis Bulling, a young man born and reared in this city, who had been separated from his wife, called at the hotel, where she was employed, and asked to see her. After a short conversation he shot her while she was kneeling by a trunk in search of a picture of their child, which Bulling had requested.

Bulling was tried, found guilty of murder in the first degree, and sentenced to be hanged. The case was appealed and remanded. A change of venue was then taken to Andrew County, and in March, 1889, the case came up for trial. The jury stood six for acquittal and six for conviction. In the following May the case was again tried and Bulling was convicted. The case was again appealed to the supreme court, which sustained the decision. The date of the execution was set for March 6, 1891, to take place at Savannah. Sheriff Berry of Andrew County secured the gallows upon which Peter Hronek had been hanged and made other preparations. However, a respite was granted to April 17, 1891. On the night of April 10, Bulling sawed the jail bars and escaped. He was captured at Chicago in the latter part of June and returned to Savannah on July 3, 1891. On the night of July 4, 1891, he made an unsuccessful attempt to suicide with morphine.

Bulling was again sentenced, and September 4 set for the date of execution. The governor's clemency was invoked, but was refused. On the night before the execution the condemned man was much disturbed in mind, although he had a slim hope that his friends would be able to secure a commutation of his sentence to life imprisonment. It was expected that the execution would take place early on the morning of September 4, but it was delayed by the sheriff. The condemned man begged for a few hours' lease of life, and the hour was set for 2 o'clock. In the meantime the militia company was called out.

Shortly before the fatal hour, Bulling, together with his spiritual adviser, went into his cell. Scarcely had the door closed before two shots were heard. Upon entering, the officers found Bulling weltering in his own blood. Both bullets had taken effect. For fear that the law would be cheated out of a victim, four stalwart men took hold of Bulling, who fought like a demon, and conveyed him to the scaffold, placing him in a chair. At 3:18 the drop fell.

* * *

Joseph Burries, known as "Dusty," a young negro, was hanged by Sheriff Andriano and his deputies at the jail on May 12, 1895. He had been convicted of criminally assaulting a little white girl on July 30, 1894. The sentence was pronounced by Judge Silas Woodson. Though a strong petition was sent to Governor Stone, the executive refused to commute the sentence, but granted a stay of execution. On the night of December 31, 1894, Burries escaped from jail, in company with Pat Crowe and three others, but instead of leaving the country, as had been planned, he could not resist the temptation of again seeing his wife, and was captured the next night while in company with her in a room on Francis street.

The last night before the execution was an eventful one within the gloomy walls of the old bastile. A number of negro ministers called, and Burries joined in the religious services with much earnestness. The colored quartette, all prisoners, sang religious songs, the singing being joined in by Burries. Between 1 and 2 o'clock the next morning, the fatal day, the condemned man awoke, sang a hymn and uttered an earnest prayer. Religious services were held that morning, and then Burries started a religious negro song entitled "I Don't Want You to Grieve After Me," in which the negroes present joined wiwth fervor. It was a weird performance. The condemned man then knelt in prayer, at the conclusion of which he marched in his stocking feet to the center of the platform where hung the fatal noose. He died without a struggle.

* * *

On Friday, June 25, 1897, James Pollard, a negro youth, was executed by James Hull, sheriff, on a scaffold erected in the jail yard. July 30, 1895, Pollard, who was born and reared in the vicinity of DeKalb, returned to that neighborhood, after an absence of some time, went to the residence of Dave Irwin, another negro, with whom he had previously had trouble, and made an attempt to kill him. In shooting at Dave Irwin he shot Joseph Irwin instead, death resulting a short time afterward.

Pollard made his escape, being at large for some time, but was finally captured at Gallatin, Mo. He was tried twice for the crime, a conviction following both times. The case was appealed to the supreme court, and a strong effort was also made for a commutation of sentence. The supreme court sustained the lower court, the governor refused to interfere, and Pollard was hanged. He was very pious during his last hours.

Charles May was hanged in the jail yard April 17, 1903, for the murder of John Robert Martin at a dance near DeKalb, on the night of December 27, 1900. He was found guilty of murder in the first degree in March, 1901, appealed to the supreme court and obtained a new trial, but was again convicted. He died protesting that he had killed Martin in self-defense.

*   *   *

Mark Dunn was hanged March 11, 1904, for murdering Alfred Fenton at Rushville on the night of July 20, 1902. He was convicted and sentenced to be hanged. The supreme court sustained the verdict, and after several respites by the governor the date of execution was set for March 11. On the morning of March 7, Dunn escaped from the county jail in a sensational manner. Having secured possession of two revolvers which were smuggled into the jail in a coal oil can with false bottom, Dunn overpowered William Henley, the death watch, and John and Walter Thomas, deputy sheriffs, and disappeared after locking the guard and deputies in the cell house. He was captured three days later at Rosendale, where he had sought refuge, being sick and exhausted, but escaped his captors in a few hours and got as far as Guilford, where his strength gave way. He was brought back to St. Joseph and executed on the day set by the governor.

CHAPTER XXIV.

SOME OF THE CASUALTIES THAT HAVE OCCURRED IN BUCHANAN COUNTY AND ST. JOSEPH—THE PLATTE RIVER BRIDGE DISASTERS—COLLAPSE OF NAVE & McCORD'S BUILDING AND DEATH OF NINE PERSONS —THE DROWNING OF FIVE GIRLS AT LAKE CONTRARY—EXPLOSION OF DANFORTH'S FLUID AND THE KILLING OF THREE NEGROES—THE EARTHQUAKE OF 1867 AND SEVERAL DESTRUCTIVE STORMS SINCE THEN—LIST OF THE MOST IMPORTANT FIRES.

A complete list of casualties that have occurred since the settlement of Buchanan County would alone make a book of considerable size. In this chapter only a few of the more notable mishaps will be briefly mentioned.

The Hannibal & St. Joseph railroad bridge over Platte River, east of the city, was the scene of several disasters. On September 21, 1859, the bridge went down under the weight of a train. Several were killed. On September 3, 1861, occurred what is generally known as the Platte River bridge disaster. The bridge had been burned, presumably by bushwhackers, who were expecting a regiment of soldiers whom they hoped to destroy by wrecking the train. Instead, however, a passenger train dashed at full speed into the chasm. Stephen Cutler, the conductor; Frank Clark, the engineer; Charles W. Moore, the fireman, two brakemen and twelve passengers were killed. Early in the following November, while a regiment was crossing the swollen stream on a pontoon bridge, a heavy log dashed against the structure, causing destruction and loss of life. Seven were drowned, among them the wives of two soldiers.

* * *

Another notable accident of the early days was the collapse of Nave & McCord's store building and the loss of life. This building, a three-story brick, stood upon the site of the building on the west side of Third street, north of Felix, occupied by C. D. Smith's wholesale grocery, and afterward by McCord & Collins' wholesale grocery. Directly north, and below the grade of the street, was a frame double-tenement, one side of which was occupied by the family of Samuel Harburger, a merchant, related to the Binswanger family of this city, and the other side by a family whose names could not be learned. On the morning of July 5, 1860, fire broke out in the upper floor of the Nave & McCord building, then occupied by that firm. There was no fire department in those days, nor were there many police, and the walls collapsed before the general alarm was given. The debris completely covered the tenement and Mr.

Harburger, his wife, two children and servant girl perished, as did also four members of the other family. Two of Nave & McCord's clerks—William Hudnut and Henry Mitchem—who slept in the second story, had a narrow escape. In the collapse the timbers had so fallen as to protect these men instead of crushing them, and they were rescued from their perilous position by volunteers. The insurance companies refused to pay the loss on the building upon the ground that the collapse had occurred before the fire. The case was tried at St. Louis, and after eight years of litigation resulted favorably to Nave & McCord. It was proved by a traveling man, representing a flour mill at Beloit, Wis., that the building was on fire for some time before the collapse. He was a guest at the Patee House, and had been unable to sleep owing to the hot weather. Seated at his window, he noticed the flames and watched the progress of the fire for some time before he heard the crash.

* * *

About 3 o'clock on the evening of May 13, 1864, a powder magazine, situated on the northern extremity of Prospect Hill, exploded. Near a hole in the ground, where the magazine had stood, the bleeding, bruised and burning body of a boy was found. Another body was found some distance away. The bodies were those of James McEnery and James Morrison. There had been several other boys in the crowd, who were more or less seriously injured. The boys had lighted a match and thrown it into a crevice in the magazine.

* * *

St. Joseph was violently shaken by an earthquake on April 24, 1867. The shock occurred at 2:35 o'clock in the afternoon. At first there was an ominous rumbling sound, then a rocking movement from east to west and west to east, which continued for twenty seconds. The alarmed populace sought the streets and there was intense excitement. The public school buildings shook, the plastering cracked, huge seams being observed in the walls; the children screamed and the teachers, being bewildered and perplexed, dismissed the frightened pupils and hastened to their homes. Never before was there such consternation in the city. In a few seconds the air was as calm, the earth as tranquil, the face of nature as placid and everything as harmonious as though nothing unusual had occurred. No damage was done to property. A second shock was felt in September of 1871, when there were fears that the old court house would collapse. A third shock was felt in the autumn of 1896.

* * *

Early on the morning of February 23, 1868, fire destroyed the Allen House stable on South Fourth street, owned by Brooks & Maupin. It was necessary to use water from an immense cistern, which was located south of the city hall. While walking around the engine, George Slocumb, engineer at Hauck's mill, fell into the cistern and drowned before assistance could reach him.

On the night of December 15, 1868, the Pacific House burned. This was regarded as one of the most expensive conflagrations up to that time.

* * *

On Sunday morning, January 23, 1870, at about 4 o'clock, fire destroyed a brick row of buildings on the west side of Second street, near a bridge which then spanned Blacksnake creek. All the inmates, with the exception of one young man, who was in an inebriated condition, in a room of a resort known as the "Rosebud," made their escape, and his body was afterward recovered, burned to a cinder. When the firemen had finished their work, and were preparing to leave, they were called back by the discovery of the remains of this victim. While engaged in removing debris, a wall fell, covering Frank Y. Heill, Arthur Colburn, Julius Sidekum, Blass Argus, Julius Gishe, all firemen, and John W. Clifford, a colored man. All were rescued, after heroic work, except Clifford, who was killed by the falling wall. Blass Argus, a member of the Hook and Ladder company, was so severely injured that he soon expired.

* * *

Perhaps the most disastrous storm in the history of St. Joseph occurred on the night of July 13, 1871. The weather had been sultry and threatening all day, but the storm did not built until at about 9 o'clock at night. Francis Street Methodist church was struck by lightning and badly damaged. The Pacific House roof was removed, the Everett, the Neeley, the Webster and the Fourth Street Colored schools were unroofed. The convent of the Sacred Heart lost a portion of its roof, as also did St. Patrick's school on South Twelfth street. The estimated damages to property were over $150,000. No lives were lost in the city, though lumber and debris of all descriptions were flying about and the people panic-stricken. A sad affair occurred in the country. At the residence of James Keiger, five miles east of the city, were a number of people, among the guests being Mrs. Lucy Lovell and her two little children. When the storm was at its height Mrs. Lovell, who was with her babes in an upper story, brought them down and placed them in the bed of Mr. and Mrs. Keiger. While kneeling in prayer for their safety a bolt of lightning laid the loving mother low. Penetrating into the hallway, the same bolt struck and killed Harry R. Blakemore of St. Joseph, who was also a guest at Mr. Keiger's.

* * *

On the night of September 3, 1873, a tornado destroyed the exposition buildings that were in the course of construction near the present site of the K. C., St. J. & C. B. shops. Other serious damage was also done.

* * *

On Sunday, July 23, 1876, a boat containing a party of pleasure-seekers, capsized in Lake Contrary and five girls were drowned.

The party was in charge of Otto Gross. Beside himself, seated in the boat were Misses Clara Kratt, Rosa Muench, Sophia Seitz, Mathilde Zimmer and Mathilde Gross, the daughter of Mr. Gross. A distance of about three miles had been traversed, and when returning, and when within less than a hundred yards from the shore which they had left, little Clara Kratt and Cora Muench, who occupied the seat in the rear of the frail craft, began to reach out and gather water lilies, causing the skiff to dip one side. This was continued until the boat capsized, and in an instant the six unfortunate persons were struggling in twelve feet of water. Mr. Gross succeeded in reaching each of the girls and placed their hands on the boat, but in their desperate efforts to regain a position in the boat it was again overturned and once more they were plunged under the treacherous waves. Mr. Gross again seized his child and attempted to save her, at least. With his burden he was making good progress, when another one of the girls seized him about the neck. This action placed him in such a position that all hope was gone, and he was compelled to free himself from both in order to save his own life. He made for the shore, but ere he reached it he was taken with cramps, and but for the timely arrival of a man in a skiff, he, too, would have drowned. The bodies were all recovered. The body of Miss Zimmer was buried from the residence of her father on the following afternoon. The funeral of the others was an impressive affair. The fire department's hook and ladder truck was improvised into a hearse, which was draped in white and black crape, and beautifully ornamented with flowers and evergreens. The procession was formed in front of Mr. Kratt's residence on Messanie street, where the first coffin was placed in position. Each house of mourning was visited in turn, and the four coffins placed side by side. The hearse was drawn by four white horses. The cortege then took its line of march to Ashland cemetery, preceded by Rosenblatt's brass band. Then came the hearse, and following this was the band wagon in which were seated a number of the girls who comprised the lake party when their companions lost their lives, each bearing in her hands a wreath of flowers. There were over 150 carriages and buggies containing sorrowing relatives and friends.

* * *

The Odd Fellow building at Fifth and Felix and the furniture store of Louis Hax, which joined it on the south, were burned on the night of January 29, 1879. The Odd Fellow building was occupied by J. W. Bailey & Co., with an extensive dry goods store. The entire loss was about $200,000. The site of these buildings is now covered by the block occupied by Townsend, Wyatt & Wall and the Louis Hax Furniture Company. The burned buildings faced Fifth street.

* * *

A grewsome accident occurred on the night of May 23, 1881. A negro resort was kept by George Cunnigan on the south side of Edmond street, between Sixth and Seventh streets, in a building owned by Dr. Wm. Leach. The basement of this building was divided into two parts, one part being used in connection with the resort and the other for the storage of an illuminant known as Danforth's fluid. On the night mentioned there were about twenty-five negroes in the saloon, playing cards and enjoying themselves. There was to be a rehearsal of a prospective minstrel troupe in the basement, and at about 8:30 John Hicks, one of the artists, went below stairs to light up the basement room. Forty barrels of the fluid had been stored in the adjoining basement room that day, and both rooms were filled with the fumes of the highly inflammable fluid. When Hicks struck a match an explosion occurred which was heard throughout the city and the shock of which was felt for quite a distance. The building was wrecked. Hicks, Billy Williams and the bartender, Charles Dunlap, who weighed 320 pounds, were killed. Fourteen negroes, congregated about the place, were more or less seriously injured, and considerable damage was done to neighboring property by the force of the explosion.

* * *

On the night of April 3, 1885, during a severe thunder storm, lightning struck the magazine of the Hazard Powder Company, located on Prospect Hill. The explosion that followed shattered many windows in the business district, the loss on plate glass having footed up over $2,000.

* * *

The following are the dates of some of the famous fires since 1880: Hannibal & St. Joseph elevator, Sixth and Lafayette streets, January 13, 1883; tank of Standard Oil Company, September 10, 1883; court house, March 28, 1885; C. D. Smith's wholesale grocery house, October 20, 1885; New Era Exposition, September 15, 1889; James Casey's sale stables, Fourth and Messanie streets, November 10, 1889; Hax furniture factory, Seventh and Angelique streets, December 13, 1890; Kennard Grocery Company, Fourth and Angelique streets, March 1, 1891; Gregg's elevator, September 23, 1891; Wyeth's hardware house, Third street, near Felix street, November 2, 1891; Union street car barns, November 30, 1891; J. B. Brady & Co., carpets, January 13, 1892; R. K. Allen's planing mill, Second and Francis, April 6, 1892.

Center block and Commercial block, at Sixth and Edmond streets, burned September 25, 1893. Center block was totally destroyed. It was occupied by the Townsend, Wyatt & Emery Dry Goods Company. North of it stood the Hoagland building, occupied by the Regnier & Shoup Crockery Company. This building and contents were also destroyed. The Commercial block, opposite Center block was partially destroyed. The Carbry block, on the east was also damaged. The total loss was over half a million dollars. The fire started on the top floor of the Townsend, Wyatt & Emery Company's store, at about 9 o'clock in the morning, and spread rapidly. There was a strong breeze and the entire business portion of the city was in danger. The department could make no headway with the fire, and it was far into the afternoon before they got it under control. The burned buildings have been replaced, though the present Center block is not so high by one story as was the original.

The Bennett Lumber Company's stock, on Middleton street and Lincoln school, burned July 24, 1894. Meierhoffer's cooper shop, South Fifth street, was totally destroyed August 27, 1894. There was a fire at Joseph Tullar's livery stable in which eight horses perished November 24, 1894. The Union Depot burned on the night of February 9, 1895. The St. Joseph pump factory, on Lake boulevard, burned May 13, 1895.

The old freight house of the Hannibal & St. Joseph railroad, located at Seventh and Olive streets, used by the Missouri Pacific road, was destroyed on Saturday morning, November 24, 1895. The office was the only portion of the building saved. This building was one of the landmarks of St. Joseph, having been built by the Hannibal & St. Joseph road in 1860.

Saturday night, February 22, 1896, the extensive feed stables and livery barn of Ducate & Grantham, on Edmond street, between Seventh and Eighth, were destroyed by fire, entailing a loss of nearly $50,000. Sixty horses and many fine carriages were burned.

The building at the corner of Ninth and Francis streets, owned by the Burnes Estate, was burned in February 1898, with a loss of $20,000, and was replaced by the King Hill building.

· The old Pinger packing house, Jules and Levee streets, was burned December 5, 1899.

On March 17, 1901, the shoe factory of Noyes, Norman & Co. burned with a loss of $75,000. Two girls, Miss Louise Blondeaü and Miss Dora Bates, were burned to death, and Miss Florence Terry, Mrs. Addie Berry and Miss Anna Gatewood were injured. The factory has been rebuilt.

Gregg Brothers' elevator, at Eighth and Oak streets, burned in October, 1902; loss, $26,000.

The Hudnut Hominy mills at Fifth and Monterey streets, burned in November, 1902; loss, $60,000. The mills were rebuilt and were again destroyed by fire January 16, 1915; loss about $100,000.

On December 23, 1902, the building occupied by G. W. Chase & Sons' candy factory, on Second street, near Felix, was burned. Misses Anna May Dakan, Rosa M. Kraus, Mattie E. Leslie, Sophia L. Mintos and Laura Crawford, employes, were injured. Miss Emma Gleich jumped from a second-story window, but was not hurt. The building was soon restored.

The most costly fire in recent years was that which destroyed a portion of the Hammond Packing Company's plant on Sunday, July 5, 1903. The loss was about $2,000,000. The plant was rebuilt and opened for business on May 20, 1904. It is not positively known that there were any fatalities, but one life is supposed to have been lost.

Following is a list of the more important fires in St. Joseph in recent years:

September 21, 1904, South Park Elevator, $42,625; May 5, 1905, Roberts Parker Mercantile Company, $192,540; September 15, 1905, Hax-Smith Furniture Company, $150,000; December 3, 1906, Nate Block Clothing Store, $47,650; January 29, 1912, I. Rothbaum Clothing Company Department Store, $24,500; December 4, 1912, American Sash & Door Co., $30,000; February 7, 1913, Jet White Laundry Company, $28,000; January 16, 1915, American Hominy Mill Company, $75,000; January 16, 1915, St. Joseph Transfer Company, $25,000; July 25, 1915, C. H. Nold Lumber Company, $45,000; August 15, 1907, Viles & Robinson Packing Plant, $50,000; September 17, 1908, Swift & Company Packing Plant; December 27, 1908, Morris & Co. Packing Plant, $125,000; January 4, 1912, Union Rendering Works, $10,000; July 17, 1915, Morris & Co. Packing Plant, $50,000.

CHAPTER XXV.

THE FAIRS OF FORMER DAYS—THE FIRST EFFORT, WHEN THE GROUNDS WERE LOCATED ON NORTH ELEVENTH STREET—THE FAIRS AT THE EAST END OF FREDERICK AVENUE—THE ELABORATE EFFORT ON LOWER SIXTH STREET—THE INTERSTATE EXPOSITION AT FOWLER'S GROVE—THE LIGHTS AND SHADOWS OF THE NEW ERA EXPOSITION—VARIOUS EFFORTS AT THE PRESENT FAIR GROUNDS.

Among the pioneers of Buchanan County were many men of intelligence, who early realized the importance of competitive exhibitions of native products in advancing the spirit of enterprise and consequent improvement of all that pertains to excellence in agricultural, mechanical and domestic pursuits. In 1854 a Fair association was formed with General Robert Wilson (afterward United States senator) as president, William M. Irvine as vice-president, Albe M. Saxton as treasurer, and Wellington A. Cunningham as secretary. Grounds were secured in what is now the northern part of the city, being on Eleventh street, south of Grand avenue, but what was then in the country. This fair was the first, and therefore a great event for the entire Platte country. Seven hundred dollars worth of gold and silver plate premiums were offered, and the world was invited to compete. September 19, 20 and 21, 1854, were the days, and *The Gazette* of September 20 says:

"Yesterday was a proud day for our county. It was the first day of the first agricultural fair ever held in the county. There was a large concourse of ladies and gentlemen present. Great interest was manifested. The St. Joseph band was there and added much to the interest of the occasion. Mr. Silas Woodson delivered a very able and eloquent address on the subject of agriculture, and, though he had but little time for preparation, he did himself and the subject great credit."

There were no races, but there was lively competition for premiums on live stock and the products of the housewife and the artisan, as will be seen by the following excerpt from the list of awards:

"Best specimen mixed jeans, a beautiful article—premium to Mrs. J. P. Bryan of Buchanan.

"Plaid linsey—premium to same lady, $2.

"White linsey—premium to William Gartin of Buchanan, $2.

"Woolen blankets, premium to Mrs. P. J. Bryan, Buchanan, $5.

"Satinet—premium to N. Buel of Buchanan, $5.

"Cotton quilt—premium to Mrs. Rosana Porter of Buchanan, $10."

There were premiums for needlework, knitting, etc. Also for the best two-horse wagon, the best set of chairs and sofa manufactured at home, best sets of harness, best saddles, best tinware, best flour, best buggy, best chickens, best butter, best fruits, vegetables, best jellies and preserves. In fact, it was a genuine old-fashioned fair, which was well attended and which pleased the people so well that it was repeated for six years in succession, the last time in the autumn of 1860.

* * *

The civil war put an end to fairs and no effort was made to revive them until July of 1867, when the St. Joseph Agricultural and Mechanical Association was organized with General Robert Wilson as president, Thos. B. Weakley as vice-president, Albe M. Saxton as treasurer and Charles B. France as secretary. The capital stock was $15,000, divided into shares of $100 each, and the money was promptly subscribed. As an incidental evidence of the political condition of those times it may be mentioned that the records of this association state that at the meeting held August 6, 1868, the oath of loyalty was signed by all the directors, which oath was filed in the office of the county clerk. A twenty-acre tract, at the head of Frederick avenue, on which had formerly been located a rope walk, was purchased from Bassett & Ensworth for $400 an acre. The fair was held four days, beginning October 29, 1867, and was pronounced a success. The association continued with various fortunes until the end of 1871, its last fair being held in December of that year. The grounds had been mortgaged to the Life Association of America and were sold under the deed of trust at the request of the stockholders. Goldsmith Maid trotted a mile in 2:18¼ on the last day of the fair.

* * *

No fairs were held at St. Joseph during 1872, but in 1873 a grand effort was made. It was no longer a plain fair, but an exposition. An association was formed with Captain George Lyon as president, I. G. Kappner as treasurer and Edward Fleischer as secretary and general superintendent. Grounds were leased southwest of the city limits, and elaborate buildings erected. Every indication pointed to success when an unexpected calamity befell. On the night of September 3, 1873, a tornado struck the exposition grounds, demolishing the main buildings and seriously damaging the art and power halls. The contractor, George Herbst, was financially ruined by the catastrophe. The demolished buildings were promptly reconstructed and the exposition opened on the appointed day, September 29.

The receipts of the week were over $28,000, and but for the tornado, there would have been a handsome net financial result. In 1874 a new corporation was formed, assuming the debts on the buildings. The officers of this association were: James N. Burnes, president; George H. Hall, vice-president; George Lyon, superintendent and manager; H. R. W. Hartwig, treasurer, and J. M.

Varnum, secretary. The exposition opened September 7, 1874, closing September 12, and the receipts were $22,500. There was a half-mile track at these grounds and there was good racing at each fair.

In 1875, with Colonel Burnes as president and J. T. Imbrie as secretary, the receipts were $20,000. The fourth exposition opened September 25, 1876, with Captain Lyon as president and J. T. Imbrie as secretary. A great feature of the exposition during its last three years was the old settlers' meeting. The association was dissolved at the close of the effort of 1877.

* * *

In 1878 Buchanan County had no fair. However, it was not in the nature of things that this should continue long. In August of 1879 the St. Joseph Exposition Association was organized with a capital stock of $12,000, divided into 1,200 shares of $10 each. The incorporators were Samuel M. Nave, John Abell, Edward Kuechle, L. G. Munger and Dr. J. M. D. France. The first officers were: Samuel M. Nave, president; H. R. W. Hartwig, vice-president; Edward J. Kuechle, treasurer, and J. T. Imbrie, secretary. A tract at the foot of Eleventh street and extending west toward Sixth, known as Fowler's grove, was leased for a term of ten years and suitable buildings and a race track were at once constructed. The grounds were accessible by two street car lines and also by railroad trains.

The first fair commenced Monday September 29, 1879, and continued for a week. Though it rained every day, the venture was considered a success by its projectors and from that time until the end of the season in 1888 a fair was held each year, generally during the first part of September. Major Hartwig succeeded Mr. Nave as president; the late Charles F. Ernst succeeded Mr. Imbrie as secretary in 1881 and continued as such until the association dissolved.

* * *

Early in 1889, when St. Joseph was proud with prosperity, when the spirit of enterprise was upon the people, and when nothing was too big to undertake, it was decided to have an exposition, the magnitude and novelty of which would overshadow not only all previous efforts at home, but elsewhere in the West. Sioux City had astonished the world with a corn palace, Denver with a mineral palace, Fort Worth, Texas, with a grass palace, and Ottumwa, Iowa, with a coal palace, but St. Joseph was to eclipse all of these with a New Era exposition.

The genius of this undertaking was H. D. Perkey, who had come here during the previous summer and who had but recently established steel car works at Brookdale. Mr. Perkey had been prominently connected with the Mineral Palace at Denver and was therefore in a position to take the leadership of this movement. On April 4, 1889, the National Railway, Electric and Industrial Exposition Association was formed, with a capital stock of one million dollars. The association was to continue for one year and was incorporated under the laws of Colorado, because these laws did not require so large a proportion of the capital stock to be paid up as the laws of Missouri. It was to have a national scope and offices were to be established in every state capital. The incorporators were G. J. Englehart, John S. Lemon, R. E. Turner, C. B. France, A. M. Saxton, John Donovan, Jr., R. L. McDonald, D. M. Steele, George W. Samuels, Louis Hax, Wm. E. Hosea, D. D. Burnes, H. R. W. Hartwig, S. C. Woodson, F. M. Posegate, T. F. Van Natta, S. A. Walker, A. M. Dougherty, W. B. Smith, Harry Keene, J. Francis Smith, R. T. Davis and Winslow Judson. The directors were John S. Emery, Chas. A. Shoup, W. J. Hobson, Herschel Bartlett, Robert Winning, J. C. Bonnell and H. D. Perkey.

A large tract of land east of the city, beyond Wyatt Park, and surrounding the Steel Car Company's plant, was secured and prepared during the summer. The car company had a building 80x960 feet, which was used as a shop. The western portion of this building, which was two stories in height, was made the main hall of the exposition. The ground were dotted with beautiful pavilions, two score in number, of quaint architecture. "Korn is King" was the motto of the enterprise, and this idea was carried into every deco- ration. The pavilions and buildings were decked with cereals in various colorings and design. The effect was entrancing, especially at night, when the grounds were fully illuminated with electric lights. The most admired of the pavilions were the "Ladies' Palace of Delights," the "Reporters' Lodge," "Pomona's Pavilion," "Cupid's Bower," "Pocahontas," "Mondamin," and "Horticultural Hall." Aside from the buildings there were artificial lakes, waterfalls, an old grist mill and other picturesque novelties. The architectural triumph, however, was the amphitheater, which had a seating capacity of eleven thousand and an arena of two acres.

The exposition opened on September 3, 1889, and continued to October 3. Bach's band, a famous musical organization of Milwaukee, was engaged for two concerts daily in the amphitheater. Capt. Jack Crawford, the "poet scout," was director of entertainments in the arena, and he had, beside a band of cowboys, several hundred Apache Indians. General Russel A. Alger of Michigan formally opened the exposition. Hon. Jeremiah Rusk, secretary of agriculture, spoke in the amphitheater on September 18th, and on September 23d Governor Larrabee of Iowa and Governor Francis of Missouri spoke there also.

The attendance was not what it should have been. If the time had been ten days instead of one month the effort might have met with better reward. Mr. Perkey doubtless had some good ideas, but they did not fit this case, and there were, consequently, disappointments. However, the difficulties might have been overcome had not an irreparable disaster visited the exposition. On Sunday night, September 15, at about 9 o'clock, just as the crowds were leaving the grounds, flames burst from the roof of the main building. The fire was beyond control from the start and the entire building, with all of its contents, excepting two pianos and a carriage in which

General Lafayette had toured Virginia, were destroyed. The loss was $193,000, upon which there was only $50,000 insurance. One life was lost. Capt. John Foster, a guard, who had quarters in the building, near where the fire broke out, was burned to death. The fire is supposed to have originated from defective wiring. At a meeting of the board of trade on the following day it was decided to at once rebuild Machinery Hall, but this was not done. The exposition continued until October 3, and then there was a benefit week for the employes.

The buildings stood until the following year and were gradually removed. There is nothing left to mark the location of the brilliant but ill-fated New Era Exposition, and it lives today only as a painful memory with those who backed it heavily.

* * *

There was no race track connected with the New Era Exposition, but this class of sport was provided by the Lake Shore Company. A half-mile track was built at Lake Contrary and a grandstand with a seating capacity of 3,000 was erected. Mayor H. R. W. Hartwig was president of the company and Capt. Charles F. Ernst secretary. The first meeting was held September 17, 18, 19 and 20, 1889. Several meetings were subsequently held, but the ventures were not profitable.

* * *

During the years 1890 and 1891 there were no fairs in St. Joseph. In the summer of 1892 the St. Joseph Fair Association was formed, with John S. Brittain as president and Homer J. Kline as secretary. The capital stock was $50,000. It was the era of fast harness horses and odd-shaped tracks and people excited over the performances of Nancy Hanks, Martha Wilkes and the other record-breakers. The association catered to the popular enthusiasm by building a mile track and offering purses of $1,000 and $500 to attract the best horses. Although a main hall was built, the fair was subordinated to the horse-race. Nancy Hanks and Martha Wilkes were both secured for exhibition work, and the best stables in the country were represented in the general entries. September 13, 14, 15, 16 and 17 were the days. The weather was perfect, the attendance was large and the turf performances were of a high character. On the first day Jim Wilkes won the 3-minute trot, $1,000 purse, in three straight heats, his best time being 2:22½. John R. Gentry won the 3:35 pace, $500 purse, in three straight heats, his best time being 2.19½. On the second day Lobasco, a magnificent horse, the property of James Ladd of Beatrice, Neb., won the free-for-all trot, $1,000. Four heats were trotted and Lobasco's best time was 2:10¾. He was driven by McHenry, and broke a great record by trotting the fastest mile heat that had been done up to that time by a stallion in a harness. On the third day, Thursday, seventy-five thousand people witnessed Hancy Hanks' effort to break her record of 2:07. The wind was a trifle too high, however, and the brave little mare did not triumph, but she made the mile in 2:07½, which was considered good enough by the crowd, and the enthusiasm was unbounded, both Nancy and her driver, Bud Doble, being covered with floral tributes. The next day Martha Wilkes went against her record of 2:08, but she, too, failed, making the mile in 2:09½. This effort was none the less appreciated by the immense crowd, however, and the floral decorations were as profuse as those that fell to Nancy Hanks. The last day was given up to unfinished harness races and jockey efforts. The association paid every obligation and was a goodly sum ahead.

In 1893 the weather was bad and the World's Fair had drained the purses, so that there was some loss connected with the fair. The association was officered as during its first effort. In 1894, with John S. Brittain as president and Matt F. Myers as secretary, a third effort was made with indifferent success. The fourth fair, with John S. Brittain as president and John Combe as secretary, was a financial success. In 1896, with James N. Burnes, Jr., as president and John Combe as secretary, the attendance was small, owing to the weather and other conditions. The association then dissolved. The grounds and buildings reverted to the owners, from whom they had been leased.

Race meetings were managed after that by W. T. Van Brunt and Palmer Clark. On October 14, 1897, Joe Patchen went a mile in 2:03 and Star Pointer covered the distance in 2:02. In 1897 and 1898 Messrs. Van Brunt and Clark successfully managed "old-fashioned fairs."

* * *

In 1899 the street railway company erected permanent exposition buildings at Lake Contrary, and for about three years held annual events there, generally in September.

* * *

In the spring of 1902 the St. Joseph Horse Show Association was formed by William E. Spratt, Morris W. Steiner, Jesse I. Roberts and others. The first show was held in August of that year at the baseball park on South Sixth street, and the second was held in July, 1903, in an especially constructed tent, and was reckoned one of the most successful events of the kind ever attempted in St. Joseph.

* * *

In 1906 the live stock interests held a stock show in South St. Joseph. It became one of the leading shows of the country, and continued until the close of the year 1911.

The grounds at Lake Contrary then attracted the attention of those interested in fall festivities. The Old Fashioned Fair, conduced by a number of public-spirited business men, was held there in 1913-14.

CHAPTER XXVI.

INDUSTRIES OF THE PAST AND WHAT SOME OF THEM·
HAVE LED TO IN THE PRESENT—HEMP RAISING,
MILLING AND PORK PACKING—BREWERIES—THE
FIRST FOUNDRY—FURNITURE FACTORIES—THE NA-
TIVE LUMBER INDUSTRY — DISTILLERIES — THE
STARCH FACTORY—THE STOVE WORKS, TOBACCO
FACTORY AND STEEL CAR WORKS—OTHER INDUS-
TRIES THAT FLOURISHED AND FADED—THE OLD-
TIME HOTELS OF ST. JOSEPH.

In reviewing the industries of the past it will not be improper
to speak of hemp first, because of the prominence of this product in
the early days. Hemp was the great staple before the war. Dr.
Silas McDonald of St. Joseph claims the distinction of having produced the first crop of hemp in the Platte Purchase. In 1840 he
procured seed from Clay County, and he sold the yield to Charles A.
Perry, who was then located at Weston, at $80 per ton. Nothing
raised in the country, either before its introduction or since its
abandonment, paid so well as hemp. The average price for years
was $100 per ton, and the average yield per acre 800 pounds. Aside
from the remunerative character of the crop, many advantages contributed to its popularity. Being invariably cut before it went to
seed, it did not, as with other crops, impoverish the soil; indeed,
it was a generally admitted fact that from the decomposition of the
foliage, old hemp land, instead of deteriorating in quality from constant cropping, steadily improved, and 1,000 pounds to the·acre on
such lands was no uncommon yield. Much of the hemp was manufactured into rope, but the most of it was shipped in bales to St.
Louis and Louisville. Hemp breaking was hard work and the abolition of slavery made it difficult to secure labor for this. Hemp
rope was formerly used as ties for cotton bales and for making
sails for ships. The invention of the hoop-iron cotton tie, the sub-
stitution of steam for sails on vessels and the introduction of
cheaper fibers for rope and twine, took hemp from the head of the
list of our staples.

* * *

Milling was the pioneer industry, and the primitive mill generally formed the nucleus of a settlement. The early mills of Buchanan County were located along the streams, water furnishing
the motive power. Going to mill in those days, when there were no
roads, no bridges, no ferries, and scarcely any convenience for traveling, was no small task, where so many streams were to be crossed,
and such a trip was often attended with great danger when the
streams were swollen. Generally the grain was packed on horses

to the mill. In cases where the mill was operated by horse power, each patron furnished his own power.

In 1838, Harrison Whetson built a mill on Platte River in Platte Township and operated it until 1843, when it was bought by John Bretz, who held it until it was consumed by fire on February 28, 1845. It was at once rebuilt on the opposite side of the river in Jackson Township. In 1857 the mill passed into the hands of William M. Matney. In 1867 it was destroyed by fire and rebuilt, and still stands, being operated yet by Mr. Matney and known as Matney's mill.

It is generally conceded that the first mill in Crawford Township was Clowser's, operated by John Clowser. The site of this mill was two miles east of Halleck. It was destroyed by a great freshet in 1858. Dr. Silas McDonald erected the first steam mill in the township, which has long since passed out of existence. Edward M. Davidson also built a steam saw and grist mill, which was destroyed by fire in 1868, after having been operated for seventeen years. In 1856 Brown & McClanahan built a steam saw mill north of Halleck. This was converted into a grist mill by Daniel Clowser, and in 1865 passed to Faucett & Ferrill, who made a famous flouring mill of it. It was destroyed by fire in 1881. Nathan Turner built a mill in 1838 in the same neighborhood, but it was not successful.

Stephen Field built the first mill in Bloomington Township in 1838. It stood three miles from DeKalb and was operated by horsepower. Later on John T. Martin built a water-power mill on Sugar Creek, which was afterward converted into a steam mill and operated by Phillip Guerner, who also carded wool. The building is still in existence. In 1860 J. H. and B. Sampson erected a mill on Contrary Creek, two miles northeast of DeKalb. A saw mill was connected therewith.

The first mill in Rush Township was built by Flannery & Son on Lost Creek, which stream supplied the power. Nothing remains of this mill, nor of a small cornmill and distillery operated during the same period of Sylvester Hays, better known in those days as "Boss." M. H. and S. F. Floyd built a good steam mill at Rushville in 1868, which burned in 1873. The McFarland mill at Rushville was built in 1875.

Agency Township had a mill as early as 1838. It was located two miles above Agency Ford, on Platte River, and was known as Dixon's mill, its builders being Benjamin and James Dixon and James Gilmore. It ceased to exist many years ago. In 1864 Smith Brothers built a mill at Agency, which afterwards passed into the hands of Boone & Yates,, and is still in operation. V. C. Cooley built a mill on Platte River, three miles southeast of Agency, which stood in 1880, but has since disappeared.

Washington Township had a mill on Contrary Creek in 1840, owned by Waymire & Gilmore, of which nothing remains. Isaac Waymire owned a mill on One Hundred and Two River in the early days, where Corby's mill now stands. The old Campbell mill on Platte River was purchased by Charles Czech in 1877 and remodeled. The proprietor failed and the mill was afterwards destroyed by fire. Corby's mill, at the crossing of One Hundred and Two River, east of the city, is the only one of the old water mills that remains as it was built. It was erected in 1852 by the late John Corby at a heavy expense. It had been an early ambition with Mr. Corby to be the owner of a good mill, such as he had seen in Ireland when a lad, where the prosperous miller was a man of high reputation in the community. When Mr. Corby had accumulated a large fortune in other lines he set about to realize the dream of his youth. The mill was the best of its kind in the West, but it never paid, owing to its location and distance from the city. Dr. Keedy built a mill south of the city in the earliest days, mention of which is made in a previous chapter.

Joseph Robidoux built a water mill on Blacksnake in 1841, the timbers of which are yet to be seen near the mouth of Blacksnake sewer. Creal & Wildbahn owned the mill afterwards. James Cargill built a steam flouring mill near the site of the Central Medical College, north of the custom house, late in the forties, which was burned after the war. Dillon's saw mill, built in 1855, was located on Blacksnake Creek, near the present site of the City Workhouse. John Fairclough built the Star mills at Second and Francis streets in 1864; the plant was burned in 1872. The Excelsior mills, at Second and Franklin streets, were built in 1865 by Hauck Bros. Northcutt & Anthony built the City mills, near Third and Louis streets, in 1860. Wm. Ridenbaugh and I. Van Riley operated them in 1868. In 1869 R. T. Davis purchased Mr. Ridenbaugh's interests and afterwards became sole proprietor. In 1882-83 Mr. Davis and Robert H. Faucett built what is now the Davis mill at Second and Edmond streets. At the completion of this plant the City mills were abandoned. The Faucett mill, at Seventh and Olive streets, now operated by the R. H. Faucett Mill Company, was built on a small scale by Captain F. B. Kercheval in 1867-68. In 1881 it was known as the Eagle mill. In 1888 it was remodeled and amplified to its present capacity. The mill at Tenth and Jackson streets was built in 1883 and was first called the Model mill. It was afterwards operated by the St. Joseph Milling Company. In 1890-94 Stephen J. Burns and others operated on oatmeal and hominy mill in what was formerly the Buell woolen mill, on Third street, north of Michel.

* * *

The Buell woolen mills, above referred to, were started in 1860 by Norman Buell and George Buell, who operated a woolen factory on North Third street. Buell & Dixon operated a flouring mill and woolen factory on Second street, between Isadore and Antoine. The same firm operated a general store at the corner of Second and Antoine streets. Norman Buell was the father of George Buell, later head of the woolen mills. The mills on Third street were enlarged and operated until 1882, when they were abandoned for the large establishment at the foot of Eleventh street, which was occupied in 1883.

* * *

Pork packing was a prominent industry in St. Joseph as early as 1846, when John Corby was engaged in the business. Fotheringham's city directory for 1861 shows the following pork packers: Carter Hughes & Co., Third street; James Hamilton, Jr., Edmond street, between Third and Fourth streets; Pinger & Hauck, Grand avenue. The latter firm also manufactured soap and candles. The firm was composed of David Pinger and Jacob Hauck. Captain Posegate's directory of 1875 shows the following: Hax & Bro. (Fred and John P.), Fourth and Mary streets; Krug & Hax, Fourth and Monterey; D. Pinger & Co., Jule and Levee streets, and the Valley Packing Company. In 1878 the E. O. Smith Packing Company was in operation in the building afterwards used for the glucose works. Connett Brothers built a house east of the Smith plant in 1881, and operated it for about ten years. Hax Brothers retired from business in 1890.

At the present time there are six meat packing houses in operation—two in St. Joseph and five at the stockyards south of the city. Those operated in the city are by the Krug Packing Company and Hoefer Packing Company, the latter being the old Pinger plant, near the mouth of the Blacksnake. At the stockyards there are five plants, two of which, those of Swift & Company and Nelson Morris, compare with the most extensive in the country. Two others are operated by the Hammond Packing Company, and the fifth by Viles & Robbins.

The development of St. Joseph as a live stock market and meat packing center is due mainly to the efforts of John Donovan, Jr. Prior to 1887 the Hannibal & St. Joseph Railroad Company had maintained stockyards on Walnut street, between Sixth and Eleventh streets. In that year the St. Joseph Stockyards Company was organized by C. B. France, Samuel M. Nave, Henry Krug, Jr., E. Lindsay, John Donovan, Jr., J. D. McNeely, M. A. Lowe and C. M. Carter. There were 440 acres in the original tract and seventy-two acres were subsequently acquired. Of this about eighty acres have been given as bonuses to packers who have erected plants. In 1888 the company erected a pork packing plant, which was leased to Allerton & Co., of Chicago. In 1890 the company erected the beef packing plant and leased it to the Anchor Packing Company. About three years after the yards had been established the company was reorganized as the St. Joseph Stockyards and Terminal Company and the capital stock was increased to $1,000,000. In 1892 the company built a third house, which was leased to the Moran Packing Company.

The Moran company failed in 1895, and the packing plant became a subject of litigation for over two years, when possession was regained by the stockyards company. In the meantime the corporation had encountered obstacles that could not be surmounted, and the yards went into the hands of receivers. John Donovan, Jr., and R. R. Conklin were appointed receivers, and as soon as the affairs of the company could be straightened out to some extent the property was sold at receiver's sale and purchased by the Jarvis-Conklin Mortgage and Trust Company for the bondholders.

The company was reorganized with a capital of $500,000, and again assumed the old name of the St. Joseph Stockyards Company. Mr. Donovan induced Swift and Company, of Chicago, to operate the Moran plant. This deal also resulted in Swift and Company purchasing a majority of the stock in the St. Joseph Stockyards Company on January 18, 1897.

In June, 1897, Nelson Morris & Co. purchased a large block of the stock in the St. Joseph Stockyards Company, and thus became interested with Swift and Company and the other packers in improving the capacity of the yards and the local market. Two months later both Swift and Company and Nelson Morris & Co. began the erection of the two largest plants at the stockyards, both of which were completed and opened for business the early part of April, 1898. The Hammond Packing Company leased the Moran house when Swift and Company vacated it, and subsequently leased the Anchor house. In 1900 the Hammonds completed the construction of the third large plant.

The people of St. Joseph celebrated the expansion of the live stock and packing industries in a jubilee, which continued for three days, May 11, 12 and 13, 1898, and which attracted thousands of people.

Since then the stockyards have been placed upon a strictly modern, high-grade basis, a bank has been organized, and a populous suburb has grown up. A live-stock exchange has been built at a cost of $100,000, and various allied industries have grown up.

* * *

Joseph Kuechle, long dead, was the pioneer brewer of St. Joseph. He had learned his art in Germany, and after working at Louisville, Ky., came to St. Joseph, arriving here per steamboat in the summer of 1849. He purchased the ground from Capt. F. W. Smith and built his brewery on the site of the ruins of what was last known as the St. Joseph brewery, on Charles, between Seventh and Eighth streets. Water for beer and also for drainage are essential to breweries, and there being neither waterworks nor sewerage, the early brewers located along the streams. Smith's branch was a lively creek in those days, flowing from the northeastern hills swiftly to the river. Kuechle's brewery was located on this stream and the pioneer brewer was fortunate in finding an inexhaustible spring of pure water on his premises. This spring still exists and is walled up in the ruins of the dismantled brewery. After Mr. Kuechle's death the plant was operated by his heirs until the formation of the St. Joseph Brewing Company, which leased the plant for some years and abandoned it in 1894. The older buildings were condemned two years afterward and torn down. The malting house and some of the others still remain, and there are several cellars in good preservation.

Henry Nunning was the second brewer. He came from La Porte, Ind., in 1854, and established himself at Eleventh and Faraon streets, also near Smith's branch. After a time business outgrew the old establishment and he built a modern brewery on Faraon street, near Fifteenth. This plant is now operated under lease by the St. Joseph Brewing Company.

In 1858 X. Aniser, Joseph Aniser and Wm. Ost built a brewery on Frederick avenue, near Thirteenth street. During the early part of the rebellion it was operated by D. W. Fritzlein, who was killed by a soldier near Wathena. Fitzlein's widow continued the business for some time. Later the plant was leased by Jacob Wingerter, but it has not been used as a brewery for many years, a carriage factory being located in the building now.

In 1859 Max & Goetz started the City brewery at Sixth and Albemarle streets. This is now one of the largest breweries in the West, having been developed by Michael K. Goetz and his sons. It is now known as the M. K. Goetz Brewing Company.

Frederick W. Islaub had a brewery on Michel street, between Main and Water streets, in 1858-60, and Peter Walter had a brewery and garden at the southwest corner of Fourth and Edmond streets during the same period. Louis Koerner, who had been Walter's brewer, started in business for himself on Main street, near Faraon, late in the sixties as a malster. Afterward he made beer and sold it by the measure at the brewery. Duemcke & Hund subsequently used his buildings as bottling works and the site is now occupied by the Chicago Great Western freight depot.

In 1865 Andreas Ohnesorg and Francis Eger formed a partnership and built the New Ulm brewery. Mr. Ohnesorg had been operating a weiss-beer brewery and garden on the north side of Felix street, near Eighth, adjoining the ground now occupied by the Hughes building. These parties also owned the grounds that were afterward known as New Ulm Park, though the park was developed by Louis Streckebein, who conducted it for sixteen years. The brewery was located on the hill east of the park and stood until 1890, when it was destroyed by fire. The cellars are still intact. It was a modern brewery in its day, representing an expenditure of $80,-000, and was operated by Ohnesorg & Eger until 1876, when it was leased to Rosemund & Schaefer, who continued it until about 1881, when it was abandoned. The property now belongs to Mrs. Margaret Burnside.

Contemporaneous with the early history of the New Ulm brewery was an effort on the part of the firm of Koehler & Diedrich, two young Germans, who had come from Palmyra, Mo., to operate an ale brewery here. They built a cellar and a plant east of Third near Louis street, costing nearly $20,000. The project failed, and all that is left of the investment is the cellar, the entrance to which, built of stone, is plainly visible from Third street.

John Jester built the Pateetown brewery at Thirteenth and Sacramento streets, in 1881, and still operates it.

* * *

One of the earliest enterprises in the way of manufactures in St. Joseph was the foundry, established on St. Joseph avenue, 1855, by T. W. Keys. This, with the exception of a small foundry at Lexington, was the first plant of the kind west of St. Louis. The power of Keys' foundry was furnished by oxen. The first pig iron melted in St. Joseph was run in 1856. This foundry was operated till 1858, when Mr. Keys erected, on the corner of Eighth and Messanie streets, the building now (1915) occupied by the foundry of Crowther & Rogers. Mr. Keys leased this in April, 1863, to John Burnside. The firm afterward became Burnside, Crowther & Co. Mr. John Burnside subsequently retired from the partnership. The foundry of J. W. Ambrose & Co., on the corner of Eighth and Monterey streets, was established in 1871.

* * *

The Louis Hax furniture factory was one of the successful and famous institutions of the city for many years. It was located at Seventh and Angelique streets from 1866 until December 13, 1890, on which date the western portion of the plant was destroyed by fire. Mr. Hax did not rebuild, but converted the eastern portion into tenements. The factory is now located at South St. Joseph.

* * *

In the days when freight rates from the north were high and when the native forests were yet rich in trees, the manufacture of native lumber was an important industry. There were two extensive saw-mills in St. Joseph during the life of the industry, both located on South Fourth street, below Messanie, near the river. James P. Hamilton operated the lower mill and Venable & Kent the one near Messanie street. Logs were brought down the river in rafts. Another saw-mill of magnitude was erected at Lake Contrary, near where the southern road strikes the lake. This was operated at one time by J. A. Piner, William Swope and John F. Tyler, who also had a lumber yard in the city. A large number of men were employed there and quite a settlement, called Lake City, sprang up near the mill. This, like the Hamilton and Venable mills, is a thing of the past.

In 1866 Edward R. Brandow, associated with other enterprising citizens, established a sorghum manufactory on lower Edmond street. It was proposed to make sugar out of the product of the cane, and farmers were urged to the importance of raising large quantities. The enterprise, after the production of a small quantity of sugar, was absorbed by larger interests.

Before the war A. M. Mitchell built a distillery upon the site of what was afterward a packing house and later a gluecose works. The venture was not profitable. Several distilleries were in operation in and near St. Joseph after the war and until about 1875. The largest was that of Edward Sheehan, on upper Blacksnake, a short distance south of New Ulm Park, which was built in 1868 and operated until 1874. Abraham Furst and S. Adler, who were for many years the leading wholesale liquor dealers in this city and St. Louis under the name of S. Adler & Co., built a re-distilling house in 1871 at Third and Louis streets, which was operated until 1876. The building is still in existence. After the enactment of the prohibitory law in Kansas, in 1880, a distillery plant was moved from Lawrence and located south of the city, below the railroad tracks on the road to the stockyards. This property was purchased in 1885 by Jacob Schloss. Subsequently it fell into the hands of the whisky trust and the plant was moved away.

* * *

The St. Joseph Steam Printing Company, which was organized by Capt. F. M. Posegate and others in 1870, and which went out of existence in February of 1892, was, in its earlier days, the best equipped, most extensive and most prosperous printing establishment between St. Louis and San Francisco.

* * *

The starch works are yet within easy memory. They were built in the summer of 1872 by O'Neill Bailey, who came here from Madison, Ind., and were operated for about four years. The works were located on a tract of ten acres, south of Messanie and east of Twenty-second street, and were both modern and pretentious, giving employment to a large number of people. The starch was made of corn, and the residue was fed to cattle. The lack of water prevented the possibility of operating the work with profit. Many wells were sunk, but with no satisfactory result, and the enterprise finally succumbed.

* * *

Among the other manufacturing enterprises that have gone out of existence Posegate's city directory for 1875 shows the following carriage and wagon makers: Gideon Miles, Edward Dutton, McBain & Fox, Ferdinand Schoen, W. E. Williams & Son, D. D. Streeter, Wm. Pape, Prawitz & Hagelin and Wiedmaier & Wildberger. Peter Habig operated a pottery at Main and Faraon streets in those days. There was also a glue factory, south of the city limits. Boellert & Schroers manufactured plows at the southeast corner of Sixth and Charles streets. C. Eichler & Co., T. H. Hail & Co., succeeded by C. M. Kingsbury, the Steam Printing Company, Swick, Wells & Co. and Woolworth & Colt were job printers. The Great Western Soap Works, L. Huggins & Co., proprietors, also existed. Wm. Gernandt operated a tannery on Frederick avenue, between Nineteenth and Twentieth streets. There were two axhandle factories, one operated by Wm. Duesler on Buchanan avenue, and another by Henry C. Middleton on Howard street. Aldrich & Scott manufactured whips at Second and Felix streets. There were also two rope factories, one operated by John Helme, on South Eleventh street, between Maple and Oak streets, and another by J. Main on Frederick avenue, near Twentieth street.

* * *

The St. Joseph Sugar Refining Company was formed in June, 1880, by A. M. Saxton, J. B. Hundley, W. W. McFarland and others for the purpose of producing glucose. John L. Motter was general manager and W. Y. Selleck chemist. The building formerly occupied by the E. O. Smith Packing Company, southeast of Calvary cemetery, was converted into a factory. It was in operation until 1889, the last manager being Van Whittaker. The building no longer exists.

* * *

In July of 1886 the St. Joseph Natatorium Association was formed by A. M. Saxton, John Demond, J. W. Hinkston, W. H. Gordon, L. C. Burnes, Joseph Andriano and E. LindJsay. The capital stock was $12,000. A building was erected at the southwest corner of Fifth and Jule streets. A natatorium was operated for several seasons. Subsequently the building was converted into a theater and called the "Bijou." This was partially destroyed by fire, and then, in the spring of 1893, remodeled throughout. It is now known as the Lyceum theater.

* * *

In 1886 Edward W. Mitchell came from Ohio and, with the assistance of local capital, built a stove foundry on the ground north of the Burlington shops, later occupied by the gas works built by the St. Joseph Light and Fuel Company. The plant was in operation for about three years, and then failed.

* * *

In 1887 the Sam Reid Tobacco Company was organized with a capital stock of $50,000, held by Sam Reid, who moved a plant here from Louisiana, Mo., and W. G. Fairleigh, John Townsend, J. D. Richardson, F. L. Sommer, M. A. Reed, G. J. Englehart, T. J. Burgess and Albert Roecker. It was a prosperous institution for three years, occupying the building owned by Daniel J. Lysaght, west of the city hall. Chewing and smoking tobacco were manufactured. In 1890 it was purchased by the tobacco trust and moved to New York.

* * *

The St. Joseph steel car plant was an institution that flourished for several months in 1889. H. D. Perkey, an eastern promoter, owned the patent of a steel car. It was cylindrical in shape and its construction was supposed to be such as to prevent it from being wrecked in collisions. Mr. Perkey had an elegant passenger coach as a sample. A stock company was formed in 1888 and the enterprise was backed by the Brookdale Land Company, which agreed to donate $50,000, the proceeds of the sale of lots. The Steel Car Company agreed to build shops and maintain them for five years. About $35,000 was paid and a building 80x900 feet was erected, equipped with machinery and set in operation during the early part of 1889. The New Era Exposition was coupled with this enterprise and a portion of the works constituted the main hall. On the night of September 15, 1889, this building was destroyed by fire. The steel passenger coach and a number of cars under construction were burned and the enterprise was fatally crippled.

* * *

Of the other prominent manufacturing enterprises that have gone out of existence were the following: August Vegely's candy factory, established in 1862; Sanders & McDonald's tinware manufactory, established 1863; Schultz, Hosea & Co., tinware manufactory, established 1863; John L. Motter's cracker factory, the first in the city, located on Main street, north of Jule; Koenig & Co.'s cracker factory, established 1874; Riley Bros.' cracker factory, located in the building now occupied by the Van Natta-Lynds Drug Co., at Third and Charles streets; Smith, Frazer & Co.'s, and Moorby & Fink's shoe factories.

* * *

The first hotel of prominence in St. Joseph was the Edgar House, a three-story building erected at the northeast corner of Main and Francis streets in 1845. It was afterward called the Planters' House. The building is still in a good state of preservation and forms a part of the Tremont House. In the following year William Fowler built the City Hotel, at the northeast corner of Main and Jule streets. This has been for many years called the Occidental, and is yet known as such. Albrecht & Huber began business as jewelers in the City Hotel in 1851. Until it dissolution a few years ago it was the oldest firm in St. Joseph. The Mansion House, which occupied the site of the Francis street depot grounds, facing Main street, was also a leading hotel in those days.

The Patee House, at Twelfth and Penn streets, was built in 1856-58, and was one of the largest and best equipped hotels in the United States in its first days. It was first kept by G. W. Allen of Philadelphia, who failed before completing his first year, and was succeeded by Colonel Minor of Chicago, who remained about a year. Major Espey was the next landlord. After keeping the house for two years he was killed by falling from one of the windows. Elijah Patee and Dougherty & Worden succeeded in turn as prioprietors. During the war the provost marshal's headquarters were located in the building and the general offices of the Missouri Valley Railroad Company were also located there in those days. At about this time Mr. Patee placed the house into a lottery. He drew it himself. In September of 1865 Rev. James H. Robinson of the M. E. Church, South, instituted a female college in the building, which existed until January, 1869. James H. Bagwell then opened the hotel, the Pacific House, of which he was landlord, having burned. In 1877 a second female academy was instituted by Rev. E. S. Dulin, a Baptist minister. This continued for four years. In the summer of 1881 Dr. S. A. Richmond leased the building. He opened what he called the "World's Epileptic Sanitarium" in a part of the building and leased the remainder to a New York firm, who for a short time conducted the "World's Hotel." The property at that time belonged to Robert W. Donnell, whose home was then in New York. After the failure of the "World's Hotel," Mr. Donnell offered the house to the city to be permanently used and maintained by the taxpayers as a female seminary; but he received no encouragement. In 1885 he sold the property to R. L. McDonald & Co., who converted the building in a factory for the production of overalls, shirts, etc.

The Pacific House was built in 1859-60 and was called the Lounsbury House, after W. B. Lounsbury, who owned it. Shackleford & Hughes were the next proprietors and changed the name to Pacific Hotel. In 1865 William K. Richardson kept the house. He was succeeded by James H. Bagwell, who was in charge when the property was destroyed by fire, December 15, 1868. The house was rebuilt and opened February 14, 1870, by Garth, Gilkey & Abell. Major Garth retired after two years and Rice D. Gilkey and John J. Abell continued the business until December, 1879. The house was their closed for repairs. April 1, 1880, it was reopened under the management of Kitchen Bros. They were succeeded by Col. Ira Wilson, and he by Charles F. Murray. In 1894 Himes & Bowman had the house, and in 1896 C. W. Johnson took charge, continuing until 1901, when the house was remodeled and made the principal part of the Hotel Metropole.

A building at the corner of Third and Jule streets was, in 1860, enlarged and converted into a hotel by E. E. Bacon, and successfully conducted by him and his family under the name of the Bacon House until 1896, when it was remodeled, converted in the Metropole and united with the building which had been called the Pacific House.

The Saunders House was another famous hostelry. It stood at the northeast corner of Third and Faraon streets, upon the site now occupied by Noyes, Norman & Co.'s shoe factory. The life of the hotel was from 1862 up to 1884. It fell from grade to grade until in its last days it was a mere rookery. From 1862 to 1877 it was conducted by Richard and John Saunders, Jr., who retired in favor of J. W. Moore and Cyrus Stahl. In its decadence the hotel had various landlords.

Fotheringham's city directory for 1860 shows the following hotels: Allen House, corner of Fourth and Sylvanie; Avenue House, corner of Frederick avenue and Sixteenth; Baechele House, east side of Eighth street, between Messanie and Locust; Blakemore House, south side of Jule street, between Main and Second; Commercial House, corner of Sixth and Angelique; City Hotel, corner of Main and Jule; Eagle Hotel, corner of Second and Sylvanie;

Huxley House, Eighth street, opposite H. & St. J. passenger depot; Missouri Hotel, south side of Edmond, west of Third; Kentucky House, east side of Third street, between Felix and Francis; Franklin House, west side of Second street, between Edmond and Charles; National Hotel, west side of Edmond street, between Fourth and Fifth; Northwestern Hotel, corner of Third and Franklin; Patee House; Pennsylvania House, Frederick avenue, between Eighteenth and Nineteenth; Planters' House, northeast corner of Second and Main streets; Sommers' Hotel, southeast corner of Second and Michel streets; St. Charles Hotel, east side of Main street, between Robidoux and Isidore; St. Joseph Hotel, west side of Second street, between Michel and Franklin; Talbott House, corner of Third and Faraon Tolson House, north side of Jule street, between Main and Second streets.

The Allen House, at the corner of Third and Angelique streets, was used as an army hospital during the civil war. It afterward became known as the Griffith House, but since 1884 has been known as the Galt House. The Commercial Hotel is still in existence, the old part having been moved to the rear. The Pennsylvania House was was kept by M. A. Ashbrook, who afterwards called it the Ashbrook House. The history of the City Hotel, Planters' House and Patee House is given. The other hotels enumerated in this list have disappeared.

The Central Hotel, at the northeast corner of Second and Edmond streets, was operated for a number of years by Wm. Kollatz. It has not been used as a hotel for over ten years.

The Missouri Valley House was quite a famous hostelry in its day. It was a frame building that stood facing east, at the northwest corner of Eighth and Edmond streets, and was surrounded by beautiful shade trees. It was kept by W. W. Clark, by Capt. O. R. Phelps, and last by Capt. M. I. Couch and S. G. Ford. The house, a large barn and several places of business were burned on the night of October 2, 1878.

Other hotels that have ceased to exist were the Michau House, on the north side of Felix sftreet, between Sixth and Seventh; the old Galt House, that occupied the site of the present general offices of the Burlington railroad; the Highly House, Nineteenth and Frederick avenue, and the Hudnut House, at Third and Felix streets. The Farmers' House, on North Second street, kept for many years by Peter Harnois, was also a noted tavern in its day. The International Hotel, at the northwest corner of Eighth and Olive streets (now Windsor), was built of the material that once constituted the Great Western Hotel at Elwood, a pretentious house that existed before the war, when Elwood had population and prospects.

In 1898 a portion of the Center block, at the northeast corner of Sixth and Edmond streets, was converted into a hotel and operated by Frank F. Harl. It was known as the Hotel Donovan, and in

May, 1904, the enterprise was abandoned. In the fall of 1904 the building was converted into a theater known as the "Lyric."

The St. Charles Hotel, at Sixth and Charles streets, was formerly conducted by C. Q. Lewis. It was rebuilt in 1902 by Charles Boone, Jr.

The Transit House, a large modern structure at the stock yards, was opened in 1904.

For many years the need of a modern hotel, of sufficient size to accommodate the better class of business, was sorely felt in St. Joseph. A number of local business men of wealth finally organized a company to build the Hotel Robidoux at Fifth and Francis streets. Work began in June, 1907, and the building was completely by the following year. It represents an investment of nearly half a million dollars and has paid good dividends from the first. The Robidoux is a nine-story structure, modern in every respect, and the equal of any hotel west of New York.

The St. Francis Hotel, Sixth and Francis streets, was built two years ago.

CHAPTER XXVII.

LODGES, BENEVOLENT, SOCIAL AND TRADE ORGANIZATIONS—FREE MASONS, ODD FELLOWS, AND OTHERS —THE TURNVEREIN, MAENNERCHOR AND OTHER GERMAN-SPEAKING SOCIETIES—TURNFESTS AND SAENGERFESTS—MUSICAL DEVELOPMENT IN ST. JOSEPH—THE ST. JOSEPH PHILHARMONIA, THE MENDELSSOHN SOCIETY AND OTHER SIMILAR ORGANIZATIONS—THE RED RIBBON CLUB.

The first fraternal organization in Buchanan County was Sparta lodge No. 46, instituted May 11, 1841, under a dispensation, and originally called Katzeel lodge. It was chartered October 8, 1841. Eli Hubbel was worshipful master, J. Brownson, senior warden, and J. A. Anthony, junior warden. R. Duncan was treasurer, T. Waymire secretary and G. Selsil tyler. This lodge was merged into DeWitt lodge, organized in St. Joseph under a dispensation in October, 1845. In 1846 the dispensation was surrendered and a charter granted, dated October 14, 1846· The name was changed to St. Joseph Lodge and the number, 78, was affixed by the grand secretary. Sinclair K. Miller was worshipful master, 1845 to 1850. This lodge is still in existence.

The following are the other Masonic bodies now existing in St. Joseph as they appear in order in the Masonic directory: Zeredetha lodge, No. 189, chartered May 28, 1859; Charity lodge, No. 331, chartered October 13, 1870; King Hill, No. 376, chartered October 13, 1870; St. Joseph chapter, No. 14, R. A. M., chartered May 23, 1849; Mitchell chapter, No. 89, R. A. M., chartered October 5, 1876; St. Joseph council, No. 9, R. and S. Masters, chartered October 6, 1871; St. Joseph commandery, No. 4, K. T., chartered October 5, 1875; Hugh de Payens commandery, No. 51, K. T., chartered May 10, 1887; Moila Temple, A. A. O. N. M. S., organized December 17, 1887; Moila court, Daughters of Isis, established October 14, 1896; St. Joseph chapter, No. 198, O. E. S., chartered May 5, 1890; Radiant chapter, No. 88, O. E. S., chartered October 1, 1897; King Hill chapter, No. 55, O. E. S., chartered May 20, 1896. There are also Masonic lodges at Saxton, Easton, Agency, DeKalb and Rushville.

The office of grand master of the state has been held by the following residents of St. Joseph: Wm. R. Penick, Joseph S. Browne, James W. Boyd and Harry Keene.

The office of grand high priest of the Royal Arch chapter has been held by Wm. R. Penick, Samuel Russell and Joseph S. Browne.

The office of most illustrious grand master of the Council of

Royal and Select Masters has been held by Joseph S. Browne, Wm. R. Penick, Wm. G. Hall, W. A. Lord, Ulrich Schneider and E. F. Hartzell.

The office of grand commander of the Knights Templar has been held by Wm. G. Hall and Joseph S. Browne.

The office of imperial potentate of A. A. O. N. M. S. of North America has been held by A. P. Clayton.

* * *

The Odd Fellows are a close second to the Masons in St. Joseph in point of age. King Hill lodge, No. 19, was instituted on October 15, 1846, at the residence of Joseph Hull, on the west side of Main street, between Francis and Jule streets. The charter members were D. B. Welding, Eli Hewitt, S. L. Leonard, Eli Bowman, C. F. Emery and Dr. J. H. Crane. In 1858 this lodge erected a three-story building, facing west, at the southeast corner of Fifth and Felix streets. The lower floor was for business, the second for lodge rooms and on the third floor was an auditorium. This was for some years the first class theater of the city and, among other notables, Edwin Forest played there. At one time there was a stock company connected with the theater. The hall was also used for social and political gatherings. During the war the property was lost by the provisions of a mortgage and was acquired by J. W. Bailey and Wm. R. Penick. When it was destroyed by fire, as mentioned in a foregoing chapter, in January of 1879, it was occupied by J. W. Bailey & Co., with a large dry goods business. In 1880, Mr. Bailey, Isaac Curd, J. B. Brady and Louis Hax built the block facing Felix street, which extends from Fifth street east to the alley.

Humboldt lodge, No. 130, was instituted April 19, 1859. This lodge works in German. Eclipse lodge, No. 143, was instituted April 18, 1860. Enterprise lodge, No. 232, was instituted April 19, 1870. During the summer of 1898 this lodge purchased the large building at Seventh and Charles streets, which had been erected by the St. Joseph Turnverein and which had been lost by that association. St. Joseph lodge, No. 432, was instituted in 1883; Invincible lodge, No. 470, in 1893, and the South Park lodge in 1898.

There have been two sessions of the state grand lodge in St. Joseph—the fifty-third session, held in 1890, and the sixtieth session, held in 1898. The office of grand master of the state was held in 1861 by Col. John Doniphan, who, however, lived at Weston at that time; in 1869, by R. J. S. Wise, of St. Joseph; in 1874, by L. T. Minturn, of Amazonia, who held his membership in St. Joseph, and in 1894, by R. M. Abercrombie, of St. Joseph.

There are five Rebekah lodges: Evening Star, No. 5, instituted in 1892; Enterprise, No. 140, 1894; Humboldt, No. 146, 1894; Eclipse, No. 157, 1894; King Hill, No. 219, 1896. There is also a branch of the Patriarchs Militant, Canton St. Joseph, No. 3, instituted in 1879. Of the encampment degrees there are two branches,

Hesperian encampment, No. 8, and St. Joseph encampment, No. 51. R. M. Abercrombie has held the office of grand patriarch of the state encampment.

* * *

The German-Americans have been prominently identified with the history and development of St. Joseph from an early day. The Turnverein, one of the most active agents in this work, was formed May 23, 1855, with Charles Zipf as first speaker, Charles Jessen as second speaker, Charles Albrecht as secretary, A. Althaus as master of property and Peter Walter as treasurer. The cornerstone of the old "Turnhalle" was laid March 29, 1860, and the building was occupied during the following August. When the Civil war broke out the Turners staunchly avowed loyalty to the Union, their hall was dubbed the "cradle of liberty" and the Stars and Stripes boldly flung to the breezes. When the mob that had taken the flag from the postoffice declared that there colors should also be torn from the staff, two Turners, Valentine Moosman and J. H. Schaefer, went upon the roof in the face of danger, guarded by Robert Bradshaw with a drawn pistol and Charles Mast with a rifle, lowered the flag and brought it safely into the building. Moosman then tore down a Confederate flag that had been hoisted on Market square. Among the St. Joseph Turners who served in the war were the following: W. Baumer went to Omaha and was made colonel of the First Nebraska infantry; Herman Lund went to Quincy and rose to the rank of captain; Charles F. Ernst and Charles Springer were in the Twelfth Missouri cavalry, the former as captain and the latter as lieutenant. Charles Weideman died from wounds received at the battle of Lexington, while Louis Graffenstein and Charles Ludi were killed at Missouri City.

The St. Joseph Turnverein was affiliated with the St. Louis Turnbezirk until May 1, 1866, when the Kansas Turnbezirk was formed. The first Turnfest of this federation was held in this city October 1-3, 1866. Leavenworth, Kansas City, Atchison, Wyandotte, Lawrence, Brunswick, Junction City and Fort Scott were represented.

In 1870 ground was purchased at the northeast corner of Eighth and Sylvanie streets for the purpose of building a new hall, and the cornerstone was laid. The project was abandoned, however, and the ground sold.

A second Turnfest of the Kansas Turnbezirk was held in St. Joseph August 6-9, 1870. In 1885 the Missouri Valley Turnbezirk was formed and the first turnfest of the new federation was held here August 14-17, 1886.

A new hall was built upon the site of the "cradle of liberty" at Seventh and Charles streets, in the summer of 1890. The cornerstone was laid with parade and appropriate ceremonies on Sunday, June, 8, 1890, and the dedication took place October 26, 1890. The new building cost $50,000. In August of 1897 the property was sold under a deed of trust and purchased by the creditors. During the summer of 1898 the property was purchased by Enterprise

Jack Ring, the Life Saver

lodge of Odd Fellows, and is now known as the Odd Fellow building. The Turnverein was without a home of its own for some
time, but in 1903 the western part of the building was purchased
from the Odd Fellows for $15,000.

*   *   *

Since the earliest times there has been a tendency in St. Joseph
toward high-class music. Rosenblatt's brass band, which was
formed by Herman Rosenblatt in 1854, was welcomed and given all
possible encouragement by the people of those days, and for many
years this organization was famous throughout the West. But
the brass band was not commensurate. There were many excellent
voices and much latent musical talent, which craved development
and expansion. In 1857 Prof. Otto Behr was induced to come to St.
Joseph. To this gentleman is due the credit of erecting and maintaining a standard of excellence which will be regarded with ad-
miration and reverence for years to come. Professor Behr was
born in Germany and educated at Leipsic. He located in New York
some years before coming to St. Joseph. In the summer of 1893
he returned to his old home, almost blind and light in purse, after
spending the best part of his life here. He had met with financial
reverses before his eyes began to dim. But he is none the less esteemed and revered in St. Joseph, where he wrought so nobly and
so successfully for his art.

In 1866 the St. Joseph Philharmonia was organized and placed
under the direction of Professor Behr. This society embraced the
best instrumental and vocal talent of the city, and there was also a
large list of honorary and contributing members. Five or six
grand concerts were generally given each season. The Philharmonia existed for about ten years.

The St. Joseph Maennerchor was another successful musical
society. It was organized May 22, 1868, and the membership was
mostly German-American. This society was affiliated with the
Pioneer Saengerbund, and two of the annual song festivals of the
federation were held in St. Joseph. The first "Saengerfest" began
on April 30, 1873, continuing several days, and formed a part of the
general festal program in honor of the completion of the bridge.
The second was held in June of 1883. Maennerchor hall was on the
third floor of the McLaughlin building, at Third and Felix streets.
Among those who served as musical directors were Prof. Felix B.
Canfield, Professor Kaiser and Prof. Wm. Plato. The Maennerchor
was merged into the Turnverein in 1888.

Professor Behr's second successful effort to organize the talent
for the exemplification of high-class music was represented in the
Mendelssohn Musical organization, which was formed in 1882, mod-
eled after the Philharmonia, and which existed until 1891. Concerts were given in the court house, where a suitable auditorium
had been prepared, until the destruction of that building by fire, in
March of 1885. Various halls were then used until the completion
of the Y. M. C. A. auditorium.

Other musical organizations of the past were the Arion, the
Apollo, Harmonia and Concordia.

*   *   *

Of the labor organizations in the city, Typographical Union
No. 40, is the oldest.   It was organized in June of 1859, and has had
a continuous existence.

*   *   *

A famous local organization in its day was the Red Ribbon Re-
form Club, which was organized December 16, 1877, by J. C. Bonte-
cue, a temperance revivalist.   There was a membership of 1,200.
The club occupied rooms in Tootle's opera house until May, 1878,
when the upper portion of the three-story building at the southeast
corner of Second and Francis streets was fitted up, with a library,
stage, etc.   Theatrical and literary entertainments were here given.
The place is yet known as Red Ribbon hall.   The organization flourished for about four years.   The first officers of the club were:
Mordecai Oliver, president; C. B. Wilkinson, first vice-president;
Thomas F. Ryan, second vice-president; William H. Wood, third
vice-president; James C. Cozine, secretary; E. A. Smith. financial
secretary; T. Van Natta, treasurer; J. A. Winsch, first marshal;
R. A. Craig, second marshal; Thomas J. Huyler, sergeant-at-arms.

The St. Joseph Mechanical and Scientific Library Association
was incorporated February 27, 1886.   George R. Mann was president and Charles A. Pfeiffer secretary and treasurer.   Charles
Nowland and F. W. Gensen were also members.   A large number of
public documents which had been collected were turned over to the
public library in 1892.

CHAPTER XXVIII.

THE BANKS AND FINANCIAL INSTITUTIONS THAT HAVE
EXISTED IN ST. JOSEPH IN THE PAST, AND THOSE
THAT LIVE IN THE PRESENT—VARIOUS ORGANIZA-
TIONS FOR THE PROMOTION OF COMMERCE AND
MANUFACTURES—A GLANCE OVER THE NEWS-
PAPER CEMETERY OF ST. JOSEPH AND THE NAMES
THAT ARE WRITTEN ON THE TOMBSTONES.

Armstrong Beattie was the first regular banker in St. Joseph.
He began business in 1852 in the City Hotel at Jule and Main
streets. He afterwards moved to Second street, north of Francis,
and finally to the west side of Third street, between Felix and Edmond, where he continued up to the period of his death, July 26,
1878.

The Farmers' and Mechanics' Savings Institution was chartered in 1853 and continued until 1865, when it was merged into the
First National bank of St. Joseph. The latter bank continued until
August, 1878, when, in consequence of a robbery of $19,700, the
mystery of which has never been solved, the directors decided to go
out of business. The bank was then located at Third and Francis
streets, south of the Pacific House, in the McLaughlin building.
Immediately after the dissolution of the First National bank the
Merchants' bank was organized and began business in the same
quarters, where it continued until the completion of the Chamber
of Commerce, March of 1885, where it remained until 1907, when
it moved to Sixth and Edmond streets. This bank was merged into
the First National bank in 1912.

A prominent bank before the war—in 1858-60—was that of
Lee & Chaffee, located on the west side of Second, between Francis
and Jule streets. The firm was composed of A. L. Lee and Jerome
B. Chaffee. When the war broke out Mr. Lee went to the front in
the Seventh Kansas Infantry regiment, and rose to the rank of
brigadier-general. After the war he located in the South. Mr.
Chaffee went to Colorado, where he prospered, rose to political emi-
nence and was elected to the United States senate.

The Western bank was organized in April, 1859, with Milton
Tootle as president, and continued until 1867, when it went into
liquidation.

The State Savings bank was organized in 1859, as a branch of
the State Bank of Missouri. It was a national bank from 1865 to
1871. From that time it was known again as the State Savings
bank until 1890, when it was again made a national bank. The
bank is now out of business.

John Colhoun & Co., bankers, commenced business in June,
1864, in the old Methodist church at the northeast corner of Third
and Felix streets.   David Pinger, who was the other member of the
firm, erected a modern building upon the site of the old church in
1865.   In 1871 the partnership expired and the business of the
bank was transferred to a new institution, known as the Colhoun
bank.   The new bank occupied the Fairleigh building at the southeast corner of Third and Felix streets.

In the meantime the German Savings bank had been organized
in the spring of 1869.   This bank purchased the building which Mr.
Pinger had erected.   It went into liquidation August 15, 1876.

The St. Joseph Savings bank was organized in June of 1873
and continued until December 1, 1875, when it consolidated with
the Colhoun bank, and the new institution was called the Colhoun
Savings bank.   On May 9, 1878, this bank ceased to exist, and its
business was turned over to Schuster, Hax & Co., bankers.   In 1899
the latter bank was reorganized as the Schuster-Hax National
bank.

The Bank of St. Joseph was organized in December, 1874, and
was first located at Fifth and Felix streets.   In August, 1876, this
corporation purchased the three-story building of the German
Savings bank, at the northeast corner of Third and Felix streets.
It was known as the National Bank of St. Joseph after 1883.   In
the fall of 1903 it took up quarters in a substantial building erected
at Fourth and Felix streets, at a cost of $150,000.   It was after-
ward absorbed by the First National Bank.

The Saxton National bank, at Fourth and Francis streets, was
organized in 1883.   In 1894 it was consolidated with the Schuster-
Hax National bank and reorganized as the National Bank of Buchanan County.

The German-American bank was organized early in 1887.   It
was located on Fifth street, opposite the Tootle theater, until the
completion of its building, at Seventh and Felix streets, in 1889.

The Commercial bank was also organized in 1887, and began
business in the Commercial block at Fifth and Edmond streets.
This bank has gone through the process of liquidation.

The bank of Tootle, Lemon & Co. was organized in July of 1889
and began business at 118 North Fourth street.   In 1894 the bank
was moved to 509-511 Felix street, where it remained until 1900,
when the massive building at the northwest corner of Sixth and
Francis streets was completed.   It became a national bank in 1902.

The Central Savings bank was organized in 1889; was first
located in the Commercial block, then in the France block, on Fifth
street, north of Edmond, and when the Commercial bank went into
liquidation, the quarters of that institution were taken.   December
31, 1898, Milton Tootle, Jr., was appointed receiver for this bank.

The Park bank was organized in 1889.   It is located at the
northeast corner of Tenth and Penn streets, opposite Patee Park.

The St. Joseph Stock Yards Bank was organized in 1898, shortly after the opening of the Live Stock Exchange, in which building it is located.

The Missouri Valley Trust Company was organized in March, 1899. It is located at Fourth and Felix Streets in the building once occupied by the State Savings Bank.

The Bank of Commerce, South St. Joseph, began business in the spring of 1901 at King Hill and Missouri avenues. It continued until January, 1907, when it was reorganized under the name of the Citizens' bank. Its business was taken over by the Drovers' and Merchants' bank in January, 1911.

The Bank of North St. Joseph was established in November, 1903, on St. Joseph avenue, to accommodate the northern end of the city.

The Farmers' and Traders' bank was organized early in 1904. It is located on upper Frederick avenue and is a great accommodation to merchants and people of that portion of the city.

The Empire Trust Company was organized October 23, 1905, by the late James N. Burnes. It was located at Fourth and Francis streets until 1910, when its present quarters at 116 South Sixth street were occupied.

The Bartlett Trust Company, 818 Frederick avenue, was organized January 2, 1906.

The First National Bank represents the merging of three banking institutions. In November, 1905, the First National Bank of Buchanan County bought the National Bank of St. Joseph, and the business of the two was consolidated, the first named moving from Fourth and Francis streets to the quarters of the latter at Fourth and Felix streets. September 12, 1912, the Merchants Bank was bought and added to the business. This bank has a capital of half million dollars, the largest capitalization in the state outside of St. Louis and Kansas City.

The Drovers and Merchants Bank, Lake avenue and Cherokee street, was organized in 1904. It has remained at this location since its organization.

The Burnes National Bank opened for business January 2, 1906, on Fifth street between Felix and Francis streets. Eighteen months later it was moved to its present quarters at Fifth and Felix streets.

The Farmers' State Bank was organized October 3, 1906; it is located at 6211 King Hill avenue.

The American Exchange Bank began business at Sixth and Messanie streets in 1907, and five years later moved to the Commercial block, Sixth and Edmond streets.

The Bank of Buchanan County opened for business at 711 Felix street October 3, 1908.

The Security Bank, 1804 Commercial street, dates its business existence from the year 1909·

The last bank established in St. Joseph was the Mechanics State Bank, located at 2331 South Sixth street.

Among the St. Joseph financial ventures of the past were two insurance companies. The Merchants Insurance Company was organized in 1866 by Thos. E. Tootle, R. L. McDonald, Arthur Kirkpatrick and others, with a capital of $200,000. A successful business was done for many years. The company is now out of existence.

The St. Joseph Fire and Marine Insurance Company was chartered December 27, 1867, by J. W. Bailey, G. W. Samuel, A. P. Goff and others. In 1879 the company wound up its business and paid back the money subscribed for stock, together with interest.

The Real Estate and Savings Association of St. Joseph was organized in 1870, and continued until 1875. The association was chartered by the state with authority to buy and sell real estate, loan money, etc., and its first officers were Arthur Kirkpatrick, president; B. S. Carter, secretary, and James Hull, treasurer.

An enterprise which shows every indication of becoming one of the most important of its kind in the country is the St. Joseph Life Insurance Company, organized November 18, 1913. The company is officered by business men of sound judgment and exceptional capabilities. At the end of the first year the company had nearly a million and a half of insurance in force, and its growth since then has been very satisfactory. Its offices are in the Schneider building, Seventh and Felix streets.

While there existed at various periods in the city's history, prior to 1871, organizations for the promotion of the commercial welfare and advancement of the community, there are so few traces of these efforts that no attempt will be made to specify them. The Improvement and Manufacturers' Aid Association of St. Joseph was formed in 1871 and continued for some years. It was largely due to the existence of this association that the bridge was built. The subject of waterworks also received attention at the hands of the organization, though the works were not built during its life.

In 1871 there was also formed a Board of Trade, which, after doing good service, was reorganized upon more substantial lines on October 19, 1878. For some years prior to 1885 the Board of Trade was located on the east side of Third street, between Felix and Francis, where daily markets were received and where a paid secretary was maintained. In 1881 a committee was appointed to formulate a plan for the erection of a suitable building. As a result the Chamber of Commerce Company was organized, and the building at the southwest corner of Third and Edmond streets, erected in 1884-85.

The following were the officers of the Board of Trade, sometimes called the Commercial Club, during its life:

For 1878-79—Thos. F. Van Natta, president; Samuel I. Smith, first vice-president; Andrew L. Kerr, second vice-president; Isaac Weil, third vice-president; George Olds, treasurer; W. A. P. McDonald, secretary.

For 1879-80—Samuel I. Smith, president; Andrew L. Kerr, first vice-president; Isaac Weil, second vice-president; John S.

Welch, third vice-president; George Olds, treasurer; W. A. P. Mc-Donald, secretary.

For 1880-81—Samuel I. Smith, president; Andrew L. Kerr, first vice-president; Isaac Weil, second vice-president; H. R. W. Hartwig; third vice-president; George Olds, treasurer; W. A. P. McDonald, secretary.

For 1882-83—J. W. Bailey, president; H. R. W. Hartwig, first vice-president; T. J. Chew, Jr., second vice-president; A. C. Dawes, third vice-president; W. A. P. McDonald, treasurer; Frank Motter, secretary.

For 1883-84—John M. Frazer, president; H. R. W. Hartwig, first vice-president; A. C. Dawes, second vice-president; Winslow Judson, third vice-president; W. A. P. McDonald, treasurer; Frank Motter, secretary.

For 1884-85—John M. Frazer, president; H. R. W. Hartwig, first vice-president; A. C. Dawes, second vice-president; Joseph A. Corby, third vice-president; W. A. P. McDonald, treasurer; Frank Motter, secretary, succeeded by Harry C. Adams.

For 1885-86—Winslow Judson, president; H. R. W. Hartwig, first vice-president; John M. Frazer, second vice-president; R. T. Davis, third vice-president; W. A. P. McDonald, treasurer; H. C. Adams, secretary, succeeded by J. L. Bittinger.

For 1886-87—Winslow Judson, president; H. R. W. Hartwig, first vice-president; E. L. Marney, second vice-president; Charles O. Shoup, third vice-president; W. A. P. McDonald, treasurer; John L. Motter, secretary.

For 1887-88—H. R. W. Hartwig, president; E. L. Marney, first vice-president; Charles A. Shoup, second vice-president; Dudley Smith, third vice-president; W. A. P. McDonald, treasurer; John L. Motter, secretary, succeeded by Fred F. Schrader.

For 1888-89—George J. Englehart, president; E. L. Marney, first vice-president; Charles A. Shoup, second vice-president; A. C. Dawes, third vice-jresident; W. A. P. McDonald, treasurer; Fred F. Schrader, secretary.

For 1889-90—E. L. Marney, president; Samuel M. Nave, first vice-president; A. C. Dawes, second vice-president; Samuel Westheimer, third vice-president; W. A. P. McDonald, treasurer; Fred F. Schrader, secretary.

For 1890-91—J. W. Walker, president; Samuel M. Nave, first vice-president; A. C. Dawes, second vice-president; N. J. Riley, third vice-president; W. A. P. McDonald, treasurer; Fred F. Schrader, secretary.

For 1891-92—J. W. Walker, president; W. C. Brown, first vice-president; S. S. McCord, second vice-president; A. P. Clayton, third vice-president; George E. Black, treasurer; James O'Shaughnessy, Jr., secretary.

In June of 1892 the Board of Trade was merged into the Commercial club, which had recently been organized. The following is a list of officers of the Commercial Club to date:

For 1892-93—R. M. Davis, president; W. C. Brown, first vice-president; R. Ford, second vice-president; W. P. Jones, third vice-president; L. L. Strong, treasurer; W. H. Dowe, secretary; James O'Shaughnessy, Jr., assistant secretary. Mr. O'Shaughnessy served until October, when he resigned and was succeeded by Hugh Bowen, who served until January 1, 1893, and was succeeded by F. W. Maxwell.

For 1893-94—H. R. W. Hartwig, president; W. P. Robinson, Jr., first vice-president; Harry J. Campbell, second vice-president; A. J. Cole, third vice-president; L. C. Burnes, treasurer; C. N. Robinson, secretary; F. W. Maxwell, assistant secretary.

For 1894-95—H. R. W. Hartwig, president; W. P. Robinson, Jr., first vice-president; J. M. Frazer, second vice-president; George L. Hammer, third vice-president; L. C. Burnes, treasurer; C. N. Robinson, secretary; F. W. Maxwell, assistant secretary.

For 1895-96—H. R. W. Hartwig, president; E. L. Marney, first vice-president; Milton Tootle, second vice-president; S. E. Crance, third vice-president; L. C. Burnes, treasurer; Purd B. Wright, secretary; F. W. Maxwell, assistant secretary.

For 1896-97—H. R. W. Hartwig, president; S. E. Crance, first vice-president; G. G. Parry, second vice-president; R. W. Powell, third vice-president; L. C. Burnes, treasurer; Samuel H. Smith, secretary; F. W. Maxwell, commissioner.

For 1897-98—A. P. Clayton, president; H. R. W. Hartwig, first vice-president; J. C. Wyatt, second vice-president; T. C. Byrne, third vice-president; C. F. Enright, treasurer; Samuel Block, secretary; F. W. Maxwell, commissioner.

For 1898-99—A. P. Clayton, president; James H. McCord, first vice-president; H. M. Hundley, second vice-president; Ed C. Smith, third vice-president; C. F. Enright, treasurer; Ed O. Wild, secretary; F. W. Maxwell, commissioner.

For 1899-1900—H. M. Hundley, president; A. P. Clayton, first vice-president; James H. McCord, second vice-president; Ed. C. Smith, third vice-president; James N. Burnes, treasurer; E. A. King, secretary; F. W. Maxwell, commissioner.

For 1900-01—H. M. Hundley, president; James N. Burnes, first vice-president; Ed. C. Smith, second vice-president; James L. Davidson, third vice-president; James N. Burnes, treasurer; E. A. King, secretary; F. W. Maxwell, commissioner.

For 1901-02—Thomas F. Van Natta, president; H. M. Hundley, first vice-president; John Donovan, second vice-president; Joshua Motter, third vice-president; J. A. Johnston, treasurer; H. J. Mueller, secretary; F. W. Maxwell, commissioner.

For 1902-03—John C. Letts, president; Thomas F. Van Natta, first vice-president; H. J. Mueller, second vice-president; J. A. Johnston, third vice-president; W. P. Graham, treasurer; E. A. King, secretary; F. W. Maxwell, secretary.

For 1903-04—T. B. Campbell, president; John C. Letts, first vice-president; J. A. Johnston, second vice-president; M. E. Mayer,.

third vice-president; Joshua Motter, treasurer; E. A. King, secretary; F. W. Maxwell, commissioner.

For 1903-04—T. B. Campbell, president; John C. Letts, first vice-president; J. A. Johnston, second vice-president; M. E. Mayer, third vice-president; Joshua Motter, treasurer; E. A. King, secretary; F. W. Maxwell, commissioner.

For 1905—Henry Krug, Jr., president; E. A. King, first vice-president; H. M. Hundley, second vice-president; W. P. McDonald, third vice-president; E. D. McAllister, treasurer; Harry L. George, secretary; F. W. Maxwell, commissioner.

For 1906—Harry L. George, president; Henry Krug, first vice-president; Samuel I. Motter, second vice-president; E. A. King, treasurer; S. M. Adsit, secretary; F. W. Maxwell, commissioner.

For 1907—W. P. Fulkerson, president; C. R. Berry, first vice-president; S. W. Hundley, second vice-president; E. L. Hart, third vice-president; directors: W. P. McDonald, H. N. Byrne, E. A. King, R. R. Clark, Otto Quentin, A. J. Brunswig; F. W. Maxwell, commissioner.

For 1908—Harry L. George, president; W. P. McDonald, first vice-president; R. R. Clark, second vice-president; E. A. King, third vice-president; A. J. Brunswig, treasurer; Otto Quentin, secretary; F. W. Maxwell, commissioner.

For 1909—R. E. Costigan, president R. E. Culver, second vice-president; R. R. Clark, third vice-president; L. M. Smith, M. L. Letts, J. A. Warner, A. L. West, J. B. O'Brien, directors; F. W. Maxwell, acting secretary.

For 1910—James M. Irvine, president; R. E. Culver, J. A. Warner, A. J. Brunswig, J. A. Rossi, T. P. Holland, L. D. W. Van Vliet, J. B. Moss, R. R. Clark, A. L. West, M. L. Letts, Dr. Jacob Geiger, J. B. O'Brien, Louis Motter, Simon Binswanger, directors; F. W. Maxwell, acting secretary.

For 1911—W. S. Lucas, president; W. P. McDonald, first vice-president; A. J. Brunswig, treasurer; D. C. Marinan, R. W. Douglas, R. Atwood, J. A. Aniser, Perry Slade, directors; E. H. Clifford, secretary; H. G. Krake, commissioner.

For 1912—R. T. Forbes, president; E. M. Lindsay, first vice-president; R. R. Clark, second vice-president; W. A. Bodenhausen, third vice-president; R. E. Culver, W. S. McLucas, J. A. Cattell, J. A. Aniser, Dr. Daniel Morton, T. R. Wall, I. A. Vant, C. D. Morris, M. F. Blanchard, T. P. Holland, R. M. Bacheller, directors; H. G. Krake, general secretary; E. H. Clifford, civic secretary.

For 1913—C. D. Morris, president; W. K. James, first vice-president; R. R. Clark, second vice-president; Harry Block, third vice-president; R. M. Bacheller, J. A. Aniser, T. R. Wall, L. H. Stubbs, Ben Phillip, M. F. Blanchard, W. A. Bodenhausen, R. T. Forbes, A. B. Swift, W. W. Head, directors; H. G. Krake, general secretary; E. H. Clifford, civic secretary.

For 1914—R. M. Bacheller, president; W. K. James, first vice-president; R. R. Clark, second vice-president; E. L. Platt, third vice-president; J. A. Aniser, M. F. Blanchard, W. A. Bodenhausen,

R. T. Forbes, M. L. Letts, C. D. Morris, F. A. Moore, J. A. Rossi, A. B. Swift, L. H. Stubbs, William M. Wyeth, directors; H. D. Ennis, secretary.

For 1915—William E. Spratt, president; P. E. Parrott, first vice-president; R. R. Clark, second vice-president; H. C. Porter, third vice-president; Frank A. Moore, J. A. Rossi, W. K. James, R. M. Bacheller, E. L. Platt, R. T. Forbes, C. D. Morris, Horace Wood, C. S. Dickey, F. R. Castle, Percy Johnson, directors; H. D. Ennis, secretary.

The Business Men's League was organized January 1, 1906, and did excellent service for its members, who were principally jobbers and business men of kindred lines. The league was merged with the commercial organizations of the city which united in the organization of the Commerce Club, December 31, 1912.

The St. Joseph Auditorium Association was formed in 1903, and as a result of several years of hard campaigning by the faithful, who would not quit until the goal was reached, the handsome Auditorium, of which every citizen of St. Joseph is proud, was built at a cost of $150,000. It is located at Fourth and Faraon streets and is one of the best appointed buildings of the kind in the country.

CHAPTER XXIX.

NEWSPAPER HISTORY—THE GAZETTE AND ITS VARIED COURSE—THE HERALD, NEWS, BALLOT, VOLKS-BLATT, PRESS AND OTHERS—TOMBSTONES IN THE NEWSPAPER GRAVEYARD OF ST. JOSEPH.

The history of St. Joseph is dotted with the graves of many newspaper ventures. The first newspaper, *The Gazette*, a weekly publication, was established in 1845, the first issue appearing on Friday, April 25. William Ridenbaugh was the proprietor and printer, and the name of Lawrence Archer, then a prominent attorney, is given as editor. It is said that the type and press were part of the equipment of the Mormon paper, published at Independence, which had been suppressed. In 1854 Holly & Carter took charge of *The Gazette*, then it passed into the hands of Gen. Lucien Eastin and next to P. S. Pfouts and J. H. R. Cundiff. In 1857 these gentlemen began the publication of *The Daily Gazette*, the first daily newspaper issued in the city. This continued until the breaking out of the war. When it became unsafe to utter such political sentiments as *The Gazette* upheld, the proprietors suspended publication, laid away the pen and went to the front to do battle for the South with the sword. June 28, 1868, *The Gazette* again appeared, Colonel Cundiff, Mr. Ridenbaugh and Peter Nugent being the publishers. In December of 1873 the paper passed into the hands of Joseph A. Corby & Co. The next publishers were F. M. Tufts, George W. Belt and J. B. Maynard. In November of 1875 Mr. Maynard was succeeded by S. A. Gilbert. In April of 1878 *The Gazette-Chronicle* appeared, *The Chronicle* having been published by M. B. Chapman. Shortly after the consolidation Charles B. Wilkinson and M. B. Chapman were announced as publishers. September 29, 1878, the "Chronicle" was dropped from the name and the paper again appeared under its ancient and original title. In November, 1878, Charles B. Wilkinson assumed sole editorial and business management. March 12, 1879, it was announced that the paper had passed into the hands of the Gazette Publishing Company, a corporation that was to be under the direction of Charles B. Wilkinson, Lewis Burnes and W. E. Smedley, the latter of New York. Colonel Wilkinson was editor until July 12, 1879, when he went to Denver, where he died in January of 1881. Lewis Burnes died November 17, 1879. Then the management of the paper was in the hands of James N. Burnes, Jr., until January 1, 1886, with the exception of a brief period, from June to September, 1883, when it was managed by George E. King. Major John N. Edwards was the editor of the paper from June, 1883, until April, 1886. Mr. Burnes was succeeded as manager by Charles F. Cochran, January 1, 1886, who, after the departure of Major Edwards, was the editor as well as the manager until he was elected to congress in 1896. He was succeeded as manager by Frank Freytag, who remained in charge until July 1, 1900, when he was succeeded by Chris L. Rutt. On August 1, 1900, *The Gazette* and *The Herald* were consolidated under the name of *The Gazette-Herald,* with Chris L. Rutt as manager and Frank B. Moore as editor. The owners were the Burnes estate and William M. Wyeth. About a month afterward the property passed into the hands of Walter B. Holmes of Memphis, Tenn., who conducted it two months and then sold it to C. B. Edgar and others, who at that time published *The Daily News.* Mr. Edgar published *The Gazette-Herald* from *The News* plant, with Chris L. Rutt as editor, until March 30, 1902, when he sold the paper to Lewis Gaylord of Colorado Springs, Colo. From the time of its consolidation until its sale to Mr. Gaylord *The Gazette-Herald* was published as an independent newspaper. Mr. Gaylord dropped the hyphen and the word "Herald," and published *The Gazette* as a Democratic paper until November, 1903, when a syndicate of Republicans bought it. E. E. E. McJimsey was editor at first, but he has since been succeeded by C. D. Morris.

The second newspaper started in St. Joseph was *The Adventure,* a Whig sheet, which made its first appearance in 1848. It was published by E. Livermore, and was at that period regarded as a worthy rival of *The Gazette,* its sole competitor in the county. In March, 1853, James A. Millan purchased the paper and changed its name, calling it *The Cycle.* It was independent. About a year after this Mr. Millan took into partnership E. C. Davis, the first state superintendent of public schools elected in Missouri. A short time after this arrangement, in consequence of difference of political sentiment, Mr. Millan being a Democrat, the partnership was dissolved, Mr. Davis buying out his associate. The latter published *The Cycle* as a Whig paper about one year, when he, in turn, sold out to Matt France, who continued to publish it as a Whig paper for another year. France then sold to A. K. Miller and Jacob T. Child, who changed the name of the paper, calling it *The Journal.* This was about 1856 or 1857. In 1858, 1859 and 1860 *The Journal* was edited and published by John P. Bruce and Jacob T. Child. This paper strongly advocated the claims of Bell and Everett during the presidential canvass. It suspended publication about 1862.

It may not be improper to state here that in the spring of 1856 the first job printing office was opened in St. Joseph. This enterprise was started by Millan & Posegate, on the south side of Francis, between Main and Second streets. Eighteen months after, Mr. Posegate, who had learned the printing business in *The Cycle* office under Mr. Millan, issued the first number of *The West.* It was a handsomely printed, eight-column weekly. His associates in the enterprise were Wellington Cunningham, Washington Jones and Edward Y. Shields. The paper, with strong Union proclivities, was independent in politics. In the spring of 1859 a daily was started in connection with *The Weekly West.* February 6, 1860, Mr. Posegate bought out his partners and became sole editor and proprietor of the paper, warmly and ably supporting Bell and Everett for the presidency. In August, 1860, he sold *The West* to James Tracy & Co. The paper, under the management, advocated the claims of John C. Breckenridge to the presidency, and boldly avowed its secession sentiments. During the winter of 1860-61 the publication of the paper was suspended.

The first German newspaper in St. Joseph was *The Volksblatt*. It was started in 1856 by Leopold Marder, who, two years after, sold the paper to J. H. Buschmann. This was in 1858. Francis Rodman, afterward secretary of state, was editor. Wednesday, March 28, 1866, the daily evening edition, a five-column paper, made it first appearance, published by Gustavus Heinrichs. In 1868 R. L. Morgenstern purchased the paper, and Leopold Marder became editor. November 8, 1868, Conrad Eichler and H. W. Kastor assumed control. The firm was styled C. Eichler & Co. Mr. Kastor was editor. November 8, 1875, Herman Brunsing purchased the interest of Mr. Eichler. Mr. Brunsing was succeeded in 1886 by Mr. George L. Hermann-Muehe. Colonel Kastor retired some years ago, since which time Mr. Muehe has had sole charge. *The Volksblatt* is the oldest continuous publication in the city.

The press and other appliances of The West Company became the property of Col. Charles B. Wilkinson, who started therewith a Republican paper, the *St. Joseph Morning Herald*. The first issue, a six-column daily, appeared Wednesday, February 12, 1862, Wilkinson & McKibbin editors and proprietors. In the issue of April 10, 1862, the proprietorship was announced under the style of Wilkinson & Co. Saturday, October 1, 1862, *The Morning Herald* appeared consolidated with *The Daily Tribune*. It continued to be published in this style until July 25, 1866, when "Daily Tribune" was dropped from its name and it again resumed its original simple title of *Morning Herald*. In 1867, F. M. Posegate took charge of the business management of *The Herald*. He remained with the paper three years, the first two as business manager for Wilkinson & Bittinger, and the third as a partner of the former, he having bought the interest of John L. Bittinger. In the summer of 1869, Wilkinson & Posegate sold out to Hallowell & Bittinger. In April, 1870, the firm became Hallowell, Bittinger & Co., C. B. Wilkinson constituting the company of the concern. When Mr. Hallowell withdrew, the firm became Wilkinson, Bittinger & Ward. July 8, 1871, Henry Ward withdrew and the firm became Wilkinson & Bittinger, continuing such till the whisky-ring developments of 1875, which wrecked the fortunes of both members of the firm. In the spring of 1876 John Severance, Wm. D. O'Toole and Major John T. Clements purchased *The Herald*. July 11, 1876, it appeared reduced from its former size, a nine-column, to an eight-column sheet, and continued to be so published till near the close of September following, when Tracy & Co. became owners of the concern, and immediately restored the paper to its former size—a nine-column folio.

The issue of September 26, 1876, was the first to appear with the announcement "Tracy & Co., Proprietors." The head of the firm was Frank M. Tracy, the company included Robert Tracy and D. W. Wilder. In 1885 the property came into the hand of Col. J. W. Strong, who represented a stock company of local capitalists. After his tragic death, in June of 1886, the paper was managed by Col. Wm. M. Shepherd, with the late George C. Smith as editor, who was succeeded by Charles Alf. Williams. In 1889 J. L. Bittinger assumed editorial charge, the paper having passed under the control of Maj. T. J. Chew and others. J. P. Knight was business manager for some years and was succeeded by W. B. Willim. Major Bittinger was succeeded in 1897 by Edward F. Trefz, who remained two years and was succeeded by Frank B. Moore, who had editorial charge until the consolidation with *The Gazette* in 1900.

Four different newspaper publications have borne the name of *The News.* The first daily evening paper issued in St. Joseph was established by Asa K. Miller in 1862. It was called *The News* and lived about two months. In the summer of 1864 Jacob T. Child and Charles M. Thompson issued, from *The Gazette* press, a campaign paper called *The Evening News.* It was published in the interest of George B. McClellan and expired after the campaign. *The Monday Morning News* was started August 20, 1877, by Isaac Pfeiffer. Colonel Wilkinson took charge of the paper after several issues and made a hit with it. The last issue of *The Monday Morning News* appeared in June, 1878, when Colonel Wilkinson assumed editorial charge of *The Gazette.* In July, 1878, a week or two after its suspension, the material and franchises of *The Monday Morning News* were purchased by George E. King, and used by him in publishing an illustrated weekly. In October following he sold out to Judge Andrew Royal and W. M. Patton, who continued its publication under the original name of *Monday Morning News.* This, some time after, was changed to *Western News.* May 3, 1879, *The Daily Evening News* was started in the office of *The Western News* by Judge A. Royal and George H. Cross. It was, at first, a small, four-column sheet. September 3 following this was enlarged. April 19, 1881, the paper was purchased by W. F. Bassett and J. W. Spencer, who enlarged and otherwise improved it. Gilbert J. Spencer succeeded W. F. Bassett in the partnership. In 1888 the paper was sold by J. W. and G. J. Spencer to Byron Dunn and George W. Martin of Maryville. In July of 1889 the property was acquired by Charles M. Palmer and E. B. Haskell. C. M. Shultz was placed in charge of the paper, and continued to manage it until August of 1894. In September of 1894 Charles B. Edgar became associated with Messrs. Palmer and Haskell, and published the paper until October, 1903, when he sold his interest to a company headed by Louis T. Golding of New York. The publication is now called *The News-Press* and represents the consolidation of *The Daily News* and *The Evening Press. The Press* was established in August, 1902, by W. H. Turner and Hobart Billman of Chicago, and was published for about fourteen months, when it was consolidated with *The Daily News*. Mr. Golding is now the publisher of *The News-Press* and Chris L. Rutt is managing editor.

The Stock Yards Journal was established by Charles Thornton soon after the stock yards were opened, and was subsequently acquired by people interested in the stock yards, who still control the paper. E. Neff was in charge for a time. W. E. Warrick became publisher in 1899 and remained until the summer of 1913, when Ewing Herbert of Hiawatha, Kan., took charge. *The Journal* was established as a live stock market report, but early in 1915 began publishing a local edition.

Of the weekly publications now in existence *The Catholic Tribune* is the oldest. It was founded in April of 1879 at Kansas City, where it was published by Wm. A. Maynard and W. W. Davis. In October of 1880 it was moved to St. Joseph, where it was published for some years by Davis & Royal. Rev. Francis Graham, pastor of St. Patrick's church, was also the publisher of the paper for a time after Davis & Royal. Peter Nugent and Michael Lawlor became the proprietors in July of 1889, and this partnership continued until 1892, when Mr. Nugent became the sole proprietor. In April of 1894 Mr. Lawlor took charge of the property and has edited and published *The Tribune* since that time.

The Journal of Commerce was founded in 1886 by Frank Witherspoon. It was subsequently published by George W. Wrenn. In 1890 J. W. Spencer, who was then the publisher, sold the paper to C. M. Shultz. Ed M. Taylor succeeded C. M. Shultz, and for a time Purd B. Wright was interested with Mr. Taylor and edited the paper. In 1897 the Combe Printing Company acquired the property and placed it under the management of Ed O. Wild. The Combe Printing Company relinquished its ownership after several years and M. M. Burns was publisher until November, 1903, when W. P. Tracy took charge and changed the name to *Western Dry Goods*. This publication was subsequently discontinued and the present *Commercial Journal*, founded by C. C. Pierce in 1908, took its place. *The Commercial Journal* is still being published by Mr. Pierce.

The *St. Joseph Observer*, a weekly Democratic newspaper, was founded September 1, 1906, by Charles Fremont Cochran and Frank Freytag. Colonel Cochran died December 19, 1906, and his interest in the paper was purchased by Mr. Freytag, who has been the sole owner ever since.

The *St. Joseph Union*, devoted to the interests of organized labor, was founded seventeen years ago by B. E. Burnham, who edited it for a time. W. P. Tracy, Clayto Riley, Frank Chaney, A. G. Roberts and W. J. Jones have edited the paper at different times. It is now published by E. L. McDonald and Glen Stevenson.

Farm and Stock, a farm paper, was established by the publishers of the *Fruit-Grower and Farmer* in 1909. Three years later it was sold to Lon Hardman, who later sold it to the New Gazette

Company, the present publishers. The name has been changed to *Profitable Farming*.

The Western Fruit-Grower was started in January of 1897 as a monthly publication devoted to horticulture. The venture met with deserved encouragement from the beginning and the increase of business has justified many improvements. The name was subsequently changed to *The Fruit-Grower and Farmer*. This publication has a national reputation and has done much to advertise St. Joseph abroad.

A glance over the tombstones in St. Joseph's newspaper cemetery reveals the following inscriptions:

Free Democrat, May 29, 1859, to April, 1861. Those connected with the paper at various times were Joseph Thompson, Earl Marble, E. H. Grant, Frank M. Tracy, D. W. Wilder, B. P. Chenoweth and Robert Tracy.

Daily Tribune, August, 1862, to October, 1864. A. K. Abeel, Philemon Bliss, Wm. M. Albin, James T. Beach and James Hunter were interested at various times.

Daily Union, December, 1864, to January, 1871. James Hunter, James T. Beach, E. J. Montague, Philomen Bliss, Willis M. Sherwood, Wm. W. Albin, Wm. Fowler, A. N. Schuster, J. W. Strong, J. W. Dinsmore, the Union Printing Company, R. D. Mitchell, Eugene Ayers, Wm. Everett, C. W. Marsh and J. B. Hinman were at various times interested in the publication. Jacob T. Child was the first local editor.

New Era, a weekly, 1862-63, Harrison B. Branch, publisher.

Vindicator, weekly, 1865, James A. Milan, publisher.

Daily Commercial, 1866; published by Jule Robidoux & Co.

Evening Tribune, 1870, Joseph Thompson and C. B. Bowman, publishers.

Daily Evening Commercial, 1872-74, Charles S. Scott, publisher.

Board of Trade Circular, 1877-83, George Rees and others.

Reflector, weekly, 1872-73, James A. Millan, publisher.

Weekly Reporter, 1875, M. B. Chapman, publisher.

The Evening Reporter, 1878, Fred F. Schrader and Max Kauffman, publishers.

The Tri-Weekly Telephone, 1878, F. M. Tufts, publisher.

The Good Way and *The Bugle and Standard*, 1879-81, Rev. J. W. Caughlin, editor.

Commercial Advicer, 1878-82, I. J. Dewitt, publisher.

Daily Anzeiger, 1879, Kurth & Schrader, publishers.

Saturday Democrat, 1880-85, George E. King, publisher.

Daily Sun, April, 1881, W. W. Davis and Phil Schmitz, publishers.

Grip, a comic weekly, 1884, Abe Steinberg and A. J. Fleming, publishers.

Daily Evening Journal, 1885-87, O. M. Gilmer and Frank Martin, publishers.

Weekly Leader, 1880-90, Joseph Crane, publisher.

The Weekly Wasp, 1889-93; H. U. Hayden, publisher; Homer J. Kline was the first editor.

Daily Ballot, 1890-91. This was a morning newspaper venture by the late Wm. Hyde of St. Louis. It involved heavy financial losses.

Weekly Argus, 1893; J. Matt Davis, editor.

The St. Joseph Republican, 1894; James T. Beach and Captain Sullivan, publishers.

The Saturday Record, established by J. W. Spencer in 1898, and later converted into a daily afternoon paper.

The Daily Times, 1897-98; George C. Crowther, Joseph Albus and O. M. Gilmer, publishers.

The Modern Farmer and Busy Bee, edited by Emerson T. Abbott.

The Daily Star was established as an evening newspaper by the Kellogg Syndicate November 27, 1905. It was published until March 22, 1909, when it died.

There have been many ephemeral publications in St. Joseph, principally weekly society ventures, whose graves are unmarked, that started briskly and with the assurance of a high-school essayist upon the road to fame and fortune, but inevitably went to pieces upon the same old financial rock.

CHAPTER XXX.

REMINISCENCES — NEGRO SLAVERY IN BUCHANAN
COUNTY—STEAMBOATS—THE TOWN OF ELWOOD—A
REMINISCENCE OF EARLY ST. JOSEPH—THE GRASS-
HOPPER SCOURGE—A FEAT IN PEDESTRIANISM—
THE FIRST FREE DELIVERY WAGON—AN EFFORT TO
SECURE WATER FROM BED-ROCK—ST. JOSEPH MEN
WHO BECAME FAMOUS.

As was stated in a previous chapter, there were over 2,000
negro slaves in Buchanan County when the war broke out. These
were owned principally in the country. The condition of the slave
here, as elsewhere, depended upon the master. It was to the slaveholder's interest, of course, to keep this class of property in good
condition that it might yield the best possible returns. The slaves,
in the main, were well cared for, and their lot was not so bad. They
were expected to work ten hours per day for the master and were
allowed half holidays on Saturday, where the conditions permitted,
and also on Sundays. They were given no education, as a rule,
though there were instances where the master taught his slaves to
read and write. This practice was frowned upon, however, by the
majority of owners. The negroes had many social privileges, but
were restricted to some extent by a pass system, which was en-
forced by a patrol. No negro could leave his master's place after
night without a pass. This he had to show to the patrol, who were
mounted and who guarded certain prescribed districts. The negroes called them "patterolers," and it was the delight of the more
venturesome youngsters to elude the vigilance of these much-hated
officers. The patrolmen were paid by private subscription. There
were licensed preachers of various Protestant denominations, and
these held religious services in different places about the country,
at stated times, and there was generally a white man present to see
that seditious utterances did not creep into the sermons. Marriages
were solemnized, and where the man and woman belonged to different estates the husband was generally permitted to visit his wife
on Saturdays and Sundays. The children always belonged to the
owner of the mother.

Slaves were paid for the work they did overtime, or as in hemp
breaking, for such work as was done over and above a stated task.
They were also given patches of ground to cultivate and could sell
the products. Men were given two suits of clothing and two pairs
of shoes per year, and women two dresses, besides other necessary
wearing apparel.

Where a slaveholder had more slaves than he could use, he let
them out for hire. The general price for a man was $150 per

year, his maintenance, medical attendance and clothing. It was prescribed how many hours he should work and that he should be paid individually for the work he did beyond the contract day. Women brought about $100 per year hire. In some instances negroes saved enough money to purchase their freedom. One case is recalled, however, where the slave fruitlessly paid over one thousand dollars. The master kept no account; neither did the slave. The master died, and when the estate was sold the slave was sold also. He had nothing to show for his payments. The slave was Alf Foutz, who was pressman on *The Gazette* before the war, and who, after the war, held a similar place on the *Atchison Champion* for many years.

The negroes, as a rule, spent their money freely and Saturday was made a busy day in St. Joseph by them.

Slaves were hired out during Christmas week for the ensuing year, and this was generally done on Market Square. The masters brought them into town and sold their services to the highest bidders.

Slaves were sold at public auction, also, but this practice was almost confined to cases where an estate was sold, though several slave buyers, who shipped their wares south, were located in St. Joseph and constantly bought up such negroes as were offered. When slavery was abolished, there were few males in bondage, most of them having been either shipped to Texas before the war or been surrendered by masters who took advantage of a bounty of $350 for every slave that was enlisted by them into the Federal army. A great many, too, had escaped to Kansas by the aid of the Jayhawkers.

Slaves held in the city were used as house servants, porters and the like, and they were either owned or hired by the masters.

* * *

In early days a great fleet of steamboats "plowed the turbid current" of the Missouri, bringing settlers and supplies for this vast virgin territory. During the '40s, '50s, and half of the '60s the river was dotted with many boats. Beyond Main street were numerous large warehouses required for the immense river traffic. They were all washed away later by encroachment. Hemp, hemp rope, hides, tallow, furs, whisky and tobacco were the principal products shipped down the river. St. Joseph was the business center for the whole river district, and from here supplies were sent all over the western mountains and plains. Here, too, most of the California pioneers of 1849, 1850 and 1851 were supplied with outfits for the long journey to the Pacific.

At times there would be as many as twenty steamboats at the wharves in one day. The city charged a wharfage of $5 for each boat, and the wharfmaster was an important personage in our early city government.

Many "mackinaw" boats would arrive about June of each year, loaded down with furs, mostly belonging to Joseph Robidoux. The cargoes would be reshipped here on steamboats if the terms were favorable, but it Uncle Joe thought the steamboat men were trying to "work" him, he would continue the trip to St. Louis with his mackinaws. Frequently these boats would be lost in passage. St. Joseph was practically the head of navigation, but in the early days a few boats would go up to the mountains each year, loaded with supplies and trinkets for the traders, consuming a whole season on the trip.

When the railroads were built there was little business left for steamboats, and they dropped out one by one, seeking other fields, until now they are a curiosity on this river.

* * *

A word of Elwood will not be amiss in these reminiscences. Fotheringham's directory for 1860 shows 166 male residents of the place. At the present estimate of population, based upon city directories—five to the name—this would show that Elwood had a population of 830 at that time. The business directory shows that there were three attorneys, one of them, D. W. Wilder, later prominently identified with the political history of Kansas and with the press of St. Joseph; another, Thomas A. Osborn, later governor of Kansas; the third, A. L. Lee, who was secretary of the town company and also interested in a bank in St. Joseph, and who subsequently gained distinction as a brigadier-general in the Union army. There were two bakeries, two blacksmiths, a brewery, a brickmaker, two butchers, six carpenters, a coffee house, a dentist, a druggist, seven general merchants, two hotels, a livery stable, two painters, three physicians, a plasterer, a restaurant, several real estate agents, five saloons, a saw-mill, a tailor, three wagon-makers, a jeweler and one dealer in stoves and tinware. There was also a newspaper, the *Elwood Free Press*, published by H. D. Hunt.

There was a city government. George W. Barr, later a resident of St. Joseph, was mayor; Dr. J. W. Robinson, clerk and recorder; Wm. H. Hugh, assessor; Thomas A. Osborn, attorney; R. S. Sayward, treasurer; Charles O. Smith, collector and city marshal. Wm. H. Hugh, D. B. Jones, J. H. Hatcher, Andrew Disque, W. L. Lewis, L. C. Booth, Wm. Luke, W. C. Groff and A. W. Tice ocmposed the city council. There was also a police force, consisting of three men.

There was an Episcopal church, and the Congregationalists held services occasionally in a hall. There was a board of public schools; also a library association and a building association.

The *New York Daily Times* of December 18, 1858, says of Elwood, that it "is one of the most promising places in Kansas, and from the eligibility of its position and great local advantages, bids fair to become the chief commercial metropolis of the future state. Situated directly opposite St. Joseph, it is placed by the Hannibal & St. Joseph railroad in direct communication with the most populous and wealthy cities of the East, and by the first of April will be within fifty hours' travel of New York. It is the starting point of the railroad chartered to Palmetto, on the South Pass route to Salt Lake and California, and of the St. Joseph & Topeka railroad, which will command a great portion of the trade of New Mexico. ^ It lies on the west bank of the Missouri River, on the verge of an extensive and thickly wooded bottom, which requires no grading,; its streets are broad and rectangular, and its levee can be approached with safety by the largest boats, and is sufficiently spacious for an immense commerce."

The war stagnated business, scattered the population and killed the prospects of this ambitious and thriving point. In rapid settlement and development of Kansas, when peace was restored, Elwood was overlooked and forgotten and went into rapid decline. The ravages of the river finished the work, and there is but little left of the ground upon which the ambitious young town stood.

* * *

The years 1866, 1867, 1874 and 1875 are known as "grasshopper" years, owing to the existence of a plague of Rocky Mountain locusts. Kansas was stricken first each time and the locusts crossed the river in September of 1866, in July of 1867, and in September of 1874. The first two visits were not so costly to the farmer as the last one. The city was deluged with the insects, however, and they were a great annoyance. The wells were polluted with their carcasses; they ate the lace curtains in the dwellings, and devoured the vegetation.

In 1874 and 1875 all the country west and north of Missouri was plagued with the locusts. The people usually referred to them as grasshoppers. Indeed, the insects greatly resembled the ordinary grasshopper. They came down from the Rocky Mountains, quickly overran Colorado, then came on through Kansas, devouring every green thing, taking every live blade of grass, every leaf on tree and bush, every flower and vegetable. In September of 1874 they struck Buchanan County. The crops having matured, they did little material damage that year. But they deposited their eggs in the ground and the warm spring weather hatched them out in great numbers. As they developed the verdure disappeared. First the young clover, then the tender bluegrass of the pastures, next the vegetables in the gardens, and finally the shrubbery and small trees; in fact, almost everything that grew fell before the greed of the insect. As they grew so did their voracity, and their depredations increased. Farmers were powerless. Some tried digging pits and driving the locusts thereinto, where they were either scalded or covered up. Others drove them into piles, where they were cremated. In fact, numerous plans for ridding the country of the pest were tried, and while untold millions of locusts were undoubtedly destroyed, others seemed to take their places immediately. It mattered not what was done, no diminution in the numbers of the hopping, creeping things was discernible. Livestock suffered greatly from the lack of food, and the farmers lost heavily by the death of cattle and hogs. When half-grown and able to fly the locusts began to disappear, and by

July they were nearly all gone. The farmers at once set to work
with energy. The seasons were favorable and the frost late. There
was a grand harvest. In fact, all over the state-there was a pro-
digious yield, and this fact served largely to alleviate the business
depression of the two previous years.

* * *

In 1869 pedestrianism was the popular athletic fad. The newspaper files contain accounts of a rather grotesque performance of
this kind in St. Joseph. One R. F. Leonard, a laundryman, agreed,
on a wager, to walk one hundred miles in twenty-four hours. His
route was on Second street, from Faraon to Isabel, a distance of
half a mile. At midnight, February 17, Leonard began his task.
The route was illuminated with torches and the pedestrian carried
in one hand a lighted lamp and in the other a bugle, upon which
he executed military signals as he marched. An immense crowd
witnessed the performance. Leonard made the first mile in thirteen minutes. The ninety-ninth mile was made in twenty-two
minutes, and the one-hundredth mile in thirteen minutes and
twenty-two seconds. Leonard covered the one hundred miles in
twenty-three hours and thirty-nine second, resting· but forty-one
seconds during the time.

* * *

In 1874 the question of waterworks was not only earnestly discussed, but a considerable sum was expended in an experiment to
obtain a supply from the bed-rock of the river. This venture was
directed by a number of influential citizens known as waterworks
commissioners. The members of this commission were Mayor I. T.
Hosea, Wm. M. Wyeth, Victor B. Buck, Bernard Patton, George H.
Hall, Milton Tootle, Winslow·Judson, Louis Hax, Charles B. France,
R. P. Richardson, George Buell, Louis Fuelling and Charles A.
Pfeiffer. These gentlemen served gratuitously and created a fund
with which to conduct the experiment. The bridge having been
recently completed, apparatus for pneumatic pressure was easily
available. A caisson was sunk and the workmen went a considerable distance below the bed of the river. However, the cherished
hope of finding a sufficient supply of pure water was not realized.

* * *

In July, 1870, the first mixed jury was impaneled in Buchanan
County. The case was before a justice, and the constable had provided a jury composed of three negroes and three white men. The
late Judge Henry S. Tutt, who had been engaged by the defendant,
refused to serve.

* * *

Buchanan County has furnished the state three governors—
Robert M. Stewart, Willard P. Hall and Silas Woodson. The office
of secretary of state was filled for two terms by Francis Rodman of
St. Joseph. Mordecai Oliver, who was appointed secretary of state

by the convention of 1861, was then a resident of Green County and did not come to St. Joseph until after the war. The office of state treasurer has had one incumbent from St. Joseph—Col. Elijah Gates. Francis Carroll Hughes of this county was appointed warden of the penitentiary by Governor Polk in 1856, and served until the exit of Governor Claiborne F. Jackson. Henry A. Vories and Philomen Bliss of Buchanan County were judges of the supreme court, and Willard P. Hall, Jr., was judge of the Kansas City court of appeals. James M. Johnson is now judge of the Kansas City court of appeals; S. S. Brown is a commissioner of the supreme court. James B. Gardenhire of St. Joseph was attorney-general. The following resident of St. Joseph have been members of congress: Willard P. Hall, Sr., James Craig, Benj. F. Loan, Isaac C. Parker, James N. Burnes, Daniel D. Burnes, George C. Crowther, Charles F. Cochran and Frank B. Fulkerson. Gen. Robert Wilson, who was appointed United States senator by Governor Hall, resided on a farm at Jimtown, in Andrew County, a short distance beyond the Buchanan County line, but was much interested here, and may be accredited to St. Joseph. Joseph K. Toole, the first governor of Montana, was a former resident of St. Joseph. Alexander W. Terrell, the first city attorney of St. Joseph, was afterward United States minister to Turkey, and Ethan Allen Hitchcock, minister to Russia, and later secretary of the interior, was a merchant in St. Joseph before the war. Jacob T. Child, minister to Siam under President Cleveland, was in the newspaper business here before and during the war, as was also E. C. Davis, the first state superintendent of public schools. James W. Porch was a resident of St. Joseph when appointed consul-general at the City of Mexico. John L. Bittinger, once consul-general at Montreal, was appointed from St. Joseph. Jerome B. Chaffe, at one time senator from Colorado, was a banker in St. Joseph before the war.

* * *

The practice of delivering groceries was established by Major H. R. W. Hartwig in 1865. At that time he was conducting a retail grocery store on Fourth street, south of Edmond street. He sent to New York for a modern delivery wagon, which he placed in active service, in charge of Chris. Hubacher, now a prominent citizen of St. Joseph.

* * *

"Voting on string" is a term that will be remembered by those who were active in politics during the reconstruction period and particularly when the odious registration law was first put into operation. Only those who were registered could vote. And only those who took the iron-clad oath were registered. There were those who were rejected by the registering officers, either for valid or political reasons, who announced that they would vote in spite of the proscription, and there were many indications of trouble. The election judges, like the registering officers, were all Republicans in those days. A council of the party leaders was called to decide upon the easiest and best way out of the impending difficulty. It was finally decided to receive all votes that were offered and to place the ballots of those who were registered in the regular box and to file the ballots of those not registered upon a string. The election was held without trouble. When an unregistered voter appeared he was greeted with courtesy, voted his ticket and departed well satisfied. But his ballot went on the string and was not counted. This trick was practiced and kept secret until the political condition had changed and the presence of Democratic judges made it unsafe for the Republicans to continue the practice.

Biographical

JOSEPH ROBIDOUX—It is proper that the following biographical sketches of the living should be preceded by those of some of the pioneers who have gone before, and whose names are prominently connected with the early history and development of Buchanan County. Joseph Robidoux, the first of these, was born in St. Louis, August 10, 1783. He was the eldest son of Joseph and Catherine Robidoux. He had five brothers —Antoine, Isadore, Francis, Michel and Louis—and one sister. Of these, Antoine, Isadore and Francis died and were buried at St. Joseph.

The father of this family was a Canadian Frenchman, who went from Montreal to St. Louis, where he located shortly after the settlement of that place by the French. He accumulated a fortune, became influential and occupied a large mansion. The first general assembly of the state of Missouri did him the honor of holding its first session at his house, in December of 1812. He educated his children as liberally as was possible in those days.

Joseph, the eldest of the boys, married Eugenie Delslille, at St. Louis, when he was eighteen years of age. There was one child by this union— Joseph E. Robidoux, who spent his life among the Indians and who died some years ago near White Cloud, Kan. Four years after this marriage the wife died. After her death the widowed husband became a wanderer. He visited New Orleans and different points along the lower Mississippi, and then went north, locating upon the present site of Chicago, as an Indian trader. He was robbed by the Indians in a short time and returned to St. Louis. Soon thereafter he made a trip up the Missouri River with one of the Chouteaus in the interest of the American Fur Company, going as far north as Council Bluffs. Robidoux returned to St. Louis, purchased a stock of goods and returned to the "Bluffs" in the fall of 1809. He traded with the Indians there for thirteen years, shipping his furs and peltries to St. Louis in keel boats.

While dwelling at the "Bluffs" in 1813, Robidoux married his second wife, who was Miss Angelique Vaudry, also of St. Louis. By this union there were six sons—Faraon, Jules C., Francis B., Felix, Edmond and Charles. There was also one daughter, who became Mrs. S. P. Beauvis. Edmond Robidoux went from here to Omaha some years ago. Mrs. Angelique Robidoux died in this city January 17, 1857.

Robidoux was so potent a rival to the American Fur Company, also established at the Bluffs, that this concern bought him out with the stipulation that he should remain away for three years. During this period Robidoux lived at St. Louis, where he operated a bakery. After three years he announced his intention of again establishing a trading post. The fur company's representative offered to place him in this neighborhood at a salary of $1,800 per year, provided he would not interfere with the trade at the Bluffs. Accepting the proposition he landed at the mouth of a creek now known as Roy's Branch, north of the city, in the fall of 1826. Shortly afterward he moved to the mouth of Blacksnake creek, where he erected a small log house. In 1830 he became the sole proprietor of the trading post. Then he erected a large house, located about where the Occidental Hotel stands, northeast of Main and Jule streets.

Robidoux's family lived at St. Louis during his early struggles here. He owned a negro named Poulite, who knew French and who attended to the household duties. Robidoux spoke the various Indian dialects fluently. His English was broken and strongly flavored with the French accent. He was

JOSEPH ROBIDOUX

a heavily built man, about five feet ten inches in height, of swarthy complexion and with piercing eyes. He was a natural trader and highly successful in his line. His manners were mild and persuasive and he was polite and hospitable. He died in this city on May 27, 1868, nearly eighty-five years of age, and was buried at Calvary cemetery, having been a Catholic. There was a public funeral. Business was suspended and the people generally participated in the last tribute to the founder of their city. Robidoux was, comparatively, a poor man at his death, having lost much of his property by unfortunate speculations.

AUSTIN A. KING, the first judge to hold court in Buchanan County, was born in Sullivan County, Tenn., Sept. 20, 1801; came to Missouri in 1830; in 1834 was chosen to the legislature; in 1837 was appointed judge of the Fifth circuit, to which Buchanan County was attached when organized; served until he was elected governor in 1848. In 1860 he was a delegate to Charleston where he supported Stephen A. Douglas. He subsequently took the ground that the war was unnecessary. In 1862 he was again made circuit judge, but resigned to go to congress, where he served 1863-65. He then devoted himself to farming and the practice of his profession. He died April 22, 1870.

PETER H. BURNETT, the first circuit attorney who prosecuted in Buchanan County, was born in Nashville, Tenn. He was appointed circuit attorney of the Fifth judicial circuit in 1837, and after serving, resigned to go to Oregon. In 1848 he went from Oregon to California, of which state he was the first governor, and afterward one of the judges of the supreme court. He published "The Path Which Led a Protestant Lawyer to the Catholic Church" (1860), "The American Theory of Government Considered With Reference to the Present Crisis" (1861), "Recollections of an Old Pioneer" (1878), and "Reasons Why We Should Believe in God, Love God and Obey God" (1884). He died May 17, 1895.

ROBERT M. STEWART, Missouri's eccentric governor, was born in Truxton, N. Y., on March 12, 1815. He taught school when he was seventeen and until he was twenty years of age.

He then went to Kentucky, studied law and was admitted to the bar at Louisville. In 1839 he came to Buchanan County and located in Bloomington township, practicing law at Sparta and at Blacksnake Hills, wherever the court happened to sit. In 1845 he was elected to the state constitutional convention and soon gained well deserved reputation as a debator. From 1846 to 1857 he was a member of the state senate. In 1857, when Governor Polk resigned, he was elected as a Democrat. He was a delegate from Buchanan County to the convention of 1861. He was not in favor of abolition, but he was against secession, and ardently supported the Union. In fact, his decided stand against secession, when so much seemed to depend upon the action of Missouri, helped to save the state to the Union, and made his action one of national consideration. He was one of the projectors of the Hannibal & St. Joseph Railroad and helped to survey the line, and by his eloquence and logic, to secure the right-of-way. He was a bachelor and a man of many eccentricities. He died September 21, 1871, and there was general suspension of business in St. Joseph upon the day of his funeral. His remains were buried at Mount Mora. The following, which appeared in the Jefferson City Tribune, as a contribution from Col. Jacob T. Child, illustrates the character of Governor Stewart: .

"When Missouri was in the turmoil of the gigantic struggle between the two great sections of the Republic, Bob Stewart of St. Joseph defeated Gen. James S. Rollins of Boone, one of the greatest men of the then West, for governor. Then Jefferson City was comparatively a small village, the gubernatorial mansion, a frail old frame building, occupying the same site where the present mansion stands. It was a time of vast changes. Everything was in an embryotic state. Stewart was a 'Bourbon' in the full sense of the word. A New Yorker, he took the Union side of the cause, but the tide of secession was so strong that he could not stem the current, and he passed down and out with but regrets. His administration was novel in the extreme for many of his actions. As soon as he was inaugurated he had his private secretary, Dr. Peabody, fill out a pardon for William Langston, a prisoner from St. Joseph, charged with aiding in the whipping of a man of worthless character to death. As soon as he could get away from the capitol he went to the penitentiary and called for Langston. The old man was employed in digging a well. Stewart went to the brink and called him up. As he stepped out of the bucket the governor slapped him on the back, exclaiming, 'Billy, old man, let me greet you as a free man for all time,' and handed him his pardon. Langston had befriended Stewart when he was an invalid and had no friends.

"Another time the governor had been 'social' with a number of friends and in the 'we sma'' hours called for his horse, rode rapidly up the stairs into the reception room, ordered his servant to open the piano and pour in on the keyboard a peck of oats, remarking, with an oath, that his horse had just as much right to food and refreshments as the balance of mankind. The hoof marks of the horse could be seen on the stairway until the old mansion had been demolished. Feeling the influence of stimulation to excess, he imagined that he had snakes in his boots, and, sending for a pint of camphor, he poured it into his shoes; he pulled them on, and by night the snakes were gone, as well as all of the skin off of his feet. His pardoning of the female convicts is known to all, and the employment of them in the mansion, where they stole things ad libitum. Notwithstanding these eccentricities, he made a good governor. While he was drinking he would never sign a state paper. He was an urgent advocate of internal improvements, and as president of the Hannibal & St. Joseph railroad, never ceased his labors in favor of that great highway till the gleaming steel connected the Mississippi and the Missouri, which aided materially in the war of the sections. His reception of the Prince of Wales in St. Louis was so courteous that Albert Edward pronounced him the most polished man he had met in the states. But the worm of the still was working in his vitals; he was his worst enemy. Prior to his death I was his major. He was appointed colonel of volunteers under Fremont, but excessive drinking caused General Halleck to relieve him of his command. After that he lived a life of Bohemianism in St. Joseph, till the dark wings of Azrael overshadowed him, passing away comparatively friendless, and if I mistake not, the grassy hillock that covers his remains has no memorial to mark the spot.

"Thus one of Missouri's most famous governors passed away, and he is mostly known for deeds that should be forgotten, rather than for those that should halo his memory. Visiting the state capitol and mingling with its progressive people, I could not help thinking when Bob Stewart was the brave fellow well-met with all, and whose name was a household word from the Ozarks to the Iowas. I offer this laurel-leaf in the columns of The Tribune to the memory of a man that might have been worthy of much to imperial Missouri, but he fell by the wayside and passed away as an arrow shot through the air."

WILLARD P. HALL — This name also figures prominently in the history of Missouri. He was born at Harper's Ferry, Va., May 9, 1820, and graduated from Yale College. In 1842 he came to Buchanan County and practiced law at Sparta. Governor Reynolds appointed him circuit attorney. In 1844 he was a Democratic presidential elector and had the honor of carrying the vote of the state electors for James K. Polk, to Washington. In 1846, while a candidate for congress against Judge Birch of Clinton County, he abandoned the campaign and enlisted as a private in the First Missouri cavalry, upon a call for troops to fight Mexico. He went with Gen. Kearney's expedition, under Col. Alexander W. Doniphan, as far as Santa Fe. He was detailed to aid Colonel Doniphan in preparing a code of laws for the government of the territory of New Mexico. While thus engaged he was notified that he had been elected to congress. As the congress to which he had been elected did not meet until December, 1847, he decided to go with General Kearney to California. He was in congress for six years. He was elected as one of the representatives of Buchanan County to the convention of 1861, and was so ardent in his opposition of secession, that when the convention assumed control of the state, he was made lieutenant-governor. During the war he was prominent in the direction of military affairs, and upon the death of Governor Gamble, January 31, 1864, General Hall was made governor, which office he filled until the inauguration of Governor Fletcher, January 2, 1865. He then resumed his law practice in St. Joseph, and was classed as one of Missouri's greatest lawyers. He died November 3, 1882. He was twice married—to his first wife, Miss Annie E. Richardson, in 1847, and to his second wife, Miss Ollie L. Oliver, in 1864.

SILAS WOODSON, the third Buchanan County man to fill the governor's chair, was born in Knox County, Ky., May 18, 1819. He worked on his father's farm, attended the log cabin school in the neighborhood and spent his leisure time in reading and study. He clerked for a time in a country store and then took up the study of law. He was admitted to the bar in 1842. In 1842 he was a member of the Kentucky legislature, and from 1843 to 1848 he was circuit attorney. In 1849 he was elected to the Kentucky constitutional convention. In 1853 he was again a member of the Kentucky legislature, and in August of 1854 he came to St. Joseph, where he opened a law office. In 1860 he was elected judge of the Twelfth judicial circuit. He was a Union man during the war and was on the staff of General Willard P. Hall. In 1872 he was nominated by the Democrats for governor and defeated John B. Henderson, the Republican candidate. At the expiration of his term he resumed the practice of law in St. Joseph. In 1885 he was appointed judge of the criminal court of Buchanan County, which position he held until 1895, when he retired owing to failing health. He died October 9, 1896. During his last illness he embraced the Catholic faith. He was married three times. His last wife was Miss Jennie Lard, daughter of Rev. Moses E. Lard, whom he married December 29, 1866, and who, with two daughters, survived him. He was a man of high character, and a powerful advocate before a jury.

M. JEFF THOMPSON — This man figured as a brilliant genius in the early history of St. Joseph. General Thompson was born at Harper's Ferry, Va., January 22, 1826. His father, Captain Merriweather Thompson, a prominent citizen of that place, was a native of Hanover County, Virginia. He was for years in the paymaster's department of the United States army at Harper's Ferry. The proper name of the subject of this sketch was Merriweather. The appellation "Jeff" was a nick-name applied in childhood, and the manner in which he acquired his middle name is somewhat amusing. It appears that in early life, the future general was anything but a studious child, indeed, was sorely addicted to playing truant, and having in numerous instances of desertion from school been found perched on the top of a scavenger's cart driven by an ancient darkey, who rejoiced in the name of Jeff Carlyle. By way of shaming the young runaway and reclaiming him from his objectionable habit, his friends called him "Jeff Carlyle." The name, however, clung to him through life and after he had attained to manhood, and emigrated from his native home to St. Joseph, many who knew him as "Jeff," and were ignorant or oblivious of the fact that it was a nick-name, continued so to address him. Powers of attorney were made out to him in this name under which, of course, he could not act, and in consequence he induced the legislature to legally affix "Jeff" to his name. On leaving home in 1846, he stopped in Liberty, Clay County, Missouri, where he clerked in a store about a year, at the end of which period he moved to St. Joseph and engaged as a clerk in the house of Middleton & Riley, remaining in the store till 1852, when he went in their interest to Great Salt Lake City. Returning in the fall, he started in partnership with Major Bogle, a grocery store in St. Joseph. He subsequently closed out his store and accompanied, in the capacity of commissary, the surveyors of the Hannibal & St. Joseph railroad. He afterward returned from Hannibal in charge of a surveying party, having acquired during his trip, by close application, a competent knowledge of practical surveying. He was entrusted with the task of constructing the western division of the Hannibal & St. Joseph railroad, and remained in that position up to the period of its completion, in February, 1859. In 1858 he filled the office of city engineer, and in 1859 was elected mayor. He was president of the Maryville or Palmetto & Roseport railroad (now St. Joseph & Grand Island), secretary of the St. Joseph & Topeka Railroad Company, now out of existence; was a member of the Elwood Town Company, and at the same time engaged in the real estate business in St. Joseph, being a member of the firm of Harbine & Thompson. He saw a great future in the railroad to the west, and had not the circumstances prevented, he might have given St. Joseph the first commercial place in this region. He was a military man also, and in 1860 and 1861 was colonel of a regiment of state guards. At the critical moment he cast his fortunes with the South and gave all of his wonderful energy and enthusiasm to that cause. The incident of taking the Union colors from the postoffice is related elsewhere in this history. He made a brilliant record as a soldier, attained the rank of brigadier-general and was known as "Swamp Fox." Toward the close of 1864, being convinced that his cause was lost, he surrendered his command to the federal authorities, and for a time was a prisoner on Johnson Island, near Sandusky, O. As soon as he was released he accepted the situation and was one of the first of the southern leaders to become reconstructed. Locating in New Orleans after the close of the war, he engaged in the grocery and liquor business for a short time, and then, through the influence of General A. L. Lee, who had been a banker in St. Joseph and president of the Elwood Town Company, General Thompson was appointed surveyor-general of Louisiana, a position which ᴜe held for eight years, and the duties of which were so arduous as to completely break down his constitution. Obtaining a leave of absence, he traveled for a time and then came to St. Joseph, where he became bedfast, and died at the Pacific House on September 5, 1876. His remains rest at Mount Mora cemetery. He was a brother to Charles M. Thompson, formerly recorder of the city, and many years deputy under Samuel D. Cowan, clerk of the circuit court, and later removed to California. Broaddus Thompson, at one time a prominent attorney here, who was noted for his refinement and culture, was also a brother. General Thompson was married at Liberty, Mo., in 1848, to Miss Emma Hays of Baltimore.

COL. ELIJAH GATES, than whom few men have been more esteemed by their countrymen, was born in Garrard County, Kentcuky, in 1827, and the greater part of his life was spent in Buchanan County and St. Joseph. He was honored with many positions of trust, all of which he filled with credit to himself and to the satisfaction of his friends. Colonel Gates died in St. Joseph March 4, 1915.

He was the son of John Gates, owner of a large plantation in Kentucky, who died when the subject of this sketch was but a year and a half old. Colonel Gates was educated in the schools of his native county, and came to Missouri when twenty years old. He located in Buchanan County in 1857 and engaged in farming, which occupation he followed until the outbreak of the Civil war.

In 1861 he enlisted in the Confederate army from St. Joseph and was soon elected captain of Company A, Missouri State Guards, Morgan's division. After three months of service he was promoted to lieutenant-colonel, and three months later was advanced to colonel.

He formed a regiment in Springfield, Mo., and served with Gen. Sterling Price until the fall of 1861. General Price once said of him: "He is the bravest man I ever knew." In the spring of 1862 he crossed the Mississippi and joined the army under Beauregard at Corinth, and continued in service east of the Mississippi until the close of the war.

Colonel Gates was taken prisoner on three occasions. At the battle of Franklin he was wounded in the left arm so badly as to lose that member. He was captured, but made his escape and went to Mobile, where he took command of a brigade and participated in the battle of Mobile. He was captured at Big Black, Miss., but eluded his captors a few days later. He was again captured at Blakely, opposite Mobile, in the last battle of the war, was incarcerated three weeks at Ship Island, and then sent to Jackson, just as General Taylor surrendered. He was in practically all of the engagement of the Missouri troops, and about half of the time was in command of his brigade.

He returned home July 5, 1865, after four years of long and hard service. He resumed the business of farming and continued until 1874, when he was elected sheriff on the Democratic ticket, in which position he served four years. He was elected state treasurer of Missouri and served four years. After returning to St. Joseph he was appointed United States marshal for the Western District of Missouri by President Cleveland during his first term. He was in the transfer and bus business in St. Joseph, as a member of the firm of Piner & Gates, for many years, but the last years of his life were spent in retirement at his home, 701 South Ninth street. He was a man representative of the highest type of character and had many warm, true friends throughout the state.

Colonel Gates was married in Livingston County, Missouri, in 1852 to Miss Maria Stamper, who was born in Monroe County, Missouri, and died December 24, 1898.

COL. ELIJAH GATES

JUDGE O. M. SPENCER comes from one of those prominent pioneer families of the West who have left such worthy examples and honorable names to their posterity. He was born on the old Spencer homestead, in Crawford Township, Buchanan County, Missouri, August 23, 1849. His father, Obadiah M. Spencer, was a native of North Carolina; his mother, Nancy Williams Spencer, a native of Kentucky. His parents came to Mis-

called "bush-whackers," and the next with the Union troops.

The boys inclined toward the cause of the South, although the father was a Union man.

In 1869, he entered the state university at Columbia. In 1871 he became a student at the Christian University at Canton, Mo., from which he was graduated with one of the honors of the institution in 1873. Subsequently he read law at Leavenworth. In 1874

JUDGE O. M. SPENCER

souri in 1837. It was Judge Spencer's good fortune to see much of life and men when he was a boy. His father, who was one of the leading citizens of the Platte Purchase, resided near the line of Platte County, in the "hot-bed" of Southern sympathizers. "Tom," as he was nick-named, and his four younger brothers were one day in the company of the rebels, commonly

he entered the law school at Harvard. The following year he opened an office for the practice of his profession at St. Joseph. Like nearly every Missouri lawyer who has made his mark on his time, Judge Spencer passed through the school of the prosecuting attorneyship. He was elected in 1880, serving the two-year term. During this time he was a member of the legal firm consisting of Willard P. Hall, Jr., and himself, known as Spencer and Hall. A decade of practice had won the favorable opinion of the people of the populous county of Buchanan. It is therefore no surprise to learn that the people acquiesced in the action of the representatives of the Democratic party when, in 1886, they nominated Mr. Spencer for circuit judge. It is a fact of special significance and which speaks eloquently of the favor with which he was viewed, that the Republican lawyers

Tootle. Her mother was a sister of James McCord. Mrs. Spencer was a lady of rare accomplishments, who died in 1880, at the age of twenty-four years, when her youngest child was only twelve months old. Two bright boys were born to Judge and Mrs. Spencer, Henry Heddens, born July 20, 1877, and who died a few years ago, and Edwin O. M., born July 4, 1879. On March 5, 1895, Judge Spencer was married to Miss Katherine Turner of Columbia, Mo., a daughter of Colonel and Mrs. S.

MAJOR H. R. W. HARTWIG

of the circuit joined him in the call and refused to nominate a candidate against him. Judge Spencer's term on the bench was characterized by capability and impartiality. He did not occupy the bench the full term, however, as at the end of four years he resigned to accept the position of general solicitor of the Burlington railroad system in Missouri, and he still occupies that place.

Judge Spencer was married in 1875 to Miss Lillian, daughter of Joseph

Turner. Their boy, whom they named Tom, was killed in an automobile accident five years ago when only fifteen years old. Their daughter, Sarah, fifteen years of age, is now in school at Washington, D. C. She is a splendid girl and is deservedly idolized by her father.

Few men are better known in Missouri than Judge O. M. Spencer, and none have made or deserve a higher standard of manhood. He is now sixty-five years old, full of life and energy, due, he says, to constant effort at some one thing or another. "Never still or idle except when asleep" is his motto. He loves home life and family ties, and next to this he loves the Burlington railroad.

ALBERT R. GOETZ, secretary-treasurer of the M. K. Goetz Brewing Company, is a native of Missouri and of St. Joseph. He was born in this city November 20, 1871. He received his education in the public schools and

DR. ELIJAH A. COLLEY

DR. ELIJAH A. COLLEY, 501½ South Sixth street, was born in Clinton County, Missouri, November 4, 1877. He was educated in the common schools of Clinton County and later attended the Plattsburg College, where he was graduated in June, 1899. In the same year he entered the medical department of the Missouri university, and received his M. D. degree in 1904. In the fall of that year he located in Plattsburg, where he began practicing. In 1908 he came to St. Joseph. He is a member of the Masonic order. He was married to Miss Elizabeth Kessler of St. Joseph, May 20, 1915.

business colleges of the city, and soon after leaving school began taking an interest in the business which his father had established some years before. He was placed in charge of the soliciting and collection departments, and in 1895 was made secretary-treasurer of the company. He has been one of the important factors in the growth and development of the business, which has become one of the most important in the city.

Mr. Goetz was married to Miss Flora Weidmaier, May 22, 1902. He has membership cards in the St. Joseph Turnverein, German Benevolent Society, Knights of Pythias, Elks and Eagles.

P. P. BUDDY BUILDING CONSTRUC-TION COMPANY

Numerous substantial public buildings and handsome private residences in St. Joseph today are lasting monuments to the constructive skill and executive ability of the P. P. Buddy Building Construction Company.

This business was first established by Philip Buddy in 1868 in a small shop at Sixth and Messanie streets.

Mr. Buddy was an eminently practical mechanic, and under his instruction his son, Philip Perry Buddy, graduated into a thorough craftsman. Philip, Jr., worked with his father as apprentice and journeyman from 1881 until 1890, when he was taken into partnership in the business. In 1902 the firm moved to the present quarters at 501-3 Main street, where a general contracting business has been followed.

P. P. BUDDY

Mr. Buddy was a master craftsman in the carpenter line, and his ability to make correct estimates on the cost of proposed buildings soon gained for him a high reputation. After ten years of successful work as a building contractor, Mr. Buddy's quarters became too small for his constantly growing business, and he moved to Second and Jule streets.

Sixteen years ago Mr. Buddy, Sr., died, and his son, Philip Perry Buddy, continued the business for seven years, when a corporation was formed with Mr. Buddy as president and treasurer, Albert T. Jones, vice-president, and Allen T. White, secretary. Mr. Jones and Mr. White had been former employes of Mr. Buddy and had risen to the positions of foreman of construction and mill work, respectively.

Among the numerous buildings in St. Joseph which bear testimony to the efficient and skillful work of the P. P. Buddy Construction Company may be mentioned the Auditorium, the Livestock Exchange, Buchanan County

(Clark) Dandurant. His parents were members of two of the oldest and best known families of this city. He has one sister, Mrs. F. Sophie Schatt also of this city.

His early education was procured at the Christian Brothers College of St. Joseph, Mo., and after graduating from this institution he took up his

LOUIS JOSEPH DANDURANT

jail, St. Patrick's Parochial School, McCord-Harlow shoe factory, the Transit House, Robidoux school, St. Francis Catholic Church of Wyatt Park, St. James' Catholic Church of South St. Joseph, German Catholic Church of the Immaculate Conception at Tenth and Angelique streets, and scores of other buildings and private residences.

LOUIS JOSEPH DANDURANT, M. D. A. B. AM. LLD., one of the leading surgeons and physicians of St. Joseph, was born in St. Joseph, Missouri, and is a son of Damas F. and Rose Ann

advanced studies in the classics and science in the noted institution of learning then known as New Engleberg College, at Conception, Mo. This college is the American branch of the ancient and famous university of Engleberg located at Engleberg, Switzerland.

From this institution he received the degree of "Bachelor of Arts" and later the degree of "Master of Arts."

He pursued his medical and surgical studies in the Central Medical College and the medical department of the University of the State of New York City graduating in the year 1898. After graduating in medicine he took up his special work in surgery in St. Vincent's hospital, the largest private hospital in New York City, as a student of Professor Herman St. John Boldt, one of America's foremost surgeons.

After graduating in medicine Dr. Dandurant began the practice of his profession in St. Joseph, Mo. Within the first year he was elected professor of chemistry, toxicology and urinalysis in the Central Medical College of

ried to Miss Cecile Agnes Buddy, daughter of Charles A. Buddy, one of St. Joseph's most substantial and best known business men.

The doctor has one child, a son born Oct. 19-12.

Dr. Dandurant has not had the disposition or time to spare for active participation in politics, however, he is a strong advocate of good government and is always ready to lend his aid to this cause. In the year 1914 he was strongly urged by many prominent and influential citizens of St.

PATRICK P. KANE

this city, and was also appointed professor of anatomy at St. Joseph's Hospital. A few years later he was appointed professor of surgery at St. Joseph's hospital, and also clinical surgery and gynecology on the staff of the Central Medical College.

Soon after beginning the practice of his profession he was appointed county physician of Buchanan county in which capacity he served several years.

Doctor Dandurant later studied advanced surgery and diagnoses in the University of Vienna, Austria, and the great clinics of Europe, pursuing special work in France, Germany, Switzerland, Austria and England.

On October 4tn, 1910, he was mar-

Joseph to become a candidate for mayor on the Democratic ticket, but the doctor felt that to fill that office properly would mean too great a sacrifice of his professional work.

In June, 1912, the degree of Doctor of Laws was conferred on him by the Christian Brother's College at St. Louis, Mo.

PATRICK P. KANE, one of the well-known and popular and respected citizens of St. Joseph, who occupies the responsible position of chief of the city fire department, was born in St. Joseph March 5, 1864, and is the son of James and Mary (Burke) Kane. He was reared and educated in St. Joseph. In early manhood he took an interest in the fire department, and, as he possessed the physique and physical courage necessary, he was admitted to membership in Hose Company No. 2 in 1882, and was transferred to Hook and Ladder Company No. 1 in October, 1884. Strict attention to duty and daring bravery in the face of danger attracted attention, and in 1885 he was appointed foreman of the Hook and Ladder No. 1 Company and was advanced to the position of assistant chief in 1891. He remained in this position until 1897, when he was made chief of the department, a

Margaret Vahey of St. Joseph, a native of England, and they have one daughter, Gertrude. Their comfortable home is located at 1807 South Eleventh street.

JOHN S. ANDREWS, real estate man, at 615 Francis street, is a native of Iowa, being born at Iowa City, September 16, 1850. He received his education in his native city. At the age of fifteen he entered the jewelry firm of O. Starchman of Iowa City, where he learned the jeweler's trade. Mr. Andrews came to St. Joseph September 16, 1871, and took charge of the

JOHN S. ANDREWS

promotion which met with the approbation of his subordinates and pleased his fellow-citizens, who had learned to trust in his fidelity. The position of chief of the fire department of St. Joseph is no sinecure, as he has sixteen engine houses and ninety-one men under his command.

In 1889 Chief Kane was married to

Jake Goodlive jewelry store at Fourth and Edmond streets, where he remained for fourteen years. In 1885 he formed a partnership with K. H. Clarke, the firm name being Clarke & Andrews. Their store was at 413 Felix street. Mr. Andrews remained with this firm four years. In 1888 he engaged in the real estate business with John L. Zeidler, the firm name being Zeidler & Andrews. In 1890 the firm of Andrews & Kelly was formed. The business is still conducted by Mr. Andrews under the name of Andrews & Kelley, although Mr. Kelley died six years ago. Mr. Andrews was married to Lillie Pinto of Chillicothe, Ohio, May 9, 1893. Fraternally Mr. Andrews is an Elk.

foreman and manager of this department in 1894, which position he still holds. Mr. Morrison was elected to the city council in 1908 for a term of four years, and served until the new charter took effect, a year later, which had the effect of legislating him out of office. He ran again in 1910, but was defeated. In 1912 he was elected again

WILLIAM DENT MORRISON

WILLIAM DENT MORRISON, president of the board of public works of St. Joseph, is a native of Iowa, having been born in Wayne county, that state, February 11, 1854. He received his education in the schools of his native county. In 1878 he went to Wyoming, where he remained for four years. In 1882 he came to Missouri, locating in Kansas City. The following year he came to St. Joseph. In March, 1889, he began work for the Wyeth Hardware & Manufacturing Company, in the collar department. He was made

by the best majority given any candidate on the Republican ticket. When the first public utilities commission was created by a city ordinance, Mr. Morrison was appointed one of the members, and served from 1910 until 1912. He has also served on the board of health and other important committees at the city hall, and has the reputation of performing his every public duty properly. He was married to Miss Lillie Story of Waynesboro, Penn., in 1877. Their family consists of a son and two daughters. Mr. Morrison is a member of the Loyal Order of Moose.

In October, 1915, Mr. Morrison resigned as councilman and was appointed by Mayor Marshall to membership on the board of public works. When that body was reorganized he was made president.

ing February 1, 1889, and entering practice at Bethany Mo., having a splendid practice, being the only osteopath in the county at that time. But the country practice being rather strenuous, he decided to locate in some city, finally deciding on St. Joseph, the City Worth While—a choice

DR. WILLIAM E. BEETS

DR. WILLIAM E. BEETS, Osteopath, at 207-8 Logan Building, is a native Missourian, his birthplace being Kirksville, the date April 5, 1868. His preliminary education was received in the public schools of his native city, after which he graduated from Humphrey's College and Business Institute, in Sullivan County. He then attended the State Normal School at Kirksville, leaving this institution to enter upon a business career. He was married to Miss Emily M. Vice of Canton, Ill. He entered the American School of Osteopathy in 1886, graduat-

he has never regretted, as his practice has been a very large one and among the very best people. He is a member of the National, Mississippi, Missouri and Kansas, State, and Northwest associations, and has been honored with a number of offices. Is a member of the Elks, M. W. A., M. B. A. and Royal Neighbors. At this writing he is taking a much-needed rest, visiting the expositions and attending the California State Osteopathic meeting at Los Angeles and the National meeting at Portland.

ENOS CRAIG was born April 27, 1829, in Millersburg, Holmes County, Ohio. He is of Scotch-Irish descent, his parents being James Craig, a lawyer, and Margaret Slater.

At the age of fourteen he removed with his parents to Farmington, Iowa, where he helped to break the prairies of the West. At the age of twenty-

coln keeper of the military prison at St. Joseph, which position he held during his term as sheriff. In 1863 he was commissioned captain to raise a company for the Union army, but while making up the company a slow, lingering illness of typhoid befell him, and he was compelled to give up his military ambitions.

ENOS CRAIG

one years he left Iowa and located in St. Joseph.

April 4, 1852, he married Emily Miranda Barnes, daughter of Joseph and Hannah Barnes, at DeKalb, Mo. Three weeks later they crossed the plains to California, where Mr. Craig prospected for several years, returning to St. Joseph in 1859.

He soon was appointed to the position of general delivery clerk in the postoffice, where he made many friends. They loyally supported him in running for sheriff of Buchanan County, to which office he was overwhelmingly elected in the fall of 1862, and was appointed by President Lin-

In 1866 he was elected city marshal, and later he was appointed the marshal of the first supreme court held in the city of St. Joseph. In 1880 he was again elected city marshal. In 1884 he was appointed deputy United States marshal for the Western District of Missouri. In 1890 he was again appointed to the same office. In 1894 he defeated Robert M. Nash by one vote for county clerk. He held the office for four or five months, but after a spirited contest, which was finally decided against him by the supreme court, he surrendered the office. In 1898 he again ran for county clerk and was defeated. In 1908, in his eightieth year, he was defeated for county judge by forty-seven votes. In his eighty-third years he was appointed city weighmaster, and when eighty-five years of age was reappointed, which position he is now holding successfully.

Mr. Craig has been a lifelong Republican and refused to recognize any faction in his party. He has always

man and designer in England. He came to America in 1870, landing in New York City. A little later he went to Patterson, N. J., and toward the end of the same year came to St. Joseph and secured work with Edward Dutton, a manufacturer of wagons at Edmond and Charles streets. After three years of this engagement he established the carriage

HARRY PARKER

—Photo by Mulvane.

abhorred treachery, deception, untruthfulness and selfishness, and has never made a promise that he did not regard as sacred.

In 1907 he lost his beloved wife, who had borne him four children, Corydon F., Morte H., Lelia M. McReynolds, and Lulu Alice.

Hs is a member of the First Baptist Church.

HARRY PARKER, carriage and ornamental painter, at 905 South Ninth street is a native of England. He was born in Coventry, March 1, 1844. He learned the trade of drafts-

and wagon painting shop at Sixth and Charles streets, where the first bus was painted for J. A. Piner. He has been in the painting business in St. Joseph ever since. He is one of the progressive, substantial business men of the city and loves his city as all good citizens should. He built the first house, at Nineteenth and Faraon streets, with funds furnished by a building and loan association in St. Joseph. Before coming to America he spent eight years in the bankruptcy department of the sheriff's office in Birmingham.

DR. FRANK PERRY WALKER, direct descendant of the Alexander and John Walker family of England, was born on a farm near Memphis, Scotland County, Missouri, in the blustering month of March, 1877.

He received his early training in the district school and graduated from the Memphis high school in 1898. During his high school course he not only carried his regular work, but taught two terms of school and graduated with his class. After graduation he continued in the teaching profession in Scotland County, and later in North Dakota, where he also proved up on a claim. During his work as a teacher he attended various teachers' training schools and took special work in Iowa City, Iowa.

In 1901 he entered the American School of Osteopathy at Kirksville, Mo., completing the course in 1903 and receiving his degree of D. O. He then located in Cando, North Dakota, where he practiced nearly three years. He removed to St. Joseph in 1905, where he entered a general practice of Osteopathy. He took the regular medical course in the Ensworth Medical College of St. Joseph, Mo., from which he received his degree of M. D., afterward passing the examination of the state medical board of Missouri. Doctor Walker spent two summers in Chicago, taking special work in operative surgery in the Post Graduate

DR. FRANK PERRY WALKER
—Photo by Mulvane.

Medical School of Chicago and at West Side Hospital.

Dr. Walker served two successive terms as president of the Missouri Osteopathic Association, and during his two years' tenure in office succeeded in organizing the state into districts. He also served as president of the Northwest Missouri Osteopathic Association and has served on the Legislative Committee of the state for several years. He was president of the Christian Endeavor Union of St

Joseph for three years, and during that time was a delegate to the International Christian Endeavor Convention in St. Paul, Minnesota. He also attended the Y. M. C. A. Conference at Lake Geneva while in the American School of Osteopathy, representing that College as a delegate.

business, and after working in the plant for ten years, attended the American Brewing Academy in 1893-95, receiving two diplomas. When the present company was formed to handle the business which Mr. M. K. Goetz had established, William L. was elected president and he has shown

WILLIAM L. GOETZ

He is a member of the First Congregational Church of St. Joseph, a Rotarian, a member of the American Osteopathic Association, belongs to the Masonic Lodge No. 78, is a member of the Country Club and also of the Commerce Club.

WILLIAM L. GOETZ, President of the M. K. Goetz Brewing Company, claims St. Joseph as the city of his nativity, having been born here June 17, 1867. He was educated in the public schools of the city and in Bryant's Business College. He served a thorough apprenticeship in the brewing

remarkable ability as an executive. He is recognized as one of the most progressive and successful business men in the city.

Mr. Goetz was married to Miss Anna B. Pape, October 19, 1898. They have two children, Wilford Lawson, aged eight, and Horace Raymond, aged seven years. Mr. Goetz is a member of the Elks, Red Men, the Country Club, the Turners, and the St. Joseph Schwabin-Verein. He is a member of the American Society of Brewing Technology, alumni association Wahl-Heninus Institute.

JACK D. ROBINSON, representative in the state legislature from the Fourth Buchanan County District, was born in Decatur, Adams County, Indiana, March 7, 1880. He was educated in the school of Decatur, graduating from the high school in 1898. The same year he entered the Indiana Law School at Indianapolis, where he stud-

in November, 1914. He introduced one-eighth of the bills that were passed by the general assembly in 1915, the most important being the school bond bill which provided adequate schools for the children of St. Joseph; also the general bond issue bill, which provided for parks, sewers, city hospital for the poor, new workhouse, improve-

JACK D. ROBINSON
—Photo by Mulvane.

ied law for two years. He was admitted to the bar at Decatur the day he was twenty-one years old, and commenced the practice of law at once. He remained in Decatur three years, and came to St. Joseph in 1907. He first engaged in the insurance business, but in 1912 returned to the practice of law, opening an office in the Corby-Forsee building. He was elected to the legislature as a Democrat

ment of electric light plant, repairing of streets, remodeling of city hall, equipping fire department with motor trucks, thereby reducing fire insurance rates, etc.

He was married to Miss Daisy McCully of St. Joseph December 12, 1907. They have one son, Calvin, five years old. Mr. Robinson is a member of the Loyal Order of Moose.

LAWRENCE BOTHWELL was born in southern Illinois, May 12, 1879, where he lived until the age of seventeen, when he went to Sedalia, Mo. He is of the Scotch and English stock, his ancestors having come from Scot-

the active practice of law ever since.

In 1913 he was nominated on the Republican ticket for prosecuting attorney of Buchanan County, but was defeated, along with the rest of the Republican ticket. He is an active

LAWRENCE BOTHWELL

land and England and settling in Pennsylvania and Ohio. While at Sedalia he lived with his uncle, the Honorable John H. Bothwell, and during his nine years' residence there he completed his high school education and then his university courses at Columbia, Mo, both the academic and law. From Sedalia he came directly to St. Joseph, where he has been in

member of the Knights of Pythias order and is one of the high officers.

On April 29, 1915, he was married to Miss Frances L. Fox, a popular young lady of St. Joseph, and whose parents formerly lived at Sedalia. Mr. Bothwell has made a pronounced success of the practice of the law, and is considered one of the leading attorneys of the Buchanan County bar.

HENRY E. GROSSER, Councilman, is a native of Illinois, having been born in Chicago, Ill. At the age of eight years he moved with his parents to Dickinson County, Kansas, where he was educated. At the age of eigh-

ness, the Warner & Grosser Lumber Company, at 1614 Commercial street.

Early in 1908 he was appointed a member of the city council by William E. Spratt, then mayor, to fill the

HENRY E. GROSSER
—Photo by Mulvane.

teen years he became a school teacher in Dickinson County, and after a time engaged in the lumber business with his father at Enterprise, in the same county. He remained there ten years, and in 1901 went to Horton, Kans., where he again became a retail dealer in lumber and kindred articles of merchandise.

Mr. Grosser came to St. Joseph in 1903 and established his present busi-

unexpired term of Dr. P. I. Leonard, who resigned. A few months later, or in April of that year, Mr. Grosser was elected to the municipal aldermanic body by a handsome majority. He served two years, and in 1914 was again elected for a four-year term.

Fraternally he holds membership in the Masons, Odd Fellows, Fraternal Aid, Woodmen of the World and Knights and Ladies of Security.

DR. A. S. J. SMITH, with offices at 710½ Felix street, was born on a farm in Vernon County, Missouri, November 5th, 1871, where he remained until 18 years of age when he entered the Christian University at began the study of medicine, after taking a scientific course at the Warrensburg State Normal. He was graduated from the Ensworth Medical College in 1905 and practiced in St. Joseph for one year before going to

DR. A. S. J. SMITH

Nevada, Missouri. Dr. Smith later spent two years in the State Normal Schools at Kirksville and Warrensburg, afterwards teaching in the public schools of Holt and Nodaway counties for eight years. The last two years of which, he was superintendent of the Skidmore schools. In 1901 he Dearborn where he remained for nine years, returning to St. Joseph in 1915. A part of the year 1911 was spent in the Post Graduate Medical School and Hospital of New York City. Dr. Smith was a popular candidate for representative of Platte County at the Democratic primary in 1914.

CHARLES F. ENRIGHT, banker, financier and managing director of the Kansas City, Clay County & St. Joseph Interurban Railway, was born in St. Joseph, Missouri, October 23, 1866, near Third and Sylvanie streets; the home place was afterwards sold by his parents to the Burlington Railway, and the south part of the present Burlington Railway General Offices in St. Joseph stands on the lot of his birth-place.

pany, becoming its vice-president and treasurer. This banking company is located on the southeast corner of Fourth and Felix streets, and is to-day one of St. Joseph's solid, prosperous banking institutions.

In 1908 Mr. Enright retired from the banking business in order to be able to devote all of his time and energies to the construction of the Kansas City, Clay County & St. Joseph Interurban Ry., of which com-

CHARLES F. ENRIGHT

In 1881 he obtained a position as collector for the National Bank of St. Joseph, known as the Burnes Bank, of which bank Col. Calvin F. Burnes was president and Hon. James N. Burnes, afterwards member of Congress, was vice-president. After various promotions he was appointed assistant cashier of the bank, and in 1894 was elected cashier, serving in that capacity until 1899.

In 1899, in connection with John J. and Milton Tootle and others, he organized the Missouri Valley Trust Com-

pany he is now the managing director.

In January, 1893, he was married to Miss Jennie Fairleigh of St. Joseph, and to this union was born one son, William Fairleigh Enright, who attained his majority in February, 1915. His son, Fairleigh, has been a student at Harvard College for the past three years, and will graduate with the class of 1916.

Mr. Enright is one of St. Joseph's most prominent citizens. He is a forceful man, of ambitious effort and tireless energy, a man of high character and strong personality, of sterling integrity, wide experience and keen knowledge of human nature. Being of a courteous and extremely obliging disposition, coupled with unusual ability, he has won many strong friends in the Missouri valley, in St. Joseph, Kansas City and St. Louis and farther away in Chicago, New York, Boston and other eastern cities.

The firm of C. F. Enright & Co. has its offices in the Corby-Forsee Building, a twelve-story modern office building, the largest and best ap-

urer and dispenser of the funds of the Charity Board of St. Joseph, and gave much of his time to the successful conduct of its affairs.

DR. EDWARD A. LOGAN, bacteriologist and chemist for the Board of Health, was born in Manhattan, Kas., March 13, 1881. He received his education in the schools of Manhattan and in 1901 entered the Kansas State Agricultural College in that city. He received his diploma in 1905, being the recipient of a degree of Bachelor of Sciences. In 1906 he

DR. EDWARD A. LOGAN
—Photo by Mulvane.

pointed office building in St. Joseph, and is one of the important enterprises successfully promoted by Mr. Enright for St. Joseph.

Always ready to contribute his time and money for the welfare of St. Joseph, one gracious word should be mentioned here that will ever stand to his credit, namely—for about twenty years Mr. Enright was treas-

re-entered the school, this time taking the veterinary course, from which department he was graduated in 1909. He came to St. Joseph in 1912 and was appointed to the position he now holds. He was married to Miss Prudie Morgan of Harrisonville, Kas., in 1906. Their family consists of two daughters. Dr. Logan is a Mason and a Woodman.

DR. GEORGE T. NETHERTON was born in Daviess County, Missouri, August 23, 1841. He received his first education in his native county. He taught school and read medical books at home, and in the office of Dr. William L. Brosius at Gallatin, Missouri. He entered the Kansas City Medical College in 1894 and graduated from that school in 1897. He first located in Gallatin, Mo., where he did a general practice for four years. In 1901

Directors of The St. Joseph Sanatorium for Rectal Diseases, now located on third floor Ballinger Building, St. Joseph, Mo., with full suite of rooms and office No. 39B. Dr. Netherton was married to Miss Hannah Everly of Daviess County, Mo., August 2, 1866. His family consists of himself and wife, and two sons and their families, towit: Dr. C. O. Netherton of Gallatin, Mo., and Dr. E. J. Netherton of St. Joseph, Mo.

DR. GEORGE T. NETHERTON

he moved to Archer County, Texas, and did a general practice in both Archer and Wichita counties for seven years. In 1908, he returned to Gallatin, Mo., and opened an office in the same building he had occupied seven years previous, but limited his practice principally to orificial diseases, where he vigorously prosecuted his specialty, until July, 1915, when he was elected physician in charge and general manager by the Board of

JOSEPH J. WYATT was one of the pioneers of St. Joseph, and one of the most worthy of our citizens during his career. He was a native of Illinois, born in St. Clair County, July 13, 1819. When two years of age his mother died and his father moved to Kentucky, where our subject spent his youth. He enjoyed good educational advantages and was a diligent student. He read law with John Cavan, a leading attorney in those days and was.

admitted to the bar. March 28, .1844 he married Miss Emily Gooding. Our subject came to St. Joseph in 1845. He was town clerk, probate judge, judge of the court of common pleas, postmaster, and held other positions of public trust and honor and he discharged every obligation with scrupulous care and fidelity. In November of 1850 he identified himself with the Christian Church and

nues, was born in St. Joseph April 27, 1888. He was educated in the schools of the city and graduated from Central High School in 1903. A year later he graduated from Gard's Business College. He began the study of medicine in the Ensworth Medical College in 1906 and was graduated from that institution in May, 1910. After receiving his diploma he was

DR. CLARENCE S. BRANSON
—Photo by Mulvane.

was in time called to the pulpit, which he filled with zeal and distinction. In fact Elder Wyatt, as he was better known, was the leader of the struggling congregation and had the satisfaction of beholding the good fruits of his earnest work before he died. His was an active life and he left a record that is without tarnish. He died suddenly April 9, 1881.

DR. CLARENCE S. BRANSON, whose office is at the northwest corner of King Hill and Missouri ave-

appointed surgeon for Swift & Co., which position he filled for a period of nine months. In May, 1911, he was appointed physician and surgeon for the Hammond and Nelson Morris packing plants and he is still serving these concerns to their satisfaction. In addition to this work he has a large private practice. He was married to Miss Cloe Manning of St. Joseph June 18, 1909. They have one child, a son. Dr. Branson is a Mason and a member of the St. Joseph Buchanan Medical Society and State Medical Society.

BENJAMIN W. TRUNK, Architect, 8-9-10 Donnell Court Building, corner Fifth and Francis streets, St. Joseph, is a native of Missouri, born in Weston, Platte County, December 2, 1872. He was educated in the schools of St. Joseph. At the age of 14, he started to study architecture with the firm of Eckel & Mann and was in their employ for eighteen years. In 1890

his design. Mr. Trunk is a member of the Academy of Designers and Inventors of Paris and holds a diploma and gold medal from that society. He is also a member of the St. Louis Architectural Club and Secretary and Treasurer of the Architects Society of this city. Mr. Trunk has been in business for himself since 1904 and is one of the leading architects of the city.

BENJAMIN W. TRUNK

the firm sent him to St. Louis, Mo., and he worked in the office of George R. Mann for ten years at the time the St. Louis City Hall was built. In 1900 he was sent to Little Rock, Ark., and remained there for about a year, at which time he helped Mr. Mann plan the State Capitol building at Little Rock. In 1893, at the time of Chicago-Columbian Exposition, Mr. Trunk entered an architectural competition open to all the draftsmen in the United States under the age of thirty, and was awarded a medal for

SIMEON KEMPER, a pioneer, and one of the first surveyors, was born in Montgomery County, Kentucky, February 5, 1799 and came to Blacksnake Hills in 1840. He made a plan of Robidoux's prospective town, but it was rejected because the streets were too wide. The people of St. Joseph today sincerely regret this. Mr. Kemper was one of the original surveyors of the Hannibal & St. Joseph Railroad, and held the office of county surveyor. He died March 11, 1882.

MORTE H. CRAIG, JR., son of Morte H. Craig and grand-son of Enos Craig, was born in Council Bluffs, Iowa, February 22, 1880. He came to St. Joseph in 1882 and made his home with his grandfather, until the time of his marriage. He attended the schools of the city until June 15, 1898, when he quit and enlisted in Co. G. Fourth Regiment Mo. Vol. Inf. He was mustered out at

St. Joseph at this time and held the office of justice of the peace four years. In 1910, at the expiration of his term of office he began the practice of his profession in South St. Joseph. Mayor Pfeiffer appointed Mr. Craig to membership on the Library Board in 1912. He is Past Chancellor Knights of Pythias and a member of Georgetown Lodge I. O. O. F.

MORTE H. CRAIG

Greenville, S. C., February 10, 1899. In the fall of that year he entered the Highland Park Law School of Des Moines, Iowa and in February, 1901, was admitted to the bar. He was married to Miss Calphurnia M. Reese of St. Joseph September 12, 1901. Mr. Craig ran for justice of the peace on the Republican ticket in 1902, but was defeated. He ran again in 1906 and was elected. He moved to South

FREDERICK W. SMITH.—Second only to Joseph Robidoux, the founder of the city of St. Joseph, in the early history of the city, and who lived to see it expand and spread out over the large body of land he preempted adjacent to the original town site, was Frederick W. Smith. Capt. Smith was born October 3, 1815, in Prussia. He received his early education in his native town and afterward entered a military academy, where he was educated as a civil engineer. When eighteen years of age he sailed for America. Landing in New York in 1833, he remained there almost a year, and then removed to New Orleans, where he was employed in a cotton press. Owing to the breaking out of yellow fever in that city, he embarked on the Mississippi River, and came to St. Louis, where soon

appointed the first postmaster of the village of St. Joseph; in 1861 he was elected mayor of the city; his last office was that of Judge of the Buchanan County Court, his term ending in 1876. He married Miss Jane Tolin, of Daviess County, Mo., in 1843. Capt. Smith died May 7, 1883. He was a public spirited man and Smith Park, which he gave to the city, perpetuates his name.

LOUIS G. GENSLER

after his arrival he was appointed Deputy City Surveyor. In 1838, or 1839 he left St. Louis for the Platte Purchase, and settled at Blacksnake Hills (now St. Joseph). Here he engaged in farming and surveying. He made the original map of St. Joseph and named it after the founder of the city, Joseph Robidoux. Capt. Smith pre-empted land, upon which a portion of the city now stands, and which has been divided and subdivided and sold at different times. He was a captain of the militia for a number of years, and was afterwards made a Major of the State Volunteers; was

LOUIS G. GENSLER, manufacturer of carriages and wagons, at 1401 South Eleventh street, was born in Saxony, Germany, June 30, 1870. When he was 11 years old his parents brought him to America. They located first in Buffalo, N. Y., where they still reside. The subject of this sketch learned his trade in Buffalo. At the age of 21 he came west, locating in St. Joseph. His first employment was with Jacob Wickenhoffer, at Fourth and Charles streets, where he remained for ten years. In 1905 he purchased a half interest in the carriage works of John Raney, at 1401

South Eleventh street. After the death of Mr. Raney in 1909 he bought the entire business. He was married to Miss Minnie Kerber, daughter of Mr. and Mrs. Henry Kerber of Garretsburg, Mo., in 1902. They have

common schools. He came to St. Joseph in 1885 and in 1887 was appointed a member of the fire department, which position he held for eight years. In 1894 he entered the Ensworth Medical College and graduated

DR. FREDERICK H. LADD
—Photo by Mulvane.

two children, a son and daughter. Mr. Gensler is a member of the Odd Fellows, Moose, Fraternal Aid Association, Woodmen of the World, German Aid Society and St. Joseph Ternverein.

DR. FREDERICK H. LADD, whose offices are in the Odd Fellows Building, at King Hill and Missouri avenues is a native Missourian. He was born in Marion County, January 31, 1870. When he was one year old his parents moved to Hamilton, Caldwell County, where he was educated in the

therefrom in 1898. He first located in Westboro, and was elected coronor of Atchison County soon after locating there. In 1901 was returned to St. Joseph and was appointed assistant city physician and was given charge of the city hospital, where he remained one year. In 1902 he went to Blockow, but one year later returned to St. Joseph and opened his present offices. He was married to Miss Asbarin Richie, of St. Joseph December 10, 1900. They have two children, a son and a daughter.

GEORGE F. LEAPER, manager of the Leaper Hardware Co., 817 Frederick avenue, is a native of Iowa; the date of his birth is October 1, 1876. At the age of five years he moved with his parents to Diller, Nebr., where he was educated. He entered the Beatrice Business College in 1891 and graduated the following year. He came to St. Joseph in 1901 and for a year was bookkeeper for Fred A. H.

ton County, Pennsylvania, February 28, 1817, went with his parents to Richland County, Ohio, when two years of age; in 1844 moved to Oregon, Mo., and began the practice of law; represented Holt County in the legislature in 1846; commanded a company in Powell's battalion in 1847; went to California in 1849, was successful and returned in 1850, locating in St. Joseph and opening a law

GEORGE F. LEAPER.

Garlichs. In 1902 he became assistant manager of the Parish-Errickson Hardware Co., which position he held for eight years. In the fall of 1910 he assumed the management of the Hinckley Hardware Co., 817 Frederick avenue and on April 1, 1913, he purchased the stock and changed the name to the Leaper Hardware Co. Mr. Leaper is a single man.

JAMES CRAIG, better known as General Craig, was born in Washing-

office; was elected district attorney in 1851; in 1856 was elected to Congress, as a Democrat, and served two terms; soon after the breaking out of the war he was commissioned brigadier general by President Lincoln; was prominent as a railroad builder and at one time president of the Hannibal & St. Joseph Company; in April, 1885, accepted the position of city comptroller and served two years. He died Oct. 21, 1888.

MAURICE EDWIN CRANE, proprietor of the department store at 1006-1008 North Third street, is a native of Kansas and was born in Atchison County, April 25, 1886. At the age of 4 years he went with his parents to Goff, Kan. When he was fourteen the family moved to Cen-

JOHN PATEE, an active pioneer, whose name is prominently connected with the early history of St. Joseph, was a native of Otsego County, New York, born Aug. 1, 1814. In 1845 he settled upon the site of the present city of St. Joseph, his holding em-

MAURICE EDWIN CRANE

tralia. He was educated in the two towns mentioned. In 1902 he came to St. Joseph and entered the employ of the Tootle-Wheeler & Motter Dry Goods Co., where he remained for ten years. In 1912 he embarked in the retail business at 911 North Second street. In September, 1913, he purchased the stock and fixtures of S. Fayman, at the location at which he is still doing business. He is one of the successful business men of the northern part of the city and an enterprising citizen. He was married to Miss Melvina Carlyle, of St. Joseph, February 2, 1907. Their family consists of a son, Marion, and two daughters, Marjorie and Marine.

bracing the various Patee additions, the price of the land being $13 per acre. He built the Patee House, after he had platted his ground into city lots, and donated terminals to the Hannibal & St. Joseph Railroad, his belief being that the business of the city would center about his hotel. Patee Park is a monument to this public spirited pioneer. He died February 14, 1868, possessed of property, the taxable value of which was $350,-000, and which is today worth several millions.

GEORGE ELERINGER, grain and fuel dealer, 326 West Missouri avenue is a native of Kansas. He was born in Doniphan County, March 26, 1873. He came to St. Joseph with his parents at the age of eight years. He was educated in the schools of this city and in 1900 began his present business. By the faithful application of the principle that honesty and square dealing is the best policy Mr. Eleringer has built up a business of

politician, was one of the most forceful men in the Democratic party in Northwest Missouri. Mr. Young was born in Bath County, Ky., in 1843 and came with his parents to Buchanan County in 1851, settling near Easton. He served on the Confederate side during the rebellion, and after the war studied law, graduating at Louisville in 1870. He was private secretary to Governor Woodson, and then represented this district in the state Sen-

GEORGE ELERINGER

which any man might well feel proud. He is accredited as being one of the most successful men in his line in St. Joseph. He has an elevator with a capacity of 25,000 bushels of grain and his facilities for handling other branches of his business are on a corresponding scale. He was married to Miss Pearl Culver of St. Joseph in 1900. Fraternally Mr. Eleringer is a K. of P.

WALLER YOUNG, lawyer and

ate, and subsequently in the legislature. He was also a member of the Board of Asylum Managers and president of the St. Joseph School Board and to his energies are due many improvements and conveniences at the Asylum and in the school system of the city. He was appointed County Clerk by Governor Stone upon the death of T. Ed. Campbell and filled out the unexpired term. Mr. Young died Nov. 17, 1896.

GEORGE G. STARMER, real estate man, at 6208 King Hill avenue, is a native of Missouri and was born near Rushville, May 9, 1871. He was educated in his native county. In 1892 he was appointed by President Cleveland as United States Deputy Marshall for the western district of Oklahoma and served four years. He re-

DR. EDMOND A. DONELAN was born at Ogdensburg, N. Y., April 25, 1824; graduated from Ohio Medical College in 1852; located at Plattsmouth, Neb., and was a member of Nebraska territorial legislature; came to St. Joseph in 1860; took a postgraduate course in Bellevue Medical College in New York city in 1870-71;

GEORGE G. STARMER

turned to St. Joseph in 1898 and served as Deputy Game and Fish Warden for the Fourth Congressional District 1905-1907. He was appointed Deputy State Factory Inspector by Governor Folk in 1907, which position he resigned to accept the superintendency of the Detention Home in St. Joseph. He remained in this position until 1909 when he organized the Starmer Land Company, in connection with Nate Block and Simon Binswanger, in which business he is still engaged. He was married to Miss Eliza E. Harman of Daviess County, Mo., January 7, 1897. Their family consists of two sons. Mr. Starmer is a Mason.

represented Buchanan county in the legislatures in 1877, 1881, 1885, 1887 and 1891 as a Democrat. He was a member of the School Board for a number of years which position he held at the time of his death.

WILLIAM RIDENBAUGH, pioneer newspaper publisher, and founder of the Gazette, was born in Bedford, Pa., on Feb. 19, 1821, and learned the printer's trade. He came to St. Joseph in the spring of 1845 and established the Gazette. He was a Democrat and prominent in political affairs. From 1852 to 1864 he was clerk of the circuit court. In 1870 he was again elected to this office, which he held at the time of his death, October 18, 1874.

MRS. ISABELLE CLARK, one of St. Joseph's interesting old ladies, was born at Grayson Court House, Wythe County, Virginia, May 10, 1831. At the age of ten years she came with her parents to Missouri. There were eight families in the party, and the trip overland was made with ox teams. They settled near Columbia. Mrs.

Two years ago she celebrated her birthday by giving a real Virginia dinner for her friends. It consisted largely of bacon, corn "pone" and the like, and Mrs. Clark superintended the cooking herself, for which she was liberally praised by her guests. Mrs. Clark's ancestors were noted for their longevity. Of her eight brothers and

MRS. ISABELLE CLARK

Clark's father, whose name was Stone, entered a homstead there and prospered as a farmer for many years. The subject of this sketch was married to M. B. Clark, who for many years was engaged in the real estate business in St. Joseph. He has been dead about twenty-five years. They came to the city from Maysville in 1867. Mrs. Clark has lived in one house, 2025 Jones street, for forty-four years, and despite her eighty-four years, she looks after the details of the household with as much vim and enthusiasm as many younger persons.

six sisters none died under the age of seventy years, except one who was killed in the Mexican war. One member of this family lived to be more than ninety years old. Mrs. Clark is the mother of seven children, Mrs. Eliza Violett of Worth County, Mo.; Mrs. Kate Kearby of Savannah, Mo.; Mrs. Belle Myers, 2025 Jones street, St. Joseph; John D. Clark, well known in St. Joseph politics; James G. Clark, Los Angeles, Calif., a Baptist minister; Mrs. Alice Buckner of Bloomington, Ill., and Albert M. Clark of St. Joseph.

DR. LOUIS F. BODE was born in Hassen, Germany, June 30, 1870. When he·was two years old his mother died and at the age of six years he was doubly orphaned by the death of his father. In 1878 his older brother, the late W. F. Bode, a resident of St. Joseph, sent for him and his brother,

by being devoted to his profession and true to his friends, for it can be said of him he is no 'fairweather friend.'

JOHN TOWNSEND, of the firm of Townsend & Wyatt, is a native of Mc-Lean County, Ill., where he was born

DR. LOUIS F. BODE
—Photo by Mulvane.

Henry, two years older, to come to America to make their home with him, so the two children made the ocean trip alone to this country, and of course not being able to speak a word of English, but everybody was kind to the two little German boys during the voyage. Dr. Bode attended the public schools of St. Joseph and is a graduate of Chapmans Business College. He attended Central Medical College four years, graduating in 1903. In the practice of medicine he is known as being thoroughly reliable and honorable both as man and as physician, and his sturdy German ancestry is shown in his every day life,

in 1837. In 1841, with his father's family he came to Buchanan County, and worked on a farm until fifteen years of age, getting such schooling as the country schools offered. He then began clerking in a dry goods store and was connected with several large houses. In 1866 he embarked in business, having several partners, until 1877, when he organized the firm of Townsend, Wyatt & Co., which now operates one of the finest department houses in the West. He is also interested in several other enterprises. He was married in 1863 to Miss Annie R. Banes of this city.

CLAYTON D. RADFORD, Councilman, was born in Winnebago City, Minn., May 24, 1874. At the age of seven years he moved with his parents to Eureka, Ill., where he received his education. Early in life he demonstrated marked ability as a sales-

important matters are under consideration. He was married to Miss Margaret Long of Carmi, Ill., December 22, 1895. He was exalted ruler of the Elks lodge, 1914-1915. He is also a member of the Moose, Eagles, M. W. A. and Turnverein.

CLAYTON D. RADFORD
—Photo by Mulvane.

man, and for ten years traveled for Chicago and Dayton, Ohio, firms. In 1889 he went to Louisville, Ky., where he engaged in the pursuit of traveling salesman. In 1905 he came to St. Joseph to become a salesman for the Olney Music Company, which position he still holds. In 1910 he was appointed by Mayor Clayton to fill the unexpired term of J. C. Wyatt, a member of the city council, who died that year. In 1914 Mr. Radford was elected to this position after making a fast race on the Democratic ticket. He takes a live interest in politics and sits in the councils of his party when

JOSEPH A. PINER, ex-mayor of St. Joseph, and member of the Missouri legislature, was born in Boone county, Ky., August 13, 1830; came to St. Joseph in 1862, and had a general store at Eleventh and Penn streets, which burned; ran a saw mill at Lake Contrary for twelve years, and then engaged in the omnibus business with Colonel Gates. Was mayor four years, and originated the city scrip. Was married in 1851 to Miss Elizabeth Maine, who died in 1861, and in 1862 to Miss Sophie Bennett, who died in 1890. Mr. Piner died in 1905.

WILLIAM E. BOWEN, banker and real estate man, is a native of Buchanan County, the date of his birth being March 5, 1866. At the age of 26 years he began teaching school, which profession he followed for five

don, of Easton, December 23, 1903. Their family consists of Virginia, age 10; Helen, 8; Dorothea, 3 and William E. Jr., 6 years.

MAJOR T. J. CHEW, capitalist and loan broker, was born in Columbus,

.... WILLIAM E. BOWEN
—Photo by Mulvane.

years. In 1903 he engaged in the fire insurance business, writing business principally among the farmers. He discontinued his efforts in this direction in 1903, when he came to St. Joseph and formed a partnership with W. A. Boyer, now a banker of Savannah, and engaged in the real estate and insurance business. They were in active business for five years and still are interested together. In 1914 Mr. Bowen bought an interest in the Security Bank and was made president. He has an interest in the First National Bank of Savannah, Mo., also. He was married to Miss Emma Gor-

O., in 1838. He received his education at the best schools of Cincinnati. After a brief stay in Iowa, he went to New York, and from 1858 till 1861, was in the insurance business there. He located in St. Joseph in 1861, and was in the wholesale grocery trade till 1874, when he engaged in the brokerage business. Major Chew served during the war, on the staff of General Willard P. Hall, and was quartermaster of the department of St. Joseph. From 1872 to 1873, he was president of the board of trade. Major Chew married Miss K. M. Forbes in 1861. Mr. Chew died April 20, 1900.

WALTER L. MACK, the well known real estate man, whose office is at the corner of Lake and Illinois avenues is a native of Kansas and was born in Pottawatomie County, October 25, 1875. He was educated in the

BENJAMIN F. LOAN, ex-Congressman, was born at Hardensburg, Ky., in 1819, and came to Buchanan County in 1838. He was a lawyer of reputation and high character and was identified with the history of St. Joseph

WALTER L. MACK

schools of his native county. He came to St. Joseph in 1898 and engaged in the barber business, which pursuit he followed for twelve years. He was a member of the Barbers' State Board of Examiners from July 7, 1906 to October 4, 1909. He sold his shop on New Years' Eve, 1910 and at once engaged in the real estate business. He is the sole agent for Klepper's Addition, secretary and treasurer of the Mack Land and Investment Company. He was married to Miss Daisy Tolliver, of Lucas, Kan., July 29, 1897. They have two children, both daughters. Mr. Mack is an active member of the Masonic order.

from the beginning up to the time of his death, which occurred March 28, 1881. In 1861 he was appointed brigadier general. In 1862 he was elected to Congress and served six years, after which he resumed the practice of law in this city.

STEPHEN S. BROWN, attorney, was born February 14, 1846, in St. Lawrence County, N. Y. Mr. Brown went to DeKalb County, Mo., in 1869, where he practiced his profession until June 1, 1882, when he came to St. Joseph. He has successfully conducted many of the most difficult cases tried in the courts of the district and state.

DR. GEORGE W. NORTHWOOD, dentist, 520 Edmond street, is a native of Canada. He was born in Ontario, April 12, 1865. He was educated in his native province. At the age of 18 years his father bound him out to a dentist of Chatham, Ontario, for a term of three years. He started without pay and in addition his father paid $300 for the privilege of learning the profession. When he had finished his apprenticeship he came to the United States and entered the Pennsylvania

DR. F. KEMPER WESTFALL, 6004½ King Hill avenue comes from the state of Illinois. He was born at Prairie City, McDonough County, January 21, 1880. He was educated in the schools of his native city. In 1899 he became a student in the Ensworth Medical College and the following year maticulated in the Hahnemarrn Medical College of Chicago, from which institution he was graduated in 1903. After graduating he

DR. GEORGE W. NORTHWOOD

Dental College at Philadelphia, where he remained for a year. After receiving his diploma he practiced in Jersey City, N. J., Rochester, N. Y., Detroit, Mich., and Elkhart, Ind. He came to St. Joseph in September, 1889, and was with Dr. J. J. Newell three years and Dr. C. S. Grant one year. In 1894 he opened his present office. He was married to Miss Rillie Bostwick of Columbus, Ohio, March 9, 1890. They have one daughter, Irene.

went to MaComb, Ill., where he practiced for five years. During the time he was in Macomb he held the chair of Diseases of Children in the Marietta Hospital there. He opened his present office in St. Joseph in 1908. He was married to Miss Dixie Hyde of St. Joseph in September, 1904. Fraternally Dr. Westfall is a Mason. He comes from a family of physicians, his father and grandfather having been successful practitioners.

Maternal Brockett Lineage.

Eunice Todd, born June 1, 1786, died March 1, 1831.

1. Eunice Todd Brockett, Grandmother.

2. Thaddeus Todd, Great Grandfather.

3. Jonah Todd, Great Great Grandfather.

Stephen Todd, married Lydia Ives.

Jonah Todd, married Lowly Harrison.

Thaddeus Todd, married Permelia Brockett, Dec. 4, 1783.

Thaddeus Todd enlisted in the 6th Continental Formation, Col. Douglass, April 16, 1777-1781, War of Revolution.

JUSTUS W. BROCKETT

4. Stephen Todd, Great Great Great Grandfather.

5. Samuel Todd, 2nd, Great Great Great Great Grandfather.

6. Samuel Todd, 1st, Great Great Great Great Great Grandfather.

7. Christopher Todd, Great Great Great Great Great Great Grandfather.

Christopher Todd and his wife, Grace, were of the original New Haven colonists, 1638. The ship Hector.

Samuel Todd 1st, married Mary Bradley.

Samuel Todd 2nd, married Susanna Tuttle.

Thaddeus Todd was a blacksmith. His shop was on his farm near Mt. Carmel north of New Haven. This farm had been in the Todd family for many generations. The farm passed to Eunice Todd, who married Justus Brockett, one of Justus Brockett's children. Justus Franklin Brockett inherited the farm and his son, Ernest Ransom Brockett, now 1909, owns and lives on the farm. Tradition in the family relates that on the forge of Thaddeus Todd, a part of the chain that was made and placed across the Hudson, to prevent the British ships from ascending the river was hammered out by Thaddeus Todd. Parts of the chain may now be seen at Newburg and West Point. Many iron relics may be dug out from the old forge stand now.

GENEALOGY JUSTUS W. BROCKETT

Brockett Lineage, Grandfather.

Brockett book, page 23. John Brockett, 1st generation in America. Born, Herts, England, 1609, emigrated to America with the New Haven colony, 1637. Was civil engineer of the colony, 1638 to 1680. Died March 12, 1690. Interment, Montowesse cemetery, headstone, near New Haven. Surveyed and platted the City of Elms, New Haven, Conn., 1638.

Brockett book, page 30. John Brockett, 2nd generation, eldest son of John Brockett 1st, was born in New Haven, 1624. Died in New Haven at Muddy River, 1720. Interment, Montoweese cemetery, headstone. Educated, England, Oxford. Education, medical and mechanical. Was physician and civil engineer. In his will, mention is made of his surveyor's instruments. He married Elizabeth Doolittle.

Brockett book, page 36. Samuel Brockett, 3d generation in America. The ninth child of John and Elizabeth (Doolittle) Brockett. Born at Muddy River, Nov. 8, 1691. Died March 3, 1775. Married Mehitabel Hill, Aug. 5, 1712. Interment, Montowesse cemetery, headstone.

Brockett book, page 45. Enos Brockett, 4th generation in America. The fourth child of Samuel and Mehitabel (Hill) Brockett. Born in New Haven, Dec. 28, 1719. Died later than 1790, exact date not known. Married Mariam Bradley, May 15, 1745, who was born in 1720 and died Jan. 12, 1809. Interment Montoweese cemetery, no headstone. In the Conn. Historical Society collections, Vol. 7, p. 220, Isaac, Munson, John, Enos and Jacob Brockett signed an agreement as volunteers in Benjamin Trumbull's Co. and enlisted for three months or longer. Original agreement in possession of Joseph Torry, Hartford.

Brockett book, page 67. Enos 2nd, 5th generation in America. The 4th child of Enos and Mariam (Bradley) Brockett. Born, Jan. 4, 1755. Died, 1828. Married Hannah Jacobs, who died Feb. 7, 1802. Interment, Montoweese cemetery, headstone. Enos 2nd was also a soldier in the Revolutionery war as well as was his father. Enos Brockett 2nd was mustered out of service, Feb. 17, 1777. He also served in war of 1812.

Brocket book, page 98. Justus Brockett, 6th generation in America. The sixth child of Enos 2nd and Hannah Jacobs Brockett. Born Dec. 23, 1790. Died May 3, 1877. He married Eunice Todd, who was born June 1, 1786. Died, March 1, 1831. She was a daughter of Thaddeus Todd, a solier of the Revolution. Interment of Justus and Eunice (Todd) Brockett, North Haven cemetery, headstone.

Brocket book, page 141. Elam Enos Brockett, 7th generation in America. The fifth child of Justus and Eunice (Todd) Brockett. Born Feb. 4, 1818, New Haven, Conn., Married Jane Bradley of Cheshire and New Haven, Oct. 2, 1846. Died at Uniontown, Kansas, Jan. 25, 1872. His widow married Capt. John L. Vidal. Elam Enos Brockett was educated in the best schools of New Haven, was a graduate, civil and nautical engineer. He made several voyages to Liverpool, South Africa, China and Japan. Interment at Uniontown, Kansas, headstone. Elam Enos and Jane E. (Bradley) Brockett had four children.

Justus Winfield Brockett, New Haven, Conn. Born, Oct. 2, 1848. Married to Catharine Vidal, daughter of Capt. John L. Vidal.

Frank Leslie Brockett, New Haven, Conn. Born, April 5, 1850. Married to Sophia Viual, daughter of Capt. John L. Vidal.

Mary Jane. Born in Hamden, Dec. 18, 1852. Died, Davenport, 1854.

Eleanor Jane. Born in Davenport, April 24, 1862. Married James B. Townsend, Davenport.

Jane E. Bradley, wife of Elam Enos Brockett, was the daughter of Sybil (Doolittle) Bradley. She married for her second husband, Capt. John L. Vidal, another seaman, voyager and soldier, Capt. Co. A, 16 Wis. Vol., war 1861. Interment, both, Mt. Ayr, Iowa, headstone.

Justus Winfield Brockett, lawyer and civil engineer, St. Joseph, Missouri, born New Haven, Conn., Oct. 2, 1848. His line of descent.

1. Elam Enos Brockett, Father.
2. Justus Brockett, Grandfather.
3. Enos Brockett 2nd, Great Grand-father.
4. Enos Brockett 1st, Great Great Grandfather.
5. Samuel Brockett, Great Great Great Grandfather.
6. John Brockett 2nd, Great Great Great Great Grandfather.

north Missouri, and of the entire building of the line from Pattonsburg to Trenton, Mo. He has located and engineered many miles of railway in north Missouri and in Illinois. He engineered much of the river and harbor work in front of the city of St. Joseph, He is still engaged in many constructive enterprises in and about St. Joseph.

JACOB ROSENTHAL
—Photo by Mulvane.

7. John Brockett 1st, Great Great Great Great Great Grandfather.

John Brockett, 1st, civil engineer, surveyed and platted the most beauti-ful city in the United States, New Haven. The college campus of Yale College is his work.

Mr. Brockett's family in America has furnished a number of artists, civil engineers and builders. Mr. Brockett, a civil engineer and lawyer has been connected with several im-portant constructive works in the state of Missouri. In St. Joseph The Union Terminal Ry., the engineering and maintenance of way for several years of the O. K. line of railroad in

JACOB ROSENTHAL, furniture dealer at 307-9-11 South Sixth street, is a native of Russia and was born December 3, 1866. He was educated in his native country. In 1890 he came to America, coming direct to St. Joseph. He engaged in the furniture business in 1891 and has been in this field of commercial activity ever since. He was married to Miss Dora Rosen-thal of Russia in 1887. They have three children—William, age twenty-five; Harry, age twenty-four, and Mar-cus, age eight. Mr. Rosenthal has been exceptionally successful in business and enjoys the respect and esteem of everyone who knows him.

GEORGE W. HINTON was the first white child born in Quindaro, Kas. Up to the time of his birth (April 23, 1857), Wyandotte papooses were the only babies born there.

He was brought by his parents to Missouri in 1860; lived on farms in the neighborhood of Horse-shoe Lake until 1868, and then in Wathena, Kas.

ing Co., of which Frank Posegate and John W. Johnson were president and secretary, respectively.

He says he owes much of his artistic ability and success, as an illustrator to the kind instructions in art given him by Herman Gerlach and William T. Keller, during a number of the many years he engraved at the

GEORGE W. HINTON
—Photo by Mulvane.

one year, where he got his first lessons in woolen mill work.

He came to St. Joseph in 1869 and worked for a while in the old Buell woolen mill, on North Third street, after which he attended the old Washington school. Miss Nye (now Mrs. Bartlett), was his teacher, while Julia Comstock (now Mrs. Eugene Field), and many who are now St. Joseph's best citizens were fellow students. He graduated in 1873, and immediately commenced the trade of wood engraving under Joseph W. Haines, at the St. Joseph Steam Print-

printing house, while they execute some of the world's best lithograph work.

Hinton has executed much creditable work, such as catalogue cuts, cartoons for our papers, buildings, machinery, and even mamoth posters, the number of all running far into the thousands and is doing engraving now (1915), at 112½ South Fourth street.

During these years he also made large numbers of patent office drawings and wrote up descriptions of invention for the procuring of patents

This part of his work grew to such proportions, that about 12 years ago, e legally qualified at Washington nd became a registered patent attorey.

Fenner, over the basement at the corner of Fifth and Edmond streets, was a fimiliar sign at the junction. These gentlemen remained partners until 1901, when the business was incorpo-

HERMAN C. FENNER
—Photo by Mulvane.

Genial, friendly, communicative, and versatile genius, he makes his work pleasure to himself and to the ones e serves.

HERMAN C. FENNER, ex-manager f the Western Dairy Company, was native of Germany. He was born n Holstein, June 19, 1867. He received his education in his native country and came to America in 1882, oming direct to St. Joseph. In 1884 e formed a partnership with John Hannefin in the milk business and for long time the sign of Hannefin &

rated under the name of the Western Dairy Company. Herman Fenner was elected president and held that important office until his death July 7, 1913. He is credited with having been the most important factor in building up the business of the Western Dairy Company, now the largest manufacturers of ice cream in the city. He was married to Miss Minnie Haas of St. Joseph in 1892. Two sons and three daughters were born to them. Mr. Fenner held membership in the Odd Fellows, Woodmen, Knights and Ladies of Security and A. O. U. W.

JOHN G. SCHNEIDER, vice-president of the German-American National Bank, has been active in the affairs of the city, both in business and in public life, continuously since 1879. He was born in St. Joseph on May 12, 1862, and is the eldest son of Ulrich and Katherine (Schott) Schneider.

John G. Schneider was educated in

Yards Company, of the Buchanan Hotel Company, of the St. Joseph and Savannah Interurban Railway Company, of the Kansas City, Clay County & St. Joseph Railway Company; and a number of other business enterprises of similar importance.

Mr. Schneider has become identified with the leading fraternal socie-

JOHN G. SCHNEIDER

the St. Joseph public schools, and when he was fifteen years of age became associated with his father in the real estate and insurance business, continuing so from 1877 to 1887. In the year last named he was one of the organizers of the German-American Bank of St. Joseph, now the German-American National Bank, and he began then to serve that bank as assistant cashier. In 1892 he became vice-president, and he has continued in that office ever since.

Mr. Schneider is a member of the directorate of the St. Joseph Stock

ties, including the A. F. & A. M., St. Joseph's Lodge No. 78; Independent Order of Odd Fellows, the Knights of Pythias, the Benevolent and Protective Order of Elks, the Woodmen of the World, the Court of Honor, and the Improved Order of Red Men. He is a member of the St. Joseph Turnverein, St. Joseph Swaben Verein, a director of the St. Joseph Country Club, a member of the Benton Club of St. Joseph, of the Lotus Club of St. Joseph, and of the St. Joseph Commerce Club.

On October 12, 1887, Mr. Schneider was married to Miss Helen Garth, a daughter of Major Samuel Garth of St. Joseph and a member of one of the pioneer families of Buchanan County.

taught school in his native county. In 1896 he was elected superintendent of schools in Platte County. Later he resigned to become principal of the Eastwood School at Marshall, Mo.

In 1898 he was elected to the

JAMES RALPH CLAY

Three children were born to Mr. and Mrs. Schneider—Ulrich Schneider, Helen, marr'ed to Henry Walker, and John G. Schneider, Jr.

JAMES RALPH CLAY, dealer in real estate, Eighth and Edmond streets, was born at Camden Point, Missouri, Platte County.

After receiving such education as the public schools provided, he spent several years in the state normals. Then he attended the Gem City Business College at Quincy, Illinois. He received his diploma from this institution in 1888. For several years he

presidency of Northwest Missouri College at Albany, Mo., which position he held until some eight years ago when he came to St. Joseph and engaged in the real estate and loan business.

Mr. Clay was married to Miss Willie E. Bywaters of Camden Point, Mo. August 24, 1890. They are the parents of three sons. All live in St. Joseph.

Mr. Clay is a man of superior literary tastes. A student of our best literature. He is a gifted public speaker. A man of rare personality. Often solicited to address assemblies where only the clearest and most dignified utterances are welcome.

DR. EDWARD DUMVILLE HOLME was born April 1, 1867 in northwestern Missouri in Andrew County, on an old negro plantation purchased by his father at the close of the Civil war.

He was born of English parentage, his father being the son of a draper of Pontefract, Yorkshire, England,

was to become a physician, havi left school once to read medicine Dr. Eli Ensor's office. On the dei of Dr. Ensor he returned to school.

After graduation from the Ame can School of Osteopathy in 1901, engaged in the practice of medicine Tarkio, Mo., to join his sister, 1 Anna Holme Hurst, his present as

DR. EDWARD DUMVILLE HOLME
—Photo by Mulvane.

and his mother, the daughter of Thomas Dumville, a woolen manufacturer of Huddersfield, England.

He was educated in the public schools of Savannah, Mo., after which he attended the Northwestern Normal, and later, Louis College, Glasgow, Mo.

After engaging in school work for some years, he took up the study of his profession from boyhood, namely —medicine, in the American School of Osteopathy. His earliest ambition

ciate and with whom he enjoys a ver; successful and lucrative practice.

Dr. E. D. Holme was elected presi dent of the first osteopathic organi zation in St. Joseph, Mo. He has beer a member of the American Osteo pathic Association since his gradua tion and is held in high esteem by the members of his profession. He also graduated from the Illinois Post Grad uate School of Medicine and Surgery Chicago, Ill., in 1915.

HERMAN K. LIBBE, born Oct. 20, 859 at Burlington, Iowa. German escent. Early education at Burlington, Iowa, and at Carman, Ills. At ne age of 14 learned telegraphy and ecame an expert in that line and in 875 was made chief clerk for the oadmasters Dept., B. & M. Ry. at incoln, Neb. In 1876 was appointed road and telegraph lines were absorb by the A. T. & S. F. Ry. March 1, 1885. On that date he went to Sprague, Washington Ferry as train master and chief dispatcher for the Northern Pacific Ry., remaining two years. In 1887 he was with the St. L., I. M. & S. at Parsons, Kas. as train dispatcher and May 1, 1888 he came to

HERMAN K. LIBBE

elief agent and operator for C. B. & Q. Ry. in Illinois for three years when n 1879 he was promoted to chief dispatcher and train master of the B. & L. W. Ry. at Burlington, Iowa when hat road was absorbed by the C. B. & Q. Ry. in 1881. He was sent as rain master and chief dispatcher to Keokuk, Iowa, for the Burlington system and while at Keokuk was appointed superintendent of telegraph by the Western Union Telegraph Co. n charge of the St. L. K. & N. & N. W. lines. In 1883 he went west to Deming, New Mexico and built the Deming, Silver City and Pacific telegraph lines from Deming to Silver City, New Mexico and became superintendent, remaining there until the St. Joseph, Mo., as trainmaster and chief dispatcher for the old Wabash Ry. and remained with them through all the changes until the system was absorbed by the A. T. & S. F. Ry. He was then transferred to Marceline, Mo., where he had charge between Kansas City and Fort Madison, Iowa as chief dispatcher until 1892, when he went to Bonne Terre, Mo., as train master and chief dispatcher of the M. R. & B. T. Ry., remaining only a year. March 4th, 1894 he established the wholesale flour company of H. H. Libbe & Co. with Mr. John Muehleisen, but for the past eight years has been sole proprietor. He is specially interested in the civic pride of St. Joseph, Mo.

DR. CARYL POTTER was born October 1, 1886 at Cameron, Missouri, and has lived in St. Joseph since he was one year of age. He was educated in the St. Joseph public schools and graduated from Central High School. He entered the University of Missouri in the fall of 1905 and received the A. B| degree in the fall of

places in New York, Roosevelt, Presbyterian and St. Luke's Hospitals in the city of New York he stood sixteenth and received the appointment to the surgical staff of Roosevelt Hospital where he served for two years, the last six months of his service holding position of House Surgeon.

DR. CARYL POTTER

1908, having received A. B. and completed one year of medicine in three years and two summer schools. While at the university he was a member of the Phi Delta Theta and Theta Nu Epsilon fraternities and a member of the University of Missouri Glee Club. He entered the second year of the medical department of Johns Hopkins University in the fall of 1908 and graduated in 1911, the only man in his class to have received A. B. and M. D. degrees in six years. While there he was a member of Nu Sigma Nu, an honorary medical fraternity.

In a joint competitive examination with 184 men from medical schools throughout the United States for 36

For two months he was an interne at the Lying-in Hospital of New York and a substitute interne in medicine at the Johns Hopkins Hospital for three months.

He is registered in the State of New York, having passed the state board examination in that state in 1911 and in the state of Missouri, having received his license before that board in 1913.

During the last year of the existence of the Ensworth Medical College, he was Professor of Medicine and has been associated with Dr. T. E. Potter in the practice of medicine and surgery since July, 1913.

DR. JOHN I. TUCKER, one of the physicians in the Swift Packing plant comes from good Missouri stock, his birthplace being Sullivan County and the date September 4, 1880. He received his early education in the schools of his native county and in 1900 entered William Jewel College where he remained one year. In 1905

Tucker was married to Miss Ethel Carter of Waldron, Kan., in 1907. They have three children, two sons and a daughter. Fraternally Dr. Tucker is an Odd Fellow.

WILLIAM M. BECKETT, real estate dealer, at 108 North Seventh street, comes from Indiana stock. He was born in Henry County, March

DR. JOHN I. TUCKER
—Photo by Mulvane.

he attended a summer term at the Northwestern, at Alva, Oklahoma. He began the study of medicine at the Ensworth Medical College in St. Joseph in 1908 and graduated from that institution in 1912. He first began practicing at Rochester, Andrew County, where he remained for seven months when he removed to South St. Joseph and was made a member of the medical staff of Swift & Co. Dr.

17, 1858. He came with his parents to Missouri in 1867, locating in Andrew County. He was educated there, after which he went to Rosendale and learned the railroad station work. In 1879 he went to King City and was the first operator on the St. Joseph & Des Moines Narrow Gauge. In August, 1881, he went to Nishnabotna as agent for the Kansas City, St. Joseph & Council Bluffs road, where he remained a year and was then transferred to Fairfax, where he remained six years. In 1888 he quit railroading and engaged in the lumber business in Tarkio. He was elected county recorder of Atchison county in 1894. Mr. Beckett located

sas, where he received a common school education. He was in the employ of the Rock Island Railroad company in New Mexico for several years. In 1907 he began the study of dentistry in the Kansas City Dental Col-

DR. OSCAR L. HUMMEL
—Photo by Mulvane.

in St. Joseph in 1901 and has been an active business man here ever since. He was married to Miss Lillian Offutt of Brown County, Kansas, in 1889. They have one child, Evelyn A., age 18 years.

DR. OSCAR L. HUMMEL, dentist, in the I. O. O. F. building, King Hill and Missouri avenues, is a native of Illinois. He was born at Lawn Ridge, February 10, 1882. At the age of two years he moved with his parents to Nortonville, Jefferson County, Kan-

lege and graduated therefrom in 1910. He first located in Lucas, Kan., where he practiced for two years. He came to St. Joseph in 1912 and opened the office in which he is now located. Dr. Hummel has been very successful as a practitioner and is one of the enterprising business men of the South Side. He was married to Mrs. Lethia Hook of Rossville, Kan., in 1908. They have one child, a son. Dr. Hummel is a K. of P. and an Odd Fellow.

JAMES B. O'BRIEN entered the shoe business in 1896 as salesman for the Geiwitz & Holland Shoe Co. at Fourth and Felix streets. A year later the firm was reorganized and Mr. O'Brien became vice-president and manager of the Holland & O'Brien

shoe stores in Northwest Missouri.

In 1910 Mr. O'Brien left the firm of the Holland & O'Brien Shoe Co. and organized the O'Brien-Kiley Shoe Co. at 516 Felix. He was president and manager of the concern for several years—when he sold out his in-

JAMES B. O'BRIEN

Shoe Co., remaining in that capacity for thirteen years. After a year at the old store at Fourth and Felix they moved into the store at 612 Felix under his management the business grew until they were compelled to take over the next store at 614 Felix, having one of the largest exclusive

terests and decided to leave the retail end and go on the road. For three years he represented the Noyes-Norman Shoe Co. of this city in Kansas and Texas, leaving them a year ago to again enter the field of retailing, taking over an interest in the Burke Shoe Co. at 614 Felix, the old store where he was so many years when it was the Holland & O'Brien Shoe Co. The firm is now Burke & O'Brien Shoe Co. and since Mr. O'Brien has come back to his first love the business has shown a very healthy increase.

the promotion of the retail interest. Governor Hadley appointed him a member of the Board of Regents of the State Normal School at Maryville, Mo., resigning when he went on the road. Jim O'Brien is widely known to the shoe trade all over the country.

EDWARD C. BURKE

Mr. O'Brien has long been active in commercial and civic affairs in St. Joseph. He was the first president of the old Ad Club and during his administration he helped to build up a membership of 1200. He was a member of the board of directors of the Retail Merchants Association for many years and always was on hand when there was anything in sight for

EDWARD C. BURKE, member of the firm of the Burke-O'Brien Shoe Company, 614 Felix street, was born in Lowell, Ind., Oct. 8, 1887. At the age of four years his parents brought him to St. Joseph and he was educated in the Christian Brothers' College, graduating in 1904. Immediately following his graduation he became identified with the Cobb Shoe Company, and left that firm in 1910 to take an interest in and participate in the management of the Battreall-Burke Shoe Company. In 1914 he purchased the Holland Bootery, which is known now as the Burke-O'Brien Shoe Company. He was married in January, 1913, to Miss Gertrude Parry, and one son has been born of the union. Mr. Burke is at this writ-

JOHN T. BURKE was born in Gallatin, Mo. Dec. 1, 1888. Came with his parents to St. Joseph, Mo. in 1893. Made his initiatory entry into school here—finishing the primary grades of school and entering the Christian Brothers College. He graduated with high honors June, 1905. He then accepted a position with the old reliable

JOHN T. BURKE

ing secretary of the Monroe Club, president of the Christian Brothers' College Alumni Association and president of the Columbus Club. He is also Deputy Grand Knight of the Knights of Columbus.

Mr. Burke is generally regarded as one of St. Joseph's leading young business men, and his record to date is considered an unusual one.

shoe concern of Holland & O'Brien Shoe Co. and shortly afterwards developed into a retail shoe salesman of great ability. Remained in capacity of shoe salesman until 1914, when he with a brother opened a first-class shoe store in the heart of the retail business district.

WILLIAM MUSE CAMPBELL, one of the leading physicians and surgeons of St. Joseph Mo., was born in Robinson, Brown County, Kansas, March 17, 1873.

His father, the Rev. William G. of Western Pennsylvania.

Our subject was éducated in the public schools, and at the age of seventeen, he began the study and practice of medicine and graduated from the Northwestern Medical Col-

WILLIAM MUSE CAMPBELL M. D.

Campbell, was a minister of the M. E. Church in Kansas-and a member of the Kansas Conference. He died in 1889. His mother's maiden name was Elizabeth Muse, and she was the daughter of Joseph Muse, a resident lege of St. Joseph in 1893. He the engaged in practice at Fairview, Kansas, where he remained two years an obtained a large practice. He the left for Philadelphia, Penna., wher he attended Jefferson Medical College and while there was elected to the Chair of Physiology in Central Medical College of St. Joseph.

He returned to St. Joseph, forming a partnership with his uncle, Dr. O. B. Campbell. In 1897 Dr. Campbell left St. Joseph and practiced his profession in Sullivan County, Missouri for a couple of years. Returning to St. Joseph, he again took up the practice of his profession. His fame, both as a physician and surgeon, is wide-

present the fruition of her prophecies and his hopes.

Dr. Campbell was married in December, 1913, to Miss Vera Marie Lechler, a daughter of Charles F. Lechler of this city.

JAMES N. NORRIS, JR., commission merchant at 214 North Second street came from New Jersey, in which state he was born at Ridgewood, May 23, 1886. At an early age

JAMES N. NORRIS, JR.

spread, and he is often called in consultation and to perform difficult operations at distant points.

In his social life, Dr. Campbell is prominent in Masonic circles, and is a member of the Odd Fellows, Elks and a number of other fraternal orders.

In his early struggles he received every encouragement and sympathy from his mother, a woman remarkable for her energy and lofty ambition, for her nobility of purpose and strength of character, and he naturally feels proud when he sees in his successful

he went to New York City where he was educated. He is a son of J. N. Norris, the pioneer commission merchant in the poultry business who began business in the early '70's. Mr. Norris came to St. Joseph in February, 1912 and took charge of the house here. He has proven one of St. Joseph's most successful business men and well deserves the success he has attained. He has demonstrated that enterprise, coupled with push and energy, will succeed where perfunctory activity will only end in disappointment.

ELLIOT MARSHALL, the twenty-ninth mayor of the city of St. Joseph, Mo., was born in New York City on April 28, 1860. He was educated at the following military schools: Westchester County, New York and the Military Academy of St. John's at Sing Sing, New York, and finished up at Columbia University, leaving in his sophomore year to accept a place with the New York branch of the Hong Kong and Shanghai Banking Corporation, of Shanghai, China.

then has claimed St. Joseph as his home. He remained with the C. B. & Q. until 1908. He was assistant general freight and passenger agent of the Burlington at St. Joseph for eight years.

In 1911 President William Howard Taft appointed him Collector of the Port of St. Joseph, but in 1913 the Port of St. Joseph was closed and consequently he was legislated out of office.

Mr. Marshall has always taken a

ELLIOT MARSHALL

Mr. Marshall comes from the old Colonial stock of New York on his mother's side, she being a great granddaughter of Lewis Morris, the signer of the Declaration of Independence, and also a descendant of Petrus Stuyvesant, the last Dutch governor of New York.

Mr. Marshall came west in 1881 with the C. B. & Q. Railroad in Burlington, Iowa. In 1883 he came to St. Joseph with the same road and since

keen interest in both civic and political affairs. In 1900 Mayor John Combe appointed him a member of the St. Joseph Library Board. In 1902 he was president of the St. Joseph Country Club. He was appointed in 1895 a major on the staff of Governor E. N. Morrill of Kansas, and in 1905 a lieutenant colonel on the staff of Governor E. W. Hoch of Kansas. At the time of these appointments, Mr. Marshall was general agent for the C. B. & Q. at Leavenworth, Kas. In 1911 Governor H. S. Hadley of Missouri appointed him a colonel on his staff.

He is a member of the Sons of the Revolution, having been president of the St. Joseph Chapter in 1903; also Society of Colonial Wars and Huguenot Society. He is a member of the Episcopal Church, and a Republican in politics.

shall and Elliot Marshall Jr.

In April 1914, he was elected mayor of St. Joseph, defeating David E. Curtin, the Democratic nominee.

JUDGE CHARLES A. LOOMIS, justice of the peace in the South Side, is a native of Buchanan County; was born September 10, 1878. He was educated in the common schools of

JUDGE CHARLES A. LOOMIS

In 1885 he married Miss Constance Blessing, daughter of the late Reverend Doctor James F. Runcie, who for eighteen years was the Rector of Christ Episcopal Church in St. Joseph; and Constance Faunt LeRoy, who was the founder of the first Womans' Club in the United States. He has two children, Jean Dale Mar-

the county. He is a son of O. M. Loomis, a well known citizen of this community. In 1910 he was elected Justice of the Peace and was re-elected in 1914. He is now the oldest justice, in point of service, in the city. Fraternally his memberships are in the Knights of Pythias and the Eagles.

JOHN M. STAUBER could trace his ancestry back to John Christian Stauber, who was born near Frankfort on the Mayne, Germany, in 1690, and whose descendants emigrated to America in 1749, twenty-seven years before the Revolutionary war.

His father, Benjamin Stauber, was born in North Carolina, in 1796, and on reaching manhood he moved to

During his life he was an active Grand Army man, at his death being a member of Custer Post, G. A. R. No. 7, St. Joseph, Missouri. At the close of the war he came west and settled in Linn County, Missouri, living there until 1887, when he removed to St. Joseph, to engage in the retail drug business, which in 1892 was incorporated as Stauber Drug Company.

His parents were members of the

JOHN M. STAUBER

Pennsylvania, where he married Elizabeth McCord, and to them were born thirteen children, John M. being their fourth child.

He was born in Bellefonte, Center County, Pennsylvania, April 8, 1830. He was married April 6, 1854, to Isabella H. McIntyre; the fruit of this union was seven children, six of whom still survive. At the age of fifteen years he entered the drug business and for sixteen years was established for himself in Lewistown, Pennsylvania. He served in the Federal army in the medical corps with the 36th and 205th Pennsylvania regiments.

Methodist Church, which he joined early in life and continued this relation to his death, for twenty-five years; he was a member of the St. Paul M. E. Church, of which he was a charter member.

He was a devoted husband, a kind father, a loyal helpful friend, and a kindly, courteous, broad-minded, generous, genial, christian gentleman.

On August 5th, 1913, at the age of eighty-three years (83), three months (3) and twenty-six days (26), he departed this life in the confident hope of the resurrection of the just to immortal life.

MRS. ELIZABETH MUSE CAMP-BELL was born in Pittsburg, Pennsylvania, August 28, 1845. She was the daughter of Joseph and Martha Wilson Muse. Her father was noted in musical circles in Western Pennsylvania, and her mother was a woman of strong yet sweet character. Mrs. Campbell has always felt very grateful to her parents for the educational advantages they gave her, for she was one of a large family, and it meant many sacrifices to them.

benefits of an education and she went resolutely to work to secure it for them. In four weeks from the time of her husbands death she was appointed postmistress at Robinson, Kansas, serving six years to the satisfaction of all the patrons of the office. She wrote for the newspapers, and became known as a literary woman of ability. The titles of some of her short stories show a delicate and artistic taste. "Lilacs" and "A Wild Rose" were published in the St. Jo-

ELIZABETH MUSE CAMPBELL

She was married to the Rev. W. G. Campbell of the Kansas Conference, Jan. 18, 1872, coming almost immediately to Kansas with her husband. Her life for the next seventeen years was much the same as all Methodist ministers' wives, having no abiding stay, and moving every two or three years.

The death of her husband in 1889 left her with a family of children and but scanty means, but she determined that her children should have the

seph Herald and "White Roses" in an Eastern publication. She then moved to Harris, Missouri, where she served another four years as postmistress, also keeping up her literary work.

Her home has been in St. Joseph since 1901. Mrs. Campbell is a woman of strong personality and high ideals. In 1904 she organized the X. X. M. D. Study Club in St. Joseph and has held it a strictly literary organization, she being president all these years, and it is now one of the leading women's clubs in the city. In 1913 she organized the Sheltering Arm's Circle, to work exclusively for the children of the Sheltering Arm's Home, and it is a great success. Mrs. Campbell believes in specializing work, claiming that more good is accomplished in that way.

Her two living children are Dr. William Muse Campbell and Walter Beverly Campbell of St. Joseph. Martha Gertrude, the only daughter,

lic schools of the city and began work in 1896, at the age of 19, for the Krug Packing Company. The firm appreciated his services so much that in a short time he was given charge of the retail department. After remaining seven years with the Krug people Mr. Brendel went into business for himself. His first venture as a retail meat dealer was at Tenth and Jackson streets in 1904. In 1908 he moved to his present location at 1701 South

JOHN BRENDEL

died in 1890, and David Clarence, who was well known in railroad circles, died August 12, 1906.

JOHN BRENDEL, member of the common council, and active in the public affairs of the city, was born in St. Joseph December 6, 1877, at Main and Robidoux streets. He has made this city his home ever since and has, by hard work and persistent effort, won a place in the business world of which he may well feel proud. He was educated in the pub-

Eleventh street, where he has built up a steady and profitable business. Mr. Brendel has always been a Republican in politics and takes a deep interest in the public affairs of his native city. He was elected councilman in 1912 for a term of four years. Mr. Brendel soon became active in the controversy with the St. Joseph Gas Company over the raise in rates. Through his efforts and those of his associates the company was prevented from charging consumers an exorbitant price for gas. When the election for the recall of Mayor Charles A. Pfeiffer was called in the summer of 1913 Mr. Brendel was nominated against him. Mayor Pfeiffer was re-elected. At the Republican convention in 1914 Mr. Brendel's name was placed before the body as a candidate for mayor. For four ballots he beat all comers, having 118 votes, with only 121 necessary to nominate. Mr. Brendel was married to Miss Minnie Cardwell of St. Joseph, May 10, 1899. They have two children, a boy and a girl.

gin the study of the law, entering the office of Judge C. M. Parke, one of the most prominent attorneys of Central New York; but after a year spent reading law the value of the broadest general education became more apparent and a return to college was decided on. After graduation he taught for a short time in New York City and spent several months traveling in the South, never, however, allowing his legal studies to be long interrupted.

In 1900 he was appointed to a posi-

ELBERT HILLES LOYD

ELBERT HILLES LOYD was born February 5, 1876, at Gloversville, New York. He was graduated from the public schools and high school in that city. At Colgate University where he was graduated with the degree A. B. in the class of 1899, he received a number of scholastic honors, among others, first prizes in chemistry and Latin and election to the honorary society Phi Beta Kappa.

After two years in college Mr. Loyd interrupted his general studies to be-

tion in the census office in Washington and until 1905 was connected with government work, principally in Washington and Boston, Mass., while in the government service he edited a number of important official publications. In spite of his official duties, Mr. Loyd from 1900 to 1904 continued to pursue his studies in law which has been begun at his former home in Gloversville, and in 1904 was graduated from Columbian (now George Washington) University with the degree LL. B. and was admitted to the bar. In 1905 he came to St. Joseph where he has since practiced his profession; specializing principally in commercial law. His office is in the Corby-Forsee Building.

On May 6, 1912, he married Miss Analee Gray of St. Joseph. They have two sons, Dewitt Clinton, born July 4, 1913, and Elbert Lee, born January 8, 1915. Mr. Loyd was a charter member of the University Club in Washington; he is a member

Mann act in this vicinity. He is a Republican in politics and in 1908 was secretary of the County Committee; but he has never been a candidate for any elective office, not caring to be diverted from a careful attention to his clients' interests. Mr. Loyd is recognized as one of the best educated men of the county, a careful counsellor, an able advocate and a lawyer whose energy and ability have brought him abundant success and hosts of satisfied clients.

DR. JOSEPH W. MAYS

of the Delta Kappa Epsilon college fraternity, of the Sons of the Revolution, of the Sons of Veterans, of the St. Joseph Bar Association, of the Commerce Club, of the Elks, and the Baptist Church.

In 1910 Mr. Loyd was appointed Supervisor of the Census for the Fourth District of Missouri; and in 1913 and 1914 he was special counsel for the United States Department of Justice for the enforcement of the

DR. JOSEPH W. MAYS, at 824 Edmond street, is a native of Missouri, having been born in Buchanan County, April 13, 1872. He was educated in the public schools of St. Joseph. In 1896 he entered the Ensworth Medical College and graduated in 1900. After receiving his diploma he located at Easton, where he practiced his profession until August 1, 1912. He then came to St. Joseph and opened his present office. In 1911 he took a post graduate course in the Chicago Polyclinic at the Chicago Post Graduate School. He was married to Miss Stella M. White, of Bolckow, Mo., June 11, 1901. Four children have been born of this marriage, three of whom are living, all sons. Dr. Mays is a Mason and an Odd Fellow. He is also an active member of the Buchanan County Medical Society and the Missouri Valley Medical Association. He is a son of Samuel M. Mays of Old Sparta.

his present business location since 1892 where he is now engaged in the sheet metal and furnace business. He belongs to the I. O. O. F., K. of P., and Woodmen of the World. He is a member of the German Evengelical Zion's Church.

CHESLEY A. MOSMAN was born in Chester, Illinois, July 29, 1842, and was educated in the High School of

WILLIAM WEHRMAN
—Photo by Mulvane.

WILLIAM WEHRMAN, tinner, 119 North Second street, was born in Germany July 15, 1858. In 1870 he came to America, locating at once in St. Joseph where he learned his trade and where he has since made his home. May 20, 1880, Mr. Wehrman was united in marriage to Miss Rosa Ann Knapp and two sons and five daughters, all living, have been born to them. Mr. Wehrman has been at

St. Louis. He served in the Union army during the Civil war, and came to St. Joseph Dec. 15, 1868. He had adopted the profession of law and in 1872 was made attorney for the Kansas City, St. Joseph & Council Bluffs road. In 1870 he was appointed to the position of solicitor for the C., B. & Q. lines. Mr. Mosman has achieved a reputation as a lawyer of superior ability. He served one term as judge of the Circuit Court as a Republican. He died in 1913.

JOHN E. DOLMAN was born in Denver, Colorado, September 18, 1865. In 1866, he removed with his parents to Tokepa, Kansas, where he was educated. He studied law in the office of Joseph G. Waters and was admitted to the Kansas bar. Afterwards attended the Albany Law School at Albany, New York and was graduated from that institution in June, 1887. On January 1, 1888, he entered the law department of the

practice of his profession in St. Joseph.

DAVID B. KELLY, contractor, was born in Grant County, Ind., July 16, 1858. His parents moved to Savannah, Mo., in 1866 and here he received his education. He read law with his father, the late Judge Henry S. Kelly at Savannah and was admitted to the bar in 1881. He was appointed postmaster at Savannah the same year.

JOHN E. DOLMAN

Chicago, Rock Island and Pacific Railway Company, at Topeka, Kansas, under Hon. M. A. Law, general solicitor for that company and was assistant attorney for that company in Missouri, Kansas, Nebraska, Colorado and Oklahoma until January 1, 1898, when he removed to St. Joseph, Mo., formed a partnership with Hon. Stephen S. Brown in the general practice of his profession under the firm name of Brown & Dolman. In April, 1911, Mr. Brown retired from the firm, having been appointed to the Supreme Bench of the State of Missouri, since which time Mr. Dolman has been alone in the general

He held this position for four years. He came to St. Joseph in 1887, and engaged in the practice of law with his father, Judge Kelly, the firm being Kelly and Kelly. The firm continued in active practice for twelve years, when, owing to failing health, Mr. Kelly engaged in the contracting business. He was secretary of the Republican City Central Committee at the time the late Major Hansen was its chairman. He was married to Miss Flora Buis, of Andrew County, in 1882, Their family consists of two sons and three daughters, one of whom is married and lives in California.

JOHN D. M'NEELY, lawyer with offices in Donnell Court, is a native Missourian. He was born in St. Joseph March 9, 1875. He was educated in the schools of St. Joseph and was graduated from the Christian Brothers College in 1892. The same year he entered the University of Missouri at Columbia, and was graduated from the law department in 1897, after which he returned to St. Joseph for the practice of his profession. He served as first lieutenant of Company

DR. L. S. LONG, the subject of this sketch was born in Longswamp, Berks County, Pennsylvania, Aug. 12, 1871. Educated in grammar schools of the township, attended Keystone State Normal School at Kutztown, Wyoming, Seminary at Kingston, Pa., University of Pennsylvania and graduate in medicine and surgery at Baltimore Medical College 1892. Came to St. Joseph and associated with an uncle, Dr. A. S. Long a pioneer physician of St. Joseph who devoted most

JOHN D. M'NEELY

G, Fourth Missouri Volunteers from May 16, 1898 to February 10, 1899, and saw some service in the Spanish-American war which was in progress at that time. In 1894 he was elected prosecuting attorney of Buchanan County and served one term. In 1909 he was appointed president of the St. Joseph Board of Police Commissioners, which position he filled until 1912. He is an active member of the Elks and was elected Exalted Ruler of that order in 1909.

of his talents to the subject of orificial surgery and rectal diseases. Married to Meta Bode 1898. Two children, Eleanor and Mildred Long. Office 822 Edmond. President Zions Evangelical German Church trustees 1914-1916. Member of American Medical Association, Missouri State Medical Association, St. Joseph-Buchanan Medical Society. Dr. Long has attended post graduate courses at Chicago Post Graduate Medical School, Laboratory of Dr. Zeit, New York Post

Graduate, New York Lying-in Hospital. Served as president Rochester Surgical Club 1913. Assistant City Health Officer St. Joseph 1897-98. Member of Mystic Shrine York Rite and Scottish Rite Masonry.

1900. He was admitted to the practice of law immediately after graduation and then became associated with the legal department of the Chicago, Burlington & Quincy Railroad Company at St. Joseph. He severed his con-

ORESTES MITCHELL

ORESTES MITCHELL, lawyer, was born in Monroe, County, Indiana, Dec. 26, 1876, being the oldest of five children of Levi Mitchell and Sarah E. Mitchell. His parents located in St. Joseph in the summer of 1888. He received his early education in the public schools of St. Joseph, afterwards studying law in the Missouri State University, from which school he graduated with honors in May,

nection with the railroad company March 1, 1907 and engaged in the general practice of the law in St. Joseph and is rated as one of the most able and influential members of the Buchanan County bar. He is a member of the American Bar Association.

Politically, he has always been an active Democrat, and in 1912 was a candidate for the nomination as judge of the Buchanan County Circuit urt, being defeated by less than a undred votes. At the spring election 1912, he was elected a member of e St. Joseph Board of Education r the term of two years and in 1914 as re-elected for another term of six ears.

He is a prominent and active Freeason, being a Thirty-third Degree ason, and an honorary member of e Supreme Council of Scottish Rite asons for the southern jurisdiction

GEORGE NEUDORFF is a native Missourian. He was born in Platte County, July 7, 1857. He came to St. Joseph with his parents in 1861. He received his education in the public schools of the city and early developed a desire to engage in business, feeling that that was his mission in life rather than serving some one else for wages. He opened the grocery

GEORGE NEUDORFF

the United States, and is also an ficer in the Grand Lodge of Masons Missouri.

Mr. Mitchell takes an active interest educational, charitable and public fairs, and in all movements for the tterment of the community.

He was married April 15, 1902 to iss Inez Altavia Samuel, and there as born of that union three children: amuel Orestes; Francis Marion, and artha Elizabeth, all of whom are ing.

store which he is still operating at 1302 North Third street in 1886. The fact that he has remained twenty-eight years in one location is excellent evidence of his sterling business qualifications and square dealing. Mr. Neudorff has always been in the front ranks when any movement calculated to benefit his native town, needed assistance. He is one of the progressive, enterprising business men who are a real benefit to the community.

KENDALL B. RANDOLPH, one of the best known and most successful lawyers of Northwest Missouri is Kendall B. Randolph, who became a member of the Missouri bar in 1882. He practiced at Maysville, DeKalb County, Missouri, until November, 1889, and then located at St. Joseph. Whether as a lawyer or through his part in public affairs, he has won a reputation for fidelity to his ideals and to the trusts which people have reposed in him. Mr. Randolph belongs to the famous Virginia family of Randolphs, and there are a number of interesting facts to be noted concerning the earlier generations.

two years. In order to have a larger field for his growing activities, he moved, in 1889, to St. Joseph, and has since been one of the leading members of the bar. He has a large general practice, taking him before all the courts of the state, and the district court, circuit court of appeals and supreme court of the United States.

On May 30, 1885, Mr. Randolph married Addie May Weatherby. They have four living children and one dead.

Mr. Randolph affiliates with Zere-

KENDALL B. RANDOLPH

ginia family of Randolphs, and there are a number of interesting facts to be noted concerning the earlier generations.

Kendall B. Randolph received his literary education chiefly at Normal, Illinois, and when nineteen years old began earning his living as a teacher. During the two years he followed that vocation he also studied law, and after his admission to the bar began practice at Maysville. In 1884 Mr. Randolph was elected prosecuting attorney of DeKalb County, and served

datha Lodge, No. 189, A. F. & A. M.; Mitchell Chapter, No. 14, R. A. M.; St. Joseph Council, No. 9, R. & S. Masters; Hugh de Payens Commandery, No. 51, Knights Templar; and Moila Temple, Nobles of the Mystic Shrine. His first presidential vote was cast for James A. Garfield in 1880, and he has ever since given loyal support to the Republican candidates and principles. In St. Joseph he was appointed city counsellor by Mayor John Combe in 1901, and served two years. Though living in a district where the

Democratic party is largely in the ascendency, he has never compromised his convictions and has vigorously supported his party in this section of the state. He was a prominent candidate before the convention which, in 1904, nominated Judge Lamb for the supreme bench in the state, and was chairman of the judicial convention which nominated Honorable James M. Johnson for judge of the Kansas City Court of Appeals, in 1904.

native of Germany. Coming to America as a young man, he located in Washington County, Maryland, in colonial days, and having purchased a tract of land, was there employed in the pursuit of agriculture until his death.

One of a family of eight children, Henry S. Smith first attended the district schools of his native town, later completing his studies at Rock Hill College, in Ellicott City, Maryland.

HENRY S. SMITH

HENRY S. SMITH, as one of the leading real estate dealers of St. Joseph, Henry S. Smith has been identified with many changes of property in this city and the surrounding country, and is widely known as a man of good judgment and honor. He was born on a farm in Washington County, Maryland, a son of Joseph M. Smith, whose birth occurred in 1822 on the same farm, while his grandfather, Michael Schmidt was born in the same county. His great grandfather, Joseph Schmidt, was a

Fitted for a professional career, Mr. Smith taught school two years in Maryland, and then went to Nemaha County, Kansas, where he continued as a teacher until 1887. Locating then in St. Joseph, Mo., Mr. Smith secured a position as clerk in a real estate and insurance office. Subsequently, in partnership with A. C. McDonald, he purchased the business of his former employer and carried it on successfully for a year as head of the firm of Smith & McDonald. W. E. Spratt was then admitted to partnership and the business was continued under the name of Smith, McDonald & Spratt until 1890. There were several changes in the firm in the years that followed, and in addition to the insurance business, more especial attention was paid to dealings in real estate and loans. In 1913 Mr. Smith became sole proprietor of the business, which is in a flourishing condition, and under his management is constantly increasing. He is also connected with other business organizations in an official ca-

DR. JOHN ANDREW FRENCH was educated in the common schools, and then began the study of medicine. He attended the Keokuk, Iowa Medical School, the Missouri Medical College at St. Louis, from which institution he was graduated in 1880. He afterward attended the Hospital Medical College and the Polycclinic and hospital in New York. He then began the practice of his profession in St. Joseph and was prominently identified with the Northwest Medical College;

DR. JOHN ANDREW FRENCH

pacity, being secretary of the Provident Building and Loan Association and secretary of the Ely Land Company.

In 1896 Mr. Smith married Gertrude Bang, who was born in Dresden, Germany, a daughter of Henry and Elise Bang. In politics Mr. Smith is a staunch supporter of the principles of the Democratic party. He is a member of the Knights of Columbus and of the Columbus Club and the Commerce Club.

and was at one time secretary and professor of gynical and rediatrics. He erected the building for the college and founded the School and Hospital for the Education of Nurses at Eighth and Sylvanie streets. He built the sanitarium on the Savannah Interurban which bears his name. The doctor served two terms as city physician and was proprietor of the St. Joseph Medical Journal. He is a member of the Buchanan County, Missouri State and other medical societies.

Dr. French was born in Gentryville, Mo., November 8, 1853 and was married to Miss Kate V.| Lewis of Andrew County, February 12, 1884.

three months he came with his parents to St. Joseph. His was one of twelve Polish families in St. Joseph thirty-six years ago. He was edu-

GEORGE KNOPINSKI

GEORGE KNOPINSKI, proprietor of the cafe and bar at 431 Illinois avenue, was born in Patterson, New Jersey, March 8, 1879. At the age of

cated in the Polish schools of St. Joseph and speaks five languages, Polish, Bohemian, German, English and Russian. He made the race for the

Democratic nomination for sheriff in 1910, but was defeated. At the age of twenty-one he was appointed to the police force, being the youngest man ever given a policeman's commission. He served five years and three months and began his present business in 1906. He was married to Miss Mary Mackowiak of St. Joseph May 23, 1900. They have three children, two daughters and a son. Mr. Knopinski has memberships in the Eagles,

laid by first graduating in pharmacy, after which he became manufacturing chemist and in 1891 graduated in medicine as an M. D. He began the practice of his profession in Harper, Iowa, and located in St. Joseph in the spring of 1902. He has at different times attended special courses of post graduate work. He is an expert electrical treatment, and is an especially capable consulting physician. Dr. Thomas' is an active member of

CONRAD E. THOMAS M. D.

—Photo by Mulvane.

the Moose, the Redmen and three Polish societies. He is a communicant of the Polish Catholic Church.

DR. CONRAD E. THOMAS, office at Suite 40 and 41 Commercial Building, is prominent among the leading physicians of St. Joseph. A native of the state of New York, he was born in Brooklyn in 1867. He received his early education in the public schools. The fundament to a thorough and practical knowledge of medicine was

the local and state medical societies and American Medical Association and is examiner for a number of old line life insurance companies. He is a member of the different Masonic bodies including the Shriners as well as of the I. O. O. F. and Knights of Pythias. He is a member of the Francis Street Methodist Church.

He has gained an interstate reputation as an opponent of the indiscriminate use of the surgeon's knife.

CHARLES ANTON PFEIFFER, than whom few men are better known in business and political circies, has been for many years one of St. Joseph's leading citizens, a distinction he bears by reason of his long years of active service in behalf of the city he loves and his unselfish devotion to every duty that has been imposed upon him. Mr. Pfeiffer is president of the Pfeiffer Stone Company, a business institution well

They arrived in New York October 2, 1849. The family resided in New York, Philadelphia and Chicago until 1860, when they came to St. Joseph, arriving here April 17th of that year.

The senior Mr. Pfeiffer immediately sought a place for his business operation, his first location being on the north side of Felix street between Fourth and Fifth streets. He remained there until 1863 doing the cut stone work for the State Bank Build-

CHARLES ANTON PFEIFFER

known throughout Missouri and adjoining states.

Mr. Pfeiffer was born in Sigmaringen, Hohenzollern, Germany, December 19, 1844. His father, Joseph Pfeiffer, came to America in 1849, arriving in New York the 9th of March. He began looking at once for a location for his business—that of ornamental carver and stone cutter. He was so well impressed with the new country that he sent for his wife and son, the subject of this sketch.

ing, Fourth and Felix streets, now the Missouri Valley Trust Company, and the stores adjoining the same. He then moved to the corner of Ninth street and Frederick avenue. In 1866 the business was changed to Sixth and Charles streets and in 1868 it was moved to Fourth and Locust streets, where it is still located. The company has extensive quarries at Batesville, Ark., on the St. Louis, Iron Mountain and Southern Railway which have established a wide reputation for the quality of stone secured there. The company has handled some of the largest contracts for building stone ever let in the United States, including the new $2,000,000 capitol building at Little Rock, Ark.

Joseph Pfeiffer died November 22, 1900, and the business of the Pfeiffer Stone Company had been incorporated in 1881, was continued with Charles A. Pfeiffer, president and E. W. Gensen, secretary and treasurer. The Batesville quarries are under the management of Joseph A. Pfeiffer, while the St. Joseph plant is under the foremanship of Otto Pfeiffer, both sons of Charles A. Pfeiffer.

Charles A. Pfeiffer in his youth attended both German and English schools, and was, therefore, thoroughly educated. After removing to St. Joseph he continued his studies in the night schools and completed the course of the Bryant & Stratton Business College. In 1864 and 1865 he served in the Civil war as a member of Company B, 87th Missouri Militia, under Capt. Louis Hax.

Very soon after attaining his majority Mr. Pfeiffer began taking an interest in politics and public affairs. He has always given of his time, ability and means to the end that his home city might prosper and in practically every instance has served the community without compensation. He was corresponding secretary of the Board of Trade in 1871 and one of the water commissioners under Mayor Hosea. He was elected on the Republican ticket as alderman at large in 1890 and served two years as chairman of the finance committee, a responsible position in those days. During this time Mr. Pfeiffer kept a duplicate set of books at his office in which every financial detail of the city government was recorded. These books are among the most highly prized treasures in his private library, which is extensive and comprehensive. In 1895 he was appointed on a commission to draft a new contract with the St. Joseph Water Company (which was not accepted). In 1898 he was nominated for mayor on the Republican ticket, but was defeated by Dr. P. J. Kirschner, largely through a factional fight in his own party. He was one of the trustees of the Hall school, a member of the Board of Directors of the Free Public Library,

of which he was secretary and treasurer for seventeen years, resigning in 1912. He has also been United States jury commissioner for seventeen years.

In the spring of 1912, Mr. Pfeiffer was again nominated for mayor and this time was successful, defeating A. P. Clayton who had held the office for two terms. Mr. Pfeiffer brought to his administration as chief executive of the city the same sterling business principles that had characterized his conduct of his private affairs and their impress were soon felt in the municipality. His manner of conducting public business was the same as though he alone were interested. This fact became known to the people soon after he was installed in office.

Certain public matters which had their inception in a previous administration—notably the proposed park and boulevard system—met with radical opposition among one element of the taxpayers and because of this an effort was made to invoke the recall law—a new feature added to the charter of the city of St. Joseph a few years previous. Notwithstanding the bitter opposition to the parks the effort to recall Mayor Pfeiffer failed and he was signally successful at the recall election. He very properly considers this one of the highest compliments ever paid him by his fellow townsmen.

L. FISCHER SR., at 423 Main street has, by integrity, fugality and painstaking effort, built up a bakery business that has few equals and no superior in St. Joseph. He has been in his present location for many years and his long service in behalf of his customers is the best testimonial to his efficiency in catering to their needs. He sells nothing but first-class goods and the first maxim on his list is "treat everybody right."

MULVANE'S PHOTOS have a reputation for quality that is not excelled anywhere. His studio at 810½ Frederick avenue is one of the best appointed in the city. His instruments and equipment are the best that money can buy and he has been in the business long enough to know how to use them. When photos come from Mulvane's they are sure to please.

THOMPSON E. POTTER, M. D., was born in Clinton County, Mo., December 18, 1849, and is the son of Thomas and Hessa (Smith) Potter. His maternal grandfather was Thompson Smith, prominently identified with the early history of Missouri. Until his 16th year, Dr. Potter attended the common schools, and then entered McGee College, located near Macon City. After graduating, he began teaching, and took up the study

Medical College of St. Joseph, which position he held for many years, and which he resigned because of his rapidly increasing practice. From 1882 to 1886 he was one of the surgeons of the Hannibal & St. Joseph railroad, and in 1883 he was, though a Democrat, appointed by President Arthur as a member of the pension examining board for the Third congressional district. Dr. Potter located in St. Joseph in 1887, and has

THOMPSON E. POTTER, M. D.

of medicine. Overcoming almost insurmountable obstacles he entered Jefferson Medical College, Philadelphia, in the fall of 1873, and graduated in March, 1875, taking a prize for the best thesis. Directly after graduating Dr. Potter returned to Missouri and located at Cameron, where he remained for about eleven years, building up a large and lucrative practice. While living at Cameron, he was called to the chair of physiology and diseases of the nervous system, in the Northwestern

achieved both success and fame in his profession. He was identified with the Northwestern Medical College for some years after coming here, and withdrew to become one of the founders of the Central Medical College. In 1880 he founded the Western Medical and Surgical Reporter, which he edited for some years.

In 1905 the Central Medical College was merged with the Ensworth and Dr. Potter held the chair of surgery in the consolidated school.

He is secretary of the Board of

Trustees and Faculty of the Ensworth Deaconess Hospital Association. He has held, at different times, the chairs of surgery in the Northwestern Central and Ensworth Medical Colleges.

In his early struggles he received every encouragement and sympathy from his mother, a woman remarkable for her energy and lofty ambition, for her nobility of purpose and strength of character, and he naturally feels proud when he sees in his successful present the fruition of her prophecies and his hopes.

versity Medical College in Kansas City five years. He graduated from that institution in 1893. He then took a full course in Rush Medical College in Chicago and received a diploma there in 1900. He specialized in Chicago for two years, during part of which time he did post graduate work in the Chicago Polyclinic. After being in the general practice in Oregon for about fifteen years he took up specialty work again in 1914. He spent nearly two years in this work studying in Tulane University in New

DR. WILLARD C. PROUD
—Photo by Mulvane.

DR. WILLARD C. PROUD, eye, ear, nose and throat specialist, with offices in the Tootle-Lemon Bank Building, is a native of Missouri. He was born in Oregon, June 28, 1873, and is the son of C. O. Proud, one of the most prominent citizens of Holt County. Dr. Proud received his early education in the public and high schools of Oregon. Then he studied pharmacy and medicine in the Uni-

Orleans, and the best institutions in Vienna, London and New York, returning a few months ago and locating in St. Joseph. He has worked in nearly all of the prominent hospitals in the country and has been exceptionally successful. He was married in Oregon, Mo., November 11, 1896, to Miss Alice Kunkel. They have three children, Kathleen, Genieve and O'Neil.

EMANUEL F. HARTELL was born near the city of Altoona, in Huntington (not Blair) County, Pennsylvania. His boyhood days were passed in the vicinity, where during the winter months he attended the best schools in the county and city; the summer months were spent in working on farms and assisting his father in his trade as carpenter and joiner in which he became quite proficient, when he entered the service of the

ing his lot with the Eight Ohio Volunteer Veteran Cavalry, in which regiment he served until it was mustered out of the service.

In August, 1866, he moved to Southeastern Missouri, among the "Ozarks" and engaged in the lumber business, but not finding it profitable he returned to Covington, Ohio, where he was married to Miss Mary E. Wise, three daughters being the fruit of this union.

EMANUEL F. HARTZELL

Pennsylvania Railroad Company.

In October, 1863, he removed with his parents to Covington, Miami County, Ohio, where he enlisted in the United States army. His time having expired in the fall of 1864, he was mustered out of the service and again accepted a position in the service of the railroad company at Altoona, Pennsylvania; but meeting with an accident he resigned his position and returned to his parents in Ohio. After his recovery, in the spring of 1865, he re-enlisted in the army, cast-

In November, 1869, he returned to Missouri and settled at St. Joseph where he first engaged in the business of contracting and building, and later traveled four years in the interest of the Forsythe Scale Company, located at Waukegan, Illinois. He then engaged in the fire insurance business which he has followed successfully for the last twenty-eight years. He has never sought or held any public office, always declining to allow his name to be used for this purpose. While intensely patriotic as an

American citizen, he is not a partizan, and does not care for the turmoil and excitement of politics—caring more for the successful administration of public affairs than for party politics. Two of his daughters are married and live in St. Joseph. The eldest, Sallie V., is the wife of Charles A. Batson, and Elsie B., is the wife of Gustave E. Hees, while the youngest, Miss Bertha D., lives with her parents.

Dearborn street as a dock hand for a year. In 1869 he went to Batavia, Ill., and engaged in the lime business for a period of four years. In 1873 he went to Kansas City and engaged in the milk business, remaining there four years. He came to St. Joseph in 1878 and again took up the business of selling milk, establishing what is now the Western Dairy and Ice Cream Company. He has done much

JOHN HANAFIN

JOHN HANAFIN, retired milk man, located at 218 South Fifth street, was born in New Fair, Niogro County, New York, December 20, 1836. His education was received in the town of his birth. In 1850 he went with his parents to Wisconsin where he lived fourteen years, following the avocation of a farmer. In 1865 he enlisted in Company B, 48th Wisconsin and was mustered out at Leavenworth, Kas., Feb. 14, 1866, and was discharged in Madison, Wis., March 1, 1866. After leaving the army he went to Chicago and worked at the foot of

to assist in the growth and development of the city and is one of its most honored and respected citizens.

J. W. CLINE, 1918 St. Joseph avenue, is one of the best jewelers and opticians in St. Joseph. He offers his trade the services of a competent men at prices perceptibly lower than is charged down town. He is out of the high rent district and gives his patrons the advantage of it. He has a good line of watches, jewelry and spectacles.

WILLIAM H. UTZ, for twenty-five years one of the successful members of the St. Joseph bar, as a lawyer, has gained a distinctive place, has been prominent in civic affairs in St. Joseph and Buchanan County, and by his own career and the associations of his family since pioneer days has a representative place in the history of Northwest Missouri.

William H. Utz was born in Crawford Township of Buchanan County, of the successful lawyers for a quarter of a century. Always an active supporter of the Democratic interests he cast his first vote for Grover Cleveland, and was assistant prosecuting attorney for Buchanan County in 1895 and 1896. For six years he served as a member of the Board of Police Commissioners in St. Joseph, having been appointed by Governor Dockery.

On May 15, 1902, Mr. Utz married

WILLIAM' H. UTZ
—Photo by Mulvane.

and acquired his early education by attending the rural schools of Buchanan County, was for one year a student in the Central College at Fayette, taught a year in the interim at Lone Star, and then entered the State University at Columbia, which graduated him LLL. B., in 1889. In July of the same year he was admitted to the bar before Judge Silas Woodson of the criminal court, and began practice at St. Joseph, where he has been one Alice A. Henry, who is a native of St. Louis. Their three children are Mary Elizabeth, Alice Ruth, and William H. Mr. Utz and wife are members of the Francis Street M. E. Church, South. His fraternal affiliations are with Zerdatha Lodge, No. 189, A. F. & A. M.; Mitchell Chapter, No. 89, R. A. M.; Hugh de Payne Commandery, No. 51, K. T.; St. Joseph Council No. 9, R. & S.; Moila Temple of the Mystic Shrine; St. Joseph Chapter No. 189, O. E. S.; Araphoe Tribe, No. 26. I. O. R. M.; St. Joseph Aerie, No. 49, F. O. E.; and St. Joseph Lodge No. 135, I. O. T. M.

DR. JACOB GEIGER, one of the leading surgeons of the west, has been a leading figure in the development of the medical profession in St. Josph. His practice is confined to surgery and he has been exceptionally successful throughout the many years he has been practicing as a specialist.

ing year he was graduated from Bryant's Business College. He then worked as a weighmaster in a packing house, reading medicine the meantime under the tutorage of Dr. Galen E. Bishop. He continued his studies while clerking in a drug store for a few years. He practiced medicine from 1868 to 1870 and then entered the medical department of the University of Louisville, from which he was graduated in 1872. He engaged in the

DR. JACOB GEIGER

Dr. Geiger was born in Wurtemberg, Germany, July 25, 1848, and is a son of Anton and Marie G. (Eberhart) Geiger. He came with his mother to America and located in Illinois in 1856. In the spring of 1858 the family moved to Brown County, Kansas, where the mother died the following November. Jacob then came to St. Joseph and worked for a dairyman until 1860, when he moved to Illinois, where he received part of his education. He returned to St. Joseph in 1865 and worked as a clerk in his brother's grocery store. The follow-

general practice of medicine in St. Joseph and since 1890 has made a specialty of surgery. Dr. Geiger was one of the organizers of the St. Joseph Hospital Medical College, in which institution he filled the chair of anatomy. He helped organize the College of Physicians and Surgeons in 1880 and after the consolidation of the two institutions in 1883 held the chair of surgery. He was dean of the faculty until 1889, when the name of the college was changed to the Ensworth. In 1890 he was one of the organizers of the Marion Sims Medical College of St. Louis and was elected to the chair of surgery. He started the Medical Herald in 1887 and is identified with numerous medical societies and organizations.

Dr. Geiger was married in 1887 to Miss Louise Kollatz. In recent years he has taken a commendable interest in the material development of his home town. He built a few years ago one of the most modern and palatial residences in the city at

ceived a common school education in his native state. When he was 14 years old his parents moved to Nebraska, locating in Oboe County. In 1877 he moved to Harlan County, Nebraska and located in Republican City where he studied medicine with Dr. H. S. Zumro for a period of four years. He graduated from the Ensworth Medical College in 1882. He practiced in Bancroft, Daviess County twelve years and in Gilman City until

DR. WILLIAM SWINT
—Photo by Mulvane.

Twenty-fifth street and Frederick avenue. The St. Francis Hotel at Sixth and Francis streets is another monument to his enterprise and pushing public spirit. Various other business enterprises have been assisted by him. His office is at 614 Francis street. Politically Dr. Geiger is a Republican, fraternally a Mason and religiously a Presbyterian.

DR. WILLIAM SWINT (in German Schwindt), is a native of Pennsylvania and was born Nov. 18, 1850. He re-

1910. He took a special course in the College of Physicians and Surgeons of St. Louis in 1884. In 1908 he received a diploma from the Kansas City Post Graduate Medical School and Hospital. He moved to St. Joseph in 1910 and took the chair of Professor of Medicine in the Ensworth Medical College. He was married to Miss Sarah Brown of Missouri in Nebraska in 1870. They have a son and two daughters. He is a Mason, Odd Fellow, K. of P. and Woodman of the World.

ALPHA WIGGLESFORTH TOOLE was born in St. Joseph, Missouri, October 28, 1862. Received his education in the public schools and high school of St. Joseph and Bryant's College, is an expert bookkeeper and accountant; was for twenty years manager of the Wood Mfg. Co., one of the largest manufacturers of clothing in the country, is a staunch Republican, is now assistant treasurer of St. Joseph, is a member of the Sons of

The Toole family was one of the pioneer families of Missouri, consisting of four brothers, Edwin, Walter, Daniel, William and three sisters, America, Nancy and Mary, sons and daughters of Dr. Daniel Toole, of Christiansburg, Shelby County, Kentucky. All came to Missouri and had large families. Edwin, born in 1808, married Lucinda Porter, and came to St. Joseph in 1887, was appointed by Austin A. King, first Circuit Clerk of

ALPHA WIGGLESFORTH TOOLE
—Photo by Mulvane.

the Revolution, Modern Brotherhood of America, Lincoln Club and Commerce Club. Married in 1891, Miss Anna Egner, daughter of Charles Egner of St. Joseph, two children by this union, Leslie, a son born in 1893, Erma a daughter born in 1895. Mrs. Toole died in 1904. Mr. Toole married his second wife, Miss Maude Curtis in 1910, a daughter of Ben F. Curtis of Doniphan County, Kansas; a daughter Vivian born in 1912 by this union.

Buchanan County in 1839, was a Justice in 1860 and in the City Council in 1871-1873. Edwin moved to Montana; one son, Joseph K. was elected governor of Montana, married a daughter of Gen. Rosecrans, and another son, Warren, became a noted railroad lawyer.

Reverend Walter Toole, born in 1820, married Virginia Lyle, settled at Macon, Missouri, and was a noted circuit preacher in the South Methodist Church.

Reverend Daniel Toole was born in 1822, married Lydia Rookwood, settled at Bloomington, Missouri, and was also a South Methodist preacher.

America Toole born in 1812, married John Bramel.

Nancy Toole born in 1814, married Robert Barkhurst.

Mary Toole born in 1824, married Wm. Woods.

Judge Wm. C. Toole, the father of A. W. Toole, came to St. Joseph in June, 1838, from Shelby County, Kentucky, where he was born in 1818. On arriving here he went to Joseph Robidoux' house to stay all night. Robidoux not having any extra beds gave him some buffalo robes and told him to roll up on the floor in front of the fireplace. Judge Toole killed wolves on the spot where the Metropole Hotel now stands and was chased by a band of Indians between St. Joseph and Savannah. Attended the first court held here, joined the Methodist Church in 1836; was ordained a minister in 1838; was charter member and preached in the first log church here in 1841.

In 1841 he married Miss Elvira Wigglesworth and had ten children. Was trustee appointed to collect money from the state to start the schools here, was superintendent of city and county schools before the war, admitted to the bar in 1848; judge of the Court of Common Pleas 1853-55, and 1870-73, city register 1856-65, city recorder 1862-64. When recorder fined Joseph Robidoux for striking his daughter-in-law; was circuit clerk 1862-64, city assesser 1855-56; 1st Lt. enrolled Mo. Militia, Co. G, assistant provost marshall 1862-63; afterwards appointed brigade commissary with rank of major by Gen. Hall, assistant post master in 1876, ran for mayor in 1880. In 1849 he drove an ox team all the way to California without swearing an oath. In 1908 he was presented with a gold headed cane by the bar of St. Joseph, on his 90th birthday, as their oldest member. Judge Toole died in St. Joseph, February 17, 1909, aged 91 years.

Dr. Daniel Toole, the father of the Toole families of Missouri, was born in Virginia in 1775, died in Savannah, Missouri, in 1850. He was the son of Wm. Toole of Culpeper County, Virginia, a planter and Revolutionary soldier. Wm. Toole's wife was Ann Roberts, daughter of Major Wm. Roberts, who commanded four companies in the Revolution; his son Roberts, was also a major in the Virginia Continental Artillery. The Toole family trace their lineage back over a thousand years through the Colonial families of Virginia, through the Milesian line of Irish kings to King Tuathal (pronounced too-all) of Ireland, whence came the name.

Mr. A. W. Toole's mother was Elvira Wigglesworth, born in 1820 in Clark County, Kentucky, married Judge Wm. C. Toole in 1841, died in St. Joseph in 1899. She was a daughter of Wm. Wigglesworth, son of James Wigglesworth of Spottsylvania County, Virginia, planter and Revolutionary soldier, whose wife was a daughter of Wm. Thompson of Richmond, Virginia, son of Samuel, son of Wm. Thompson of Blair Manor, Ayrshire, Scotland. This Wm. Thompson of Richmond had a son, Gen. David Thompson, who was in the war of 1812, and was commander of the 2nd battalion at the battle at the River Thames in Canada, where Tecumsen was killed. Col. Manlius V. Thompson, son of Gen. David was colonel of the 3rd Kentucky Volunteers in the war with Mexico, was in the battle of Beuna Vista and the fall of the City of Mexico, was Lt. Gov. of Kentucky in 1840. President of the Baptist College at Georgetown, Kentucky. His body lies buried in the college campus where an elegant monument is erected to his memory. Gen. David Thompson moved to Missouri in 1833. This Wm. Thompson of Richmond, Virginia, married Ann Rodes, daughter of John Rodes, of Amhurst County, Va., who is third in descent from Baron Francis Rodes of England. John Rodes' wife was Mary Crawford, daughter of Capt. David Crawford of Amhurst County, Virginia, who lived to be 100 years old and belonged to the Earls of Crawford of Scotland. Francis Crawford, wife of Cornelius Vanderbilt belongs to this family.

The Wigglesworth family are old English stock from the town of Wigglesworth in Yorkshire, England. Edward born in 1604 in England came to America in ship James of Bristol in 1638, with his family; his son Michael was known as the Puritan Poet, author of "The Day of Doom" which had a larger circulation than the Bible in its day. Michael's son Edward was professor of divinity at Harvard College; a grandson Edward also a professor at Harvard; a great-grandson one of the editors of the Encyclopedia Americana. Eleven sons of the Wigglesworth family were graduates of Harvard College. John Quincy Adams stayed at the Wigglesworth home while attending Harvard girls. The Wigglesworth branch runs back to Abbot De Wigglesworth in the year 1100.

Mr. A. W. Toole's grandmother was Frances Bush, born 1789 in Clark County, Ky., wife of Wm. Wigglesworth and died in St. Joseph in 1870; was the daughter of Phillip Bush Jr., a Virginia planter and Revolutionary soldier of Orange County, Virginia. The Bush family was the first to settle in Kentucky. Wm. Bush came to Kentucky with Daniel Boone in 1774, then went back and gathered together forty families, all relations, including the families of the five brothers, Phillip Bush, Wm. Bush, John Bush, Ambrose and Francis Bush, and started back to Kentucky in 1780, fighting Indians every step until they reached the garden spot of Kentucky called Clark County. They were all Baptists and built the first church in Kentucky. Captain Wm. Bush was with Gen. Geo. Roger Clark in the conquest of the northwest, fought at Kaskaskia and Vincennes. William and John were in Lord Dunmore's war with the Indians and fought at Point Pleasant; all of the brothers were in the Revolution. On the tombstone at the grave of Capt. Wm. Bush is engraved these words, "The Friend and Companion of Daniel Boone." The Bush family descend from John Bush who came from England in the ship Neptune in 1618, having bought 300 acres of land from the Virginia Land Company in England before starting. He settled in the corporation of Elizabeth City, Virginia.

Sarah Bush, cousin of Frances Bush, was the second wife of Thomas Lincoln, the father of Abraham Lincoln, made his clothes and reared him and taught him to be one of the greatest men in the world. Abe's mother, Nancy Hanks, died when Abe was nine years old. Dennis Hanks, brother of Nancy, gives Sarah Bush great praise in the rearing of Abe.

JOHN ALBUS was born Oct. 4, 1860 on a farm in Leavenworth County, Kansas a few miles from Fort Leavenworth. With his parents he came to St. Joseph, Mo., in 1863. His education was limited to the grammar grades of our public schools.

He sold newspapers as a boy on the street corners and was a carrier on the "Old St. Joseph Gazette" when Eugene Field was the city editor. He was later connected with Ernst &

now a prominent member of the party. In 1902 President Roosevelt appointed him surveyor of customs at this port to succeed W. L. Buechle and in 1908 reappointed for another term. He remained in the office a total of nine years and three months. He was for thirteen years a stock holder and member of the Combe Printing Company, having charge of the stationery department.

From 1891 to 1896 he served on the

JOHN ALBUS

Brill in the book and stationery business. For several years he was in partnership with Dr. A. V. Banes in the manufacture of special medicines

In 1888 he was selected as a delegate to the National Republican Convention, which convention nominated General Benjamin Harrison as the Republican candidate for president and who defeated President Grover Cleveland in the November election. He has served on the Republican city, county, congressional and state committees on diferent occasions and is

Board of Education. He is now located at 811 Edmond street, Moss Building, where he represents the St. Joseph Stock Yards Journal and the Daily Journal as advertising manager and also represents several fire insurance companies.

He resides at 728 North Twenty-second street. In lodge and other orders he belongs to the Masonic order, being a life member of Charity Lodge No. 331, A. F. and A. M.; is a member Woodmen of the World, Elks Lodge No. 40, B. P. O. E., St. Joseph

Press Club, The Ad Club, Knights and Ladies of Security, The Turnve'ein, German-American Alliance, Commerce Club, North West Missouri Press Association and the Lincoln Club.

C. T. M'QUINN, secretary and manager of the McQuinn Clothing Co., was born at Bloomington, Ill., Dec. 12, 1868. He attended the public and parochial schools of Bloomington until he was 19 years of age, when he

during the eight years he was connected with the company here, he increased that number to 5000, this being the largest number of accounts held by any of the credit stores in the city.

In the spring of 1911 he entered business for himself under the name of the McQuinn Clothing Co. and in the same year he incorporated with his sisters, Annie McQuinn and Mary F. McQuinn. Notwithstanding that

C. T. M'QUINN

removed to Kansas City where he entered the wall paper and paint business which business he remained in until 1900 when he accepted a position with one of the large credit companies and in 1902 was sent to Leavenworth, Kas. as manager of the company's store, where he remained for one year and was transferred to St. Joseph in May, 1903.

When he came to St. Joseph the company had about 800 accounts and

the past four years have been very bad from a business standpoint, he has succeeded in building up a very large business and claims the honor of having more individual accounts on his books than any other concern in the city.

It has been said by a very prominent attorney, who expressed himself before a court, that of all the credit men in the city, Mr. McQuinn was king of them all.

Mr. McQuinn has been very active in fraternal organizations, being state treasurer for four years of the Ancient Order of Hibernians, faithful navigator of the St. Joseph assembly Knights of Columbus, delegate to the state convention at St. Louis of the Catholic Knights of America and also a member of tne Columbus Club and Modern Woodmen of America.

Mr. McQuinn resides at 2717 Renick street and besides his wife there are

and came to America in 1885. He went first to California and located in Marysville. He stayed there four years and in 1889 came to St. Joseph and opened his present place of business. He was elected a member of the city council in 1906 and again in 1910, serving six years in all. He built the Hickory theater, a two-story brick building, in 1914. It is one of the finest buildings in the southern part of the city and the place has en-

JOHN EGLI
—Photo by Mulvane.

two children, Miss Marie, who is a graduate of the Cathedral High School and also of the Normal, and at present a teacher at Hosea School. Miss Margaret is a student at the Sacred Heart Academy.

JOHN EGLI, dealer in meats and provisions, at 2310 South Eleventh street, is a native of Switzerland, in which country he was born in 1867. He was educated in his native country

joyed a good patronage from the first.

G. D. SHAFFER, plumber and gas fitter, 1018 Frederick avenue, is one of the newer men in business in St. Joseph, and has already given evidence of his ability to hold his own against the fiercest competition. He is a practical man in his line, a good workman and insists that every piece of work turned out shall bear the stamp of quality.

E. F. HARTWIG—The wholesale liquor house of E. F. Hartwig, 212 South Third, is known all over the west as one of the leaders in that line of business and the name has come to be a synonym for merit. For personal integrity and sterling worth no man stands higher than Ernst F. Hartwig, a position which he has attained by many years of business experience, in which his motto has always been fair dealing. This house was originally founded in 1864 by Maj. H. R. W. Hartwig, brother of E. F. Hartwig, the latter becoming a member of the firm of H. R. W. Hartwig & Co. in 1869, and this firm, by the exercise of strict business integrity and unbounded energy, forged steadily and rapidly to the front and achieved remarkable success. In 1887 Major Hartwig, who had meantime served as mayor of St. Joseph, retired, and since then the business has been conducted by Mr. E. F. Hartwig, and is accompanied by the same success that marked the career of the original firm. Mr. Hartwig was born in the Province of Hessen, Germany, where he was trained in the grocery business. In 1862 he came to America and was bookkeeper in the dry goods house of Stix, Eckhart & Co. of St. Joseph for seven years prior to joining his brother in the business which he now conducts, and which he has brought to the high standing it now occupies in the business world. Mr. Hartwig was married March 18, 1868, to Miss Emma Friedrich, and they have had five children.

E. F. HARTWIG
—Photo by Mulvane.

HENRY O. HARTWIG, 212 South Third street, associated with his father, Ernest F. Hartwig, in the wholesale liquor business, is a native of Missouri. He was born in St. Joseph November 5, 1868. He received his education in the schools of the city. He entered the business house of his father in 1886 in the capacity of bookkeeper. He is now manager only those whose memory is good can remember when it first began business. There is a reason for the long continued prosperity of this store. It is due to the straight-forward, fair and impartial treatment the trade has received from the first day this store opened. The indications are that the same policy will make possible the continuance of good business at this stand for many years to come.

HENRY O. HARTWIG
—Photo by Mulvane.

of the house and has been a potential factor in its success.

He was married to Marie Louise Wenz, a daughter of Fred Wenz, June 20, 1897. They have two children, Caroline E. E., fifteen, and Elizabeth, nine years old. Fraternally Mr. Hartwig is a Mason.

SCHENEKER'S DRUG STORE at the corner of Third and Franklin streets has been there so long that

JOHN BERGEN, whose bakery is at 1608 Frederick avenue, appeals to the buying public as a man who keeps his goods in first-class condition and sells them at right prices. This inspires confidence and confidence means more and better business. Mr. Bergen is developing an excellent trade by treating his patrons right and he deserves the success he has attained.

EUGENE AYRES, son of Reuben and Maria S. Ayres, was born near New Brunswick, New Jersey, Nov. 15, 1843 and is of Scotch-English ancestry. In early boyhood his parents removed to New York City. He graduated from the Mount Washington Collegiate Institute in that city in 1860. He then entered Rutgers College at New Brunswick, N. J., and later studied law in the offices of Col.

Susan Morton of Bordentown, N. J., were united in marriage December 18, 1867, Mrs. Ayres being a graduate of the Bordentown Female College. They have two sons, Clarence Morton Ayres, who is a civil engineer residing in Tuscaloosa, Alabama, and Eugene Bruce Ayres residing at Hartford, Conn,; their only daughter, Helen May, died in early girlhood. All the family is connected with the Protestant Episcopal Church. Mr. Ayres is

EUGENE AYRES
—Photo by Mulvane.

Garrett S. Cannon at Bordentown, N. J. and attended lectures in the Philadelphia Law School. He was admitted to practice as an attorney and counselor at law and solicitor in chancery by the Supreme Court of New Jersey at Trenton, Nov. 9, 1865, and settled in St. Joseph in May, 1866, being admitted to practice in this state by the late Judge Wm. Heren. Mr. Ayres and Miss Margaret R. Morton, daughter of Jacob and

also a member of two fraternal organizations, the Delta Kappa Epsilon with which he became connected in college, and the Ancient Order of United Workmen of Missouri. Mr. Ayres ranks as the leading lawyer in Saint Joseph in Government practice: he is registered in the United States Patent Office and for many years has given large attention to the prosecution of Patent applications in both the United States and Foreign countries, as also to claims in the Pension Bureau.

In politics Mr. Ayers is independent, although for many years he has been favorable to prohibition and a few years since was the nominee of the Prohibition Party for Judge of the Supreme Court of Missouri.

DR. FRANK X. HARTIGAN was born in Horton, Kas., in 1888 and moved to St. Joseph in 1895 and received his education in the public

Dr. Hartigan has been practicing medicine and surgery in St. Joseph since his return and for two years taught anatomy at Ensworth Medical College and has been chief anaesthetist at St. Joseph's Hospital for three years.

He is a member of the Buchanan County and State societies and is secretary of the Academy of Surgery.

His office is at 710½ Felix street.

DR. FRANK X. HARTIGAN
—Photo by Mulvane.

schools and graduated from Christian Brothers College in 1906. In the fall of 1906 he entered Ensworth Medical College and graduated in 1910. Immediately he received the appointment of house physician and surgeon at St. Alexis Hospital in Cleveland, Ohio, which position he occupied until June, 1911, then received appointment as house physician in St. Ann's Maternity Hospital and Infant Asylum in Cleveland, Ohio.

DAVID L. LITTLE, while a comparative new comer in the business world in this part of the city, has been at 1503 North Third street a sufficient length of time to become permanently established. He carries a line of the choicest groceries that can be procured anywhere and he sells them at the lowest possible prices consistent with good merchandising. His methods are such that his popularity is bound to increase.

ORVILLE M. SHANKLIN, attorney at law, was a son of Col. John H. Shanklin, of Trenton, Mo. Was born at Trenton September 16, 1854, reared in his native city, whose public schools supplied his education, and after studying in his fathers office,

cuting attorney. In 1902 Mr. Shanklin came to St. Joseph, and has since been in the active practice of law, making a specialty of real estate and probate practice, and is now title examiner for the Bartlett Bros. Land & Loan Company, as well as in the general practice of those branches of law.

ORVILLE M. SHANKLIN

was admitted to practice by Judge Burgess, in the Circuit Court at Trenton in January, 1877, and began the practice of law at Jamesport in Daviess County, Mo., and after a short residence there returned to his native town. While at Trenton he also held the offices of city attorney, justice of the peace, and assistant prose-

September 19, 1877, he married Miss Dora A. Newton, who was born in Grundy County, a daughter of Obediah G. and Mary G. Newton. Five children were born of this marriage, the two now living are John H. and Mary. John H. married Ruth Peterson and resides with his father. Marry married Samuel Z. Weaver, and they reside at Toronto, Ontario, Dominion of Canada, Mr. Weaver being head of a department of Swift's Canadian Company. Mr. Shanklin was reared in the Christian Church, while his wife is a member of the Huffman Methodist Episcopal Church. He has always been active in fraternal affairs; he joined Adelphia Lodge, Knights of Pythias, at Trenton in 1885, and is now a member of Golden Cross Lodge No. 143, of which he served as chan-

1956. He attended the schools of his native city and came to St. Joseph in 1881. He engaged in the hardware business with Sanders & McDonald on Fourth street between Edmond and Charles streets, where he remained two years. In 1884 he went with the R. H. Jordan Hardware Company on Fourth street between Felix and Edmond streets. He was with this firm

JACOB B. DAVIS

cellor three successive years, and has served as outer and inner guard and master-at-arms in the Grand Lodge of Missouri. He is also a member of the Woodmen of the World, the Woodmen's Circle, and the Sons of Veterans.

JACOB B. DAVIS, manager of the Curtin & Clark Hardware Company's business at 209-211 South Sixth street, was born in Hillsboro, Ohio, July 3,

nineteen years and became one of the leading men of the concern. In 1903 h accepted the position of manager of the Curtin & Clark Hardware Company, and after twelve years of service seems good for as many more. He was married to Miss Josseta Richards of St. Joseph, April 1884. They have three children, two sons and one daughter. Mr. Davis is a Mason and Odd Fellow.

LUCIAN J. EASTIN, one of the prominent lawyers and a leader of his profession in the St. Joseph bar, is properly mentioned, even though somewhat briefly, in a work of the nature and purpose of this publication. His legal activities, for the most part, since he launched out into the practice of his profession, have been carried on in Buchanan County, and he is widely and favorably known hereabouts.

Mr. Eastin has been active as an Odd Fellow, has been grand master of the Grand Lodge of Missouri, and has since 1908 represented that body in the Sovereign Grand Lodge, of which he is an active member.

On October 4, 1904, Miss Janet Strong, a daughter of Col. James W. Strong, became the wife of Mr. Eastin. Mr. and Mrs. Eastin have one son, Robert Strong Eastin, and the family home is at No. 202 South Twentieth street.

LUCIAN J. EASTIN

He was born in Clay County, Missouri, on July 12, 1868. He graduated from the law department of the University of Michigan, in 1894, and came direct to St. Joseph and began practice, and he has since been occupied in legal work in the city and county.

In November, 1908, he was elected judge of the Circuit Court of Buchanan County, and he served from January 1, 1909, to January 1, 1911, when he resigned to return to the practice.

HENRY W. McCOOL is a native of Kentucky and was born in Louisville April 5, 1875. He came to St. Joseph in 1899. He was appointed to a position on the St. Joseph Fire Department in 1906. He has been in the employ of the city in this capacity for seven years. He was married to Miss Ida West of Lyons, Kans., in 1903. Their family consists of one son. Mr. McCool is one of St. Joseph's most highly respected and honored citizens.

WILLIAM E. SPRATT, a prominent and old-established real estate man of St. Joseph, has been identified with this city in a successful and public spirited manner for many years, and is numbered among the citizens who have been instrumental in helping to promote many projects for the up-building and progress of the community. Mr. Spratt has the distinction of being the third Democratic

ette County, in 1867. Deprived of his mother when he was two years old, caused the placing of William E. Spratt in tne home of his grand-parents at St. Joseph, where he spent the first nine years of his life, and from 1876 he lived for several years in his father's home at Hamilton. He was sent away to school, and altogether was absent from St. Joseph for a period of eleven years. In 1886, having graduated from the St. James

WILLIAM E. SPRATT

candidate elected to the office of mayor of St. Joseph in a period of twenty-two years. His real estate business conducted at 213 North Seventh street has really been in continuous existence ever since the close of th Civil war, having been founded by the late Col. John F. Tyler, his uncle, and continued as Tyler & Co., until 1911.

William E. Spratt is a native Missourian, born at Lexington, in Lafay-

Military Academy at Macon City, Mr. Spratt returned to St. Joseph, and in the spring of the following year engaged in the real estate business with his uncle, Col. John F. Tyler, who had been both a lawyer and real estate man of St. Joseph since the close of the Civil war. In 1887 the firm became John F. Tyler & Company, and to the large and growing real estate interests of the firm Mr. Spratt gave his undivided attention. At Colonel

Tyler's death, in 1911, the firm name was changed to W. E. Spratt.

In 1902, Mr. Spratt was first candidate for the office of mayor on the Democratic ticket. His defeat was accomplished by only eight votes although the city was normally between six and eight hundred Republican. This was a high personal tribute to Mr. Spratt's popularity and ability. and in 1904, having been renominated by his party by acclamation, he was

and societies. In 1890 Mr. Spratt married Effie L. Cowgill, who was born in Indiana. Mr. and Mrs. Spratt are the parents of three children: Tyler, who died in infancy; Elliot Cowgill Spratt, and Leah Spratt.

JOHN M. CRAWFORD, chief deputy in the county assessor's office, was born in St. Joseph April 8, 1870. He was educated in the Christian Brothers College, from which in-

JOHN M. CRAWFORD
—Photo by Mulvane.

triumphant by eight hundred majority, and as already stated, was one of the few Democratic mayors in a period of more than twenty-two years. Mr. Spratt is a director of the Auditorium Association, and has identified himself in a public spirited manner with every organization and measure for the benefit of his home city. His fraternal affiliations are with the Odd Fellows, the Benevolent and Protective Order of Elks, and other lodges

stitution he was graduated in 1883. In 1896 he was a deputy in the county collector's office under E. J. Breen. He went into the assessor's office in the fall of 1898 and has been identified with this office ever since. For seventeen years Mr. Crawford has made up the tax books for the county and has frequently been called upon to assist in this work at the city hall. He was married to Miss Loretta Lysaght of St. Joseph January 24, 1914.

WALTER W. HEAD—As cashier of the German-American National Bank of St. Joseph, Walter W. Head is reckoned among the rising young bankers of Northwest Missouri, as well as one of the most enterprising and valuable citizens the city claims today. He was born at Adrian, Hancock County, Illinois, on December 10, 1877, and is the son of Alfred W. and Margaret (Lambert) Head. The County and was graduated therefrom in 1894, with the highest honors of his class. He then entered Stanberry Normal School, and in 1897 was graduated. During the five years that followed he was engaged in teaching in the schools of DeKalb and Buchanan Counties, and during the last year of his pedagogic work he was principal of the DeKalb public schools. While teaching, Mr. Head took a very prominent part in the work of Teachers In-

WALTER W. HEAD

father was a man of Scotch and German descent, while the mother comes of English parentage, her family having long been established in Lancashire, England. In 1885 the parents of the subject came to Missouri, settled in DeKalb County, and there they have continued to reside. They are now living retired after active lives devoted to the farming industry.

Walter W. Head had his early education in the schools of DeKalb stitute, and instructed institutes in the years 1900 and 1901. One of them was in DeKalb and the other was in Buchanan County, and each of them was attended by a hundred teachers of the respective counties. His educational work was of a high order and gained much praise for him during the brief space he devoted to it. Had he elected to continue in the teaching profession, it is more than probable that he would have reached a high place in educational circles as the exponent of public school instruction, but he chose another field for the exercise of his talents.

In 1903 Mr. Head served for ten months as receiving teller in the German-American National Bank of St. Joseph, that service being preliminary to his acceptance of the post of cashier of the DeKalb State Bank of DeKalb, Missouri, a new organization that entered upon its business career August 21, 1904, and to which he had been elected cashier despite the fact of his very limited banking experience.

In June, 1906, Mr. Head resigned his position as cashier of the DeKalb State Bank, having been appointed by Honorable John E. Swanger, secretary of the state of Missouri, to the office of bank examiner for a term of four years. In June, 1908, he resigned the office of bank examiner to accept the position of cashier of the German-American National Bank of St. Joseph, which position he still holds.

He is at the present time chairman of the agricultural committee of the Missouri Bankers Association, serving his second year as such. Is also chairman of the executive committee of the Third Annual Agricultural and Industrial Congress, which meetings are held in the St. Joseph Auditorium in December each year. Is also president of the Young Men's Christian Association of St. Joseph.

Other banking connections of Mr. Head's are the vice-presidency of the Drovers and Merchants Bank of St. Joseph and a number of smaller banks throughout the state, which claim his attention as stockholder or official, or both. He is vice-president of the St. Joseph Life Insurance Company.

Mr. Head is a member of the Republican state committee. He attends the First Christian Church of St. Joseph and is prominently identified with numerous fraternal and purely social orders. The Masonic fraternity claims his as a member in many of its bodies and he has held offices in practically all of them. He is past master of DeKalb Lodge No. 22, A. F. & A. M.; past high priest of Ringo Chapter No. 6, Royal Arch Masons; member of Hugh De Payens Commandery No. 51, Knights Templars; past potentate of Moila Temple, Ancient Arabic Order of the Nobles of the Mystic Shrine; member of St. Joseph Council No. 9, Royal and Select Masters; member of all the Scottish Rite bodies and a member of St. Joseph Consistory No. 4, A. A. S. R., of Thirty-second Degree Masons. He is past noble grand of DeKalb Lodge No. 191, Independent Order of Odd Fellows; past consul of DeKalb Camp No. 5256, Modern Woodmen of America; member of Charity Camp No. 220, Knights of Pythias; member of the Benevolent Protective Order of Elks No. 40, of St. Joseph, and a life member of St. Joseph Lodge No. 315, Loyal Order of Moose. Those organizations of St. Joseph of a purely social nature with which he is identified are the St. Joseph Country Club, the Highland Golf and Country Club of St. Joseph, the Benton Club of St. Joseph, and the St. Joseph Automobile Club. He is also a member of the St. Joseph Commerce Club, was elected president of the club in December, 1913, but owing to an injury of the knee, sustained from an accident, could not serve; and he was president of the St. Joseph Interstate Fair Association in 1913 and 1914. In all of these clubs and societies he is popular and prominent, and he has a wider circle of friends in the city than perhaps any other man who might be mentioned by reason of his many sterling traits of character, his genial good fellowship, and his hearty and wholesome interest in all matters that make for the betterment of local conditions along whatever lines.

On March 7, 1900, Mr. Head was married to Miss Della E. Thompson, a daughter of John J. and Roxcelana (Dittemote) Thompson, who were among the early pioneer families of Buchanan County. Mr. and Mrs. Head have one daughter, Audrey Vernelle.

B. H. CRAMER, at the corner of St. Joseph avenue and Monroe street, has been supplying residents of that part of the city with the best groceries on the market long enough that his name has become a household word with his patrons. They know he will do just as he says he will and for that reason place dependence in him. The reliability of his goods and the low prices at which he sells them brings him the business.

B. M. ACHTENBERG, born March 13, 1884, was brought to St. Joseph, by his parents, in the spring of 1889. He was educated in the public schools in this city, being graduated from the St. Joseph High School with the class of 1903. During the following year he engaged in the mercantile business and although he had several lucrative offers to follow that line he was bent on further education and in the fall

the St. Joseph Bar Association; he is a member of the judiciary and legislative committee of the Commerce Club and almost since the day he reached manhood he has been intimately connected with every Jewish charitable, benevolent and philantropic organization in this city. In his private life he has often made the boast that he has not a single enemy.

AL KLENK, at the corner of Sixth

B. M. ACHTENBERG
—Photo by Mulvane.

of 1904 he entered the law school of the University of Michigan, graduating in June of 1907. On July 13, 1907, he received his license to practice law in the state of Missouri and within a few days thereafter he was admitted to practice in the courts of this county, and soon built up a lucrative practice. He has been an active member of every organization with which he has been connected. For three years he has been trasurer of

and Messanie streets, is an applicant for popular favor who goes on the principle that that which is right is bound to bring returns. He applies this principle to his business and by treating his trade according to the dictates of the golden rule he has enlarged his business materially until now he has one of the best places in the city. In addition to his bar he makes a specialty of lunches at reasonable prices.

HARRY W. MANNING, real estate dealer, at 505 Francis street, was born in Warren County, Ohio, January 4, 1854. He was educated in his native state. In 1876 he left Ohio for the Black Hills country where he remained for about six months. In July, 1876, he went to Memphis, Tenn. He was in the south for ten years and in 1886 came to St. Joseph and became

Miss., November 23, 1883. Fraternally Mr. Manning is a K. of P.

WALTER R. COBB, retail shoeman, at 413 Felix street, comes from that old Virginia stock that invariably makes good citizens. He was born in Bedford City, Va. After attending the schools in his birthplace he removed to St. Joseph where his educa-

HARRY W. MANNING
—Photo by Mulvane.

the manager for the New Home Sewing Machine Co. In 1887 he went to Wichita, Kas., and engaged in the sewing machine business on his own account. In 1890 he returned to St. Joseph and became a real estate man. In 1896 he went to Kansas City and engaged in the same business, but returned to St. Joseph two years later and the firm of Manning & Dyer was formed. He was married to Miss Annelle H. Hudson of Columbus,

tion was completed. He came here in 1882 with his parents and in 1889 entered the employ of A. N. Schuster & Co., clothiers. He remained with this firm until 1894 when he became identified with the Tootle, Wheeler & Motter Dry Goods Co., with which firm he remained until 1897 when he engaged in the retail shoe business, which has claimed his time and attention ever since. Fraternally Mr. Cobb is a Mason and an Odd Fellow.

CHARLES E. DICKEY, member of the Board of Public Works, is a native of Kansas. He was born in Independence June 8, 1873. He attended the schools of his native county and came to St. Joseph in 1896. He at once engaged in the furniture and hardware business in South St. Joseph and has been successful in building up one of the most substantial business enterprises in the city. He has

well as giving attention to decorating, glazing and graining. Mr. Myer has been identified with the trade in St. Joseph for sixteen years. He has been with some of the leading firms in this line of work in the city and has built up a patronage of which he may well feel proud. Since engaging in business for himself, two years ago; he has been unusually successful because he knows what his trade re-

CHARLES E. DICKEY

always taken much interest in public affairs and because of this fact was selected by Mayor Marshall for membership on the Board of Public Works in October, 1915. Mr. Dickey was married to Miss Anna B. Newman of St. Joseph in 1894. They have three children—two sons and a daughter. Fraternally Mr. Dickey is an Odd Fellow.

THE H. A. MYER PAINTING COMPANY, 1115 Frederick avenue, does a general house painting business as

quires and always supplies the want to the satisfaction of all.

I. F. RAMSEY & CO. is the name of the undertaking concern at Ninth and Olive streets. This is the only colored undertaking establishment in the city, and is in the hands of professionals. Mr. Ramsey has been in business many years and his success is not to be wondered at when it is considered that he always gives the best of attention to every call and that his prices are as low as consistent with good business.

M. A. DEAKINS was born in Buchanan County, Missouri, January 4, 1891. He resided in St. Joseph until 1904, when he removed to South Dakota, where he remained two years. In 1907 he returned to St. Joseph and lived here until February 12, 1910, when he went to Lincoln, Neb. March 7, the same year he enlisted in the United States navy at Omaha, Neb. Decatur, a torpedo boat destroyer. He remained with the Decatur a short time, visiting China in 1910, Japan in 1911. He also visited Russia, France, Germany, England, Holland, Turkey, Greece, Sidney, Australia; New South Wales, Melbourne, Australia; and returned to China late in 1912. He remained in that country nearly two years and returned to Manila, P. I., in 1914. He sailed for the United

M. A. DEAKINS
—Photo by Mulvane.

He was sworn in by Lieut. Duncan in the month of July and sailed on the U. S. Buffalo for an Asiatic station, arriving at Honolulu July 14. Two days later he sailed for Guam at which port he arrived July 30. The following day he sailed for Manila and the good ship anchored in Manila Bay August 6. One month from anchorage he was transferred to the U. S. S. States, February 15, 1914, and March 17, of that year was discharged from the navy at Mare Island, Cal., having served four years and ten days. At 4.45 o'clock of the afternoon of his discharge he was on his way to St. Joseph, arriving here March 21. He has been in business in this city ever since. At the present time he is a stockholder in and secretary of the Boyer Sales Co., with offices in the German-American Bank Building.

VINTON PIKE has been a member of the St. Joseph bar for more than forty years, and is regarded as one of the leading lawyers of the state. Descended from an old family in New England, Vinton Pike was born in the town of Cornish, York County, Maine.

Vinton Pike as a boy attended the schools in his native locality and the Bridgetown Academy at North Bridgeton, Maine. His uncle, Bennet Pike,

a member of the Christian Church. Mr. Pike affiliates with Lodge No. 189, A. F. & A. M.; belongs to the Country Club and is a member of the American Society of Social and Political Science. He held the office of city counselor of St. Joseph in 1882-84, and served on the local utilities commission of his city, and is a member of the State Board of Law Examiners.

A. E. UELIGGER, at Tenth and Sac-

VINTON PIKE

was a lawyer in St. Joseph, which fact brought Vinton at an age of eighteen to that place, where he took up the study of law in the office of his uncle, and in 1872 was admitted to the bar. Since that time he has been in active practice, a period of more than forty years.

In 1878 Mr. Pike married Minnie Hereford, a daughter of Dr. Richard and Amanda (Tracy) Hereford. Mrs. Pike died in 1908, leaving two sons and one daughter, Vinton Jr., Hereford, and Katherine. Mrs. Pike was

ramento streets, has one of the best conducted places in the city where refreshments are served. Contrary to the general impression, it requires more than ordinary tact to so conduct a business of this character that it will continue to grow in favor with the trade. Mr. Ueligger seems to know just how to do it, and the fact that his business grows from month to month is proof that he has made good use of his knowledge.

JOHN P. STRONG, publisher of the St. Joseph Daily Courier, was born in Jacksonville, Ill., April 18, 1858. He came with his parents to St. Joseph in 1864, and was educated in the schools of the city. He was graduated from the St. Joseph High School in 1875. The same year he was admitted to Harvard College, class of '79, and attended three years. In 1882 he was graduated from the St.

organization he is now the president. Mr. Strong was married in 1895 to Miss Emma Geiger, daughter of Stephen Geiger. Mrs. Strong died in January, 1910. In 1882 Mr. Strong joined Childe Harold lodge Knights of Pythias and in 1910 the St. Joseph Lodge of Elks No. 40, of which he is still an active member.

NATHAN KAUFMAN is a native of Russia, in which country he was born December 20, 1869. He came to

JOHN P. STRONG

Louis Law, and practiced law for three years. From 1885 to 1889 he was editor of the St. Joseph Daily Herald. In 1889 he was appointed city assessor and held the office until 1895, when he was appointed city comptroller, and served two years. In July, 1901, he bought the St. Joseph Daily Courier, of which he is still the sole owner. In 1904 he was elected to membership on the St. Joseph Board of Education, of which

America when a young man, arriving in New York City December 1, 1889. He remained there for two years, but finding the big city lacking in opportunities for him he came to St. Joseph in 1891. He opened his present place of business at 3106 St. Joseph avenue in 1909. It is a general store, one of the better kind, where all customers are treated alike. He has built up a very satisfactory business by his honesty and integrity.

JOHN W. HOLTMAN

JOHN W. HOLTMAN, president of the common council of St. Joseph, was born in Quincy, Ill., Nov. 7, 1867. He was educated in the common schools of Quincy. In 1887 he went to Kansas City and engaged in the live stock business. He remained there ten years and came to St. Joseph in 1897, continuing in the same field of endeavor, in which he has been exceptionally successful. He is manager of the Crider Brothers Live Stock Commission Company, with offices in the Exchange Building in South St. Joseph. Mr. Holtman was elected to the city council in 1910 and re-elected in 1914, and is now serving his third year as president of tnat body. He was married to Miss Dora W. Fleir of Quincy in 1889. They have six children, two sons and four daughters. Mr. Holtman is a 33rd degree Mason and a member of the Woodmen.

DR. ELMER F. KEARNEY, room 34, Commercial Building, is a native

Kearney is a Mason and an Odd Fellow. He was married to Miss Mabel Moore of St. Louis January 16, 1908.

STAR DRY CLEANING AND DYE WORKS, 903 Frederick avenue, is one of those business concerns of which St. Joseph citizens like to boast. It is one of the firmly established and enduring institutions the like of which would be a valuable addition to the

DR. ELMER F. KEARNEY

Missourian. He was born in Holt County April 22, 1880. He first attended the schools of his native county and in 1902 entered Barnes Medical College of St. Louis, and graduated there in 1906. He served an internship at the Centenary Hospital of St. Louis and in 1907 located at New Point, Mo., where he practiced his profession until August, 1913, when he came to St. Joseph. Dr.

industries of any city. The proprietors, Mr. G. S. Harris and Mr. Rowland McDonald has been on the job here for twelve years and it seems that the longer they stay the better their trade likes them. They allow nothing but the best of workmanship to leave their store and perhaps to this fact more than anything else is their success due.

DR. EMMETT F. COOK was born on a farm near Stewartsville, Mo., August 5, 1873. His early education was received from the country schools, after which he graduated from The Plattsburg College, Plattsburg, Mo. in 1888, and from William Jewell College, Liberty, Mo. in 1892. His medical education was received from The American Medical College, St. Louis,

phy. Dr. Cook is a member of the Buchanan County Medical Society, the Missouri State Medical Society, and the Academy of Surgery. Dr. Cook was married to Miss Laura L. Bennett, of Clarksdale, Mo., April 28, 1898 with whom he now lives in their beautiful home at 2506 Lafayette street.

His offices are located in the Long Building, 710 Felix street.

DR. EMMETT F. COOK

Mo, and the St. Louis City Hospital, entering these institutions in 1893 and graduating in 1897. Immediately after graduating he located at Frazier, Mo. and after four years he took a post graduate course at Chicago and then located in St. Joseph in 1901 where he practiced general medicine and surgery. Every two years since Dr. Cook took post graduate work in surgery at the Cook County Hospital and at the clinic of Dr. John B. Mur-

PENNEY & PENNEY do a wholesale business in feed, grain and hay at 813-15-17 South Seventh street. They have been in the business for eighteen years, and their reputation is well established for fair and honest dealing and good service. They give special attention to keeping up the quality of the merchandise they sell and their growing business shows conclusively that this policy is a correct one.

ROBERT C. BELL, Lawyer, Corby-Forsee Building, is a native Missourian, having been born in Cass County, November 1, 1880. In 1882 his parents moved to Caldwell County where he was reared on a farm. He was educated in the common schools and at Kidder Institute, Kidder, Missouri, where he graduated. He taught school for three years, after which, in

HUNT BROTHERS FRUIT COMPANY, one of the progressive firms of the city, was organized in 1904. James E Hunt is president, George W. Hunt, vice-president; and Luther H. Hunt, secretary. All members of the company were born in Brookfield, Mo., and have been successful business men from the start. James E. Hunt came to St. Joseph in 1894, George W. in 1907 and Luther H. in 1904. The

ROBERT C. BELL

September, 1905, he entered the University of Missouri. He graduated in law June, 1908, receiving the degree of LL. B., and soon thereafter was admitted to the bar. He began practicing law in St. Joseph, September, 1908. He married Mamie B. Collins November, 1911, and has two children, Robert C. Jr., and Maryann. He is now Exalted Ruler of St. Joseph Lodge No. 40 of the Benevolent and Protective Order of Elks.

company does a general fruit and produce business and, having been founded on sound business principles, has prospered and grown until it is now one of the leading concerns of the kind in the city. The company also is engaged in the apple growing and shipping business, being the largest operator of this kind in the Missouri valley. Secretary Wilson once said that the greatest benefactor is the man who makes two blades of grass grow where one grew before. He might have added that in the same class should be placed the man who makes two apples grow where one grew before and if he had he should have placed Hunt Brothers at the top of the honor roll, for they have proven their ability to increase the yield of apple orchards. Realizing the value of spraying to the apple growing industry the company has encouraged that enterprise among other growers

leyan College of Cameron. In the fall of 1909 he entered the Ensworth Medical College, in St. Joseph and completed his course in 1913. He was intern in the hospital for one year after graduation and then began practicing in St. Joseph. He is one of the coming practitioners of the city and is enjoying a good business. Fraternally Dr. Conrad is a Mason. He was married to Miss Ruth Wait, of Rock Island, Ill., June 12, 1915.

DR. HARRY S. CONRAD

and can justly claim to be the most ardent and enthusiastic advocates of this means of destroying insects and germs.

DR. HARRY S. CONRAD, physician and surgeon, with offices in the Ballinger Building, was born in Maryville, Mo., June 25, 1886. He attended the schools of Maryville, and was graduated from the High School there, the State Normal and the Missouri Wes-

C. W. REID'S REPAIR SHOP, at 311 South Eighth street, is where everybody goes when they need the services of an expert locksmith. He will make a key for any kind of lock in the world, but that is not all. He does a general repairing business besides. He is an excellent workman and his prices are never exorbitant. His many years' experience are a valuable asset to his business.

DR. FRANKLIN G. WEARY, whose office is at 5024½ King Hill avenue was born in Stephanson County, Ill., March 20, 1862. He was educated in the schools of his birthplace and came to St. Joseph with his parents in 1874, locating near Bethany in Harrison County. In 1880 he entered the Bennett Medical College at Chicago and was graduated in 1883. He first located in Humenston, Iowa,

grocery business in St. Joseph, at Second and Isidore streets, where, on December 8, 1868, he opened a general store.

Today the business is an incorporated concern, employing sixty people, and doing a wholesale as well as retail business at 701-3 Edmond street and 113-15-17-18-19-21-23-25 South Seventh streets.

The firm occupied successively locations at Fourth and Charles, 213-15

DR. FRANKLIN G. WEARY

where he began his professional career. In 1887 he returned to Harrison County and practiced in Eagleville until 1899, when he came to St. Joseph. He has been ministering to the needs of the sick in South St. Joseph for sixteen years and has a reputation second to none in the city.

S. S. ALLEN

Nearly half a century has elapsed since S. S. Allen embarked in the

South Fourth and on South Sixth streets, but has been at its present place of business for twenty years. A house system of telephones is in use, and eighteen delivery wagons handle the daily retail business. Staple groceries are bought in carload lots, the house maintains its own bakery for pastries and bread, runs an extensive meat market in connection and does its own coffee roasting.

The incorporation of the business

dates from March 20, 1903, the officials at this time being S. S. Allen, president and treasurer; J. Q. Morrow, vice-president and manager, and Charles Dillon, secretary.

S. S. Allen, founder of the house, is a Kentuckian by birth, where, in January, 1835, he was born. Missouri became his adopted home in 1841, and he has lived in St. Joseph sixty-one years. On January 1, 1861, he was united in marriage with Emmeline

He was married to Fanny Armstrong here on September 4, 1895.

Mr. Morrow has been identified with the Allen store during the past thirty years.

CHARLES BISHOFF, proprietor of the stamp and stencil works at 408 Felix street, comes from that sturdy German stock that has done much to assist in the development of the western country. He was born in Baden,

CHARLES BISHOFF

Dillon. Mr. and Mrs. Allen are enjoying a hale old age, having celebrated their golden wedding anniversary several years ago. Mr. Allen retired from active management of the great business he built up, some fifteen years ago.

J. Q. Morrow, who directs the activities of the house now, has been manager since Mr. Allen's retirement. He was born in Bath, Ill., in 1871, and came to Missouri in 1885.

July 25, 1836. He came to America in 1857 and located in New York City where he learned the business of engraver. He came to St. Joseph in 1865 and set up as a jewelry engraver. He did the work for all of the jewelry houses here for twenty-five years. He started in the rubber stamp business in 1870. He was married to Miss Carrie Pather of Quincy, Ill., in 1865. Mr. Bishoff has a family of five children.

DR. SIDNEY LAWSON, located at King Hill and Missouri avenues, is a native of Missouri and was born at DeaKlb, October 22, 1882. He was educated at the Gaylord Institute at Platte City, and the State Normal at Chillicothe. He matriculated in the Kentucky University in 1904, where he remained for two years. In 1906 he began the study of medicine in the Ensworth Medical College of St. Jo-

FRANK DOWLING'S saloon at Eighth and Charles streets is not a new comer in the community. It has been there a long time, and if the present good service and good goods are maintained it will be there for many years to come. It is one of the places where all customers receive the same treatment, and it is believed that it is upon this one feature that the success of the business has been built.

DR. SIDNEY LAWSON

seph, and received his degree in 1908. After graduating he began the practice of his profession at DeSoto, Kas., where he remained four years, when he moved to Springfield, Mo., and practiced two years. He came to St. Joseph March 1, 1915, and opened his present office. He was married to Miss Grace Richardson of West Plains, Mo., in 1910. They have one son. Fraternally Dr. Lawson is an Odd Fellow.

F. C. Bolliger at 1834 Frederick avenue, is one of the best business men in St. Joseph. His horse-shoeing shop is the center for those who want the best to be had and want it promptly. He realizes that service as well as workmanship is essential to success, and he acts upon his knowledge in this respect. There are few men in this line anywhere who can claim superiority to Mr. Bolliger.

DR. P. I. LEONARD devotes his practice exclusively to the diseases of the eye, ear, nose and throat. He graduated from Bellevue Hospital Medical College, New York City, practiced general medicine and surgery for six years in this city, and studied his specialty in Europe in 1890 and 1891. In 1906 he was elected councilman for the eighth ward, and became the president of the board of

Frederick Boulevard, and his office is at 710 Felix street.

T. I. BOGGS, proprietor of the St. Joseph Fence Company at 1021 Mitchell avenue, is one of the substantial business men of the southern part of the city. He has been making fences for a number of years and knows all the details of the business thoroughly. His reputation for integrity and hon-

DR. P. I. LEONARD

health for 1906-7-8. Dr. Leonard was married in 1897 to Miss Annie L. Good and they have an only son, P. I. Jr., who is now thirteen years old. The doctor is a member of the Buchanan County, State and the American Medical Association. He was president of the Buchanan County Medical Society in 1905. He taught ophthalmology and oto-laryngology at the Ensworth Medical College for twenty years. Dr. Leonard lives at 3006

est dealing is unsurpassed in St. Joseph, and every piece of fencing turned out of his factory is the best that skill can make.

GEHR'S SHEET METAL WORKS has been at 1019 South Tenth street for a number of years. The business is well established and is conducted along modern lines. Good workmanship is the motto of this concern and the prices are always made reasonable. A specialty is made of furnace installation, tin and galvanized iron work. No mistake has ever been made in patronizing the Gehr Sheet Metal Works. Mr. G. H. Gehrs is the manager.

WILLIAM H. SHERMAN, attorney at law, 123 Donnell Court was born in Oakland, Ill., June 25, 1876. While quite young he moved to Sullivan, Ill.,

member of the committee which revised the Missouri Statutes. In 1911 he was appointed assistant prosecuting attorney, and served four years. He was married to Miss Marie Eden of Sullivan, Ill., and they have three children, all boys.

E. GIBSON is one of the prosperous and enterprising business men of Frederick avenue. He prospers because he invariably gives his patrons

WILLIAM H. SHERMAN

where his education was begun. After graduating from the Sullivan High School he entered the University of Illinois, at Urbana, in 1896. He took two years in the collegiate course and then entered the law department. He received his degree June 1, 1901. He was admitted to the Buchanan County bar by Judge A. M. Woodson the same year. He was elected to the lower house of the legislature in 1906 and again in 1908. He was a

their money's worth. His place at 1529 Frederick avenue is headquarters for the best wines and liquors and the choicest cigars and smoker's supplies.

GEORGE W. WALKER of 609 North Third street, is a native of Kentucky, in which state he was born January 20, 1854. He came to St. Joseph at the age of three years and has lived here ever since. He has for many years been connected with the St Joseph Railway, Light, Heat & Power Company. Mr. Walker was married to Miss Nellie A. Barnett, December 6, 1904.

DR. F. G. BEARD was born in Cowley County Kansas Dec. 11, 1889; moved to Oklahoma when he was six years old, where he spent the most of his time on a cattle ranch owned burden of his responsibilities far beyond the expectations of his most ardent admirers. It has been said of him by the mayor and city council that he is the most efficient city physician that St. Joseph ever had. On May 1, 1915, his salary was increased one third. Dr. Beard is high in his praise of all the city officials for he says it is to them and his wife that he owes the success he has enjoyed.

DR. F. G. BEARD
—Photo by Mulvane.

by his stepfather; he was married to Miss Frances McKee of Sheridan, Mo., May 27, 1911. Graduated from the medical department of the Valpraiso University at Chicago, Ill., in May, 1914; was appointed City Physician, Police Surgeon and Health Officer of St. Joseph, July, 1914, although he is the youngest physician ever appointed to such office he has borne the

WILLIAMS & TYMON, watchmakers and jewelers, at 508 Edmond street, have been established in St. Joseph for about a quarter of a century. They have a trade that has been cemented to them by their efficient workmanship, square dealing and good service. In addition to expert watch and jewelry repairing, a well-selected stock of down-to-date jewelry is carried at all times.

DR. CHARLES G. GEIGER was born in Champaign County, Illinois, in 1865; he went to Kansas in 1869, where he grew up on a farm and attended the common schools. In 1886 he came to St. Joseph and graduated from the St. Joseph Medical College, took an honorary degree at the Ensworth and then graduated with high honors from the Jefferson Medical College, Philadelphia, and subse-

FRED WHITTEN, 1720 Messanie street, prides himself that he has one of the best bars in the city, barring none. He knows his business well and uses his knowledge intelligently, with the result that his friends get the best, and it costs no more. He keeps his goods in first-class condition —an important feature in this line of business. Naturally his business is growing steadily.

DR. CHARLES G. GEIGER

quently attended lectures in Vienna. Dr. Geiger held important chairs in the Ensworth College, and has memberships in several medical societies. About a year ago he began the manufacture of surgical instruments of his own invention. This venture has been remarkably successful. His instruments are used by some of the greatest surgeons in the United States. He was married to Miss Ethel Elizabeth Welty of St. Joseph April 5, 1910.

L. ANDERSON, ladies' tailor, at 713 Francis street, has a well-established reputation for honest goods and fair treatment. One of the cardinal principles upon which this business has been built is that every piece of work that leaves the place must be entirely satisfactory to the customer. In addition to tailoring, a general dress making business is conducted by the enterprising proprietor.

CHARLES R. BERRY, assistant vice-president of the Chicago Great Western Railway Company, was born in Collins County, Texas, and came to St. Joseph in 1869. He attended the schools of the city and began his railroad career in 1879, with the Kansas City, St. Joseph & Council Bluffs road. His first position was that of telegraph operator. In 1881 he was operator for the St. Joseph & Des

THE WESTERN PRINTING COMPANY at 401 Francis street is one of those long-established concerns that bids for the patronage of the public on quality of product and fair dealing. George Maxfield, the proprietor, has been known to the trade in St. Joseph for thirty years. He was with Lon Hardman for a time, and went into business for himself twelve years ago. Few men anywhere enjoy a better rep-

CHARLES R. BERRY

Moines, a narrow gauge line, with which he remained until 1883. He then went with the Chicago, Rock Island & Pacific, in the traffic department. He was with that road until January 1, 1888, when he changed to the Chicago Great Western, taking the position of general agent. He was later assistant general freight agent and a few years ago was made assistant vice-president.

utation for honest dealing and few have the confidence of those who know them to a greater degree than George Maxfield.

THE CHAPMAN PRINTING COMPANY, 411 Francis street, is one of the pronounced successes of the city. It has stood the test of many years and seems to grow better as time passes. The company makes a specialty of best quality office stationery and supplies. In addition, a general printing business is conducted along modern, up-to-date lines, and the Chapman quality is known to discriminating patrons beyond the confines of the city of St. Joseph. L. C. Chapman has been in business here for twenty-three years, and has a thorough knowledge of the needs and requirements of his customers. F. E. Wise, the junior

born. He came to St. Joseph December 20, 1889, and at once engaged in the piano business, giving his attention both to the wholesale and retail branches of the business. He has continued in this field of activity to the present time. At the primary election last year he was a candidate for the office of county clerk. Mr. Martin is one of those progressive citizens of which no city has too many.

RUFUS H. MARTIN
—Photo by Mulvane.

member, has been connected with the company for four years, and is one of the most enterprising men engaged in the printing business in St. Joseph.

RUFUS H. MARTIN, music dealer, is a native of Caldwell County, North Carolina, where he was born August 31, 1863. His education was from the schools of the county in which he was

THE ELITE RESTAURANT, 103 Francis street, has been newly furnished throughout, and its appearance greatly helped thereby. It is one of the reliable places in the city because the proprietor, G. L. Burroughs, insists that none but the best service will do for his customers. He serves meals at all hours and gives every patron his money's worth.

JOSEPH I. McDONALD, lawyer, 903 Corby-Forsee Building, was born in Concordia, Kan., Jan. 27, 1890. He came to St. Joseph with his parents at the age of 5 years and was educated in the Catholic schools of the city. He graduated from the Brothers College in 1905. He then attended St. Marys College, St. Marys, Kan., where he completed the academic course. Then he entered the law department of the St. Louis University,

THE PARISIAN DRY CLEANING COMPANY at Fourth and Francis streets, is a leader in dry cleaning; in fact, it is the only concern of the kind in the city. Its product has a distinction that cannot be attained by imitators, and for this reason it enjoys the patronage of the people who will be satisfied with nothing short of the best. This company has been in business for a good many years

JOSEPH I. McDONALD

graduating in 1911. After practicing a year in St. Louis he returned to St. Joseph in 1912. He was appointed police commissioner April 28, 1914, to fill the unexpired term of E. L. Hart, resigned. He was again appointed April 28, 1915, for a term of three years. He is a member of the Elks and Knights of Columbus. His father is W. P. McDonald, vice-president of the Noyes-Norman Shoe Company.

and seems to grow in favor with its customers as time passes. '

THE INDEPENDENT FRUIT AND PRODUCE COMPANY, 204 Edmond street, is one of those reliable, dependable concerns which appeals to the buyer because of the uniform courtesy with which all customers are served. The management is careful that everything that leaves the house is first class and that it is carefully handled. This accounts for the exceptional business success of the Independent.

DR. CHARLES C. DUTTON, dentist, at 412 Felix street, was born in Mt. Pleasant, Iowa, November 22, 1872. He attended the schools of his native city and in 1896 entered the Iowa Wesleyan of Mt. Pleasant, where

as professional ability and is rated as one of St. Joseph's most substantial citizens. He was married in the fall of 1899 to Miss Blanche M. Payne, a daughter of the Hon. C. W. Payne. To them has been born one child, Margaret, age six years. Mrs. Dutton died December 13, 1914.

FOGARTY, KNEIB & CO., 1404 South Twelfth street, have a well es-

DR. CHARLES C. DUTTON

he studied three years. In 1893 he went to the Iowa State University at Iowa City and took a two-year course in dentistry. He completed his education in his profession at the Chicago College of Dental Surgery in 1896. Dr. Dutton practiced in Chicago until 1899 and in the autumn of that year came to St. Joseph. He has been practicing here continuously since that time. Dr. Dutton has demonstrated that he has business as well

tablished business in feed and fuel. It has been brought to its present high state of development by the sterling business principles that have been strictly applied from the outset. There is no article in their line that cannot be supplied on short notice, and at prices that are always pleasing. The service, too, is worthy the consideration of purchasers.

DR. LEROY BECK, at 301-302 Lincoln Building, was born in Waverly, Iowa, Nov. 16, 1873. He was educated in his native city. In 1891 he entered Highland Park College of Des Moines, Iowa, and was graduated therefrom in 1894. In 1903 he came to St. Joseph and entered the Ensworth Medical College, from which institution he received a diploma in 1907. After graduation he took the

Beck is a Mason, an Odd Fellow and a Woodman.

THE CRYSTAL BAR AND CAFE, M. G. Curry and Son, proprietors, corner of Fourth and Edmond streets, has proven its popularity through many years of successful management. It is one of the places in the city where a man feels at home, and to which he likes to return. The

DR. LEROY BECK
—Photo by Mulvane.

chair of anatomy, which he held until the Ensworth College went out of business. He began the practice of medicine in St. Joseph in 1907. He was appointed surgeon for the Swift Packing plant, which position he now holds, a short time later, and in 1913, was appointed surgeon for the St. Joseph Stock Yards Company. He was married to Miss Minnie Kathka, of St. Joseph August 31, 1907. They have one child, a son. Fraternally Dr.

management claims to provide the best popular-priced lunch in the city. A specialty is made of fish dinners, for which the place has attained quite a reputation.

MILLER & BERKLEY, dry cleaners and costumers, 314 Francis street, have always stood out as the exponents of honest dealing and good values for the customer's money. It is this policy that has built up their business until now they have one of the best institutions of the kind in the city. They know what their patrons need and are always ready to supply it. They also do pressing and repairing and assure every customer of entire satisfaction.

GEORGE W. WINNEMORE, proprietor of the bakery at 817 Francis street, was born in Ottawa, Ill., March

erly be classed among the successful business men of St. Joseph and his success is due solely to his own efforts. He was married to Miss Kate Redmond, of Muscatine, Iowa, October 27, 1885. They have one daughter, Anna, living and a son dead. Mr. Winnemore's fraternal membership is with the Knights of Pythias.

MARSHALL & DUNN, grocers, at

GEORGE W. WINNEMORE
—Photo by Mulvane.

20, 1858. When he was three years old his parents moved to Muscatine, in which city he was educated, and where he also learned the trade of baker. He came to St. Joseph in February, 1889, and worked as a carpenter for Hugh H. King for nine years. In 1898 he started his present business, which has proven a pronounced success. Mr. Winnemore may prop-

the corner of Ninth street and Frederick avenue, may very properly claim to be "old timers" in the grocery business. They have been established many years and their record is one of which any firm might boast. They have given their customers good values and unexcelled service and that is why their business has increased steadily year after year.

FRED A. H. GARLICHS was born)ctober 1, 1866, in St. Joseph, Mo. He eceived his education in the grammar chools, high school, the Christian 3rothers College and Ritner's Commercial College of this city.

In 1881 he went to Chicago, entering the John A. Tolman Wholesale 3rocer Co., where he worked three ears in the credit department, from

seph, with the idea of starting a building and loan association. The Midland Building Association, organized April 1, 1890, was the result of this effort.

Taking up fire insurance as an adjunct to the building and loan association, he soon built up one of the largest fire insurance businesses in the city of St. Joseph, and has represented forty companies since that time.

Mr. Garlichs acquired by purchase

FRED A. H. GARLICHS
—Photo by Mulvane.

ere going into the Union Trust Comny Bank, corner Dearborn and adison streets, where he remained e years, filling various positions, m clearings clerk to general bookeper.

While working at the bank he studl auditing and checking of commerll accounts, being auditor of three al building and loan associations in icago, doing the work at night.

n 1889 he left Chicago for St. Jo-

the agencies of Clagget & Fowler, Wienman & Christ, C. J. Wisser, Jas. Hull & Co., R. R. Calkins, and Clark & Harmon.

In 1893 Mr. Garlichs took charge of the safe deposit vault, also took the management of the Safe Deposit Building, and the Commercial Block. This removed the office from the First National Bank to Sixth and Edmond streets, where it has remained ever since.

EDWIN MASON SWARTZ

EDWIN MASON SWARTZ was born at Greenville, Ohio, April 1, 1865.

His parents' names were Mahlon T. Swartz and Sarah Hoofnagle. His mother was born in Westmoreland County, Virginia, in the Lee neighborhood, near the birthplace of Washington.

His paternal grandmother was Zeller, related to the great philoso pher and preacher, Prof. Eduard Zeller, of Wurtemburg, Germany. He is related through his mother with the Mason family of Virginia.

Mr. Swartz read law at Kansas City and has practiced at Kansas City, Chillicothe, St. Louis and St. Joseph, Mo.

He is a friend of the laborer and a tribune of the people. He has always fought on the side of the people

13, 1871. He came to Buchanan County with his parents when but two years old. They located on the Ashland Road, near the county line. He was educated in the schools of Buchanan County. He is the son of J. C. Bigham, a retired farmer. He came to St. Joseph in 1898 and worked for the Standard Oil Company five years. He engaged in his present business in 1903. He was married to Miss Maude McIntyre of St. Joseph.

BIRD B. BIGHAM
—Photo by Mulvane.

against corporate influences on all public questions.

Mr. Swartz is a leading Democrat and politician and is considered one of the able lawyers of St. Joseph.

Mr. Swartz has one son, Edwin M. Swartz. Jr., born October 28, 1902, at 2848 Lafayette avenue, St. Louis, Mo.

BIRD B. BIGHAM, real estate dealer at 116 North Eighth street, was born in Wyandotte County, Kas., Oct.

JOHN F. NICHOLAS is a native of the state of Illinois. He dates his induction into the world back to November 17, 1873. He was educated in the schools of his native state and came to Missouri in 1898. He first stopped in Lathrop, where he began learning the drug business in the store of N. E. Owen. He removed to Cameron in 1906, where he engaged in the drug business. He prospered there and became one of the leading citizens of the town. But in 1913 he had what he considered a good chance to dispose of his holdings, and he took advantage of the opportunity. Later he came to St. Joseph. Mr. Nicholas is a registered pharmacist, and stands high in his profession. His place of business is at 301 Middleton street, and is one of the most presentable stores in the city. The building is invariably neat and tidy, and

in Higginsville, Lafayette County, Mo., Sept. 3, 1885. At the age of 9 he went with his parents to Independence, Kan., where he was educated. In 1904 he entered the Western Dental College at Kansas City, Mo., and was graduated from this school in 1907. Dr. Hutchason opened an office for the practice of his profession in St. Joseph in 1911, and has been successful almost from the start. He is a Mason and an Elk.

DR. CLARENCE E. HUTCHASON
—Photo by Mulvane.

the stock is fresh and clean. In addition to a nice line of drugs, he carries the usual complement of toilet articles and sundries to be found in a first-class drug store. He was married in Lathrop, Feb. 18, 1898, to Miss Ethel J. Parshall. Mr. and Mrs. Nicholas have an interesting family of four children, three boys and one girl.

DR. CLARENCE E. HUTCHASON, dentist, 710½ Felix street, was born

WILLIAM LEE MARKS, druggist, 2610 St. Joseph avenue, was born near Canton, Mo., in 1858, the son of John W. and Elizabeth (Blackburn) Marks. His father was a carpenter and farmer. Our subject studied under Dr. Marchand near Monticello, Mo., and first established himself in business at Avillo, Kan., in 1886, where his stock was destroyed by a cyclone. In 1891 he located in St. Joseph, and by close and successful business methods has built up a patronage of which many of the older druggists would be proud. In 1886 he was married to Miss Ella Owens, born at Maysville, Ky. They have four daughters living, Maggie, Mary, Josie and Ruby. A son died. Mr. Marks is a Democrat, a Baptist and belongs to the Knights of Pythias and Modern Woodmen.

RALPH ELMER SQUIRES, general secretary of the Y. M. C. A., is a native of Wisconsin, in which state he

endowment for the same of $45,000. He came to St. Joseph in April, 1912 to open the new St. Joseph building and to organize the new work here. He was married to Miss Alice Howe of Brooklyn, Minn., in 1902. They have two children, a son and a daughter. Fraternally Mr. Squires is a Mason and his church affiliation is with the Baptist denomination.

JAMES W. LEHR, contractor and builder, is a native of Indiana, where he was born Dec. 21, 1855. His

RALPH ELMER SQUIRES

was born September 8, 1876. He was educated in the school of St. Paul and was graduated from the University of Minnesota with the class of 1902. In the fall of that year he began his Y M. C. A. work as an assistant secretary. From Minneapolis he was transferred to Winona where he was general secretary and where he was instrumental in inaugurating a movement that resulted in the erection of a $65,000 building and in securing an

father, Samuel, was a contractor, and after attending school our subject learned the carpenter's trade. He came west in 1880 and located at Bethany, Mo., where he remained till 1886, when he came to St. Joseph. He has done a great deal of work here and has a first-class reputation in his line. He was married March 1, 1880, in McPherson, Kan., to Miss Helen L. Sharp, who has borne him two children, a boy and a girl.

DR. WILLIAM J. HUNT, rooms
1212-1215 Corby-Forsee Building, is a
Missourian. He was born in St. Joseph January 19, 1891. He was first
educated in the schools of the city
and then entered the Ensworth Medical College in 1908. He received his
diploma in 1912, at the age of 21
years. He first opened an office in
St. Joseph for the practice of his
profession and in 1913 was appointed

AGNES C. GLEITZ is a native of
Germany, in which country she was
born December 14, 1854. She was educated in her native country In 1868
she came to America, locating in
Evansville, Ind., where she was married to Louis Engel in 1869, where
two children were born, Louis and
Emma. In company with her husband
she returned to Germany in 1872 and
remained there for seven years. Two

DR. WILLIAM J. HUNT

assistant pathologist at State Hospital for Insane No. 2. He remained
there one year and returned to the
city and established an office in the
Logan Building. In January, 1915,
he was appointed county physician,
which position he still holds. He was
married to Miss Marguerite Bryan of
St. Joseph, September 15, 1914. Dr.
Hunt is an Elk and also holds membership in the state and county medical associations as well as the American Medical Association.

boys were born in Germany. Otto and
Hugo. In 1879 they returned to
America and located in Leavenworto,
Kans. The family came to St Joseph
in 1880. Mr. Engel died in this city
in 1883. In 1886 the subject of this
sketch was married to H. F. Gleitz.
She took charge of the Occidental
Hotel at Main and Jule streets the
same year, which hostelry she conducted for ten years. She then took
charge of the Greentree Hotel, and
remained there until 1907, when she

became the proprietor of the Windsor Hotel at Eighth and Olive streets. She is still in active charge there and has built up a very satisfactory business. Six children were born of her first marriage—five sons, Louis, Hugo, Otto, Phillip and John, and one daughter, Emma, who was married to Fred Mast, son of Christ Mass. To the second marriage were born two children, Elmer and Antoinette, the latter being now an actress. Mrs. Gleitz

he has been practicing medicine and surgery in this city. He is a member of the Buchanan County State and American Medical Association; also of the Academy of Surgery of St. Joseph, Mo.

DAVID H. HATFIELD, former constable of Washington Township, was born in Ross County, Ohio, Feb. 12, 1847. He attended school in Ohio, and Sept. 3, 1861, enlisted in the 31st Ohio

DR. J. S. FORSEN
—Photo by Mulvane. ·

peaks four languages—German, English, French and Flemish.

DR. J. S. FORSEN was born in Clinton County, May 15, 1885 and received his early education at the Lower high school and the Kansas City central. He entered Ensworth Medical College in 1906 and graduated in 1910. He was an entern at the St. Joseph Hospital for 2 years and since

Infantry, serving until July 20, 1865. He was in twenty-one general engagements, among them the battle of Chickamauga. He came to St. Joseph March 17, 1872, and was in the livery and horse dealing business until 1890. He then acted as special police till 1897. In the fall of 1898 he was elected constable on the Republican ticket. He was married to Miss Susan Epperson Oct. 3, 1873, and they have three children, two sons and a daughter.

FRANK W. STOUT, druggist, at 1308 South Sixth street, is an Iowan. He was born in Corydon, July 12, 1870. At the age of five years he moved with his parents to Putnam County, Mo., where he received a common school education. In 1883 he went to Chicago, where he remained two years. In 1887 he entered the drug store of E. M. Morrison, at Unionville.

MARAN S. HORN, transfer man, claims Missouri as the state of his nativity. He was born in Jackson County, March 4, 1864. He came to St. Joseph in 1904 and engaged in the transfer business. He is one of the substantial business men of the city and his success has been due to his determination to give his patrons at all times the best of service at reasonable rates.

FRANK W. STOUT
—Photo by Mulvane.

Mo., where he learned the business. In 1891 he went to Muskogee, Okla., where he remained a year and then located in Sikeston, Mo. for a year. He came to St. Joseph in 1893 and established the business he is now conducting. He was married to Miss Mary Hildebrandt of St. Joseph in 1895. Two children, a son and a daughter, have been born to them. Fraternally Mr. Stout is a Mason and an Elk.

THEODORE BASSAR, meat market, 1314 North Fourth street, was born in Buchanan County, Nov. 22, 1847. His father was Francis Bassar, born at Paris, France, who came here in an early day, who was on terms of warm friendship with Joseph Robidoux, and who operated the first horse-power grist mill in the county. Our subject was for twelve years with the St. Joseph Gas Company as lamp ighter, and then entered his present ine. He was married in 1869 to Miss 3erena Sharp of Nodaway County and .hey have one son and two daughters. Mr. Bassar has by his thrift and business ability accumulated handsome property. He is a Republican.

DON C. KINNAMAN, proprietor of he restaurant at 618 Edmond street s a native of Illinois. He was born n Mercer County April 28, 1861. At

Woodmen, Knights of Pythias and the Independent Order of Forresters. Religiously Mr. Kinnaman is a Latter Day Saint.

ABRAHAM DAVIS, ex-member of the Missouri legislature, was born in Buchanan County, July 3, 1844, the son of Joseph and Sarah (Sheckel) Davis, on a farm that is now part of St. Joseph Extension Addition, in the

DON C. KINNAMAN
—Photo by Mulvane.

he age of fifteen years, he moved ith his parents to Stewartsville, Mo., here his education was finished. He ame to St. oJseph in 1889 and engaged in various occupations. He began the restaurant business in 1897 { 715 Edmond street and moved to 'is present location in 1910. He was larried to Miss Elizabeth Lewis of t. Joseph in 1899. They have five hildren, three sons and two daughters. He has membership in the

northwestern part of the city. In his early days he worked on a steamboat that ran to New Orleans, and was for many years in the ice business. He was elected as Democrat to the legislature in 1880 and again in 1890. September 16, 1879, he was married to Miss Jennie Robbins, born in New York state; both are members of the Baptist Church. Mr. Davis is now in the real estate business.

WILLIAM F. KIRKPATRICK, jewler at 721-723 Felix street, is a native of Kansas. He was born at Garnett, April 6, 1869. His education was received in the schools of his native town, where he also learned the trade of jeweler. In 1889 he went to Parsons, Kan., where he worked at his trade for a time. He came to St. Joseph in 1890 and worked at his trade for two years, after which he

counselor, is a native of St. Joseph, having been born in this city Sept. 11, 1872. He was educated in the city schools after which he read law in the offices of Charles M. Street, for three years. He was admitted to the bar in 1902 by Judge W. K. James. In 1905 he was appointed assistant prosecuting attorney by John D. McNeely, then prosecutor of Buchanan County. Mr. Hess was appointed to his present position in 1913. He is unmarried.

WILLIAM F. KIRKPATRICK

engaged in business. He started at 616 Edmond street in 1892. He moved to his present location in 1894, and has enjoyed his full share of prosperity, his business having developed until it is one of the largest of the kind in the country. He was married to Miss Lenora K. Ahern of Hiawatha, Kan., September 23, 1897. He is a member of the Elks.

HERMAN HESS, assistant city

TILLMAN H. SINCLAIR, blacksmith for the Board of Public Works, is a native Missourian. He was born in 1852 and has resided in St. Joseph since 1902. He was appointed to his present position in 1908, and has served through the various administrations and changes since that time. His services are in demand because is a competent and painstaking workman. He is also one of St. Joseph's representative citizens.

JOHN D. CLARK is a native of Missouri. He was born in Daviess County, January 21, 1858. His father, Marion D. Clark, was at one time a real estate dealer in St. Joseph. Our subject's mother, Mrs. Isabelle Stone Clark, was born in Virginia. Mr. Clark came to St. Joseph, with his parents, in 1867, and was educated in the public schools of the city. He was in charge of the circulation of the board were Charles J. Borden and W. A. Bodenhausen. Mr. Clark is an active Republican and has served on the city, county and state committees. He was elected to the state committee four times, serving two years each term. He still takes an active interest in the affairs of his party. He is vice-president of the St. Joseph Brewing Company. Mr. Clark was married October 23, 1879 to Miss Frances

JOHN D. CLARK
—Photo by Mulvane.

Daily News for about five years and later drifted into politics. He was elected alderman from the Second Ward in 1893 and in 1895 was appointed city license inspector, holding the position until 1897. He was elected a member of the first board of public works in the city, which was dissolved by a supreme court decision in 1900, it being held that the law creating it was not properly passed. The other members of this M. Echtler, who was born in St. Joseph in 1873.

DANIEL D. DARROW, subscription book publisher, 322 South Sixth street, was born in Crawford County, Pennsylvania, Nov. 22, 1856, and came to St. Joseph in 1887, engaging in his present line, and by his energy and sagacity has built up a business of large proportions. Mr. Darrow married Miss Adella L. Anderson at Lind-boro, Pa., April 9, 1883, by whom he has two boys. Mr. and Mrs. Darrow take great interest in the order of Knights and Ladies of Security, and are both high in its circles.

F. CLAUDE DAVIS, engaged in the real estate business, Seventh and Francis streets, was born in Platte County, Missouri, February 22, 1858.

Our subject attended the common schools of Platte and Buchanan counties, and at the age of twelve years moved to St. Joseph with his parents and for a period of seven years, together with his brother, the late Dr. W. B. Davis, who was two years his senior, engaged in the dairy and ice business under the firm name of Davis Bros., after which time his brother graduated from the Missouri Medical College and practiced medicine, when

F. CLAUDE DAVIS

His grandparents on both his mother's and father's sides were natives of Kentucky. His father was the Reverend John C. C. Davis, who was one of the pioneer Methodist ministers of this section of the county, being a member of the Missouri Conference of the M. E. Church, South. His mother is Mary G. (Clay) Davis. Her parents, Johnson and Rebecca Clay, came from Kentucky and settled in Platte County among the earliest settlers.

Mr. F. Claude Davis associated himself with his uncle, the late R. T. Davis (who was in the milling business), as sales manager, and was very successful in building the brands manufactured by Mr. R. T. Davis throughout the entire country. Shortly after the death of R. T. Davis, he severed his relations with the milling business and associated himself with hith brothers, Marvin M. and Robert L., in the real estate business, in which he is now engaged under the firm name of Davis Bros. To his credit are placed many of the large transactions in St. Joseph real estate.

Mr. Davis was married November 27, 1888, to Miss Fannie Dean Popple, who was a native of Illinois, and to this union were born three children, Fannie Lee, Ruth and F. Claude, Jr.

Mr. Davis is a member of the Methodist Episcopal Church, South, and is a Mason.

business. He was married to Miss Elizabeth Fondermann in November, 1901. They _ave six children, five daughters and one son. Mr. Fenner's fraternal affiliations are with the Redmen, the Odd Fellows and Knights and Ladies of Security.

WILLIS GILBERT BRINSON, manager of the Postal Telegraph Co., was born on a farm near St. Joseph, Sept.

AUGUST H. FENNER
—Photo by Mulvane.

AUGUST H. FENNER, manager of the Western Dairy Co., is a native of Holstein, Germany, where he was born June 29, 1878. He was educated in Germany and at the age of 16 years came to St. Joseph. He at once became associated with his brother, the late Herman C. Fenner in the conducting of the affairs of the Western Dairy Co. Herman Fenner died in July, '1913' and the subject of this sketch was made manager of the

18, 1867, and was educated in the public schools of St. Joseph. He learned telegraphy and before he became of age was made manager of the Postal Telegraph Company's office in this city, which position he has held ever since and by strict attention to business has secured his company a large share of the telegraph traffic of the city. Mr. Brinson is an earnest Republican in politics, but has never aspired to office.

WILLIAM J. BETTIS

WILLIAM J. BETTIS was born in Nashville, Tenn., November 27, 1866. At the age of five years he came with his parents to St. Joseph, and received his education in the schools of the city.

He went to work for the old Citizens' Street Railway Company at the age of eighteen years. Cars were pulled by horses in those days, and Mr. Beattie was a driver for a number of years. When the street railway lines were electrified he was a driver on the Union line. One Saturday, when he took his faithful mule team to the barns, he received orders to take out the first-regular electric car over the road. Accompanied by Mr. J. H. VanBrunt, now general manager of the street railway system in St. Joseph, he made the trip amid the cheers of an interested and startled public. For twenty-seven years he remained in the service of the street railway company, twenty-two years of which time he was a conductor on the Union line. He was at all times considered one of the most trustworthy men in the service, and became a warm personal friend of Mr. Van Brunt, with whom he made the initial trip on the electric car. In 1908 he was a candidate for the Republican nomination for sheriff at the primary election, and was beaten by the late Joseph Albus by the narrow margin of fifty votes. In 1912 he received the Republican nomination for sheriff, but was defeated at the general election

the law department of Yale University in 1906-07. He was admitted to the bar in 1908, after a thorough examination by the Missouri State Board, May 25th, 1908, and has since practiced his profession successfully in this city. He is one of the promising young attorneys of St: Joseph, his success being due to his thorough knowledge of his profession coupled with willingness to work hard.' He is a son of Benjamin Goldman, a

JOSEPH GOLDMAN
—Photo by Mulvane.

by C. H. Jones by a majority of 125 votes.

He was married to Miss Neva Mc-Natt of Topeka, Kan., November 22, 1894. They have five children, three girls and two boys.

JOSEPH GOLDMAN, attorney at law, 401-402 German-American Bank Building. He came to St. Joseph while yet young. After being educated in the city schools he attended

pioneer merchant of this city.

KESSLER BROTHERS, 102 Francis street, are known to their trade as men of reliability. They never misrepresent an article and their customers know it. They have a well established and growing business and bid fair to prosper as the years go by. Their industry and attentiveness entitle them to the success they have achieved.

DAVID FELTENSTEIN, head of the D. Feltenstein Liquor Company, and one of the most successful business men St. Joseph has ever developed, is a native of New York. He was born there October 22, 1873. He came to St. Joseph with his parents when a lad of 10 years. Mr. Feltenstein was educated in the public schools of this city. His predilection of a mercantile career manifested itself early in

rooms, known to the trade as the Blue Front Department Store. After eight years, each more successful than the one preceding, he sold his interest in the Blue Front Store and embarked in the wholesale, retail and mail order liquor business. He started in one room at 315 Edmond street, but this soon proved inadequate to the needs of his growing business. He needed more room and first one then another adjoining room was secured until he

DAVID FELTENSTEIN

his life for when he was but 18 years old he started in the dry goods business at Third and Poulin streets. He remained at this location for two years. In 1893 he moved to Market Square, where he started in a small room in a modest way and began building the business that was destined to be a monument to his memory for years to come. His growth in business was steady and rapid. In a few years he occupied four large

now occupies three full store buildings, both ground and second floors. In 1913 he bought the half block on Edmond street immediately west of Fourth street, in which his place of business is located. With characteristic enterprise Mr. Feltenstein immediately began making plans for remodeling the property. When he had finished it had been transformed into one of the most presentable looking business properties in the city. But not alone in this instance has he proven his enterprising spirit. He owns other pieces of valuable property, including the building occupied by the George Cooke Crockery Company on Third street. It, too, was remodeled by the new owner and made into a modern business structure of which any city might well feel proud. He believes that it pays to improve any piece of real estate he owns, and the success he has accomplished

in the buggy business established by his father, Walter C. Beardsley, in 1869. Few firms are better known throughout the western country and the fact that it has withstood the competition of nearly half a century is evidence that it was established on the right basis and managed according to sound business principles. Mr. Beardsley was married to Miss Fannie Johnson of Atchison, Kas., in August, 1896. He is a member of the Elks.

HERBERT C. BEARDSLEY
—Photo by Mulvane.

proves the correctness of his theory. Mr. Feltenstein was married to Miss Roe Cohen of St. Joseph. They have a family of three sons, all living.

HERBERT C. BEARDSLEY, carriage dealer, at 218 South Fourth street, is a native of St. Joseph, having been born here May 10, 1871. He was educated in the public schools, and at an early age became interested

JOHN M. WITT, that whom there are few better and more prosperous business men in the city, is proud of the fact that he is a native Missourian. He was born in Buchanan County, March 19, 1877. His education covered the entire range of the schools of the county and later he attended the State Normal School in Chillicothe, from which institution he was graduated with honors in 1899. After leaving school he entered the railway mail service in 1903. He remained in the service for three years and in 1906 was transferred to the St. Joseph postoffice where he was assigned to duty as a city distributor. He held this position for four and one-half years, when he was made postmaster of Station E. His assignment to this position dates from May 12, 1911. He is still on the job at this station and gives general satisfaction to the pa-

law, 716 Corby-Forsee Building, was born in St. Joseph June 20, 1882. He was educated in the city schools and was graduated from the Christian Brothers College in 1898. The following five years he spent in study at the St. Mary's College, St. Mary's, Kansas. He received his diploma from this school in 1903. The same year he entered the law department

PHIL A. SLATTERY.
—Photo by Mulvane.

trons of the office. Mr. Witt was married June 10, 1903, to Miss Emma G. Creek of Stewartsville, Mo. They have four children, two sons and two daughters. Mr. Witt is an active member of the Odd Fellows organization. His father, James M. Witt, was born in Platte Township, on a farm where he lived and died at the age of 70 years.

PHIL A. SLATTERY, attorney at

of Georgetown University at Washington, D. C. and was graduated in 1906. He began practicing in St. Joseph at once and in 1908 was elected city attorney, as a Democrat. The office was discontinued by the charter of 1909, the duties being performed by an attache of the city counselor's office. Mr. Slattery was appointed to this place and served three years.

DR. ALBERT R. HAROLD, dentist, at 2004 St. Joseph avenue is a native of Kansas. He was born at Axtell, January 12, 1888. He was educated in Axtell, and in 1910 entered the Kansas City Dental College, from which school he was graduated in 1913. He first located in Blue Springs, Kansas, where he practiced his profession with success for a period of eight years. In 1914 he came to St. Joseph

ning twenty-four years ago to its present magnificient proportions. The customers of this modern establishment not only include every class of people within the confines of the city but also embrace the residents in numerous other cities and towns throughout Missouri and adjacent states.

The business of Hirsch Brothers Dry Goods Company was originally established at 319 Felix street in 1891

DR. ALBERT R. HAROLD

and became associated with Dr. James Ross where he remained for about a year. In May, 1915, he opened his present office and has been enjoying a profitable practice. Dr. Harold's fraternal affiliation is with the Masons.

THE HIRSCH BROTHERS DRY GOODS COMPANY is one of St. Joseph's leading department stores which has grown from a small beginning

under the firm title of the NEW YORK RACKET STORE. During the twenty-four years that have elapsed since then the managing partners have been remarkably successful although obliged to change location three different times.

The nucleus of the present Hirsch Brothers Dry Goods Company was formed by Sol and Morris Hirsch and they are still the sole proprietors and executive managers of this extensively popular establishment. Their expert business acumen coupled with strict personal integrity has been one of the controlling factors in their unqualified mercantile success.

Five years after the opening of the New York Racket store by the Hirsch Brothers the business had prospered so well that they sought more commodious quarters at the southwest corner of Fourth and Felix streets, familiarly known to old residents of St. Joseph as "The Old Corner" which had for many years been occupied by Young, Townsend & Frazer. For five years more the Hirsch Brothers conducted a successful and rapidly growing business there until they were obliged to relinquish the premises when the First National Bank bought the property in order to erect the present imposing building now the headquarters of that great financial institution.

After having been forced to leave the Old Corner the Hirsch Bros. moved into temporary quarters at 411 Felix street where they remained until the present building at Eighth, Felix and Frederick avenue had been completed for their occupancy. Upon the removal of the business there fourteen years ago the style of the firm was changed to that of HIRSCH BROTHERS DRY GOODS COMPANY, under which title the business has multiplied to its present immense dimensions under careful and judicious management.

A fair idea of the magnitude of the Hirsch Brothers trade and its comprehensive details may be gained from the fact that there are thirty different departments conducted in a strictly up-to-date manner under the same roof. These include the silk department, dress goods department, cotton piece goods department, linen department, lining department, handkerchiefs, ribbons, gloves, neckwear, laces and embroideries, hosiery, blankets and comforts, patterns, notions, shoes, gents furnishings, underwear, millinery, art goods, infants wear, corsets, muslin underwear, curtains and draperies, toys, drug sundries, fancy novelties, leather goods and bric-a-brac, trimmings and buttons, and last but not least women's and misses' ready-to-wear and millinery departments.

The building occupied by the Hirsch Brothers Dry Goods Company is admirably situated in the heart of the St. Joseph shopping district. It has the advantage of having the benefit of traffic from three streets, Frederick avenue, Eighth street and Felix street. It is a solid buff brick structure, 120x140 feet, and contains two stories and a basement. The front is a veritable field of glass, the huge show windows giving the establishment every opportunity to have at all times an attractive and splendid display for the edification of the public.

The Hirsch Brothers store is equipped with all the latest modern conveniences calculated to prove beneficial to its patrons and employes alike. There is an automatic sprinkler system in operation which cannot be excelled by any of the large department stores in any metropolitan cities of the country. One of the most delightful and attractive features of the store is the ladies' rest rooms where either customers or employes may find comfort when tired or fatigued. The ventilation throughout the entire store is superb and every kind and character of improvement is installed there, which may be found in any first class department store.

The Hirsch Brothers Dry Goods store enjoys an excellent patronage in St. Joseph and from cities, towns and country districts throughout the states of Missouri, Kansas, Nebraska and Iowa. This trade was built up principally on the record made for the high grade values given the patrons of the store, and likewise for the uniform courtesy which is the guiding spirit of every employe in the establishment.

The Hirsch Brothers Dry Goods Company is composed of Sol Hirsch, president and treasurer; and Morris Hirsch, vice-president and secretary. There are over one hundred and fifty employes in the different departments and six attractive delivery wagons give prompt service to the patrons all over the city. The management also conducts an extensive mail order business which has increased ten fold since the inauguration of the parcel post service in the United States.

HUND & EGGER BOTTLING COM-
PANY.—The city of St. Joseph has
many prosperous business enterprises
dating back to the early days, but
few can equal the successful career of
the Hund & Egger Bottling Company.

It is more than two generations ago
since the nucleus of the present firm
was started by Dumke & Gleitz at
Main and Faraon streets. In 1881
William Hund, now active executive

required that property for trackage
purposes. Hund & Egger selected the
old Aniser & Ost brewery site at
Thirteenth and Frederick avenue as
the base of their immediate operations. They remained in that location
two years and then erected their
present building at 421-423 North
Second street, where the firm is now
doing a fine business.

In addition to making and bottling
every variety of soft drinks the Hund

WILLIAM HUND
—Photo by Mulvane.

head of the company, purchased Mr.
Gleitz's interest and the firm name
was changed to Dumke & Hund.
Seven years later Mr. Dumke sold his
partnership interest to Louis Egger in
1888 and the firm name was changed
to Hund & Egger, the present name
of the corporation.

Shortly after Mr. Dumke retired the
bottling works was obliged to move
from the old location at Main and
Faraon streets because the railroad

& Egger company are sole agents in
St. Joseph for Pabst Milwaukee beer
either in bottles or by the keg. The
plant is one of the finest in the west
and nothing is lacking in modern machinery to bring it up-to-date in every
respect. With motor delivery trucks
and several wagons the business of
the Hund & Egger Bottling Company
has extended to the remotest confines
of the city and to a number of towns
throughout adjacent states.

After the death of Mr. Egger on February 10, 1908, Mr. Hund organized a company and he was unanimously elected president of the corporation. Mr. Hund is favorably known to the old residents of St. Joseph, and even the young ones have a keen liking for Hund & Egger's bottled goods.

DR. WESLEY GOOD, dentist, at 409½ Edmond street, was born August

He was married to Miss Harriet B. Brown of King City, Mo., December 29, 1892. The family consists of a son and a daughter. Mrs. Good died in October, 1912.

Doctor Good is a member of the Modern Woodmen, Modern Brotherhood, Court of Honor and Knights of the Maccabees.

HARRY C. SEVERNS claims Missouri as his native state and is quite

DR. WESLEY GOOD
—Photo by Mulvane.

4, 1865, in York County, Pennsylvania. He was educated in the common schools of his native county, and in 1886 came to St. Joseph and entered the dental offices of his uncle, Dr. J. B. Good, at the same location in which he is now practicing. In 1890 he entered the Philadelphia Dental College, and was graduated in 1892. He returned at once to St. Joseph and continued the practice of his profession with his uncle.

proud of this fact. He was born in Mound City August 26, 1885. He removed to St. Joseph in 1887 and received his education in the schools of the city. He was married to Miss Rose Vedder of Savannah, Mo., December 1, 1914. Mr. Severns has always taken a lively interest in the growth and development of St. Joseph and is proud to claim this city as his home.

THE ARTCRAFTS ENGRAVING COMPANY is a corporation composed of five practical men in that line of business. Mr. W. H. Guenther, president and manager of the concern, born in Illinois, learned his trade and worked in some of the largest and best engraving plants in Chicago and other cities.

Mr. Leslie L. Forgrave, vice president, born in Leon, Iowa, completed a course in Chicago Academy of Fine Arts and worked in some of the best plants in the southwest.

connected with several successful plants.

These gentlemen are working on strictly business principles and have the most successful plant ever established in St. Joseph.

LOWENBERG'S MILLINERY STORE, 718-720 Francis street, is one of those stores with a reputation well-established for good goods and low prices. They do a wholesale, as well as a retail business, and enjoy a good patronage. Mr. Lowenberg has been in the millinery business in St. Joseph

THE ARTCRAFTS ENGRAVING CO.

Mr. J. E. Blacet, secretary of the company and foreman of shop was born in Illinois, for several years was foreman of one of the largest plants in Iowa, and has thorough knowledge of engraving in all its branches.

Mr. Holly Markle, born and raised in Illinois, completed a course in the Chicago Art Institute and is one of the most capable and experienced retouchers in the west.

Mr. O. Lambert, born and raised in Illinois has followed the engraving business for some time and has been

for over thirty years and knows its every detail thoroughly.

CYRUS P. MILLER is a native of Pennsylvania. He was born in that state April 12, 1851. He early learned the trade of shoemaker, and became quite proficient in that field of endeavor. Mr. Miller came to St. Joseph in 1891 and engaged in the mercantile business soon afterward. He is one of the city's enterprising business men and assists anything that will help in the upbuilding of his home town.

WILLIAM HENZE, boot and shoe merchant at 1602 St. Joseph avenue, is a native of Germany. He was born in that country October 27, 1849. After receiving a liberal education in his native country he was apprenticed as a shoe maker, and he learned the trade thoroughly, as all Germans learn trades. While yet a young man he came to America, arriving in St. Joseph November 5, 1872. After ac-

because he has never deviated from the business principles learned in the old country, the essence of which, is that honesty is invariably the best policy. Mr. Henze was married to Miss Mary Rusler of St. Joseph in 1874. They have four children, two boys and two girls.

FREDERICK C. KUEHL, merchant tailor, was born in Oldenburg, Holstein, March 8, 1850. He was edu-

WILLIAM HENZE
—Photo by Mulvane.

quainting himself with the demands of the shoe business in this city he opened his present place of business in 1875. For thirty-nine years he has been in business at this location. It is doubtful if his record can be excelled in St. Joseph. Nearly half a century of merchandising without a move certainly is an excellent recommendation for any man. And, moreover, Mr. Henze grows in popular favor as he grows in years. This is

cated and learned his trade in his native country; also worked in a wholesale grocery in Hamburg. He came to New York in 1868, going thence to Chicago, St. Louis, Memphis, New Orleans, Cheyenne and Omaha. He came to St. Joseph in 1870 and began his present business in 1871. He was elected to the council in 1897, and was chairman of the finance committee. Mr. Kuehl was married April 10, 1872, to Miss Bertha Volk.

ROBERT (ROY) H. STAUBER, druggist and pharmacist, was born January 15, 1859, in Lewiston, Pa. In 1868 he moved to St. Catherine, Linn County, Mo. Here he attended the public school in the winter and worked in the woolen mill located there in the summer. In 1877 he was employed in the only drug store in the village. In the winter of 1879-80 he taught the Lineberry school in Linn County, at

In 1891 he became the treasurer of the Stauber Drug Company, a retail drug business founded by his father, John M. Stauber, in 1888. At the death of his father, in 1913, he became the head of the business, having been actively connected with it from 1899, and becoming a registered pharmacist in 1910.

His forefathers were Methodists in religion, and Republican in politics, and he was reared in their faiths.

ROBERT (ROY) H. STAUBER

the close of which he clerked in a dry goods store in Brookfield, Mo, for the next three years. After a short experience in a grocery store in Topeka, Kans., in 1883, he came to St. Joseph, where, in the following sixteen years, he received a thorough business training in the offices of the Regnier & Shoup Crockery Company, the Nave-McCord Mercantile Company, the St. Joseph Gas Company, and the Doniphan Candy Company.

For years he has been a member of the Independent Order of Foresters, the Modern Woodmen of America, the Knights of the Maccabees, the Masonic order, and the Independent order of Odd Fellows, and through them contributing to the general good of society through the benefits and charities distributed by these fraternal and benevolent orders.

He was commissioned as a notary public in 1901, and has served the public in this capacity for over four-teen years.

HENRY VERAGUTH is a native of Switzerland and was born February 14, 1836. He received his education in his native country. In 1854 he came to America in a sailing vessel. He takes pleasure in telling his friends that at the time he came over it took 55 days to cross the Atlantic. This

and at once became identified with the growth and development of the City Worth While. He has at all times been in the front ranks of those business men who stand for the progress and prosperity of the city. He has lived in retirement from business for several years but his advice and counsel is sought by younger men on many occasions. He was married to Miss Ida Burger of Baden, Germany, in 1866. Six children have been born

HENRY VERAGUTH

seems incredibly slow compared with the fast ships of the present day. Mr. Veraguth first located in Dubuque, Iowa, where he remained for two years. He moved to Sioux City in 1856, where he engaged in farming. When the Civil war broke out he enlisted in Company I, Seventh Iowa cavalry and remained in the service for three years. He was mustered out in Sioux City in November, 1865. Mr. Veraguth came to St. Joseph in 1866

of this marriage, four boys and two girls. Mr. Veraguth is a member of Custer Post, G. A. R.

OSCAR A. PASH is a native of Ohio, in which state he was born May 10, 1873. He came with his parents to St. Joseph in 1879. He was educated in the schools of St. Joseph. He has been in the decorative business in this city for sixteen years. He was married to Miss Nellie Hall of St. Joseph, Mo., July 24, 1892. They have two children, a son and a daughter. Mr. Pash gives particular attention to high-class interior decorating in St. Joseph and immediate vicinity and carries a complete line of up-to-date wall paper. All of the modern appliances which tend to make merchandising satisfactory to patrons are to be found in Mr. Pash's store. He was one of the first men in St. Joseph to use the auto delivery. He, is a promi-

for your years. When the St. Joseph Star was established in 1905, Mr. Smith came here, and remained with that paper during the period of its existence. He then went with the Wheeler-Motter Mercantile Company, with which concern he was identified seven years in the shipping and packing department. He was appointed probation officer in 1912. He was married to Miss Kittie Morris of St. Louis in 1896. They have three chil-

THOMAS J. P. SMITH
—Photo by Mulvane.

nent member of the Elks and Knights of Pythias lodge.

THOMAS J. P. SMITH, former Probation Officer, is a native Missourian. He was born in St. Louis, January 6, 1870. He was educated in that city, and in 1886 went to Kansas City, where he engaged in newspaper work. He held responsible reportorial positions with The Star and The Post

dren. Religiously Mr. Smith is a Roman Catholic.

JOHN M. COBB is a native Missourian, his place of birth being Andrew County and the date Sept. 29, 1872. He was educated in the schools of his native county and came to St. Joseph in 1887. Soon after coming here he engaged in the mercantile business and has been more than ordinarily successful. He is a live, wide-awake business man, thoroughly familiar with the details of his trade and a man in whom his patrons have confidence. He is yet in the prime of life and promises to be one of the exceptional success of the future. He was married to Miss Laura A. Waltrip, of St. Joseph, March 3, 1903. They have a family of four boys.

JOHN J. KAMLER is a native of Missouri. He was born in Gasconade

his day. This was in 1887, and during the following years he devoted himself assiduously to mastering the details of the tinner's trade. In a comparatively short time he became recognized as one of the best workmen in his field of endeavor in the city.

In 1901, feeling that he had the necessary knowledge and experience to assure success, he established himself in business in his present location, 1139 Frederick avenue. He has been

JOHN J. KAMLER

County, October 21, 1868. At the age of seven years he moved with his parents to Bigelow, Holt County, Missouri. The family came to St. Joseph in 1881. Mr. Kamler was educated in the schools of St. Joseph and was so attentive to his studies that at an early age he felt fully equipped educationally to enter business. His first engagement was with C. H. Boller, the veteran hardware merchant, who was one of the leading business men of

exceptionally successful, due to his excellent early training, good judgment and close attention to the details of his business. Mr. Kamler is a member of the Eagles, Moose, St. Stephens Society, St. Cecilia Society, and th Turnverein. He was married to Mis Mary Walkowski of St. Joseph, Jun 21, 1891, and to this union have bee born six children, two sons and fou daughters. Mr. Kamler is a communi cant of the Catholic church.

WILLIAM AUGUST ZIEMEN-DORFF, humane officer of the city of St. Joseph, was born in Richardson County, Neb., December 21, 1864. His father, William H., was a native of Germany and was a lawyer. Mr. Ziemendorff attended the public schools in Nebraska, and, having decided to become a druggist, attended the University of Buffalo, N. Y., where he graduated in pharmacy in

made probate officer in addition to his duties as humane officer. He held this position until the law was changed in 1909. He was married in this city May 15, 1894, to Miss Maud Harding, who is dead. Mr. Ziemendorff was again married July 11, 1914, to Miss Leda Hull. Two sons were born of the first marriage.

FRED D. HENNESSY, druggist and business man has been one of the live

WILLIAM AUGUST ZIEMENDORFF

the class of 1890. He first came to St. Joseph in March, 1882, and clerked for some time in some of the leading drug stores. From 1896 to 1898 he held the position of steward at the city hospital, and January 1, 1899, was appointed by the Humane Society and Board of Police Commissioners to the position he now holds, that of humane officer. When the legislature in 1907 created the juvenile court Mr. Ziemendorff was, by the terms of the law,

ones in St. Joseph for many years. He came here with his parents in 1879. He is a native of Iowa, where he was born Feb. 6, 1876. He was educated in the grammar schools of St. Joseph. He was married to Miss Lolla M. Nusser, May 17, 1900. They have one son, Robert E. Mrs. Hennessy is a daughter of John Nusser, former editor of the St. Joseph Volksblatt. Mr. Hennessy is a business man of sterling qualities—one of those men of whom no city has a sufficient number.

. WILLIAM F. GARRETT is a native of Missouri, having been born in St. Joseph October 20, 1884. He was educated in the public schools of the city, and .embarked in the grocery business in 1910. His store at 301 East Highland avenue is one of the

poration, one of the very. largest of this country's breweries. was established twenty-two years ago, when Adolph Rettig took charge of its affairs at its location on South Second street, where it .has continuously occupied since that time.

The agency has been in charge, successively, of Charles F. Dienger, 1895-98; Louis Streckbein, Jr., 1899; Frank Schmidt, 1900-03, and Henry W. Schmidt, the present popular manager,

WILLIAM F. GARRETT
—Photo by Mulvane.

best conducted business houses in the city. Mr. Garrett has manifested his public spirit in many ways and always helps any enterprise or undertaking that will benefit his home town. He was married in 1909 to Miss Elizabeth Angold. They have one son, Wilfred.

KANSAS CITY BREWERIES COMPANY

The local agency for this great cor-

from 1903 to the present time.

The Kansas City Breweries Company was formerly known as the Fred Heim Brewing Company. That company's business and that of the Imperial and the Rochester Brewing companies was consolidated under the corporate name. and organization of the Kansas City Breweries Company.

The company's product is distributed throughout the West and Middle West, its chief brand, "Old Fashioned

Lager Beer," being almost a household word where good beer is drank and its qualities appreciated. It is made under every sanitary precaution that will insure its absolute purity when it reaches the consumer, and from the choicest and best of materials.

The growth of the company's business in St. Joseph has been extremely gratifying, having increased under the agency of Mr. H. W. Schmidt, the present manager, from four thousand barrels in 1903 to twelve thousand barrels during the last year. Mr. Schmidt's own personality has been a very material factor in this pleasing growth. In his genial, whole-souled and courteous way he has made a large and constantly growing circle of friends in this community. He has given the great company he represents a high standing here, and has made for himself an enviable place among the widely known, substantial and progressive business men of the city.

Mr. Schmidt was born in Illinois and educated in St. Joseph. His business life also began here, and this has always been his home.

He has developed the business to the entire satisfaction of all concerned. He is regarded as one of the most successful men in this industry in the city. This agency has grown until now it has fourteen men on its pay roll, and four teams are required to make deliveries in the city.

DR. THOMAS REDMOND
—Photo by Mulvane.

DR. THOMAS REDMOND, 403 Corby-Forsee Building, was born in Indiana August 29, 1874. He was educated in the common schools of his native county. He entered the State University at Bloomington, Ind., in 1900. In 1902 he entered the Rush Medical College at Chicago and after graduation he came to St. Joseph and identified himself with St. Joseph's Hospital as house physician, where he remained for two years. He entered the general practice in 1908. He is a member of the Buchanan County and American Medical Associations. He was married to Miss Margaret Storey of Ontario, Canada, in February, 1909. They have three sons, Arthur age 4, William age 3, John age 1.

lished the business in which he is now engaged. He was married to Miss Lena Ettenson, of St. Joseph, Sept. 19, 1894. One son has been born to them, Basil Lionel, now eighteen years old, who has just entered the law department of the Michigan-Ann Arbor University. Mr. Kaufmann is a Mason.

DR. J. FRANCIS SMITH, the only living male descendant of Major Fred

JACOB KAUFMANN
—Photo by Mulvane.

JACOB KAUFMANN, wholesale liquor dealer, 108 South Third street, was born in Zeltingen, Germany, May 23, 1864. He was educated in Germany and at the age of eighteen came to America. He stopped in New York for a year and in 1883 went to Nashville, Ill., where he remained two years. He removed to Kansas City in 1885 and stayed there until 1895, when he came to St. Joseph and estab-

W. Smith, an illustrious pioneer, who made the plat of the original town of St. Joseph and who gave Smith Park to the city. Mr. Smith was born in St. Joseph December 12, 1846, and this has been his home ever since. He studied medicine and graduated from Jefferson Medical College, Philadelphia, in 1869, but has not practiced his profession for many years, devoting his time to the management of his estate and to real estate generally.

DR. CHARLES GREENBERG, Eighth and Edmond streets, is a native of Boston, Mass., where he was born December 23, 1888. At the age of three he went with his parents to Capetown, South Africa, where he remained until he was seventeen. He was educated in the Wynberg High School for Boys at Wynberg, Cape Colony. This is one of the most famous schools in South Africa. After

Marchain's Restaurant, 408 Edmond street, has back of it the ripening experience of thirty years in this line of business. That advantage is being taken of the knowledge is evident from the fact that no matter what other changes may take place, Marchain's is still the popular word with those who want a good place to eat, where they can get satisfactory service and the best the market affords.

DR. CHARLES GREENBERG
—Photo by Mulvane.

serving several years .in the. British civil .service he returned to Boston in 1905. In 1907 he entered the University of Louisville, medical department, and graduated in May, 1911. He served as senior intern at the National Jewish Hospital for. Consumptives, at Denver, for one year, and for a like period was one of the house physicians at the Louisville City Hospital, Louisville, Ky. He located in St. Joseph in 1914.

Ask anyone to name the principal business concerns in the northern part of the city and the name of Bassar & Moskau will be well toward the top of the list. They are at 2110-2112 St. Joseph Avenue, and the firm is one of the most enterprising and wide-awake in the city. They occupy two buildings; connected. In one building is the grocery stock under the able management of Mr. Bassar, who keeps his stock fresh and pure at all times and sells at prices that attract customers. In the other building Mr. Moskau has charge of the dry goods department. Here may be found an unsurpassed selection of dry goods and kindred lines, always up-to-date and priced right. The firm has been in business fifteen years and its patronage is large, and it deserves to be.

ELMER A. GURLEY, 2207 Olive

ter. Mr. Gurley is a member of the Woodmen of the World and the Eagles.

One of the most prospeous drug stores in St. Joseph is that of Bandel Brothers, at the corner of Third and Isabelle Streets. They have been at this location for many years. Their success in business is due to their policy of honesty and fair dealing from which they have never allowed

ELMER A. GURLEY
—Photo by Mulvane.

street, is a native Missourian, having been born in Springfield, Dec. 26, 1877. He was educated in the public schools of Springfield and came to Buchanan County in 1898, locating at DeKalb. He came to St. Joseph July 3, 1900 and for a number of years was engaged in the brewery business. He opened his present business Dec. 15, 1913. He was married to Miss Vernie Monday of Springfield, Oct. 3, 1900. Their family is four sons and a daugh-

anything to swerve them. They carry a line that is complete in every detail and are prepared at all times to handle prescription work satisfactorily.

Just about everybody in the north end knows E. F. White, the enterprising hardware merchant at 2706 St. Joseph Avenue. He carries a complete line of hardware, stoves, cutlery, and household goods. He has a well appointed and admirably managed tin shop in connection and guarantees his workmanship to be the equal of any in the city. Mr. White has been in business in St. Joseph four years and in that time has established one of the most substantial houses in the city.

FREDERICK WENZ is one of the pioneer shoe dealers in St. Joseph. He is a native of Germany. He came

has been commander of Custer Post, G. A. R. In politics he is a Republican. He was married in 1871 to a daughter of Jacob Schwaderer. Mr. and Mrs. Wenz have three children, a son and two daughters.

· One of the most substantial business men in St. Joseph is D. W. Sher, whose store at 1117-1119-1121-1123 North Third Street has long been

FREDERICK WENZ
—Photo by Mulvane.

to St. Joseph on July 6, 1860. When the Civil war was at its height he enlisted, in 1864, as a private in Company A, Forty-third Missouri Volunteer Infantry. Upon being mustered out he returned to St. Joseph and has been a shoe merchant practically ever since. His store on Edmond street is one of the best known in the city. Mr. Wenz is an Odd Fellow, a Mason and a Red Man. He is a life member of the Nobles of the Mystic Shrine,

known as the house of bargains in Furniture, Carpets, Stoves and kindred articles of merchandise. He carries a large stock and sells for cash or credit, as occasion and circumstances require. Mr. Sher knows the needs and requirements of his customers and is at all times ready to supply them with good values at prices that cannot be equaled elsewhere.

HENRY W. SCHMIDT, local agent for the Kansas City Breweries Co., at 226 South Second street, is a native of Sonora, Ill., where he was born, August 22, 1878. At the age of 11 years he came with his parents to St. Joseph and was educated in the schools here. After finishing his education he entered the employ of the brewing company with which he is

Housewives living within a radius of a good many blocks of 2604 St. Joseph Avenue, have found that it is to their best interest to buy their groceries and provisions from W. E. Travis & Co. They have been at this location for a good many years, and have had a successful business career to which they can justly point with considerable pride. This is one of the most substantial firms in this part of St. Joseph.

HENRY W. SCHMIDT
—Photo by Mulvane.

now connected. He began as an office boy and has by industry, aptitude and business ability, risen to the position of manager. He has been with this company since June 11, 1896 and is considered one of the best men identified with the company's large interests. He was married to Miss Wilhelmina Zerbst of St. Joseph in 1897. They have two children, Arthur, age 17; Helen, age 12.

When two men continue in partnership for ten years it is pretty good evidence that they possess the necessary qualifications for success and that they have given their patrons the kind of treatment that makes for the upbuilding of the business in which they are engaged. This may be said of Veraguth & Moskau, who have been at the corner of Fillmore Street and St. Joseph Avenue for one-tenth of a century. They have two rooms connected, in one of which choice wines and liquors are dispensed, and the other is devoted to a clean, well-kept pool hall. None but white customers are served in either room, and the large business that has been built up among the better class of people is proof positive of the popularity of this firm.

GEORGE M. VOLTZ, president of the Voltz Manufacturing Company,

Among those who always know the right things to provide for their friends and patrons, none stands higher than W. P. Ellis, whose thirst emporium at Fourth and Albemarle Streets is a favorite meeting place for those who want to spend a pleasant hour amid surroundings that are agreeable and congenial. He has one-of the best conducted places in St. Joseph.

GEORGE M. VOLTZ

914-916 Penn street, was born in Norwich, N. Y., October 11, 1858. He is an expert machinist and came to St. Joseph in 1877, where he has since followed his trade. For many years he made a specialty of plating and more recently has given attention to universal sash bar and store fronts, a device of superior merit. Mr. Voltz was at one time a member of the St. Joseph Board of Public Schools.

Just about everybody in the north end knows Martin Nelson, proprietor of the Narrow Gauge Restaurant, at 1219½ North Third Street. And everyone who knows him has a good word for him. He gives his customers a good meal for their money and from the fact that his business is a success it may be taken for granted that they appreciate it. He has at all times a full line of tobacco and cigars.

HARRY ROSENTHAL, one of those enterprising young business men of whom no city has an over-supply, was born in St. Joseph, March 22, 1891. He received a thorough education in the schools of the city and after leaving school took up the furniture business with his father, J. Rosenthal, 307-309-311 South Sixth street. The subject of this sketch has demonstrated **that he has** business ability of the better sort by the material assistance which he has been to his father in building up one of the best concerns

ways given his patrons the best of workmanship and has observed the golden rule in his treatment of them. Mr. Jesberg has been in St. Joseph for thirty-one years and is one of the city's most respected citizens.

For many years John Sebus had charge of the Old Narrow Gauge place at Sixth and Messanie Streets. But later he determined to change locations and is now at Second and Robidoux Streets. He is well known to the trade for the courteous treatment he gives his patrons and seems to grow

HARRY ROSENTHAL

in this line of merchandising in the city. He is popular with his associates and admired by all who have the pleasure of his acquaintance. Fraternally Mr. Rosenthal is a K. of P.

It always speaks well for any business institution to have it said "he has been at that location for a long term of years." This applies with force to William Jesberg, the tinner, who has been at 1212 North Third Street for twenty years. He has al-

better in this respect as he grows older. His wines and liquors are always kept in proper condition and served in the best manner possible.

One year ago there opened for busi ness at 1006-1008 North Third Stree Crane's Department Store. From th first it was evident that this ventur was destined to be a success. Th people soon showed their appreciatio of down-to-the-minute business meth ods and patronized the store liberally

That their confidence, manifested at the outset has not been misplaced is evident from the fact that this store's business has grown steadily from the day it opened.

FRANK J. STAEDTLER, representative from the Second Buchanan County District, is a native of Germany. He was born July 6, 1869, and came to America with his parents in 1882. The family first located in New York, and in 1882 removed to Chicago.

the Second District in the fall of 1914 by a majority of 675. He was married to Miss Amelia Mayer in St. Joseph in 1895.

CHARLES E. ROESELE was born in Switzerland in 1844. He came to America in 1864, landing in New York City. Two years later he came on to St. Joseph and has made this city his home ever since. In 1910 he was appointed bookkeeper at the city workhouse, which position he still holds.

FRANK J. STAEDTLER

The following year the subject of this sketch came to St. Joseph. He was engaged as head baker at the Hospital for Insane No. 2, under Dr. C. R. Woodson's supervision, in 1888, which position he held for seven years. In 1895 Mr. Staedtler engaged in the bakery business on his own account and has been a successful business man. He was elected representative from

He married Miss Margaret Kort, of Brooklyn, N. Y. in 1868. They have twelve children, six sons and six daughters.

RUDOLPH PHARMACY.—There is something more to the drug business than merely filling prescriptions and dealing out cigars at a nickel apiece. It is required that the man behind the counter be a business man in

every sense of the word. When one
of such is found the fact soon becomes known, for business will drift
that way in spite of opposition. This
applies to the Rudolph Pharmacy at
the corner of Fifteenth and Penn
Streets.

JAMES E. GATES, general contractor, 1024 Francis street, was born
in Chelsie, Mass., May 26, 1855. He
received his education in his native

Frank Long at Nineteenth and Oliv
streets. Mr. Gates was married
Miss Gussie Brink, of St. Josep
March 14, 1896. He is a Woodma
of the World and an Odd Fellow.

KALIS SUPPLY COMPANY. — (
all the mail order houses in the ci
none stands better, with the trade tha
the Kalis Supply Company, northea
corner of Second and Felix Street
This concern deals in high-grade whi

JAMES E. GATES

—Photo by Mulvane.

town and learned the trade of carpenter there. He came to St. Joseph
in 1878 and for five years worked for
John DeClue and R. K. Allen, well
known contractors in the early days.
In 1883 he began contracting on his
own account and is perhaps the oldest
contractor, in a business sense, in the
city. He has built some of the best
buildings in St. Joseph as well as in
other cities. At the present time he
is engaged on the theater building for

keys, wines and beers, and custom
invariably get the value of the mo
they spend. When this house
established it was upon the basis t
the man who got the value of
dollar would remain a customer,
time has proven the correctness
this reasoning. The company p
express charges on all shipments.

McMILLAN TAILORING COMPA
—Who does not know of McMilla
pants? He has been making th

$3.50 for so long that they have most become a household word. His op at 308 Francis Street is always led with work because he invariably ves 100 cents of value for every llar spent with him—and in some ses more. That's the reason his nts are so well and favorably own.

ALVA F. LINDSAY, attorney at law, mes from good Missouri stock, hav-

opened his present office. Fraternally Mr. Lindsay is a Mason and Yeoman.

SAFFERN BROS.—One of the largest and best selected stocks of merchandise in the city in that of the Blue Front Department Store (Saffern Bros.), 207-11 Felix Street, and fronting on Market Square. Here may be found a well-selected stock of millinery and women's ready-to-wear gar-

ALVA F. LINDSAY

—Photo by Mulvane.

ng been born in Davies County, September 23, 1891. His early education as in the schools of his home county. hen he went to the Trenton College rom which school he was graduated n 1911. In the fall of that year he nrolled as a student in the law department of the Kansas State University, from which he was graduated vith honors in 1914. In July of that rear he came to St. Joseph and

ments, the equal of any in the city. A well-balanced line of dry goods is also carried. This store has a steady and substantial patronage.

H. W. GOLDBERG.—The demands made upon the skill and efficiency of a ladies' tailoring establishment are many and varied. It may properly be said that only an artist can meet all requirements with success. But H. W. Goldberg, 111 North Eighth Street, has solved the problem. He is one of St. Joseph's successful business men, and it is all due to his capable and painstaking management.

FRANK M. LEMMON, city comptroller, was born in Cincinnati, O., January 4, 1858, the son of Alexander H. and Caroline (Reynolds) Lemmon. His father was a native of New London, Pa., and his mother was born in Cincinnati. Mr. Lemmon came to

treasurer February 14, 1914, to succeed George H. Wyatt who had resigned when the affairs of his office became tangled. Mr. Lemmon brought order out of the mix-up and April 24 the same year, was appointed city comptroller by Mayor Elliot Marshall.

SHEPPARD'S FISH & OYSTER MARKET.—When a man has been at one stand for a period equal to an ordinary lifetime he is justified in

FRANK M. LEMMON

—Photo by Mulvane.

St. Joseph in 1882. He has always taken an active interest in the political affairs of the city, being an earnest, hard working Republican. In 1896 he was elected to the city council from the Third Ward and served as president of that body. At one time he was special deputy surveyor of customs and in 1906 was elected justice of the peace for Washington township. He was appointed city

claiming a distinction peculiarly his own. This may be said truthfully of Sheppard's Fish and Oyster Market on Market Square. The waters of two oceans, the great lakes, and many of the larger rivers give up their finny tribe that Sheppard's customers may be supplied with fish for their tables. And Sheppard knows how to satisfactorily supply their needs, too.

LORREN W. GARLICHS, son of Fred A. H. Garlichs, proudly claims St. Joseph as the city of his nativity. He was born here May 11, 1893. His early education was received in the public schools of the city. In the fall of 1911 he went to the Wharton School of Finance and Commerce, in the University of Pennsylvania, at Philadelphia. He remained there two years. On his return to St. Joseph he en-

Edmond Street, has established itself in the business world in St. Joseph by many years of successful merchandising, and its success has been due to its square deal policy which has been strictly adhered to from the day the firm started in business.

OSCAR KLEINBRODT. — The man who does not know Oscar Kleinbrodt does not know what he has missed. He is the owner and boss of the Coney

LORREN W. GARLICHS

—Photo by Mulvane.

gaged in business with his father, taking charge of the insurance department. He is one of the enterprising young men of St. Joseph on whom the city must depend for its growth in the next generation.

H. GRONEWEG CIGAR COMPANY. When any business house has been in existence for a long period of time it attracts to itself a prestige that cannot be secured in any other way. The H. Groneweg Cigar Company, 420

Island Buffet at 314 Edmond Street. Oscar is always around the place, giving his personal attention to the wishes and demands of his customers. He knows how to meet their requirements and takes a pleasure in humoring their whims. It is very easy, therefore, to understand why he is popular.

PHIL KALIS.—There are few better fellows in the refreshment business than Phil Kalis, at 622 South

Sixth Street. It just seems that he knows how, and that tells the whole story. He is always alert to get for his trade the best the market supplies. And then he knows how to serve it, too. The excellent business he has built up is the best evidence of the truth of these statements.

EDGAR G. HUDDLESTON, proprietor of the Transfer Meat Market,

Spencer of St. Joseph in 1908. They have one son. Mr. Huddleston is an Eagle, a Moose, an Odd Fellow and an Elk.

MRS. C. BASSING. — The world looks approvingly upon a business woman, particularly if she has been successful. When she has demonstrated that she is able to cope with the men in the struggle for business, they are ready to applaud her efforts

EDGAR G. HUDDLESTON

—Photo by Mulvane.

214 South Fifth street, is a Tenneseean. He was born in Knoxville, March 22, 1881. He was educated in the schools of his native town and later engaged in various fields of endeavor which gave him an excellent business education. He came to St. Joseph in 1901 and the following year established the Transfer Meat Market, which has been one of the phenomenal business successes of the city. He was married to Miss Jennie

generously. Such a woman is Mrs. C. Bassing, at Seventeenth and Messanie Streets. For many years she has been in the grocery business at this location, and it is one of the most prosperous stores in the city.

BERT MASSON.—One of the boys who knows what the other boys want is Bert Masson, at the corner of Seventeenth and Messanie Streets. His buffet is not excelled, and he maintains a restaurant in connection that is up to date in all of its appointments. His service is good and he always has a pleasant smile for his patrons. That helps to make things pleasant and agreeable.

RAYMOND R. CALKINS, vice-president of the German-American National Bank, is a Missourian. He was born in St. Joseph, November 13, 1876. He was educated in the schools of the city

cashier through his efforts and ability. He was made vice-president in 1908. In 1912-13 he was treasurer, vice-president and president of the Missouri Bankers' Association. He is a member of the Country Club, the Benton Club and the Commerce Club. Mr. Calkins served one term as president of the St. Joseph Clearing House. Fraternally he is a Mason and an Elk.

RAYMOND R. CALKINS

and was graduated from Central High School in 1893. In 1897 he took a position as messenger with the German-American National Bank. He advanced to the positions of bookkeeper, paying teller, assistant cashier, and

W. H. SUMMERS.—For more than five years W. H. Summers has been selling meats and groceries at 2109 Messanie Street. He carries an exceptionally good stock as regards quality as well as quantity, and his prices are as low as consistent with good merchandising. He only asks a living profit, depending more on patronage than high prices for his success. His store is one of the best in this section of the city.

CLAUDE F. WIATT, real estate dealer, room 10 old Corby Building, is a native of Harrison County, Mo. He was born November 18, 1874 and was educated in the common schools of

been very successful. He was married in 1898 to Miss Eva Mahon, of Rockbridge, Mo. Three children, a son and two daughters, have been born to them. Mr. Wiatt is a Mason, an Odd Fellow and an Elk.

A. T. HOPPE.—Reliability is the watchword at the store of A. T. Hoppe, proprietor of the Patee Park Grocery at 1021-23 South Tenth Street. He has been in business here for many

CLAUDE F. WIATT

—Photo by Mulvane.

Harrison County. Later, in 1890, he entered the Stanberry Normal School, from which institution he was graduated in 1893. He was admitted to the bar by Judge W. N. Evans, of the 20th judicial circuit, at West Plains, Mo., in 1902. The following year he began traveling for the Simmons Hardware Company of St. Louis and remained with this firm for several years. He began his real estate business in St. Joseph in 1913 and has

years and seems to be good for many more. He has a substantial patronage and holds his own with his competitors because he insists that none but reliable goods shall leave his store. His excellent business proves that his policy is the right one.

M. M. NELSON.—Of all the grocery stores in St. Joseph none can boast of better goods at right prices that M. M. Nelson, at the corner of Ninth and Olive Streets. A full and complete line of the best groceries the market affords is carried at all times. A milk depot is maintained in connection with the store. This firm enjoys a growing trade, and it is due to the fact that it treats its trade right at all times.

LOUIS V. STIGALL, the subject of this sketch, was born in Stewartsville, Mo., July 9, 1882, was graduated with the degree of Bachelor of Arts at

Knights of Pythias, and order of Elks, and is at present the national president of the Phi Delta Phi honorary law fraternity.

A. F. DEVORSS.—It takes a man with a reasonably good memory to remember the time when A. F. Devorss started in the hardware and tin business at 627 South Eighth Street. He has been at this place for twenty-five years and has, therefore, a long

LOUIS V. STIGALL

William Jewel College, at twenty years of age; after some years spent in teaching school he entered the law department of the University of Missouri, from which he was graduated in 1910, since which time he has been engaged in the practice of law in St. Joseph, Mo.; now being associated with Merrill E. Otis in the firm of Stigall & Otis, which is rapidly growing into one of the leading law businesses in this city. Stigall is an active member of the Masonic fraternity,

business career, which he can point to with justifiable pride. Mr. Devorss was born in St. Joseph and has been an active participant in its growth and development. He is admittedly one of the best tin and metal workers in the city. His excellent business attests this fact.

OSCAR SANDUSKY. — Among the business enterprises in St. Joseph which have had a speedy growth since being started, none has eclipsed Oscar Sandusky's automobile and machine, shop at 619 South Seventh Street. Mr. Sandusky is a mechanic of exceptional ability, has had the experience necessary to enable him to give to his trade unexcelled service and knows how to treat his patrons right.

ARTHUR FREDERICK SCHLAGLE was born October 3, 1889, in St. Joseph, Mo. His father was John Ferdinand Schlagle, who for twenty-five years was foreman of the composing

Islaub, conducted a brewery at Dewey avenue and Michel street before the Civil war.

J. A. SCHELHAMER. — Some men engaged in the drug trade are merely storekeepers, while others are druggists and business men. In the latter class should be placed J. A. Schelhamer, whose place of business, conducted under the name of the Schelhamer Pharmacy, is at 629 South

ARTHUR FREDERICK SCHLAGLE

—Photo by Mulvane.

room of the St. Joseph Herald, and one of the best known men in the printing fraternity in the west at that time. The subject of this sketch was educated in the Crosby school and at the age of fifteen years entered the employ of the Kansas City Breweries Co., as office boy. His position is now that of bookkeeper and cashier. His mother's name was Clara I. Islaub. His grandfather, Frederick

Eighth Street. Mr. Schelhamer has reason to be just a little proud of the success he has made in business, as he began at the bottom and has climbed to the top by sound business methods and close attention to details.

S. MAIER.—For more than a quarter of a century S. Maier, 612 South Seventh Street, has been in the marble business in St. Joseph. He knows the needs and requirements of the people and also knows how to supply them in a satisfactory manner. His business is one of the most substantial concerns in the city, and no one who has bought a monument from him has been disappointed.

LYMAN W. FORGRAVE, justice of the peace, was born in Ohio, July 10, 1844. After attending school in Ohio he came west, locating in Iowa, and at the breaking out of the Civil war entered the volunteer service as a

was elected justice of the peace to fill the unexpired term of Henry W. Burke, who died in office. In 1914 Mr. Forgrave was re-elected by a handsome majority.

JOSEPH SANGER.—Often times a man likes to find a place where he can get the real, old-fashioned lager beer—like father used to get. When he finds such a place, he seldom strays away, but gives it his patron-

LYMAN W. FORGRAVE

member of what was known as Gen. Dodge's band of the Third Brigade, Fourth Division, Fifteenth Army Corps. He was mustered out in Louisville in 1865 and engaged in the contracting business. He came to St. Joseph in 1888 and in 1896 was appointed building inspector. He held this office for ten years. In 1912 he

age because he feels assured that what he gets is O. K. This is the kind of place kept by Joseph Sanger at 606 Messanie Street. He has a good lunch room in connection, which is proving very popular.

SEAMAN & SCHUSKE METAL WORKS COMPANY.—There is no denying the fact that a certain amount of prestige goes with a firm that has weathered the storms of a number of years in business. It inspires confidence, and rightly so. Seaman & Schuske Metal Works Company is entitled to the confidence of the trade because of its long career as tin and metal contractor. This firm has one of the largest plants in the city engaged in this line of work, and the business shows a healthy growth each

count for the past eight years. He is one of the successful young business men of the city and the future seems bright for him. He is a good booster for the town in which he lives and never fails to support anything that will aid in its advancement. He was married to Miss Ada B. Marr, of Taylorsville, Ill., in 1901.

J. G. DUNLAP.—Few men in St. Joseph know better than J. G. Dunlap

J. P. GARVEY

year. This was a pioneer company in the metal contracting business in St. Joseph and the proprietors may well be proud of their success.

J. P. GARVEY, plumber, at 511 South Sixth street, is a native of Ireland. He was born in Limerick, May 31, 1876. At the age of 11 years he came to America, coming direct to St. Joseph. He was educated in this city. He served his apprenticeship under the direction of M. W. Jackson. He has been in business on his own ac-

how to cater to the wants of a discriminating public. He has been at the business so long that he instinctively feels what should be done and then he does it, His place of business at 1911 Frederick Avenue is one of the best in the city, because he takes a pride in keeping it that way. His stock of wines and liquors is unexcelled anywhere.

SCHAEFER & CLAUS.—For a number of years Schaefer & Claus have been selling groceries at 2007 Frederick Avenue. Apparently, the longer they stay in business the better their customers like them. There is, of course, a reason for this. It is because they treat the trade right, both with respect to quality and price. Moreover, the service this firm gives is one of its strong points.

JAMES LIMBIRD, attorney at law, was born at Bicker, Lincolnshire, England, July 24, 1843, the son of James

customs at St. Joseph, serving four years.

A. DEPPEN & SON.—Anyone passing up or down Frederick Avenue cannot but notice the handsome store of A. Deppen & Son, at the corner of Seventeenth Street. They have a room well filled with an excellent stock of hardware, stoves and kindred articles, as well as a complete furniture and carpet department the equal of any in

JAMES LIMBIRD

and Elizabeth (Lane) Limbird. In 1854 he came to Delphos, Ohio, and worked about from place to place till the war, when he enlisted in company I, 27th Ohio Infantry, being discharged in 1862 for disability, but later he enlisted in a cavalry company, serving till the war closed. Was twice prosecuting attorney for Holt County, once in the legislature, three years city counselor of St. Joseph, and in March, 1890, was made surveyor of

the city. The stock throughout has the appearance of being fresh and new, and this inspires confidence in the prospective customer.

SCHREIBER & ENGEL.—Most men like to drop in occasionally and meet a friend who also likes a refreshing drink. The pleasure is greatly enhanced when the place is well kept, clean and inviting. In fact, this has come to be one of the requirements of the trade. This fact is recognized by Schreiber & Engel, whose thirst parlor at 1011 North Third Street is enjoying the patronage of those who care.

FRANK SIEMENS, Superintendent of Buildings, is a native of St. Joseph, the date of his birth being March 13, 1867. He was educated in the city schools. He is a son of Dr. C. J. Siemens, an old and respected citizen of St. Joseph Mr Siemens was ap-

and he wants to go to place where the surroundings are congenial and the service satisfactory. When he finds the place that suits him he goes again. That is why A. K. Godsey, 1415 Frederick Avenue, retains such a good hold on his trade. His wines and liquors bear the mark of quality and he knows how to serve them.

GEORGE F. LEAPER.—One always admires a young, ambitious and enter-

. .. SIEMENS.

—Photo by Mulvane.

pointed to his present office in April, 1914, by Mayor Elliot Marshall. October 1' 1904, he was appointed deputy collector of internal revenue, which position he resigned to accept his present office He was married to Miss Cecelia Schumacher of St. Joseph, March 27, 1901. They have two children, two sons.

A. K. GODSEY.—Occasionally the average ma . li' es to spend a half hour away f' ... the cares of business,

prising business man—one who has the sterling qualities necessary to make a success of that which he undertakes. Such a man is George F. Leaper, of the Leaper Hardware Company at 817 Frederick avenue. He began as manager of the business for others, but in a short time had advanced to a place where he could claim it as his own. Mr. Leaper has reasons to be proud of his success.

GEORGE WASHINGTON WEBB was born January 20, 1856, in Albia, Monroe County, Iowa, the only son of John Webb, Jr., and Julia Ann Rowles. His father, John Webb, Jr., was captain of Company K, Thirty-sixth Iowa infantry during the war of 1861-5, and died at the mouth of White River, Arkansas, September 7, 1863. His mother had previously died August 9, 1860. His parental grandfather, John Webb, was born in Louden County,

and his first work here was that of an engineer on the construction of a temporary bridge across the Missouri River at St. Joseph on which to transfer cars for the railroads terminating in St. Joseph to the one railroad then terminating in Elwood, Kans., known as the St. Joseph & Denver City railroad. The transfer of these cars had previously been done by boats until navigation was closed by the ice and made the temporary bridge necessary.

GEORGE WASHINGTON WEBB

Virginia, and served as a soldier in the war of 1812. He was a son of Adrian Webb, who was the son of Cuthburt Webb, who was a descendant of William Webb, who was born at Dorchester, England, in 1582 and came to America in 1629, settling at Isle of Wight, Virginia. William Webb and his three brothers were the progenitors of the Webb family in the United States.

George W. Webb came to Buchanan County, Missouri, in the fall of 1872,

In 1873 Mr. Webb enlisted in Company G, Third United States Infantry, at Fort Leavenworth, and served two years in Colorado, his regiment being engaged in protecting the settlers from Indian depredations.

Soon after retiring from the army he settled in Florida, engaging in orange growing until the fall of 1888, when he returned to St. Joseph and had charge of the construction of some large business structures, including the C. D. Smith Drug Company building.

In the fall of 1889 he was engaged by the contractors who consolidated the street railway systems of St. Joseph into one corporation and system and changed it from mule transportation to that of electricity, St. Joseph being the first city in the United States to make this complete change, as electrical traction was just being born. He then went to Denver in January, 1890, and took charge of the

the First Reformed Church, and for over twenty years has been its secretary and treasurer. He has always been a champion of fraternal societies, especially those that furnish insurance to its members, and, besides holding his membership in a number of them, he has served in various offices of trust in them, especially those offices having to do with records and finances. He also is a member of the Lincoln Club.

CHARLES F. OGDEN

—Photo by Mulvane.

opening of the first electric railway in Denver, known as the South Broadway, of which he was superintendent and electrician until his health broke down and he was obliged to seek a lower altitude, and so returned to St. Joseph where he has resided continuously since. Since the year 1890, when he returned to St. Joseph from Denver, he has been engaged almost continuously in the real estate and insurance business.

Mr. Webb is a charter member of

Mr. Webb has been married twice, his first wife being Julia M. Merritt of Janesville, Wis., who died in 1913. His present wife was Mrs. Lorena Jane Earll, whose maiden name was Jackson, a native born Missourian, her family being among the early settlers of St. Joseph, and she herself born in what was then known as Blacksnake Hills.

CHARLES F. OGDEN was born in Ralls County, Missouri, July 19, 1868. At the age of seven he was taken by his parents to live at Hannibal, Mo., where he was educated. In June, 1886, he came to St. Joseph, and was in the employ of the Badger Lumber Company for two years. In 1888 he accepted a position with E. W. Ray & Son, lumber dealers, which he retained thirteen years. For nine years he was the company's foreman. In 1900 he was elected, at large, as a member of the city council, which office he held two years. Mr. Ogden has a wide acquaintance in St. Joseph.

perintendent of the street railway lines. He held this position for fifteen years, during which time he had active charge of all outside work. Mr. VanBrunt has been a potent factor in building up the street railway system of St. Joseph, which at the time he came here was in a very distressed condition. That St. Joseph has now one of the best transportation systems in the country, size of town considered, is admittedly true. That this state of near perfection is

JOHN H. VAN BRUNT

JOHN H. VAN BRUNT, vice-president and general manager of the St. Joseph Railway, Light, Heat & Power Company and president of the Savannah Interurban Railway Company, is a native son of New York and was born in Redbank, September, 1868. His early education was received in the schools of his native town; later he attended some of the best schools in New York City. He came to St. Joseph in March, 1889, to become su-

due in great part to Mr. VanBrunt's untiring energy is equally true. When the Clarke syndicate bought the plant in 1892, Mr. VanBrunt was made vice-president and general manager, which position he has held continuously since that date.

He was married to Miss Pearle Dougherty, only daughter of A. M. Dougherty. They have a family of three sons.

JOSHUA MOTTER, vice-president of the Wheeler-Motter Mercantile Company, comes from the good state of Maryland, and from one of the oldest families of that commonwealth. He was born in Williamsport, and was educated in the Penn College at Gettysburg. He came to St. Joseph in 1867 and first engaged with the old Colhoun Bank, as bookkeeper. He held this position for several years to the complete satisfaction of his employers. In 1875 he embarked in the dry goods business, as a traveling salesman for Tootle, Craig & Co. Later he sold goods for Tootle, Hosea & Co. for a period of eight years. He quit the road in 1883, his advancement having been so rapid that he was taken into the firm some years prior to that date. In 1893 the house of Tootle, Wheeler & Motter was organized, and continued in business under that name until 1899, when its scope was considerably enlarged and the Tootle, Wheeler & Motter Mercantile Company was incorporated. The name was changed to the Wheeler & Motter Mercantile Company.

Mr. Motter was married to Miss Gussie Barrow, daughter of Major John E. Barrow, December 2, 1873. Their family consists of three children, Samuel I. and John Barrow Motter of St. Joseph, and Mary Catherine Hall of Kansas City. Mr. Motter is a Mason.

JOSHUA MOTTER

JOHN COMBE came to St. Joseph in 1858. He learned bookbinding, and in 1879 started in business, the firm being Combe & McCreary. To Mr. Combe's tireless energy and business tact the present establishment stands as a credit. Mr. Combe is a Republican and represented the Sixth Ward in the council in 1892-94. He was mayor of St. Joseph from 1900 to 1902.

MAURICE G. CURRY, formerly a member of the city fire department, was born in Springfield, Ill., July 28, 1864. In March, 1873, he came with his parents to St. Joseph, where. he received his education. In 1890 he was appointed a member of the St. Joseph fire department, in which capacity he served for eight years. In 1898 he retired, to accept a position as fire marshal for Swift & Company. After serving four months he was in-

ciation and the Red Men.

The morning after the Kennard fire, in March, 1892, The Gazette reported that Mr. Curry had been burned to death. The report was erroneous, and Mr. Curry enjoyed the joke along with his friends.

REV. SADIE GIBBONS EVALSON, was born in Ringgold, Pa., February 20, 1864, and lived in Illinois, Iowa and Kansas before coming to St. Joseph in 1913. She was educated in

MAURICE G. CURRY

—Photo by Mulvane.

jured by the falling of a wall. This mishap occurred on his birthday. During the succeeding three years he was incapacitated for work. In 1901 he resumed his connection with Swift's, and remained in their service until 1907.

In 1889 he was married to Miss Agnes O'Donough of St. Joseph. There were four children of the union, two boys and two girls. Mr. Curry is a life member of the Eagles, and a member of the Central Protective Asso-

the common schools of Iowa and in Ashland College, Ohio. She was married to Charles Gibbons October 27, 1887, who died the following month. The subject of this sketch was in business as a dressmaker in Milledgeville, Ill.,. and later followed nursing and missionary.work in Chicago. She was married to John W. Evalson of St. Joseph September 7, 1915. Rev. Evalson has been active in the ministry of the Brethren church for many years.

VINCENT E. BURCH, tonsorial artist, whose shop is in the German-American Bank building, was born in Bloomfield, Ind., December 13, 1869. He went to Maryville, Mo., in 1881 and came to St. Joseph in 1890 and embarked in the business he now follows and in which he has been successful. In 1900 he was appointed by Governor Stephens a member of the state board of examiners for barbers,

farm. His father, Henry S. Hill, was a lieutenant in company D, Fifth Missouri cavalry, and our subject accompanied his father through the entire campaign of that regiment. Subsequently he learned the printer's trade at Brownville, Neb., and came to St. Joseph in March of 1877 to take the popsition of foreman of the Gazette composing room, in which position he continued until the organization of

VINCENT E. BURCH

and was reappointed by Gov. Dockery in 1903. He was named to a place on the same board by Governor Major. Mr. Burch is an enterprising and progressive citizen, and his work on this important board has always been most satisfactory. He was married November 28, 1893, to Miss Anna Tolson of St. Joseph. Mr. Burch is an Odd Fellow and a member of several other secret societies.

BENJAMIN F. HILL was born in Atchison County, Missouri, Sept. 13, 1850, and spent his early years on a

the Press Printing company in 1893. Mr. Hill is now with the Combe Printing company.

JAMES NELSON BURNES, who represented this district in congress from 1882 to 1889, was one of the ablest men in the history of Missouri. He was born in Indiana Aug. 22, 1827, and came to the Platte Purchase in 1837 with his father, James Burnes; was educated in the best schools of the section and then went to Harvard, graduating from the law school in 1852. Locating at Weston in Platte

County he soon took front rank in his profession, and was elected circuit attoroney in 1855. He had a great talent for business and was interested in various enterprises, notably in projecting and building railroads, bridges and waterworks in this section, and in the promotion of public interests generally. In 1869 he was elected judge of the court of common pleas of Platte County, which he held until

St. Joseph, was born in Buchanan County, Oct. 23, 1862. When he was two years old his parents moved to the city, where he was educated. At an early age he began carrying papers on the old St. Joseph Gazette, which was then published in the second story of the building now occupied by Nevin & Schwein on Felix street. Mr. Cameron soon developed unusual business acumen for a newspaper

WILLIAM H. CAMERON

1872, when he resigned and located in St. Joseph. In 1882 he was elected to congress and re-elected in 1884, 1886 and 1888. He served with distinction and was one of the foremost members on the Democratic side. On Jan. 23, 1889, he was stricken with paralysis while uttering the first words of a speech on the floor of the house, and died at his hotel in Washington on the following day.

WILLIAM H. CAMERON, than whom few men are better known in

man and engaged in the distribution and sale of the leading publications of the country. He is now local agent for the Curtis Publishing Company and other similar concerns of national reputation.

GEN. DONIPHAN—Alexander W. Doniphan, whose military exploits are briefly chronicled in a previous chapter, was closely identified with the early history of Buchanan County. He practiced law at Sparta and at St. Joseph. He was born in Mason county, Kentucky, July 9, 1808, and came to Missouri in 1830, locating at Lexington. In 1837 he moved to Liberty, where he made his home for thirty years, and then moved to Richmond, where he died Aug. 8, 1887. His first military exploits were against the Mormons, and his second was the famous expedition to Mexico. He was most successful as a criminal lawyer. Nature had endowed him munificent-

has gained a reputation as a first-class apothecary. His store is one of the best in the city. He was married October 4, 1881, to Miss Julia Dio, a native of Alabama, and they have one boy and three girls living.

THOMAS J. CARSON was one of the pioneers of the Platte Purchase. Mr. Carson was born in Cocke County, Tenn., Dec. 24, 1825, where his father was also born. He married

ANTON BURVENICH

—Photo by Mulvane.

ly; his presence was magnetic and his speech fascinating, and he exercised a great and wholesome influence in a broad sphere.

ANTON BURVENICH, Eighteenth and Frederick avenue, is the oldest druggist in St. Joseph, with forty-nine years practice to his credit. He was born in Germany March 7, 1852, and came to St. Joseph in 1857. He began in the drug business in 1865 and

Miss Sarah Easterhay, Nov. 19, 1846, and in 1851 came with his wife and small children to Platte County, later removing to Buchanan, where he was for many years a successful farmer. His wife died March 22, 1882, having borne him nine children, among them T. Jeff Carson, formerly a member of the local police force. Our subject died March 31, 1899.

THOMAS J. DUNCAN, real estate agent, is a native of Missouri, having been born in Gentry County, May 25, 1859. When six years of age he removed with his parents to Buchanan County, and he received his education in the schools of this county. In 1892 he was appointed road overseer of District 24 by the late Judge Thomas Brown. This position he held for ten years. In 1906 he made the race for

parents to Kansas, where he attended grade and high schools at Leavenworth, Peabody and Holton. He graduated from Northwestern College, Naperville, Ill., in 1904, since which time he has served as pastor of different churches in Kansas and Missouri. He was appointed to St. Joseph in 1914.

Rev. Kliphardt served many years as secretary of the Kansas Confer-

THOMAS J. DUNCAN

—Photo by Mulvane.

sheriff, and again participated in this contest in 1908, but was defeated in both elections. In 1914 he made the race for presiding judge of the county court and was defeated by Judge T. J. Hill. He is a member of the Odd Fellows and the Eagles.

CHARLES F. KLIPHARDT, pastor of First Church of the Evangelical Association, Sixteenth and Locust streets, was born at Wallace, Ontario, Dominion of Canada, May 11, 1878. At the age of nine he moved with his

ence Missionary Society, an organization carrying on extended work throughout Missouri, Kansas, Oklahoma and Colorado. He did editorial work on the first volume of the History of the Kansas Conference, published in 1915, and has been honored by his conference with appointment on some of her most important committees. For two years he was treasurer and a member of the executive committee of the Kansas Conference Branch young people's organization of his church.

He was married July 17, 1906, to Miss Lydia Abbuehl of Valley Falls, Kans., and has one child, Annetta Kliphardt.

E. W. DIENGER, proprietor of "Badischer Hof," 614 Messanie street, was born in Baden, Germany, Dec. 17, 1844, and received a good education; came to St. Joseph in 1867, worked at various occupations and then engaged

born near Pevely, Jefferson County, Missouri, July 22, 1888, as the first son of the Rev. F. E. Rothe, an Evangelical Lutheran pastor. In 1902 he entered St. Paul's College at Concordia, Mo., where he completed a six years' course in 1908. The same year he entered Concordia Seminary, St. Louis, Mo., where he completed a three years' theological course in June, 1911. He accepted a call from St. Peter's

E. W. DIENGER

—Photo by Mulvane.

in gardening for eight years; kept the Charleston House until 1888, when he moved to his present location, which he owns. August 21, 1871, he married Caroline Beck, who died Sept. 10, 1888, leaving five children. Oct. 21, 1890, he married Emma Aniser, born in St. Joseph.

REV. OTTO ROTHE, pastor of the Evangelical Lutheran St. Peter's church at Fourth and Dolman, was

Evangelical Lutheran congregation, arriving in St. Joseph in August, 1911. Mr. Rothe was married April 18, 1912, to Miss Hulda Schaefer of St. Louis, Mo. The first child, Vera, was born Dec. 15, 1914. Mr. Rothe preaches regularly in the German and in the English language and also conducts a German-English parochial school. He has always been a member of th Evangelical Lutheran church, but ha never joined any lodges or secret societies. He resides in St. Peter's parsonage, 415 Dolman Street.

ARTHUR O. LEWARS, of the firm of Snyder & Lewars, painters, is a native of St. Joseph. He was born May 14, 1875 and has spent his life in St. Joseph. He comes from one of the oldest families in this section-- the kind of people that make a community worth while. He took up the

Missouri. His father came here in the early "forties." Mr. Petree spent his entire boyhood in Andrew County. He taught school in Andrew and Gentry Counties and January 24, 1892, married Rhoda B. Richardson of Gentry County. In 1895 he entered the ministry of the Methodist church. His first charge was Cosby, a few miles northeast of St. Joseph. He later was pastor at Union Star, King City, Mays-

ARTHUR O. LEWARS
—Photo by Mulvane.

painter's trade in 1895 and has never found it necessary to change. His present partnership was formed four years ago. He is a member of the Odd Fellows and Modern Woodmen of America.

REV. CHARLES E. PETREE was born near Savannah, Mo., Oct. 1, 1869. His parents were pioneers in the Platte Purchase. His mother was born at Liberty Landing in 1837, and from infancy has lived in Northwest

ville and Marceline. Then he served four years as superintendent of the Kirksville district of the Methodist Episcopal church. In October, 1913, he was appointed pastor of the Huffman Memorial church of St. Joseph. He has been active in temperance movements, local and otherwise. He has a family of two sons and four daughters. His eldest son, Leo H, served one year as principal of the

Maxwell school, St. Joseph. The second son, Noel H., is principal of the Central ward school of Trenton, Mo.

WILLIAM L. SCHRAAG, contractor and builder, 2906 Francis street, is a Kansan. He was born in Atchison, July 20, 1881. He was educated in Atchison and at the age of 16 years enlisted in the Twenty-second Kansas Infantry. November 3, 1899, he enlisted in the First United States

REV. JAMES EDGAR DILLARD, D. D., pastor of the First Baptist Church was born in Danville, Va., June 3, 1879, and came to St. Joseph in February, 1915. After being educated in William Jewell College and Washington University he took special work in other universities, specially fitting him for his life's work. He has taken an active interest in educational matters and held the position of presi-

WILLIAM L. SCHRAAG

—Photo by Mulvane.

Infantry and served three years in the Philippines. He was mustered out November 22, 1902. Mr. Schraag came to St. Joseph several years ago and has built up a profitable business as a contractor. He has been the successful bidder for some of the most important jobs let in this section of the country in recent years. He was married to Miss Minnie Haulthaus, of Atchison, March 10, 1900. He is a member of the First Baptist Church.

dent of Clarksburg College 1901-0(Entering the ministry he became pas tor of Tabernacle Baptist Churcl Kansas City, Mo., and later held th pastorate of Delmar Avenue Baptis Church, St. Louis. He came fror that city to St. Joseph, and althoug he has been a resident here for les than one year his energy and abilit have advanced him to the front ran among the city's progressive and su cessful ministers. Aside from a worl

g interest in educational institu-
ns for fifteen years he has found
ne to devote to literary work. He
s written several books and has
en a contributor to some of the
ading magazines and newspapers.
v. Dillard has also done much lec-
re work and in this field his success
s been marked. He was married to
ss Lillian Lee Madison and they
ve an interesting family of two chil-

law department of the Missouri University the same year. He was graduated from the state law school in
1912 and began practicing in St. Joseph the same year. He formed a
partnership with Joseph Goldman in
January, 1913.

REV. J. F. LE CLERE, minister of
the gospel, pastor of the First United
Presbyterian church, Twelfth and
Felix Streets, was born in Dubuque

BENJAMIN L. LIBERMAN

—Photo by Mulvane.

n, James Edgar, Jr., and Lillian
is.

BENJAMIN L. LIBERMAN, lawyer,
s born in Russia, Nov. 17, 1886. He
me with his parents to America
en he was but 7 years old. They
me direct to St. Joseph and young
erman was educated in the city
ools, graduating from Central High
ool in 1906. He took his B. A. de-
e at Yale in 1910 and entered the

County, Iowa, Feb. 24, 1881. He grad-
uated from Monmouth College, Mon-
mouth, Ill., in 1906, and from the
Pittsburg Theological Seminary of the
United Brethren Church of North
America, in 1909. The first year of
his ministery was spent in Jeannette,
Westmorland County, Pennsylvania.
In 1911 he took charge of the Rix
Mills United Presbyterian Church of
New Concord, Ohio, where he re-

mained until the fall of 1914, when he accepted the pastorate of the local church. He was married June 12, 1911, to Miss Edna Chalfant of Jeannette, Pa.

DR. JOHN H. SAMPSON, physician and surgeon, whose office is in the Corby block, Fifth and Edmond, was born in Buchanan County, Jan. 29, 1857. His father, Benjamin, is a farmer and miller and was born in Illinois, while his mother Eliza (Ewell) Sampson is a native of Ray County,

that he might have a more extended field of operation and his success in the city has been in keeping with his expectations. Dr. Sampson was married Aug. 7, 1878 to Miss Mary J. Parnell of Buchanan County. One boy and four girls, all now living, have been born to them.

REV. GEO. S. MURPHY, D. D., pastor of the First English Lutheran church, Tenth and Charles Streets, was born in Reedsville, Penn., March 4, 1865. He graduated at Wittenberg

Dr. Thomas   Nellie

FAMILY GROUP OF BENJAMIN SAMPSON

Standing (Left to Right)—Richard, Dr. Benjamin, Charles, Albert, William, Belle, Grant, Dr. Clarence. Sitting (Left to Right)—Magdeline, James, Father and Mother, Dr. John, Jesse.

Mo. Our subject early decided on the profession of medicine as the one best suited to him and he prepared himself by attending the Missouri Medical College at St. Louis, graduating in 1881; also with a post-graduate course in 1891. On his graduation, in 1881, he located at New Market, in Platte County, Mo., where he built up a large practice and where he still has many patrons. March 15, 1885 he located in DeKalb, remaining in DeKalb for 11 years. February 19, 1896 Dr. Sampson located in St. Joseph

College, Springfield, Ohio, in 1893, with second honors, and was a member of the faculty of his alma mater from graduation until 1903, when he resigned the chair of Greek to enter the work of the active ministry. His first charge was near Mansfield. In 1906 he was called to Peabody, Kans., where he soon led the congregation in building the finest church in that section of the state. In March, 1912, he came to his present field and before a year had passed he was again leading his people in a building enterprise resulting in the fine stone church and brick parsonage at Tenth and Charles.

He was married in 1906 to Miss Rebecca Weber, of Penn's Grove, N. J., who has the unique distinction of being descended from Roger Williams, through his second as well as his first marriage. George W. Murphy, the only child, is a sophomore at Central High School.

Dr. Murphy is a member of the Phi Hill Avenue, is a native of the state of Illinois. He was born at Astoria, June 8, 1868. At the age of twelve years he went with his parents to Sabetha, Kans., where he was educated. He came to St. Joseph in August, 1906. The Farmers' State Bank was organized October 30, 1906, and Mr. Klepper was elected cashier. The growth of this bank has been steady since the day it began business, and

WILLIAM J. KLEPPER

Kappa Psi Fraternity. He is a Knight Templar, a Shriner, and 32° Mason. The Supreme Council, Ancient and Accepted Scottish Rite, conferred upon him the honorary degree of Knight Commander Court of Honor, at the recent meeting in Washington. In 1914, Midland College conferred upon him the honorary degree of Doctor of Divinity.

WILLIAM J. KLEPPER, cashier of the Farmers' State Bank, 6211 King this has been due largely to the business ability and enterprise of the cashier.

Mr. Klepper was married to Miss Ida Belle Dunlap of Sabetha, Kans., May 22, 1888. They have one daughter. Mr. Klepper is a Mason and an Odd Fellow.

FREDERICK C. KLICK, pastor of Zion's Evangelical Church, Ninth and Jule Streets, was born Dec. 29, 1879, in Pinckneyville, Ill., the oldest son

of Rev. J. F. Klick and Magdalene.
Buechle. He spent his childhood days
in St. Louis, where he received his
education in the parochial and public
schools. He is a graduate of Walther
College, St. Louis; of Elmhurst Col-
lefe, Elmhurst, Ill.; of Eden Theological Seminary, St. Louis, and took post-
graduate work at Washington University, St. Louis. In 1903 he was ordained to the ministry and took up

DR. AMEDEE DeCOUAGNÉ, de
tist, at 2518 Frederick Avenue, is
native of Canada. He was born
Montreal, March 11, 1859. He w
educated in his native country. I
was graduated from the St. Lawren
College in 1879. He studied dentist
in Montreal. In 1885 he entered t
Harvard School and attended the de
tal clinics. In 1887 he located in F
River, Mass., where he first practic

DR. AMEDEE DeCOUAGNE

active work near Chicago. In 1908
he was called to St. Joseph to become
pastor of Zion's Evangelical Church.
In 1915 he was elected president of
the West Missouri district of his denomination, which comprises thirty-
seven congregations, being the youngest man who has ever been elected
to this position.

In June, 1906, he married Etta
Hunnig, of St. Louis, and has one son,
Wilfred H., and two daughters, Elsie
M. and Audrey.

his profession. He came to St.
seph in 1897, and has been success
in building up a lucrative practi

He was married to Miss Jen
Sweet of St. Joseph in October, 19
They have one child, a son.

REV. W. D. BOLTON, a Bapt
minister, was born near Jeffers
City, Mo., Oct. 6, 1865. He taught
the country schools four years, beg
ning when 19 years old. He graduat
from the business college at Sedal
Mo., then entered William Jewell C

ʒe as a student for the ministry. At is college he was for four years one the editors of the College Maga- ıe, and won the medals in the ora- rical and debate contests.

In 1896 he graduated and entered e Southern Baptist Theological Sem- ary at Louisville, Ky., from which graduated in 1899. The same year was married to Miss Margaret ʒan of Mt. Sterling, Ky., and came

years. Located in St. Joseph, Novem- ber, 1913, connecting with Ehrlich Mfg. Co. and later establishing the Boyer Sales Co., which firm is en- gaged in the selling of household goods, advertising novelties, advertis- ing service and office supplies.

ELDER WALTER CASH, pastor of the Krug Park Primitive Baptist Church, was born near Bucklin, Linn County, Missouri, Sept. 2, 1856. After

CLIFFORD F. BOYER

St. Louis as pastor of the Baptist urch there. He was pastor at Bowl- ʒ Green six years, and came to St. ʒeph as pastor of the Savannah enue Baptist Church eight years ʒ. In this city he was president of ʒ Baptist Ministers' Alliance for two ars and president of the General ʒnisters' Alliance one year.

CLIFFORD F. BOYER, born in Chi- ʒo, Ill. Came to St. Joseph from St. ʒuis where he resided for seven

attending the common schools and the Kirksville State Normal he began teaching school and taught for ter years.

He was married to Miss Ellen P. Hardin, August 19, 1875, who died Feb 8, 1876. March 4, 1877, he was mar- ried to Miss Emma Bentley, and to them have been born ten children, of whom there are five daughters and four sons living.

Mr. Cash united with the Primitive

Baptist Church when in his seventeenth year and was ordained to the ministry in May, 1880, having then been preaching as a licensed preacher for four years. Ever since his ordination he has had the pastoral care of churches and has held the pastorate of the church he first united with for thirty-five years continuously. He served as moderator of the association of which his church was a mem-

While in Marceline he owned and published the "Marceline Mirror," a weekly newspaper, and was twice elected mayor of that city, resigning the office when he came to St. Joseph to live. He is the author of several books on religious subjects.

FREDERICK J. WENZ, JR., shoe merchant at 423 Edmond Street, claims St. Joseph as the town of his nativity. He was born here January

FREDERICK J. WENZ

—Photo by Mulvane.

ber for fifteen years.

In 1890 he began editorial work on the "Messenger of Peace," a semi-monthly religious paper which is published for the Primitive Baptists of Missouri and the West, and one year later bought the paper and moved it to Marceline, Mo. For the last ten years he has published the paper in St. Joseph, Elder Cash having made his home here since 1903.

21, 1872. He attended the schools the city, and after receiving his education, engaged in business with h father, Fred Wenz, the veteran sh dealer of St. Joseph. He has bee thus engaged since 1890. He takes live interest in the public affairs the city and may always be depend upon to help any worthy cause.

Mr. Wenz was married to Miss Le Duye of St. Joseph in 1897. Frater ally he holds memberships in the Odd Fellows, Red Men and Sons of Veterans.

PAUL KREUGER is a native of Germany, having been born in that country December 12, 1868. He received his education in his native country and came to America in 1884. St. Joseph was the first city in which he settled, and he has been here ever since. He first opened a saloon at

New Albany, Ind., November 15, 1882. He was educated in the University of Cincinnati and also in the Hebrew Union College of the same city. He spent most of his life before coming to St. Joseph, in Omaha, Neb., where his parents still reside. He came here August 15, 1906, and has been wonderfully successful in his work with his congregation. The consummation of the plans for the building

I'AUL KREUGER

—Photo by Mulvane.

eighth and Messanie streets, and remained there for six years. In 1890 he moved to 1508 St. Joseph avenue, where he opened the place of business he is now conducting. He is one of the liberal and potential business men of the northern part of the city. Mr. Kreuger was married to Miss Anna Semtner, of Germany, in 1910.

RABBI LOUIS BERNSTEIN, of Temple Adath Joseph, was born in

of the handsome new church edifice at Seventeenth and Felix Streets was due in large measure to his efforts. Rabbi Bernstein takes great interest in charitable work and is an advanced thinker in this field. He was appointed a member of the State Board of Charities and Corrections by Governor Hadley, but later resigned. He is a member of the executive committee of the National Conference of

Charities and Corrections and is connected with many other organizations of similar character, both local and national. Fraternally he has memberships in the various Masonic bodies, including the Shrine and the Independent Order B'nai B'rith.

JUDGE THOMAS J. HILL, presiding judge of the county court, is a prominent farmer of Bloomington township. He was born in this town-

in its prosperity. He has always been interested in the improvements of the highways of the county, having served five years as road overseer.

Judge Hill was united in marriage to Florence B. Garton in 1878. They have no children. Religiously, they are members of the Missionary Baptist Church. They have a fine residence on a hill commanding a fine view of the surrounding country. The

JUDGE THOMAS J. HILL

ship May 23, 1858, and is a son of Thomas and Margaret (Norris) Hill. Judge Hill was educated in the district schools and the DeKalb school. Generally he has devoted himself exclusively to farming. He was elected judge of the county court in 1898, and served until 1902. He was elected presiding judge of that tribunal in 1912, and is still serving.

He has an excellent farm of 207 acres, and takes commendable pride

judge is a stanch Democrat in politics, and was a delegate to the state convention in 1896, and served as county central committeeman for four years. Fraternally he is a member of DeKalb Lodge, No. 191, I. O. O. F., and Missouri Camp, No. 1893, M. W. A., of St. Joseph.

MIDLAND PRINTING COMPANY, printers and publishers, Board of Trade building, is one of the older printing establishments in St. Joseph.

It was started nearly a quarter of a century ago by Charles E. Thornton, who had associated with him H. W. Beard and Herman Rose. Mr. Rose retired after a few years, but Beard and Thornton continued the business until 1911, when they sold to E. L. McDonald and W. J. Jones. This partnership continued until June, 1915, when Mr. Jones retired and the business was incorporated, the stockholders being E. L. McDonald, Frank Frey-

New York City, and graduated in 1905. In 1910 he matriculated in the American School of Osteopathy at Kirksville, Mo., and graduated in 1913. He then went back to New York and practiced one year under Dr. Fechtig. He opened his office in St. Joseph in 1914.

REV. DUNCAN BROWN, was born in Hannibal, Mo., June 6, 1844. At the age of 12 years he moved with his parents to a farm in Shelby coun-

DR. IBER WEBSTER MERVINE

—Photo by Mulvane.

tag and Glen Stevenson. The company specializes on publication work and is the home of the St. Joseph Observer, the St. Joseph Union and several other publications.

DR. IBER WEBSTER MERVINE, room 35, Ballinger Building, was born at Gordon, Penna., April 22, 1885. He was educated in the common schools of his native town. In 1903 he entered the Mills Training School in

ty, where his early education was received. He enlisted in the Union army, first in St. Joseph in 1861 and later at Palmyra, Mo., in 1862. At that time and place he attached himself to Glover's Third Missouri Cavalry Volunteers and served until the end of the war. Rev. Brown received his college education at Pardee College and graduated with the degree of A. B. in 1868. He was educated for the ministry in Princeton Theological Seminary, graduating in 1871. He has been at work in the gospel ministry ever since. He has held charges in St. Joseph, Mound City, Craig and Tarkio. He was president of the Highland (Kansas) College and the Brookfield (Missouri) College from 1885 to 1891. He received the degree of D. D. from the first mentioned college in 1884. On account of failing health he went to Arizona several

dent of the Missouri State Sunday School Association. He has held various other minor offices in connection with the religious work of the state in which nearly all of his life has been spent. Rev. Brown was married August 25, 1874, to Miss Mattie T. Lewis. Their family consists of five children. His fraternal connections are confined to Custer Post, G. A. R. of which organization he is the chaplain.

RALPH M. STAFFORD
—Photo by Mulvane.

years ago and preached there for a year and a half. For nearly four years he preached in Mexico City. Rev. Brown returned to St. Joseph in 1913 and is now living at 1810 North Twenty-second Street. Most of his activities have been in the Presbyterian Church, but he is now supplying the pulpit of the Plymouth Congregational Church. He has held the important office of moderator of the Presbyterian Synod of Missouri and was presi-

RALPH M. STAFFORD, real estate dealer at the northeast corner of Eighth and Edmond Streets, is of Missouri stock, Buchanan County being his birthplace and the date June 3, 1874. After receiving his education in the county schools, he engaged in the grocery business in St. Joseph in 1896, which field of activity claimed his attention for eleven years, during which time he was active in the Retail Grocers', Butchers' and Bakers'

Association and served as its president. In 1911 he embarked in the real estate business, and his success has been such that he does not believe he will make any more changes. He was married to Miss Mary K. Bailey of St. Joseph, March 19, 1893. They have two children, both boys.

WILLIAM H. OSWALD, justice of the peace, is a native of St. Joseph. He was born here September 8, 1882,

years, until the fall of 1914, when he was elected justice of the peace for Washington township. He is a Democrat in politics.

HARRY L. GRAHAM, solicitor for the Combe Printing Company, is a native of St. Joseph, where he was born June 10, 1861, and where he has lived ever since. He was educated in the public schools and has been actively

WILLIAM H. OSWALD

and was educated in the schools of the city and graduated from the St. Joseph Business University in 1899. The following year he was made chief signal operator at Central Police Station. This position he held for fifteen

engaged in business since boyhood, mostly as a salesman and solicitor. He was married October 1, 1884, to Miss Hannah J. Hayward, daughter of Joseph and Mary Hayward of St. Joseph. They have two children.

MR. R. T. FORBES, president of the First National Bank and the First Trust Company of St. Joseph, was born at Port Lavaca, Texas, on March 4, 1868. Having been deprived of schooling facilities he entered the employ of the Galveston City Railway Company at a very early age as office boy, one of his duties being to "rob" the street car boxes of the fares, it being in the days when passengers were required to deposit their nickels serving that institution in the capacity of a mail teller. The line of work not affording any particular experience or education, he decided to enter a country institution and accepted a position with Ritter & Doubleday, private bankers, at Columbus, Kansas, where he was permitted to serve in a general capacity, remaining until 1889, when the First National Bank of Las Vegas, New Mexico, tendered him a position as teller, which he accepted,

R. T. FORBES

in the cash boxes instead of having conductors. This was the beginning of his taste for financial matters and which led him into the banking business.

After leaving Galveston, his parents settled at Dallas, where he entered the service of the American National Bank in 1884 as messenger at a salary of $2.50 per week. After remaining with the Dallas banks until 1887 he was called by Dr. W. S. Woods to the Bank of Commerce, Kansas City, remaining there until the summer of 1891, when he purchased an interest in the Stephens Lithographing and Engraving Company of St. Louis, Mo., and as president of that company, he piloted it most successfully through the panic of 1893. The effect of this panic was most severe and in a measure impaired his health, so in 1896 he determined to relieve himself of the strenuous task of managing a manufacturing business and to return to his first love, which was that of banking, and in 1896 sold his holdings in the lithographing company and established the American Trust and Savings Bank at Cedar Rapids, Iowa, which bank in a very short time grew to large proportions, and in 1904 he was chosen cashier of the Citizens National Bank of Cedar Rapids in conjunction with the management of the savings bank. Both banks under his management trebled in the space of three years' time.

The rapid growth of these banks attracted the attention of bankers throughout the country, and on January 1, 1907, he was invited to accept the position of vice-president of the Drovers' Deposit National Bank of Chicago, which position he accepted, taking up the duties on January 8, just in time to become familiar with the customers and business of this great institution, which permitted him to successfully cope with the panic of that year. The progress made by the Drovers' Deposit National Bank was of such a character that in June, 1908, he was elected to the position of president. On May 16, 1910, he was chosen president of the First National Bank of St. Joseph, and May 17 took up his residence in St. Joseph.

Mr. Forbes has a personal acquaintance among the bankers of the United States extending from coast to coast and from Canada to Mexico, who have been loyal to him and assisted him in building up the various institutions with which he has been connected. Strange as it may seem, every change he has ever made has been a promotion unsolicited and never has he been compelled to seek a place or advancement.

Aside from his business career, he served through the period of the Spanish-American war as first lieutenant of the Fifth Iowa Volunteer Light Artillery. He was mustered in the United States service at Camp McKinley, Iowa, on July 5, 1898. The board of directors of his bank, of which he was then cashier, passed a unanimous resolution granting him a leave of absence extending through the Spanish-American war.

He is a prominent Mason, having served that fraternity as master of the lodge, high priest of the chapter, commander of the Commandery Knights Templar, grand captain general of the Grand Commandery of the State of Iowa, most wise master of the Rose Croix Chapter Scottish Rite, being a 32° Mason. He is also a life member of the Benevolent and Protective Order of Elks.

He is a member of the Sons of the Revolution, holding his membership as a descendant of General Wm. Davidson of North Carolina, and has served as president of the Iowa society; is a member of the Protestant Episcopal church, which he has served as vestryman and treasurer for many years. He is a member of the following clubs: Union League Club, South Shore Country Club, of Chicago; the St. Joseph Country Club, Benton Club and Commerce Club of St. Joseph.

On June 28, 1910, he married Miss Coudrey Palmer at Algona, Iowa, which union has been blessed with three sons, Richard Tasker Forbes, Jr., Robert Palmer Forbes, and Randolph Mitchell Forbes.

SMITH-STULL TYPESETTING CO. —With the perfecting of typesetting machines, doing away with the old method of setting books, magazines, newspapers and advertising matter by hand, a new industry was born which has proven a success from its inception—the trade composition office. One well equipped typesetting plant can supply the demands of every printing office in Buchanan county, and still have time to set up and deliver the type for several newspapers in Kansas, Iowa and Nebraska and well as the adjacent counties in Missouri. Such an institution is the Smith-Stull Typesetting Company of St. Joseph, which was started by Marshall W. Smith in 1911, under the name of the Smith Typesetting Company. In April, 1914, W. R. H. Stull, superintendent of the mechanical department of the Gazette, entered into a partnership with Mr. Smith, forming the Smith-Stull Typesetting Company. In July, 1914, Mr. Smith died, and his interests were taken over by C. L. Smith. The firm is well known throughout Missouri, Kansas, Iowa and Nebraska, and is the only independent typesetting company in this part of Missouri.

B. RALEIGH MARTIN was born at Macomb, McDonough County, Illinois, July 6, 1872. His paternal ancestry were among the early settlers of Marion County, Kentucky, and his maternal ancestry resided in Randolph County, Virginia.

The subject of this sketch removed with his parents in early boyhood to Maryville, Nodaway County, Missouri, where he grew to manhood, receiving his education in the Maryville public

practice of his profession in Maryville until January, 1910, when, seeking a wider field of labor, he removed to the metropolis of Northwest Missouri and became a citizen of St. Joseph where he now resides.

In 1912 Mr. Martin became a candidate for the Democratic nomination for congress against Congressman Charles F. Booher and was defeated by a small majority. He has been very active in Democratic politics for

B. RALEIGH MARTIN

schools and the Maryville Seminary, from which he graduated in 1892, and during which time he pursued the study of the classical languages under private instructors. Mr. Martin is widely read in the classics, a finished scholar and a master of English. He studied law and was admitted to the bar in 1893, and in 1897 was elected prosecuting attorney of Nodaway County, Missouri, serving four consecutive years. At the expiration of his term of office he continued the

twenty years. He is an able lawyer enjoying a large practice, and is recognized as one of the most brilliant orators in the state. Before a jury he has few equals and he has been engaged in some of the most celebrated cases in Northwest Missouri, and in many noted cases in the central western states. While being engaged in the general practice of law, Mr. Martin has made a specialty of will cases, and has appeared as counsel in many memorable will contests in this and other states.

In politics Mr. Martin is a Democrat and has been a hard worker for his friends and party during his public career. He has delivered speeches in many parts of the country under the direction of the National Democratic Committee, and is always found ready to lend a helping hand in his home and surrounding counties to the local tickets in every campaign. He has legion of friends who predict that

clerk, and, later, worked in the same capacity for the S. S. Allen Grocery Company. At the end of three years he went with the News-Press as solicitor and followed this position with one on the Gazette as circulation manager, in which capacity he spent several years. He left the Gazette to go to the St. Joseph Star, but remained only a short time, returning to the Gazette as advertising manager. Eight years ago he founded the Com-

CLARENCE C. PIERCE

as a reward for his faithful services to his party he would receive whatever honors he might ask should he become an aspirant for political preferment. Mr. Martin is a Shriner, Elk, Eagle, Moose, Knight of Pythias, Woodman, K. & L. of S., Yeoman and a member of other orders. In religion he is a Presbyterian. He resides with his family consisting of his wife, daughter, Pauline, and son, Marion, at his residence, 1202 Ashland avenue, St. Joseph, Mo.

CLARENCE C. PIERCE was born in Remington, Indiana, in 1873. He came to St. Joseph in 1892 and went into the employ of the Rainalter Grocery Company at 712 Felix Street, as

mercial Journal, a trade paper devoted to the interests of manufacturer, wholesaler and retailer. This publication, of which he is the publisher and owner, recently absorbed the Retailer, a trade paper of Kansas City; became the official organ of the Free Service Bureau of St. Joseph, and has started on a career of uncommon usefulness to the middle west territory.

Mr. Pierce is quite a lodge man, being a 32° Mason and a Shriner. He is a charter member of the Scottish Rite Masons; a charter member of the Elks; a member of the United Commercial Travelers; has been secretary of the Humane Society for six years; is a director in the Union Gospel Mission, in which he takes a great interest; and is a member of the White Temple (M. E.) church. He is deeply interested in sociological work for the alleviation of the condition of the poor and for their general uplift.

THOMAS BUFORD ALLEN, judge of the circuit court, was born in Fredericktown, Mo., March 26, 1868. He is

county for twenty years. His mother, whose maiden name was Sarah Bollinger, was born in Bollinger County, Missouri. Mr. Allen was educated in the public schools of Fredericktown and at the state university at Columbia. After teaching school in Madison county and reading law with Hon. B. B. Cahoon of Fredericktown, he en-

THOMAS BUFORD ALLEN

the son of Judge N. B. Allen, a native of Madison County, Missouri, who was judge of the probate court of that

tered the Georgetown University Law School at Washington, D. C., graduating in the class of 1891 and the post-graduate class of 1892. From October, 1892, to August, 1893, he was a law clerk in the office of the judge advocate general, war department, at Washington, appointed after competitive examination under the civil service law. This position he resigned to begin the active practice of his profession in St. Joseph. He was a member of the firm of Sherwood & Allen from August, 1893, to July, 1898. He has achieved both fame and a lucra-

Division No. 1, in the fall of 1914, and is dean of the Y. M. C. A. law school.

Mr. Allen was married at New Madrid, Mo., November 10, 1892, to Miss Emma Hunter, daughter of Joseph Hunter.

EDMOND J. ECKEL, architect, was born in Strasboarg, Alsace, France, June 22, 1845. He studied architecture in Paris at the Ecole des Beaux Arts, where he graduated in 1868. He came to America, landing in St. Jo-

EDMOND J. ECKEL

tive practice since coming to St. Joseph. For several years after 1897 he was attorney for the county collector and for a long time was connected with the faculty of the Ensworth Medical College, as lecturer on medical jurisprudence. In 1906 he was appointed to membership on the state board for the examination of applicants for admission to the bar. He was elected judge of the circuit court,

seph July 3, 1869. He at once obtained employment as a draughtsman with the firm of Stigers & Boettner, becoming a partner in 1872. In 1880 the firm became Eckel & Mann, and in 1892 it was dissolved, Mr. Eckel continuing the business. In 1910 he associated himself with his son, Geo. R. Eckel, and Will S. Aldrich, the firm name now being Eckel & Aldrich. Some of the finest structures in this and other large cities were designed by Mr. Eckel. He was married in 1875 to Miss M. L. Schroers, who bore him four children.

WILLIAM A. BODENHAUSEN, clothier, of the Derge-Bodenhausen Clothing Company, 621-623 Felix Street, is a native of Missouri. He was born in St. Joseph October 25, 1870, and was educated in the public schools of the city. In 1890 he attended the Iowa Wesleyan University er serving two years he resigned. He was third vice-president of the Commerce Club at its inception and served on the board of directors the second year of its existence. He has been on some of the most important committees of that organization ever since. Mr. Bodenhausen began his business career with the John S. Brittain Dry Goods Company. After a connection with that firm of fourteen years he engaged in the retail clothing business

WILLIAM A. BODENHAUSEN

at Mt. Pleasant, Iowa. He was elected to the city council from the First ward in 1899; two years later he was elected a member of the first board of public works in St. Joseph. The law creating this board was held invalid by the supreme court. In 1904 he was appointed to the board of public works, as at present constituted. Aft- with the firm of Perkins & Derge, then located at Fourth and Felix Streets. Later the style of the firm was changed to the Derge-Bodenhausen Clothing Company. Fraternally he is a Mason, K. of P., Moose, Elk and Odd Fellow. Mr. Bodenhausen was married September 15, 1903, to Miss Clara Bauman of St. Joseph.

W. A. BODENHAUSEN

SAFEI
W. H. GORDON

W, D. WEBB

H. E. MOOERS is a native of Virginia, coming to St. Joseph in 1883 from his birthplace in Charles City County. For four years he made his home with his aunt, Mrs. C. P. Kingsbury, and worked in the Kingsbury printing plant at 408 Felix Street. In 1886 he became a member of the old Board of Trade, located at Third and Edmond streets, Mr. W. D. B. Motter being the secretary. Mr. Mooers had the distinction of being the youngest

once left the city to enter the field of country newspaper work as owner and publisher, in which he was engaged for over twenty-two years, his last venture being at Florence, Ala., where he published the Florence Herald for five years.

During all of this time the call of St. Joseph was sounding in the ears of Mr. Mooers, and in 1909 he obeyed the summons and moved back to this city. At the time he left he possessed

H. E. MOOERS

member of the club at that time. During the time of his stay in St. Joseph he was an active worker in the Y. M. C. A., then located at the northwest corner of Fifth and Edmond streets, now occupied by a saloon. J. W. Hansel was the secretary. He was a member of Christ Church, and took an active part in its affairs, being one of the ushers.

In 1887 Mr. Mooers married Miss Mary E. Crowley, the then youngest daughter of Judge and Mrs. Thomas M. Crowley of Andrew County, and at

only a wife and a stout heart, and he brought back with him a family of two sons and two daughters, the daughters and one son now being married, with homes of their own.

Soon after his return to St. Joseph, Mr. Mooers accepted the position of manager of the Trust Book & Credit Company, which he retained until February 15, 1914, when he resigned to accept the position of industrial commissioner of the Commerce club, which position he now holds. In this work he has been remarkably successful, having been instrumental in bringing a number of valuable industries to the city, as well as assisting materially in the upbuilding and progress of St. Joseph, in which he has had the hearty co-operation of a live committee.

Mr. Mooers has always been associated with the Northwest Missouri Press Association ever since his starting in the newspaper work, and is now a member of the local associa-

St. Joseph, was born February 7, 1832, in Jassamine County, Kentucky, and is a great-great-grandson of Jacob Sodowski (as the name was spelled in the early days), who was the founder of Sandusky, Ohio. The subject of this sketch attended the rural schools when young, and on the home farm learned the various branches of agriculture. He came to St. Joseph in 1855, when this city was on the extreme frontier. He worked on a

OLIVER A. SANDUSKY, SR.

tion. He is a member of the Francis Street Methodist Church, a member of the board of stewards, chairman of ushers, and in charge of the public comfort of the church.

Mr. Mooers is a booster for St. Joseph, first, last and all the time, and can ever be found in the forefront of everything pertaining to the growth, progress and upbuilding of the city.

OLIVER A. SANDUSKY, SR., a retired and respected business man of

farm in Andrew County for a time, and after his marriage to Serelda A. Potter, in 1857, he took up farming as an occupation. In a few years they were owners of a well-stocked farm. Mr. Sandusky enlisted in Company M of the Ninth Regiment, Union army, in 1863, was captured at Glasgow, Mo., paroled at St. Louis, and was honorably discharged at the end of the war. He immediately returned to this city and opened a grocery store. In 1867 he embarked in the fruit and produce business and built up an extensive and profitable trade. He retired from active business in 1913.

Mr. and Mrs. Sandusky have no children of their own, but have brought up and educated a nephew and a niece. The nephew, Oliver A. Sandusky, Jr., is now a business man in St. Joseph, and the niece, now Mrs. James S. Polk, also lives in the city.

Mr. and Mrs. Sandusky celebrated

Jamesport, Mo. He came to St. Joseph in 1906 and has been connected with some of the leading wholesale and retail drug houses in the city. He has been largely instrumental in bringing the city health department up to its present state of efficiency, being considered one of the most tactful men who ever held the position of clerk of that department. Fraternally Mr. Harrington is a Mason and an Elk. He is unmarried.

WILLIAM E. HARRINGTON

their golden wedding in 1907. They are members of the Francis Street Methodist Church.

WILLIAM ELLIS HARRINGTON, clerk of the board of health, was born in Christian county, Illinois, Sept. 14, 1881. He was reared on a farm and came with his parents to Missouri when a lad. After receiving his education he took up the study of pharmacy in 1900, and later engaged in the drug business in King City and

ALBERT B. DUNCAN, judge of the probate court and one of the prominent members of the Buchanan County bar, was born in a log house in Green township, Platte County, Missouri, April 17, 1862. He is a lineal descendant of John Duncan, a Scotchman who immigrated to Virginia at an early date and founded one of the best families of that commonwealth. His father, Richard F. Duncan, one of the pioneers in Platte county, was born in Culpepper County, Virginia. His mother, whose maiden name was Sara A. St. John, was born in Platte County, Missouri.

graduated in June, 1886, with the degree of A. B. He came to St. Joseph the same year and associated himself with the law firm of Woodson &

Judge Duncan was educated in the public schools and in William Jewell College, from which institution he was Woodson. He was elected a member of the city council in 1891, and served two years. He was prosecuting attor.

ney from 1894 to 1896.

In 1900 he was elected to the legislature, and was re-elected in 1902. He was one of the leaders in both sessions, and still has many friends throughout the state, which he made while serving in the state's law-making body. Besides serving on some of the most important committees, he was speaker pro tem of the house during the last session he served. He was elected probate judge in Novem-

ERNEST V. CUMBERFORD, cashier of the Security Bank of South Park, is a native of Missouri, having been born in Platte County, October 22, 1876. He attended the schools of the community in which he was reared, and later attended the Chillicothe Normal School, where he graduated in 1894. In 1895 he went to Edgerton and engaged in the banking business. He remained there eight years, and in 1903 went to Hill City,

ERNEST V. CUMBERFORD

ber, 1914, which office he is now holding.

He was married to Mrs. Emma Witherspoon, September 9, 1900. They have one daughter, Alta. Judge Duncan has memberships in the various Masonic bodies, being past potentate of Moila Temple, the Eagles, Elks, Red Men and Modern Brotherhood of America.

Kan., where he was connected with a bank for six years. He came to St. Joseph in 1911, and was made cashier of the Security Bank.

He was married to Miss Mabel Sturgis of Terrin, Mo., in 1900. Their family consists of three sons. Fraternally, Mr. Cumberford is a Mason an Odd Fellow, a Red Man and Woodman.

MURRAY C. KALIS, pharmacist and chemist, conducts two modern, twentieth century drug stores, the Kalis Pharmacy, situated near the stockyards at 403 Illinois Avenue, and the Bartlett Park Pharmacy at 1310 South Twenty-seventh Street. Mr. Kalis began his apprenticeship in a retail drug store at the early age of thirteen. He studied pharmacy at the St. Louis College of Pharmacy, 1896-7.

Aside from his activities as a retail druggist, Mr. Kalis is probably best known as a manufacturer of pharmaceutical preparations. His pharmaceutical laboratory is considered one of the best equipped in Northwest Missouri.

He is regarded by his many friends as a man of sterling character and genial disposition. "Keep on the sunny side of the street" is a favorite slogan

MURRAY C. KALIS

Later he attended the St. Louis College of Physicians and Surgeons. He tired of the dissecting room and clinics, and journeyed to New York City, where he took a post-graduate course in chemistry. Returning to St. Louis in 1900, he engaged in the retail drug business, in which he was successful. Ten years later he moved to St. Joseph.

with him, and he practices what he preaches—most of the time. Books and out-door recreations are his hobbies. When you fail to find him at home or either place of business, you probably will locate him somewhere out in the open, absorbed in some volume of Plutarch's Lives, Emerson's Essays or Hubbard's Little Journeys.

G. M. BRINTON was born March 10, 1854, on a farm in Dallas County, Texas, and moved with his parents, Bryant and Emily Brinton, to Jefferson County, Kansas, in 1855. The family moved to Buchanan County in 1861 and located near Agency in the neighborhood known as "The Pocket." They moved to Johnson County, Nebraska, in 1865; back to Buchanan County in 1867, and lived on a farm

He came to St. Joseph in the spring of 1898, leaving his family in Warrensburg until their education was complete. He was first employed by the Artesian Ice Company and in July, 1900, went with the John S. Brittain Dry Goods Company, with which concern he has been identified ever since. Mr. Brinton's family consists of four sons and three daughters, five of whom are living. Mr. Brinton is

G. M. BRINTON

near Agency until the subject of this sketch was twenty-one, when he went to Doniphan County, Kansas, and engaged in farming with his brother. He moved to Andrew County, Missouri, in 1876, and in December of the following year was married to Miss Maggie Lewis of Union Star, Mo. Mr. Brinton moved to DeKalb County in 1885 and in 1897 went to Warrensburg to obtain the educational advantages of that town for his children.

president of the Central Taxpayers' League and of Taxpayers' League No. 1, organized in March, 1913, for the purpose of defeating the proposed establishment of Prospect Park and the park and boulevard system in St. Joseph. The league, through his efforts, was successful in this as well as in preventing the issue of bonds in 1915 for public improvements. He was an independent candidate for mayor on the Taxpayers' ticket in the spring of 1914, but was unsuccessful.

JOHN L. ZEIDLER, real estate and insurance agent and concrete contractor, at Fourth and Francis Streets, is a native of Pennsylvania. He was born at Scranton, December 24, 1861. He was educated at Hoboken Academy, New Jersey, and Muehlenberg College at Allentown, Pa. He came to St. Joseph in 1881 and engaged in business for himself in 1885 and has since been active in the business life of the city. He was married to Jose-

for sewers and road culverts and has developed a satisfactory pipe in size from six inches to six feet in diameter, both plain and reinforced concrete. He was the inventor of the machine using a revolving head for making bell and spigot end plain concrete sewer pipe. It is known as the Pioneer Process, and the machine is made by the Pioneer Manufacturing Company of Waterloo, Iowa. Mr. Zeidler is president of this company.

JOHN L. ZEIDLER

—Photo by Mulvane.

phine Wanger in May, 1885. Fraternally he is a Mason, an Eagle, and an Elk. He holds a life membership in the St. Joseph Gymnastic Society.

Mr. Zeidler learned the baker's trade in Scranton with his father, but never followed it, as he preferred other fields of activity. Since 1909 he has given much time and attention to the manufacture of concrete pipe

He is the man who first suggested to the owners of the Union Street Railway Company in 1887 that electricity be used as the motive power. Mr. Steinacker, then general manager of the traction company, became interested and made a trip to Scranton to investigate the proposition. He was so well pleased with what he saw that Mr. Zeidler's plan was adopted.

DR. HARRISON S. FORGRAVE was born in Richland, Iowa, September 13, 1873. He lived at Leon, Iowa, until 1890, when he removed with his parents to St. Joseph. He was graduated from Central high school in this city in 1893. He studied medicine for four years, graduating from Central Medical College in St. Joseph in 1897. He first located in Corning, Mo., where he gained his first experience as a College). After a prolonged course of study he returned to St. Joseph and re-entered the practice of medicine and surgery. In 1913, accompanied by his wife and three children, he went abroad and spent a year in the famous clinics of Europe, studying in London, Paris, Berne, Berlin and Vienna. The doctor's work is largely confined to surgery and gynecology and consultation. He was president of the

DR. HARRISON S. FORGRAVE

practitioner. He was married in October, 1907, to Miss Jessie Chesney, daughter of Dr. J. Portman Chesney, a prominent physician of St. Joseph. He practiced in Corning for two years and then after an extensive post graduate course in New York and Baltimore he located in St. Joseph. In 1906 he removed, temporarily, with his family to Chicago, where he entered the medical department of the Chicago University (Rush Medical St. Joseph-Buchanan County Medical Society in 1908. He is a member of various other medical and surgical societies. The doctor is also surgeon for the Chicago, Rock Island & Pacific Railway Company and attending surgeon at the Ensworth and St. Joseph hospitals. The doctor and Mrs. Forgrave have three children, Harrison S., Mary C., and John R., all of whom were born in St. Joseph.

HOMER C. KING, attorney, rooms 15-16, Donnell Court, was born in Ohio, February 4, 1890. He came with his parents to St. Joseph while yet quite young, and was educated in the common schools. In 1910 he entered the Kansas City School of Law and was graduated from that institution in 1913. He came at once to St. Joseph, and began practicing, and has been one of the most active members of the

County, Michigan, July 3, 1846. His father was the Rev. Paul Shepherd, and his mother's maiden name was Asenath Mack. Mr. Shepherd received his education in Dover and Adrain, Mich., and for five years clerked in a drug store in Adrain. In 1870 he went to Troy, Kansas, where he opened a drug store, which he conducted for five years. He then came to St. Joseph and was business manager of the

HOMER C. KING

—Photo by Mulvane.

Buchanan County bar ever since. He is one of those live, energetic, young fellows, who allows nothing to daunt his aspirations and hopes, and who expects nothing in this life but success. Fraternally Mr. King is an Odd Fellow.

WILLIAM M. SHEPHERD, three times mayor of St. Joseph, and a prominent Republican politician in his day, was born at Nedina, Lenawee

Herald for several years. In 1880 he was appointed assistant postmaster under Col. Tracy, where he remained until 1884, when he again assumed control of the business affairs of the Herald. He was elected mayor of St. Joseph as a Republican in 1890. He gave such good satisfaction that he was re-elected in 1892 and again in 1894. Retiring from office Mr. Shepherd became connected with the Barber Asphalt Company until 1898, when he was appointed deputy revenue collector. Mr. Shepherd stood high in Masonic circles and was a member of the Chapter, Royal and Select Masters, Knights Templar and Nobles of the Mystic Shrine. He died in Denver, Colo., Sept. 20, 1899.

CHAS. L. WIEHL was born at St. Louis, Mo., on the 17th day of April, 1853, and came with his parents to

with Robt. Douglas he held a junior partnership, which was dissolved on Dec. 31, 1888.

During the summer of 1889 Chas. L. Wiehl, with the counsel and assistance of the late Col. B. B. Frazer, organized and established the Park Bank of St. Joseph, Mo., at the corner of Tenth and Penn Streets. He was elected cashier of the bank and served as its cashier until the death of

CHARLES L. WIEHL

St. Joseph in the summer of 1856. He has resided here continuously ever since. On February 18, 1867, he went to work for the Robt. Douglas & Bro. glass and queensware concern, and remained with Robt. Douglas, the senior member, for twenty-two years, the last eleven years of his association

Col. B. B. Frazer on Aug. 30, 1899, when he was elected to serve as president of the bank, and is acting in that capacity at this time.

Mr. Wiehl was married on May 22, 1888, to Cora V. Gerard, the eldest daughter of Dr. S. W. Gerard, at Hopkins, Nodaway County, Missouri.

WILLIAM EDWARD PENTZ, M. D., was born in St. Joseph, April 3, 1874, and attended the public schools of this city and Ensworth Medical College. He served two years in the Missouri State Hospital for the Insane No. 2 and in 1901 received appointment to the British Transport Service (during Boer war). Dr. Pentz made two trips to South Africa as chief surgeon for the transports Drayton Grange and Mechanician; returning to London he

reer.

His mother, whose maiden name was Euphema Dougherty, was born at Danville, Kentucky. Her father was a practicing physician and Baptist minister.

ROBERT MONROE ABERCROMBIE, secretary and manager of the Abercrombie Stone Company, was born in New York City, Janu. 14, 1856, the son of James Abercrombie. He attended schools in New York City, Hol-

DR. WILLIAM E. PENTZ

spent seven months in hospital service there.

John Edward Pentz, father of the subject of this sketch, was one of the pioneer business men of St. Joseph, coming here from the city of his birth, York, Penn., in 1872. He had taken up the study of medicine with an uncle who was a practicing physician of Philadelphia and had taken one term at Jefferson Medical College, but gave up medicine for a business ca-

brook, Long Island, Montreal, St. Joseph and Breckenridge, Mo. He came to Missouri in 1866 and lived at Breckenridge till 1878, when he removed to St. Joseph, going into the stone-cutting business with his father. He was for four years a member of the St. Joseph city council; was appointed a member of the State Board of Charities for the second time in January, 1899; served one term as representative in the State Legislature. Mr. Abercrombie is a prominent Odd Fellow and has held every office in the order, including grand maste of the Grand Lodge of Missouri. He married Miss Rosaline M. Bailey of Breckenridge.

THOMAS F. RYAN, judge of the Criminal Court of Buchanan County, was born in Ireland, and when but a small boy came with his parents to Missouri.

Mr. Ryan's father engaged in farming in Andrew County. Thomas re-

chise ordinance granted to the street railway company to operate its cars by electricity and the contract for the electric lighting of the city were prepared. In 1893 Governor Francis appointed him police commissioner for the term of three years. At the expiration of that term he was reappointed to the same office by Governor Stone. He was elected judge of the criminal court for a term of four years in 1908, and was re-elected

JUDGE THOMAS F. RYAN

ceived his early education in the district schools, and later graduated from the Christian Brothers College of St. Joseph. After his graduation, he took up the study of law, and was admitted to the St. Joseph bar in 1874. In 1882 he was elected prosecuting attorney of Buchanan County, which office he filled with marked ability. In 1886 he was appointed city counselor by Dr. Thomas H. Doyle, then mayor of St. Joseph. Under his supervision as city counselor the fran-

to the same office in 1912, having no opposition for the nomination and receiving the largest majority ever given to a judicial officer in this county.

In politics Judge Ryan is a Democrat and has ever been active and loyal in the support of his party.

He is a logical and forcible speaker and possesses a keen anaalytica mind. He has the faculty for analyz ing facts and applying reasoning and precedent to them. He has strong executive ability and is universally known as a man of undoubted courage and rugged honesty, and in the discharge of every public trust reposed in him his aim has ever been to ascertain what was right, and then to fearlessly perform his duty regardless of whether or not his action met with popular approval.

It is generally conceded that Judge Ryan is one of the ablest judges that has ever presided over the Criminal

diction as judge of the Juvenile Court, have won for him the name of friend and father of the unfortunate boys and girls.

JOHN S. BOYER, attorney-at-law, 805 Corby-Forsee Building, is a native Missourian and was born in Buchanan County, December 28, 1870. His common school education was received in the community in which he was reared. Later he graduated from the Christian Brothers College at St. Jo-

JOHN S. BOYER

Court of Buchanan County. But it is his work as judge of the Juvenile Court that appeals to him most strongly—for it is there that he feels he has done his most effective work and accomplished the greatest results for the uplift of humanity. His kindness of heart and his strong common sense so wisely exercised in the disposition of the thousands of cases of unfortunate and neglected children that have been settled under his juris-

seph, the Missouri University, and the law department of Washington University at St. Louis. He began practicing in St. Joseph in partnership with John D. McNeely. He is now referee in bankruptcy for the St. Joseph division of the United States District Court. He has served one term as city attorney, and has also held the position of assistant prosecuting attorney for one term.

DR. FREDERICK ELISCU, 720 Francis Street, was born in Roumania, in 1868. He is the son of Samuel and Julia (Sharaga) Eliscu, and is one of a family of eight children, all of whom became prominent in the professions. The eldest, Dr. Eugenie R. Eliscu of New York City, is a physician and psychologist of national reputation; a sister, Fernanda Eliscu, tragedian of national reputation; Edmund Eliscu has attained fame as a playwright and

New York Post-Graduate in 1898, and in the New York Polyclinic in 1907. He occupied the chair of chemistry and diagnosis at the Central Medical College, St. Joseph. He is a member of the Masonic fraternity and the B'nai B'rith society. Doctor Eliscu has practiced in St. Joseph since the fall of 1893. He enjoys a good general practice, and has a reputation as a diagnostician all over America.

He was married in 1906 to Miss

DR. FREDERICK ELISCU

—Photo by Mulvane.

a writer of short stories; a brother, Julius, and a sister, Rose, are artists of distinction. Doctor Eliscu, after receiving his education at Stefan, Cel Mare, Roumania, came to the United States in 1898. He received the degree of Ph. G. from the New York College of Pharmacy and Chemistry in 1891, and of M. D. from the Northwestern Medical College in 1893. He took the post-graduate course at the

Rose Speer of Lincoln, Nebr., to which union three daughters have been born.

PURD B. WRIGHT, former librarian of the Free Public Library, was born near Weston, Platte County, Missouri, Sept. 4, 1860. His father died in 1865, and, with his mother, he moved in 1867 to Cameron, where he went to school and worked on a farm until sixteen, when he learned the printers' trade and was for nine years on the

Vindicator, as printer, reporter and editor. He came to St. Joseph in 1883 and was city editor of the Herald, resigning in April of 1885 to become city clerk, which position he held until 1895, under Mayors Hartzig, Doyle, Englehart and Shepherd. He was instrumental in establishing the Free Public Library; was secretary of the Commerce Club in 1895-96; and was librarian for three years. He was married to Miss Lulu M. Floyd at

ber, was a native of Virginia. Mr. Stauber attended Lewis College, Glasgow, Mo., from which he was graduated in 1879. He read law and practiced first in Brookfield, but in 1883 came to St. Joseph, where for many years he has been the senior member of the firm of Stauber, Crandall & Strop, which has a very extensive and lucrative practice. Mr. Stauber is an active Republican and is prominent in politics. Never asking for an office

RALPH O. STAUBER
—Photo by Mulvane.

oux City, Iowa, in 1885. Mr. Wright now in charge of the public library Kansas City.

RALPH O. STAUBER, attorney, is native of Martinsburg, Va., where was born June 2, 1859. His father, l. T. J. Stauber, was an editor, and mother, Margaret (Burwell) Stau-

for himself, he is a power in his party, and in the past has been very close to national administrations, where his judgment and sagacity were esteemed.

Mr. Stauber was married June 20, 1888, to Miss Anna M. Carter of St. Joseph. Their family consists of two daughters.

OZRO H. MULVANE

OZRO H. MULVANE, photographer, at 810 Frederick Avenue, is a native of Ohio. He was born in Newcomerstown, and with his parents moved to Newman, Ill., at the age of six years. In 1875 he went to Lincoln, Neb., where he served an apprenticeship in photography. He has been in bus ness in St. Louis and Kansas City, Mo., Cedar Rapids, Iowa, and Lead, S. D. He came to St. Joseph from Kansas City in 1911, and began business at his present location.

He was married to Miss Jennie Sinclair of Lincoln, Neb., in 1909. Fraternally he is a Woodman of the World.

GEORGE G. STARMER, politician, at 1612 Commercial Street, is a native of Worth County, Missouri, where he

In 1900 he went to the stockyards and was made chief of police at the Hammond packing plant. He remained there a year and a half, and then engaged in business on his own account at his present location. He is a Red Man and a Woodman of the World.

CHARLES BLOOMFIELD EDGAR is a native Missourian and was born in St. Louis, where he attended the public schools, and later the Transyl-

GEORGE G. STARMER

—Photo by Mulvane.

was born April 6, 1852. In 1866 he came with his parents to Buchanan County, where he was educated. In 1879 he went to Bozeman, Montana, where he remained seven years. In 1886 he returned to St. Joseph and ngaged in business as a plastering ontractor. In 1896 he was appointed eputy in the office of Sheriff Hull, hich position he held for four years.

vania University of Lexington, Ky. He began his editorial career in the university, where he was editor of The Collegian, the monthly publication of the students.

Mr. Edgar was educated for the ministry, and preached for some years in Missouri, Kentucky, and Brooklyn, N. Y., but during those years he was always connected with the press. In

October, 1894, he became president and editor of The Daily News (now The News-Press) of St. Joseph. At that time the paper was losing money and was but a small affair of about 4,000 circulation, but under his management it grew to be the largest and best paper in the city. In 1898 The News purchased the two morning papers, The Gazette and The Herald, and hyphenated them, publishing them as the morning edition of The

Aurora, daughter of Judge W. B. Drescher of Hannibal, Mo. They have a daughter, Miss Helen, and a son, Joseph Carl Edgar.

WILLIAM GORDON was born in Aledo, Ill., in the year 1877. He attended the schools of his native state, and in 1894 removed with his parents to Iowa, where his education was completed. In 1900 he came to St. Joseph and was employed as a draughtsman in the office of E. J. Eckel, architect,

WILLIAM GORDON

News for more than a year, when Mr. Edgar sold them to Lewis Gaylord and associates.

In 1905 Mr. Edgar sold his interest in The News, which thereafter was consolidated with The Press, and bought an interest in The Star of Lincoln, Neb. Four years later he sold that interest and bought three afternoon papers in Oklahoma City, which he consolidated in one, The Times.

Mr. Edgar married, in 1882, Miss

and later with Eckel & Mann. After a few years he associated himself with Ben. W. Trunk. They opened an office on South Eighth Street. The firm of Trunk & Gordon now has offices in Rooms 8, 9 and 10, Donnell Court building, where they have been located since 1909. The firm enjoys a large practice from the surrounding country in Missouri, Iowa, Kansas and Nebraska, as well as in St. Joseph where they have been employed for many public and private buildings.

SAMUEL I. MOTTER, attorney-at-law, rooms 712-14-16 Corby-Forsee Building, is a native of St. Joseph, the date of his birth being November 7, 1874. He attended the public schools the autumn of that year he entered the University of Michigan's law department, and was graduated in 1899, receiving the degree of LL.B. He returned to St. Joseph and was admit_

SAMUEL I. MOTTER

of the city, and was graduated from Central High School in 1891. He entered Yale the same year, and received the degree of A.B. in 1896. In ted to the bar in the fall of 1899, and at once entered the practice of law in St. Joseph, and is now engaged in the general practice. He was appointed assistant prosecuting attorney in 1901, and was appointed member of the public library board in 1910. He was elected member of the school board in 1914, and is still an active member of that board.

Mr. Motter was married to Miss Susan Jane Brittain of St. Joseph in 1910. They have one daughter, Susan Brittain Motter. He has membership cards in the Masons, Elks and Red Men.

been successful in building up a large and profitable business. He gives of his time and means to the promotion and advancement of any worthy public enterprise and delights in seeing St. Joseph become more and more a better town. He was married to Miss Allie M. Carnes of Galt, Mo., in 1897. Fraternally he is a member of the Knights of the Maccabees. He is a son of the late Joseph McInerny, a prominent citizen and politician.

DR. JOSEPH M. McINERNY

DR. JOSEPH M. McINERNY, 515½ Edmond Street, was born in St. Joseph, February 19, 1873. After attending the primary schools he went to the Christian Brothers College in St. Joseph and St. Mary's College in Atchison, Kansas. Then he entered the Northwestern Medical College in St. Joseph and received his diploma in 1893. Two years later he took a post-graduate course in Rush Medical College of Chicago. He began practicing in St. Joseph in 1898 and has

WILLIAM D. RUSK, attorney, was born in Woodford County, Kentucky June 15, 1850, and his parents were also Kentuckians. He came to St. Joseph in 1856 and after going through the high school completed a course at Phillips' College, Exeter, New Hampshire, graduating in 1872. Returning to St. Joseph, he taught in the high school for six years, being principal from 1877 to 1882. He began practicing law in 1882, and was married October 16, 1884.

HENRY KRUG, JR., was born in St. Joseph, July 9, 1861. Educated in the public and high schools of St. Joseph, he entered the packing business when but sixteen years of age, and gained the benefit of the excellent training under the supervision of his father and uncle. He was one of the organizers of the German-American Bank in 1887, when he was made vice-president, a position which he continued to hold until 1913, in that year No. 1105 Krug Park Place.

On May 18, 1892, Mr. Krug was married to Miss Selma Hegner of St. Joseph, prominent in the social life of the city. Mr. and Mrs. Krug have no children, but have reared two children whom they adopted.

DR. ARTILEUS V. BANES was born near Zanesville, Ohio, February 19, 1845, where he received his primary education; came to St. Joseph in April, 1858, with his step-father, the

HENRY KRUG, JR.

succeeding to the presidency. He was one of the organizers of the St. Joseph Stock Yards Company in 1887, and is also largely interested in a number of important commercial enterprises. Mr. Krug is a deacon in the First Presbyterian Church, of which the family have always been members. His social connections include membership in the St. Joseph, Country, Benton and Commerce Clubs. The pleasant family home is located at late Judge John A. Dolman. He took a classical course with Professor E. B. Neely of St. Joseph, and in 1860 went to Denver and later to Montana, where he was successful in mining for four years. Returning to St. Joseph, he read medicine, was graduated from Jefferson College, Philadelphia, in 1868, and has become celebrated in his profession. He was married in Philadelphia, March, 1873, to Miss Bessie Davis.

JOHN P. FREEMAN, JR., was born in Winfield Junction, Queens County, Long Island, New York, November 15, 1865. He came to St. Joseph in August, 1885, and at once took up the plumber's trade, serving his apprenticeship with M. E. Herbert, at 616 Felix Street. He was married to Miss Mary G. Conniff in the St. Joseph Cathedral, September 29, 1892. Mr. Freeman removed to Mexico, Mo., in 1893, where he engaged in business, Quebec, Canada, Nov. 30, 1841. His father, David Lawlor, a carriage maker, and his mother, whose maiden name was Margaret Sullivan, were born in Ireland, and came to the province in 1830. After learning the printers' trade, Mr. Lawlor went to New York and thence to Liberty, Clay County, Missouri. He came to St. Joseph in 1872 and entered the employ of the Steam Printing Company, where he worked first as compositor

JOHN P. FREEMAN, JR.

but returned to St. Joseph in 1901. For many years he was identified with the union labor movement, serving as president of the plumbers' organization and also of the Central Labor Council. He was appointed city plumbing inspector by Mayor William E. Spratt in April, 1905. He was re-appointed by Mayors Clayton and Pfeiffer and served until the spring of 1915.

MICHAEL LAWLOR, publisher of the Catholic Tribune, was born at and then as superintendent. In 1893 he purchased a half interest in the Catholic Tribune, which he retained for three years. In 1894 he became the sole proprietor of this publication, which has prospered under his able guidance. At Liberty, Mr. Lawlor married Miss Margaret McCormick, daughter of Thomas and Dorothea (Alexander) McCormick. Nine children—four boys and five girls—were born into this union.

WILLIAM T. LETTS, proprietor of box factory and cooperage works, is a native of England, where he was born May 17, 1851. His parents were George T. and Mary (Knight) Letts. Mr. Letts was schooled and learned his trade of box making in England and came to America in 1882, locating in Chicago, where he remained two years and then came to St. Joseph, where he has since built up a profitable business in the manufacture of

only to Joseph Robidoux, the founder of the City of St. Joseph, in the early history of the city, and who lived to see it expand and spread out over the large body of land he pre-empted adjacent to the original town site, was Frederick W. Smith. Captain Smith was born October 3, 1815, in Prussia. He received his early education in his native town and afterwards entered a military academy, where he was educated as a civil engineer. When eigh-

WILLIAM T. LETTS

—Photo by Mulvane.

all kinds of packing boxes and cooperage. Mr. Letts is one of the most enterprising of St. Joseph's citizens. Before leaving England Mr. Letts met and married Miss Elizabeth Palmer, in 1871. Of this union nine children were born, six boys and three girls. Mrs. Letts died in 1899. In 1900 Mr. Letts married Mrs. Reid Arnnol of St. Joseph.

FREDERICK W. SMITH, second

teen years of age he sailed for America. Landing in New York in 1833, he remained there almost a year, and then removed to New Orleans, where he was employed in a cotton press. Owing to the breaking out of the yellow fever in that city, he embarked on the Mississippi River, and came to St. Louis, where soon after his arrival he was appointed Deputy City Surveyor. In 1838, or 1839, he left St.

Louis for the Platte Purchase and settled at Blacksnake Hills (now St. Joseph). Here he engaged in farming and surveying. He made the original map of St. Joseph and named it after the founder of the city, Joseph Robidoux. Captain Smith pre-empted lands, upon which a portion of the city now stands, and which has been divided and sub-divided and sold at different times. He was a captain of of the militia for a number of years,

public spirited man, and Smith Park, which he gave to the city, perpetuated his name.

CHARLES L. FAUST, attorney-at-law, was born April 24, 1879, in Logan County, Ohio. He moved with his parents to Kansas when a year and a half old, and his early years were spent on a farm near Highland. He began his education in the common schools of the community in which he was reared, and attended Highland

CHARLES L. FAUST

and was afterwards made a major of the state volunteers; was appointed the first postmaster of the village of St. Joseph; in 1861 he was elected mayor of the city; his last office was that of judge of the Buchanan county court, his term ending in 1876. He married Miss Jane Tolin, of Daviess County, Missouri, in 1843, who died shortly before her husband. Captain Smith died May 7, 1883. He was a

University from 1892 to 1898. He taught the Winona district school, three miles west of Highland, from 1898 to 1900, and in the latter year entered the State University of Kansas, graduating from the law department in 1903. He finished the course with honors, being president of his class at graduation. During two years of the time spent in the University, and during vacation periods, he studied in the office of Judge John Q. A. Norton, leader of the Douglas County bar. Mr. Faust came to St. Joseph in October, 1903, and has practiced law here uninterrruptedly since that date. He was appointed city counselor in April, 1915. Fraternally he is a Mason and an Elk.

LEWIS C. GABBERT, lawyer, in the Corby-Forsee Building, was born January 21, 1874, in Platte County. He is the son of George B. and Alice

latter being given him as winner of the Kentucky Inter-Collegiate contest in 1895. He was elected prosecuting attorney of Buchanan County in 1902, and during the year 1907 was president of the Monroe Club, the local Democratic organization. He was married in Louisville, October 5, 1897, to a daughter of Judge N. Sandifer of Lancaster, Ky. They have three children, Benton S., Lewis C., Jr., and Virginia Lee.

LEWIS C. GABBERT

—Photo by Mulvane.

Layton Gabbert. He finished his college education in 1897 from the Center College, Danville, Ky., having previously attended the Missouri State University and William Jewel College. Mr. Gabbert gained distinction as an orator at college, receiving two gold medals and a cash prize of $50, the

CHARLES M. BETTS, real estate agent, 716½ Edmond Street, was born in Otsego County, N. Y., June 27, 1852. His father, Roderick C. Betts, a farmer, was born in Maryland. His mother's maiden name was Johanna P. Wilson; she was a native of New York State. The family went to

Bloomington, Ill., in September of 1865, and returned to New York in August of 1873. Our subject was educated in the district and common schools and then learned the machinists' trade; came to St. Joseph March 13, 1875, and has resided here continuously since, with the exception of two years; worked as a machinist in the shops of the Kansas City, St. Joseph & Council Bluffs Railroad Company for ten years, and then went to Wal-

the sophomore class of the University of Chicago in October, 1897. Mr. Betts is a Republican in politics, though not a strict partisan.

FRANCIS W. BRAND, plumbing inspector, was born in Pierce City, Mo., October 23, 1875, and came with his parents to St. Joseph in 1884. He was educated in this city and in Portland, Ore., where the family afterward lived. He began his apprenticeship in the plumbing trade in 1893, and

FRANCIS W. BRAND

nut, Texas, where he remained for two years; returned to St. Joseph in 1887 and embarked in the real estate business, in which he has been successful. Was married Oct. 10, 1876, in St. Joseph, to Miss Mary A. Estes, born Jan. 15, 1855. They have one child, Otie E. born Dec. 14, 1877, who graduated from the St. Joseph high school, class of 1896; entered the freshman class of the Northwestern University, at Evanston, Ill., in September, 1896, and

for several years worked here and in Omaha, until April, 1915, when he was appointed city plumbing inspector, which office he is filling quite acceptably. He was married in 1899 to Miss Anna Marie Falk. They have a family of three children. Fraternally Mr. Brand is an Odd Fellow and Woodman of the World. He has always taken an interest in organized labor, and holds the office of secretary of the St. Joseph Central Labor Council.

CHARLES C. CROW

A former St. Joseph attorney, now of Kansas City, and a candidate for judge of
the Kansas City Court of Appeals.

FREDERICK NEUDORFF, president of the Neudorff Hardware Company, 114 South Fourth Street, St. Joseph, Mo., was born in Platte county, Mo., July 5, 1859. His father, Louis Otto, was born in Germany, and his mother, whose maiden name was Arnold, was born in Alsace, then a province of France. About 1863 he was brought to St. Joseph and has resided here ever since. He attended the public schools until 11½ years old, and for forty-five years has been located in the same block as employe and owner —since 1887 in business for himself. Mr. Neudorff served two terms on the school board, vice-president one term. He has been a member of the park board, and for practically fifteen years he has been president of the St. Joseph Retail Merchants Association, as well as numerous other semi-public positions without pay. He is independent in thought about religion, politics and public duty, a positive optimist, believes in service and humility. Mr. Neudorff was married to a daughter of Rev. H. Fiegenhaum and at her decease married his present wife, a daughter of Frederick Bauer. He is the father of six living children. He loves his home, friends, music, literature and art in its various expressions, and has been considered by his friends as a fairly useful citizen. Dewey Avenue Boulevard and the extension of Blacksnake sewer are largely due to his faith and energy. Mr. Neudorff is a positive man who loves sincerity, dislikes sham and pretense.

FREDERICK NEUDORFF.

HARRY E. WYATT, president of the Drovers and Merchants Bank, Lake Avenue and Cherokee Street, was born in Atchison county, May 1, 1869. He was educated in the schools of his native county and in 1886 served a year in the office of the probate judge in Rock Port. Having a desire to become a banker he engaged with the Bank of Atchison County in 1888 in the capacity of clerk and book-keeper. He held this position until

union. He was again married April 9, 1913, to Mrs. Mary Baker of St. Joseph. They have one child, an interesting little daughter. Fraternally Mr. Wyatt has memberships in the Elks, Masons and Knights of Pythias. He has been an important factor in the growth and upbuilding of the Drovers and Merchants Bank, of which a recent writer said: "The wide experience of its officers in the making of careful loans is of inestim-

HARRY E. WYATT

1902, when he was promoted to the office of cashier. He held this post until 1908, when he came to St. Joseph to accept the presidency of the Drovers and Merchants Bank, which office he still holds, to the general satisfaction of the large number of patrons of the bank.

Mr. Wyatt was married to Miss Mary Sly of Atchison county, June 24, 1891, who died in July, 1909. Two children, both sons, were born to this

able value to the bank's patrons. The officers are well known and have the highest standing in business and financial circles of the state, and are ever ready to offer responsible persons financial service of the highest character."

REV. WILLIAM HARMON LITTLE, Baptist minister, was born in Buchanan county, September 7, 1868, one mile northwest of what is now the town of

Dearborn, then known as Lick Skillet. After completing the work of the common schools he finished his education in William Jewel College at Liberty, Mo. While yet a young man he learned the trade of carpenter and later served as constable of Center Township. He was a deputy under Sheriff Andriano in 1900. Rev. Little lived on a farm one mile north of Old Sparta for twenty years and was for a time assistant to the postmaster at Adams postoffice.

and Missouri Avenues, is a native of Illinois. He was born in Bloomington, July 12, 1873. His parents moved to Denver when he was ten years of age and most of his early education was received there. In 1890 he entered the Louisville Medical College and graduated from this school in 1894. After graduation he entered the St. Luke's Hospital in Denver as an interne, where he remained one year, and in 1895 he located in La Junta,

DR. ARTHUR R. TIMMERMAN

He was married to Miss Jennie Laston in 1896. They have two children, Gladys and William Jewell. Fraternally he is a Mason and an Odd Fellow. He has been in the ministry since 1903 and was pastor of the Baptist church at Beloit for three years.

DR. ARTHUR R. TIMMERMAN, physician and surgeon, with offices in the Odd Fellows building, King Hill

Colo., where he was engaged in the practice of his profession for ten years. He came to St. Joseph in 1904 and opened his present office. He was surgeon for the Stock Yards Company 1906-08. He was married to Miss Leonora Hall, of Pueblo, Colo., in 1895. They have one son, Arthur, fourteen years old. Fraternally Dr. Timmerman is a Mason and Knight of Pythias. He is a member of the Buchanan County, Missouri State, Missouri Valley and American Medical Societies and of the Academy of Surgery of St. Joseph.

VICTOR SCHWIEN, dealer in fancy groceries and liquors at 416 Felix Street, is a native of Alsace, France, and his parentage was German and French. He was born August 1, 1865. He came with his parents to America in 1866, first locating in Chicago, Ill.,

to Miss Amiela Dietz of Weston, Mo. They have five children, all sons.

RANDOLPH T. DAVIS, one of the foremost men of the community in his day, was born December 26, 1837, in Buchanan County, the son of Ishmael and Nancy (McDaniel) Davis, who were among the first settlers of Buchanan County. Our subject attended such schools as there were in those days, and at the age of sixteen entered the Western high school to prepare for

VICTOR SCHWIEN

where he was educated. He came to St. Joseph in 1880 and engaged with H. C. Boller in the hardware business for four years, and later was associated with James Horigan in a plumbers' supply business. He devoted five years to this last mentioned pursuit. In 1888 he and Patrick Nevin purchased the business of Textor Brothers, at the present location of Nevin & Schwien.

Mr. Schwien was married in 1893

college, but his father having lost heavily by the default of an official upon whose bond he was, the young man was disappointed. Having aided his father in recovering the homestead our subject then purchased the Union Mills in Platte County, and this venture was successful. Desiring wider field, he sold the Union Mills and came to St. Joseph, purchasing an interest in the City Mills at Third and Antoine Streets, forming a partnership with Isaac Van Riley; in 1876 he became the sole proprietor. In 1883 the present large modern mill of the R. T. Davis Mills Company was built and Mr. Davis was at the head of this business until his death. Politically, Mr. Davis was a staunch Democrat. He was county collector in 1878-82, and was elected to the state senate in 1882, but resigned after serving in one session. He took great interest in the advancement of St. Joseph and

ilies of which Buchanan county is justly proud. He was born on a farm near DeKalb, September 19, 1883. His early education was in the schools of Buchanan county, and in 1901-2-3 he attended the Warrensburg State Normal school. The following year he took up school teaching in Doniphan, Kans. Later he taught one year in Buchanan county, Mo. In 1905 he went with the DeKalb State Bank as bookkeeper, which position he held for one

WILLIAM E. THOMPSON

was a leader in movements for the public welfare. It was his ambition to be mayor, and he made unsuccessful efforts in 1888 and in 1890. He was married first in February, 1859, to Miss C. L. Bordston, who died in 1861, and again in 1863 to Miss Mary J. Bordston, his first wife's sister. He died Dec. 14, 1894.

WILLIAM E. THOMPSON, cashier of the Drovers and Merchants Bank, comes from one of those splendid fam-

year. In 1906 he was elected cashier of the Bank of Faucett, Faucett, Mo., in which capacity he served two years. In 1908, when the Drovers and Merchants Bank needed a careful, thorough and conservative man for cashier, Mr. Thompson was elected, and he has since filled the office to the entire satisfaction of all concerned. He was married to Miss Mary E. Albus of St. Joseph in 1910. They have one child, a son. Fraternally Mr. Thompson is a Mason, an Elk and Knight of Pythias. Of the bank with which he is connected a recent publication said: "Guided and managed by citizens of sterling worth, character and integrity, properly describes the Drovers and Merchants Bank. This reliable financial institution has had a steady growth in strength and usefulness since its inception, and today is recognized as one of the best banking institutions in our city.

vania, June 28, 1859. His father, Ellis Chandlee, was a school teacher and also a native of Pennsylvania. Mr. Chandlee was educated in the common schools of York county, and learned the trade of paper hanger. He came to St. Joseph in 1877 and worked at his trade for a time. Later he engaged in business for himself. He is a Democrat, and his political experience is confined to membership in the city council, where he once repre-

EDMUND G. CHANDLEE

"This bank does a general banking business and is equipped with every service and convenience for the accurate handling of all the business entrusted to its care, and enjoys the confidence of our citizens in every walk of life."

EDMUND G. CHANDLEE, proprietor of one of the largest and best wall paper and paint stores in the city, was born in York County, Pennsyl-

sented the Sixth ward.

Mr. Chandlee was married in 1883 to Miss Catherine Stern.

THEODORE STEINACKER, civil engineer, born May 4, 1853, at St. Louis; came to St. Joseph in 1858 and was educated in St. Joseph High school and Rensselaer Polytechnic Institute, Troy, N. Y., graduating from the latter in 1873. Mr. Steinacker was county surveyor from 1881 to 1888, and was again elected in 1896.

MAX ANDRIANO was born at Mannheim, Germany, in 1855, and after obtaining his education, came directly to St. Joseph to live with his uncle, Albert Andriano. He remained here until 1874, when he moved to the East, and in 1875 he entered the United States army, where he spent five years on the northwestern frontier, then known as Dakota Territory. He served under General Otis at Standing Rock, Indian Agency, and at

(By Max Andriano)

God bless St. Joe, the Pearl of the West,
The Real City Worth While.
For of all kind hosts she has proved the best,
To extend the glad hand with a cheerful smile.
Her fame extends beyond her bounds By miles and miles of space.
No matter where man makes his rounds,

MAX ANDRIANO

Fort Abraham Lincoln as headquarters clerk, also as chief clerk in the quartermaster's department under General J. Franklin Bell; also at Fort Rice. After the terrible massacre of General Custer's command in 1876, he helped to disarm the Sioux Indians.

Mr. Andriano has been continually engaged in the banking business in St. Joseph since 1881, and is now connected with the First National Bank of this city in an official capacity.

He cannot find a better place.
When nature planned for mother earth
A glorious resting place to find—Where hope and faith might find its birth,
To bless the choice of human kind.
The compass with Utopian guide Placed in Dame Fortune's hand,
Pointed quickly with most gleeful pride
Upon God's chosen land.

For the God of the winds whispered
  to the Dame—
"Where the waves of the great Missouri flow,
The good, the brave and the faithful
  shall go
  To dwell forever in glory and
  fame."
Where the grass is green the whole
  year long,
  The breezes on angel's wings bring
  health;

This cradle of heroes and princes of
  trade,
  Of men fit for life's every station;
And women, whom God, like lilies in
  beauty has made,
  None better in all this great nation.
Such is our great city, in short called
  St. Joe,
  The best spot in all this great land;
Where peace and plenty, good cheer
  and content,
  Forever go hand in hand.

JOHN T. OVERBECK

—Photo by Mulvane.

Where the heart is thrilled by the
  feathered tribes' song,
  Where honest labor brings comfort
  and wealth.
Where the spirit of love is breathed
  in the air,
  And friendship extends its brotherly
  hand
To the downtrodden races of every
  land,
  And God's blessing hand is felt
  everywhere.

I have now resolved forevermore
  To keep my mind and heart content,
To bask in the sun of Missouri's shore,
  Where kind Dame Fortune has
  pitched my tent.
December 18.

JOHN T. OVERBECK, dealer in
fancy groceries at 901 Frederick Avenue, is a native of Platte County and
was born November 17, 1875. He was
educated in the schools of Platte
County, and came to St. Joseph in

1894. He was first engaged by the Schuster-Hax Bank, and later by the First National, as clerk. He held this position for four years, and in 1898 began railroading, which pursuit he followed for ten years. He engaged in his present business enterprise in 1914. Fraternally Mr. Overbeck belongs to the Elks, Moose, Eagles and Knights of Pythias.

DR. LOUIS C. BAUMAN, with offices in the Lincoln Building, is a na-

cians of the city and as his success has come wholly through his own efforts, it is well deserved. He was in the drug trade here for twelve years, commencing in 1889 with the Van Natta-Lynd Drug Company.

ELWOOD L. McDONALD, president of the Midland Printing Company, his literally grown up in the printing and publishing business. He was born in Holt County, Missouri, August 21, 1869, and was educated in a district

DR. LOUIS C. BAUMAN

tive Missourian, St. Joseph being his birthplace, and the date January 19, 1875. He was educated in the schools of St. Joseph and in 1896 graduated from the Northwestern University of Chicago, pharmacy department. In 1900 he entered the Central Medical College, from which institution he was graduated in 1904. He began the practice of his profession in St. Joseph at once and has been here ever since. He is one of the rising young physi-

school. When but a lad he did odd jobs to earn enough money to buy a small hand-lever printing press, a crude little affair which he still retains as a souvenir as his early efforts. In 1889 he began a regular apprenticeship in the office of the Holt County Sentinel, at Oregon, Mo. Later he came to St..Joseph and worked in the principal shops in the city until 1895 when he changed to the news gathering and editorial branch of the business. His first reportorial work was done on the Daily News. Then he changed to the Gazette and participated in the stirring campaign of 1896, when the late Col. Cochran, then editor of that paper, was elected to congress. In 1899 he was made city editor of the Gazette, and later served as Sunday editor and managing editor. He was appointed deputy city clerk in 1901 and in 1911 engaged in the printing business as one of the pro-

116 South Sixth Street, is a native of Andrew County, Missouri. He came to St. Joseph in 1905 and began his business career with the Empire Trust Company the same year. He is one of the exceptionally successful young business men of St. Joseph and his future is full of promise.

FRANK W. BEACH was born in St. Joseph, June 8, 1869, his parents being James T. and Harah H. (Foote) Beach. Mr. Beach was educated in

CHARLES E. WRIGHT

prietors of the Midland Printing Company and has been active in the development of the concern since that date. From 1913 to 1915 he was also in the printing business in South St. Joseph. He was married November 17, 1896, to Miss Ida V. Kunkel of Oregon. Their family consists of a son, Daniel K., and two daughters, Mary Madeliene and Lillian Josephine.

CHARLES E. WRIGHT, vice-president of the Empire Trust Company,

St. Joseph, and has held several important positions. He was deputy sheriff under Joseph Andriano, and in 1898 was nominated by the Republican party for representative from the Second district. He made a very creditable race in a strong Democratic district, being defeated by a very small majority. He was appointed city clerk by Mayor Combe in 1901 and served until 1905. He is now a resident of Texas.

GRAHAM G. LACY, vice-president of the Tootle-Lemon National Bank, was born in Spootsylvania county, Virginia, August 8, 1858. He is the son of Major James Horace Lacy, and comes from one of the most representative and distinguished Virginia families. Mr. Lacy was reared on the old homestead plantation, and his early education was received under the direction of private tutors. He attended the Virginia Military Institute at Lexing-

When the business was reorganized and incorporated as the Tootle-Lemon National Bank in 1912, he became vice-president, which position he still occupies. Mr. Lacy is also president and treasurer of the St. Joseph & Grand Island Railway Company, and a director in the St. Joseph & Savannah Interurban Railway Company and the Aunt Jemima Milling Company, and president of the Westminister Improvement Company of St. Joseph. He

GRAHAM G. LACY

ton, and came to Missouri in 1880. He first located in Sedalia, where he read law and was admitted to the bar in 1882. He came to St. Joseph the same year and engaged in the practice of his profession. In 1889 he associated himself with the private banking house of Tootle, Lemon & Company, which was organized in July of that year. He was first assistant cashier, and the following year was advanced to the important position of cashier.

is a member of the Benton Club, the Country Club and the Highland Golf Club, and an elder in the First Presbyterian Church. Mr. Lacy was married November 11, 1886, to Miss Ellen Bell Tootle, daughter of Thomas E. and Ellen (Bell) Tootle of St. Joseph. They have six children, Agnes Churchill, wife of Ericc Moore of Rochester, N. Y.; Mary Graham, wife of George E. Porter of St. Louis, Mo.; Lucy L., Bibi E., Ellen Tootle and Graham Gordon, Jr.

CHARLES DILLON MORRIS, publisher of the St. Joseph Gazette and a man of marked attainments and wide experience, has achieved success in his work and gained a position of note among his fellow men solely by his own efforts. He is a native of Ohio and was born at Buena Vista, Scioto county, where he spent his boyhood days. He attended the common schools of Ohio until fifteen years old, when he came to Missouri and attended a

he published for thirteen years as a daily and weekly newspaper. In 1904 he once more sought a larger field of endeavor and in company with E. E. McJimsey and John E. Swanger bought the St. Joseph Gazette. He has since purchased nearly all of the stock of his former partners and is the sole manager and publisher of the paper. The Gazette has prospered under his management as has every other newspaper with which he has

CHARLES D. MORRIS

private school at Quitman, Nodaway County, earning his board by doing chores for August Johnson, with whom he made his home. He began teaching at the age of eighteen and after one term in a district school became principal of the Quitman schools, where he served two years. He then purchased the Quitman Record and published it for three years. Desiring a larger field, he sold the Record and bought the Trenton Tribune, which

been connected. Mr. Morris was married December, 1889, to Miss Mary Gladdice Cox, a daughter of Rev. John H. and Nannia Cox. Mr. and Mrs. Morris have two children, Earl D., and Edwin L. Mr. Morris cast his first presidential vote for James G. Blaine, and for many years has been active in local, state and national politics. He has been chairman of the city, county, congressional and state Republican committees. Missouri went

Republican three times while Mr. Morris was connected with the state committee. He was appointed postmaster at Trenton by President McKinley and re-appointed by President Roosevelt, but resigned before the end of his term in order to devote his time to his personal affairs. He has been president of the St. Joseph Commerce Club and has always been in the forefront of any move calculated to advance the interests of his chosen city.

Vegas, New Mexico, and engaged in the banking business. He remained there four years and was reckoned one of the most successfu' men in this field of endeavor in that part of the country. Desiring a change, however, he accepted a position as traveling salesman, which avocation claimed his attention and efforts until 1901, when he went to East St. Louis and again engaged in banking. He came to St. Joseph in 1911 to accept the office of

JAMES E. COMBS

Fraternally Mr. Morris is an Elk, a Mason, an Odd Fellow and a Knight of Pythias.

JAS. E. COMBS, cashier of the First National bank, was born in Collinsville, Ill., May 6, 1867. His early education was in the schools of his native city and he was graduated from the Carbondale State Normal in 1887. After leaving college he went to Las

cashier in the First National Bank, the position he holds. He was married to Miss Nannie Powell, a daughter of Dr. A. M. Powell, of Collinsville, Ill., April 30, 1891. They have an interesting family of three children, two sons and one daughter. Fraternally Mr. Combs has membership cards in the Masons, Elks, Royal Arcanum, Modern Woodmen, Red Men and Knights of Pythias.

WILLIS H. SHERWOOD, insurance agent, at 402 Francis Street, is a native of North Carolina. He was born at Wilmington. His parents were Willis M. and Charles C. Sherwood. They were New Yorkers and removed with their family to St. Joseph in 1858. Here the subject of this sketch was educated. In 1864 he entered the tin shop of Jack Fraley, on the west side of Market Square, where Chase's matic coffee and tea economizer and distiller. In 1877 he returned to St. Joseph and engaged in the manufacture and sale of his tea and coffee urn and afterwards placed the manufacture of the same with Manning & Bowman of Meriden, Conn., and with Duparquet & Hus of New York. He took a position as traveling salesman with Manning & Bowman. He remained on the road for ten years and

WILLIS H. SHERWOOD

—Photo by Mulvane.

candy factory now is located. He served an apprenticeship as coppersmith, heavy sheet iron worker and tinner. In 1873 he was foreman for C. H. Schultz, afterwards Schultz & Hosea. In 1874 he went to Waco, Tex., and took charge of the large hardware and tin house of Fred Quarles, and remained two years. While there he patented the great Sherwood auto- then returned to St. Joseph and took charge of the insurance business of his father, Willis M. Sherwood, which business has claimed his attention ever since. He was married Feb. 4, 1912. He resides at 1822 Jones Street in a lovely home built on ground that was originally a part of the old Sherwood home place.

EMORY M. PLATT, principal of
Platt's Commercial College, in the
Bartlett Building, was born in Manhattan, Kans., November 4, 1865. He
attended the State Agricultural College at Manhattan and later took a
course in a college in Oberlin, Ohio.
He removed to Topeka, where he remained until 1891, when he came to
St. Joseph and engaged in the sale of
typewriters, later establishing the

ly upon the success of these in later
years for their reputation and standing in the educational world. Such
methods cannot help but leave a lasting and pleasing effect upon the
people.

Every parent of our city should con-
gratulate themselves because of being
a resident in the vicinity of Platt's
Commercial College, at which their
boy or girl may be equipped for life's

EMORY M. PLATT

Platt Commercial College, of which he
is president. He is a man of culture,
fully competent to assume charge of
the important position, and has served
in this capacity with ease and given
the utmost satisfaction to all concerned.

The Platt Commercial College has
made it a policy to give the young
people such a sound and thorough education and training, depending large-

struggles.

In politics Mr. Platt is a Republican.
He was married in St. Joseph, August
9, 1891, to Miss Elizabeth Landon
Prescott, and they have two children,
Emory Melzar Platte, Jr., and Evart
Platt.

PHILLIP STROP is a native of
Ohio. His father, Christopher Strop,
a baker, was a native of Germany.
His mother, whose maiden name was

Margareth Klein, was a native of France. Mr. Strop was engaged in brickmaking here for many years, and has furnished the material for many of the best buildings in the city. He is the father of Hon. Charles F. Strop, ex-judge of the circuit court.

GEORGE ADNEY NELSON, cashier of the Burnes National Bank, is a native of Missouri. He was born near Weston, in Platte County, April 3,

tail, he applied himself assiduously to every task given him, and the inevitable result was a rapid rise to more important positions. As a result of this rigorous early training he is now reckoned one of the best men in the banking business, not only in St. Joseph but in the Middle West. So well was his ability recognized that when the Burnes National Bank was organized in 1906 he was selected for

GEORGE ADNEY NELSON

1871. His early education was received in the public schools of Platte county and later he attended the High school in St. Joseph and the Missouri State University. In 1893 he began his business career, filling the meek and lowly position of messenger for the State Bank, which institution he served faithfully and well until it quit business. Determined to learn the business thoroughly in its every de-

the important position of cashier, and his efforts have been a material factor in the growth of this financial institution. Mr. Nelson was married to Miss Lucy E. Merriam of St. Joseph, June 17, 1896. They have four children, Fred M., Emma E., Nora C., and Roy F. He is a Mason, an Elk and a Woodman. He is a member of the Benton Club, Country Club and Monroe Club.

DR. GEORGE M. BOTELER, with offices at 825 Frederick Avenue, is a native of Missouri, and was born in St. Joseph June 10, 1887. In 1897 he went with his parents, Dr. and Mrs. William C. Boteler, to Frederick, Maryland, where he was educated. In 1906 he entered the Central Medical College and was graduated from that institution in 1910. He at once began practicing in St. Joseph, and in 1911-12 was city physician. He was also

announcement that this industry is to revived after an idleness of several years, brings Mr. Buell's early activities to the fore.

Mr. Buell's father was a manufacturer of woolens and it was in his father's mill that he mastered the details of the industry. He came to St. Joseph in 1848 and first started a small sawmill on the Blacksnake. Later he had a flour mill at Weston. This did not agree with his health and

DR. GEORGE M. BOTELER

physician for the Social Welfare Board for three years. He is a grandson of George W. McCrary, who was secretary of war under President Hayes.

GEORGE W. BUELL, one of the men who have made St. Joseph industrially, was born in Rodman, Jefferson County, New York, and died in St. Joseph July 4, 1900. He was the founder of the Buell Woolen Mills on South Eleventh Street, and the recent

he returned to St. Joseph and started a woolen mill on the site of his old sawmill. It proved profitable from the beginning.

At the solicitation of John S. Lemon, who had acquired a woolen mill at Blue Rapids, Kans., and others, Mr. Buell incorporated the Buell Manufacturing Company, of which he became president and held the office until his death. Though Mr. Buell was handicapped in many ways by the lack

)f experience on the part of the other directors, his skillful management proved equal to all emergencies and the company soon had a capital stock of $200,000. The products of this mill were sold in every part of the United States and Alaska. The plant used a million pounds of wool a year and gave employment to 175 men and women. A new plant costing a quarter of a million dollars was erected in 1882. It covers seventeen acres and

again, and there appears no reason why its prosperity of a few years ago should not be duplicated.

BERNARD MORAN, capitalist, 731 South Fifteenth street, is a native of Connecticut. He was born December 10, 1847. At the age of three years he went with his parents to Berlin, Wis., where he was educated. He was pilot on the Mississippi River from Warsaw, Wis., to St. Louis, Mo., and Dubuque, Iowa, for ten years. He came

BERNARD MORAN

or many years was one of the leading industries of St. Joseph.

After the death of Mr. Buell the property fell into other hands, and owing to difficulty in securing raw material and for other reasons, its operation was discontinued. Recently a company, headed by some eastern men of experience, has been formed, with ample capital to start the mill

to Missouri in 1869, locating in Maryville. He first engaged in farming, in which he was more than ordinarily successful. He served as road-overseer for eight years, and in 1890 was elected sheriff of Nodaway county for one term of two years. Mr. Moran was married to Laura E. Beckett of Maryville, October 16, 1867. To them has been born six children, five of whom are living. Mr. Moran is a Woodman of the World and is prominent in his activity in behalf of the Catholic church, of which he is a communicant. Since coming to St. Joseph he has been one of the most enterprising citizens here and has ever shown his interest in the growth and advancement of the city of his adoption.

EUGENE H. ZIMMERMAN, cashier of the Tootle-Lemon National Bank,

The Central Savings Bank was located on Edmond Street between Sixth and Seventh, and Mr. Zimmerman went to it as its assistant cashier. He remained with this institution until it liquidated in 1898. The following year he accepted the position of assistant cashier of Tootle, Lemon & Company, private bankers, and when this business was nationalized in 1904 under the name of the Tootle-Lemon National Bank. Mr. Zimmerman was ap-

EUGENE H. ZIMMERMAN

was born in St. Joseph, Missouri, June 12, 1871. He attended the public schools of this city and entered the banking businss with Schuster, Hax & Company, Bankers, at Third and Felix Streets, in 1887, as a messenger boy. He remained with this bank until 1890, then went with the Central Savings Bank, an institution affiliated with the Schuster-Hax National Bank, which had succeeded to tue private banking business of Schuster, Hax & Company.

pointed its cashier.

Mr. Zimmerman was married in February, 1901 to Miss Rufina McDonald, of St. Joseph.

Fraternally he is an Elk and holds memberships in the Commerce Club and the Country Club. He served as president of the St. Joseph Clearing House in 1913, and is now president of the St. Joseph Credit Men's Association and a director in the Y. M. C. A.

WILLIAM L. PATRICK, at 420 South Sixth Street, is a native of Missouri. He was born in Oregon, Holt County, February 13, 1865. At the age of thirteen he went west, locating in Nemeha County, Nebraska, where he received his education. He came to St. Joseph in December, 1899. He entered the employ of Graham, Lake & Stringfellow, as machinist, and remained with them seven years. In 1896 he went with the Hudnut Mill-

for many years general manager of the Townsend & Wyatt Dry Goods Company. He was born in St. Joseph August 11, 1845, and died here in November, 1911. He was the son of Hon. Joseph J. and Emily M. (Gooding) Wyatt.

Mr. Wyatt received his educational training in the public schools of St. Joseph, and in 1860, embarked in business. In 1875 he became a member of the firm of Townsend & Wyatt, which

WILLIAM L. PATRICK

ing Company, remaining one year. In 1897 he began business on his own account.

Mr. Patrick holds membership cards in the K. of P., Eagles, Moose and Red Men. He was married to Miss Clara Ramsey of Johnson, Neb., in 1889. They have four children, three daughters and a son.

JOHN CAVAN WYATT, a prominent and successful business man, was

in 1890 was reorganized as the Townsend & Wyatt Dry Goods Company, and has since been changed to the Townsend, Wyatt & Wall Dry Goods Company. This establishment is classed with the great department stores of Missouri. It was to the wise management of Mr. Wyatt that much of its development was due. His ability as a business man was universally recognized and honest business methods gained for him the highest respect of the people. He served as a member of the Board of Education and the City Council, was a trustee in the Y. M. C. A., president of the Robidoux Building and Loan Association and president of the Mt. Mora Cemetery Association. He was an active member of the First Christian Church and served faithfully as a member of its board of trustees.

Mr. Wyatt was married to Miss Kate

was educated in Georgetown University, where he studied for the priesthood. He studied law in the office of Judge Edwards and his brother, James Moran.

He came to St. Joseph in 1880 and plunged at once into the thick of politics and law. He was elected to the state senate in 1887. After serving four years he retired voluntarily, refusing to make the race again. He

MICHAEL G. MORAN

Girrard, in 1875, in Lexington, Ky. Mrs. Wyatt died in St. Joseph in 1889.

MICHAEL G. MORAN, for years a noted figure in the public life of St. Joseph, and a lawyer and politician with a fame that was almost nation wide, was born in Berlin, Wisconsin, January 5, 1858, and died in St. Joseph, August 30, 1915.

Senator Moran came with his parents to Nodaway County in 1869. He

ran for the Democratic nomination for congress twice, but was defeated. While in the state legislature he was the author of the law creating the metropolitan police system. He was an active figure in the campaign when the present city charter was adopted and in the only recall election ever attempted in St. Joseph, when an effort was made to recall Mayor Pfeiffer

LEE C. BROOM, proprietor of Lee Broom's Restaurant at 420 Francis Street, was born in Zanesville, Ohio, November 9, 1879. At the age of two years he came west with his parents, locating in Topeka, Kans., where he was educated. He has engaged in the restaurant business since the age of fifteen years. His first position was that of bell boy at the Benton Club. Before coming to St. Joseph the second time he was superintendent of

Shelbyville, Ill., in 1901. They have one child, a son.

CELSUS C. CALVERT, city editor of the News-Press, was born on a farm near Weston, Mo., Feb. 25, 1862. His father, James M. Calvert, and an uncle, were the proprietors of the St. George Hotel at Weston, one of the famous hostelries of Missouri river steamboating days. His father afterward conducted the old Virginia House in Platte City, and in 1871 the

LEE C. BROOM

he eating houses on the Gould System of the Iron Mountain and Missouri Pacific railroads. Mr. Broom first came to St. Joseph when fourteen years old. His first position was that f day clerk at the Benton Club. He hen went to Kansas City and was uperintendent of service at the Kanas City Club. Later he opened the niversity Club in that city, where he emained until he went with the Gould ystem. He returned to St. Joseph nd was married to Miss Sylvin of

family removed to Atchison, Kans. When he was sixteen years old Celsus Calvert entered upon a newspaper career, starting as city circulator of the Atchison Patriot, a Democratic afternoon daily published by H. Clay Park and Thomas J. Stivers. Displaying a fondness for news gathering and writing, he soon was made a reporter. After two years of newspaper experience, he entered the Atchison postoffice as register clerk. Two years later, although of pronounced Democratic ancestry, friendship with the late Senator John James Ingalls of Atchison obtained for him an appointment as railway postal clerk on the old Atchison & Nebraska (Burlington)˙ road, between Atchison and Columbus, Neb. Although he was not of age, Calvert enjoyed the distinction of being the only person of Democratic antecedents in the mail service in Kansas—possibly in the United States—for it was fashionable at that

covered the Thirty-fifth Missouri General Assembly, in 1891, for the paper, when Colonel Cochran was serving his first session as state senator from Buchanan County. In August, 1891, he went to the St. Joseph Daily News, of which C. M. Shultz was publisher, and, with the exception of one year spent in the south as a representative of the Illinois Central Railroad Company, has been employed by the Daily News and the News-Press as reporter

DR. E. A. GUMMIG

time to appoint only tried and true Republicans to these much-coveted positions. But the newspaper instinct asserted itself and he resigned after two years on the road to return to the Patriot as city editor. In May, 1888, he was offered a position as reporter on the St. Joseph Gazette, by the late Col. C. F. Cochran, who was publishing that newspaper then, and who had known Calvert as a boy in Atchison. Calvert worked for the Gazette something more than three years, having

or city editor continuously ever since He was married June 10, 1895, to Miss Emma K. Gates of St. Joseph, and one child was born to them, which died in infancy.

DR. E. A. GUMMIG, room 121 Corby-Forsee building, was born i Wathena, Doniphan County, Kansas September 14, 1883. He attended th schools of Wathena and graduate from the Wathena high school in 190 and graduated from the St. Joseph Business University in 1905. In 191

ie entered the Ensworth Medical Col.
ege and graduated therefrom April
0, 1914. He was interne in the Ens.
vorth Hospital from March 1, 1913, to
arch 1, 1914, as junior, from the lat.
er date until March 1, 1915, as senior.
ifter graduating, he commenced prac.
cing, and the future looks bright for
im. His lodge memberships are in
ie Odd Fellows and Woodmen of the
orld. He is a member of the Bu-

of employment to take up the surplus
energy with which all ambitious boys
are endowed. He decided that the
street railway company offered ex.
cellent advantages and in 1902 became
connected with the company in the
capacity of clerk. That he was not
mistaken in his decision that there
was a chance for advancement in the
company's service is evident from the
fact that in a few years he had been

CHARLES E. FOSTER

ianan County and the Missouri State
edical Societies and the American
edical Association.

CHARLES E. FOSTER, secretary
d treasurer of the St. Joseph Rail-
y, Light, Heat & Power Company.
a native Missourian. He was born
Chillicothe, February 20, 1877. He
ne with his parents to St. Joseph in
i9 and here his education was com-
ted. When he had finished school
began casting about for some form

promoted to the post of assistant sec-
retary-treasurer and in 1913 was made
the head of this important department.
Mr. Foster was married to Miss Anna
Sims, of Platte City, in 1899. One son,
Charles E. Jr., has been born to them.
Fraternally he is an Elk and a Mason.
He is a member of the Patee Park
Baptist church. He is the son of W. T.
Foster whose reliable weather fore-
casts have made him famous.

WALTER H. ROBINSON, comes
from an old and prominent family of
Virginia. He was born in Rappahan-
nock County, March 4, 1862, and traces
his lineage back to one of the best
families in Scotland. He received his
early education in the rural schools
and also attended Flint Hill Academy.

in the automobile business, making a
remarkable success of that venture.
Mr. Robinson was married to Miss Ida
L. Yocum in 1890. They are the
parents of two sons, Kenneth and Edwin Bryan. Mr. Robinson was appointed a member of the Board of Police   Commissioners   by   Governor

WALTER H. ROBINSON

He began teaching school at eighteen
and in 1881 came to St. Joseph. He
first engaged as a salesman for the
Brady Carpet Company and advanced
to the position of manager. Later he
and his brother, Benjamin C. Robinson, succeeded to the business. Mr.
Robinson sold out in 1909 and engaged

Stephens and reappointed by Governor
Dockery. He has served two terms
as president of the Monroe Club and
at the present time is a very promising
candidate for the Democratic nomination for Mayor of St. Joseph. Fraternally he is a Mason, K. of P. and an
Elk.

ADOLPH GOERMAN, vice-president of the Sturgess, Ellingwood & Goerman Dry Goods Co., is a native of Germany. He was born in Ham province, Westphalia, May 30, 1861. He was educated in Germany and served an apprenticeship in the mercantile business in that country. He came to America in November, 1881, coming direct to St. Joseph. He started with the Townsend & Wyatt Dry Goods Company, January 4, 1882, with which

the Turners.

SOLOMON LEONARD, a pioneer judge of the circuit in which Buchanan County was located, was born in Ohio in 1811 and was one of the early settlers in Platte County. He was first a school teacher and then a lawyer and farmer in Platte County. In 1843 the state of Missouri was entitled to 500,000 acres of public land, and our subject was one of the commissioners to select this land. Subse-

ADOLPH GOERMAN

concern he remained twenty-four years and three months. He worked himself up from cash boy to stockholder in this company in a period of eight years. In 1906 he became identified with his present company. He was married to Miss Elizabeth Wildberger of St. Joseph in 1888. They have one ---d, a daughter. Mr. Goerman is a member of the Odd Fellows, Elks and

quently he located in Buchanan County, a few miles east of St. Joseph. In 1845 he was appointed judge of the circuit court upon the resignation of Henderson Young, and served until 1852. He then formed a law partnership with Bela M. Hughes. In October of 1861 he was drowned near Fort Gibson, I. T., while journeying on horseback to Texas.

DR. L. S. LONG, the subject of this sketch, was born in Longswamp, Berks County, Pennsylvania, August 12, 1871. Educated in the grammar schools of the township, attended the Keystone State Normal school at Kutztown, Wyoming Seminary at Kingston, Pa., University of Pennsylvania, and graduated in medicine and surgery at Baltimore Medical College in 1892. Came to St. Joseph and associated with an uncle, Dr. A. S. Long, a pio-

Chicago Post Graduate Medical School Laboratory of Dr. Zeit, New York Post Graduate, New York Lying-in Hospital. Served as president of the Rochester Surgical Club in 1913. Assistant City Health Officer of St. Joseph 1897-98. Member of Mystic Shrine, York Rite and Scottish Rite Masonry.

CHARLES J. L. MAY, who has been engaged in newspaper work in St. Jo-

DR. L. S. LONG

neer physician of St. Joseph, who devoted most of his talents to the subject of orficial surgery and rectal diseases. Married to Meta Bode, 1898. Two children, Eleanor and Mildred Long. Office 822 Edmond. President Zions Evangelical German Church, trustees 1914-1916. Member of American Medical Association, Missouri State Medical Association, St. Joseph-Buchanan Medical Society. Dr. Long has attended post-graduate courses at

seph a number of years, was born in Brunswick, Mo., July 28, 1874, and has been a resident of Missouri all his life. He was married to Miss Mary Albright of Kansas City, Kans., April 2, 1902. Five children were born, Frederick W., Elmer Lawrence, Alice Nona, Elizabeth H., and Carl Grogg May. Alice died in her eighth year. The others survive. May attended the public school of St. Joseph and is a graduate of Central high school.

CAVAN G. WYATT, of the Wyatt Fuel Company is a native of Missouri. He was born in Boone County, on the Bill Anderson battlefield, September 14, 1877. He came with his parents, Cavan Wyatt and wife, to St. Joseph when a child. He was educated in the schools of St. Joseph and immediately after leaving school, took up the active affairs of business and has been uncommonly successful. He was with the Townsend & Wyatt Dry Goods

daughters. Mr. Wyatt is a member of the First Christian church.

HON. CHARLES F. COCHRAN, member of congress from the Fourth District from 1896 to 1904, was born in Kirksville, Mo., September 27, 1848. The family moved to Lancaster and Weston, Mo., and Atchison, Kan., before our subject grew to manhood. In each of these points he attended the public schools and then learned the printers' trade. He continued to be

CAVAN G. WYATT

Company for nineteen years and participated in the growth and development of the business during that time. In 1911 he disposed of his interests there and engaged in the fuel business, taking charge of the Wyatt Fuel Company, 721-723 South Eight Street, and has been doing an excellent business ever since. He was married to Miss Catherine Hartwig, daughter of Ernest F. Hartwig, in 1901. They have an interesting family of two children, both

interested in newspaper work, as compositor or editor, until 1872, when he was elected justice of the peace in Atchison. He had spent his spare time studying law. He was elected prosecuting attorney of Atchison County, Kansas, in 1884, and served two terms. He early became interested in politics and espoused the cause of democracy with much zeal and fervor. He soon became known as one of the hardest-working Democrats in this section, and later, when he was sent to congress, he jumped at once into national prominence because of his exceptional ability as a debater and because of his comprehensive knowledge of public affairs. He became part owner and manager of the St. Joseph Gazette in 1886 and continued to direct its policy until 1896 when he was first elected to congress. He was elected to the state senate in 1890 and served four years.

of that city. In 1895 he embarked in the furniture business in Marion, which business he continued with success for fourteen years. He came to St. Joseph in 1908 and opened the store which he is still conducting. His success here has been due to his painstaking efforts, a determination to please every customer and to the strict adherence to sound business principles. He was married to Miss Francis E. King of Canada, in 1900.

SWAYZE A. LYON

Congressman Cochran was married to Miss Louisa M. Webb in 1874. They reared one son, Charles W., who is still a resident of St. Joseph. Congressman Conchran died in this city in 1906.

SWAYZE A. LYON, proprietor of the Lyon Furniture Company, Seventh and Charles Streets, is a native of Indiana. He was born in Loogootee, August 28, 1872. When yet an infant his parents moved to Marion, Ohio, where he was educated in the schools

Fraternally he is an Elk. Religiously he is a member of the Francis Street Methodist church.

CHARLES F. KLIPHARDT, pastor of First Church of the Evangelical Association, Sixteenth and Locust streets, was born at Wallace, Ontario, Dominion of Canada, May 11, 1878. At the age of nine he moved with his parents to Kansas, where he attended grade and high schools at Leavenworth, Peabody and Holton. He graduated from Northwestern College,

Napierville, Ill., in 1904, since which time he has served as pastor of different churches in Kansas and Missouri. He was appointed to St. Joseph in 1914. Rev. Kliphardt served many years as secretary of the Kansas Conference Missionary Society, an organization carrying on extended work throughout Missouri, Kansas, Oklahoma and Colorado. He did editorial work on the first volume of the History of the Kansas Conference, pub-

spot where the Metropole Hotel now stands. His father, Prestor T. Moss, was a Kentuckian; his mother (Susan Henry Beattie) was from Virginia. Mr. Moss has been engaged in the lumber business for many years and is a member of the Dougherty & Moss Lumber Company at Tenth Street and Mitchell Avenue. He was married in 1891 to Miss Mary Wood Leach, daughter of Lewis and Ellen J. W. Leach of St. Joseph; one girl, Cather-

JAMES B. FARBER

lished in 1915, and has been honored by his conference with appointment on some of her most important committees. For two years he was treasurer and a member of the executive committee of the Kansas Conference Branch young people's organization of his church. He was married July 17, 1906, to Miss Lydia Abbuehl of Valley Falls, Kansas, and has one child, Annetta Kliphardt.

JOSIAH BEATTIE MOSS, lumberman, was born in St. Joseph on the

ine Corby, and one boy, Preston Leach, were born of this union.

JAMES B. FARBER, seed dealer, at 725 South Fourth Street, is a native of Iowa. He was born in Chariton, September 16, 1856. He was educated in the schools of the town of his birth and came to St. Joseph in 1883. He engaged in the implement and seed business, the firm being known as Chesmore & Farber. He is now in the seed business exclusively. He was married to Miss Alice Ashford of St.

Joseph. They have one son, Reuel A. Farber, age 18, whose halftone appears on this page. Fraternally Mr. Farber belongs to the Knights of Pythias.

AUGUSTUS W. HORN, former city assessor and until recently a member of the board of public works, was born in St. Joseph in 1854 and is the son of the late John A. and A. L. (Horning) Horn. In 1870 Mr. Horn went to Kansas City, where he accepted a clerkship in a grocery store

subject of our sketch in 1890, and placed upon the market. It represents a considerable portion of the southeastern part of the city and much of the growth of that part of St. Joseph is due to his development efforts. He was first elected to the city legislative body in 1900. Later he served eight years as City Assessor and was appointed member of the Board of Public Works in the spring of 1915. This office he resigned eight months later

REUEL A. FARBER

and engaged in the clothing business a few years later. After thirteen years in this line he embarked in the grain and commission business, dealing also in real estate, and was recognized as a shrewd, reliable and leading business man of Kansas City. He returned to St. Joseph in 1892, as he had been made the executor of his father's estate. That part of the city known as "Horn Heights" was platted by the

on account of failing health. Fraternally Mr. Horn is a member of the Masons, Odd Fellows, Knights of Pythias, Red Men, Modern Woodmen and Ancient Order of United Workmen. Mr. Horn was married to Miss Lillie E. Bruce of Kansas City, who died a few years ago. One son, John A., lives in Omaha, where he has an important position with Swift & Company.

DR. WILLIAM W. WALKER, whose offices are in rooms 10, 11 and 12 of the Commercial Building Sixth and Edmond Streets, was born in Marion County, Illinois, June 29, 1861. He was educated in the common schools of Charleston, Ill., and later entered the Chiropractic School of Oklahoma City, from which institution he was graduated in 1908. After graduation he began practicing in Lincoln, Neb., where he remained six years. In 1914

was graduated from Coe College, Cedar Rapids, Iowa, in 1908, and after teaching two years in Earlham Academy, Earlham, Iowa, entered the Presbyterian Theological Seminary at Omaha, Nebr., where he graduated in 1913, and came to St. Joseph, Mo., as pastor of the Third Street Presbyterian church. He is now on a leave of absence from his church, taking work preparatory to the degree of Bachelor of Divinity.

DR. WILLIAM W. WALKER

he came to St. Joseph and opened his present offices. He was married to Miss Mattie McCracken, of Oklahoma City, in 1895. They have a family of five daughters. He is a member of the Masons, Odd Fellows, and the Brotherhood of Locomotive Firemen.

REV. E. J. NICKERSON, Presbyterian clergyman, pursuing post-graduate study in the Princeton Theological Seminary at Princeton, N. J., was born at Inman, Nebr., August 12, 1884. His boyhood days were spent in various towns in Nebraska, South Dakota and Iowa, completing the high school course at Malvern, Iowa, in 1903. He

DICK KLEINBRODT. — There are few men in the city better known among the good fellows than Dick Kleinbrodt. His buffet, the Sterling, at 416 Francis Street, is headquarters for those who care. It has a reputation for selling none but first-class goods, and the patronage it enjoys is proof positive that Mr. Kleinbrodt's methods are correct. Few men in the city have a larger circle of warm friends than he, and once a man becomes a friend of Dick Kleinbrodt he never has occasion to regret it. Mr. Kleinbrodt has the finest collection of deer, elk and buffalo heads in the city, which adds very materially to the attractiveness of his place and helps make it more homelike.

ORRILLIS E. SHULTZ, lawyer, was born in Henry County, his father being a farmer. He attended school at the Northwest Missouri College, at Albany, and at Clarence, Mo. Later he took a course in the Missouri State University, from which institution he was graduated in 1898. He came to

He was born at New Athens, Ohio, January 10, 1848. The Kennard family is of English origin and some of its members were among the early settlers of Pennsylvania. Our subject's father was a member of the Society of Friends, from which he was expelled for marrying out of the meeting.

George A. Kennard was quite young when he was taken by his parents to Omaha, Neb., where he grew to ma-

ORRILLIS E. SHULTZ

St. Joseph in June 1898, and at once began the practice of law. He was appointed assistant prosecuting attorney January 1, 1899, and served four years. January 1, 1907, he was appointed assistant city counselor by W. B. Norris and served until April, 1913. He has since been engaged in the general practice of law.

GEORGE A. KENNARD, deceased, was a prominent citizen of St. Joseph, where he was engaged in the wholesale grocery business for many years.

turity. He attended the common schools and later completed a course in bookkeeping. While a young man he located in Chicago, with Marshall Field & Company, with whom he remained until 1874, when he came to St. Joseph. Here he accepted a position as bookkeeper and served as such until 1877, when he embarked in the tea and spice business, as the senior member of the firm of Kennard, Willson, & Company. They transacted a large wholesale business and continued with success for a number of years. He then engaged in the wholesale grocery business, first in association with William G. Fairleigh and later by himself. He established an extensive patronage and continued the business for some time, then he sold out to good advantage to the Roberts-Parker Mercantile Company of St. Joseph. After disposing of his business he lived in retirement until his death on May 28, 1903.

was sent to school at St. Benedict's then a primitive academy, but which has since become famous in the West as a college. After having acquired the rudiments of English, German and Latin, he left school early in his thirteenth year, and went to work in a brickyard. Subsequently he labored in a boiler shop, was helper to a plumber, tried book-binding and the drug trade, and finally found congenial employment as "devil" in the com-

CHRISTIAN L. RUTT

CHRISTIAN LUDWIG RUTT, compiler and editor of the first History of Buchanan County, was born in Milwaukee, Wis., October 8, 1859, the son of Christian and Eva Katherine Gaiss) Rutt. His parents were both German, from the neighborhood of Stromberg, in Rhenish Prussia, a short distance from Bingen, on the opposite side of the Rhine. In September, f 1865, the family removed to Kansas, locating at Atchison. The boy

posing room of the Atchison Champion, then a prosperous morning newspaper, edited and published by the late Col. John A. Martin, afterwards governor of Kansas. As a journeyman printer, he traveled about the country after the manner of the journeymen printers of those days, until November of 1881, when he forsook the "case" for the editorial room, having been made telegraph editor of the Leavenworth Standard, then a morning paper, edited by ex-United States Senator Edgar G. Ross of Kansas. Subsequently he served in a similar capacity on the Leavenworth Times, under the late D. R. Anthony. In the summer, of 1882 he published a weekly paper at Atchison—the Sunday Morning Call—in partnership with Luther L. Higby. It was a losing venture, and he returned to Leavenworth and was city editor of 'the Standard until January of 1883, when he came to St. Joseph, Mo., and served as telegraph editor of the Gazette until the following June, when he accepted an offer from the Fort Worth (Texas) Gazette. He remained in Texas until the following December, holding positions on the San Antonio Express, the Galveston News, the Austin Statesman, and the Waco Examiner.

made manager of the Gazette-Herald, and when the paper was sold he was retained as managing editor, which place he held until August of 1902, when he resigned to take charge of a political department in the Daily News. In October, 1902, he was appointed managing editor of the Daily News, which place he retained at the consolidation of the News and Press, and which he holds at this time.

Mr. Rutt was married May 11, 1887, to Annie Herbst, daughter of George and Theresa Herbst. Mrs. Rutt is a native of St. Joseph. Like her husband, she is of German descent. Our subject's parents are dead, the father having died in St. Louis, Mo., December 29, 1895, and his mother in Boonville, Mo., December 21, 1900.

ROY A. LINDSAY

iner. Malaria sent him north, and he found a welcome at the Gazette, where he served as telegraph editor and city editor until May 1, 1887, when he was appointed secretary of the board of police commissioners, which position he held for thirteen years, during which period, however, he maintained a connection with the Gazette as editorial writer. In March, 1900, he was made editor-in-chief of the Gazette, and in June of that year was made manager of that paper. Two months afterward when the Gazette and Herald were consolidated, he was

Mr. Rutt is a Roman Catholic, and is a member of the Knights of Columbus, the Catholic Order of Foresters, St. Joseph's benevolent society organizations of that faith. He is also an active member of the Monroe Club (Democratic), and an honorary member of the Typographical Union.

ROY A. LINDSAY, attorney at law, was born in Davis County, Mo., September 21, 1888. He received a common school education in his native county and graduated from the Gilman High School in 1907. The same year he matriculated in the Kirksville

Normal and graduated therefrom in 1909. In 1910 he entered the law department of the Kansas State University from which institution he received his diploma in 1913. After leaving school he went to Springfield, Mo., where he opened an office, remaining there until January 1, 1914. He came to St. Joseph in June, 1914, and opened an office in Donnell Court. Mr. Lindsay is a Mason.

hanging. He came to America in 1854 and stopped first in Cincinnati. He worked at his trade for four months, and then went to New Orleans. He came from that city to St. Joseph by boat in 1855. He worked at his trade until 1860, when he engaged in business for himself. At the outbreak of the Civil War he suspended operations for a couple of years, but began again in 1863. His sons have grown

HENRY VOSS

—Photo by Mulvane.

HENRY VOSS, pioneer wall paper merchant of St. Joseph, has been in active business for upward of half a century. He has watched with satisfaction the growth of the city of his adoption from a mere village to a modern metropolis. Mr. Voss was born in the village of Pinneberg, Holstein, Germany, August 9, 1831. He attended school until he was sixteen years old, when he began an apprenticeship in upholstering and paper

up in the business and are now associated with him, the business having been incorporated in 1893 as the Henry Voss Wall Paper Company, with Mr. Voss as president. He was married in 1863 to Miss Katie Kitzel, who came with her mother from Germany and settled in Nebraska City, Nebraska. Their family consists of four sons and one daughter.

MAURICE HICKEY—The death of Maurice Hickey, which occurred April

26, 1902, removed one of the old pioneer citizens and useful, honored and successful business men of St. Joseph. Mr. Hickey was born in May, 1835, in County Tipperary, Ireland, a member of an old family of tenant farmers.

At the age of 16 years the youth left home in search of the proverbial fortune, in which he was more successful than many; for he became, across the Atlantic, a prominent citizen of his

Joseph secured her admirable waterworks system, one which he mainly originated and zealously promoted.

The late Mr. Hickey was a devout Catholic, being one of the leading members of the Cathedral parish, and his remains were laid to rest in Mount Olivet cemetery. He belonged to an old generation which is rapidly passing away, but the records of their honorable and useful lives remain.

WALTER H. COBB

adopted country and one of the capitalists of his chosen city of residence. After a short season spent at Litchfield, Conn., in 1858, he came to St. Joseph, Mo., entering into business here, in which he continued to be actively engaged until he retired in 1892. Mr. Hickey was a man of character, and he became a leading factor in the ci y's affa rs. He long held a seat in the city council and was a member of that honorable body at the time St.

WALTER H. COBB, retail shoeman at 413 Felix Street, comes from that old Virginia stock that invariably makes good citizens. He was born at Bedford City, Va. After attending the schools in his birthplace, he removed to St. Joseph, where his education was completed. He came here in 1882 with his parents, and in 1889 entered the employ of A. N. Schuster & Co., clothiers. He remained with this firm until 1894, when he became identified with the Tootle, Wheeler & Motter Dry Goods Company, with which firm he remained until 1897, when he engaged in the retail shoe business, which has claimed his time and attention ever since. Fraternally Mr. Cobb is a Mason and an Odd Fellow.

DAVID EDGAR HEATON, president of the Heaton-BeGole Undertaking Co., one of the oldest undertakers in point of service in the cty, was born in St.

the same. In 1881 he purchased his father's interest in the business and it was continued as the D. E. Heaton Undertaking Company until January, 1911, when he incorporated his business under the name of Heaton-BeGole Undertaking Company, and it continues as such at this time.

David E. Heaton was married on the 5th day of October, 1882 The family consists of two daughters,

DAVID E. HEATON

Joseph, Mc., April 17 1855, and was the son of David Johnson Heaton and Lucinda (King) Heaton, who started the business in 1842 as furniture and undertaking and continued as such until 1859 when it was destroyed by fire. Since that time it has been continued as an undertaking business only. In 1872 David E. Heaton became an apprentice in his father's business and in 1874 purchased an interest in

Hazel E. and Bessie D. (now Mrs. Geo. C. Gordon and Mrs. J. O. Wilson, both of Kansas City, Missouri.)

Politically Mr. Heaton is a Democrat, and has served as president of the Monroe Club, the central organization of his party. He is also president of the St. Joseph Auditorium Co., and has always been active in any public enterprise worthy of support. He is a member of the various

branches of the Masonic order, and
also belongs to the Elks, Odd Fellows
and a number of the fraternal organizations.

GEORGE W. MARLOW, one of the
pioneer business men and honored
citizens of St. Joseph, died at his home
in this city, November 16, 1893. Mr.
Marlow was born December 14, 1838,
in Loundoun County, Virginia, and
was one of a family of fourteen chil-

til his decease.

The late Mr. Marlow was noted for
his innate courtesy and for the gentle-
manly instincts that marked his bearing on all occasions. He possessed at-
tributes which called forth the respect
of all who knew him. He was an honorable, upright business man, one who
took a deep interest in all that per-
tained to St. Joseph, was valued in his
church relations and was beloved in

LEWIS C. BURNES

dren born to his parents, George W.
and Mary (Smith) Marlow.

The subject of this sketch was well
educated and had many social advantages, but he was left, like many others after the Civil war, with the necessity of entering into a business life.
He came to St. Joseph in 1869 and established himself here in the boot and
shoe business, becoming proprietor of
the "Elephant Shoe Store," and continued to be interested in this line un-

his home.

LEWIS C. BURNES was born and
reared in Missouri. He is a member
of one of the oldest and best-known
families in the Platte Purchase, if not
in Missouri. He is president of the
Burnes National Bank, and by reason
of long training and a careful study
of the business has come to be recognized as one of the leading bankers in
the Middle West.

SIMON BROUSE—It requires a man of varied accomplishments and thoroughly versed in modern business methods to successfully manage the extensive interests in St. Joseph of that great manufacturing concern, the Val Blatz Brewing Company, and thereby sustain the fair name and great reputation of the product that "made Milwaukee famous;" therefore when the Blatz interests sought for a

under the control of Mr. Brouse. There is no point or detail of the business with which Mr. Brouse is not thoroughly familiar, and the success of his management is largely due to these essentials.

Mr. Brouse was born in Leavenworth, Kansas, on the New Year's Day, 1880, and was given a classical and business education in the best institutions of that state. After com-

SIMON BROUSE

man in whom they could feel that their interests were safe and competent hands, they selected Simon Brouse, and in 1912 gave him the management of the St. Joseph Branch. That they made no mistake is shown by the added popularity of their famous brew in this section and the constant and substantial increase in the volume of business, not only in St. Joseph but in the large territory tributary to this city which is also

pleting his education, he associated himself with the Blatz interests and rose rapidly to his present position. He was married to Miss Rose Wienberg, of St. Joseph, in 1911. They have two children, both sons. Mr. Brouse is an Eagle, a Moose, and Beneigherouth.

RT. REV. MAURICE FRANCIS BURKE, bishop of the diocese of St. Joseph, is one of the most venerated of the ecclesiastics of the Catholic church in Missouri, and was born in Ireland, May 5, 1845. He is one of eight children born to his parents, Francis N. and Hohanna (Casey) Burke, native of Ireland.

The family came to America in 1849 and settled at Chicago, Ill., then a city of small area with but 23,000 population. However, a parochial school had been established, and this the youth attended, subsequently taking a com-

Chicago. After three years of faithful service there he was appointed pastor of St. Mary's church, Joliet, Ill., where he remained nine years.

In 1887 he was made Bishop of Cheyenne, Wyo., by His Holiness Pope Leo XIII. In June, 1893, he was transferred to the diocese of St. Joseph.

RICE McDONALD, treasurer of the Empire Trust Company, 116 South Sixth Street, was educated in the pub-

RICE McDONALD

mercial course at Bryant & Stratton's Business College and later attended St. Mary's University.

In 1866 he completed his literary course and education at Notre Dame, Ind., and the same year went to Rome to pursue his philosophical and theological studies in the American College. He was ordained to the priesthood at Rome, May 22, 1875, by Cardinal Patrizi. Upon his return to the United States he was assigned an assistant pastor of St. Mary's church,

lic schools of the city. His education being completed he began his business career with the R. L. McDonald Dry Goods Company of this city. He became identified with the Empire Trust Company in 1912 and was made treasurer.

COL. JOSEPH A. PINER, one of the best known citizens of St. Joseph, of which city he was mayor four years, was born in Boone County, Kentucky, in 1820, and died in this city January, 1905. He spent his boyhood days in

Kentucky, after receiving his education in the common schools. In the early '40's he was appointed sheriff of Campbell County, Kentucky, by the governor, and subsequently was elected to that office.

Col. Piner was engaged in the banking business in Campbell County until 1860, and two years later came to St. Joseph, where he started a general store. He had the misfortune to lose

ing mayor of St. Joseph, served his party and his county as representative in the legislature.

MARTIN L. KULLMAN, M. D., is prominently engaged in the practice of medicine in St. Joseph, where he has resided since 1896. He was born in Wisconsin in 1865.

He was reared in Wisconsin, and there received his early education. He later attended the Chillicothe Normal

MARTIN L. KULLMAN, M. D.

his store through a destructive fire and subsequently engaged in various business enterprises.

He purchased and operated saw mills at Lake Contrary and several years later embarked in the transfer and omnibus business. This he conducted alone for some time and then took as a partner Col. Elijah Gates, the firm becoming Piner & Gates. The business was sold to Amos M. Brown in the '80's, and is now conducted under the name of the Brown Transfer and Storage Company, one of the largest concerns of the kind in the country. In politics Col. Piner was always a consistent Democrat and besides be-

School of Chillicothe, Missouri, from which he was graduated in 1892. He came to St. Joseph the following year and attended the Central Medical College, graduating therefrom in 1896. He then entered upon his practice in this city, and has since continued with a great deal of success, establishing a large and well-paying practice.

In 1890 Doctor Kullman was united in marriage with Betty Herrth, a native of Missouri, and they have one daughter, Clara, who was born in Chillicothe. The doctor is a member of Enterprise Lodge, No. 22, I. O. O. F., and Modoc Tribe, No. 29, Improved

Order of Red Men. In politics he has always been a loyal supporter of the Republican party.

PETER M. EGGER, at 114 North Second Street, proprietor of the Colorado House was born in Davenport, Iowa, August 28, 1855. He went to St. Louis in 1873 and engaged in the bakery business, for a period of thirteen years. He came to St. Joseph in 1886 and entered the employ of Som-

densburg, New York, February 21, 1845, and died at his home in St. Joseph, April 7, 1890. He received his primary education in the public schools of the state of New York. Later he became a student at Hamilton College at Clinton, New York, and was subsequently graduated there, and then entered the Albany Law School at Albany, New York, where he completed the prescribed course. He came

PETER M. EGGER

mer-Richardson Co., now the National Biscuit Co., where he remained for sixteen years. He took charge of the Colorado House August 2, 1902. He was married to Miss Mollie Jones of St. Louis in 1883. Four children have been born to them, two of whom, a son and a daughter are living. Mr. Egger is a Redman and an Eagle; in the latter lodge he is a member of the board of trustees.

WINSLOW JUDSON, one of the great lawyers and public spirited citizens of St. Joseph, was born at Og-

to St. Joseph in 1867 and entered upon the practice of law, and this city continued to be his place of residence during the whole of his subsequent career.

Perhaps it was as a promoter of great business enterprises that Mr. Judson was best known. In this he benefitted both himself and the city for which he was so loyal and persistent a worker. He was at the head of a number of movements which resulted in the erection of large buildings, the construction of many miles of railroad and the development of a pleasure resort that has since become one of the favorite spots for summer recreation seekers in the West.

The Board of Trade Building is a monument to the enterprise of Mr. Judson. It was to his unceasing efforts that the shops of the St. Joseph Terminal Company were built. The yards and freight house of this company were built under his personal

present popularity of that place is due, primarily, to his efforts.

JOHN W. PATT, merchant tailor at 511 Francis Street, was born in Rhine Province, Germany, November 2, 1869. He was educated in his native country. He came to America in 1883, locating first in New York where he remained three years. In 1886 he went to Sedalia, Mo., in which city he resided for three years. Mr. Patt came to St.

JOHN W. PATT

supervision. Mr. Judson is the man who convinced the officials of the Santa Fe railroad that they ought to own a line into St. Joseph. He purchased what was then the St. Joseph & St. Louis railroad, from St. Joseph to Lexington Junction, Missouri. This property was sold to the Santa Fe in 1885 and is still a part of that great railroad system. Soon after this he took up the development of Lake Contrary as a pleasure resort and the

Joseph in 1892 and established the merchant tailoring business of Patt brothers, his brother being associated with him. He was married in 1893 to Miss Stella M. Reiplinger of St. Joseph. Their family consists of one daughter and two sons. Fraternally Mr. Patt is a Mason and an Elk. He is a man for whom the glamor and glory of politics has no attraction, having recently declined to accept the appointment of member of the city council,

MERRILL E. OTIS, the subject of this sketch, was born near Hopkins, in Nodaway County, Missouri, July 7, 1884. He remained on the farm until he entered the University of Missouri. Having graduated from the university with the degrees of Bachelor of Arts, Master of Arts, and Bachelor of Laws, Mr. Otis began the practice of law in St. Joseph, Mo., in November, 1911, and shortly afterward entered into a

Ashland College, Ohio. She was married to Charles Gibbons October 2?, 1887, who died the following month. The subject of this sketch was in business as a dressmaker in Milledgeville, Ill., and later followed nursing and missionary work in Chicago. She was married to John W. Evalson of St. Joseph September 7, 1915. Rev. Evalson has been active in the ministry of the Brethren church for many years.

MERRILL E. OTIS

partnership with Mr. Louis V. Stigall, under the firm name of Stigall and Otis. Mr. Otis was the Republican candidate for congress in the Fourth District of Missouri at the November election in 1914. He is a member of the Lincoln Club, of the Masonic and Knights of Pythias lodges, of the Phi Delta Phi Legal Fraternity, and of the Phi Beta Kappa Society.

REV. SADIE GIBBONS EVALSON was born in Ringgold, Pa., February 20, 1864, and lived in Illinois, Iowa and Kansas before coming to St. Joseph in 1913. She was educated in the common schools of Iowa and in

BENJAMIN F. MIDDAUGH, proprietor of the Victoria Hotel and Restaurant, 622-624 South Sixth Street, a native of Missouri. He was born at Cameron, April 22, 1860. He came to St. Joseph in 1898. In 1890 opened the Victoria and has been very successful in this venture. He was married to Miss Rosa E. Powell Cameron, in 1879. They have fo children. Mr. Middaugh believes the future of the city of his adopti and always aids every worthy ent prise that is calculated to build up Joseph and make it a better place which to live.

DR. ROLLA H. BROWN, osteopath, Room 28, Ballinger Building, is a native of Kansas, having been born at Huron, December 31, 1883. He received his education in the schools of his native town, and in the fall of 1912 entered the American School of Osteopathy at Kirksville. He graduated from this school in June, 1915. He came at once to St. Joseph and began practicing.

to St. Joseph in 1912. He was educated in the public schools, and finished the classical-theological course in Central Wesleyan College at Warrensburg, Mo. He was married to Miss Ida Goebe of Kansas City in 1897. Four children were born to them. Rev. Buechner is a trustee of his alma mater. He served the churches at Cosby, Mo., four years.; Sedalia, Mo., seven years; Higgins-

DR. ROLLA H. BROWN

Doctor Brown was married to Miss Ruby Klostermeier of Atchison, Kans., June 15, 1915. He is a Mason and an Odd Fellow and a member of the First Baptist Church. He is one of those determined, progressive young men that are bound to succeed, and his future looks exceptionally bright.

REV. SAMUEL BUECHNER, clergyman, pastor of the First German Methodist Episcopal Church, at Third and Robidoux streets, was born at Cameron, Mo., July 12, 1873, and came

ville, Mo., four years, and the St. Joseph church four years.

H. ROLEAU KAULL, newspaper reporter, is a native of St. Joseph, having been born here March 12, 1890. He received his education in the local public schools and the Central High school. When seventeen years old he went with his parents to live in Cleveland, Ohio, but returned a year later. He is now city hall reporter for the News-Press.

JOHN FISKE BARNARD, who died in this city a few years ago, was one of the men who made railroad history in the early days. He was born in Worcester, Massachusetts, April 23, 1829, and came from a family which had its origin in England. His forbears were among the early settlers in New England, and the family is now scattered all over the United States, some members of which have become distinguished in the varied

career in which his mechanical abilities might have play, and this resulted in his entering the Rensselaer Polytechnic School at Troy, New York, where he tok a course in civil engineering, graduating from that institution in 1850.

He was almost immediately engaged as chief engineer of the St. Lawrence & Atlantic Railroad, now a part of the Grand Trunk Railway of Canada, to go to the Dominion, where he re-

J. W. BOYD
Attorney and Counselor at Law

walks of life.

Mr. Barnard was reared on a farm and until he was seventeen enjoyed only the educational advantages of the country schools during the winter months. In 1847, however, his prospects changed and he entered the State Normal School at Bridgewater, Massachusetts. His special talents attracted the attention of his teachers, who suggested to him the wisdom of thoroughly preparing himself for a

mained until the spring of 1857, when he took charge of a short road on the banks of the Ottawa river in Canada. After filling several other important positions acceptably, he came back to the United States in 1869 and took charge of the Missouri Valley Railroad as chief engineer and superintendent. In 1870 the Missouri Valley and the Council Bluffs & St. Joseph roads were consolidated and he was retained as chief engineer. In 1871

ie went with the St. Joseph & Denver
Iity Railroad as chief engineer, and
xtended the construction of the road
ifty miles westward. In August, 1872,
ie was appointed superintendent of
he Kansas City, St. Joseph & Coun-
il Bluffs Railroad, which position he
etained until he was made general
nanager of the same upon its pur-
hase by the Chicago, Burlington &
Juincy Railroad in 1880. In the au-
umn of 1884 he was also made gen-

much proficiency in his line as any
other man of his time.

EDWARD A. PRINZ, proprietor of
Prinz's Academy of Dancing, of St.
Joseph, and probably one of the best
instructors in the terpsichorean art in
this section of the state, was born in
St. Joseph, October 3, 1872.

He received his education at Father
Linnencamp's parochial school in St.
Joseph, and, as a little lad, began his
career by carrying a newspaper route

EDWARD A. PRINZ

al manager of the Hannibal & St.
seph. He continued to manage these
o properties until 1886, when he
came president and general man-
er of the Ohio & Mississippi Rail-
ad Company. He remained with this
mpany until 1892 and during the
lowing five years was receiver for
e Omaha & St. Louis Railroad. He
sed a busy and successful railroad
·eer in the capacity of president of
e St. Clair, Madison & St. Louis
ilroad. He probably attained as

for the St. Joseph Herald. Later he
became connected with the business
department of that paper and continued in the business employ for five
years. During all this period he had
improved every opportunity to study
dancing as a graceful art, in preparation to embracing it as a career. In
1891 he opened his first school of
instruction in dancing, in old Younger
Hall at the corner of Eighth and Edmond streets. After one season, during which he received much encour-

agment, he moved to the Samuels Building at Sixth and Charles streets, and in 1898 to more commodious quarters in Columbia Hall in the Irish-American building. His reputation has grown to such an extent as a teacher of deportment and the graceful and useful art of dancing, that his pupils invariably refer with pride to the fact that they have been tutored by him. He has several private classes in dancing, and for years he has been in-

common schools of the city. He was graduated from the St. James Academy of Macon, Mo., in 1885. He attended the Pennsylvania Military College in Chester, Pa., in 1886-87. Mr. Fairleigh was married to Miss Forrestine Cavalier McDonald of St. Joseph, in 1895. They have one child, a son.

WILLIAM H. BARTLETT, a pioneer citizen, who was engaged in the real estate business in St. Joseph

J. O. FAIRLEIGH

structor at the Blees Military Academy at Macon, Mo. His methods are those recognized by polite society all over the world, and his careful instruction covers every form of the subject.

J. O. FAIRLEIGH, capitalist, with offices at 814 Corby-Forsee Building, was born in St. Joseph, August 12, 1868. His early education was in the

for forty years, passed out of life September 19, 1904. Mr. Bartlett was born on a farm in Ripley County, Indiana, June 26, 1845, and was one a family of five children born to David L. and Phoebe (Elsworth) Bartlett. His parents moved to Atchison County, Missouri, in 1858, where attended school and became a teacher himself, when but sixteen years age. He came to St. Joseph in 18 and found employment in the record-er's office in this city. In 1864 he associated with his brother, Herschel, in the real estate business; a third brother, Latham, entering the firm in 1874. About this time the scope of their business enlarged and they began to loan money for eastern investors on real estate security. For forty years the brothers continued together, our subject's death making the first break in a closely united business and

G. R. ECKEL, architect, is the son of E. J. Eckel, and a member of the firm of Eckel & Aldrich, architects. He was born in the city of St. Joseph, December 30, 1882, where he was reared and educated in the public schools. He is an alumni of the Massachusetts Institute of Technology of Boston, where he studied architecture. In 1910 the firm of Eckel & Aldrich, of which he is a member, was organized, and since that time he has been

G. R. ECKEL

fraternal union.

The late Mr. Bartlett was a man of great determination and persistent energy. By strict attention to business and ever adhering to his unswerving standard of business ethics, he lived to see his firm, founded in the city's early days, become one of the leading institutions in its line in the state. He was a man of acute perceptions, a great reader and a competent judge of men and affairs.

actively and intimately connected with the practice of his profession in this city and the surrounding country.

ETHELBERT M. CLAYPOOL, reporter St. Joseph Gazette, was born January 9, 1892, at Montesano, Chehalis county, Washington, the son of a Methodist minister. Resided in Washington until 1898, when he removed to Iowa with his parents. His early schooling was received in the Iowa public schools. The first two years of his high school course were spent in Holton, Kans., although he was graduated from Central High School, Kansas City, Mo., in 1910. He spent two years in Wesleyan university, Middletown, Conn.

As a "devil" on the Holton (Kansas) Recorder, he first entered the newspaper field in 1905. From that time on he was connected in various capacities with several dailies, doing reportorial work on the Hannibal Courier-

taken an active interest in politics and is firm in the belief that his democracy is not surpassed by anyone anywhere. He sought the Democratic nomination for circuit clerk in 1910, but was unsuccessful. He is one of the live wires of the South Side and one of the progressive citizens of St. Joseph.

WALTER D. LADD, city editor of the Gazette, was born in St. Joseph, October 1, 1891, and is the son of Dr.

ISAAC T. KEYWOOD

Post, the Springfield (Missouri) Republican, the Springfield, (Missouri) Leader, and the St. Joseph Gazette.

ISAAC T. KEYWOOD, whose place of business is at 401 Illinois avenue comes from Andrew County, where he was born May 29, 1856. He came with his parents to St. Joseph at the age of six years. He was educated in the schools of the city and then took up the harness makers trade, serving his apprenticeship with Israel Landis, whose employ he entered in 1874. After serving this trade for fifteen years Mr. Keywood sought other fields of activity. He has always

and Mrs. Fred H. Ladd. He has lived here practically all his life, and received his education in the St. Joseph schools. He graduated from Central High School in 1910. Mr. Ladd went into newspaper work as a cub reporter on the Gazette just after leaving high school, became telegraph editor in the spring of 1912 and took the city desk in the spring of 1914. He was married May 29, 1912, to Miss Inez I. Chittenden of St. Joseph.

FORD M. PETTIT, telegraph editor of the Gazette, was born at Flushing Mich., Sept. 9, 1888. He was educated at the Jackson, Mich., high school, an

Kalamazoo college. He went into newspaper work when still in college, and has been connected with the following newspapers: The Kalamazoo (Michigan) Gazette, Jackson (Michigan) Morning Patriot, Fort Madison (Iowa) Gem City, Illinois State Journal, Springfield, Ill.; Kansas City Post, Kansas City Times, St. Louis Globe-Democrat, and St. Joseph Gazette. He went to the Gazette Dec. 26, 1913.

OTTO THEISEN, former sheriff of

party and staunchly supports his friends at all times. Mr. Theisen holds membership cards in the Woodman, Eagles and Red Men.

REV. DUDLEY M. CLAGETT, D. D., was born December 31, 1875, at Palmyra, Mo. Graduated from Westminster College, Fulton, Mo., with A. B. degree, June, 1895, and from Princeton Theological Seminary, May, 1900. Received A. M. degree from Princeton University, '01. Held three pas-

OTTO THEISEN

hanan County, is a native of St. eph. He was born here February 1873, and was educated in the ools of the city. He has always a active in the affairs of the city, an enterprising citizen. Politics claimed considerable of his time attention and in 1908 he was ted sheriff of Buchanan County, he Democratic ticket. He has also been one of the leaders of his

torates in Presbyterian church—Longwood, Mo., 1900-03; Sedalia, 1903-10, and Westminster Presbyterian church, St. Joseph, since that time. He was chosen moderator of Synod of Missouri of Presbyterian Church, U. S. A., 1913. Received Doctor of Divinity degree from Park College, June, 1914. He was married in December, 1903, to Nora Robertson, Marshall, Mo. They have two living children,

Robertson, born July 18, 1908, and Eleanor, born June 29, 1910.

LOUIS KLEINBRODT was born April 14, 1839, in Baden, Germany. He came to America in 1881, locating in St. Joseph. He was employed by the Hax Furniture Company for twenty years and assisted greatly in the growth and advancement of that business. He was the father of five children.

went to Kentucky, where he studied law and was admitted to the bar at Louisville. He came to Buchanan County in 1839, locating in Bloomington Township, and practicing wherever court happened to sit—at Sparta or Blacksnake Hills—the seat of justice was not very firmly established in those days. So able and brilliant was he that in 1845 he was elected to the State Constitutional Convention

LOUIS KLEINBRODT

HON. ROBERT M. STEWART, one time governor of Missouri, a man of winning manner, brilliant intellect and compelling influence, whose greatest achievements were somewhat clouded by his personal eccentricities, began life as a farmer boy, born near Truxton, New York, March 12, 1815.

From the age of seventeen until the age of twenty, Mr. Stewart taught school in his native locality, and then

and from 1845 to 1857 he served in the state senate. In the latter year he was elected to succeed Governor Polk, upon the latter's resignation.

Governor Stewart was elected delegate from Buchanan County to the famous convention of 1861. He ardently supported the Union and decried secession, and he helped to save Missouri to the Union, an action which was of a national character. He was one of the projectors of the Hannibal & St. Joseph Railroad, helping to survey the line. It was mainly through his eloquence and logic that the right of way was secured.

Governor Stewart never married. His death occurred September 21, 1871, and there was a general suspension of business in St. Joseph on the day of the funeral. His remains were laid away in Mount Mora cemetery and for many years his grave was unmarked, except by a pine slab, left there by the undertaker. But after

ried to Miss Josephine Nix, of Autrian, January 18, 1886. They have four children, all daughters. Mr. Weiss is an Odd Fellow, a Moose, a Red Man and a Woodman.

HUGO GREBEL, one of the most prominent business men of St. Joseph, is manager of the Anheuser-Busch Brewing Association for this city, doing an exclusive wholesale business. Mr. Grebel was born in Zittau, Saxony, Germany, August 8, 1856, and came to America first in 1888, as traveling representative of a Leipsic type

GEORGE WEISS

many years of effort a suitable monument was erected to his memory by friends and public spirited persons who desired to honor the ex-governor's memory, though he was somewhat erratic in his lifetime.

GEORGE WEISS, whose place of business is at the corner of Tenth and Jackson streets, is a native of Switzerland, in which country he was born October 23, 1862. He was educated in his native country and came to America in 1882, arriving in St. Joseph April 3, that year. He was mar-

foundry. He was well impressed with this country and a second visit in 1890 resulted in his locating here. He has been with the Anheuser-Busch people since 1891.

In 1892 Mr. Grebel was married to Miss Bertha Wezler, who came of a prominent St. Louis family. He is a highly educated gentleman, of a genial temperament and pleasant manner. His social circle is wide and he is a very highly esteemed citizen of St. Joseph.

INDEX

INDEX

INDEX

INDEX

INDEX

.